Stanley Gibbons
Stamp Catalogue

Switzerland

Including Liechtenstein and
United Nations Office at Geneva

1st Edition 2019

By Appointment to
Her Majesty The Queen
Philatelists
Stanley Gibbons Ltd,
London

1st edition – 2019

Published by Stanley Gibbons Ltd
Editorial, Publications Sales Offices
7 Parkside, Christchurch Road, Ringwood,
Hants BH24 3SH

© Stanley Gibbons Ltd 2019

Copyright Notice

The contents of this Catalogue, including the numbering system and illustrations, are fully protected by copyright. No part of this publication may be reproduced, stored in a retrieval system, or transmitted in any form or by any means, electronic, mechanical, photocopying, recording or otherwise, without the prior permission of Stanley Gibbons Limited. Requests for such permission should be addressed to the Catalogue Editor. This Catalogue is sold on condition that it is not, by way of trade or otherwise, lent, re-sold, hired out, circulated or otherwise disposed of other than in its complete, original and unaltered form and without a similar condition including this condition being imposed on the subsequent purchaser.

British Library Cataloguing in
Publication Data.
A catalogue record for this book is available from the British Library.

Errors and omissions excepted. The colour reproduction of stamps is only as accurate as the printing process will allow.

ISBN-13: 978-1-911304-48-7

Item No. R 1419-19

Printed by
Cambrian Printers, Wales

Stanley Gibbons Foreign Catalogue

ABOUT THIS EDITION

It is over 35 years since the present split into 'Parts 2 to 22' was announced, dividing up what had up to then been an alphabetical listing of European and Overseas countries over seven large volumes into handy-sized catalogues, bringing together countries or groups of countries, generally united by geography or political affiliations.

Back in 1979 the new 'Parts' catalogues proved to be very popular with collectors, but over time these volumes have grown in size, with the ever increasing numbers of new issues.

In 2015 Stanley Gibbons celebrated 150 years of catalogue production and it seemed the right time to take a look at the structure and break down of our Foreign catalogue range.

- Prices have been thoroughly revised and brought up to date, by leading experts in the field.
- Specimen stamps have been included for the first time
- Design indexes for Liechtenstein and Switzerland have been updated, and are designed to aid the collector in identifying and cataloguing their stamps.

New issue listings have been updated:

- Switzerland – March 2019
- Liechtenstein – November 2018
- United Nations Office at Geneva – March 2017

The first supplement to this catalogue appeared in *Gibbons Stamp Monthly* for March 2020.

We would like to thank James Bendon for his advice with the Specimen (UPU) lisings.

Addresses for specialist societies for this area are on page iv.

Clare de la Feuillade, Editor
Hugh Jefferies, Consultant
Sue Price, New Issues Listings
Barbara Hawkins, Pricing Assistant
Leslie Fuller, Proof Reader
Emma Fletcher, Designer and page layout

NUMBERS ADDED

SWITZERLAND
Z4a
1109b
O381As/O389As
O390s/O398s
386s

PRO JUVENTUTE CHARITY STAMPS
J92a

INTERNATIONAL ORGANISATIONS SITUATED IN SWITZERLAND
A. League of Nations
LN45As/LN46As
LN48As/LN49As
LN51As/LN51Acs
LN47Bs
LN50Bs
LN52Bs/LN55Bs

B. International Labour Office
LB27as
LB40As
LB41Ads/LB42As
LB43Acs/LB46s
LB39Bs
LB41Bs
LB43Bs
LB47Bs
LB48s/LB51s
LB52s/LB55s
LB56s/LB58s

LICHTENSTEIN
53Aa
O119As
O118Bs
O120Bs/O121Bs
O123Bs/O125Bs
O122Cs
O127a
O176

NUMBERS ALTERED

SWITZERLAND

OLD	NEW
O174	O173
Z4	Z1
Z5	Z2
Z1	Z3
Z2	Z4
Z3	Z5
12a	13
13	14
14	15
1676	1674
1677	1675
1678	1676
1679	1677
1680	1678

LIECHTENSTEIN

OLD	NEW
O174	O173
O175	O174
O176	O175

PHILATELIC SOCIETIES

Helvetia Philatelic Society

Secretary: Neville Nelder
76 Greenaways
Ebley Wharf
Stroud
GL5 4UQ

Email: secretary@swiss-philately.co.uk
Website: swiss-philately.co.uk

Contents

Stanley Gibbons Holdings Plc vi	H. United Nations 99
General Philatelic Information and Guidelines to the Scope of Stanley Gibbons Foreign Catalogues vii	I. International Telecommunication Union 100
Abbreviations xiv	J. World Intellectual Property Organisation 101
International Philatelic Glossary xv	K. International Olympic Committee 101
List of Catalogues xix	
Guide to Entries xx	**LIECHTENSTEIN** — **102**
The Strubel stamps of Switzerland, 1854 to 1862 xxii	I. Issues of the Austrian Post Office 102
	II. Issues of Principality of Liechtenstein 102
SWITZERLAND — **1**	Machine Labels 160
I. Cantonal Administrations 1	**Design Index** 161
II. Transitional Period 1	
III. Federal Administration 1	**UNITED NATIONS OFFICE AT GENEVA** — **164**
Postcard Stamps 76	Stamp Booklets 217
Machine Labels 76	
Stamp Booklets 77	
Pro patria stamp booklets 79	
'Pro juventute' charity stamps 79	
'Pro juventute' Stamp Booklets 89	
Postcard Stamp Booklets 89	
Design Index 90	
INTERNATIONAL ORGANISATIONS SITUATED IN SWITZERLAND — **95**	
A. League of Nations 95	
B. International Labour Office 96	
C. International Bureau of Education 97	
D. World Health Organisation 98	
E. International Refugees Organisation 98	
F. World Meteorological Organisation 98	
G. Universal Postal Union 99	

Stanley Gibbons Holdings Plc

Stanley Gibbons Limited,
Stanley Gibbons Auctions
399 Strand, London WC2R 0LX
Tel: +44 (0)207 836 8444
Fax: +44 (0)207 836 7342
E-mail: help@stanleygibbons.com
Website: www.stanleygibbons.com
for all departments, Auction and
Specialist Stamp Departments.
Open Monday–Friday 9.30 am to 5 pm
Shop. Open Monday–Friday 9 am to
5.30 pm and Saturday 9.30 am
to 5.30 pm

Stanley Gibbons Publications,
Gibbons Stamp Monthly and
Philatelic Exporter
7 Parkside, Christchurch Road,
Ringwood, Hampshire BH24 3SH.
Tel: +44 (0)1425 472363
Fax: +44 (0)1425 470247
E-mail: help@stanleygibbons.com
Publications Mail Order.
FREEPHONE 0800 611622
Monday–Friday 8.30 am to 5 pm

Stanley Gibbons Publications Overseas Representation
Stanley Gibbons Publications are represented overseas by the following

Australia
Renniks Publications PTY LTD
Unit 3 37-39 Green Street,
Banksmeadow, NSW 2019, Australia
Tel: +612 9695 7055
Website: www.renniks.com

Canada
Unitrade Associates
99 Floral Parkway, Toronto,
Ontario M6L 2C4, Canada
Tel: +1 416 242 5900
Website: www.unitradeassoc.com

Germany
Schaubek Verlag Leipzig
Am Glaeschen 23, D-04420
Markranstaedt, Germany
Tel: +49 34 205 67823
Website: www.schaubek.de

Italy
Ernesto Marini S.R.L.
V. Struppa, 300, Genova, 16165, Italy
Tel: +3901 0247-3530
Website: www.ernestomarini.it

Japan
Japan Philatelic
PO Box 2, Suginami-Minami,
Tokyo 168-8081, Japan
Tel: +81 3330 41641
Website: www.yushu.co.jp

Netherlands (also covers Belgium
Denmark, Finland & France)
Uitgeverij Davo BV
PO Box 411, Ak Deventer, 7400
Netherlands
Tel: +315 7050 2700
Website: www.davo.nl

New Zealand
House of Stamps
PO Box 12, Paraparaumu,
New Zealand
Tel: +61 6364 8270
Website: www.houseofstamps.co.nz

Philatelic Distributors
PO Box 863
15 Mount Edgecumbe Street
New Plymouth 4615, New Zealand
Tel: +6 46 758 65 68
Website: www.stampcollecta.com

Norway
SKANFIL A/S
SPANAV. 52 / BOKS 2030
N-5504 HAUGESUND, Norway
Tel: +47-52703940
E-mail: magne@skanfil.no

Singapore
C S Philatelic Agency
Peninsula Shopping Centre #04-29
3 Coleman Street, 179804, Singapore
Tel: +65 6337-1859
Website: www.cs.com.sg

Sweden
Chr Winther Sorensen AB
Box 43, S-310 20 Knaered, Sweden
Tel: +46 43050743
Website: www.collectia.se

General Philatelic Information and Guidelines to the Scope of Stanley Gibbons Foreign Catalogues

These notes reflect current practice in compiling the Foreign Catalogue.

The *Stanley Gibbons Stamp Catalogue* has a very long history and the vast quantity of information it contains has been carefully built up by successive generations through the work of countless individuals. Philately itself is never static and the Catalogue has evolved and developed during this long time-span. These notes apply to current policy – some of the older listings were prepared using slightly different criteria – and we hope you find them useful in using the catalogue.

THE CATALOGUE IN GENERAL

Contents. The Catalogue is confined to adhesive postage stamps, including miniature sheets. For particular categories the rules are:
(a) Revenue (fiscal) stamps or telegraph stamps are listed only where they have been expressly authorised for postal duty.
(b) Stamps issued only precancelled are included, but normally issued stamps available additionally with precancel have no separate precancel listing unless the face value is changed.
(c) Stamps prepared for use but not issued, hitherto accorded full listing, are nowadays footnoted with a price (where possible).
(d) Bisects (trisects, etc.) are only listed where such usage was officially authorised.
(e) Stamps issued only on first day covers and not available separately are not listed but priced (on the cover) in a footnote.
(f) New printings, as such, are not listed, though stamps from them may qualify under another category, e.g. when a prominent new shade results.
(g) Official and unofficial reprints are dealt with by footnote.
(h) Stamps from imperforate printings of modern issues which also occur perforated are covered by footnotes or general notes, but are listed where widely available for postal use.

Exclusions. The following are excluded:
(a) non-postal revenue or fiscal stamps;
(b) postage stamps used fiscally;
(c) local carriage labels and private local issues;
(d) telegraph stamps;
(e) bogus or phantom stamps;
(f) railway or airline letter fee stamps, bus or road transport company labels;
(g) cut-outs;
(h) all types of non-postal labels;
(i) documentary labels for the postal service, e.g. registration, recorded delivery, airmail etiquettes, etc.;
(j) privately applied embellishments to official issues and privately commissioned items generally;
(k) stamps for training postal officers;
(l) specimen stamps. (except those distributed by the UPU)

Full listing. 'Full listing' confers our recognition and implies allotting a catalogue number and (wherever possible) a price quotation.

In judging status for inclusion in the catalogue broad considerations are applied to stamps. They must be issued by a legitimate postal authority, recognised by the government concerned, and must be adhesives valid for proper postal use in the class of service for which they are inscribed. Stamps, with the exception of such categories as postage dues and officials, must be available to the general public, at face value, in reasonable quantities without any artificial restrictions being imposed on their distribution.

We record as abbreviated Appendix entries, without catalogue numbers or prices, stamps from countries which either persist in having far more issues than can be justified by postal need or have failed to maintain control over their distribution so that they have not been available to the public in reasonable quantities at face value. Miniature sheets and imperforate stamps are not mentioned in these entries.

The publishers of this catalogue have observed, with concern, the proliferation of 'artificial' stamp-issuing territories. On several occasions this has resulted in separately inscribed issues for various component parts of otherwise united states or territories.

Stanley Gibbons Publications have decided that where such circumstances occur, they will not, in the future, list these items in the SG catalogue without first satisfying themselves that the stamps represent a genuine political, historical or postal division within the country concerned. Any such issues which do not fulfil this stipulation will be recorded in the Catalogue Appendix only.

For errors and varieties the criterion is legitimate (albeit inadvertent) sale over a post office counter in the normal course of business. Details of provenance are always important; printers' waste and fraudulently manufactured material is excluded.

Certificates. In assessing unlisted items due weight is given to Certificates from recognised Expert Committees and, where appropriate, we will usually ask to see them.

New issues. New issues are listed regularly in the Catalogue Supplement in *Gibbons Stamp Monthly*, then consolidated into the next available edition of the Catalogue.

Date of issue. Where local issue dates differ from dates of release by agencies, 'date of issue' is the local date. Fortuitous stray usage before the officially intended date is disregarded in listing.

Catalogue numbers. Stamps of each country are catalogued chronologically by date of issue. Subsidiary classes (e.g. postage due stamps) are integrated into one list with postage and commemorative stamps and distinguished by a letter prefix to the catalogue number.

The catalogue number appears in the extreme left column. The boldface type numbers in the next column

Information and Guidelines

are merely cross-references to illustrations. Catalogue numbers in the *Gibbons Stamp Monthly* Supplement are provisional only and may need to be altered when the lists are consolidated. Miniature sheets only purchasable intact at a post office have a single MS number; sheetlets – individual stamps available – number each stamp separately. The catalogue no longer gives full listing to designs originally issued in normal sheets, which subsequently appear in sheetlets showing changes of colour, perforation, printing process or face value. Such stamps will be covered by footnotes.

Once published in the Catalogue, numbers are changed as little as possible; really serious renumbering is reserved for the occasions when a complete country or an entire issue is being rewritten. The edition first affected includes cross-reference tables of old and new numbers.

Our catalogue numbers are universally recognised in specifying stamps and as a hallmark of status.

Illustrations. Stamps are illustrated at three-quarters linear size. Stamps not illustrated are the same size and format as the value shown unless otherwise indicated. Stamps issued only as miniature sheets have the stamp alone illustrated but sheet size is also quoted. Overprints, surcharges, watermarks and postmarks are normally actual size. Illustrations of varieties are often enlarged to show the detail.

CONTACTING THE CATALOGUE EDITOR

The editor is always interested in hearing from people who have new information which will improve or correct the Catalogue. As a general rule he must see and examine the actual stamps before they can be considered for listing; photographs or photocopies are insufficient evidence. Neither he nor his staff give opinions as to the genuineness of stamps.

Submissions should be made in writing to the Catalogue Editor, Stanley Gibbons Publications, 7 Parkside, Christchurch Road, Ringwood, Hants BH24 3SH. The cost of return postage for items submitted is appreciated, and this should include the registration fee if required.

Where information is solicited purely for the benefit of the enquirer, the editor cannot undertake to reply if the answer is already contained in these published notes or if return postage is omitted. Written communications are greatly preferred to enquiries by telephone or e-mail and the editor regrets that he or his staff cannot see personal callers without a prior appointment being made.

The editor welcomes close contact with study circles and is interested, too, in finding local correspondents who will verify and supplement official information in overseas countries where this is deficient.

> We regret we do not give opinions as to the genuineness of stamps, nor do we identify stamps or number them by our Catalogue.

TECHNICAL MATTERS

The meanings of the technical terms used in the Catalogue will be found in *Philatelic Terms Illustrated*, published by Stanley Gibbons (Price £14.95 plus postage).

1. Printing

Printing errors. Errors in printing are of major interest to the Catalogue. Authenticated items meriting consideration would include background, centre or frame inverted or omitted; centre or subject transposed; error of colour; error or omission of value; double prints and impressions; printed both sides; and so on. Designs *tête-bêche*, whether intentionally or by accident, are listable. *Se-tenant* arrangements of stamps are recognised in the listings or footnotes. Gutter pairs (a pair of stamps separated by blank margin) are excluded unless they have some philatelic importance. Colours only partially omitted are not listed, neither are stamps printed on the gummed side.

Printing varieties. Listing is accorded to major changes in the printing base which lead to completely new types. In recess-printing this could be a design re-engraved, in photogravure or photolithography a screen altered in whole or in part. It can also encompass flat-bed and rotary printing if the results are readily distinguishable.

To be considered at all, varieties must be constant. Early stamps, produced by primitive methods, were prone to numerous imperfections; the lists reflect this, recognising re-entries, retouches, broken frames, misshapen letters, and so on. Printing technology has, however, radically improved over the years, during which time photogravure and lithography have become predominant. Varieties nowadays are more in the nature of flaws and these, being too specialised for a general catalogue, are almost always outside the scope. We therefore do not list such items as dry prints, kiss prints, doctor-blade flaws, blanket set-offs, doubling through blanket stretch, plate cracks and scratches, registration flaws (leading to colour shifts), lithographic ring flaws, and so on. Neither do we recognise fortuitous happenings like paper creases or confetti flaws.

Overprints (and surcharges). Overprints of different types qualify for separate listing. These include overprints in different colours; overprints from different printing processes such as litho and typo; overprints in totally different typefaces, etc.

Overprint errors and varieties. Major errors in machine-printed overprints are important and listable. They include overprint inverted or omitted; overprint double (treble, etc.); overprint diagonal; overprint double, one inverted; pairs with one overprint omitted, e.g. from a radical shift to an adjoining stamp; error of colour; error of type fount; letters inverted or omitted, etc. If the overprint is handstamped, few of these would qualify and a distinction is drawn.

Varieties occurring in overprints will often take the form of broken letters, slight differences in spacing, rising spacers, etc. Only the most important would be considered for footnote mention.

Sheet positions. If space permits we quote sheet positions of listed varieties and authenticated data is solicited for this purpose.

2. Paper

All stamps listed are deemed to be on 'ordinary' paper of the wove type and white in colour; only departures from this are mentioned.

Types. Where classification so requires we distinguish such other types of paper as, for example, vertically and horizontally laid; wove and laid bâtonné; card(board); carton; cartridge, enamelled; glazed; GC (Grande Consommation); granite; native; pelure; porous; quadrillé; ribbed; rice; and silk thread.

The 'traditional' method of indentifying chalk-surfaced papers has been that, when touched with a silver wire, a black mark is left on the paper, and the listings in this catalogue are based on that test. However, the test itself is now largely discredited, for, although the mark can be removed by a soft rubber, some damage to the stamp will result from its use.

The difference between chalk-surfaced and pre-war ordinary papers is fairly clear: chalk-surfaced papers being smoother to the touch and showing a characteristic sheen when light is reflected off their surface. Under good magnification tiny bubbles or pock marks can be seen on the surface of the stamp and at the tips of the perforations the surfacing appears 'broken'. Traces of paper fibres are evident on the surface of ordinary paper and the ink shows a degree of absorption into it.

The various makeshifts for normal paper are listed as appropriate. They include printing on: unfinished banknotes, war maps, ruled paper, Post Office forms, and the unprinted side of glossy magazines. The varieties of double paper and joined paper are recognised.

Descriptive terms. The fact that a paper is hand-made (and thus probably of uneven thickness) is mentioned where necessary. Such descriptive terms as 'hard' and 'soft'; 'smooth' and 'rough'; 'thick', 'medium' and 'thin' are applied where there is philatelic merit in classifying papers.

Coloured, very white and toned papers. A coloured paper is one that is coloured right through (front and back of the stamp). In the Catalogue the colour of the paper is given in italics, thus

black/*rose* = black design on rose paper.

Papers have been made specially white in recent years by, for example, a very heavy coating of chalk. We do not classify shades of whiteness of paper as distinct varieties. There does exist, however, a type of paper from early days called toned. This is off-white, often brownish or buffish, but it cannot be assigned a definite colour. A toning effect brought on by climate, incorrect storage or gum staining is disregarded here, as this was not the state of the paper when issued.

Safety devices. The Catalogue takes account of such safety devices as varnish lines, grills, burelage or imprinted patterns on the front or moiré on the back of stamps.

Modern developments. Two modern developments also affect the listings, printing on self-adhesive paper and the tendency, philatelic in origin, for conventional paper to be reinforced or replaced by different materials. Some examples are the use of foils in gold, silver, aluminium, palladium and steel; application of an imitation wood veneer; printing on plastic moulded in relief; and use of a plastic laminate to give a three-dimensional effect. Examples also occur of stamps impregnated with scent; printed on silk; and incorporating miniature gramophone records.

3. Perforation and Rouletting

Perforation gauge. The gauge of a perforation is the number of holes in a length of 2 cm. For correct classification the size of the holes (large or small) may need to be distinguished; in a few cases the actual number of holes on each edge of the stamp needs to be quoted.

Measurement. The Gibbons Instanta gauge is the standard for measuring perforations. The stamp is viewed against a dark background with the transparent gauge put on top of it. Though the gauge measures to decimal accuracy, perforations read from it are generally quoted in the Catalogue to the nearest half. For example:

Just over perf.
12¾ to just under perf. 13¼ = perf. 13
Perf. 13¼ exactly, rounded up = perf. 13½
Just over perf.
13¼ to just under perf. 13¾ = perf. 13½
Perf. 13¾ exactly, rounded up = perf. 14

However, where classification depends on it, actual quarter-perforations are quoted.

Notation. Where no perforation is quoted for an issue it is imperforate. Perforations are usually abbreviated (and spoken) as follows, though sometimes they may be spelled out for clarity. This notation for rectangular stamps (the majority) applies to diamond shapes if 'top' is read as the edge to the top right.

P 14: perforated alike on all sides (read: 'perf. 14').

P 14×15: the first figure refers to top and bottom, the second to left and right sides (read: 'perf. 14 by 15'). This is a compound perforation. For an upright triangular stamp the first figure refers to the two sloping sides and the second to the base. In inverted triangulars the base is first and the second figure refers to the sloping sides.

P 14-15: perforation measuring anything between 14 and 15: the holes are irregularly spaced, thus the gauge may vary along a single line or even along a single edge of the stamp (read: 'perf. 14 to 15').

P 14 irregular. perforated 14 from a worn perforator, giving badly aligned holes irregular spaced (read 'irregular perf. 14').

Information and Guidelines

P *comp(ound)* 14×15: two gauges in use but not necessarily on opposite sides of the stamp. It could be one side in one gauge and three in the other, or two adjacent sides with the same gauge (Read: 'perf. compound of 14 and 15'). For three gauges or more, abbreviated as 'P 14, 14½, 15 or compound' for example.

P 14, 14½: perforated approximately 14¼ (read: 'perf. 14 or 14½'). It does not mean two stamps, one perf. 14 and the other perf. 14½. This obsolescent notation is gradually being replaced in the Catalogue.

Imperf: imperforate (not perforated).

Imperf×P 14: imperforate at top and bottom and perf 14 at sides.

P 14×*imperf* = perf 14 at top and bottom and imperforate at sides.

Such headings as 'P 13×14 (vert) and P 14×13 (horiz)' indicate which perforations apply to which stamp format – vertical or horizontal.

Some stamps are additionally perforated so that a label or tab is detachable; others have been perforated suitably for use as two halves. Listings are normally for whole stamps, unless stated otherwise.

Other terms. Perforation almost always gives circular holes; where other shapes have been used they are specified, e.g. square holes; lozenge perf. Interrupted perfs are brought about by the omission of pins at regular intervals. Perforations have occasionally been simulated by being printed as part of the design. With few exceptions, privately applied perforations are not listed.

Perforation errors and varieties. Authenticated errors, where a stamp normally perforated is accidentally issued imperforate, are listed provided no traces of perforation (blind holes or indentations) remain. They must be provided as pairs, both stamps wholly imperforate, and are only priced in that form.

Stamps merely imperforate between stamp and margin (fantails) are not listed.

Imperforate-between varieties are recognised, where one row of perfs has been missed. They are listed and priced in pairs:

Imperf between (horiz pair): a horizontal pair of stamps with perfs all around the edges but none between the stamps.

Imperf between (vert pair): a vertical pair of stamps with perfs all around the edges but none between the stamps.

Where several of the rows have escaped perforation the resulting varieties are listable. Thus:

Imperf vert (horiz pair): a horizontal pair of stamps perforated top and bottom; all three vertical directions are imperf – the two outer edges and between the stamps.

Imperf horiz (vert pair): a vertical pair perforated at left and right edges; all three horizontal directions are imperf – the top, bottom and between the stamps.

Straight edges. Large sheets cut up before issue to post offices can cause stamps with straight edges, i.e. imperf on one side or on two sides at right angles. They are not usually listable in this condition and are worth less than corresponding stamps properly perforated all round. This does not, however, apply to certain stamps, mainly from coils and booklets, where straight edges on various sides are the manufacturing norm affecting every stamp. The listings and notes make clear which sides are correctly imperf.

Malfunction. Varieties of double, misplaced or partial perforation caused by error or machine malfunction are not listable, neither are freaks, such as perforations placed diagonally from paper folds. Likewise disregarded are missing holes caused by broken pins, and perforations 'fading out' down a sheet, the machinery progressively disengaging to leave blind perfs and indentations to the paper.

Centering. Well-centred stamps have designs surrounded by equal opposite margins. Where this condition affects the price the fact is stated.

Type of perforating. Where necessary for classification, perforation types are distinguished. These include:

Line perforation from one line of pins punching single rows of holes at a time.

Comb perforation from pins disposed across the sheet in comb formation, punching out holes at three sides of the stamp a row at a time.

Harrow perforation applied to a whole pane or sheet at one stroke.

Rotary perforation from the toothed wheels operating across a sheet, then crosswise.

Sewing-machine perforation. The resultant condition, clean-cut or rough, is distinguished where required.

Pin-perforation is the commonly applied term for pin-roulette in which, instead of being punched out, round holes are pricked by sharp-pointed pins and no paper is removed.

Punctured stamps. Perforation holes can be punched into the face of the stamp. Patterns of small holes, often in the shape of initial letters, are privately applied devices against pilferage. These 'perfins' are outside the scope. Identification devices, when officially inspired, are listed or noted; they can be shapes, or letters or words formed from holes, sometimes converting one class of stamp into another.

Rouletting. In rouletting the paper is cut, for ease of separation, but none is removed. The gauge is measured, when needed, as for perforations. Traditional French terms descriptive of the type of cut are often used and types include:

Arc roulette (percé en arc). Cuts are minute, spaced arcs, each roughly a semicircle.

Cross roulette (percé en croix). Cuts are tiny diagonal crosses.

Line roulette (parcé en ligne or en ligne droite). Short straight cuts parallel to the frame of the stamp. The commonest basic roulette. Where not further described, 'roulette' means this type.

Rouletted in colour or coloured roulette (percé en lignes colorees or en lignes de coleur). Cuts with coloured edges, arising from notched rule inked simultaneously with the printing plate.

Saw-tooth roulette (percé en scie). Cuts applied zigzag fashion to resemble the teeth of a saw.

Serpentine roulette (percé en serpentin). Cuts as sharply wavy lines.

Zigzag roulettes (percé en zigzags). Short straight cuts at angles in alternate directions, producing sharp points on separation. US usage favours 'serrate(d) roulette' for this type.

Pin-roulette (originally *percé en points* and now *perforés trous d'epingle)* is commonly called pin-perforation in English.

4. Gum

All stamps listed are assumed to have gum of some kind; if they were issued without gum this is stated. Original gum (o.g.) means that which was present on the stamp as issued to the public. Deleterious climates and the presence of certain chemicals can cause gum to crack and, with early stamps, even make the paper deteriorate. Unscrupulous fakers are adept in removing it and regumming the stamp to meet the unreasoning demand often made for 'full o.g.' in cases where such a thing is virtually impossible.

Until recent times the gum used for stamps has been gum arabic, but various synthetic adhesives – tinted or invisible-looking – have been in use since the 1960s. Stamps existing with more than one type of gum are not normally listed separately, though the fact is noted where it is of philatelic significance, e.g. in distinguishing reprints or new printings.

The distinct variety of grilled gum is, however, recognised. In this the paper is passed through a gum breaker prior to printing to prevent subsequent curling. As the patterned rollers were sufficient to impress a grill into the paper beneath the gum we can quote prices for both unused and used examples.

Self-adhesive stamps are issued on backing paper from which they are peeled before affixing to mail. Unused examples are priced as for backing paper intact. Used examples are best kept on cover or on piece.

5. Watermarks

Stamps are on unwatermarked paper except where the heading to the set says otherwise.

Detection. Watermarks are detected for Catalogue description by one of four methods:

(1) holding stamps to the light;
(2) laying stamps face down on a dark background;
(3) adding a few drops of petroleum ether 40/60 to the stamp laid face down in a watermark tray; or
(4) by use of the Stanley Gibbons Detectamark, or other equipment, which works by revealing the thinning of the paper at the watermark. (Note that petroleum ether is highly inflammable in use and can damage photogravure stamps.)

Listable types. Stamps occurring on both watermarked and unwatermarked papers are different types and both receive full listing.

Single watermarks (devices occurring once on every stamp) can be modified in size and shape as between different issues; the types are noted but not usually separately listed. Fortuitous absence of watermark from a single stamp or its gross displacement would not be listable.

To overcome registration difficulties the device may be repeated at close intervals (a **multiple watermark**), single stamps thus showing parts of several devices. Similarly a large **sheet watermark** (or all-over watermark) covering numerous stamps can be used. We give informative notes and illustrations for them. The designs may be such that numbers of stamps in the sheet automatically lack watermark; this is not a listable variety. Multiple and all-over watermarks sometimes undergo modifications, but if the various types are difficult to distinguish from single stamps notes are given but not separate listings.

Papermakers' watermarks are noted where known but not listed separately, since most stamps in the sheet will lack them. Sheet watermarks which are nothing more than officially adopted papermakers' watermarks are, however, given normal listing.

Marginal watermarks, falling outside the pane of stamps, are ignored except where misplacement causes the adjoining row to be affected, in which case they may be footnoted.

Watermark errors and varieties. Watermark errors are recognised as of major importance. They comprise stamps intended to be on unwatermarked paper but issued watermarked by mistake, or stamps printed on paper with the wrong watermark. Watermark varieties, on the other hand, such as broken or deformed bits on the dandy roll, are not listable.

Watermark positions. Paper has a side intended for printing and watermarks are usually impressed so that they read normally when looked through from that printed side.

Illustrations in the Catalogue are of watermarks in normal positions (from the front of the stamps) and are actual size where possible.

Differences in watermark position are collectable as distinct varieties. In this Catalogue, however, only normal sideways watermarks are listed (and 'sideways inverted' is treated as 'sideways'). Inverted and reversed watermarks have always been outside its scope: in the early days of flat-bed printing, sheets of watermarked paper were fed indiscriminately through the press and the resulting watermark positions had no particular philatelic significance. Similarly, the special make-up of sheets for booklets can in some cases give equal quantities of normal and inverted watermarks.

6. Colours

Stamps in two or three colours have these named in order of appearance, from the centre moving outwards.

Four colours or more are usually listed as multicoloured.

In compound colour names the second is the predominant one, thus:

orange-red = a red tending towards orange;
red-orange = an orange containing more red than usual.

Standard colours used. The 200 colours most used for stamp identification are given in the Stanley Gibbons Colour Key. The Catalogue has used the Key as a standard for describing new issues for some years. The names are also introduced as lists are rewritten, though exceptions are made for those early issues where traditional names have become universally established.

Determining colours. When comparing actual stamps with colour samples in the Key, view in a good north daylight (or its best substitute: fluorescent 'colour-matching' light). Sunshine is not recommended. Choose a solid portion of the stamp design; if available, marginal markings such as solid bars of colour or colour check dots are helpful. Shading lines in the design can be misleading as they appear lighter than solid colour. Postmarked portions of a stamp appear darker than normal. If more than one colour is present, mask off the extraneous ones as the eye tends to mix them.

Errors of colour. Major colour errors in stamps or overprints which qualify for listing are: wrong colours; one colour inverted in relation to the rest; albinos (colourless impressions), where these have Expert Committee certificates; colours completely omitted, but only on unused stamps (if found on used stamps the information is footnoted).

Colours only partially omitted are not recognised.

Colour shifts, however spectacular, are not listed.

Shades. Shades in philately refer to variations in the intensity of a colour or the presence of differing amounts of other colours. They are particularly significant when they can be linked to specific printings. In general, shades need to be quite marked to fall within the scope of this Catalogue; it does not favour nowadays listing the often numerous shades of a stamp, but chooses a single applicable colour name which will indicate particular groups of outstanding shades. Furthermore, the listings refer to colours as issued: they may deteriorate into something different through the passage of time.

Modern colour printing by lithography is prone to marked differences of shade, even within a single run, and variations can occur within the same sheet. Such shades are not listed.

Aniline colours. An aniline colour meant originally one derived from coal-tar; it now refers more widely to colour of a particular brightness suffused on the surface of a stamp and showing through clearly on the back.

Colours of overprints and surcharges. All overprints and surcharges are in black unless otherwise in the heading or after the description of the stamp.

7. Luminescence

Machines which sort mail electronically have been introduced in recent years. In consequence some countries have issued stamps on fluorescent or phosphorescent papers, while others have marked their stamps with phosphor bands.

The various papers can only be distinguished by ultraviolet lamps emitting particular wavelengths. They are separately listed only when the stamps have some other means of distinguishing them, visible without the use of these lamps. Where this is not so, the papers are recorded in footnotes or headings. (Collectors using the lamps should exercise great care in their use as exposure to their light is extremely dangerous to the eyes).

Phosphor bands are listable, since they are visible to the naked eye (by holding stamps at an angle to the light and looking along them, the bands appear dark). Stamps existing with and without phosphor bands or with differing numbers of bands are given separate listings. Varieties such as double bands, misplaced or omitted bands, bands printed on the wrong side, are not listed.

8. Coil Stamps

Stamps issued only in coil form are given full listing. If stamps are issued in both sheets and coils the coil stamps are listed separately only where there is some feature (e.g. perforation) by which singles can be distinguished. Coil strips containing different stamps *se-tenant* are also listed.

Coil join pairs are too random and too easily faked to permit of listing; similarly ignored are coil stamps which have accidentally suffered an extra row of perforations from the claw mechanism in a malfunctioning vending machine.

9. Booklet Stamps

Single stamps from booklets are listed if they are distinguishable in some way (such as watermark or perforation) from similar sheet stamps. Booklet panes, provided they are distinguishable from blocks of sheet stamps, are listed for most countries; booklet panes containing more than one value *se-tenant* are listed under the lowest of the values concerned.

Lists of stamp booklets are given for certain countries and it is intended to extend this generally.

10. Forgeries and Fakes

Forgeries. Where space permits, notes are considered if they can give a concise description that will permit unequivocal detection of a forgery. Generalised warnings, lacking detail, are not nowadays inserted since their value to the collector is problematic.

Fakes. Unwitting fakes are numerous, particularly 'new shades' which are colour changelings brought about by exposure to sunlight, soaking in water contaminated with dyes from adherent paper, contact with oil and dirt from a pocketbook, and so on. Fraudulent operators, in addition, can offer to arrange: removal of hinge marks; repairs of thins on white or coloured papers; replacement of missing margins or perforations; reperforating in true or false gauges; removal of fiscal cancellations; rejoining of severed pairs, strips and blocks; and (a major hazard) regumming. Collectors can only be urged to purchase from reputable sources and to insist upon Expert Committee certification where there is any doubt.

The Catalogue can consider footnotes about fakes where these are specific enough to assist in detection.

PRICES

Prices quoted in this Catalogue are the selling prices of Stanley Gibbons Ltd at the time when the book went to press. They are for stamps in fine condition for the issue concerned; in issues where condition varies they may ask more for the superb and less for the sub-standard.

All prices are subject to change without prior notice and Stanley Gibbons Ltd may from time to time offer stamps at other than catalogue prices in consequence of special purchases or particular promotions.

No guarantee is given to supply all stamps priced, since it is not possible to keep every catalogued item in stock. Commemorative issues may, at times, only be available in complete sets and not as individual values.

Quotations of prices. The prices in the left-hand column are for unused stamps and those in the right-hand column are for used.

Prices are expressed in pounds and pence sterling. One pound comprises 100 pence (£1 = 100p).

The method of notation is as follows: pence in numerals (e.g. 10 denotes ten pence); pounds and pence up to £100, in numerals (e.g. 4·25 denotes four pounds and twenty-five pence); prices above £100 expressed in whole pounds with the '£' sign shown.

Unused stamps. Prices for stamps issued up to the end of the Second World War (1945) are for lightly hinged examples and more may be asked if they are in unmounted mint condition. Prices for all later unused stamps are for unmounted mint. Where not available in this condition, lightly hinged stamps are often available at a lower price.

Used stamps. The used prices are normally for stamps postally used but may be for stamps cancelled-to-order where this practice exists.

A pen-cancellation on early issues can sometimes correctly denote postal use. Instances are individually noted in the Catalogue in explanation of the used price given.

Prices quoted for bisects on cover or on large piece are for those dated during the period officially authorised.

Stamps not sold unused to the public but affixed by postal officials before use (e.g. some parcel post stamps) are priced used only.

Minimum price. The minimum catalogue price quoted is 10p. For individual stamps prices between 10p and 95p are provided as a guide for catalogue users. The lowest price charged for individual stamps purchased from Stanley Gibbons Ltd. is £1.

Set prices. Set prices are generally for one of each value, excluding shades and varieties, but including major colour changes. Where there are alternative shades, etc, the cheapest is usually included. The number of stamps in the set is always stated for clarity.

Where prices are given for *se-tenant* blocks or strips any mint price quoted is for the complete *se-tenant* strip or block. Mint and used set prices are always for a set of single stamps.

Repricing. Collectors will be aware that the market factors of supply and demand directly influence the prices quoted in this Catalogue. Whatever the scarcity of a particular stamp, if there is no one in the market who wishes to buy it it cannot be expected to achieve a high price. Conversely, the same item actively sought by numerous potential buyers may cause the price to rise.

All the prices in this Catalogue are examined during the preparation of each new edition by expert staff of Stanley Gibbons and repriced as necessary. They take many factors into account, including supply and demand, and are in close touch with the international stamp market and the auction world.

GUARANTEE

All stamps are guaranteed genuine originals in the following terms:

If not as described, and returned by the purchaser, we undertake to refund the price paid to us in the original transaction. If any stamp is certified as genuine by the Expert Committee of the Royal Philatelic Society, London, or by B.P.A. Expertising Ltd, the purchaser shall not be entitled to make claim against us for any error, omission or mistake in such certificate. Consumers' statutory rights are not affected by this guarantee.

The establishment Expert Committees in this country are those of the Royal Philatelic Society, 41 Devonshire Place, London W19 6JY, and B.P.A. Expertising Ltd, PO Box 1141, Guildford, Surrey GU5 0WR. They do not undertake valuations under any circumstances and fees are payable for their services.

Abbreviations

Printers

A.B.N. Co.	American Bank Note Co, New York.
B.A.B.N.	British American Bank Note Co. Ottawa
B.D.T.	B.D.T. International Security Printing Ltd, Dublin, Ireland
B.W.	Bradbury Wilkinson & Co, Ltd.
Cartor	Cartor S.A., La Loupe, France
C.B.N.	Canadian Bank Note Co, Ottawa.
Continental	Continental Bank Note Co. B.N. Co.
Courvoisier	Imprimerie Courvoisier S.A., La-Chaux-de-Fonds, Switzerland.
D.L.R.	De La Rue & Co, Ltd, London.
Enschedé	Joh. Enschedé en Zonen, Haarlem, Netherlands.
Format	Format International Security Printers Ltd., London
Harrison	Harrison & Sons, Ltd. London
J.W.	John Waddington Security Print Ltd., Leeds
P.B.	Perkins Bacon Ltd, London.
Questa	Questa Colour Security Printers Ltd, London
Walsall	Walsall Security Printers Ltd
Waterlow	Waterlow & Sons, Ltd, London.

General Abbreviations

Alph	Alphabet
Anniv	Anniversary
Comp	Compound (perforation)
Des	Designer; designed
Diag	Diagonal; diagonally
Eng	Engraver; engraved
F.C.	Fiscal Cancellation
H/S	Handstamped
Horiz	Horizontal; horizontally
Imp, Imperf	Imperforate
Inscr	Inscribed
L	Left
Litho	Lithographed
mm	Millimetres
MS	Miniature sheet
N.Y.	New York
Opt(d)	Overprint(ed)
P or P-c	Pen-cancelled
P, Pf or Perf	Perforated
Photo	Photogravure
Pl	Plate
Pr	Pair
Ptd	Printed
Ptg	Printing
R	Right
R.	Row
Recess	Recess-printed
Roto	Rotogravure
Roul	Rouletted
S	Specimen (overprint)
Surch	Surcharge(d)
T.C.	Telegraph Cancellation
T	Type
Typo	Typographed
Un	Unused
Us	Used
Vert	Vertical; vertically
W or wmk	Watermark
Wmk s	Watermark sideways

(†) = Does not exist
(–) (or blank price column) = Exists, or may exist, but no market price is known.
/ between colours means 'on' and the colour following is that of the paper on which the stamp is printed.

Colours of Stamps
Bl (blue); blk (black); brn (brown); car, carm (carmine); choc (chocolate); clar (claret); emer (emerald); grn (green); ind (indigo); mag (magenta); mar (maroon); mult (multicoloured); mve (mauve); ol (olive); orge (orange); pk (pink); pur (purple); scar (scarlet); sep (sepia); turq (turquoise); ultram (ultramarine); verm (vermilion); vio (violet); yell (yellow).

Colour of Overprints and Surcharges
(B.) = blue, (Blk.) = black, (Br.) = brown, (C.) = carmine, (G.) = green, (Mag.) = magenta, (Mve.) = mauve, (Ol.) = olive, (O.) = orange, (P.) = purple, (Pk.) = pink, (R.) = red, (Sil.) = silver, (V.) = violet, (Vm.) or (Verm.) = vermilion, (W.) = white, (Y.) = yellow.

Arabic Numerals
As in the case of European figures, the details of the Arabic numerals vary in different stamp designs, but they should be readily recognised with the aid of this illustration.

٠ ١ ٢ ٣ ٤ ٥ ٦ ٧ ٨ ٩
0 1 2 3 4 5 6 7 8 9

International Philatelic Glossary

English	French	German	Spanish	Italian
Agate	Agate	Achat	Agata	Agata
Air stamp	Timbre de la poste aérienne	Flugpostmarke	Sello de correo aéreo	Francobollo per posta aerea
Apple Green	Vert-pomme	Apfelgrün	Verde manzana	Verde mela
Barred	Annulé par barres	Balkenentwertung	Anulado con barras	Sbarrato
Bisected	Timbre coupé	Halbiert	Partido en dos	Frazionato
Bistre	Bistre	Bister	Bistre	Bistro
Bistre-brown	Brun-bistre	Bisterbraun	Castaño bistre	Bruno-bistro
Black	Noir	Schwarz	Negro	Nero
Blackish Brown	Brun-noir	Schwärzlichbraun	Castaño negruzco	Bruno nerastro
Blackish Green	Vert foncé	Schwärzlichgrün	Verde negruzco	Verde nerastro
Blackish Olive	Olive foncé	Schwärzlicholiv	Oliva negruzco	Oliva nerastro
Block of four	Bloc de quatre	Viererblock	Bloque de cuatro	Bloco di quattro
Blue	Bleu	Blau	Azul	Azzurro
Blue-green	Vert-bleu	Blaugrün	Verde azul	Verde azzuro
Bluish Violet	Violet bleuâtre	Bläulichviolett	Violeta azulado	Violtto azzurrastro
Booklet	Carnet	Heft	Cuadernillo	Libretto
Bright Blue	Bleu vif	Lebhaftblau	Azul vivo	Azzurro vivo
Bright Green	Vert vif	Lebhaftgrün	Verde vivo	Verde vivo
Bright Purple	Mauve vif	Lebhaftpurpur	Púrpura vivo	Porpora vivo
Bronze Green	Vert-bronze	Bronzegrün	Verde bronce	Verde bronzo
Brown	Brun	Braun	Castaño	Bruno
Brown-lake	Carmin-brun	Braunlack	Laca castaño	Lacca bruno
Brown-purple	Pourpre-brun	Braunpurpur	Púrpura castaño	Porpora bruno
Brown-red	Rouge-brun	Braunrot	Rojo castaño	Rosso bruno
Buff	Chamois	Sämisch	Anteado	Camoscio
Cancellation	Oblitération	Entwertung	Cancelación	Annullamento
Cancelled	Annulé	Gestempelt	Cancelado	Annullato
Carmine	Carmin	Karmin	Carmín	Carminio
Carmine-red	Rouge-carmin	Karminrot	Rojo carmín	Rosso carminio
Centred	Centré	Zentriert	Centrado	Centrato
Cerise	Rouge-cerise	Kirschrot	Color de ceresa	Color Ciliegia
Chalk-surfaced paper	Papier couché	Kreidepapier	Papel estucado	Carta gessata
Chalky Blue	Bleu terne	Kreideblau	Azul turbio	Azzurro smorto
Charity stamp	Timbre de bienfaisance	Wohltätigkeitsmarke	Sello de beneficenza	Francobollo di beneficenza
Chestnut	Marron	Kastanienbraun	Castaño rojo	Marrone
Chocolate	Chocolat	Schokolade	Chocolate	Cioccolato
Cinnamon	Cannelle	Zimtbraun	Canela	Cannella
Claret	Grenat	Weinrot	Rojo vinoso	Vinaccia
Cobalt	Cobalt	Kobalt	Cobalto	Cobalto
Colour	Couleur	Farbe	Color	Colore
Comb-perforation	Dentelure en peigne	Kammzähnung, Reihenzähnung	Dentado de peine	Dentellatura e pettine
Commemorative stamp	Timbre commémoratif	Gedenkmarke	Sello conmemorativo	Francobollo commemorativo
Crimson	Cramoisi	Karmesin	Carmesí	Cremisi
Deep Blue	Blue foncé	Dunkelblau	Azul oscuro	Azzurro scuro
Deep bluish Green	Vert-bleu foncé	Dunkelbläulichgrün	Verde azulado oscuro	Verde azzurro scuro
Design	Dessin	Markenbild	Diseño	Disegno

International Philatelic Glossary

English	French	German	Spanish	Italian
Die	Matrice	Urstempel. Type, Platte	Cuño	Conio, Matrice
Double	Double	Doppelt	Doble	Doppio
Drab	Olive terne	Trüboliv	Oliva turbio	Oliva smorto
Dull Green	Vert terne	Trübgrün	Verde turbio	Verde smorto
Dull purple	Mauve terne	Trübpurpur	Púrpura turbio	Porpora smorto
Embossing	Impression en relief	Prägedruck	Impresión en relieve	Impressione a relievo
Emerald	Vert-eméraude	Smaragdgrün	Esmeralda	Smeraldo
Engraved	Gravé	Graviert	Grabado	Inciso
Error	Erreur	Fehler, Fehldruck	Error	Errore
Essay	Essai	Probedruck	Ensayo	Saggio
Express letter stamp	Timbre pour lettres par exprès	Eilmarke	Sello de urgencia	Francobollo per espresso
Fiscal stamp	Timbre fiscal	Stempelmarke	Sello fiscal	Francobollo fiscale
Flesh	Chair	Fleischfarben	Carne	Carnicino
Forgery	Faux, Falsification	Fälschung	Falsificación	Falso, Falsificazione
Frame	Cadre	Rahmen	Marco	Cornice
Granite paper	Papier avec fragments de fils de soie	Faserpapier	Papel con filamentos	Carto con fili di seta
Green	Vert	Grün	Verde	Verde
Greenish Blue	Bleu verdâtre	Grünlichblau	Azul verdoso	Azzurro verdastro
Greenish Yellow	Jaune-vert	Grünlichgelb	Amarillo verdoso	Giallo verdastro
Grey	Gris	Grau	Gris	Grigio
Grey-blue	Bleu-gris	Graublau	Azul gris	Azzurro grigio
Grey-green	Vert gris	Graugrün	Verde gris	Verde grigio
Gum	Gomme	Gummi	Goma	Gomma
Gutter	Interpanneau	Zwischensteg	Espacio blanco entre dos grupos	Ponte
Imperforate	Non-dentelé	Geschnitten	Sin dentar	Non dentellato
Indigo	Indigo	Indigo	Azul indigo	Indaco
Inscription	Inscription	Inschrift	Inscripción	Dicitura
Inverted	Renversé	Kopfstehend	Invertido	Capovolto
Issue	Émission	Ausgabe	Emisión	Emissione
Laid	Vergé	Gestreift	Listado	Vergato
Lake	Lie de vin	Lackfarbe	Laca	Lacca
Lake-brown	Brun-carmin	Lackbraun	Castaño laca	Bruno lacca
Lavender	Bleu-lavande	Lavendel	Color de alhucema	Lavanda
Lemon	Jaune-citron	Zitrongelb	Limón	Limone
Light Blue	Bleu clair	Hellblau	Azul claro	Azzurro chiaro
Lilac	Lilas	Lila	Lila	Lilla
Line perforation	Dentelure en lignes	Linienzähnung	Dentado en linea	Dentellatura lineare
Lithography	Lithographie	Steindruck	Litografía	Litografia
Local	Timbre de poste locale	Lokalpostmarke	Emisión local	Emissione locale
Lozenge roulette	Percé en losanges	Rautenförmiger Durchstich	Picadura en rombos	Perforazione a losanghe
Magenta	Magenta	Magentarot	Magenta	Magenta
Margin	Marge	Rand	Borde	Margine
Maroon	Marron pourpré	Dunkelrotpurpur	Púrpura rojo oscuro	Marrone rossastro
Mauve	Mauve	Malvenfarbe	Malva	Malva
Multicoloured	Polychrome	Mehrfarbig	Multicolores	Policromo
Myrtle Green	Vert myrte	Myrtengrün	Verde mirto	Verde mirto
New Blue	Bleu ciel vif	Neublau	Azul nuevo	Azzurro nuovo
Newspaper stamp	Timbre pour journaux	Zeitungsmarke	Sello para periódicos	Francobollo per giornali
Obliteration	Oblitération	Abstempelung	Matasello	Annullamento
Obsolete	Hors (de) cours	Ausser Kurs	Fuera de curso	Fuori corso

International Philatelic Glossary

English	French	German	Spanish	Italian
Ochre	Ocre	Ocker	Ocre	Ocra
Official stamp	Timbre de service	Dienstmarke	Sello de servicio	Francobollo di
Olive-brown	Brun-olive	Olivbraun	Castaño oliva	Bruno oliva
Olive-green	Vert-olive	Olivgrün	Verde oliva	Verde oliva
Olive-grey	Gris-olive	Olivgrau	Gris oliva	Grigio oliva
Olive-yellow	Jaune-olive	Olivgelb	Amarillo oliva	Giallo oliva
Orange	Orange	Orange	Naranja	Arancio
Orange-brown	Brun-orange	Orangebraun	Castaño naranja	Bruno arancio
Orange-red	Rouge-orange	Orangerot	Rojo naranja	Rosso arancio
Orange-yellow	Jaune-orange	Orangegelb	Amarillo naranja	Giallo arancio
Overprint	Surcharge	Aufdruck	Sobrecarga	Soprastampa
Pair	Paire	Paar	Pareja	Coppia
Pale	Pâle	Blass	Pálido	Pallido
Pane	Panneau	Gruppe	Grupo	Gruppo
Paper	Papier	Papier	Papel	Carta
Parcel post stamp	Timbre pour colis postaux	Paketmarke	Sello para paquete postal	Francobollo per pacchi postali
Pen-cancelled	Oblitéré à plume	Federzugentwertung	Cancelado a pluma	Annullato a penna
Percé en arc	Percé en arc	Bogenförmiger Durchstich	Picadura en forma de arco	Perforazione ad arco
Percé en scie	Percé en scie	Bogenförmiger Durchstich	Picado en sierra	Foratura a sega
Perforated	Dentelé	Gezähnt	Dentado	Dentellato
Perforation	Dentelure	Zähnung	Dentar	Dentellatura
Photogravure	Photogravure, Heliogravure	Rastertiefdruck	Fotograbado	Rotocalco
Pin perforation	Percé en points	In Punkten durchstochen	Horadado con alfileres	Perforato a punti
Plate	Planche	Platte	Plancha	Lastra, Tavola
Plum	Prune	Pflaumenfarbe	Color de ciruela	Prugna
Postage Due stamp	Timbre-taxe	Portomarke	Sello de tasa	Segnatasse
Postage stamp	Timbre-poste	Briefmarke, Freimarke, Postmarke	Sello de correos	Francobollo postale
Postal fiscal stamp	Timbre fiscal-postal	Stempelmarke als Postmarke verwendet	Sello fiscal-postal	Fiscale postale
Postmark	Oblitération postale	Poststempel	Matasello	Bollo
Printing	Impression, Tirage	Druck	Impresión	Stampa, Tiratura
Proof	Épreuve	Druckprobe	Prueba de impresión	Prova
Provisionals	Timbres provisoires	Provisorische Marken. Provisorien	Provisionales	Provvisori
Prussian Blue	Bleu de Prusse	Preussischblau	Azul de Prusia	Azzurro di Prussia
Purple	Pourpre	Purpur	Púrpura	Porpora
Purple-brown	Brun-pourpre	Purpurbraun	Castaño púrpura	Bruno porpora
Recess-printing	Impression en taille douce	Tiefdruck	Grabado	Incisione
Red	Rouge	Rot	Rojo	Rosso
Red-brown	Brun-rouge	Rotbraun	Castaño rojizo	Bruno rosso
Reddish Lilac	Lilas rougeâtre	Rötlichlila	Lila rojizo	Lilla rossastro
Reddish Purple	Poupre-rouge	Rötlichpurpur	Púrpura rojizo	Porpora rossastro
Reddish Violet	Violet rougeâtre	Rötlichviolett	Violeta rojizo	Violetto rossastro
Red-orange	Orange rougeâtre	Rotorange	Naranja rojizo	Arancio rosso
Registration stamp	Timbre pour lettre chargée (recommandée)	Einschreibemarke	Sello de certificado lettere	Francobollo per raccomandate
Reprint	Réimpression	Neudruck	Reimpresión	Ristampa
Reversed	Retourné	Umgekehrt	Invertido	Rovesciato
Rose	Rose	Rosa	Rosa	Rosa
Rose-red	Rouge rosé	Rosarot	Rojo rosado	Rosso rosa
Rosine	Rose vif	Lebhaftrosa	Rosa vivo	Rosa vivo
Roulette	Percage	Durchstich	Picadura	Foratura
Rouletted	Percé	Durchstochen	Picado	Forato
Royal Blue	Bleu-roi	Königblau	Azul real	Azzurro reale

xvii

International Philatelic Glossary

English	French	German	Spanish	Italian
Sage green	Vert-sauge	Salbeigrün	Verde salvia	Verde salvia
Salmon	Saumon	Lachs	Salmón	Salmone
Scarlet	Écarlate	Scharlach	Escarlata	Scarlatto
Sepia	Sépia	Sepia	Sepia	Seppia
Serpentine roulette	Percé en serpentin	Schlangenliniger Durchstich	Picado a serpentina	Perforazione a serpentina
Shade	Nuance	Tönung	Tono	Gradazione de colore
Sheet	Feuille	Bogen	Hoja	Foglio
Slate	Ardoise	Schiefer	Pizarra	Ardesia
Slate-blue	Bleu-ardoise	Schieferblau	Azul pizarra	Azzurro ardesia
Slate-green	Vert-ardoise	Schiefergrün	Verde pizarra	Verde ardesia
Slate-lilac	Lilas-gris	Schierferlila	Lila pizarra	Lilla ardesia
Slate-purple	Mauve-gris	Schieferpurpur	Púrpura pizarra	Porpora ardesia
Slate-violet	Violet-gris	Schieferviolett	Violeta pizarra	Violetto ardesia
Special delivery stamp	Timbre pour exprès	Eilmarke	Sello de urgencia	Francobollo per espressi
Specimen	Spécimen	Muster	Muestra	Saggio
Steel Blue	Bleu acier	Stahlblau	Azul acero	Azzurro acciaio
Strip	Bande	Streifen	Tira	Striscia
Surcharge	Surcharge	Aufdruck	Sobrecarga	Soprastampa
Tête-bêche	Tête-bêche	Kehrdruck	Tête-bêche	Tête-bêche
Tinted paper	Papier teinté	Getöntes Papier	Papel coloreado	Carta tinta
Too-late stamp	Timbre pour lettres en retard	Verspätungsmarke	Sello para cartas retardadas	Francobollo per le lettere in ritardo
Turquoise-blue	Bleu-turquoise	Türkisblau	Azul turquesa	Azzurro turchese
Turquoise-green	Vert-turquoise	Türkisgrün	Verde turquesa	Verde turchese
Typography	Typographie	Buchdruck	Tipografia	Tipografia
Ultramarine	Outremer	Ultramarin	Ultramar	Oltremare
Unused	Neuf	Ungebraucht	Nuevo	Nuovo
Used	Oblitéré, Usé	Gebraucht	Usado	Usato
Venetian Red	Rouge-brun terne	Venezianischrot	Rojo veneciano	Rosso veneziano
Vermilion	Vermillon	Zinnober	Cinabrio	Vermiglione
Violet	Violet	Violett	Violeta	Violetto
Violet-blue	Bleu-violet	Violettblau	Azul violeta	Azzurro violetto
Watermark	Filigrane	Wasserzeichen	Filigrana	Filigrana
Watermark sideways	Filigrane couché	Wasserzeichen liegend	Filigrana acostado	Filigrana coricata
Wove paper	Papier ordinaire, Papier uni	Einfaches Papier	Papel avitelado	Carta unita
Yellow	Jaune	Gelb	Amarillo	Giallo
Yellow-brown	Brun-jaune	Gelbbraun	Castaño amarillo	Bruno giallo
Yellow-green	Vert-jaune	Gelbgrün	Verde amarillo	Verde giallo
Yellow-olive	Olive-jaunâtre	Gelboliv	Oliva amarillo	Oliva giallastro
Yellow-orange	Orange jaunâtre	Gelborange	Naranja amarillo	Arancio giallastro
Zig-zag roulette	Percé en zigzag	Sägezahnartiger Durchstich	Picado en zigzag	Perforazione a zigzag

Stanley Gibbons Stamp Catalogues

Commonwealth & British Empire Stamps 1840–1970 (122nd edition, 2020)

King George VI (9th edition, 2018)

Commonwealth Country Catalogues
Australia & Dependencies (11th Edition, 2018)
Bangladesh, Pakistan & Sri Lanka (3rd edition, 2015)
Belize, Guyana, Trinidad & Tobago (2nd edition, 2013)
Brunei, Malaysia & Singapore (5th edition, 2017)
Canada (6th edition, 2016)
Cyprus, Gibraltar & Malta (5th edition, 2019)
East Africa with Egypt & Sudan (4th edition, 2018)
Eastern Pacific (3rd edition, 2015)
Falkland Islands (8th edition, 2019)
Hong Kong (6th edition, 2018)
India (including Convention & Feudatory States) (5th edition, 2018)
Indian Ocean (3rd edition, 2016)
Ireland (7th edition, 2019)
Leeward Islands (3rd edition, 2017)
New Zealand (6th edition, 2016)
Northern Caribbean, Bahamas & Bermuda (4th edition, 2016)
St. Helena & Dependencies (6th edition, 2017)
Southern & Central Africa (2nd edition, 2014)
West Africa (2nd edition, 2012)
Western Pacific (4th edition, 2017)
Windward Islands & Barbados (3rd edition, 2015)

Stamps of the World 2019
Volume 1 Abu Dhabi – Charkhari
Volume 2 Chile – Georgia
Volume 3 German Commands – Jasdan
Volume 4 Jersey – New Republic
Volume 5 New South Wales – Singapore
Volume 6 Sirmoor – Zululand

Great Britain Catalogues
2019 Collect British Stamps (70th edition, 2019)
Collect Channel Islands & Isle of Man (30th edition, 2016)
2019 GB Concise (34th edition, 2019)

Great Britain Specialised
Volume 1 Queen Victoria (16th edition, 2011)
Volume 2 King Edward VII to King George VI (14th edition, 2015)
Volume 3 Queen Elizabeth II Pre-decimal issues (13th edition, 2019)
Volume 4 Queen Elizabeth II Decimal Definitive Issues – Part 1 (10th edition, 2008)
          Queen Elizabeth II Decimal Definitive Issues – Part 2 (10th edition, 2010)

Foreign Countries
Antarctica (2nd edition, 2012)
Arabia (1st edition, 2016)
Austria and Hungary (8th Edition 2014)
Belgium & Luxembourg (1st edition, 2015)
Central America (3rd edition, 2007)
China (12th edition, 2018)
Czech Republic and Slovakia (1st edition, 2017)
Denmark and Norway (1st edition, 2018)
Finland and Sweden (1st edition, 2017)
France, Andorra and Monaco (1st edition, 2015)
French Colonies (1st edition, 2016)
Germany (12th edition, 2018)
Japan & Korea (5th edition, 2008)
Middle East (1st Edition, 2018)
Netherlands & Colonies (1st edition, 2017)
North East Africa (2nd edition 2017)
Poland (1st edition, 2015)
Russia (7th edition, 2014)
South-East Asia (5th edition, 2012)
Southern Balkans (1st edition, 2019)
Spain and Colonies (1st edition, 2019)
United States of America (8th edition, 2015)

We have catalogues to suit every aspect of stamp collecting

Our catalogues cover stamps issued from across the globe - from the Penny Black to the latest issues. Whether you're a specialist in a certain reign or a thematic collector, we should have something to suit your needs. All catalogues include the famous SG numbering system, making it as easy as possible to find the stamp you're looking for.

BY APPOINTMENT TO
HER MAJESTY THE QUEEN
PHILATELISTS
STANLEY GIBBONS LTD
LONDON

STANLEY GIBBONS
THE HOME OF STAMP COLLECTING

STANLEY GIBBONS | 399 Strand | London | WC2R 0LX
www.stanleygibbons.com

 @StanleyGibbons    /StanleyGibbonsGroup    @StanleyGibbons

Guide to Entries

Ⓐ Country of Issue – When a country changes its name, the catalogue listing changes to reflect the name change, for example Cambodia was formerly known as Kampuchea, the stamps in South East Asia are all listed under Cambodia, but spilt into Kampuchea and then Cambodia. When a country spilts, for example Czechoslovakia split into Czech Republic and Slovakia, there will be a listing for Czechoslovakia and then separate sections for Czech Republic and Slovakia.

Ⓑ Currency – Details of the currency, and dates of earliest use where applicable, on the face value of the stamps.

Ⓒ Country Information – Brief geographical and historical details for the issuing country.

Ⓓ Illustration – Generally, the first stamp in the set. Stamp illustrations are reduced to 75%, with overprints and surcharges shown actual size.

Ⓔ Illustration or Type Number – These numbers are used to help identify stamps, either in the listing, type column, design line or footnote, usually the first value in a set. These type numbers are in a bold type face – **123**; when bracketed (**123**) an overprint or a surcharge is indicated. Some type numbers include a lower-case letter – **123a**, this indicates they have been added to an existing set. New cross references are also shown in bold.

Ⓕ Date of issue – This is the date that the stamp/set of stamps was issued by the post office and was available for purchase. When a set of definitive stamps has been issued over several years the Year Date given is for the earliest issue. Commemorative sets are listed in chronological order. Stamps of the same design, or issue are usually grouped together, for example one of the French Marianne definitive series' was first issued in 2002 but includes stamps issued to the end of 2004.

Ⓖ Number Prefix – Stamps other than definitives and commemoratives have a prefix letter before the catalogue number. Their use is explained in the text: some examples are A for airmail, E for East Germany or Express Delivery stamps.

Ⓗ Footnote – Further information on background or key facts on issues.

Ⓘ Stanley Gibbons Catalogue number – This is a unique number for each stamp to help the collector identify stamps in the listing. The Stanley Gibbons numbering system is universally recognised as definitive. Where insufficient numbers have been left to provide for additional stamps to a listing, some stamps will have a suffix letter after the catalogue number (for example 214a). If numbers have been left for additions to a set and not used they will be left vacant. The separate type numbers (in bold) refer to illustrations (see **E**).

Ⓙ Colour – If a stamp is printed in three or fewer colours then the colours are listed, working from the centre of the stamp outwards (see **R**).

Ⓚ Design line – Further details on design variations

Ⓛ Key Type – Indicates a design type on which the stamp is based. These are the bold figures found below each illustration, for example listed in Cameroun, in the Germany catalogue is the Key type A and B showing the ex-Kaiser's yacht *Hohenzollern*. The type numbers are also given in bold in the second column of figures alongside the stamp description to indicate the design of each stamp. Where an issue comprises stamps of similar design, the corresponding type number should be taken as indicating the general design. Where there are blanks in the type number column it means that the type of the corresponding stamp is that shown by the number in the type column of the same issue. A dash (–) in the type column means that the stamp is not illustrated. Where type numbers refer to stamps of another country, e.g. where stamps of one country are overprinted for use in another, this is always made clear in the text.

Ⓜ Coloured Papers – Stamps printed on coloured paper are shown – e.g. 'brown/*yellow*' indicates brown printed on yellow paper.

Ⓝ Surcharges and Overprints – Usually described in the headings. Any actual wordings are shown in bold type. Descriptions clarify words and figures used in the overprint. Stamps with the same overprints in different colours are not listed separately. Numbers in brackets after the descriptions are the catalogue numbers of the non-overprinted stamps. The words 'inscribed' or 'inscription' refer to the wording incorporated in the design of a stamp and not surcharges or overprints.

Ⓞ Face value – This refers to the value of each stamp and is the price it was sold for at the Post Office when issued. Some modern stamps do not have their values in figures but instead shown as a letter, shown as a letter, for example Great Britain use 1st or 2nd on their stamps as apposed to the actual value.

Ⓟ Catalogue Value – Mint/Unused. Prices quoted for pre-1945 stamps are for lightly hinged examples.

Ⓠ Catalogue Value – Used. Prices generally refer to fine postally used examples. For certain issues they are for cancelled-to-order.

Prices
Prices are given in pence and pounds. Stamps worth £100 and over are shown in whole pounds:

Shown in Catalogue as	Explanation
10	10 pence
1·75	£1·75
15·00	£15
£150	£150
£2300	£2300

Prices assume stamps are in 'fine condition'; we may ask more for superb and less for those of lower quality. The minimum catalogue price quoted is 10p and is intended as a guide for catalogue users. The lowest price for individual stamps purchased from Stanley Gibbons is £1.
Prices quoted are for the cheapest variety of that particular stamp. Differences of watermark, perforation, or other details, often increase the value. Prices quoted for mint issues are for single examples. Those in *se-tenant* pairs, strips, blocks or sheets may be worth more. Where no prices are listed it is either because the stamps are not known to exist (usually shown by a †) in that particular condition, or, more usually, because there is no reliable information on which to base their value.
All prices are subject to change without prior notice and we cannot guarantee to supply all stamps as priced. Prices quoted in advertisements are also subject to change without prior notice.

Ⓡ Multicoloured – Nearly all modern stamps are multicoloured (more than three colours); this is indicated in the heading, with a description of the stamp given in the listing.

Ⓢ Perforations – Please see page ix for a detailed explanation of perforations.

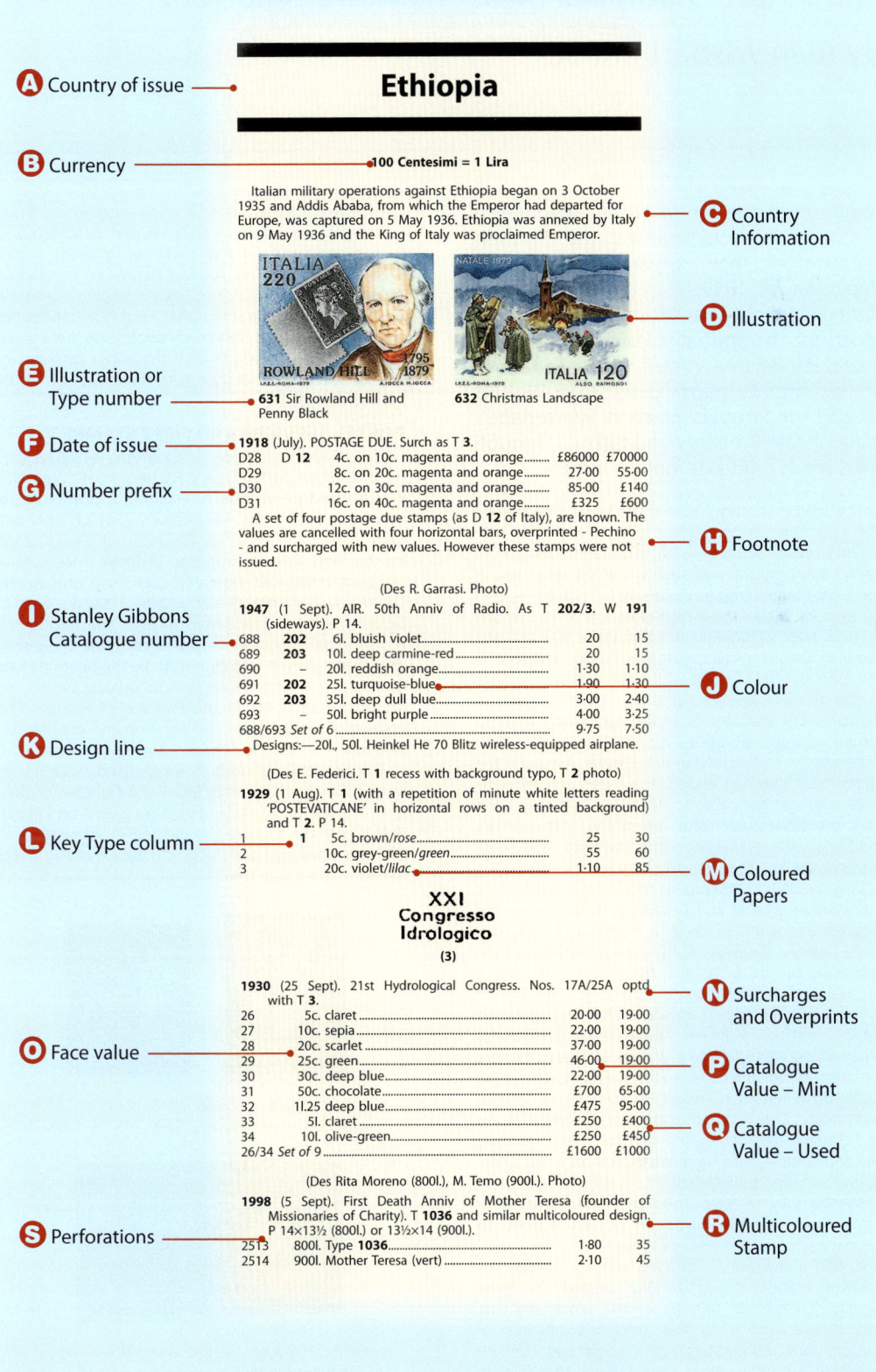

The Strubel stamps of Switzerland, 1854 to 1862
By Alan Wishart FRPSL

Although the design of 1854–1862 stamps of Switzerland, nicknamed the Strubels because of their apparent wild-haired depiction of Helvetica, did not change during its eight-year lifespan, there is still much for the specialist collector to study, especially when it comes to the variations in the security paper used. Alan Wishart reveals the Strubels' place in Switzerland's early philatelic history and talks us through the various printings that were made.

Switzerland as we know it came into being with the Old Swiss Confederacy, which was formed in the late 14th century. From 1353 to 1481 it was a confederation of eight cantons which was able to use any weakness in the Holy Roman Empire in central Europe to expand its territory. It became a confederation of 13 cantons in 1515 after victories in the Burgundy War and the Swabian War. The Reformation in Europe led to civil war amongst the cantons, which avoided involvement in the Thirty Years War, although, at the Treaty of Westphalia in 1648, the Swiss delegation was granted formal recognition of the confederacy as a state independent of the Holy Roman Empire. Although the Thirty Years War had ended, there was still religious strife amongst the cantons, which did not really end until the Napoleonic Wars. From the 15th century the Swiss were relatively neutral, but until 1860 Swiss mercenaries fought in almost every European war.

The French had taken over small parts of the Swiss Confederacy in 1793, but in 1798, with the aid of the Republican faction in Vaud, a French Revolutionary Army invaded the Swiss Confederacy. There was little resistance by the Swiss and the French proclaimed the Helvetic Republic on 12 April 1798. The French introduced a centralised administration that had been established throughout France and the occupied areas. When all the cantonal and private postal services were replaced by the French system the Swiss began to resist, especially when Austrian and Russian troops entered Switzerland. This resulted in the Act of Mediation on 19 February 1803 when the cantons were restored and Switzerland became a confederation once again, but now made up of 19 cantons. In 1815, the Congress of Vienna fully re-established the independence of Switzerland and the European powers agreed to permanently recognise its neutrality.

In 1847 a civil war – *Sonderbundskrieg* – broke out between Protestant and Catholic cantons. The Swiss quickly realised that this made little sense and that they should show unity and strength to the rest of Europe. The war lasted less than a month and a debate was begun to draw up a new federal constitution.

The Federal Constitution of 1848 established Swiss citizenship in addition to cantonal citizenship; a federal central government was set up along with a central judiciary. The Federal Assembly introduced a uniform postal service in 1849; a single currency in 1852; a telegraph system in 1851; weights and measures were unified and in 1854 roads and canals were taken under federal control. In 1859 the mercenary service (*Reisläuferei*) was abolished with the exception of the Vatican Guard.

POSTAL SERVICES AND FIRST STAMPS

As Switzerland was divided into cantons, postal services were localised. In 1675, Beat Fischer von Reichenbach was granted permission to establish a private postal service in Bern – the 'Fischerpost' – which operated until 1832. Beate Fischer von Reichenbach was knighted by the Holy Roman Emperor, Leopold I, for setting up postal services between Germany and Spain. Other services existed and in June 1799 the Seat of Government was transferred to Bern and the Central Post Administration was established there. Some time after that, Lucerne was chosen to be the headquarters of all the mail at the Central Post Bureau, which was under the authority of the Minister of Finance. The volume of official mail was very high and private mail very low.

The first stamps used in Switzerland were issued by the Cantons of Zürich, Basel and Geneva for their own use. The Zürich 4r. and 6r. were issued on 1 March 1843 (*Fig 1*); the 'Double Geneva' (*Fig 2*) was issued on 30 September 1843 and the 2½r. 'Basel Dove' (*Fig 3*) was issued on the 1 July 1845.

Fig 1 The 1843 4r. and 6r. cantonal administration issue of Zurich

Fig 2 The 'Double Geneva' issue released on 30 September 1843

The Strubel stamps of Switzerland, 1854 to 1862

Fig 3 The 2½r. 'Basel Dove' town post issue of 1845

After the adoption of the federal constitution in 1848, it became possible for stamps to be issued which could be used throughout the confederation. These stamps were issued in 1850 with a Swiss cross and a posthorn in the design and either inscribed 'ORTS-POST' in German or 'POSTE LOCALE' in French with the value in 'RAYON' (*Fig 4*). On 1 January 1852, a single currency was introduced with the Swiss franc consisting of 100 rappen, which replaced the many former currencies in the cantons.

Fig 4 The 1850 2½r. issue of the Federal Administration

THE STRUBELS

In late 1851, Dr Kuster, the Director of the Federal Mint, visited Paris and London to research methods of stamp production. It is said that whilst visiting the Perkins Bacon Printing Works, he saw the designs of stamps for Barbados, Mauritius and Trinidad, which featured 'Britannia' and that these may have been the inspiration for the design of the Strubel stamps. A seated figure of Helvetia, the symbolic mother of Switzerland, featured on the design of the stamps, which were produced using a letterpress printing process with an uncoloured embossed printing of Helvetia and the text (*Fig 5*).

Fig 5 The 1854 definitives were produced by letterpress with the a seated figure of Helvetia, the symbolic mother of Switzerland, and the text embossed

The Strubel issue was printed on Dickinson paper. This had an embedded coloured silk thread running horizontally through the paper which acted as an anti-counterfeiting measure. They were all printed imperforate.

The Dickinson paper was produced by John Dickinson Stationery Limited, which was founded by John Dickinson (29 March 1782–11 January 1869). At the age of 15, he began an apprenticeship as a stationer with Messrs Harrison and Richardson in London and he was admitted to the Livery of the Stationers' Company in 1804. He established paper mills at Apsley, Nash Mill and Croxley in Hertfordshire with the backing of publisher, George Longman. John Dickinson patented methods of mechanising paper production as well as the making of paper containing silk threads for security purposes. In 1850, he also started mechanical envelope production which made gummed envelopes.

Strubel stamps were valid for postage from 15 September 1854 until 31 July 1863, when they were replaced by a new design.

The design shows a seated figure of Helvetia wearing a laurel wreath with a spear and shield. It is the effect of the wreath which caused the issue to be jokingly referred to as the 'Strubel' issue. This is a reference to Struwwelpeter – a frizzy-haired character from a popular mid-19th-century children's book.

Der Struwwelpeter

Der Struwwelpeter is a German children's book written by Heinrich Hoffman, which was originally published in 1845 under the title *Funny Stories and Droll Pictures*. It comprises of ten stories, which contain a strong moral based on the consequences of bad behaviour. The first story was entitled 'Struwwelpeter', which translates as 'shock-headed Peter' or 'Shaggy Peter' and describes a boy who does not comb his hair. The first edition was published privately in 1845 and was

xxiii

the first to use chromolithography to produce the multicoloured illustrations. The name was changed to *Der Struwwelpeter* for the third edition published in 1858 (*Fig 6*).

Fig 6 The nickname for the Strubels comes from the wild-haired book character, 'Struwwelpeter', created by Heinrich Hoffman in 1845

Heinrich Hoffmann (13 June 1809–20 September 1894), was born in Frankfurt am Main and studied medicine in Heidelberg and Halle. He became the doctor at the lunatic asylum in Frankfurt where he became a caring psychiatrist. He published poetry and satirical works before writing Struwwelpeter, which was followed by other popular children's books. Hoffmann was a well-connected member of Frankfurt society, belonging to several non-political public bodies including the Mozart Foundation. In Frankfurt there is a Heinrich-Hoffmann-Museum and a statue of Struwwelpeter stands in the centre of Frankfurt am Main.

THE STAMP ISSUE
Although the design stayed the same and all of the stamps are imperforate, the Strubels offer much for the specialist philatelist, including changes in printer and paper.

A total of seven values were issued between 1854 and 1862: 2r., 5r., 10r., 15r., 20r., 40r., and 1f. The first printing was produced by the University Print Office, Munich, in sheets of 10×10. Not long after, production of the stamps moved to the Swiss Federal Mint, Bern, which initially printed in sheets of 5×5 and then, from 1857, 10×5.

MUNICH PRINT
The first stamps printed in Munich were printed on thin to medium thick paper with emerald green silk threads:
• 5r. yellow-brown – however, a rare orange-brown shade is known (*Fig 7*), as is a colour error produced in blue.
• The 10r. bright blue
• 15r. rose.
• 40r., pale green – a rare pale yellow-green shade is also recorded in the Stanley Gibbon Catalogue.

According to the Swiss Zumstein catalogue, there is also a second Munich printing. This is virtually identical to the first Munich printing except for some variations, such as the hand-engraved frame lines being uniform, very good embossing, sharp and clear lozenges, and fresher colours.

Fig 7 A rare orange-brown shade of the 5r. produced during the first Munich print

BERN PRINTS
The first printings from Bern comprised four values printed on medium-weight paper with green silk threads. This printing was made with plates of 25 positions with orderly arrangement and variable spacing. In this printing, the frame lines are variable, with good to excellent embossing.
• 5r. grey-brown (issued 4.11.1854).
• 10r. milky blue (29.5.1855).
• 15r. pale rose (29.1.1855).
• 20r. orange (14.10.1854) (*Fig 8*).

Fig 8 The 20r. value from the first Bern with green thread Dickinson paper

The Strubel stamps of Switzerland, 1854 to 1862

These values were also reprinted in 1856 and 1857 on thin paper with bright green silk threads. Again, this printing was made with plates of 25, with orderly arrangement and variable spacing. The frame lines are also variable with fair embossing.
• 5r. grey-brown (6.56).
• 10r. blue (1857).
• 15r. rose (4.57).
• 20r. orange (6.56)

SECOND BERN PRINTING
A second printing period between 1855 and 1857 was made on thick paper with different coloured silk threads. The plates have 50 positions with a misaligned arrangement and narrow spacing. The printing shows variable frame lines with good to fair embossing.
• 5r. yellow brown with yellow silk threads (30.5.1855) – a deep brown shade with the same thread is also catalogued.
• 10r. blue with carmine silk threads (31.12.1855) – a pale blue shade is also catalogued.
• 40r. yellow-green with red thread (17.2.1855) (Fig 9).
• 1f. grey lilac with black thread (17.2.1855) – a lilac shade with black thread is also known.
The second printing also includes several values with changed colours of the silk threads:
• 5r. pale brown with black thread (1.56) – a deep brown shade with black thread is also catalogued.
• 10r. blue with carmine silk threads (1857) (Fig 10) – a pale blue shade with carmine thread is also catalogued.
• 15r. rose with blue silk thread (4.7.57) – a pale rose shade with blue thread is also catalogued.
• 1f. grey-lilac with yellow thread (1856) – a lilac shade with yellow thread is also known.

Fig 9 An 1855 40r. yellow-green, from the second Bern printing with red thread Dickinson paper

Fig 10 A 10r. blue with carmine silk threads from the second Bern printing

Another printing was made at Bern as part of the the second printing. This was on thin (so-called silk) paper and again with different coloured silk threads. The plates have 25 positions with orderly arrangement and variable spacing. The printing shows variable frame lines and fair embossing.

• 10r. pale blue with carmine thread (1857)
• 1f. grey-lilac with yellow thread (1857) – a lilac shade is also catalogued.

THIRD BERN PRINTING
The final printing was on thick paper with bright green silk thread:
• 5r. brown (4.58) – a deep brown and purple brown shades are also catalogued.
• 10r. blue (16.6.1859) – a deep blue shade is also catalogued.
• 15r. rose (1858) – a pale rose shade is also catalogued.
• 20r. orange (26.8.1857)
• 40r. green (1858) – a yellow green shade is also catalogued.

On 1 January 1862, an additional 2r. grey value was issued to pay the newspaper rate (Fig 11). It was printed at Bern on thick paper with green silk thread.

Fig 11 An additional 2r. grey Strubel was added on 1 January 1862 to pay the newspaper rate

THE POSTMARKS
The most common postmarks used to cancel the 'Strubel' stamps were diamond-shaped *Rautenstempel* postmarks, and then circular datestamps. The diamond-shaped postmarks were in use throughout Switzerland, with different designs indicating different post offices. Not all were applied in black ink (Fig 12).

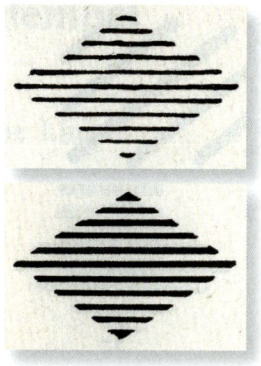

The Strubel stamps of Switzerland, 1854 to 1862

Fig 12 Examples of the diamond-shaped Rautenstempel postmarks. The slightly different designs indicated different post offices

The first circular datestamps were large double-ring versions with no time of day indication. These were introduced in the pre-philatelic period. Most of these cancellations were made around 1832/1833 in Paris and are very similar to the French postmarks issued around that time. The month names can be found in French even for postmarks produced in the German and Italian-speaking areas of Switzerland. However, in 1839 most of the post offices of the cantons of St Gallen and Glarus had German month names.

There can be subtle differences in the size of these postmarks, the fonts used, and the colour of these marks – most are black, then blue or red and, rarely, brown or green. There can also be a variety of ornamentation on these postmarks such as cantonal Coat of Arms, posthorns or floral motifs. Smaller sized double-ring circular datestamps can be found with a Swiss cross in the design (*Fig 13*).

Fig 13 Examples of the various postmarks in use during the period of validity of the Strubel issue

Your SWISS Specialist in the U.K.

My stock consists of an almost complete run of all Swiss stamps from 1850 to the latest issues, mint, unmounted mint and used – singly and in sets. Thousands of cards, covers, items of postal history also available, including airmails, Bundesfeier cards, military material and other side-lines and specialities such as picture postcards. I also stock a range of Liechtenstein stamps.

MY SERVICES TO YOU:

- Free 48-page price-list with SG and SBK/Zumstein numbers
- Wants-list and approval services
- Regular "Werner's Treasure Trove" list of offers 8-10 times a year
- Help with identifying difficult stamps and forgeries for regular clients

Werner Gattiker

7 Friars Oak Rd, Hassocks, West Sussex BN6 8PT
Telephone: 01273 845 501 – E-mail: werner@swisstamps.co.uk

THE BEST OF STANLEY GIBBONS' DIGITAL OFFERING IN ONE PLACE

SG DIGITAL

- Our online PDF of the world famous Stanley Gibbons Catalogues
- Access priceless information wherever you may go
- Access to single country catalogues, Great Britain, Commonwealth catalogues, etc.
- Purchase individually or as a collection

MY COLLECTION

- The digitised copy of Stamps of the World
- Your collection with you wherever you go
- Create your wishlist
- Add your own stamps, including stamps not featured in Stamps of the World
- Less than £4/Month

GSM ONLINE

- First choice for stamp collectors since 1890
- Latest News from the philatelic world
- Regular updates from our catalogue editor Hugh Jefferies
- Available on Android devices, Apple devices and online

To order www.stanleygibbons.com/SGDigital

STANLEY GIBBONS
THE HOME OF STAMP COLLECTING

STANLEY GIBBONS | 399 Strand | London | WC2R 0LX
www.stanleygibbons.com

 @StanleyGibbons   /StanleyGibbonsGroup   @StanleyGibbons

CORINPHILA - TRADITION AND EXPERIENCE IN CLASSIC PHILATELY SINCE 1919

FOUNDED IN 1919

OUTSTANDING RESULTS FROM RECENT CORINPHILA SALES 2007 - 2019 *

- CHF 788,700 CHINA 1897, 1 dollar mint block of 15 (October 2008)
- CHF 720,000 BRAZIL 1843, 60 reis, the unique mint sheet (June 2013)
- CHF 605,000 CHINA 1897, 1 dollar ‚Small Dollar' mint (June 2018)
- CHF 573,600 SWITZERLAND 1850, The ‚Winterthur' block of 8 on cover (June 2009)
- CHF 523,600 CHINA 1897, 5 dollar mint pair with inverted overprint (December 2007)
- CHF 406,300 ZURICH ‚4' mint strip of 5 (June 2009)
- CHF 384,000 BASLE 1845, the ‚Renan Cover' (June 2017)
- CHF 324,000 GENEVA 1846, Large Eagle block of 20 (April 2012)
- CHF 314,600 WESTERN AUSTRALIA 1854, 4d., ‚Inverted Swan' (June 2018)
- CHF 259,600 SWITZERLAND 1850, ‚Waadt 5' and Rayon II (2) on cover (Febr. 2007)
- CHF 239,000 CANADA 1851, 12 Pence mint (March 2010)

PLUS ANOTHER 37 REALISATIONS *
BETWEEN CHF 100,000 AND 320,000 !

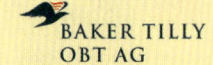

BAKER TILLY OBT AG
All realisations in 2007 - 2019 over CHF 100,000 hammer prices confirmed by Certified Swiss Accountant !
Full Accountant's report online on www.corinphila.ch

The ‚Renan Cover'
1845, Basle Dove (pair) mixed franking with Rayon II on cover

CHF 384.000,-*
in June 2017

* Hammer Prices incl. Buyer's Premium (excl. tax)

CORINPHILA AUKTIONEN AG
WIESENSTR 8 · 8032 ZURICH
SWITZERLAND
Phone +41-44-3899191
www.corinphila.ch

CORINPHILA VEILINGEN BV
AMSTELVEEN · NETHERLANDS
Phone +31-20-6249740 · www.corinphila.nl

CORINPHILA AUCTIONS

As the oldest stamp auction house in Switzerland, situated in the international financial centre of Zürich, we at Corinphila really know the market.

The most specialised philatelic knowledge, fastidious presentation and an international customer base with strong purchasing power guarantee the highest prices.

We are quite willing to discuss larger holdings in your own home.

Switzerland

100 Rappen = 1 Franken
100 Centimes = 1 Franc
100 Centesimi = 1 Franco

These are expressions of the same currency in three languages

CONDITION. The condition of all issues of the Cantonal Administrations and Federal stamps up to No. 51 is an important factor in establishing catalogue value. The prices are for stamps in good condition with four margins, but the stamps in very fine condition with large margins all round are worth very much more, whilst medium and close-cut copies are supplied at lower prices.

I. CANTONAL ADMINISTRATIONS
ZÜRICH

C **1**   C **2**

(Litho Orell, Füssli & Co, Zürich)

1843 (1 Mar)–**46**. Types C **1** (inscr 'Local-Taxe') and C **2** (inscr 'Cantonal-Taxe'). Imperf.

(a) Ground of vertical red lines (1843)

			Un	Used	On Cover
Z1	C 1	4r. black	£24000	£24000	£47000
Z2	C 2	6r. black	£8000	£2250	£5500

(b) Ground of horizontal red lines (1846)

Z3	C 1	4r. black	£22000	£29000	£63000
Z4	C 2	6r. black	£2500	£2000	£4750
Z4a	C 2	6r. black (with damaged background below 'ZU' in 'ZURICH' (pos. 98))	†	–	†

(c) Retouched background (1846)

| Z5 | C 2 | 6r. black (pos. 98) | £4500 | £4250 | £7500 |

The damaged background on No. Z4a shows breaks in the criss-cross pattern below the letters 'ZU' in the word 'ZURICH' in the top margin. No. Z5 is the re-touched version of this flaw.
There are five varieties of each value.
In October 1862, reprints were made of both values on thinner paper and without red lines.
A 4r. and a half of a 4r. are known used *On Cover* for a 6r.
Forgeries of both values are known

GENEVA

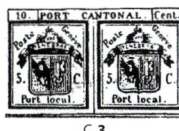  

C **3**   C **4**   C **5**

(Litho C. A. Schmid, Geneva)

1843 (30 Sept). Black impression. Imperf.
G1   C **3**   5c. +5c. on *yellow-green* £89000 £51000 £94000

Varieties.
(i) Half-stamp used separately as 5c.
G2   C **3**   5c. on *yellow-green* £29000 £11000 £23000

(ii) Pairs cut wrong way
G2a C **3**   5c. +5c. on *yellow-green*
        (horiz) £87000 £170000
G2b   5c. +5c. on *yellow-green*
        (vert) £190000

No. G2a is a horizontal pair with right half at left and left half at right. No. G2b is a vertical pair comprising either two left halves or two right halves.

(Litho C. A. Schmid, Geneva)

1845 (1 Apr). Small Eagle. Black Impression. Imperf.
G3   C **4**   5c. on *yellow-green* £3750 £2250 £4250

1846–48. Large Eagle. Black impression. Imperf.
G4   C **5**   5c. on *yellow green* (20.12.46) £2750 £2250 £4250
G5   5c. on *blue green* (22.8.48) £5000 £3750 £7000

1849 (1 June). Similar design, printed on white paper.
G6   C **5**   5c. yellow-green £550 £4500 £25000

This is an envelope stamp cut out and used as an adhesive, as there was little demand for the entire envelopes.

BASEL
TOWN POST

C **6** Dove of Basel

(Des M. Berri. Eng (Eagle embossed), Krebs, Frankfurt-am-Main)

1845 (1 July). Imperf.
B1   C **6**   2½r. carmine, black and blue ... £19000 £18000 £38000
   a. *Carmine, black and bright
      blue* £23000 £21000 £42000

The stamp with vermilion centre, and *green* background in the four corners, is a proof (*Price* £8500).

II. TRANSITIONAL PERIOD
GENEVA

T **1**   T **2**   T **3**

(Litho C. A. Schmid, Geneva)

1849 (22 Oct). Imperf.
L1   T **1**   4c. black and red £51000 £26000 £54000

(Litho C. A. Schmid, Geneva)

1850 (22 Jan). Imperf.
L2   T **2**   5c. black and red £3250 £2250 £4250

The numeral of each stamp on the plate of the 4c. was altered by hand into a 5c.; there are consequently 100 varieties of the numeral of the higher value. Both these stamps were formerly attributed to Vaud.

(Litho C. A. Schmid, Geneva)

1851 (9 Aug). Imperf.
L3   T **3**   5c. black and red £13000 £4750 £9000

This stamp was formerly attributed to Neuchâtel. In Nos. L1 to L3 the background of the central portion of the stamp is in the second colour.

ZÜRICH

T **4**

(Drawn by F. Muller. Typo)

1850 (25 Feb). Background in second colour. Imperf.
L4   T **4**   2½r. black and red £8000 £4750 £63000

This stamp was formerly attributed to Winterthur.

III. FEDERAL ADMINISTRATION

1   2   3

www.robstine-stamps.com
A fantastic array of fine used stamps is now available!
Comprehensive stocks of fine used Switzerland, especially 1907-2015
Pro Juventute, Pro Patria, Airs, Mini sheets etc.
Extensive stocks of the International Bureaux.
Thorough coverage of Liechtenstein 1912-2003.
Many more countries in stock. Please visit my web site
See also www.robstineextra.com for scans of selected stamps
www.robstine-stamps.com
EXCELLENT QUALITY ✦ PROMPT SERVICE

Scott Starling Stamps
www.scottstarling.com.au
Australia | Great Britain |
Europe | British Commonwealth

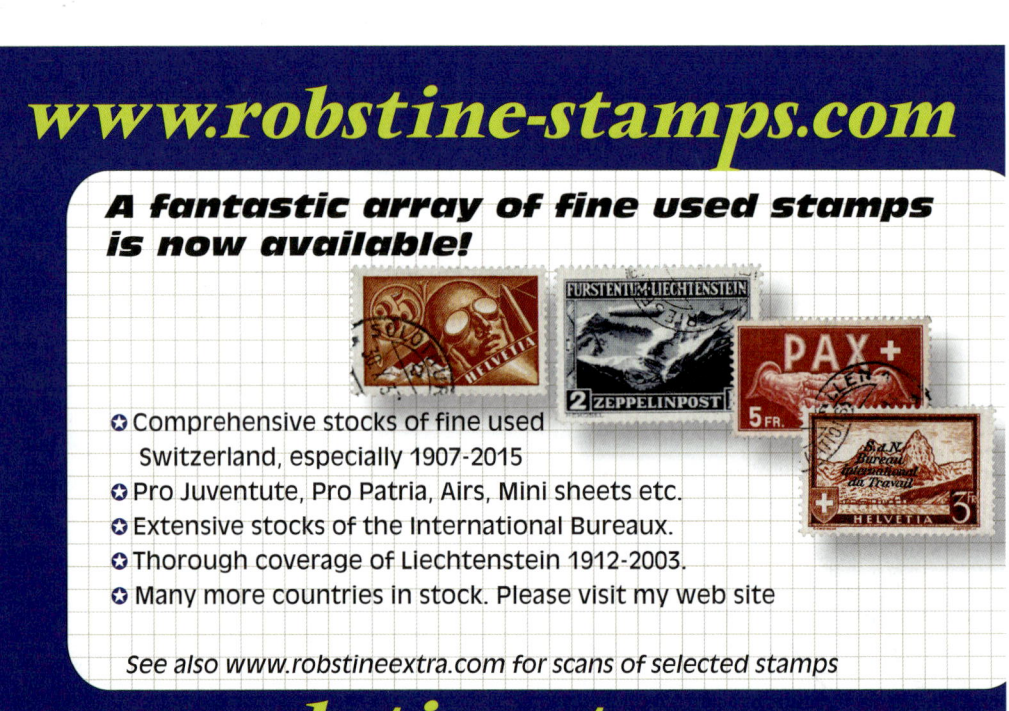

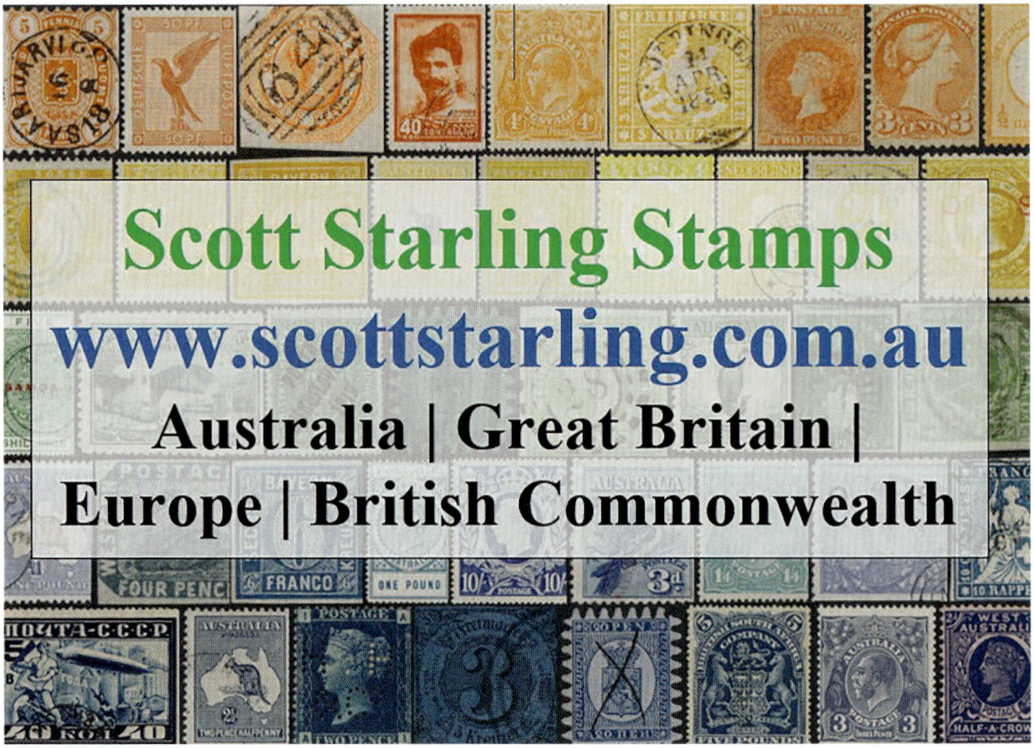

1850 SWITZERLAND

(Litho M. Durheim, Bern)

(a) Central cross with black frame (or blue frame on No. 12a)
(b) Central cross without frame

1850–51. 40 varieties in the plate. Imperf.

(I) Inscr 'ORTS POST'

			Un	Used
1	1	2½r. black and red (a) (16.7.50)	£3750	£1900
2		2½r. black and red (b) (18.5.50)	£7000	£3500

(ii) Inscr 'POSTE LOCALE'

3	2	2½r. black and red (a) (1.10.50)	£3250	£1900
4		2½r. black and red (b) (1851)	£55000	£31000

1850 (1 Oct). 40 varieties in the plate. Imperf.

(i) Inscr 'RAYON I'

5	3	5r. red, black and blue (a)	£6500	£1600
6		5r. red, black and blue (b)	£2500	£750
7		5r. red, black and deep blue (a)	£6500	£1600
8		5r. red, black and deep blue (b)	£5500	£1400

(ii) Inscr 'RAYON II'

9		10r. red, black and orange-yellow (a)		£164000
10		10r. red, black and yellow (b)	£1200	£180
11		10r. red, black and orange yellow (b)	£1300	£400
		a. Carton paper	£3000	£400
12		10r. red black and brownish yellow (b)		£7000

1851 (30 Mar). Colours changed. Imperf. Inscr 'RAYON I'.

13	3	5r. red and pale blue (a)		£243000
14		5r. red and pale blue (b)	£700	£180
15		5r. red and deep blue (b)	£1700	£400

Nos. 16/19 are vacant.

4 5 6

(Litho M. Durheim, Bern)

1852 (1 Jan). Inscr RAYON III. Small figures of value. Ten varieties in the plate. Imperf.

20	4	15r. vermilion	£23000	£900
21		15c. rose	£21000	£1300
22		15c. vermilion	£23000	£900

(Litho M. Durheim, Bern)

1852 (Apr). Ten new varieties of the 15r. with larger figures of value. Imperf.

23	5	15r. rose	£3000	£180
24		15r. vermilion	£3000	£180
		a. Printed both sides		

PRINTINGS OF TYPE 6.
Munich Details of background clear, with the lines of the lozenges distinctly visible, especially beneath the right arm of Helvetia.
Berne Printing of background far less distinct than in Munich printings, lines in lozenges tend to run together, especially beneath the right arm. The figure is surrounded by a band of thick colour, not present on the Munich printings.

(Eng E. Vogt, Munich Embossed)

1854 (15 Sept). Printed by J. G. Weiss, Munich. Thin paper. Emerald-green silk thread. Imperf.

25	6	5r. yellow-brown	£700	£190
		a. Orange-brown	£12000	£2000
		b. Error 5r. blue		
26		10r. bright blue	£1000	£100
27		15r. rose	£1500	£225
28		40r. pale green	£1800	£400
		a. Pale yellow-green	£14000	£1500

No. 25b is on paper with silk thread.
The 5r. in blue on paper without thread is from a trial printing.

1854 (14 Oct)–**62**. Printed at Mint Bern. Imperf.

A. Green silk thread. Thin to medium paper

29	6	5r. grey-brown (4.11.54)	£850	£200
30		10r. blue (shades) (29.5.56)	£2000	£140
31		15r. pale rose (29.1.55)	£1200	£130
32		20r. orange (14.10.54)	£1800	£225

B. Different coloured threads for each value

(a) Thick paper

33	6	5r. yellow brown (yellow thread) (5.55)	£700	£130
		a. Deep brown (yellow thread)	£700	£130
34		5r. pale brown (black thread) (1.56)	£400	45·00
		a. Deep brown (black thread)	£1100	£275
35		10r. blue (carmine thread) (9.56)	£375	55·00
		a. Pale blue (carmine thread)	£1400	£275
36		15r. rose (blue thread) (7.57)	£650	80·00
		a. Pale rose (blue thread)	£650	80·00
37		40r. yellow-green (red thread) (4.55)	£1300	£130
38		1f. grey lilac (black thread) (2.55)	£1800	£1200
		a. Lilac (black thread)	£1800	£1200
39		1f. grey-lilac (yellow thread) (1856)	£1800	£1200
		a. Lilac (yellow thread)	£1800	£1200

(b) Thin paper

40	6	10r. pale blue (carmine thread) (1857)	£6000	£550
41		1f. grey-lilac (yellow thread) (1857)	£25000	£9000
		a. Lilac (yellow thread)	£25000	£9000

C. Bright green silk thread

(a) Thin paper

42	6	5r. grey-brown (6.56)	£6000	£1300
43		10r. blue (1857)	£8000	£1200
44		15r. rose (4.57)	£4000	£400
45		20r. orange (6.56)	£4750	£325

(b) Thick paper

46	6	2r. grey (1.1.62)	£325	£650
		a. Bisected and used with No. 45 (on piece)		£7000
47		5r. brown (4.58)	£275	29·00
		a. Deep brown	£275	29·00
		b. Purple-brown	£275	29·00
		c. Bisected (on piece)		£1800
48		10r. blue (6.59)	£300	29·00
		a. Deep blue	£300	29·00
49		15r. rose (1858)	£475	80·00
		a. Pale rose	£475	80·00
50		20r. orange (26.8.57)	£600	90·00
51		40r. green (1858)	£550	£110
		a. Yellow-green	£550	£110

No. 46a was allowed to do duty as a 1r. value to make-up the printed matter rate to Italy. Most known examples were used to frank newspapers.
No. 47c was accepted by the Geneva postal authorities from mid-1861 to June 1862 as payment for printed matter in excess of 20 copies which was charged at half rate (2½r.).

7 8 8a

WATERMARK. There are two types of the impressed watermark. In T **8a** the arms of the cross are longer and narrower while the oval frame lines are so close that they usually appear to be one.

FOR WELL CENTRED COPIES ADD 35%

(Des J. Riess, Munich. Typo Bern)

1862 (1 Oct)–**64**. Wmk **8** (impressed). P 11½.

52	7	2c. grey	£200	5·50
53		3c. black	18·00	£180
54		5c. brown (8.12.62)	4·50	1·10
		a. Yellow-brown	£160	2·75
		b. Purple-brown	4·50	1·10
		c. Blackish brown	£170	17·00
		d. Double impression, one inverted	£5000	£550
55		10c. blue	£850	1·10
		a. Deep blue	£850	1·10
		b. Double impression, one inverted		£9500
56		20c. pale orange	3·00	4·50
		a. Deep orange	3·00	4·50
		b. Orange-yellow (5.3.63)	£450	4·50
57		30c. vermilion	£2250	55·00
58		40c. green (30.6.63)	£2000	90·00
59		60c. copper-bronze (18.5.63)	£1800	£250
60		1f. bronze-gold (18.5.63)	£2000	£550
		a. Gold (1864)	£1900	£650

See also Nos. 61/67 and 105/113.

1867 (Mar)–**78**. Colours changed and new values. W **8** (impressed). P 11½.

61	7	2c. light bistre-brown (1.2.74)	3·00	2·30
		a. Bistre	3·00	2·30
		b. Red-brown	£850	£325

SWITZERLAND 1878

62		10c. rose	10·00	1·40
		a. Pale rose	10·00	1·40
63		15c. lemon-yellow (1.1.75)	8·25	55·00
64		25c. blue-green (1.9.68)	2·10	5·50
		a. Deep green	7·50	25·00
		b. Yellow-green	60·00	40·00
		c. Double impression, one inverted	—	£1400
65		30c. blue	£2750	£300
		a. Ultramarine	£700	18·00
66		40c. grey (5.4.78)	2·10	£200
		a. Pale grey	2·10	£200
67		50c. purple	70·00	90·00
		a. Deep purple	70·00	90·00

Nos. 68/88 are vacant.

D 9   D 10

I   II (normal)   II (inverted)

T D **10**. Two types of frame:
I. Corner triangles complete below winged wheel in all corners.
II. Corner triangle broken below wheel in one corner. This type is found normal with broken triangle in top right-hand corner, or inverted with broken triangle in bottom left-hand corner.

(Des and Eng J. Durussel. Typo Stämpfli & Co, Bern until 1906 and then at the Mint)

1878 (1 July)–**80**. POSTAGE DUE. White paper. Figures in deep blue. W **8** (impressed). P 11½.

(a) Frame Type I
A. Normal

D89A	D **9**	1c. blue	2·75	2·20
D90A	D **10**	2c. blue	2·75	2·20
D91A		3c. blue (31.1.80)	26·00	30·00
D92A		5c. blue	25·00	16·00
D92Aa	D **9**	5c. blue		
D93A	D **10**	10c. blue	£300	13·00
D94A		20c. blue	£325	12·00
D95A		50c. blue	£550	29·00
D96A		100c. blue	£750	22·00
D97A		500c. blue	£650	36·00

B. Inverted

D89B	D **9**	1c. blue	19·00	25·00
D90B	D **10**	2c. blue	3·00	2·75
D91B		3c. blue (31.1.80)	26·00	27·00
D92B		5c. blue	36·00	18·00
D93B	D **10**	10c. blue	£300	24·00
D94B		20c. blue	£325	16·00
D95B		50c. blue	£600	43·00
D96B		100c. blue	£800	25·00
D97B		500c. blue	£750	40·00

(b) Frame Type II
A. Normal

D98A	D **10**	3c. blue (31.1.80)	18·00	17·00
D99A		5c. blue	25·00	12·00
D100A		10c. blue	£250	10·00
D101A		20c. blue	£300	8·00
D102A		50c. blue	£600	33·00
D103A		100c. blue	£1500	£190
D104A		500c. blue	£700	£100

B. Inverted

D98B	D **10**	3c. blue (31.1.80)	20·00	18·00
D99B		5c. blue	23·00	10·00
D100B		10c. blue	£250	10·00
D101B		20c. blue	£325	9·00
D102B		50c. blue	£600	43·00
D103B		100c. blue		£3000
D104B		500c. blue	£700	70·00

There are many shades of Nos. D89/D104.
A single cancelled example of No. D92a with rayed background is known.

FOR WELL CENTRED COPIES ADD 30%
(Nos. 111/113 only)

1881. Granite paper. W **8** (impressed). P 11½.

105	**7**	2c. ochre	70	35·00
		a. Double impression, one inverted	£450	
106		5c. black-brown	70	18·00
		a. Double impression, one inverted	32·00	£550
107		10c. bright rose	6·00	18·00
108		15c. lemon-yellow	12·00	£200
109		20c. brown-orange	70	£200
110		25c. green	70	£130
111		40c. slate	2·10	£4500
112		50c. purple	25·00	£700
		a. Double impression, one inverted	£325	£6000
113		1f. gold	24·00	£1600

Stamps of this issue are found with forged postmarks.

1882. POSTAGE DUE. Granite paper. Figures In deep blue. W **8** (impressed). P 11½.

A. Frame Type II (normal)

D116A	D **10**	10c. blue (7.1.82)	£250	60·00
D117A		20c. blue (6.3.82)	£550	70·00
D118A		50c. blue (2.5.82)	£3500	£800
D119A		100c. blue (2.5.82)	£1100	£600
D120A		500c. blue (12.6.82)	£21000	£325

B. Frame Type II (inverted)

D116B	D **10**	10c. blue (7.1.82)	£275	60·00
D117B		20c. blue (6.3.82)	£600	90·00
D118B		50c. blue (2.5.82)	£3500	£900
D119B		100c. blue (2.5.82)	£1200	£700
D120B		500c. blue (12.6.82)	£23000	£350

See also Nos. D188/D199 and D268/D273.

9   10   40c. Nos. 136, 142, 149, 158

FOR WELL CENTRED COPIES ADD:
35% for Nos. 121/125; 30% for Nos. 126/133

(Des C. Hasert. Eng E. Burger. Typo Stämpfli & Co, Bern)

1882 (1 Apr)–**99**. Impressed watermark. P 11½.

*(a) Plain wove paper. W **8***

121	**9**	2c. olive-bistre	£600	£475
122		5c. maroon	£1600	£140
123		10c. pink	£3250	85·00
124		12c. pale ultramarine	£350	35·00
125		15c. orange-yellow	£450	£425

The 15c. was formerly listed tête-bêche but it is doubtful if this is a genuine variety.

*(b) Granite paper. A. W **8** (1882–1893)*

126A	**9**	2c. olive-bistre	45·00	6·25
		c. Bronze-brown	48·00	6·75
		d. Olive-brown	50·00	7·00
127A		3c. purple-brown	70·00	75·00
		c. Drab	70·00	75·00
128A		5c. maroon	£110	3·50
		c. Tête-bêche (pair)	£14000	—
130A		10c. pink	£130	2·30
		c. Rose	£750	13·50
		d. Carmine (1893)	£130	2·30
131A		12c. pale ultramarine	£180	7·25
		c. Ultramarine	£180	8·00
132A		15c. lemon	£200	45·00
		b. Deep yellow	£200	45·00
		ba. Tête-bêche (pair)	£14000	£21000
		c. Orange-yellow	£22000	£6000
133A		15c. purple (15.12.89)	£550	36·00

*B. W **8a** (1884–1899)*

126B	**9**	2c. olive-bistre	2·75	1·40
		c. Bronze-brown	3·50	2·30
		d. Olive-brown	2·75	1·40
127B		3c. purple-brown	12·00	16·00
		c. Drab	3·50	18·00
128B		5c. maroon	27·00	90
		d. Claret (1894)	38·00	

129B		5c. deep green (1899)	13·50	1·00
		c. Pale green	12·00	1·00
130B		10c. rose	10·50	90
		d. Carmine (1893)	12·00	2·75
		e. Scarlet (1897)	13·50	5·50
131B		12c. ultramarine	13·00	1·40
		d. Dull blue (1894)	£450	49·00
		e. Bright blue (1894)	13·00	1·40
133B		15c. dull violet (1894)	90·00	5·00
		c. Deep violet (1894)	£130	18·00

See also Nos. 194/199.

FOR WELL CENTRED COPIES ADD:
30% for Nos. 134/139
40% for Nos. 140/144
30% for Nos. 145/154

(Des and Eng and recess printed until 1886 by Müllhaupt & Son. Bern; from 1886 by Max Girardet, Bern)

1882–1903. Plain wove paper. Impressed watermark.

*(a) Perf 11¾. W **8** (1882–1901)*

134	**10**	20c. yellow-orange	£400	8·50
		a. Orange	£400	8·50
135		25c. blue-green	£550	11·00
		a. Pale yellow-green	£225	6·25
		b. Deep yellow-green	£225	6·25
136		40c. grey	£350	70·00
137		50c. pale blue	£350	31·00
		a. Deep blue	£325	28·00
138		1f. maroon	£550	18·00
		a. Claret	£550	18·00
139		3f. yellow-brown (1891)	£375	36·00
		a. Brown-orange	£375	36·00
		b. Wmk **8a** (1901)	—	£8500

*(b) Perf 9½. W **8** (1888)*

140	**10**	20c. yellow-orange	£1300	£140
		a. Orange	£1300	£140
141		25c. deep yellow-green	£275	27·00
		a. Green	£225	27·00
142		40c. grey	£1300	£1100
143		50c. pale blue	£1900	£500
		a. Deep blue	£1900	£500
144		1f. maroon	£1500	£130
		a. Claret	£1500	£130

*(c) Perf 11½×11. W **8** (1891–1898)*

145A	**10**	20c. orange	£1100	13·50
146A		25c. yellow-green	£400	10·00
		c. Green	£375	9·00
148A		30c. deep brown (1892)	£700	80·00
		c. Pale brown	£700	80·00
149A		40c. grey	£1400	£190
150A		50c. pale blue	£800	44·00
		c. Deep blue	£850	50·00
152A		1f. maroon	£1300	36·00
		c. Claret	£1500	40·00
154A		3f. yellow-brown (1898)	—	£26000

*(d) W **8a** (1894–1902)*

145B	**10**	20c. orange	£200	2·75
		c. Yellow-orange (1895)	£225	3·50
146B		25c. yellow-green	22·00	2·75
		c. Green	24·00	3·00
		d. Grey-green	25·00	3·50
147B		25c. blue (1899)	24·00	7·25
148B		30c. deep brown (1892)	50·00	2·75
		c. Pale brown	50·00	2·75
149B		40c. grey	£120	8·50
150B		50c. pale blue	80·00	27·00
		c. Deep blue	80·00	27·00
151B		50c. yellow-green (1899)	£120	60·00
		c. Grey-green	£120	60·00
152B		1f. maroon	70·00	7·25
		c. Claret	70·00	7·25
		d. Rosy mauve (1895)	£180	9·00
153B		1f. carmine (1902)	£140	14·00
		c. Rose-carmine	£180	37·00
		d. Bright carmine	£475	37·00
154B		3f. yellow-brown (1898)	£250	44·00

*(e) Perf 11½×12. W **8a** (1901–1903)*

155	**10**	20c. orange	55·00	2·75
		a. Yellow-orange	90·00	4·50
156		25c. deep blue	31·00	2·40
		a. Blue	22·00	1·80
157		30c. deep brown	60·00	3·25
		a. Pale brown	50·00	3·00
		b. Lake-brown	50·00	3·00
158		40c. grey	£140	55·00
159		50c. green	95·00	22·00

160		1f. claret	£3250	£400
161		1f. carmine (1903)	£800	65·00
162		3f. brown (1902)	£300	36·00

The 25c. is known imperforate but this is probably an essay. See also Nos. 193 and 200/224.

1883–1908. POSTAGE DUE. Granite paper. Impressed watermark. P 11½.
A. Frame Type I
B. Frame Type II (normal)
C. Frame Type II (inverted)

*(a) Pale blue green. Figures in carmine W **8** (1883)*

D163B	**D 10**	5c.	£160	£275
D164B		10c.	£275	£180
D165B		20c.	£475	£160
D166B		50c.	£600	£450
D167B		100c.	£1600	£1900
D168B		500c.	£3000	£1100
D163C		5c.	60·00	43·00
D164C		10c.	90·00	35·00
D165C		20c.	£160	31·00
D166C		50c.	£190	95·00
D167C		100c.	£550	£475
D168C		500c.	£1100	£275

*(b) Dull green Figures in carmine W **8** (1884–1887)*

D169B	**D 10**	5c.	35·00	35·00
D170B		10c.	55·00	8·75
D171B		20c.	55·00	9·75
D172B		50c.	£140	80·00
D173B		100c.	£275	£200
D174B		500c.	£475	£140
D169C		5c.	35·00	45·00
D170C		10c.	55·00	8·75
D171C		20c.	55·00	13·50
D172C		50c.	£130	65·00
D173C		100c.	£250	£200
D174C		500c.	£475	£120

*(c) Yellow-green (shades). Figures in carmine W **8** (1887–1888)*

D175A	**D 10**	5c.	£1200	£700
D176A		10c.	£1200	£700
D177A		20c.	£1600	£650
D178A		50c.	£2500	£1400
D179A		100c.	£2500	£1400
D180A		500c.	£3000	£1900
D175B		5c.	40·00	16·00
D176B		10c.	45·00	10·50
D177B		20c.	£200	10·50
D178B		50c.	£400	£140
D179B		100c.	£400	£180
D180B		500c.	£800	70·00
D175C		5c.	35·00	13·00
D176C		10c.		10·50
D177C		20c.		10·50
D178C		50c.	£350	£130
D179C		100c.	£375	£140
D180C		500c.	£750	70·00

(d) Olive-green (shades). Figure in carmine
*I. W **8** (1889–1893)*

D181A	**D 10**	3c.	£600	£450
D182A		5c.	£550	£400
D183A		10c.	£650	£400
D184A		20c.	£550	£400
D185A		50c.	£750	£475
D186A		100c.	£750	£475
D187A		500c.	£1200	£600
D181B		3c.	7·25	8·00
D182B		5c.	35·00	4·50
D183B		10c.	45·00	3·50
D184B		20c.	40·00	2·75
D185B		50c.	£140	7·25
D186B		100c.	£160	31·00
D187B		500c.	£180	19·00
D181C		3c.	8·00	16·00
D182C		5c.	31·00	27·00
D183C		10c.	40·00	27·00
D184C		20c.	45·00	10·50
D185C		50c.	£120	22·00
D186C		100c.	£160	18·00
D187C		500c.	£180	27·00

*II. W **8a** (1894–1896)*

D188A	**D 10**	5c.	£500	£325
D189A		10c.	£650	£350
D190A		20c.	£550	£325
D191A		50c.	£1400	£700
D192A		100c.	£1400	£850
D188B		5c.	23·00	6·25
D189B		10c.	31·00	8·75

SWITZERLAND 1900

D190B	20c.		31·00	13·50
D191B	50c.		£140	£110
D192B	100c.		£275	£325
D188C	5c.		18·00	3·50
D189C	10c.		24·00	3·50
D190C	20c.		26·00	4·50
D191C	50c.		90·00	27·00
D192C	100c.			60·00

*(e) Olivish green to grass-green. Figures in vermilion W **8a** (1897)*

D193A	D **10**	1c.	£900	£900
D194A		5c.	£650	£650
D195A		10c.	£900	£650
D196A		20c.	£1100	£650
D197A		50c.	£1300	£950
D198A		100c.	£1400	£1500
D199A		500c.	£3250	£1900
D193B		1c.	55·00	31·00
D194B		5c.	35·00	18·00
D195B		10c.	£160	23·00
D196B		20c.	£160	23·00
D197B		50c.	£160	49·00
D198B		100c.	£160	£130
D199B		500c.	£200	95·00
D193C		1c.	£180	£140
D194C		5c.	£140	£110
D195C		10c.	£475	£140
D196C		20c.	£350	£140
D197C		50c.	£325	£275
D198C		100c.	£400	£400
D199C		500c.	£400	£475

*(f) Olive-green (shades). Figures in vermilion W **8a** (1897–1908)*

D200A	D **10**	1c.	£300	£300
D201A		5c.	£325	£350
D202A		10c.	£300	£250
D203A		20c.	£325	£200
D204A		50c.	£550	£300
D205A		100c.	£900	£475
D206A		500c.	£2250	£1500
D200B		1c.	95	95
D201B		5c.	2·30	95
D202B		10c.	5·25	1·40
D203B		20c.	13·50	1·80
D204B		50c.	19·00	6·25
D205B		100c.	23·00	4·50
D206B		500c.	£250	£325
D200C		1c.	1·20	3·50
D201C		5c.	2·30	2·75
D202C		10c.	5·50	2·75
D203C		20c.	13·50	5·50
D204C		50c.	19·00	6·25
D205C		100c.	23·00	13·50
D206C		500c.	£250	£250

Some of the shades of Nos. D200/D206 can only be distinguished from the true shade of Nos. D193/D199 by the worn appearance of the print and the generally faint and dull colours of the numeral. Dated cancellations prior to 9.11.97 indicate stamps belonging to Nos. D193/D199.

    11   **A**   **B**

FOR WELL CENTRED COPIES ADD 30%

(Des E. Grasset. Eng F. Florian, Paris. Recess M. Girardet. Bern)

1900. 25th Anniversary of Universal Postal Union. W **8a** (impressed). P 12×11½ (harrow or line).

(a) Figures of value solid, as A (2 July)

188	**11**	5c. green	75·00	7·75
		a. Line perf	43·00	3·50
189		10c. rosine	22·00	3·50
		a. Line perf	13·00	3·50
190		25c. blue	43·00	70·00
		a. Line perf	34·00	55·00
188/190	Set of 3		£130	75·00
188a/190a	Set of 3		80·00	55·00

(b) Re-engraved. Horizontally-lined background clearer. Figures of value lined, as B. Top telegraph wire thinner than in the original plate

191	**11**	5c. green (1.8.00)	4·50	3·50
192		10c. rosine (10.00)	70·00	65·00

The 25c. was also re-engraved, but was not issued for use, although a few specimens were obtained by favour. (*Price* £1100 *un*, £1900 *used*)

 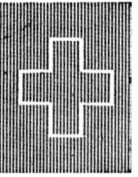 

   12   **13**   **14**

1904. T **12** (T **10** redrawn). W **8a** (impressed). P 11¾.

193	**12**	40c. pearl-grey	60·00	43·00

The 40c., T **12**, may be distinguished from T **10** by the shape and size of the figures of value (see illustration above No. 121).

(Typo Stämpfli & Co, Bern and after summer 1906 by The Mint, Bern)

1905–07. W **13**.

I. Granite paper. P 11½ (Aug 1906)

194	**9**	2c. olive-brown	10·50	3·25
195		3c. drab	12·00	£160
196		5c. pale green	11·50	90
		a. Yellow-green	11·50	90
197		10c. red-orange	10·50	90
		a. Vermilion	19·00	3·50
198		12c. blue	16·00	5·25
		a. Deep blue	18·00	7·00
199		15c. purple	£110	30·00
		a. Reddish purple	£450	£250

II. Plain white paper (printed by Gicardet, Bern)

(a) P 11½×11 (Aug 1905–1906)

200	**10**	20c. orange	7·25	4·50
201		25c. blue	13·50	18·00
202		30c. brown	13·50	3·50
		a. Pale brown	18·00	4·50
203	**12**	40c. pearl-grey	£225	£275
204	**10**	50c. grey-green	£110	18·00
205		1f. deep carmine	£180	7·25
206		3f. bistre-brown (8.06)	£400	£275

(b) Redrawn. P 11½×11 (1906)

207	**14**	25c. pale blue	10·50	3·25

(c) Redrawn. P 11½ (1906)

208	**14**	25c. blue	£225	16·00
209	**12**	40c. pearl-grey	55·00	27·00

The 25c., T **14**, is T **10** redrawn, the stars in the frame are larger, the background under FRANCO is netted instead of being composed of straight and curved lines, and the numerals in the upper corners are altered in shape.

(d) P 11½×12 (1907)

210	**10**	20c. orange	12·50	10·50
211		50c. grey-green	90·00	36·00
212		1f. carmine	£160	21·00
213		3f. bistre-brown	£500	£350

Nos. 200/213 on plain white paper are also found in many shades on a kind of oiled paper.

III. Granite paper (printed by Benziger & Co. Einsiedeln) (1907)

(a) P 11½×12

214	**10**	20c. orange-yellow	4·50	7·25
		a. Red-orange	25·00	17·00
215	**14**	25c. blue	27·00	27·00
216	**10**	30c. brown	10·50	36·00
217	**12**	40c. pearl-grey	36·00	90·00
218	**10**	50c. green	9·00	36·00
		a. Deep green	50·00	22·00
219		1f. carmine	55·00	18·00
219a		3f. yellow-brown		£18000

(b) P 11½×11

220	**14**	25c. blue	21·00	13·50
221	**10**	30c. brown	£300	£600
222	**12**	40c. pearl-grey		£23000
223	**10**	1f. carmine	£23000	£9000
224		3f. bistre-brown	£200	£130

15 Tell's Son   **16**   **17**   **18**   **19**

(a)   (b)   **18a**   **18b**   **18c**

T **18a**. Cord passes in front of crossbow stock
T **18b**. Cord is behind stock; loop at top is thin
T **18c**. Cord is behind stock; loop is thick, also other differences

(Des A. Welti (T **15**), C. L'Eplattenier (T **16**). Typo Mint, Bern)

1907 (11 Nov). Granite paper. W **13**. P 11½.

225	**15**	2c. olive-yellow	45	1·80
226		3c. cinnamon	45	18·00
227		5c. green	5·50	90
228	**16**	10c. rose-red	2·75	90
229		12c. ochre	45	7·25
230		15c. mauve	5·50	23·00
225/230	*Set of 6*		13·50	47·00

> **GRILLED GUM.** Some of the paper used during the period 1932 to 1944 was passed through a gum breaker, prior to printing, to prevent subsequent curling. The machinery used impressed a grill into the gum by means of patterned rollers. Sufficient force was exerted for this grill to be transferred to the paper beneath the gum and, in consequence, we quote prices for both unused and used examples.

(Des C. L'Eplattenier. Typo Mint, Bern)

1908 (Aug)–**40**. Granite paper (ordinary). W **13**. P 11½.

(i) Designer's name in full on rock (a)

231	**17**	40c. orange-yellow and purple	10·50	£140

(ii) Initials C.L. only on rock (b)

232	**17**	20c. yellow and red	3·75	1·80
233		25c. light blue and deep blue	3·25	1·30
		a. Tête-bêche (pair)	36·00	£225
		b. pale green and pale blue	£3750	
234		30c. pale green and yellow-brown	2·50	90
235		35c. yellow and green	3·25	4·00
		a. Chalk-surfaced paper. Grilled gum (1933)	1·80	24·00
236		40c. orange-yellow and purple	19·00	1·80
237		40c. light blue (3.21)	10·00	3·50
238		40c. blue (4.22)	2·50	90
239		40c. yellow-green and deep magenta (1.25)	60·00	90
		a. Chalk-surfaced paper. Grilled gum (1933)	50·00	2·75
240		50c. yellow-green and deep green	18·00	90
		a. Chalk-surfaced paper. Grilled gum (1933)	11·50	2·75
		b. Chalk-surfaced paper. Smooth gum (1940)	16·00	£150
241		60c. orange-brown (11.18)	16·00	1·80
		a. Chalk-surfaced paper. Grilled gum (1933)	15·00	2·75
		b. Chalk-surfaced paper. Smooth gum (1940)	19·00	£170
242		70c. orange-yellow and chocolate	90·00	31·00
243		70c. buff and violet (10.24)	23·00	6·25
		a. Chalk-surfaced paper. Grilled gum (1934)	22·00	7·00
244		80c. buff and olive-grey (11.16)	15·00	3·25
		a. Chalk-surfaced paper. Grilled gum (1933)	18·00	7·25
		b. Chalk-surfaced paper. Smooth gum (1940)	19·00	£500
245		1f. pale green and claret	13·50	90
		a. Chalk-surfaced paper. Grilled gum (1933)	26·00	11·50
246		3f. pale yellow and yellow-bistre	£475	4·50
231/246	*Set of 16 (cheapest)*		£650	£180

> **BOOKLET PANES.** Those panes which have two values *se-tenant*, or include *se-tenant* labels, are now listed and can be found under the lowest value stamp included in each pane.
> Most booklet panes were also available to collectors as uncut sheets. Many combinations not occurring in normal panes can be found from such sheets but, with the exception of *tête-bêche* pairs of the same value, these are not listed.
> A checklist of booklets is given at the end of the country.

(Des A. Welti (T **18**), C. L'Eplattenier (T **19**). Typo Mint)

1908–33. Granite paper. W **13**. P 11½–12.

(a) Types **18/19** *(1908–1909)*

247	**18a**	2c. bistre (28.12.08)	45	2·30
		a. Tête-bêche (pair)	4·00	60·00
248		3c. deep violet (1.09)	45	25·00
249		5c. green (1.09)	13·50	65
		a. Tête-bêche (pair)	40·00	£100
250	**19**	10c. carmine (1.09)	1·80	90
		a. Tête-bêche (pair)	8·00	30·00
251		12c. yellow-brown (1.09)	90	1·80
252		15c. mauve (1.09)	44·00	1·80
		a. Deep mauve	50·00	1·80

(b) T **18b** *(1910–1933)*

253	**18b**	2c. bistre (3.10)	14·00	12·00
254		3c. deep violet (3.11)	45	90
		a. Tête-bêche (pair)	5·50	20·00
255		3c. orange-brown (1.17)	45	50
		a. Tête-bêche (pair)	17·00	38·00
256		3c. ultramarine/buff (7.30)	3·25	12·50
		a. Grilled gum (8.33)	8·25	39·00
257		5c. green (7.10)	32·00	12·50
		a. Tête-bêche (pair)	£180	£600
258		7½c. grey (7.18)	1·50	50
		a. Tête-bêche (pair)	22·00	£100
259		7½c. green/buff (6.27)	45	6·00

(c) Redrawn T **18c** *(1911–1933)*

260	**18c**	2c. ochre (9.11)	45	90
		a. Tête-bêche (pair)	6·00	28·00
261		2½c. claret (12.17)	45	2·30
262		2½c. bistre/buff (1.28)	45	4·50
263		5c. green (3.11)	1·30	50
		a. Tête-bêche (pair)	7·00	30·00
264		5c. orange/buff (10.21)	30	30
		a. Booklet pane. No. 264×5 and No. 280 (1921)	35·00	
265		5c. violet-grey/buff (6.24)	30	30
		a. Booklet pane. No. 265×5 and No. 280 (1924)	30·00	
266		5c. deep claret/buff (6.27)	30	30
		a. Booklet pane. No. 266×5 and No. 280 (1927)	55·00	
		b. Booklet pane. No. 266×5 and No. 281 (1928)	25·00	
267		5c. deep green/buff (7.30)	45	70
		a. Booklet pane. No. 267×5 and No. 282 (1930)	65·00	
		b. Grilled gum (1933)	95	10·00
		ba. Booklet pane. No. 267b×5 and No. 282b (1933)	£110	
268		7½c. grey (1.18)	5·50	5·50

See note on grilled gum below No. 230.

1908–10. POSTAGE DUE. Granite paper. Figures in vermilion. W **13**. P 11½.

A. Greenish olive (1908)

D269A	D **10**	5c.	5·00	2·75
D270A		10c.	5·00	2·75
D271A		20c.	15·00	19·00
D272A		50c.	75·00	£250

B. Brown-olive (shades) (1909–1910)

D268B	D **10**	1c.	45	1·60
D269B		5c.	1·20	1·30
D270B		10c.	4·25	3·25
D271B		20c.	17·00	8·00
D272B		50c.	70·00	1·80
D273B		100c.	£110	3·50

Nos. D269A/D273B also come frame inverted.

SWITZERLAND 1910

D 21   F 21

(Des C. L'Eplattenier. Die Eng A. Geel Typo
PTT Printing Bureau, Bern)

1910 (1 Sept). POSTAGE DUE. Value, shield and flowers in red. Granite paper. W **13**. P 11½.

D274	D **21**	1c. blue-green	20	20
D275		3c. blue-green	20	20
D276		5c. blue-green	20	20
D277		10c. blue-green	16·00	45
D278		15c. blue-green	1·10	1·80
D279		20c. blue-green	28·00	45
D280		25c. blue-green	1·80	90
D281		30c. blue-green	1·80	90
D282		50c. blue-green	2·20	1·80
D274/D282 Set of 9			46·00	6·25

See also Nos. D299/D302.

21a Small Figures   **21**b Large Figures

(Des C. L'Eplattenier. Typo Mint)

1911–26. FRANK. Blue granite paper. W **13**. P 11½.

(a) Small black control figures at top

F268	F **21**	2c. red and olive-green	25	25
F269		3c. red and olive-green (1916)	3·25	85
F270		5c. red and olive-green	1·60	25
F271		10c. red and olive-green	2·00	25
F272		15c. red and olive-green (1919)	29·00	5·75
F273		20c. red and olive-green (1921)	5·50	85
F268/F273 Set of 6			37·00	7·50

(b) Large control figures at top (1.26)

F274	F **21**	5c. red and olive-green	18·00	6·50
F275		10c. red and olive-green	10·50	5·00
F276		20c. red and olive-green	13·50	5·75
F274/F276 Set of 3			36·00	16·00

These stamps were issued to charity hospitals for the free transmission of their mails, and are generally found with black control numbers at the top. They were also made available to collectors, both mint and cancelled-to-order, either numbered or without control number (*Price for set of 6 without control numbers: £43 mounted mint, £475 us*).

See also Nos. F335/F337.

21 William Tell

(Des R. Kissling. Die Eng J. Springer. Typo Mint)

1914 (July)–**33**. Granite paper. W **13**. P 11½.

278	**21**	10c. red/buff (a)	2·50	33·00
279		10c. red/buff (b)	50	50
		a. *Tête-bêche* (pair)	3·50	18·00
		b. Booklet pane. No. 279×5 and No. 285 (1918)	42·00	
280		10c. green/buff (2.21)	25	25
		a. *Tête-bêche* (pair)	1·30	3·50
281		10c. blue-green/buff (6.27)	45	25
		a. *Tête-bêche* (pair)	1·80	5·50
282		10c. reddish violet/buff (7.30)	1·20	50
		a. *Tête-bêche* (pair)	7·75	8·50
		b. Grilled gum (1933)	5·50	2·75
		ba. *Tête-bêche* (pair)	28·00	90·00
283		12c. yellow-brown/buff	50	8·00
284		13c. olive-green/buff (9.15)	2·30	90
285		15c. purple/buff	3·50	90
		a. *Tête-bêche* (pair)	£140	£250
		b. Deep violet/buff	55·00	1·50
286		15c. brown-lake/buff (6.27)	4·50	8·00
		a. Grilled gum (1933)	70·00	95·00
287		20c. purple/buff (exc. O302)	2·50	50
		a. *Tête-bêche* (pair)	8·50	18·00
288		20c. orange-red/buff (7.24)	90	90
		a. *Tête-bêche* (pair)	5·50	23·00
289		20c. scarlet/buff (3.25)	50	25
		a. *Tête-bêche* (pair)	4·50	5·50
		b. Grilled gum (1932)	9·00	2·75
		ba. *Tête-bêche* (pair)	£950	£3250
290		25c. orange-red/buff (1.21)	1·80	3·75
291		25c. scarlet/buff (10.22)	90	1·80
292		25c. yellow-brown/buff (9.25)	4·75	2·75
		a. Grilled gum (1933)	£130	65·00
293		30c. blue/buff (10.24)	17·00	90
		a. Grilled gum (1932)	90·00	4·50

There are two dies of the 10c.: in (*a*) the bar of the H is exactly half way, in (*b*) it is nearer the top.

See note on grilled gum below No. 230.

22 The Myth   **23** The Rutli

24 The Jungfrau

(Des E. Grasset. Eng A. Burkhard (5f.), J. Sprenger (others).
Recess Survey Dept, Bern)

1914 (July)–**18**. Granite paper. W **13**. P 11½ (comb).

294	**22**	3f. deep blue-green	£1000	10·50
295		3f. rose-carmine (2.18)	£140	2·75
296	**23**	5f. deep ultramarine	55·00	4·50
297	**24**	10f. deep mauve	£140	4·50

For T **23** redrawn see No. 336. See also No. 337.

(25)	(26)	(27)	(28)
1	13 / 13	80	80

1915 (26 Jan–Oct). Surch as Types **25** to **28**.

298	**18b**	1c. on 2c. ochre	25	2·30
299	**19**	13c. on 12c. yellow-brown	25	19·00
300	**21**	13c. on 12c. yellow-brown/buff	25	1·50
301	**17**	80c. on 70c. orange-yellow and chocolate (10.15)	44·00	35·00
298/301 Set of 4			40·00	50·00

10	Industrielle Kriegs- wirtschaft	Industrielle Kriegs- wirtschaft	
(29)	(O 29)	(O 30)	(30)

1916–24. POSTAGE DUE. Old values cancelled with fancy pattern in red on which new value as T **29** is surch in black.

D299	D **21**	5c. on 3c. red and blue-green	25	25
D300		10c. on 1c. red and blue-green (1924)	45	12·50
D301		10c. on 3c. red and blue-green (1924)	40	2·10
D302		20c. on 50c. red and blue-green (1924)	1·20	2·10
D299/D302 Set of 4			2·10	15·00

1918. OFFICIAL. Contemporary stamps opted by Hermann Stolz, Bern.

*(a) With T O **29** (23 July)*

O299	**18b**	3c. orange-brown	£170	£400
O300	**18c**	5c. green	14·50	65·00
O301	**18b**	7½c. grey	£450	£950
O302	**18c**	7½c. grey	£850	£1800
O303	**21**	10c. red/buff (b)	22·00	80·00
O304		15c. purple/buff	18·00	95·00
O305	**17**	20c. yellow and red	£180	£750
O306		25c. light blue and deep blue	£180	£750
O307		30c. pale green and yellow-brown	£180	£750
O299/O307 Set of 8 (exc. O302)			£1100	£3500

*(b) With T O **30** (3 Sept)*

O308	**18b**	3c. orange-brown	5·25	55·00
O309	**18c**	5c. green	15·00	80·00

O310	**18b**	7½c. grey...	5·25	38·00
O311	21	10c. red/*buff* (b)...............................	65·00	£140
O312		15c. purple/*buff*................................		£130
O313	**17**	20c. yellow and red...........................	12·50	85·00
O314		25c. light blue and blue....................	12·50	85·00
O315		30c. pale green and yellow-brown......	20·00	£140

The above stamps were for the use of the official departments dealing with the import and export of war material. No. O312 was not issued, the stock being sold with the remainders of the other values. Forgeries exist.

Stamps used *on cover* are worth considerably more than the used prices quoted.

1919 (30 Apr)–**20**. AIR. Optd with T **30** in red.

302	**17**	30c. pale green and yellow-brown (11.20)..	£180	£1800
303		50c. yellow-green and deep green.........	60·00	£190

Beware of forgeries.

31

32

33

(34)

(Des E. Vallet, P. Robert and O. Baumberger.
Eng J. Sprenger, Typo Mint)

1919 (1 Aug). Peace Celebration. P 11½.

304	**31**	7½c. grey-olive and black.......................	1·30	3·50
305	**32**	10c. yellow and red................................	1·80	13·00
306	**33**	15c. yellow and reddish violet................	3·25	4·50
304/306		Set of 3	5·75	19·00

1921 (Jan)–**30**. Surch as T **25** or T **27** or with T **34** (No. 315).

307	**18b**	2½c. on 3c. orange-brown..................	25	1·80
		a. *Tête-bêche* (pair)..............................	1·30	9·00
308	**18c**	3c. on 2½c. bistre/*buff* (6.30)..........	25	5·50
309		5c. on 2c. ochre (R.)...........................	25	8·00
310	**18b**	5c. on 7½c. grey (R.)...........................	45	90
		a. *Tête-bêche* (pair)..............................	8·00	£120
311	**18c**	5c. on 7½c. grey (R.)...........................	£3500	£8500
312	**18b**	5c. on 7½c. green/*buff* (6.30)............	45	18·00
313	21	10c. on 13c. olive-green/*buff* (R.).....	45	4·50
314		20c. on 15c. purple/*buff* (B.).............	3·50	11·00
		a. Surch in black...................................	90	4·50
		b. Do. *Tête-bêche* (pair).......................	3·50	£130
315	**17**	20c. on 25c. light blue and deep blue..	45	90
		a. *Tête-bêche* (pair)..............................	2·75	20·00
307/315		(*exc.* 311) Set of 8 (*cheapest*)................	3·00	40·00

35 Monoplane

36 Pilot

37

38 Biplane

39 Icarus

40

(Des K. Bickel (Nos. 317/319, 320, 321/322).
P. Vibert (others). Typo PTT Printing Bureau, Bern)

1923 (1 Mar)–**40**. AIR. Granite paper (ordinary). W **13**. P 11½.

316	**35**	15c. yellow-green and dull scarlet........	4·50	12·50
317		20c. green and deep green (5.25)..........	2·00	8·50
		a. Chalk-surfaced paper. Grilled gum (6.37)...	45	95
		b. Chalk-surfaced paper. Smooth gum (1940)......................................	95	70·00
318		25c. bluish grey and deep dull blue......	12·00	35·00
		a. Chalk-surfaced paper. Grilled gum (1.34)..	8·50	80·00
319	**36**	35c. cinnamon and light brown.............	18·00	80·00
320	**37**	35c. lake-brown and brown-ochre (1.7.29)...	23·00	80·00
		a. Chalk-surfaced paper. Grilled gum (11.33)..	13·50	80·00
321	**36**	40c. slate-lilac and dull violet.................	22·00	90·00
322	**37**	40c. blue and apple green (1.7.29)........	85·00	£140
		a. Chalk-surfaced paper. Grilled gum (11.33)..	60·00	£120
323	**38**	45c. red and indigo.................................	2·75	18·00
		a. Chalk-surfaced paper. Grilled gum (8.37)..	3·25	75·00
324		50c. black and red..................................	23·00	30·00
		a. *Deep grey green and red* (chalk-surfaced paper, grilled gum) (6.35)..	1·80	3·50
325	**39**	65c. slate-blue and deep turquoise-blue (13.5.24)...................................	6·50	42·00
		a. Chalk-surfaced paper. Grilled gum (1937)...	4·50	13·00
326		75c. red-orange and claret (13.5.24)......	22·00	£110
		a. Chalk-surfaced paper. Grilled gum (1936)...	34·00	£275
327		1f. reddish lilac and purple (13.5.24).....	70·00	75·00
		a. Chalk-surfaced paper Grilled gum (1933)...	2·30	5·25
328	**40**	2f. chestnut, sepia and grey-brown (5.7.30)...	£140	£160
		a. Chalk-surfaced paper. Grilled gum (7.35)..	13·00	26·00
316/328		Set of 13 (*cheapest*)..............................	£160	£550

See note on grilled gum below No. 230.

D **41**

41

(Des L. Salzmann. Typo PTT Printing Bureau, Bern)

1924–**34**. POSTAGE DUE. Granite paper (ordinary). W **13**. P 11½.

D329	D **41**	5c. red and olive-green.....................	1·10	45
		a. Grilled gum (1934).........................	95	90
D330		10c. red and olive-green...................	4·50	65
		a. Grilled gum (1934).........................	3·50	1·60
D331		15c. red and olive-green (1926)........	4·00	90
D332		20c. red and olive-green....................	9·75	45
		a. Grilled gum (1934).........................	7·00	2·40
D333		25c. red and olive-green....................	4·50	90
		a. Grilled gum (1934).........................	10·50	£110
D334		30c. red and olive-green....................	4·50	1·20
D335		40c. red and olive-green (1926)........	6·25	1·10
D336		50c. red and olive-green....................	6·25	1·10
D329/D336		Set of 8 (*cheapest*)............................	33·00	6·00

Printings with grilled gum (see note below No. 230) are on chalk-surfaced paper.

(Des L. Salzmann. Typo)

1924 (1 Oct)–**40**. Shield and value in red. Granite paper (ordinary). W **13**. P 11½.

329	**41**	90c. deep green and green....................	26·00	4·50
		a. Chalk-surfaced paper. Grilled gum (1933)...	31·00	5·50
		b. Chalk-surfaced paper. Smooth gum (1940)......................................	26·00	90·00
330		1f.20 brown-lake and salmon-pink........	8·50	8·50
		a. 'HFLVETIA'.......................................	28·00	£140
		b. Chalk-surfaced paper. Grilled gum (1934)...	85·00	9·50
		c. Chalk-surfaced paper. Smooth gum (1940)......................................	26·00	£130
331		1f.50 blue and greenish blue..................	70·00	10·50
		a. Chalk-surfaced paper. Grilled gum (1934)...	55·00	10·50
		b. Chalk-surfaced paper Smooth gum (1940)......................................	26·00	£1000

SWITZERLAND 1924

332		2f. black and olive-grey	80·00	11·50
		a. Chalk-surfaced paper. Grilled gum (1933)	48·00	14·50
329/332 Set of 4 (cheapest)			£100	32·00

See note on grilled gum below No. 230.

42 Seat of First UPU Congress

43 The Mythen

(Des A. Tieche (20c.), W. Stettler (30c.). Eng J. Sprenger. Recess Survey Dept, Bern (20c.), Orell, Füssli & Co, Zürich (30c.).)

1924 (9 Oct). 50th Anniversary of Universal Postal Union. Granite paper. T **42** and similar vert design. W **13**. P 11½.

333	–	20c. red	90	12·00
334	**42**	30c. deep blue	1·80	9·25

Design: 20c. Similar to T **42** but with different frame.

1927 (Jan)–**34**. FRANK. Large control figures. White granite paper. W **13**. P 11½.

F335	F **21**	5c. orange-red and light green	6·75	65
F336		10c. orange-red and light green	3·25	40
		a. Grilled gum (1934)	£400	£1100
F337		20c. orange-red and light green	4·75	40
F335/F337 Set of 3			13·50	1·30

10c. with grilled gum (see note below No. 230) is on chalk-surfaced paper. This was placed on sale at the National Stamp Exhibition post office.

See note below No. F276.

(Des E. Cardinaux (3f.), E. Grasset (others). Eng J. Sprenger. Recess)

1928–31. Granite paper. W **13**. P 11½.

335	**43**	3f. red-brown (1931)	75·00	8·50
336	**23**	5f. deep blue	£190	18·00
337	**24**	10f. deep grey-green (12.2.30)	£325	65·00
335/337 Set of 3			£550	80·00

On No. 336 the engraver's name, J. Sprenger, appears at right bottom corner instead of A. BURKHARD as in T **23**. The whole design is redrawn.

PRINTERS. Early in 1932 the stamp printing department of the Mint was taken over by the PTT Printing Bureau.

44 Symbol of Peace

45 After the Darkness, Light

(Des M. Barraud; Eng G. Matter, typo PTT Printing Bureau, Bern (T **44**). Des G. Fustier, photo Courvoisier (T **45**).)

1932 (2 Feb). International Disarmament Conference. Granite paper with grilled gum. P 11½.

(a) W 13

338	**44**	5c. blue-green	45	90
339		10c. bright orange	45	50
340		20c. magenta	45	50
341		30c. bright blue	3·25	2·75
342		60c. bistre-brown	26·00	16·00

(b) No wmk

343	**45**	1f. olive-grey and blue	26·00	17·00
338/343 Set of 6			50·00	34·00

46 Peace and the Air Post

47 Louis Favre (engineer)

48 Staubbach Falls

(Des O. Braumberger. Typo PTT Printing Bureau, Bern)

1932 (2 Feb). AIR. International Disarmament Conference. Granite paper with grilled gum. W **13**. P 11½.

344	**46**	15c. light green and black	85	4·00
345		20c. flesh and scarlet	1·70	5·00
346		90c. light blue and blue	9·50	65·00
344/346 Set of 3			11·00	65·00

(Des and Eng K. Bickel, Recess Orell Füssli, Zürich)

1932 (31 May). 50th Anniversary of St Gotthard Railway. T **47** and similar vert portraits. Granite paper. W **13**. P 11½.

347		10c. chestnut	30	25
348		20c. orange-red	45	45
349		30c. royal blue	90	5·25
347/349 Set of 3			1·50	5·25

Designs: 10c. T **47**; 20c. Alfred Escher (President of Railway): 30c. Emil Welti (founder).

(Des E. Jordi. Typo PTT Printing Bureau, Bern)

1934 (2 July). As T **48** (landscapes). Granite paper with grilled gum. W **13**. P 11½.

350		3c. yellow-olive	40	5·75
351		5c. blue-green	25	25
		a. Tête-bêche (pair)	4·25	6·75
352		10c. deep mauve	55	45
		a. Tête-bêche (pair)	3·75	7·50
353		15c. orange	70	65
		a. Tête-bêche (pair)	4·25	15·00
354		20c. bright scarlet	1·10	85
		a. Tête-bêche (pair)	5·25	14·00
355		25c. orange-brown	10·50	13·00
356		30c. ultramarine	39·00	3·50
350/356 Set of 7			47·00	27·00

Designs: 3c. T **48**; 5c. Mount Pilatus; 10c. Chillon Castle and Dents du Midi; 15c. Grimsel Pass; 20c. Landwasser Viaduct, Filisur (St Gotthard Railway); 25c. Viamala Gorge; 30c. Rhine Falls near Schaffhausen.

1934 (29 Sept). National Philatelic Exhibition, Zürich (NABA). Sheet 62×72 mm.

MS357 Nos. 351/354	£600	£1100

F **49** Deaconess

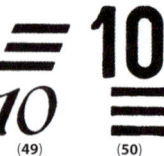

(49)   (50)

51 Freiburg Cowherd

(Des K. Bickel. Typo PTT Printing Bureau, Bern)

1935 (1 Jan)–**43**. FRANK. Designs as T F **49**. W **13**.

A. Granite paper with, grilled gum (1935)
B. Granite paper (ordinary) (1943). P 11½

(a) With large control figures

F358A	5c. green	4·25	2·50
F359A	10c. violet	4·25	2·50
F360A	20c. scarlet	4·50	2·50
F358B	5c. green	3·25	12·00
F359B	10c. violet	3·25	12·00
F360B	20c. scarlet	3·25	16·00

(b) Without control figures

F361A	5c. green	22·00	90
F362A	10c. violet	22·00	45
F363A	20c. scarlet	22·00	90
F361B	5c. green	2·00	13·00
F362B	10c. violet	2·00	13·00
F363B	20c. scarlet	2·00	13·00

Designs: 5c. T F **49**; 10c. Sister of the Ingenbohl Order, 20c. Henri Dunant (founder of Red Cross).
See note on grilled gum below No. 230.

1935–37. AIR. Nos. 316 and 344/346 surch.

*(a) Surch with T **49***

358	**35**	10c. on 15c. yellow-green and dull scarlet	7·00	60·00

*(b) Surch as T **50***

359	**46**	10c. on 15c. light green and green	45	90
		a. Surch inverted	£10000	£14000
360		10c. on 20c. flesh and scarlet (9.9.36)	50	3·00
361		30c. on 90c. light blue and blue (9.9.36)	4·00	29·00
362		40c. on 20c. flesh and scarlet (1937)	5·25	29·00
363		40c. on 90c. light blue and blue (R.) (1.8.36)	4·50	29·00
358/363 Set of 6			20·00	£140

1936 SWITZERLAND

(Des from picture by F. Hodler. Photo Courvoisier)
1936 (1–26 Oct). National Defence Fund. Granite paper (No. **MS**367 with grilled gum). P 11½.

364	**51**	10c. +5c. reddish violet	90	1·80
365		20c. +10c. orange-red	1·30	7·00
366		30c. +10c. ultramarine	6·00	33·00
364/366	Set of 3		7·50	38·00
MS367	109×102 mm. Nos. 364/366 (26.10.36)		70·00	£325

52 Staubbach Falls   **52A** I   **52A** II

I. No diagonal lines through o.
II. Two diagonal lines through o and railway track heavier.

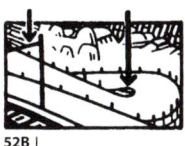 

52B I   **52B** II

Type I: Kerbstone beneath the gantry does not reach the crossbar. Small shading line in bend angled up (higher on the left, lower on the right).
Type II: All Kerbstones are larger and bolder. Small shading line in bend angled differently (lower on the left, higher on the right).

(Des and Eng K. Bickel. Recess PTT Printing Bureau, Bern)
1936 (Nov)–**42**. As T **52** (landscapes as 1934 issue but redrawn with figure of value in line with 'HELVETIA' at bottom).

A. Smooth white non granite paper. P 11½

368A	3c. yellow-olive	25	30
369A	5c. blue-green	25	30
	c. Tête-bêche (pair)	55	1·10
370A	10c. bright purple (I)	1·40	95
	c. Tête-bêche (pair)	5·25	8·75
	d. Type II (1938)	1·40	95
	dc. Tête-bêche (pair)	2·75	3·25
371A	10c. red-brown (1939)	40	45
	c. Tête-bêche (pair)	1·40	2·75
372A	10c. chestnut (1942)	30	30
	c. Tête-bêche (pair)	95	2·30
373A	15c. orange	65	1·80
374A	20c. scarlet (St Gotthard) (I)	£140	44·00
	d. Type II (1937)	6·00	45
	dc. Tête-bêche (pair) (II)	33·00	70·00
375A	20c. scarlet (17.9.38) (Lugano)	35	40
	c. Tête-bêche (pair)	1·10	1·40
376A	25c. yellow-brown	85	1·80
377A	30c. dull ultramarine	1·30	45
378A	35c. bright green	1·70	3·50
379A	40c. grey	8·00	45
368A/379A	Set of 12 (cheapest)	19·00	10·00

B. Non granite paper with grilled gum

368B	3c. yellow-olive	90	13·00
369B	5c. blue-green	30	30
	c. Tête-bêche (pair)	65	2·30
370B	10c. bright purple (I)	65	95
	c. Tête-bêche (pair)	3·25	4·50
	d. Type II (1937)	1·40	45
	dc. Tête-bêche (pair)	1·80	7·00
371B	10c. red-brown (1939)	1·90	42·00
373B	15c. orange	45	1·90
374B	20c. scarlet (St Gotthard) (I)	8·50	2·75
	d. Type II (1937)	7·75	45
	dc. Tête-bêche (pair) (II)	26·00	60·00
375B	20c. scarlet (17.9.38)	45	1·80
	c. Tête-bêche (pair)	2·50	26·00
376B	25c. yellow-brown	1·40	7·00
377B	30c. dull ultramarine	1·30	45
378B	35c. bright green	2·00	6·00
379B	40c. grey	12·00	95

Designs: 3c. T **52**; 5c. Mount Pilatus; 10c. (Nos. 370/372) Chillon Castle and Dents du Midi; 15c. Grimsel Pass; 20c. (No. 374), Landwasser Viaduct, Filisur (St Gotthard Railway); 20c. (No. 375), Lake Lugano and Mount San Salvatore; 25c. Viamala Gorge; 30c. Rhine Falls; 35c. Mount Neufalkenstein and Klus; 40c. Mount Santis and Lake Seealp.

Nos. 368A, 369A, 370Ad, 371A, 372, 373A, 375A and 376A/379A were also issued in coils. The 5c., 10c. (all colours), 20c. and 30c. values had a control letter and figures on the back of every fifth stamp in the roll.

See note on grilled gum below No. 230.
See also No. **MS**387*a* and Nos. 489/494.
Copies of No. 374 are known with a worn impression, these are from printings using worn dies of Type I, and were previously listed as No. 347c. The die was re-engraved in 1937, see No. 374d.

5
(D **53**)   **53** Mobile PO

1937 (1 June). POSTAGE DUE. Nos. D334, D337 and D339 surch as T D **53**.

D380	D **41**	5c. on 15c. red and olive-green	1·30	5·75
D381		10c. on 30c. red and olive-green	1·30	2·20
D382		20c. on 50c. red and olive-green	2·30	7·00
D383		40c. on 50c. red and olive-green	3·50	18·00
D380/D383	Set of 4		7·50	30·00

(Des B. Reber. Photo Courvoisier)
1937 (5 Sept). Granite paper. P 11½.

380	**53**	10c. yellow and black	45	95

This stamp was for use on mail posted at mobile post offices.
For redrawn type, issued in 1946, see No 471.

D **54**   (O **54**)   (**54**)

(Des W. Weiskönig. Eng G. Matter. Recess PTT Printing Bureau, Bern)
1938 (1 Feb). POSTAGE DUE.

A. Smooth white non granite paper. P 11½

D384A	D **54**	5c. scarlet	60	30
D385A		10c. scarlet	85	20
D386A		15c. scarlet	1·80	3·00
D387A		20c. scarlet	1·40	45
D388A		25c. scarlet	2·10	3·00
D389A		30c. scarlet	2·00	1·80
D390A		40c. scarlet	2·30	65
D391A		50c. scarlet	2·75	3·25
D384A/D391A	Set of 8		12·50	11·50

B. White non granite paper with grilled gum

D384B	D **54**	5c. scarlet	95	2·75
D385B		10c. scarlet	1·00	1·80
D386B		15c. scarlet	2·30	5·25
D387B		20c. scarlet	1·80	90
D388B		25c. scarlet	2·50	22·00
D389B		30c. scarlet	2·30	6·00
D390B		40c. scarlet	3·25	5·25
D391B		50c. scarlet	4·00	8·50
D384B/D391B	Set of 8		16·00	47·00

See note on grilled gum below No. 230.
From 1954 ordinary postage stamps were used in place of Postage Due stamps and Nos. D384/D391 were withdrawn in March 1956.

1938. OFFICIAL. Various issues optd as T O **54**.

*(a) As T **52** (Landscape types. Recess)*

A. Smooth white non-granite paper

O381A	3c. yellow-olive	45	45
O382A	5c. blue-green	45	45
O383A	10c. bright purple (II)	1·30	65
O384A	15c. orange	45	2·75
O385A	20c. scarlet (No. 375)	70	45
O386A	25c. yellow-brown	70	2·20
O387A	30c. dull ultramarine	90	1·60
O388A	35c. bright green	90	2·00
O389A	40c. grey	90	1·60
O381A/O389A	Set of 9	6·00	11·00

SWITZERLAND 1938

B. Non-granite paper with grilled gum

O381B		3c. yellow-olive	6·50	70
O382B		5c. blue-green	1·90	50
O383B		10c. bright purple (II)	2·20	90
O384B		15c. orange	4·00	1·80
O385B		20c. scarlet (No. 375)	2·20	1·10
O386B		25c. yellow-brown	£110	12·00
O387B		30c. dull ultramarine	3·50	1·60
O388B		35c. bright green	2·75	3·25
O389B		40c. grey	3·50	1·60
O381B/O389B		*Set of 9*	£120	21·00

(b) Helvetia seated

O390	17	50c. yellow-green and deep green	3·50	2·20
O391		60c. orange-brown	3·50	4·00
O392		70c. buff and violet	3·50	6·50
O393		80c. buff and olive-grey	3·50	5·25
O394		1f. pale green and claret	4·50	5·25

(c) Arms type Shield and value in vermilion

O395	41	90c. deep green and green	4·50	5·25
O396		1f.20 brown-lake and salmon-pink	4·50	7·00
O397		1f.50 blue and greenish blue	7·75	9·50
O398		2f. black and olive-grey	8·75	11·00
O390/O398		*Set of 9*	40·00	50·00
O381As/O389As and O390s/O398s. *Optd* 'SPECIMEN' *Set of 18*			£900	

See note on grilled gum below No. 230.

1938 (Apr). AIR. No. 325a surch with T **54**.
381	39	10c. on 65c. slate-blue and deep turquoise-blue	45	95

See also No. **MS**387a.

55 International Labour Bureau

(Des H. Fischer. Photo Courvoisier)

1938 (2 May). T **55** and similar horiz designs. Granite paper. P 11½.
382		20c. red and buff	45	45
383		30c. blue and pale blue	75	45
384		60c. brown and buff	3·00	4·50
385		1f. black and buff	11·00	29·00
382/385 *Set of 4*			13·50	31·00

Designs: 20c. T **55**; 30c. Palace of League of Nations (inscr SDN); 60c. Inner Courtyard of Palace of League of Nations (inscr SDN); 1f. International Labour Bureau (*different*).

(59)

1938 (22 May). AIR. Special Flights. No. 324a surch with T **59**.
386	38	75c. on 50c. deep grey-green and red		9·50
		s. Specimen		£800

This stamp was affixed to letters handed to Post Offices, or sold cancelled but not unused.

60 William Tell's Chapel

(Des H. Thöni. Photo Courvoisier)

1938 (15 June). National Fête. Fund for Swiss Subjects abroad. Yellow borders. Granite paper. P 11½.
387	60	10c. +10c.violet	50	3·25
		a. Grilled gum*	30·00	£160

*See note below No. 230.

1938 (17 Sept). National Philatelic Exhibition, Aarau and 25th Anniversary of Swiss Air Mail Service. Sheet 74×87 mm Granite paper.
MS387a Nos. 375 (pair) and 381 (*sold at* 1f.50) .... 50·00 60·00

61 First Act of Federal Parliament   **62** Symbolical of Swiss Culture

(Des and Eng K. Bickel. Recess PTT Printing Bureau, Bern)

1938 (1 Feb)–**54**. As T **61** (Symbolic designs). Granite paper with black and red fibres. Yellowish gum. P 11½.

A. Buff paper with bluish surface coating

388A	3f. red-brown	18·00	16·00
389A	5f. slate-blue	12·00	10·50
390A	10f. green	95·00	95·00

B. Buff paper (May 1942)

388B	3f. red-brown	34·00	1·80
389B	5f. slate-blue	16·00	1·80
390B	10f. green	49·00	4·50

C. White paper with blue and red fibres (July 1954)

388C	3f. red-brown	5·00	1·80
389C	5f. slate-blue	7·25	1·80
390C	10f. green	14·50	6·00

Designs: 3f. T **61**; 5f. The Assembly at Stans; 10f. A polling booth.
On the first issue the bluish coating is sensitive to light and water and has often disappeared, particularly on used examples.
The third issue, which appeared in July 1954, is on white paper with blue and red fibres, a yellowish surface coating and white gum, this coating is also prone to disappearance.

(Nos. 391/392. Des and Eng K. Bickel. Design recess; Coat of Arms photo PTT, Bern. No. 393. Des V. Surbek. Photo Courvoisier)

1939 (1 Feb). National Exhibition, Zürich. T **62** and similar types. Coat of Arms in scarlet. Grilled gum (20c., 30c.). P 11½.

A. Inscribed in French

391A	10c. deep violet	45	45
392A	20c. carmine	1·00	45
393A	30c. blue and buff	3·75	13·50

B. Inscribed in German

391B	10c. deep violet	45	45
392B	20c. carmine	75	45
393B	30c. blue and buff	3·75	5·00

C. Inscribed in Italian

391C	10c. deep violet	45	45
392C	20c. carmine	6·00	45
393C	30c. blue and buff	3·00	16·00

Designs: 10c. Group symbolic of Swiss Industry and Agriculture; 20c. T **62**; 30c. Piz Rosegg and Tschirva Glacier.

64 Crossbow and Floral Branch   **65** Laupen Castle

(Des V. Surbek. Photo Courvoisier)

1939 (6 May). National Exhibition, Zürich. Smooth white granite paper. P 11½.

A. Inscribed in French

(a) Smooth white granite paper

394Aa	5c. green	65	4·50
395Aa	10c. blackish brown	70	4·50
396Aa	20c. scarlet	1·40	6·25
397Aa	30c. royal blue	3·75	17·00

(b) Grilled paper

394Ab	5c. green	1·40	6·25
395Ab	10c. blackish brown	1·70	9·25
396Ab	20c. scarlet	3·75	27·00

B. Inscribed in German

(a) Smooth white granite paper

394Ba	5c. green	65	4·50
395Ba	10c. blackish brown	70	3·00
396Ba	20c. scarlet	1·40	3·75
397Ba	30c. royal blue	3·50	14·00

(b) Grilled paper

394Bb	5c. green	1·60	8·75
395Bb	10c. blackish brown	2·10	9·75
396Bb	20c. scarlet	3·50	26·00

1939 SWITZERLAND

C. Inscribed in Italian
(a) Smooth white granite paper

394Ca	5c. green		90	6·75
395Ca	10c. blackish brown		70	5·75
396Ca	20c. scarlet		1·50	8·75
397Ca	30c. royal blue		3·75	18·00

(b) Grilled paper

394Cb	5c. green		1·60	7·00
395Cb	10c. blackish brown		1·80	9·75
396Cb	20c. scarlet		4·00	28·00

No. 395Bb, the 30c. and all grilled gum varieties were issued in sheets, the remainder in coils. The coils were issued both with and without control numbers on the back of every fifth stamp in the roll.

No. 395Bb can be distinguished by the length of 'COURVOISIER S A' which is longer and extends to beyond the base of the 'V' of 'HELVETIA', whereas in the coil stamps the imprint extends to just before the 'V'.

See note on grilled gum below No. 230.

(Des P. Bösch. Photo Courvoisier)

1939 (15 June). National Fête. Fund for Destitute Mothers. Coat of Arms In scarlet. Granite paper. P 11½.

398	**65**	10c. +10c. brown and grey	45	2·30

66 Geneva   **67** Les Rangiers

(Des A. Yersin. Photo Courvoisier)

1939 (22 Aug). 75th Anniversary of Geneva (Red Cross) Convention. Cross In scarlet. Granite paper. P 11½.

399	**66**	20c. red and buff	45	50
400		30c. bright blue and grey	45	4·75

(Des C. Liner (5c.), B. Reber (10c., 20c.), Ch. L'Eplattenier (30c.) Photo Courvoisier)

1940 (20 Mar). National Fête and Red Cross Fund. As T **67** (memorial types inscr 'FETE NATIONALE 1940' in German (5c., 20c.), Italian (10c.), and French (30c.)). Coat of Arms in scarlet. Granite paper. P 11½.

401		5c. +5c. black and green	45	1·80
402		10c. +5c. black and orange	45	1·40
403		20c. +5c. black and red	3·50	2·20
		a. Redrawn design	7·00	12·00
404		30c. +10c. black and blue	2·30	13·00
401/404 Set of 4			6·00	17·00
MS404a 125×65 mm. Nos. 401/402, 403a/404 Imperf (sold at 5f.) (16.6.40)			£450	£950

Battle memorials: Sempach (5c.), Giornico (10c.), and Calven (20c.).

No. 403. The inscription at the base of the statue is enclosed in a white rectangular tablet.

No 403a. The inscription is on a grey background forming part of the statue.

68 William Tell (Ferdinand Hodler)   **69** Ploughing

(Des and Eng Karl Bickel. Recess PTT, Bern)

1941 (15 Jan)–**59**. As T **68** (historical types). Granite paper. P 11½.

405		50c. deep violet-blue/blue-green	7·50	45
406		60c. reddish-brown/cinnamon	13·00	45
407		70c. deep reddish purple/mauve	3·25	2·75
408		80c. black/olive-grey	75	45
408a		80c. black/mauve (29.10.58)	3·50	85
409		90c. scarlet/pink	80	45
409a		90c. scarlet/buff (22.6.59)	4·50	4·50
410		1f. myrtle green/blue-green	1·30	45
411		1f.20 plum/olive-grey	1·30	45
411a		1f.20 purple/reddish lilac (29.10.58)	5·25	95
412		1f.50 indigo/buff	2·30	45
413		2f. brown-lake/pink	2·75	45
413a		2f. brown-lake/cream (22.6.59)	7·75	95
405/413 Set of 13			49·00	12·00

Designs: (Works of art)—50c. *Oath of Union* (James Vibert); 60c. T **68**; 70c. *Kneeling Warrior* (Ferdinand Hodler); 80c. *Dying Ensign* (Hodler); 90c. *Standard-bearer* (Niklaus Deutsch). (Portraits)—1f. Colonel Louis Pfyffer; 1f.20, George Jenatsch; 1f.50, Lieutenant-General Francois de Reynold; 2f. Colonel Joachim Forrer.

(Des A. Patocchi. Photo Courvoisier)

1941 (21 Mar). Agricultural Development Plan. Granite paper. P 11½.

414	**69**	10c. chocolate and buff	45	90

70 Douglas DC-2 and The Jungfrau   **71** Chemin Creux, near Kussnacht

(Des and Eng A. Yersin. Recess PTT, Bern)

1941 (1 May).–**48**. AIR. T **70** (landscapes). Granite paper. P 11½.

415		30c. ultramarine/salmon	95	45
415a		30c. slate-blue/salmon (1.10.48)	13·00	22·00
416		40c. grey/salmon	95	45
416a		40c. ultramarine/salmon (1.10.48)	90·00	4·50
417		50c. olive/salmon	95	45
418		60c. yellow-green/salmon	1·30	45
419		70c. violet/salmon	95	95
420		1f. blue-green/buff	2·75	95
421		2f. lake/buff	7·00	6·00
422		5f. deep blue/buff	31·00	26·00
415/422 Set of 10			£130	55·00

Designs: 30c. T **70**; 40c. Valais; 50c. Lac Lemon; 60c. Alpstein; 70c. Ticino; 1f. Vierwaldstattersee (Lake Lucerne); 2f. Engadin; 5f. Churfirsten.

1941 (12 May). AIR. Special (Buochs–Payerne) Flights. No. 420 with 'PRO AERO/28.V.1941' added.

423		1f. blue-green/buff	8·50	32·00

(Des P. Bösch and C. L'Eplattenier. Photo Courvoisier)

1941 (15 June). National Fête and 650th Anniversary of Foundation of Swiss Confederation. T **71** and another design dated 1291–1941. Granite paper. P 11½.

424		10c. +10c. blue, scarlet and yellow	45	1·80
425		20c. +10c. scarlet, brown-red and buff	45	3·25
		a. Scarlet, brown and buff	6·00	£160

Designs: 10c. Relief map of Lake Lucerne with Arms of Uri, Schwyz and Unterwalden around it; 20c. T **71**.

Premium in aid of Public Utility Funds.

72 Arms of Berne, Masons laying Corner-stone and Knight   (O **73**)

(Des P. Bösch. Photo Courvoisier)

1941 (6 Sept). 750th Anniversary of Foundation of Bern. Granite paper. P 11½.

426	**72**	10c. black, yellow, scarlet and olive	45	1·80

1942 (25 Feb)–**43**. OFFICIAL.

*(a) Nos. 368/379 optd with T O **73**. Smooth white non-granite paper.*

O427	3c. yellow-olive	45	3·50
O428	5c. blue-green	45	45
O429	10c. red-brown (No. 371)	90	90
O430	10c. chestnut (No. 372) (1943)	45	70
O431	15c. orange	90	3·25
O432	20c. scarlet (No. 375)	90	70
O433	25c. yellow-brown	90	3·50
O434	30c. dull ultramarine	1·40	1·40
O435	35c. bright green	1·80	4·50
O436	40c. grey	1·80	90
O427/O436 Set of 10		9·00	18·00

(b) Nos. 405/413 with larger opt

O437	50c. deep violet-blue/blue-green	6·00	7·00
O438	60c. reddish-brown/cinnamon	7·00	7·00
O439	70c. deep reddish purple/mauve	7·75	13·00
O440	80c. black/olive-grey	2·10	2·75
O441	90c. scarlet/pink	2·75	3·50
O442	1f. myrtle green/blue-green	2·75	2·75
O443	1f.20 plum/olive-grey	3·50	4·50
O444	1f.50 indigo/buff	3·50	5·25
O445	2f. brown-lake/pink	4·50	6·00
O437/O445 Set of 9		37·75	46·50

SWITZERLAND 1942

73 To survive, collect salvage

(Des A. Yersin. Photo Courvoisier)

1942 (21 Mar). Salvage Campaign. As T **73**. Inscr in French (F), German (G). or Italian (I). Value and Coat of Arms in scarlet, tablets In blue. Granite paper. P 11½.

427F		10c. brown	45	1·80
427G		10c. brown	45	90
427I		10c. brown	7·75	8·00
427F/427I Set of 3			7·75	9·75

Inscriptions: T **73** (F); Zum Durchhalten/Altstoffe sammeln (G); PER RESISTERE/RACCOGLIETE/LA ROBA VECCHIA (I).

74 View of Old Geneva   **75** Soldiers' Memorial at Forch, near Zürich

(Des A. Yersin and O. Rüegg. Photo Courvoisier)

1942 (15 June). National Fête. National Relief Fund and Second Millenary of Geneva Coat of Arms in scarlet. Granite paper. P 11½.

428	**74**	10c. +10c. black and yellow	45	1·30
429	**75**	20c. +10c. red and yellow	45	3·75
MS429a 105×62 mm. Nos. 428/429 Imperf (sold at 2f.)			85·00	£400

76

76a

(Eng A. Yersin. Recess PTT Printing Bureau, Bern)

1943 (26 Feb). Centenary of First Swiss Cantonal Postage Stamps. Background of horiz red lines. P 11½.

430	**76**	10c. (4+6) black	45	45

Miniature Sheets

MS430a 164×140 mm. No. 430 (block of 12) Imperf (sold at 5f.) .... 80·00 95·00

(Litho Orell Füssli, Zürich)

MS430b 70×75 mm. Type **76a** 4 and 6 (c.) black Imperf (sold at 3f.) .... 75·00 95·00

77 Intragna (Ticino)   **77a** Double Geneva

(Des A. Yersin and P. Burkhard. Photo Courvoisier)

1943 (15 June). National Fête and Youth's Vocational Training Fund. T **77** (and another design inscr 'FESTA NAZIONALE 1943'). Coat of Arms and values in scarlet. Granite paper. P 11½.

431		10c. +10c. grey-black and buff	45	1·40
432		20c. +10c. brown-red and buff	45	4·00

Designs: 10c. T **77**; 20c. Federal Palace, Berne.

1943 (13 July). AIR. Special Flights. 30th Anniversary of First Flight across Alps by Oscar Bider. As No. 432, but optd 'PRO AERO/13.VII.1943' and value in black.

433	1f. brown-red and buff	3·50	18·00

(Des B. Reber. Photo Courvoisier)

1943 (17 Sept). National Philatelic Exhibition, Geneva (GEPH) and Centenary of Geneva Cantonal Stamp. Sheet 72×73 mm. Imperf.

MS433a **77a** 5c. black and yellow green (sold at 3f.) . 80·00 70·00

78 Apollo of Olympia   **79** Heiden

(Des Mme Maya Allenbach (after H. R. von der Mühll). Photo Courvoisier)

1944 (21 Mar). Olympic Games Jubilee. Granite paper. P 11½.

A. Yellowish gum with long granite threads

434A	**78**	10c. black and orange	45	1·80
435A		20c. black and carmine	45	1·80
436A		30c. black and light blue	90	14·00
434A/436A Set of 3			1·60	16·00

B. Thick white gum with short granite threads

434B	**78**	10c. black and orange	3·00	65·00
435B		20c. black and carmine	2·20	55·00
436B		30c. black and light blue	1·80	40·00
434B/436B Set of 3			6·25	£140

(Des O. Rüegg (5c.), W. Koch (10c.), A. Juon (20c.), P. and B. Artaria (30c.). Photo Courvoisier)

1944 (15 June). National Fête and Red Cross Fund. As T **79** (views, inscr 'FESTA NAZIONALE 1944/BUNDES FEIER 1944/FETE NATIONALE', or similar inscr). Coat of Arms in scarlet. Granite paper. P 11½.

437	5c. +5c. green and buff	45	4·00
438	10c. +10c. grey and buff	45	90
439	20c. +10c. carmine and buff	45	1·80
440	30c. +10c. blue and buff	3·25	30·00
437/440 Set of 4		4·25	33·00

Designs: 5c. T **79**; 10c. St Jacques on the River Birs; 20c. Castle ruins, Mesocco; 30c. Basel.

80 Haefeli DH-3 Biplane

(Des O. Baumberger (10c. to 30c.), H. R. von der Mühll (1f.50). Photo Courvoisier)

1944 (1 Sept). AIR. 25th Anniversary of National Air Post. T **80** and similar horiz designs. Granite paper. P 11½.

441	10c. bistre-brown and sage green	45	90
442	20c. rosine and stone	45	90
443	30c. ultramarine and blue	45	3·25
444	1f.50 agate, grey brown and vermilion	8·75	30·00
441/444 Set of 4		9·00	32·00

Aircraft: 10c. T **80**; 20c. Fokker F.VIIb/3m; 30c. Lockheed 9B Orion of Swissair; 1f.50, Douglas DC-3 HB-IRI Swissair.

No. 444 was only on sale until 18 September and was only valid for use on the special commemorative flight from Zürich to Geneva and back on 20 September.

81 Symbolical of Faith, Hope and Charity   **81a** Lifeboat

1945 SWITZERLAND

(Des N. Stoeklin (T **81**), V. Surbek (T **81a**). Photo Courvoisier)
1945 (20 Feb). War Relief Fund. Granite paper. P 11½.
445	**81**	10c. +10c. blackish olive, black and grey	45	90
446		20c. +60c. scarlet, black and grey	1·40	10·50
MS446a	70×110 mm. Imperf. Type **81a** 3f.+7f. indigo...		£180	£350

81b Basel Dove

(Des E. and M. Lenz. Typo and Dove embossed. PTT, Bern)
1945 (14 Apr). Centenary of Basel Cantonal Stamp Issue. Sheet 71×63 mm. Granite paper. Imperf.
MS446b **81b** 10 (c.) grey-green, red and black
(sold at 3f.) .... 90·00 £150

82 *Trans* Peace to men of good will   **83** Olive Branch

(Des N. Stoecklin (5c. to 40c.), A. Patocchi and H. Steiner (50c. to 2f.); photo Courvoisier. Des and Eng K. Bickel, recess PTT, Bern (3c. to 10f.))
1945 (9 May). Peace. Granite paper. As Types **82/83** (symbolic designs inscr 'PAX'). P 11½.
447	5c. green and grey	45	90
448	10c. brown and grey	45	40
449	20c. carmine and grey	45	40
450	30c. ultramarine and grey	70	5·25
451	40c. orange and grey	2·00	19·00
452	50c. brown red and buff	3·00	40·00
453	60c. dark and light grey	2·75	27·00
454	80c. red and buff	5·50	£130
455	1f. blue and buff	8·75	£150
456	2f. brown and buff	28·00	£275
457	3f. green/*buff*	35·00	£140
458	5f. red-brown/*buff*	£130	£475
459	10f. violet/*buff*	£100	£180
447/459 Set of 13		£275	£1300

Designs: As T **82**—5c. to 40c., Numerals. As T **83**, 38×22½ mm—50c. T **83**; 60c. Keys, 80c. Horn of Plenty; 1f. Dove; 2f. Spade and flowers in ploughed field As T **83**, but 38×21 mm and 'PAX' in large outlined capital letters—3f. Crocuses; 5f. Clasped hands; 10f. Aged couple.

84   **85** Silk weaving

(Des N. Stoecklin. Photo Courvoisier)
1945 (9 May). Red Cross. Cross and premium in red. Granite paper. P 11½.
460 **84** 5c. +10c. green .... 45 1·40

(Des P. Boesch, Eng A. Yersin; recess and photo PTT Bern (5c.) Des Faustina Iselin (10c.), H. Zaugg (20c.), F. Deringer (30c.); photo Courvoisier)
1945 (15 June). National Fête. T **85** and similar horiz designs. Coat of Arms in scarlet. Granite paper (10c. to 30c.). P 11½.
461	5c. +5c. blue-green	45	3·50
462	10c. +10c. brown and grey	45	1·40
463	20c. +10c. brown-red and buff	90	1·40
464	30c. +10c. blue and grey	8·75	80·00
461/464 Set of 4		9·50	80·00

Designs: 5c. T **85**; 10c. and 20c. Jura and Emmental farmhouses; 30c. Timbered house.

86 Pestalozzi   **87** Zoglic Instructional Glider

(Des and Eng Karl Bickel, from a relief by J. M. Christen. Recess, PTT Bern)
1946 (12 Jan). Birth Bicentenary of Johann Heinrich Pestalozzi (educational reformer). P 11½.
465 **86** 10c. purple 45 40

(Des O. Baumberger. Photo Courvoisier)
1946 (1 May). AIR. Special (Lausanne, Lucerne, Locarno) Flights. Granite paper. P 11½.
466 **87** 1f.50 red and grey .... 43·00 47·00
No. 466 was valid for postage only on the special postal flights of 22nd and 23rd May, 1946.

88 Cheese-making   **89** Chalet in Appenzell

(No. 467. Des P. Boesch. Eng A. Yersin. Design recess; Coat of Arms photo, plain paper, PTT, Bern Des No. 468, F. Iselin, Nos. 469/470 Des W. Koch. Photo Granite paper Courvoisier)
1946 (15 June). National Fête and Fund for Swiss Citizens Abroad. T **88** and designs as T **89**, inscr 'I. VIII 1946'. Coat of Arms in scarlet. P 11½.
467	5c. +5c. green	1·40	5·25
468	10c. +10c. sepia and buff	90	1·40
469	20c. +10c. red and buff	1·40	4·00
470	30c. +10c. blue and blue-grey	13·00	22·00
467/470 Set of 4		15·00	27·00

Designs: 5c. T **88**; 10c. Châlets in Vaud; 20c. T **89**; 30c. Engadine.

1946 (6 July). T **53** redrawn. Granite paper. P 11½.
471 10c. yellow and black .... 5·50 1·80
No. 471 measures 38×22½ mm. as against No. 380's 37×21 mm. The most outstanding difference is that in No. 471 there are eight lines of horizontal shading above the highest white peak at the top right of the design, whereas in No. 380 there are only three.

90 Douglas DC-4 of Swissair, Statue of Liberty and St Peter's Cathedral, Geneva

(Des B. Reber. Photo Courvoisier)
1947 (17 Mar). AIR. First Geneva–New York Swissair Flight. Granite paper. P 11½.
472 **90** 2f.50 deep blue, pale blue and red.......... 30·00 35·00
No. 472 was valid for postage only on 2nd May for use on the first Swissair flight between Geneva and New York.

91 Platelayers   **92** Rorschach Station

(5c. Des P. Boesch, Eng A. Yersin; recess PTT, Bern 10c., 20c. Des W. Koch, 30c. Des H. Thöni; photo Courvoisier)
1947 (14 June). National Fête. Professional Education of Invalids and Anti-Cancer Funds. As Types **91/92** (horiz designs inscr 'I. VIII 1947'). Granite paper. Coat of Arms in scarlet. P 11½.
473	5c. +15c. green	95	4·50
474	10c. +10c. black and buff	1·80	1·40
475	20c. +10c. carmine and buff	1·80	1·80
476	30c. +10c. blue and grey	13·00	21·00
473/476 Set of 4		16·00	26·00

Designs: 5c. T **91**; 10c. T **92**; 20c. Luen-Castiel; 30c. Fluelen Railway Stations.

SWITZERLAND 1947

93 *Limmat*, First Swiss Steam Locomotive

(Des 5c. B. Reber. 10c. O. Baumberger, 20c., 30c. O. Rüegg. Photo Courvoisier)

1947 (6 Aug). Centenary of Swiss Railways. As T **93** (horiz designs Inscr '1847–1947'). Granite paper. P 11½.
477	5c. green, yellow and black	1·80	90
478	10c. black and brown	1·80	90
479	20c. scarlet, buff and lake	95	90
480	30c. blue, grey and light blue	4·50	4·50
477/480	Set of 4	8·25	6·50

Designs: 5c. T **93**; 10c. Steam freight locomotive, 20c. Electric train crossing Melide causeway; 30c. Railway bridge.

95 Sun of St Moritz   **96** Ice Hockey

(Des 5c., 10c. A. Diggelmann; 20c., 30c. W. Weiskönig. Photo Courvoisier)

1948 (15 Jan). Fifth Winter Olympic Games. As Types **95/96** (designs inscr 'ST. MORITZ OLYMPIA 1948') Granite paper. P 11½.
481	5c. +5c. brown, yellow and green	95	2·75
482	10c. +10c. blue, light blue and brown	95	1·80
483	20c. +10c. yellow, black and claret	1·80	3·50
484	30c. +10c. black, light blue and blue	6·00	10·50
481/484	Set of 4	8·75	17·00

Designs: 5c. T **95**; 10c. Snow crystals; 20c. T **96**; 30c. Ski-runner.

97 Johann Rudolf Wettstein   **99** Frontier Guard

(Des 5c., 10c., 20c., Hermann Eidenbenz; 30c. Maya Allenbach. Photo Courvoisier)

1948 (27 Feb). Tercentenary of the Treaty of Westphalia and Centenaries of the Neuchâtel Revolution and Swiss Federation. T **97** and designs inscr '1848–1948'. Granite paper. P 11½.
485	5c. green and dark green	45	90
486	10c. grey-black and grey	45	40
487	20c. carmine and rose	90	45
488	30c. blue, grey-blue and brown	1·80	2·75
485/488	Set of 4	3·25	4·00

Designs: 5c. T **97**; 10c. Neuchâtel Castle; 20c. Symbol of Helvetia; 30c. Symbol of Federal State.
See also No. **MS**498*a*.

1948 (1 Mar–1 Oct). As Nos. 369/379, but colours changed and new design (25c.).
489	5c. reddish brown	45	30
	a. *Tête-bêche* (pair) (1.10.48)	3·50	3·75
490	10c. green	45	30
	a. *Tête-bêche* (pair) (1.10.48)	3·75	5·50
491	20c. chestnut	55	30
	a. *Tête-bêche* (pair) (1.10.48)	5·00	6·25
492	25c. scarlet	3·25	1·40
493	30c. deep turquoise-blue	18·00	13·00
494	40c. deep blue	55·00	19·00
489/494	Set of 6	70·00	19·00

Designs: 5c. Mount Pilatus; 10c. Chillon Castle and Dents du Midi; 20c. Lake Lugano and Mount San Salvatore; 25c. National Park; 30c. Rhine Falls; 40c. Mount Sands and Lake Seealp.

The 5c., 10c., 20c. and 30c. values were also issued in coils with a control letter and figures on the back of every fifth stamp in the roll. The 40c. was also issued in coils but without control numbers.

(5c. Des and Eng, K. Lieven. Recess Plain paper PTT, Bern, 10c. Des F. Iselin, 20c. W. Koch, 30c. P. Chatillon. Photo Granite paper. Courvoisier)

1948 (15 June). National Fête and Anti-Tuberculosis Fund. T **99** and horiz designs as T **89**, inscr 'I. VIII 1948'. Coat of Arms in scarlet. P 11½.
495	5c. +5c. green	1·40	2·20
496	10c. +10c. slate and grey	90	1·40
497	20c. +10c. brown-red and buff	1·30	1·80
498	30c. +10c. ultramarine and grey	7·00	13·00
495/498	Set of 4	9·50	17·00

Designs: 5c. T **99**; (Typical houses in)—10c. Fribourg; 20c. Valais; 30c. Ticino.

1948 (21 Aug). National Philatelic Exhibition. Basel (IMABA). Sheet 110×61 mm. T **97**. Granite paper. P 11½.
MS498*a*	10c. reddish purple and grey; 20c. bluish grey and grey (sold at 3f.)	£140	£110

101 Glider   **102** Posthorn

(Des H. Erni. Eng A. Yersin. Design recess, background typo PTT, Bern)

1949 (11 Apr). AIR. Special (La Chaux de-Fonds, St Gallen, Lugano) Flights. P 11½.
499	**101** 1f.50 purple and yellow	70·00	70·00

No. 499 was valid for postage only on the special postal flights of 27 and 28 April, 1949.

(Des W. Weiskönig. Photo Courvoisier)

1949 (16 May). Centenary of Federal Post. T **102** and similar types inscr '1849/1949' Granite paper. P 11½.
500	5c. yellow pink and grey	45	90
501	20c. yellow, violet and grey	45	45
502	30c. yellow, brown and grey	1·80	15·00
500/502	Set of 3	2·40	14·50

Designs: 5c. T **102**; 20c. Mail coach drawn by five Horses; 30c. Postal motor coach and trailer.

103 Main Motif of UPU Monument, Berne   **104** Postman

(Des H. Thöni. Photo Granite Paper. Courvoisier)

1949 (16 May). 75th Anniversary of Universal Postal Union. T **103** and similar horiz designs. P 11½.
503	10c. green (Type **103**)	45	90
504	25c. claret (Globe and ribbon)	95	10·50
505	40c. blue (Globe and Pigeons)	1·80	12·00
503/505	Set of 3	3·00	21·00

(5c. Des W. Koch, Eng K. Lieven. Recess Plain paper. PTT, Bern. 10c. Des F. Deringer, 20c. H. Zaugg, 40c. W. Koch, Photo Granite paper. Courvoisier)

1949 (15 June). National Fête and Aid to Youth Fund. T **104** and various horiz designs as T **89**, inscr 'I. VIII. 1949'. Coat of Arms in scarlet. P 11½.
506	5c. +5c. purple	1·40	2·75
507	10c. +10c. blue-green and buff	90	1·40
508	20c. +10c. brown and buff	1·30	1·40
509	40c. +10c. blue and light blue	9·50	24·00
506/509	Set of 4	12·00	27·00

Designs: 5c. T **104**; (Typical houses in)—10c. Basel; 20c. Lucerne, 40c. Prättigau.

106 High-tension Pylons   **107** Sitter Viaducts near St Gall

1949 SWITZERLAND

107A I.

107B II.

Type II: (a) Two clear horizontal lines instead of three between shore and top of rocks. (b) horizontal line inserted to mark base of building. (c) Cross-hatching extended above '20 H'.

(Des and Eng Karl Bickel. Recess PTT, Bern)

1949 (1 Aug)–**50**. Types **106**/**107** and similar designs. P 11½.

510	3c. grey-black	4·75	4·75
511	5c. orange	55	30
	a. Tête-bêche (pair) (1.3.50)	1·40	45
512	10c. yellow-green	45	30
	a. Tête-bêche (pair) (1.3.50)	1·40	45
513	15c. turquoise	90	90
514	20c. maroon (I)	£5500	£120
	a. Type II	65	30
	b. Tête-bêche (pair) (II) (1.3.50)	2·20	1·80
515	25c. scarlet	55	30
516	30c. olive	90	30
517	35c. brown	1·80	1·80
518	40c. blue	4·50	45
519	50c. bluish grey	4·50	45
520	60c. blue-green	14·00	1·40
521	70c. violet	4·50	90
510/521	Set of 12 (cheapest)	34·00	11·00

Designs: 3c. T **106**; 5c. T **107**; 10c. Mountain cog railway, Rochers de Naye; 15c. Rotary snowplough; 20c. Grimsel reservoir; 25c. Lake Lugano and Melide railway causeway; 30c. Verbois hydroelectric power station; 35c. Alpine road (Val d'Anniviers); 40c. Rhine harbour, Basel; 50c. Suspension railway, Säntis; 60c. Railway viaduct. Landwasser; 70c. Survey mark. Finsteraarhorn.

The 5c., 10c., 25c., 30c. and 40c. values were also issued in coils with a control letter and figures on the back of every fifth stamp in the roll and the 20c. Type II in coils with or without controls.

1950 (1 Feb). OFFICIAL. Nos. 511/521 optd with T O **73**.

O522	5c. orange	90	1·80
O523	10c. yellow-green	1·80	1·80
O524	15c. turquoise	14·50	26·00
O525	20c. maroon (II)	5·25	1·80
O526	25c. scarlet	8·75	16·00
O527	30c. olive	6·00	7·00
O528	35c. brown	8·75	18·00
O529	40c. blue	7·00	7·75
O530	50c. bluish grey	10·50	12·00
O531	60c. blue-green	13·00	13·00
O532	70c. violet	40·00	39·00
O522/O532	Set of 11	£100	£130

110 First Federal Postage Stamps

111 Putting the Weight

(5c. Des B. Reber, Eng. K. Bickel. Recess (Coat of Arms photo) Plain paper PTT, Bern. Others Des H. Fischer. Photo Granite paper Courvoisier)

1950 (1 June). National Fête, Red Cross Fund, and Centenary of First Federal Postage stamps. T **110** and sporting types as T **111** inscr 'I.VIII 1950' Coat of Arms in scarlet. P 11½.

522	5c. +5c. black	90	1·40
523	10c. +10c. green and greenish grey	2·40	1·40
524	20c. +10c. brown-olive and grey	3·00	1·80
525	30c. +10c. magenta and grey	8·50	39·00
526	40c. +10c. blue and grey	13·00	22·00
522/526	Set of 5	25·00	60·00

Designs: 5c. T **110**; 10c. T **111**; 20c. Wrestling; 30c. Sprinting; 40c. Ritle-shooting.

112 Arms of Zürich

113 Valaisan Polka

114 Telegraph

(5c. Des P. Boesch. Eng A. Yersin. Recess (Coat of Arms photo). Plain paper. PTT, Bern. Others, Des H. Fischer. Photo Granite paper Courvoisier)

1951 (1 June). National Fête. Mothers' Fund and Sixth Centenary of Zürich. T **112** and national activities as T **113** inscr 'I.VIII 1951'. Coat of Arms in scarlet. P 11½.

527	5c. +5c. black	95	1·40
528	10c. +10c. green and grey	95	90
529	20c. +10c. brown-olive and grey	2·00	2·20
530	30c. +10c. magenta and grey	9·00	22·00
531	40c. +10c. blue and grey	13·00	26·00
527/531	Set of 5	23·00	47·00

Designs: 5c. T **112**; 10c. T **113**; 20c. Flag-waving; 30c. Homussen (National Game); 40c. Blowing alphorn.

1951 (29 Sept). National Philatelic Exhibition, Lucerne (LUNABA). Sheet 74×57 mm. As No. 529. Imperf.

MS531a	40c. multicoloured (sold at 3f.)	£400	£300

(Des P. Gauchat. Photo Granite paper. Courvoisier)

1952 (1 Feb). Swiss Telecommunications Centenary. Designs as T **114** inscr '1852 1952'. P 11½.

532	5c. red-orange and yellow (Type **114**)	45	1·80
533	10c. emerald and pink (Telephone)	45	30
534	20c. magenta and lavender (Radio)	1·80	30
535	40c. blue and pale blue (Television)	4·50	11·50
532/535	Set of 4	6·50	12·50

115 Arms of Glarus and Zug

116 River Doubs

(5c. Des P. Boesch. Eng A. Yersin. Recess (Coat of Arms photo). Plain paper PTT, Bern. Others. Des O. Baumberger. Photo Granite paper. Courvoisier)

1952 (31 May). Pro Patria. Cultural Funds and 600th Anniversary of Glarus and Zug joining Confederation. T **115** and horiz designs as T **116**. P 11½.

536	5c. +5c. scarlet and black	90	1·80
537	10c. +10c. blue-green and cream	90	90
538	20c. +10c. claret and pink	90	90
539	30c. +10c. brown and buff	6·00	18·00
540	40c. +10c. blue and pale blue	8·50	16·00
536/540	Set of 5	15·00	34·00

Designs: 5c. T **115**; 10c. T **116**; 20c. St Gotthard Lake; 30c. River Moesa; 40c. Marjelen Lake.

117 Arms of Berne

118 Rapids, River Reuss

SWITZERLAND 1953

(5c. Des P. Boesch. Eng A. Yersin. Recess (Coat of Arms photo).
Plain paper. PTT, Bern. Others. Des O. Baumberger.
Photo Granite paper. Courvoisier)

1953 (1 June). Pro Patria. Emigrants' Fund and 600th Anniversary of Berne joining Confederation. T **117** and various horiz designs as T **118**. P 11½.

541	5c. +5c. scarlet and black	1·40	1·40
542	10c. +10c. blue-green and cream	90	90
543	20c. +10c. claret and pink	1·40	1·40
544	30c. +10c. brown and buff	8·50	18·00
545	40c. +10c. blue and pale blue	10·50	16·00
541/545	Set of 5	20·00	34·00

Designs: 5c. T **117**; 10c. T **119**; 20c. Lake Sihl; 30c. Aqueduct Bisse; 40c. Lac Léman.

119 Zürich Airport   **120** Alpine Postal Coach and Winter Landscape

(Des E. and M. Lenz. Photo Granite paper. Courvoisier)

1953 (29 Aug). Inauguration of Zürich Airport. P 11½.

546	**119**	40c. blue, grey-blue, grey and scarlet	8·00	18·00

(Des H. Thöni. Photo Granite paper. Courvoisier)

1953 (8 Oct). Mobile PO Issue. T **120** and similar horiz design. P 11½.

547	10c. yellow, grey-green and emerald	90	45
548	20c. yellow, brown-lake and scarlet	90	45

Design: 10c. T **120**; 20c. Alpine postal coach and summer landscape.

121 Ear of Wheat and Flower   **122** Map of Rhine

(Des H. Hartmann (10c.), B. Reber (20c.), N. Stoecklin (25c.), H. Schwarzenbach (40c.). Photo Granite paper. Courvoisier)

1954 (15 Mar). Publicity Issue. Designs as Types **121/122**, inscr '1954'. P 11½.

549	10c. yellow, cerise, bronze-green and green	45	30
550	20c. buff, slate-blue, black and brown-lake	2·75	45
551	25c. bronze-green, pale blue and vermilion	1·80	4·50
552	40c. blue, yellow and black	5·75	6·00
549/552	Set of 4	9·75	10·00

Designs: Horiz—10c. T **121** (Agricultural Exhibition, Lucerne); 20c. Winged spoon (Cookery Exhibition, Berne); 40c. Football and world map (World Football Championship). Vert—25c. T **122** (50th Anniversary of Navigation of River Rhine).

123 Opening Bars of Swiss Hymn

(5c. Des and Eng K. Lieven. Recess Plain paper. PTT. Bern.
Others. Des P. Chatillon. Photo Granite paper. Courvoisier)

1954 (1 June). Pro Patria. Youth Fund and Centenary of Death of Father Zwyssig (composer of *Swiss Hymn*). T **123** and horiz designs as T **118** but inscr '1954'. P 11½.

553	5c. +5c. deep turquoise-green	90	1·80
554	10c. +10c. blue-green and turquoise	90	90
555	20c. +10c. maroon and cream	1·80	90
556	30c. +10c. brown and buff	6·75	14·50
557	40c. +10c. deep blue and pale blue	7·50	18·00
553/557	Set of 5	16·00	32·00

Designs: 5c. T **123**; 10c. Lake Neuchâtel; 20c. River Maggia; 30c. Taubenloch Gorge Waterfall, River Scliuss; 40c. Lake Sils.

124 Lausanne Cathedral   **125** Alphorn Blower

(Des A. Rosselet (5c.), M. Allenbach (10c.), P. Boesch (20c.), K. Wirth (40c.) Photo Granite paper. Courvoisier)

1955 (15 Feb). Publicity Issue. Designs as Types **124/125**, inscr '1955'. P 11½.

558	5c. black, scarlet, yellow and bistre-brown	90	1·40
559	10c. yellow, red, bistre and emerald	90	90
560	20c. sepia and red	2·20	90
561	40c. rose, black and blue	5·75	5·25
558/561	Set of 4	8·75	7·50

Designs: Horiz—5c. T **124** (National Philatelic Exhibition, Lausanne); 10c. Vaud girl's hat (Vevey Winegrowers' Festival); 40c. Car steering-wheel (25th International Motor Show, Geneva). Vert—20c. T **125** (Alpine Herdsman and Costume Festival, Interlaken).

1955 (15 Feb). National Philatelic Exhibition, Lausanne. Sheet 103×52 mm. T **124**. Imperf.

MS561a	10c. and 20c. multicoloured (sold at 2f.)	£150	£140

126 Federal Institute of Technology, Zürich

(5c. Des E. and M. Lenz. Eng A. Yersin. Recess
Plain paper. PTT, Bern. Others. Des F. Fedier.
Photo Granite paper. Courvoisier)

1955 (1 June). Pro Patria. Mountain Population Fund and Centenary of Federal Institute of Technology T **126** and horiz designs as T **118** but inscr '1955'. P 11½.

562	5c. +5c. slate	90	1·40
563	10c. +10c. deep blue green and cream	90	90
564	20c. +10c. lake and pink	1·80	1·40
565	30c. +10c. deep brown and buff	6·00	11·00
566	40c. +10c. deep bright blue and pale blue	6·25	14·00
562/566	Set of 5	14·50	26·00

Designs: 5c. T **126**; 10c. Grandfey railway viaduct, River Saane; 20c. Lake Aegeri; 30c. Grappelensee; 40c. Lake Bienne.

127 Road Safety   **128** Fokker F.VIIb/3m and Douglas DC-6 Aircraft

(Des B. Reber (5c.), U. Huber-Bavier (10c.) E. Hauri (20c.), P. Gauchat (40c.). Photo Granite paper. Courvoisier)

1956 (1 Mar). Publicity Issue. Designs as Types **127/128**, inscr '1956'. P 11½.

567	5c. yellow, black and grey-olive	55	40
568	10c. grey-black, emerald and red	90	45
569	20c. yellow, black, vermilion and carmine red	2·75	90
570	40c. blue and red	4·00	3·50
567/570	Set of 4	7·50	4·75

Designs: Horiz—5c. First postal motor coach (50th Anniversary of postal motor coach service); 10c. Electric train emerging from Simplon Tunnel and Stockalper Palace (50th Anniversary of opening of Simplon Tunnel); 20c. T **127** Vert—40c. T **128** (25th Anniversary of Swissair).

1956 SWITZERLAND

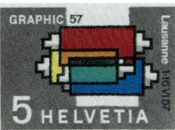

129 Rose, Scissors and Tape-measure
130 Printing Machine's Inking Rollers

(Des E. and M. Lenz. Eng A. Yersin. Recess Plain paper. PTT, Bern (5c.). Des P. Togni. Photo Granite paper. Courvoisier (others))

1956 (1 June). Pro Patria. Swiss Women's Fund. T **129** and horiz designs as T **118** but inscr '1956'. P 11½.

571	5c. +5c. deep turquoise-green		90	2·20
572	10c. +10c. deep emerald and pale green		90	90
573	20c. +10c. claret and pink		1·80	1·40
574	30c. +10c. deep brown and light brown		4·50	10·50
575	40c. +10c. deep bright blue and pale blue		5·50	13·50
571/575 Set of 5			12·00	26·00

Designs: 5c. T **129**; 10c. River Rhone at St Maurice; 20c. Katzensee; 30c. River Rhine at Trin; 40c. Walensee.

(Des E. Witzig (5c.), W. Mühlemann (10c.), E. and M. Lenz (20c.), D. Brun (40c.) Photo Granite paper. Courvoisier)

1957 (27 Feb). Publicity Issue. Designs as T **130**, inscr '1957'. P 11½.

576	5c. carmine, yellow, blue, black and grey	45	30
577	10c. brown, deep bluish green and turquoise-green	4·50	45
578	20c. deep grey and orange-red	45	90
579	40c. yellow-olive, maroon, green and blue	2·75	1·80
576/579 Set of 4		7·25	3·00

Designs: 5c. T **130** (Graphic 57 International Exhibition, Lausanne); 10c. Electric train crossing bridge (75th Anniversary of St Gotthard Railway), 20c. Civil Defence shield and Coat of Arms (Civil Defence), 40c. Munatius Plancus, Basel and Rhine (Bimillenary of Basel).

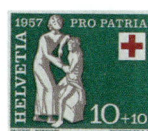

131 Shields of Switzerland and the Red Cross
132 Charity

(Des 5c. E. and M. Lenz. Eng A. Yersin. Recess Plain paper. PTT. Bern. Others. Des P. Gauchat and K. Mannhart. Photo Granite paper. Courvoisier)

1957 (1 June). Pro Patria. Swiss Red Cross and National Cancer League Funds. Designs as Types **131/132**. P 11½.

580	**131**	5c. +5c. red and deep slate	45	1·40
581	**132**	10c. +10c. dull purple, deep emerald green and carmine	90	45
582		20c. +10c. grey, red and carmine	90	90
583		30c. +10c. grey-blue brown and carmine	5·00	7·75
584		40c. +10c. ochre, blue and carmine	6·00	10·50
580/584 Set of 5			12·00	19·00

133 Symbol of Unity
134 Nyon Castle

(Des W. Weiskönig. Eng H. Heusser. Recess PTT, Bern)

1957 (15 July). Europa. P 11½.

585	**133**	25c. scarlet	1·40	1·40
586		40c. blue	4·75	1·40

(Des P. Perret (5c.), M. Allenbach 10c., 40c.), R. Bircher (20c.) Photo Granite paper. Courvoisier)

1958 (5 Mar). Publicity issue. Horiz designs as T **134**, inscr 1958. P 11½.

587	5c. blackish violet, pale buff and yellow olive	45	30
588	10c. blackish green, red and green	45	30
589	20c. carmine, lilac and vermilion	90	40
590	40c. indigo, crimson, deep blue and light blue	1·80	2·20
587/590 Set of 4		3·25	3·00

Designs: 5c. T **134** (Bimillenary of Nyon), 10c. Woman's head with unions (Saffa Exhibition, Zürich); 20r. Crossbow (25th Anniversary as symbol of Swiss manufacture); 40c. Salvation Army bonnet (75th Anniversary of Salvation Army in Switzerland).

135 Needy Mother
136 Fluorite

(Des D. Brun. Eng A. Yersin. Recess Plain paper. PTT. Bern (5c.). Des N. Stoecklin. Photo Granite Paper. Courvoisier (others))

1958 (31 May). Pro Patria. For Needy Mothers. T **135** and horiz designs of minerals, rocks and fossils as T **136**, inscr 'PRO PATRIA 1958'. P 11½.

591	5c. +5c. brown-purple	45	45
592	10c. +10c. yellow green and black	95	45
593	20c. +10c. bistre, red and black	1·10	1·30
594	30c. +10c. bright purple, ochre and black	3·75	7·50
595	40c. +10c. pale turquoise-blue, ultramarine and black	3·75	8·50
591/595 Set of 5		9·00	16·00

Designs: 5c. T **135**; 10c. T **136**; 20c. *Lytoceras fimbriatus* (Ammonite); 30c. Garnet; 40c. Rock crystal.

137 Atomic Symbol
138 Modern Transport

(Des H. Schwarzerbach. Photo Granite paper. Courvoisier)

1958 (25 Aug). Second United Nations Atomic Conference, Geneva. P 11½.

596	**137**	40c. orange-red, blue and cream	90	90

(Des C. Piatti (5c., 20c.), E. and M. Lenz (10c.). B. Cuendet (50c.) Photo Granite paper. Courvoisier)

1959 (9 Mar). Publicity issue. Horiz designs as T **138**, inscr '1959'. P 11½.

597	5c. red, green, yellow, black and slate-purple	55	30
598	10c. yellow, pale drab and green	55	30
599	20c. blue, bistre-brown and red	90	45
600	50c. blue, violet and light blue	1·80	1·40
597/600 Set of 4		3·50	2·20

Designs: 5c. T **138** (Opening of The Swiss House of Transport and Communications); 10c. Lictor's fasces of the Coat of Arms of St Gall and posthorn (NABAG National Philatelic Exhibition, St Gall); 20c. Owl, Hare and Fish (Protection of Animals); 50c. J. Calvin, Th. de Beze and University building (Fourth centenary of University of Geneva).

1959 (9 Mar). National Philatelic Exhibition, St Gallen (NABAG) Sheet 94×57 mm. As No. 598. Imperf.
MS600*a* 10c. and 20c. multicoloured (*sold at* 2f.) .... 22·00   22·00

139 Swiss Citizens Abroad
140 Europa
(**141**)

(Des B. Reber. Eng K. Bickel, junior. Recess Plain paper. PTT Bern (5c.) Des N. Stoecklin. Photo Granite paper. Courvoisier (others))

1959 (1 June). Pro Patria. For Swiss Citizens Abroad. T **139** and horiz designs of minerals, rocks and fossils as T **136**, inscr 'PRO PATRIA 1959'. P 11½.

601	5c. +5c. red and greenish grey	45	90
602	10c. +10c. red, orange, yellow green and black	45	90
603	20c. +10c. turquoise, yellow, magenta and black	90	90
604	30c. +10c. bluish violet, brown and black	3·00	5·25
605	40c. +10c. grey-blue greenish blue and black	3·25	5·25
601/605 Set of 5		7·25	12·00

Designs: 5c. T **139**; 10c. Agate; 20c. Tourmaline; 30c. Amethyst; 40c. Fossilised Giant Salamander.

SWITZERLAND 1959

(Des H. Schwarzenbach. Eng H. Heusser. Recess PTT, Bern)

1959 (22 June). Europa. P 11½.
606	**140**	30c. red	1·80	90
607		50c. blue	2·75	1·80

1959 (22 June). European PTT Conference, Montreux. No. 606/607 optd with T **141**.
608	**140**	30c. red (B.)	22·00	10·00
609		50c. blue (R.)	22·00	10·00

Postal validity of the above stamps was restricted to mail posted at special post offices in the Conference Hall and at Palace Hotel, Montreux, for the duration of the Conference, and also at the Philatelic Agency, Berne, until 31 July, 1959.

142 Campaign against Cancer

(Des E. Ruder (10c.). M. Allenbach (20c.), P. Jacopin (50c.), E. and M. Lenz (75c.) Photo Granite paper. Courvoisier)

1960 (7 Apr). Publicity Issue. Horiz designs as T **142**, inscr '1460–1960' (20c.) or '1960' (others). P 11½.
610	10c. red, pale green and green	90	30
611	20c. yellow, black, brown and cerise	90	30
612	50c. yellow, ultramarine and blue	90	1·80
613	75c. red, black and light blue	6·00	6·00
610/613	Set of 4	7·75	7·50

Designs: 10c. T **142** (50th Anniversary of Swiss National League for Cancer Control); 20c. Charter and sceptre (500th Anniversary of Basel University); 50c. Uprooted tree (World Refugee Year); 75c. Douglas DC-8 (Swissair enters the jet age).

143 15th-century Schwyz Cantonal Messenger **143a** Lausanne Cathedral

143b 614 **143c** 615 **143d** 617 **143e** 622

I. Sheet stamps

143f 614b **143g** 615c **143h** 617b **143i** 622b

II. Coil stamps

PHOSPHORESCENT PAPER. In 1963 phosphorescent paper, which reacts under a UV lamp, was introduced. Up to 1973 these can be distinguished without a lamp by the violet fibres in the paper. Non-phosphorescent granite paper has red and blue fibres.

(Des W. Weiskönig (5c., 10c., 15c., 20c., 25c., 40c., 70c., 80c., 1f.20); H. Hartmann (others). Eng H. Heusser (5c. to 20c.), A. Yersin (others). Recess PTT, Bern)

1960 (10 May)–**76**. As T **143** (postal history) and T **143a** (Architectural Monuments (1st series)). P 11½.

(a) Ordinary paper (10.5.60)
614	5c. new blue (I)	30	20
	a. Tête-bêche (pair) (24.10.60)	45	45
	p. Phosphor granite paper (3.10.63)	30	20
	pa. Tête-bêche (pair) (24.6.68)	45	45
	b. Type II (coils) (6.60)	1·70	1·70
	bp. Phosphor granite paper* (1.65)	2·20	2·20
615	10c. bluish green (I)	30	20
	a. Tête-bêche (pair)	45	45
	p. Phosphor granite paper (3.10.63)	30	20
	pa. Tête-bêche (pair) (24.6.68)	45	45
	pb. Booklet pane. No. 615p×2 plus two labels (1968)	90	
	c. Type II (coils)	1·80	45
	cp. Phosphor granite paper* (1.65)	1·80	1·80
616	15c. Venetian red	30	20
	p. Phosphor granite paper (3.10.63)	95	90
617	20c. cerise (I)	45	30
	a. Tête-bêche (pair) (24.10.60)	90	70
	p. Phosphor granite paper (3.10.63)	45	30
	pa. Tête-bêche (pair) (24.6.68)	90	90
	b. Type II (coils) (6.60)	2·00	1·80
	bp. Phosphor granite paper* (1.65)	2·00	1·80
618	25c. emerald	95	30
	p. Phosphor granite paper (3.10.63)	45	30
619	30c. vermilion	95	30
	p. Phosphor granite paper (3.10.63)	55	30
	pa. Tête-bêche (pair) (24.6.68)	1·10	90
620	35c. orange-red	1·40	1·40
621	40c. purple	1·20	30
	p. Phosphor granite paper (1967)	70	30
	pa. Tête-bêche (pair) (1976)	1·40	1·40
622	50c. ultramarine (I)	1·50	40
	a. Tête-bêche (pair)	2·75	2·75
	p. Phosphor granite paper (3.10.63)	1·40	90
	b. Type II (coils) (6.60)	5·25	5·25
	bp. Phosphor granite paper* (1.65)	6·75	6·75
623	60c. bright rose-red	1·80	45
	p. Phosphor granite paper (1967)	1·80	45
624	70c. orange	1·90	1·90
625	75c. greenish blue	2·75	1·80
	p. Phosphor granite paper (1968)	2·75	1·80
626	80c. brown-purple	2·50	45
	p. Phosphor granite paper (3.10.63)	1·80	45
627	90c. deep yellow-green	1·90	45
	a. Double print	£950	
	p. Phosphor granite paper (1967)	1·80	45
628	1f. yellow-orange	1·90	30
	p. Phosphor granite paper (1967)	3·50	90
629	1f.20 brown-red	2·40	40
	p. Phosphor granite paper (1968)	5·25	5·25
630	1f.50 bright emerald	3·00	90
	p. Phosphor granite paper (1968)	5·25	5·25
631	2f. blue	4·50	1·80

(b) Non phosphorescent granite paper (blue and red fibres) (4.2.63)
632	1f.30 orange-brown/lilac	2·30	45
633	1f.70 purple/lilac	3·00	45
634	2f.20 blue-green/green	4·00	1·80
635	2f.80 red-orange/pale orange	5·00	1·80

Designs: (Postal History) Horiz—5c. 17th-century Fribourg Cantonal Messenger; 10c. T **143**; 15c. 17th-century Mule-driver; 20c. 19th-century mounted postman. (Monuments) Vert—25c. T **143a**; 30c. Grossmunster, Zürich; 35c., 1f.30, Woodcutters Guildhall, Bienne; 40c. St Peter's Cathedral, Geneva; 50c. Spalentor (gate). Basel; 60c. Zeaglockenturm (clock tower), Berne; 70c. Collegiate Church of St Peter and St Stephen, Bellinzona; 75c. Kapellbrucke (bridge) and Wasserturm, Lucerne; 80c. St Gall Cathedral; 90c. Munot Fort, Schaffhausen; 2f.80, as 70c. but redrawn without bell-tower on Collegiate Church. Horiz—1f. Fribourg Town Hall; 1f.20, Basel Gate, Solothurn; 1f.50, Ital Reding's House, Schwyz; 1f.70, 2f., 2f.20, Abbey Church, Emsiedeln.

* These phosphorescent stamps in Type II were first issued in coils only (numbered on the back of every fifth stamp). In 1966 they were reissued in the coil printing-sheets (with every fifth row or column numbered on the back) but can only be distinguished thus in blocks or with sheet margins.

The 40c., 60c., 90c., 1f. and Nos 623/625, on both ordinary and phosphor granite paper, were also issued in coils with control figures on the back of every fifth stamp in the roll.

For similar Buildings see Nos. 698/713 and 1276.

144 Symbols of Occupational Trades **144a** Conference Emblem

(Des H. Kümpel. Eng H. Heusser. Photo, background recess PTT, Bern (50c.). Des N. Stoecklin. Photo Courvoisier (others). Granite paper)

1960 (1 June). Pro Patria. For Swiss Youth. T **144** and horiz designs inscr 'PRO PATRIA 1960'. P 11½.
636	5c. +5c. yellow-brown, pale blue and sepia	95	1·50
637	10c. +10c. salmon-pink, green and black	95	95
638	20c. +10c. olive-yellow, bright purple and black	95	95
639	30c. +10c. blue, orange-brown and black	4·25	7·25
640	50c. +10c. gold and blue	4·75	7·00

1960 SWITZERLAND

636/640 *Set of 5* .... 10·50 16·00
Designs: 5c. Smoky quartz; 10c. Orthoclase (feldspar); 20c. Devil's Toenail (fossilised shell); 30c. Azurite; 50c. T **144** (50 Years of the National Day Collection).

1960 (1 June). 50th Anniversary of Pro Patria Charity Fund. Sheet 85×75 mm. As No. 640. Imperf.
MS641 **144** 50c.+10c. gold and blue (block of 4)
  (sold at 3f.) .... 55·00 32·00

(Des P. Rahikamen. Eng H. Heusser. Recess PTT, Bern)

1960 (19 Sept). Europa. P 11½.
642 **144a** 30c. red .... 1·20 60
643   50c. blue .... 1·80 1·70

145 Aid for Development

146 Cultural Works of Eternity

(Des E. & M. Lenz (5c.), H. Neuberg (10c.), J. & L. Ongaro (20c.), B. Reber (50c.). Photo Granite paper. Courvoisier)

1961 (20 Feb). Publicity Issue. Horiz designs as T **145** inscr 'MARS 1961' (20c.) or '1961' (others). P 11½.
644   5c. red, turquoise-blue and grey 60 35
645   10c. yellow and greenish blue 60 25
646   20c. greenish yellow, deep brown, grey and
         carmine .... 3·50 1·20
647   50c. carmine, grey-green and ultramarine .... 2·40 2·30
644/647 *Set of 4* .... 6·50 3·75

Designs: 5c. T **145** (Aid to countries in process of development); 10c. Circular emblem (Hyspa Exhibition of 20th-century Hygiene. Gymnastics and Sport, Berne); 20c. Hockey stick (World and European Ice Hockey Championships, Geneva and Lausanne); 50c. Map of Switzerland with telephone centres as wiring diagram (inauguration of Swiss fully automatic telephone service).

(Des H. Schwarzenbach. Eng K. A. Bickel junior. Recess Plain paper. PTT, Bern (5c.). Des N. Stoecklin. Photo Courvoisier (others). Granite paper)

1961 (1 June). Pro Patria. For Swiss Cultural Works. T **146** and horiz designs of minerals, rocks and fossils inscr 'PRO PATRIA 1961'. P 11½.
648   5c. +5c. blue .... 60 1·20
649   10c. +10c. bright purple, green and black .... 1·20 80
650   20c. +10c. bright carmine, grey-blue and
         black .... 1·20 90
651   30c. +10c. turquoise-blue, orange and
         black .... 3·00 5·25
652   50c. +10c. bistre, blue and black .... 3·50 7·00
648/652 *Set of 5* .... 8·50 13·50

Designs: 5c. T **146**; 10c. Fluorite; 20c. Fossilised fish; 30c. Lazulite; 50c. Fossilised fern.

147 Doves

148 St Matthew

(Des T. Kurpershoek and H. Thöni. Eng K. Bickel, jun. Recess PTT, Bern)

1961 (18 Sept). Europa. P 11½.
653 **147** 30c. red .... 1·20 60
654   50c. bright blue .... 1·80 1·70

(Des Agathe Bagnoud. Eng H. Heusser. Recess Granite paper. PTT, Bern)

1961 (18 Sept). T **148** and similar vert designs showing wood carvings from St Oswald's Church, Zug. P 11½.
655   3f. crimson (Type 148) .... 7·00 60
656   5f. Prussian blue (St Mark) .... 11·00 60
657   10f. sepia (St Luke) .... 22·00 60
658   20f. brown-red (St John) .... 44·00 7·00
655/658 *Set of 4* .... 75·00 8·00

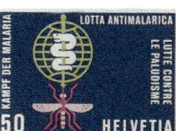
149 World Health Organisation Emblem and Mosquito

150 Rousseau

151 Schwyz Gold Ducat

(Des P. Perret (5c.), H. Hartmann (50c.). D. Brun (others) Photo Granite paper, Courvoisier)

1962 (19 Mar). Publicity issue Horiz designs as T **149**. P 11½.
659   5c. red, buff, black and grey-black .... 1·20 60
660   10c. bistre, bright purple and blue-green .... 1·20 60
661   20c. slate, violet-grey, bistre and mauve .... 4·75 1·20
662   50c. green, magenta and deep blue .... 2·40 2·30
659/662 *Set of 4* .... 8·50 4·25

Designs: 5c. Electric train (introduction of Trans-Europe Express); 10c. Oarsman (World Rowing Championship Lucerne); 20c. Jungfraujoch and Mönch (50th Anniversary of Jungfraujoch Railway Station); 50c. T **149** (Malaria eradication).

(Des and Eng K. Bickel. Recess Plain paper. PTT, Bern (5c.). Des C. Piatti. Photo Granite paper. Courvoisier (others)

1962 (1 June). Pro Patria. For Old People's Homes and Swiss Cultural Works. T **150** and vert designs of old Swiss coins as T **151**, inscr 'PRO PATRIA 1962'. P 11½.
663   5c. +5c. blue 60 60
664   10c. +10c. grey-blue, black and green 60 60
665   20c. +10c. olive-yellow, black and carmine .. 1·20 1·20
666   30c. +10c. green, grey-blue and orange-red . 1·80 3·50
667   50c. +10c. slate-violet, black and bright
         blue .... 1·80 3·50
663/667 *Set of 5* .... 5·50 8·50

Coins: 5c. T **150**; 10c. Obwalden Silver Half-taler; 20c. T **151**; 30c. Uri batzen; 50c. Nidwalden batzen.

152 Europa Tree

153 Campaign Emblem (Freedom from Hunger)

(Des Lex Weyer. Photo Granite paper. Courvoisier)

1962 (17 Sept). Europa. P 11½.
668 **152** 30c. orange-yellow, greenish yellow
         and red-brown .... 1·50 1·40
669   50c. blue, light turquoise-green and
         red-brown .... 2·40 1·70

(Des E. Poncy (5c.), H. Auchli (10c.), H. Thöni (20c.), E. & M. Lenz (30c.), W. Baumberger (50c. No. 674), H. Hartmann (50c. No. 675). Photo Granite paper. Courvoisier)

1963 (21 Mar). Publicity Issue. Horiz designs as T **153**. P 11½.
670   –   5c. yellow-brown, carmine-red and
         grey-blue 60 45
671   –   10c. carmine-red, grey and bronze-
         green .... 1·20 35
672   –   20c. lake, carmine-red and pale grey .... 4·00 60
673 **153** 30c. pale yellow, ochre and dull green. . 1·80 1·70
674   –   50c. red, silver and blue .... 2·50 2·40
675   –   50c. grey, rose, greenish yellow and
         ultramarine .... 3·25 3·00
670/675 *Set of 6* .... 12·00 7·75

Designs: 5c. Boy scout (50th Anniversary of Swiss Boy Scout League); 10c. Badge (Centenary of Swiss Alpine Club); 20c. Luegelkinn Viaduct (50th Anniversary of Lötschberg Railway); 50c. (No. 674), Jubilee emblem (Red Cross Centenary); 50c. (No. 675), Hôtel des Pastes, Paris, 1863 (Paris Postal Conference).

1963 (21 Mar). International Red Cross Centenary. Sheet 100×80 mm. As No. 674. Imperf.
MS675a 50c. fluorescent blue, red, deep blue and
   cobalt (block of four) (*sold at 3f.*) .... 11·50 11·00

154 Dr. Anna Heer (nursing pioneer)

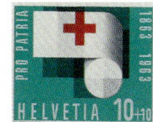
155 Roll of Bandage

(Des and Eng K. Bickel. Recess Plain paper. PTT, Bern (5c.).
Des K. Wirth. Photo Granite paper, Courvoisier (others))

1963 (1 June). Pro Patria. For Swiss Medical and Refugee Aid. T **154** and horiz designs of Red Cross activities as T **155**, inscr 'PRO PATRIA 1963'. P 11½.

676		5c. +5c. blue..	60	60
677		10c. +10c. red grey and blue-green................	60	60
678		20c. +10c. red grey, deep violet and pink.....	1·20	60
679		30c. +10c. red, carmine, sepia and orange...	1·80	3·25
680		50c. +10c. red, indigo and light blue.............	2·40	3·25
676/680 Set of 5			6·00	7·50

Designs: 5c. T **154**; 10c. T **155**; 20c. Gilt parcel; 30c. Blood plasma; 50c. Red Cross brassard.

156 Glider and Jet Aircraft **157** Co-operation

(Des R. Gerbig. Photo Granite paper. Courvoisier)

1963 (1 June). AIR. 25th Anniversary of Swiss Pro Aero Foundation, and Special Flights. P 11½.

681	**156**	2f. yellow, red, blue and silver...............	7·00	6·25

No. 681 was valid for postage only on the special Berne–Locarno or Langenbruck–Berne (helicopter feeder) flights of July 13th, 1963.

(Des A. Holm, B. Reber. Photo Granite paper. Courvoisier)

1963 (16 Sept). Europa. P 11½.

682	**157**	50c. ochre and blue..................................	1·20	1·10

158 Exhibition Emblem **159** Great St Bernard Tunnel

(Des P. Monnerat (T **158**), A. Hofmann (others). Photo Courvoisier)

1963 (16 Sept). Swiss National Exhibition, Lausanne. T **158** and similar horiz designs. Granite paper. P 11½.

683	**158**	10c. emerald and deep olive....................	60	25
684	–	20c. red and lake-brown...........................	60	25
685	–	50c. ultramarine, grey and red................	1·20	60
686	–	75c. reddish violet, grey and red............	1·80	1·40
683/686 Set of 4			3·75	2·30

Designs: 50c. Outlook (emblem on globe and smaller globe); 75c. Insight (emblem on large globe).

(Des B. Reber (5c.), H. Erni (10c.), E. & M. Lenz (20c.), W. Grandjean (Bodjol) (50c.) Photo Granite paper. Courvoisier)

1964 (9 Mar). Publicity Issue. Horiz designs as T **159**. P 11½.

687		5c. blue, vermilion and yellow olive............	60	25
688		10c. turquoise-green and blue......................	60	25
689		20c. multicoloured...	90	35
690		50c. multicoloured...	2·75	2·30
687/690 Set of 4			4·25	2·75

Designs: 5c. T **159** (Opening of Great St Bernard Road Tunnel); 10c. Ancient use of the waters (Protection of water supplies); 20c. Swiss soldiers of 1864 and 1964 (Centenary of Swiss Association of Non-commissioned Officers); 50c. Standards of Geneva and Swiss Confederation (150th Anniversary of arrival of Swiss in Geneva).

PHOSPHORESCENT PAPER. See note after T **143**.

160 J G. Bodmer (inventor) **161** Europa Flower

(Des and Eng K. Bickel. Recess PTT, Bern (5c.).
Des J. F. Liengme. Photo Courvoisier (others))

1964 (1 June). Pro Patria. For Swiss Mountain Aid and Cultural Funds. T **160** and vert designs of old Swiss coins as T **151**. Non-phosphorescent granite paper (50c.), phosphorescent paper (others). P 11½.

691		5c. +5c. greenish blue................................	50	35
692		10c. +10c. drab, black and bluish green ...	50	35
693		20c. +10c. grey-blue, black and magenta......	70	60
694		30c. +10c. grey-blue, black and orange	1·20	1·20
695		50c. +10c. olive-yellow, brown and blue.......	1·80	1·70
691/695 Set of 5			4·25	3·75

Designs: 5c. T **160**; 10c. Zürich copper; 20c. Basel doppeldicken; 30c. Geneva silver cater; 50c. Berne half gold florin.

(Des G. Bétemps and E. Witzig. Eng K. Bickel jun. Recess PTT, Bern)

1964 (14 Sept). Europa. Phosphorescent paper. P 11½.

696	**161**	20c. red...	1·20	60
697		50c. blue..	2·40	1·20

(Des W. Weiskönig (10c., 15c., 20c., 50c.), H. Hartmann (others) Eng A. Yersin. Recess PTT, Bern)

1964–73. Architectural Monuments (2nd series). Designs As T **143a**. Phosphorescent, slightly greyish toned paper. P 11½.

698		5c. cerise (12.9.68).................................	40	15
699		10c. ultramarine (12.9.68)......................	40	15
		a. Tête-bêche (pair) (18.6.70)...............	60	60
		b. Booklet pane. No 699×2 plus two labels (1970)....................................	85	
700		15c. bright chestnut (12.9.68)................	40	15
		a. Tête-bêche (pair) (8.1.73)................	70	60
701		20c. blue green (12.9.68).........................	40	15
		a. Tête-bêche (pair) (18.6.70)...............	95	65
702		30c. vermilion (12.9.68)..........................	70	25
		a. Tête-bêche (pair) (18.6.70)...............	1·70	1·40
703		50c. new blue (12.9.68)............................	1·20	35
704		70c. brown (18.9.67).................................	1·70	35
705		1f. bluish green (12.9.68).......................	2·40	35
706		1f.20 brown lake (12.9.68).....................	3·00	45
707		1f.30 ultramarine (21.2.66)....................	3·00	2·30
708		1f.50 emerald (12.9.68)..........................	3·50	60
709		1f.70 dull vermillion (21.2.66)..............	4·00	2·75
710		2f. orange (18.9.67).................................	4·75	60
711		2f.20 blue-green (14.9.64).....................	5·25	2·50
712		2f.50 blue-green (18.9.67).....................	6·00	70
713		3f.50 purple (18.9.67)..............................	8·25	80
698/713 Set of 16			41·00	11·50

Buildings: Horiz—5c. Lenzburg Castle; 10c. Freuler Mansion, Näfels; 15c. Mauritius Church, Appenzell; 20c. Planta House, Samedan; 30c. Town Square, Gais; 50c. Neuchâtel Castle and Collegiate Church. Vert—70c. Lussy 'Höchnus', Wolfen-schiessen; 1f. Riva San Vitale Church; 1f.20, Payerne Abbey Church; 1f.30, St Pierre-de-Clages Church; 1f.50, Gateway, Porrentruy; 1f.70, Frauenfeld Castle; 2f. Castle Seedorf (Uri); 2f.20, Thomas Tower and Arch, Liestal; 2f.50, St Oswald's Church, Zug; 3f.50, Benedictine Abbey, Engelberg.

The 15c. was also issued in coils with a control number on the back of every fifth stamp.

162 Swiss 5r. Stamp of 1854 with Lozenge Cancellation

(Des E. & M. Lenz (5c.), A. Flückiger (10c.), A. Oertle (20c.), H. Thöni (50c.). Photo Courvoisier)

1965 (8 Mar). Publicity Issue. T **162** and similar horiz designs. Non-phosphorescent granite paper (50c.), phosphorescent paper (others). P 11½.

714		5c. black, red and light blue...................	35	15
715		10c. brown, blue and emerald................	50	20
716		20c. multicoloured..................................	60	25
717		50c. red, black and greenish blue.........	1·20	70
714/717 Set of 4			2·40	1·20

Designs: 5c. Nurse and patient (Nursing); 10c. T **162** NABRA 1965 National Stamp Exhibition, Berne); 20c. WAC officer (25th Anniversary of Women's Army Corps); 50c. World telecommunications map (centenary of International Telecommunications Union).

(Des A. Flückiger. Photo Courvoisier)

1965 (8 Mar). National Philatelic Exhibition, Berrie (NABRA). Sheet 94×61 mm. As T **162**. Granite paper. Imperf.
MS718 10c. orange, blue and green (20r.) 20c. green blue and claret (40r.) (sold at 3f.) .... 3·50 2·00

163 Father T. Florentini **164** Fish-tailed Goose (Evil)

(Des and Eng H. Heusser. Recess PTT, Bern (5c.)
Des H. Schwarzenbach. Photo Courvoisier (others))

1965 (1 June). Pro Patria. For Swiss Abroad and Art Research. T **163** and vert designs as T **164**, inscr 'PRO PATRIA 1965'. Phosphorescent paper. P 11½.

719	**163**	5c. +5c. blue	35	25
720	**164**	10c. +10c. multicoloured	35	25
721	–	20c. +10c. multicoloured	60	25
722	–	30c. +10c. brown and blue	1·10	1·00
723	–	50c. +10c. blue and orange brown	1·20	1·20
719/723	Set of 5		3·25	2·75

Designs: Ceiling paintings in St Martin's Church, Zillis (Grisons)—20c. One of Magi Journeying to Herod; 30c. Fishermen; 50c. The Temptation of Christ.

165 Swiss Emblem and Arms of Cantons

166 Matterhorn

(Des A. Rosselet. Photo Courvoisier)

1965 (1 June). 150th Anniversary of Entry of Valais, Neuchâtel and Geneva into Confederation. Granite paper. P 11½.

724	**165**	20c. multicoloured	60	45

(Des E. Hauri. Photo Courvoisier)

1965 (1 June). Mobile PO Issue Non-phosphorescent granite (10c.) or phosphorescent (30c.) paper. P 11½.

725	**166**	10c. black, grey bluish green and red	1·20	25
726		30c. black, grey, red and bluish green	2·40	1·70

No. 726 is inscribed 'CERVIN'.

167 Europa Sprig

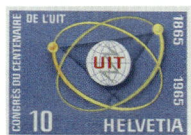
168 ITU Emblem and Satellites

(Des W. Mühlemann, after H. Karlsson. Photo Courvoisier)

1965 (14 Sept). Europa Phosphorescent paper. P 11½.

727	**167**	50c. emerald and light blue	1·20	60

(Des A. Rosselet. Photo Courvoisier)

1965 (14 Sept). International Telecommunications Union Centenary Congress, Montreux. T **168** and similar horiz design phosphorescent (10c.) or non-phosphorescent granite (30c.) paper. Multicoloured. P 11½.

728		10c. Type **168**	35	25
729		30c. Symbols of world telecommunications	70	35

PHOSPHORESCENT PAPER. All stamps from No. 730 to No. 926 are printed on phosphorescent paper, with violet fibres, *unless otherwise stated.*

169 Figure Skating

170 River Kingfisher

(Des W. Haettenschweiler. Photo Courvoisier)

1965 (14 Sept). World Figure Skating Championships, Davos. P 11½.

730	**169**	5c. multicoloured	60	45

(Des B. Waltenspül (10c.), D. Brun (20c.)
H. Kümpel (50c.) Photo Courvoisier)

1966 (21 Feb). Publicity Issue. Horiz designs as T **170**. Multicoloured. P 11½.

731		10c. Type **170**	35	15
732		20c. Mercury's helmet and Laurel twig	50	20
733		50c. Phase in nuclear fission and flags	1·20	45
731/733	Set of 3		1·80	70

Publicity events: 10c. Preservation of natural beauty; 20c. 50th Swiss Industrial Fair, Basel (MUBA); 50c. International Institute for Nuclear Research (CERN).

171 H. Federer (author)

172 Society Emblem

173 Europa Ship

(Des and Eng K. Lievin. Recess PTT, Bern (5c.)
Des H. Schwarzenbach. Photo Courvoisier (others))

1966 (1 June). Pro Patria. For Aid to Mothers. T **171** and vert designs as T **164**, inscr 'PRO PATRIA 1966' Nos. 735/738 rnultcoloured. P 11½.

734		5c. +5c. greenish blue	55	15
735		10c. +10c. Joseph's dream	55	15
736		20c. +10c. Joseph on his way	60	35
737		30c. +10c. Virgin and Child	1·10	1·00
738		50c. +10c. Angel pointing the way	1·20	1·20
734/738	Set of 5		3·50	2·50

Designs: T **171**. The designs of Nos. 735/738 represent the Flight into Egypt and are taken from ceiling paintings in St Martin's Church, Zillis (Grisons).

(Des A. Flückiger. Photo Courvoisier)

1966 (1 June). 50th Anniversary of New Helvetic Society for Swiss Abroad. P 11½.

739	**172**	20c. vermilion and bright blue	60	35

(Des G. and J. Bender. Eng A. Yersin. Recess PTT, Bern)

1966 (26 Sept). Europa. P 11½.

740	**173**	20c. rose red	60	60
741		50c. blue	1·20	60

174 Finsteraarhorn

175 White Stick and Motorcar Wheel (Welfare of the Blind)

(Des H. Thöni. Photo Courvoisier)

1966 (26 Sept). Swiss Alps. P 11½.

742	**174**	10c. multicoloured	60	30

(Des J. Mauerhofer (10c.), R. Mumprecht (20c.). Photo Courvoisier)

1967 (13 Mar). Publicity Issue. T **175** and similar horiz design. P 11½.

743		10c. multicoloured	35	15
744		20c. multicoloured	50	20

Designs: 10c. T **175**; 20c. Flags of European Free Trade Area countries (abolition of EFTA tariffs).

176 CEPT Emblem and Cogwheels

177 Theodor Kocher (surgeon)

178 Cogwheel and Swiss Emblem

(Des J. Mauerhofer, after O. Bonnevalle. Eng A. Yersin. Recess PTT, Bern)

1967 (13 Mar). Europa. P 11½.

745	**176**	30c. grey-blue	1·30	60

(Des and Eng K. Lieven Recess PTT, Bern (5c.). Des H. Schwarzenbach. Photo Courvoisier (others))

1967 (1 June). Pro Patria. For National Day Collection. T **177** and vert designs as T **164** inscr 'PRO PATRIA 1967'. P 11½.

746		5c. +5c. new blue	35	15
747		10c. +10c. multicoloured	40	20
748		20c. +10c. multicoloured	60	25
749		30c. +10c. multicoloured	1·10	1·00
750		50c. +10c. multicoloured	1·20	1·20
746/750	Set of 5		3·25	2·50

Designs: 5c. T **177**. Ceiling paintings in St Martin's Church, Zillis (Grisons)—10c. Annunciation to the shepherds; 20c. Christ and the woman of Samaria; 30c. Adoration of the Magi; 50c. Joseph seated on a throne.

SWITZERLAND 1967

(Des H.-R. Lauterburg (10c.), H. Kümpel (20c.), B. Waltenspül (30c.), W. Mühlemann (50c.) Photo Courvoisier)

1967 (18 Sept). Publicity Issue. T **178** and similar horiz designs. Multicoloured. P 11½.

751	10c. Type **178**	25	15
752	20c. Hour-glass and Sun	40	25
753	30c. San Bernardino highway	60	35
754	50c. OCTI emblem	1·20	90
751/754 Set of 4		2·20	1·50

Publicity events: 10c. 50th Anniversary of Swiss Week; 20c. 50th Anniversary of Aged People Foundation; 30c. Opening of San Bernardino road tunnel; 50c. 75th Anniversary of Central Office for International Railway Transport (OCTI).

179 Stylised Mountains and Swiss Emblem   **180** Maius

(Des A. Flückiger (10c.), H. Schwarzenbach (20c.), R. Geiser (30c.), M. Gallay (50c.). Photo Courvoisier)

1968 (14 Mar). Publicity Issue T **179** and similar horiz designs. P 11½.

755	10c. red, cobalt, deep green, green and light green	35	20
756	20c. yellow, brown and greenish blue	95	60
757	30c. bright ultramarine, ochre and yellow-brown	50	25
	a. Missing blue	£4500	£4500
758	50c. red, deep greenish blue and light blue	60	50
755/758 Set of 4		2·20	1·40

Designs and events: 10c. T **179** (50th Anniversary of Swiss Women's Alpine Club); 20c. Europa key (Europa); 30c. Staunton rook and chessboard (18th Chess Olympiad Lugano); 50c. Dispatch satellites and aircraft tail fin (inauguration of new Geneva Air Terminal).

(Des E. Witzig. Photo Courvoisier)

1968 (30 May). Pro Patria. For National Day Collection. T **180** and similar vert designs, inscr 'PRO PATRIA 1968'. Multicoloured. P 11½.

759	10c. +10c. Type **180**	60	20
760	20c. +10c. Leo	70	25
761	30c. +10c. Libra	1·20	45
762	50c. +20c. Pisces	1·80	1·20
759/762 Set of 4		3·75	1·90

The designs of Nos. 759/762 are symbols of months and the signs of the zodiac taken from stained-glass panels in the rose window, Lausanne Cathedral.

181 Protective Helmet   **182** Guide Camp and Emblem

(Des E. Küng (10c.), P. Birkhäuser (20c.), B. la Roche (30c.), J. Mauerhofer (50c.). Photo Courvoisier)

1968 (12 Sept). Publicity Issue. T **181** and similar horiz designs. Multicoloured. P 11½.

763	10c. Type **181**	35	15
764	20c. Geneva and Zürich stamps of 1843	40	20
765	30c. Part of Swiss map	60	25
766	50c. Six Stars (countries) and anchor	1·20	60
763/766 Set of 4		2·30	1·10

Events: 10c. 50th Anniversary of Swiss Accident Insurance Company; 20c. 125th Anniversary of Swiss stamps; 30c. 25th Anniversary of Swiss Territorial Planning Society; 50c. Centenary of Rhine Navigation Act.

(Des E. Meier (10c.), H. Erni (20c.), P. Monnerat (30c.), H. Leupin (50c.), E. and M. Lenz (2f.). Photo Courvoisier)

1969 (13 Feb). Publicity Issue. T **182** and similar horiz designs Multicoloured. P 11½.

767	10c. Type **182**	60	25
768	20c. Pegasus constellation	1·20	35
769	30c. Emblem of Comptoir Suisse	70	25
770	50c. Emblem of Gymnastrade	1·20	90
771	2f. Haefeli DH-3 biplane and Douglas DC-8	4·75	3·25
767/771 Set of 5		7·50	4·50

Events: 10c. 50th Anniversary of Swiss Girl Guides' Federation; 20c. Opening of first Swiss Planetarium, Lucerne; 30c. 50th Anniversary of Compton Suisse, Lausanne; 50c. Fifth Gymnastrada, Basel; 2f. 50th Anniversary of Swiss Airmail Services.

183 Colonnade   **184** St Francis of Assisi preaching to the Birds (Abbey-church, Königsfelden)

(Des L. Gasbarra, G. Belli and H. Hartmann. Photo Courvoisrer)

1969 (28 Apr). Europa. P 11½.

772	**183** 30c. multicoloured	70	60
773	50c. multicoloured	1·20	1·00

(Des E. Witzig. Photo Courvoisier)

1969 (29 May). Pro Patria. For National Day Collection. T **184** and similar vert designs, showing stained-glass windows. Multicoloured. P 11½.

774	10c. +10c. Type **184**	55	15
775	20c. +10c. The People of Israel drinking (Berne Cathedral)	60	35
776	30c. +10c. St Christopher (Läufel-fingen Church, Basel)	1·20	60
777	50c. +20c. Madonna and Child (St Jacob's Chapel, Gräpplang, Flums)	1·80	1·20
774/777 Set of 4		3·75	2·10

See also Nos. 793/796 and 813/816.

185 Kreuzberge   **186** Huldrych Zwingli (Protestant reformer)

(Des H. Thöni (50c.), E. Hauri (others). Photo Courvoisier)

1969 (18 Sept). Publicity and Swiss Alps (20c.) Issue. T **185** and similar horiz designs. P 11½.

778	20c. Type **185**	95	25
779	30c. Children crossing road	70	25
780	50c. Hammersmith	1·20	60
778/780 Set of 3		2·50	1·00

Events: 30c. Road Safety campaign for children; 50c. 50th Anniversary of International Labour Organisation.

(Des G. Humair. Eng H. Heusser. Recess PTT, Bern)

1969 (18 Sept). Swiss Celebrities. T **186** and similar horiz designs. P 11½.

781	10c. reddish violet	35	15
782	20c. emerald	50	20
783	30c. carmine	60	25
784	50c. new blue	1·20	90
785	80c. chestnut	1·80	1·40
781/785 Set of 5		4·00	2·50

Designs: 10c. T **186**; 20c. General Henri Guisan; 30c. Francesco Borromini (architect); 50c. Othmar Schoeck (composer); 80c. Germaine de Stael (writer).

187 Telex Tape   **188** Flaming Sun

(Des E. & M. Lenz (20c.), E. Bosshart (30c. No. 787), D. Brun (30c. No. 788), H. Thöni (50c.), H. Hartmann (80c.) Photo Courvoisier)

1970 (26 Feb). Publicity Issue. T **187** and similar horiz designs. Multicoloured. P 11½.

786	20c. Type **187**	60	15
787	30c. Fireman saving child	95	20

788	30c. Chained wing emblem	70	25
789	50c. UN emblem	1·20	1·10
790	80c. New UPU Headquarters	1·90	1·70
786/790 Set of 5		4·75	3·00

Events: 20c. 75th Anniversary of Swiss Telegraphic Agency; 30c. (No. 787) Centenary of Swiss Firemen's Assocation; 30c. (No. 788) 50th Anniversary of Pro Infirmis Foundation; 50c. 25th Anniversary of United Nations Organisation; 80c. inauguration of new Universal Postal Union headquarters, Bern.

(Des L. le Brocquy, adapted P. Kräuchi. Eng A. Yersin. Recess PTT, Bern)

1970 (4 May). Europa. P 11½.
| 791 | **188** | 30c. red | 85 | 45 |
| 792 | | 50c. new blue | 1·20 | 60 |

(Des C. Piatti. Photo Courvoisier)

1970 (29 May). Pro Patria. For National Day Collection. Vert designs similar to T **184**, but showing glass by contemporary artists and inscr '1970'. Multicoloured. P 11½.
793	10c. +10c. Sailor (G. Casty)	55	45
794	20c. +10c. Architectonic composition (C. Piatti)	60	45
795	30c. +10c. Bull, symbol of Marduk, from The Four Elements (H. Stocker)	1·20	60
796	50c. +20c. Man and Woman (M. Hunziker & K. Ganz)	1·80	1·20
793/796 Set of 4		3·75	2·40

189 Footballer (75th Anniversary of Swiss Football Association)

190 Numeral

(Des B. Schorderet (10c.), H. Burgin (20c.), A. Diggelmann (30c.), J. Mauerhofer (50c.) Photo Courvoisier)

1970 (17 Sept). Publicity and Swiss Alps (30c.) Issue. T **189** and similar horiz designs. Multicoloured. P 11½.
797	10c. Type **189**	1·20	25
798	20c. Census form and pencil (Federal Census)	60	35
799	30c. Piz Palu, Grisons	1·20	60
800	50c. Conservation Year Emblem (Nature Conservation Year)	1·20	1·10
797/800 Set of 4		3·75	2·10

(Des A. Hofmann. Eng M. Müller. Recess PTT, Bern)

1970 (17 Sept). Coil Stamps. P 11½.
801	**190**	10c. carmine	25	15
802		20c. bronze-green	40	20
803		50c. bright blue	1·20	35
801/803 Set of 3		1·70	65

These stamps were also available in sheets of 50 from philatelic sales counters. All stamps in such sheets, and every fifth stamp in the coils, bear control numbers on the reverse, at first this number was in the colour of the stamp but from 1987 the 10c. and 50c. were issued with black numbers. The 50c. exists on both phosphorescent (coloured numbers) and fluorescent (black numbers) paper, unnumbered stamps can only be distinguished under a UV lamp. The 10c. and 20c. values were issued on phosphorescent paper only.

191 Female Gymnasts (Youth and Sport)

192 Rayon I Stamp of 1850

(Des A. Diggelmann (Nos. 804/805), H. Bauer (20c.), H. Hartmann (50c.), A. Flückiger (others). Photo Courvoisier)

1971 (11 Mar). Publicity Issue. T **191** and similar horiz designs. P 11½.
804	10c. multicoloured	95	60
	a. Pair Nos. 804/805	2·00	1·30
805	10c. multicoloured	95	60
806	20c. multicoloured	60	60
807	30c. multicoloured	70	60
808	50c. ochre and royal blue	1·20	1·10
809	80c. multicoloured	2·20	2·30
804/809 Set of 6		6·00	5·25

Designs and events: 10c. (No. 804) T **191**, (No. 805), Male athletes (Youth and Sport constitutional amendment); 20c. Stylised Rose (child welfare); 30c. Rayon II stamp of 1850 and basilisk (NABA Philatelic Exhibition, Basel); 50c. Co-operation symbol (aid for technical development); 80c. *Intelsat 4* (International Telecommunications Union Space Conference).

Nos. 804/805 were issued together in *se-tenant* pairs within the sheet.

(Des E. Schnell. Typo PTT, Bern)

1971 (11 Mar). NABA 1971 Stamp Exhibition. Basel. Sheet 61×75 mm. Imperf.
| MS810 | **192** | 50c.×4 red black and blue (*sold at 3f.*) | 4·75 | 4·25 |

Issued with tri-lingual inscription on the reverse.

193 Europa Chain

194 Telecommunication Services (50th Anniversary of Radio-Suisse)

(Des H. Haflidason, adapted W. Mühlemann. Eng A. Yersin. Recess PTT, Bern)

1971 (3 May). Europa. P 11½.
| 811 | **193** | 30c. orange-yellow and magenta | 70 | 60 |
| 812 | | 50c. orange-yellow and new blue | 1·20 | 1·10 |

(Des C. Piatti. Photo Courvoisier)

1971 (27 May). Pro Patria. For National Day Collection. Vert designs similar to T **184**, but showing glass by contemporary artists and inscr '1971'. Multicoloured. P 11½.
813	10c. +10c. Religious Abstract (J.-F. Comment)	50	45
814	20c. +10c. Cockerel (J. Prahin)	60	50
815	30c. +10c. Fox (K. Volk)	1·20	60
816	50c. +20c. Christ's Passion (B. Schorderet)	1·80	1·60
813/816 Set of 4		3·75	2·75

(Des E. Hauri (30c.) H. Thöni (40c.). Photo Courvoisier)

1971 (23 Sept). Publicity and Swiss Alps (30c.) Issue. T **194** and similar horiz design. P 11½.
| 817 | 30c. plum, blue-grey and mauve | 1·20 | 35 |
| 818 | 40c. multicoloured | 1·20 | 1·10 |

Designs: 30c. Les Diablerets, Vaud; 40c. T **194**.

195 Alexandre Yersin (bacteriologist)

196 Warning Triangle and Wrench (75th Anniversaries of Motoring Organisations)

(Des G. Humair. Eng M. Müller. Recess PTT, Bern)

1971 (23 Sept). Famous Physicians. T **195** and similar horiz portraits. P 11½.
819	10c. deep olive	30	15
820	20c. blue green	40	20
821	30c. carmine red	70	25
822	40c. new blue	95	1·10
823	80c. purple	1·90	1·70
819/823 Set of 5		3·75	3·00

Portraits: 10c. T **195**; 20c. Auguste Forel (psychiatrist); 30c. Jules Gonin (ophthalmologist); 40c. Robert Koch (German bacteriologist); 80c. Frederick Banting (Canadian physiologist).

(Des H. Lauterburg (10c.), H. Auchli (20c.), R. Hirter (30c.), C. Piatti (40c.). Photo Courvoisier)

1972 (17 Feb). Publicity Issue. T **196** and similar horiz designs. P 11½.
824	10c. multicoloured	40	15
825	20c. multicoloured	60	25
826	30c. yellow-orange, orange-red and carmine-red	70	35
827	40c. reddish violet, green and new blue	95	80
824/827 Set of 4		2·40	1·40

Designs and events: 10c. T **196**; 20c. Signal-box switch-table (125th Anniversary of Swiss Railways); 30c. Stylised radio waves and girl's face (50th Anniversary of Swiss Broadcasting); 40c. Symbolic tree (50th Swiss Citizens Abroad Congress).

SWITZERLAND 1972

197 Swissair Boeing 747-100   **198** Communications

(Des B. Waltenspül. Photo Courvoisier)

1972 (17 Feb). AIR. Pro Aero Foundation and 50th Anniversary of North Atlantic and International Airmail Services. P 11½.
828   **197**   2f.+1f. multicoloured .... 4·75   4·25
Issued for compulsory use on the special Geneva–New York and Geneva–Zürich–Nurnberg flights. The stamp could also be used for other mail.

(Des P. Huovinen and C. Piatti. Photo Courvoisier)

1972 (2 May). Europa. P 11½.
829   **198**   30c. multicoloured 70   60
830   40c. multicoloured .... 1·10   1·00

199 Late Stone Age Harpoon Heads   **200** Civil Defence Emblem

(Des E. and M. Lenz. Photo Courvoisier)

1972 (1 June). Pro Patria. For National Day Collection. Archaeological Discoveries (1st series). T **199** and similar vert designs. Multicoloured. P 11½.
831   10c. +10c. Type **199** 50   35
832   20c. +10c. Bronze water vessel, c 570 BC 60   45
833   30c. +10c. Gold Bust of Marcus Aurelius, 2nd-century AD .... 1·20   60
834   40c. +20c. Alemannic disc, 7th-century AD ..... 3·00   2·75
831/834 Set of 4 .... 4·75   3·75
See also Nos. 869/872, 887/890 and 901/904.

(Des J. Mauerhofer (10c.), E. Hauri (20c.), R. Gerbig (30c.), M. Hunziker and C. Piatti (40c.) Photo Courvoisier)

1972 (21 Sept). Publicity and Swiss Alps (20c.) issue. T **200** and similar horiz designs. Multicoloured. P 11½.
835   10c. Type **200** 40   15
836   20c. Spannörter .... 1·20   45
837   30c. Sud Aviation SE 3160 Alouette III rescue helicopter .... 1·40   60
838   40c. The Four Elements (53×31 mm) 95   1·10
835/838 Set of 4 .... 3·50   2·10
Subjects: 10c. Swiss Civil Defence; 20c. Tourism; 30c. Swiss Air Rescue Service; 40c. Protection of the environment.

201 Alberto Giacometti (painter)   **202** Satellite Transmitter

(Des H. Erni. Eng K. A. Bickel. Recess & photo PTT, Bern)

1972 (21 Sept). Swiss Celebrities. T **201** and similar vert portraits. P 11½.
839   10c. black and buff 30   15
840   20c. black and pale bistre 60   20
841   30c. black and pink 70   25
842   40c. black and pale blue 95   1·10
843   80c. black and pale reddish purple .... 1·90   1·20
839/843 Set of 5 .... 4·00   2·50
Portraits: 10c. T **201**; 20c. Charles Ramuz (novelist); 30c. Le Corbusier (architect); 40c. Albert Einstein (physicist); 80c. Arthur Honegger (composer).

(Des H. Thöni (15c.); E. and M. Lenz (30c.); J. Mauerhofer (40c.). Photo Courvoisier)

1973 (15 Feb). Publicity Issue. T **202** and similar horiz designs. Multicoloured. P 11½.
844   15c. Type **202** 60   45
845   30c. Quill pen 70   40
846   40c. Interpol emblem 95   90
844/846 Set of 3 .... 2·00   1·60
Events: 15c. Construction of Satellite Earth Station, Leuk-Brentjong; 30c. Centenary of Swiss Association of Commercial Employees; 40c. 50th Anniversary of International Criminal Police Organisation (Interpol).

203 Sottoceneri   **204** Toggenburg Inn Sign

(Des H. Wetli (Nos. 847/857). H. Hartmann (others). Eng H. Heusser (Nos. 847, 849/851, 854), P. Schopfer (Nos. 848, 853, 855/857) K. Bickel, junior (Nos. 852, 866a), M. Müller (No. 866b), A. Yersin (others). Recess and photo (Nos. 847/857) or recess PTT. Bern)

1973 (15 Feb)–**80**. Phosphorescent paper. P 11½.

(a) T **203** and similar vert designs. Fibre-less paper
847   5c. blue and yellow-ochre (30.8.73) 30   15
848   10c. bronze-green and bright purple (30.8.73) 35   15
849   15c. ultramarine and salmon (30.8.73) 35   20
850   25c. bluish violet and bright green (30.8.73) 50   25
851   30c. deep violet and red (30.8.73) 70   35
852   35c. bluish violet and red-orange (27.11.75) 85   60
853   40c. deep greenish grey and new blue (30.8.73) 95   55
854   50c. deep green and light orange (30.8.73) .... 1·20   60
855   60c. yellow-brown and grey (30.8.73) .... 1·40   60
856   70c. myrtle-green and dull purple (30.8.73) .... 1·70   65
857   80c. rose-red and bright emerald (30.8.73) ..... 1·90   1·10

(b) T **204** and similar horiz designs. Fibre-less paper (3f., 3f.50) or paper with fibres (others)
858   1f. deep purple (19.9.74) .... 2·40   55
    a. Fibre-less paper (24.8.78) .... 4·75   2·75
859   1f.10 deep green-blue (27.11.75) .... 2·75   55
860   1f.20 rose-red (19.9.74) .... 3·00   60
861   1f.30 yellow-orange .... 3·00   60
862   1f.50 emerald (19.9.74) .... 3·50   60
863   1f.70 slate .... 4·00   60
864   1f.80 orange-red .... 4·25   60
865   2f. blue (19.9.74) .... 4·75   60
    a. Fibre-less paper (24.8.78) .... 8·50   5·25
866   2f.50 light brown (11.9.75) .... 6·00   60
866a   3f. brown-lake (6.9.79) .... 7·25   1·20
866b   3f.50 deep olive (21.2.80) .... 8·50   1·70
Designs: Vert—5c. T **203**; 10c. Grisons; 15c. Central Switzerland; 25c. Jura; 30c. Simmental; 35c. Houses, Central Switzerland; 40c. Vaud; 50c. Valais; 60c. Engadine; 70c. Sopraceneri; 80c. Eastern Switzerland. Horiz—1f. Rose window, Lausanne Cathedral; 1f.10, Gallus portal, Basel Cathedral; 1f.20, Romanesque capital, St-Jean-Baptiste Church, Grandson; 1f.30, T **204**; 1f.50, Medallion, St Georgen Monastery, Stein am Rhein; 1f.70, Roman Capital, Jean-Baptiste Church, Grandson; 1f.80, Gargoyle, Berne Cathedral; 2f. Oriel, Schaffhausen; 2f.50, Weathercock, St Ursus Cathedral, Solothurn; 3f. Font, St Maurice Church, Saanen; 3f.50, Astronomical clock, Berne.
The 2f.50 was issued on non-phosphorescent paper with violet fibres in 1984.

 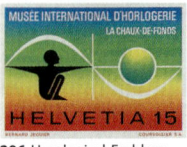

205 Europa Posthorn   **206** Horological Emblem

(Des L. F. Anisdahl. Eng K. A. Bickel. Recess PTT, Bern)

1973 (30 Apr). Europa. P 11½.
867   **205**   25c. yellow and lake 95   55
868   40c. yellow and ultramarine .... 1·40   1·10

(Des E. and M. Lenz. Photo Courvoisier)

1973 (29 May). Pro Patria. For National Day Collection. Archaeological Discoveries (2nd series). Designs as T **199**, but horiz. Multicoloured. P 11½.
869   15c. +5c. Rauraric jar 60   45
870   30c. +10c. Head of a Gaul (bronze) .... 1·20   55

871	40c. +20c. Almannic Fish brooches		2·40	2·20
872	60c. +20c. Gold bowl		3·00	2·75
869/872	Set of 4		6·50	5·25

(Des B. Jéquier (15c.), L. Grendene (30c.), P. Ferret (40c.) Photo Courvoisier)

1973 (30 Aug). Publicity Issue. T **206** and similar horiz designs. Multicoloured. P 11½.

873	15c. Type **206**		60	45
874	30c. Skiing emblem		70	45
875	40c. Face of child		1·10	85
873/875	Set of 3		2·20	1·60

Subjects: 15c. Inauguration of International Horological Museum, Neuchâtel (1974); 30c. World Alpine Skiing Championships, St Moritz (1974); 40c. Terre des Hommes (Child-care organisation).

207 Global Hostels

208 Cantonal Messenger (Basel)

(Des C. Piatti (15c.), H. Schelbert (30c.), H. Bürgin (40c.). Photo Courvoisier)

1974 (29 Jan). Publicity Issue. T **207** and similar horiz designs. Multicoloured. P 11½.

876	15c. Type **207**		60	25
877	30c. Gymnast and hurdlers		70	35
878	40c. Pistol and target		1·40	85
876/878	Set of 3		2·40	1·30

Subjects: 15c. 50 Years of Swiss Youth Hostels; 30c. Centenary of Swiss Workmen's Gymnastics and Sports Association (SATUS); 40c. World Shooting Championships, 1974.

(Des F. Boscovits. Photo Courvoisier)

1974 (29 Jan). Internaba 1974 Stamp Exhibition, Basel. Sheet 83×73 mm containing T **208** and similar vert designs, showing cantonal messengers. Multicoloured. P 11½.

MS879 30c. Type **208**; 30c. Zug; 60c. Uri; 80c. Schwyz (sold at 3f.) .... 7·00 6·75

209 Continuity (Max Bill)

210 Eugene Borel (first Director of International Bureau UPU)

(Des M. Bill. Photo Courvoisier)

1974 (28 Mar). Europa. Swiss Sculptures. T **209** and similar vert design. P 11½.

880	30c. black and red		1·20	55
881	40c. brown, blue and black		1·60	1·10

Designs: 30c. T **209**; 40c. *Amazone* (Carl Burckhardt).

(Des E. Kassner. Eng M. Müller. Recess and photo PTT, Bern)

1974 (28 Mar). Centenary of Universal Postal Union. T **210** and similar vert portraits. P 11½.

882	30c. black and pink		70	35
883	40c. black and light grey		95	55
884	80c. black and pale yellow-green		1·90	1·60
882/884	Set of 3		3·25	2·30

Portraits: 30c. T **210**; 40c. Heinrich von Stephan (founder of UPU); 80c. Montgomery Blair (US Postmaster-General and initiator of 1863 Paris Postal Conference).

211 View of Berne

212 *Oath of Allegiance* (sculpture) (W. Witschi) (Centenary of Federal Constitution)

(Des F. Witzig. Photo Courvoisier)

1974 (28 Mar). 17th Universal Postal Union Congress, Lausanne. T **211** and similar horiz design. Multicoloured. P 11½.

885	30c. Type **211**		95	55
	a. Pair Nos. 885/886		2·00	1·20
886	30c. View of Lausanne		95	55

Nos. 885/886 were issued together in *se-tenant* pairs within the sheet.

(Des E. and M. Lenz. Photo Courvoisier)

1974 (30 May). Pro Patria. For National Day Collection. Archaeological Discoveries (3rd series). Designs as T **199**, but horiz. Multicoloured. P 11½.

887	15c. +5c. Glass bowl		60	45
888	30c. +10c. Bull's head (bronze)		1·20	55
889	40c. +20c. Gold brooch		1·80	1·20
890	60c. +20c. Bird vessel (clay)		2·40	2·20
887/890	Set of 4		5·50	4·00

(Des H. Hartmann (No. 891), H. Scheller (No. 892), E. Bosshart (No. 893). Photo Courvoisier)

1974 (19 Sept). Publicity Issue. T **212** and similar horiz designs. P 11½.

891	15c. deep brown-olive, yellow-olive and lilac		60	20
892	30c. multicoloured		70	25
893	30c. multicoloured		60	20
891/893	Set of 3		1·70	60

Designs: No. 891, T **212**; No. 892, Foundation emblem (Aid for Swiss Sports Foundation); No. 893, Posthorn and postal transit arrow (125th Anniversary of Federal Posts).

No. 893 was issued on fibre-less paper.

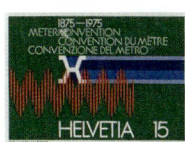

213 Metre and Krypton Line (Centenary of Metre Convention)

214 *The Mönch* (F. Hodler)

(Des R. Hirter (15c.), H. Erni (30c.), H. Hartmann (60c.), B. Waltenspül (90c.). Photo Courvoisier)

1975 (13 Feb). Publicity Issue. T **213** and similar horiz designs. Fibre-less paper. P 11½.

894	15c. orange, ultramarine and deep green		60	45
895	30c. red-brown, claret and yellow		70	45
896	60c. vermilion, black and bright blue		1·40	55
897	90c. multicoloured		2·40	1·80
894/897	Set of 4		4·50	3·00

Designs: 15c. T **213**; 30c. Heads of women (International Women's Year); 60c. Red Cross flag and barbed-wire (Humanitarian International Law Conference, Geneva); 90c. Astra airship *Ville de Lucerne* (Aviation and Space Travel exhibition, Transport and Communications Museum, Lucerne).

(Des H. Kümpel. Photo Courvoisier)

1975 (28 Apr). Europa Paintings T **214** and similar vert designs. Multicoloured. Fibre-less paper. P 12×11½.

898	30c. Type **214**		70	55
899	50c. *Still Life with Guitar* (R. Auber-jonois)		1·20	85
900	60c. *L'effeuilleuse* (M. Barraud)		1·40	1·30
898/900	Set of 3		3·00	2·40

(Des E. and M. Lenz. Photo Courvoisier)

1975 (30 May). Pro Patria. Archaeological Discoveries (4th series). Vert designs as T **199**. Multicoloured. Fibre-less paper. P 11½.

901	15c. +10c. Gold brooch, Oron-le-Châtel		95	55
902	30c. +20c. Bacchus (bronze statuette), Avenches		1·40	55
903	50c. +20c. Bronze daggers, Bois-de-Vaux, Lausanne		2·40	1·90
904	60c. +25c. Coloured glass decanter, Maratlo		2·75	2·30
901/904	Set of 4		6·75	4·75

215 Disabled Person in Wheelchair being dragged up Steps (Eliminate Obstacles!)

216 Forest Scene (Centenary of Federal Forest Laws)

SWITZERLAND 1975

(Des C. Piatti (15c.), W. Beutter (30c.), P. Besson (50c.), Courvoisier (60c.)). Photo Courvoisier

1975 (11 Sept). Publicity Issue. T **215** and similar horiz designs. Fibre-less paper. P 11½.
905	15c. black, bright green and lilac		60	45
906	30c. black, rosine and orange-red		70	55
907	50c. reddish brown and yellow-bistre		1·20	1·10
908	60c. multicoloured		1·40	1·10
905/908	Set of 4		3·50	3·00

Designs: 15c. T **215**; 30c. Organisation emblem (Interconfessional Pastoral care by Telephone Organisation); 50c. EAHY emblem (European Architectural Heritage Year); 60c. Beat Fischer von Reichenbach (founder) (300th Anniversary of Fischer postal service).

(Des A. Rosselet (No. 909), B. Kühne (No. 910). C. Piatti (No. 911), A. Cserno and J.-J Chevalley (No. 912). Recess PTT, Bern (No. 912) Photo Courvoisier (others))

1976 (12 Feb). Publicity Issue. T **216** and similar horiz designs. P 11½.
909	20c. multicoloured		1·20	55
910	40c. multicoloured		95	55
911	40c. black, salmon and claret		95	55
912	80c. black and pale blue		1·90	1·60
909/912	Set of 4		4·50	3·00

Designs: No. 909, T **216**; No. 910, Fruit and vegetables (campaign to promote nutriments as opposed to alcohol); No. 911, African child (fight against leprosy); No. 912, Early and modern telephones (telephone centenary).

Nos. 909/911 were issued on fibre-less paper.

217 Floral Embroidery   **218** Kyburg Castle, Zürich

(Des H. Hartmann. Eng M. Müller. Recess PTT, Bern)

1976 (3 May). Europa. Handicrafts. T **217** and similar vert design. P 11½.
913	40c. yellow, red-brown and pink		1·20	55
914	80c. blue, rose-red and yellow-ochre		3·00	1·60
	a. Red spot near '5'		24·00	23·00

Designs: 40c. T **217**; 80c. Decorated pocket watch.

No. 914 was issued on fibre-less paper.

(Des A. Oertle. Photo Courvoisier)

1976 (28 May). Pro Patria. Swiss Castles (1st series). T **218** and similar horiz designs. Multicoloured. Fibre-less paper. P 11½.
915	20c. +10c. Type **218**		1·20	60
916	40c. +20c. Grandson castle, Vaud		1·80	70
917	40c. +20c. Murten castle, Fribourg		1·80	70
918	80c. +40c. Bellinzona castle, Ticino		5·00	4·00
915/918	Set of 4		8·75	5·50

See also Nos. 932/935, 955/958 and 977/980.

219 Roe Deer Fawn, Frog and Barn Swallow (World Federation for Protection of Animals)   **220** Oskar Bider and Blériot XI

(Des P. Bergmaier (No. 919), U. Knoblauch (No. 920), E. Hauri (No. 921), W. Haettenschweiler (No. 922). Photo Courvoisier)

1976 (16 Sept). Publicity Issue. T **219** and similar horiz designs. Fibre-less paper. P 11½.
919	20c. black, deep brown and yellow-green		1·20	55
920	40c. black, yellow and rosine		95	45
921	40c. multicoloured		1·40	55
922	80c. rosine, deep violet and blue		1·90	1·70
919/922	Set of 4		5·00	3·00

Designs: No. 919, T **219**; No. 920, Sun and inscription (Save Energy campaign); No. 921, St Gotthard mountains (Swiss Alps); No. 922, Skater (World Speed Skating Championships, Davos).

(Des K. Wirth. Eng K. Bickel, junior. Recess PTT, Bern)

1977 (27 Jan). Swiss Aviation Pioneers. T **220** and similar horiz designs. P 11½.
923	40c. black, magenta and red		1·20	60
924	80c. black, deep reddish purple and new blue		3·00	1·30
925	100c. black, grey-olive and bistre		2·40	1·70
926	150c. black, brown and blue-green		4·25	2·00
923/926	Set of 4		9·75	4·50

Designs: 40c. T **220**; 80c. Eduard Spelterini and balloon basket; 100c. Armand Dufaux and Dufaux IV biplane; 150c. Walter Mittelholzer and Dormer Do-B Merkur seaplane *Switzerland*.

> **PHOSPHORESCENT PAPER.** All stamps from No. 927 are printed on phosphorescent, fibre-less paper, *unless otherwise stated.*

221 Blue Cross (Centenary of Swiss Blue Cross (society for care of alcoholics))   **222** St Ursanne

(Des C. Mojonnet (20c.). Bornand, Gaeng and Monod (40c.), D. Froidevaux (80c.). Photo Courvoisier)

1977 (27 Jan). Publicity Issue. T **221** and similar horiz designs. P 11½.
927	20c. blue and grey-brown		65	45
928	40c. multicoloured		1·00	50
929	80c. multicoloured		2·00	1·80
927/929	Set of 3		3·25	2·50

Designs: 20c. T **221**; 40c. Festival emblem (Vevey vintage festival); 80c. Balloons carrying letters (Juphilex 1977 youth stamp exhibition, Berne).

(Des and Eng K. Oberli (40c.), K. Bickel, junior (80c.), Recess and photo PTT, Bern)

1977 (2 May). Europa. Landscapes. T **222** and similar horiz design. Multicoloured. P 11½.
930	40c. Type **222**		1·00	60
931	80c. Sils-Baselgia		2·00	1·80

(Des A. Oertle. Photo Courvoisier)

1977 (23 May). Pro Patria. Swiss Castles (2nd series). Horiz designs as T **218**. Multicoloured. P 11½.
932	20c. +10c. Aigle, Vaud		65	50
933	40c. +20c. Pratteln, Basel-Landschaft		1·20	60
934	70c. +30c. Sargans, St Gallen		2·75	3·00
935	80c. +40c. Hallwil, Aargau		3·75	3·50
932/935	Set of 4		7·50	6·75

223 Factory Worker   **224** Sternsingen, Bergün

(Des R. Hirter (20c.), W. Mühlemann (40c.), H. Bürgin (80c.). Photo Courvoisier)

1977 (25 Aug). Publicity Issue. T **223** and similar horiz designs. Multicoloured. P 11½.
936	20c. Type **223**		65	50
937	40c. Ionic capital		1·00	60
938	80c. Association emblem and Butterfly		2·00	1·80
936/938	Set of 3		3·25	2·50

Subjects: 20c. Centenary of Federal Factories Act; 40c. Protection of cultural monuments; 80c. Swiss Footpaths Association.

(Des S. Moser. Eng H. Heusser (30c., 40c., 70c., 90c.); P. Schopfer (others). Recess PTT, Bern)

1977 (25 Aug)–84. Regional Folk Customs. T **224** and similar horiz designs. P 11½.
939	5c. deep blue-green		30	15
	a. Perf two or three sides. Booklets (1.2.84)		1·00	1·00
	ab. Booklet pane. No. 939a×2 (1.2.84)		4·25	
940	10c. red		30	15
	a. Perf two sides. Booklets (5.1.79)		1·10	1·10
	ab. Booklet pane. No. 940a×2 plus two labels (5.1.79)		2·30	
	ac. Booklet pane. No. 940a×4 (1.2.84)		4·75	
941	20c. red-orange		50	30
	a. Perf two or three sides. Booklets (5.1.79)		90	85
	ab. Booklet pane. No. 941a×4 (5.1.79)		3·75	
941b	25c. reddish brown (11.9.84)		65	50
941c	30c. emerald (25.11.82)		90	45

1978 SWITZERLAND

942	35c. deep olive		90	50
	a. Perf two or three sides. Booklets (1.2.84)		2·40	2·40
	ab. Booklet pane. No 942a×4 (1.2.84)		9·75	
943	40c. deep claret		1·00	50
	a. Perf two or three sides. Booklets (5.1.79)		1·20	1·20
	ab. Booklet pane. No 943a×4 (5.1.79)		5·00	
	b. Granite paper (24.8.78)		2·40	2·40
943c	45c. indigo (11.9.84)		1·20	95
944	50c. brown-red		1·20	50
	a. Perf two or three sides Booklets (1.2.84)		2·40	2·40
	ab. Booklet pane. No 944a×4 (1.2.84)		9·75	
	ac. Booklet pane. No 944a×2 plus two labels (1.2.84)		5·00	
944b	60c. sepia (11.9.84)		1·60	1·20
945	70c. deep rose-lilac		1·70	50
946	80c. Prussian blue		1·90	1·80
947	90c. purple-brown		2·40	2·40
939/947 Set of 13			13·00	9·00

Designs: 5c. T **224**; 10c. Sechseläuten, Zürich; 20c. Silvesterkläuse, Herisau; 25c. Chesstete, Solothurn; 30c. Röllelibutzen, Alstätten; 35c. Gansabhauet, Sursee; 40c. Escalade, Geneva; 45c. Klausjagen, Küssnacht; 50c. Achetringele, Laupen; 60c. Schnabelgeissen, Offenbach; 70c. Processions storiche, Mendrisio; 80c. Vogel Gryff, Basel; 90c. Roitschäggätä, Lötschental.

The booklet panes have their outer three edges imperforate, giving stamps with one or two adjacent sides imperf.

40c. printed in litho is a forgery.

225 Mailcoach Route Plate, Vaud Canton **226** *La Suisse*, Lake Geneva

(Des E. Witzig (20c.), A. Flückiger (40c.), A. M. Petitmaitre (70c.), J. Hägeli (80c.) Photo Courvoisier)

1978 (9 Mar). Publicity Issue. T **225** and similar horiz designs. Multicoloured. P 11½.

948	20c. Type **225**		60	30
949	40c. View of Lucerne		1·60	80
950	70c. Title page of book *Mélusine*		1·80	1·70
951	80c. Stylised camera and lens		2·00	1·90
948/951 Set of 4			5·50	4·00

Events: 20c. Lemanex 78 National Stamp Exhibition; 40c. 800th Anniversary of Lucerne; 70c. 500th Anniversary of Printing in Geneva; 80c. Second International Triennial Exhibition of Photography, Fribourg.

(Des C. Piatti. Photo Courvoisier)

1978 (9 Mar). Lemanex 78 National Stamp Exhibition, Lausanne. Sheet 133×149 mm containing T **226** and similar horiz designs, showing lake steamers, with four labels. Multicoloured. P 11½.

MS952	20c. Type **226**; 20c. *Il Verbano*; 40c. *Gotthard*; 40c. *Ville de Neuchâtel*; 40c. *Romanshorn*; 40c. *Le Winkelried*; 70c. *Loetschberg*; 80c. *Waedenswil* (sold at 5f.)	8·75	8·50

227 Stockalper Palace, Brig **228** Abbé Joseph Bovet (composer)

(Des K. Oberli. Eng M. Müller. Recess and photo PTT. Bern)

1978 (2 May). Europa. T **227** and similar horiz design. P 11½.

953	40c. multicoloured		1·30	60
954	80c. cobalt, yellow-brown and black		2·50	1·80

Designs: 40c. T **227**; 80c. Old Diet Hall, Berne.

(Des A. Oertle. Photo Courvoisier)

1978 (26 May). Pro Patria. Swiss Castles (3rd series). Horiz designs as T **218**. Multicoloured. P 11½.

955	20c. +10c. Hagenwil, Thurgau		65	50
956	40c. +20c. Bergdorf, Berne		1·30	60
957	70c. +30c. Tarasp, Graubünden		3·00	3·00
958	80c. +40c. Chilton, Vaud		4·25	3·50
955/958 Set of 4			8·25	6·75

(Des M. Boegli Eng K. Bickel, junior. Recess PTT, Bern)

1978 (14 Sept). Celebrities. T **228** and similar vert designs. P 11½.

959	20c. dull green	65	50
960	40c. brown-purple	1·00	60
961	70c. olive-grey	1·80	1·70
962	80c. grey-blue	1·90	1·90
959/962 Set of 4		4·75	4·25

Designs: 20c. T **228**; 40c. Henri Dunant (founder of Red Cross); 70c. Carl Gustav Jung (psychiatrist); 80c. Auguste Piccard (physicist).

229 Worker wearing Goggles **230** Arms of Switzerland and Jura

(Des B. Mäder. Photo Courvoisier)

1978 (14 Sept). Safety at Work. T **229** and similar horiz designs. Multicoloured. P 11½.

963	40c. Type **229**	1·50	95
	a. Strip of 3 Nos. 963/965	4·75	
964	40c. Worker wearing respirator	1·50	95
965	40c. Worker wearing safety helmet	1·50	95
963/965 Set of 3		4·00	2·50

Nos. 963/965 were issued together in *se-tenant* strips of three within the sheet.

(Des and photo Courvoisier)

1978 (25 Sept). Creation of Canton of Jura. P 11½.

966	**230**	40c. bright scarlet, black and yellow-ochre	1·00	70

231 Rainer Maria Rilke (writer) **232** Othmar H. Ammann and Verrazano Narrows Bridge

(Des H. Erni. Eng P. Schopfer. Recess PTT, Bern)

1979 (21 Feb). Celebrities. T **231** and similar vert designs. P 11½.

967	20c. deep dull green	65	50
968	40c. red	95	60
969	70c. red-brown	1·80	1·70
970	80c. Prussian blue	1·90	1·90
967/970 Set of 4		4·75	4·25

Designs: 20c. T **231**; 40c. Paul Klee (artist), 70c. Herman Hesse (novelist and poet); 80c. Thomas Mann (novelist).

(Des H. Thöni (20c.), W. Haettenschweiler (40c.), K. Wirth (70c.), H. Bürgin (80c.). Photo Courvoisier)

1979 (21 Feb). Publicity Issue. T **232** and similar horiz designs. Multicoloured. P 11½.

971	20c. Type **232**	65	50
972	40c. Target and marker	1·00	60
973	70c. Hot-air balloon *Esperanto*	1·80	1·70
974	80c. Aircraft tail fins	2·00	1·90
971/974 Set of 4		5·00	4·25

Subjects: 20c. Birth centenary of O. H. Ammann (engineer); 40c. 50th Federal Riflemen's Festival, Lucerne; 70c. World Esperanto Congress, Lucerne; 80c. Basel-Mulhouse Airport.

233 Old Letter Box, Basel **234** Gold Stater

(Des K. Oberli. Eng M. Müller. Recess and photo PTT, Bern)

1979 (30 Apr). Europa. T **233** and similar vert design. P 11½.

975	40c. multicoloured	1·30	70

SWITZERLAND 1979

976	80c. deep grey-blue, pale blue and yellow-ochre		3·25	1·90

Designs: 40c. T **233**; 80c. Alpine relay station on Jungfrauloch.

(Des A. Oertle. Photo Courvoisier)

1979 (25 May). Pro Patria. Swiss Castles (4th series). Horiz designs as T **218**. Multicoloured. P 11½.

977	20c. +10c. Oron, Vaud	65	50
978	40c. +20c. Spiez, Berne	1·30	60
979	70c. +30c. Porrentruy, Jura	3·25	3·00
980	80c. +40c. Rapperswil, St Gallen	4·50	3·50
977/980 Set of 4		8·75	6·75

(Des E. and M. Lenz (20c.), F. Bauer (40c.), R. Gerbig (70c.), H. Auchli (80c.). Photo Courvoisier)

1979 (6 Sept). Publicity Issue. T **234** and similar designs. Multicoloured. P 11½.

981	20c. Type **234**	65	50
982	40c. Child on a Dove (horiz)	1·00	60
983	70c. Morse key and satellite (horiz)	1·80	1·70
984	80c. Ariane rocket	2·00	1·90
981/984 Set of 4		5·00	4·25

Subjects: 20c. Centenary of Swiss Numismatic Society; 40c. International Year of the Child; 70c. 50th Anniversary of Swiss Radio Amateurs; 80c. European Space Agency.

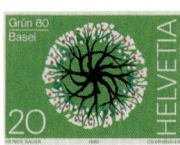
235 Tree in Blossom

236 Johann Konrad Kern (politician)

(Des H. Bauer (20c.), E. and M. Lenz (40c.), A. Flückiger (70c.), J. Ongaro (80c.). Photo Courvoisier)

1980 (21 Feb). Publicity Issue. T **235** and similar horiz designs. Multicoloured. P 11½.

985	20c. Type **235**	65	50
986	40c. Carved milk vessel	1·00	60
987	70c. Town Hall, Winterthur	1·80	1·70
988	80c. Pic-Pic car	2·00	1·90
985/988 Set of 4		5·00	4·25

Subjects: 20c. Horticultural and Landscape Gardening Exhibition, Basel; 40c. 50th Anniversary of Arts and Crafts Centre; 70c. Centenary of Society for Swiss Art History; 80c. 50th International Motor Show, Geneva.

(Des and Eng P. Schopfer. Recess PTT, Bern)

1980 (28 Apr). Europa. T **236** and similar horiz design. Granite paper. P 11½.

989	40c. flesh black and rose	1·00	60
990	80c. flesh, black and blue	2·00	1·80

Designs: 40c. T **236**; 80c. Gustav Adolf Hasler (communications pioneer).

237 Mason and Carpenter

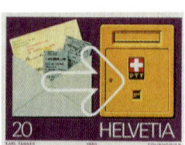
238 Girocheque and Letter Box

(Des P. Schiegg (20c., 80c.), G. Rimensberger (others). Photo Courvoisier)

1980 (29 May). Pro Patria. Trade and Craft Signs. T **237** and similar vert designs. Multicoloured. P 11½.

991	20c. +10c. Type **237**	65	50
992	40c. +20c. Barber	1·30	60
993	70c. +30c. Hatter	3·25	2·40
994	80c. +40c. Baker	3·75	3·50
991/994 Set of 4		8·00	6·25

(Des A. Flückiger, Eng M. Müller; recess and photo PTT Bern (70c.). Des K. Tanner; photo Courvoisier (others))

1980 (5 Sept). Swiss PTT Services. T **238** and similar horiz designs. P 11½.

995	20c. multicoloured	65	50
996	40c. multicoloured	1·00	60
997	70c. drab, black and lavender	1·80	1·70
998	80c. multicoloured	2·50	1·90
995/998 Set of 4		5·25	4·25

Designs: 20c. T **238**; 40c. Postbus; 70c. Transfer roller (50th Anniversary of PTT postage stamp printing office); 80c. Telephone and flowers (Centenary of telephone in Switzerland).

239 Weather Chart

240 Granary from Kiesen

(Des P. Kräuchi (20c.), R. Hirter (40c.), W. Haettenschweiler (80c.). Photo Courvoisier)

1980 (5 Sept). Publicity Issue. T **239** and similar horiz designs. Multicoloured. P 11½.

999	20c. Type **239** (Centenary of Swiss Meteorological Office)	65	50
1000	40c. Figures and cross (Centenary of Swiss Trade Union Federation)	1·00	60
1001	80c. Motorway sign (Opening of St Gotthard road tunnel)	3·25	1·90
999/1001 Set of 3		4·50	2·75

(Des A. Wittmer (20c.), R. Mösch (40c.), E. Hauri (80c.), K. Wirth (110c.). Photo Courvoisier)

1981 (9 Mar). Publicity Issue. T **240** and similar multicoloured designs. P 11½.

1002	20c. Type **240** (Ballenberg Open-air Museum)	65	50
1003	40c. Disabled figures (International Year of Disabled Persons)	1·00	60
1004	70c. The Parish Clerk (Albert Anker, 150th birth anniversary) (vert)	1·80	1·70
1005	80c. Theodolite and rod (16th International Federation of Surveyors Congress, Montreux)	2·00	1·90
1006	110c. Tail of DC-9-81 (50th Anniversary of Swissair)	3·75	2·40
1002/1006 Set of 5		8·25	6·25

241 Figure leaping from Earth

242 Dancing Couple

(Des H. Erni. Photo Courvoisier)

1981 (9 Mar). AIR. 50th Anniversary of Swissair. P 11½.

1007	**241** 2f.+1f. reddish lilac, deep dull violet and lemon	5·00	4·75

No. 1007, printed in sheets of eight, was for compulsory use on Swissair Jubilee flights to Chicago, Helsinki, Djakarta and Buenos Aires; it was also valid on other mail.

(Des W. Haettenschweiler. Photo Courvoisier)

1981 (4 May). Europa. T **242** and similar vert design. Multicoloured. P 11½.

1008	40c. Type **242**	1·30	60
1009	80c. Stone putter	3·25	2·40

243 Aarburg Post Office Sign, 1685

244 Seal of Fribourg

(Des E. Witzig. Photo Courvoisier)

1981 (27 May). Pro Patria. Postal Signs. T **243** and similar vert designs. Multicoloured. P 11½.

1010	20c. +10c. Type **243**	65	50
1011	40c. +20c. Mail coach sign of Fribourg Cantonal Post	1·90	60
1012	70c. +30c. Gondola post office sign (Ticino Cantonal Post)	2·50	2·40
1013	80c. +40c. Splugen post office sign	3·75	3·50
1010/1013 Set of 4		8·00	6·25

(Des E. Witzig. Eng M. Müller (80c), K. Bickel, junior (others). Recess and photo PTT, Bern)

1981 (3 Sept). 500th Anniversary of Covenant of Stans. T **244** and similar horiz designs. P 11½.
1014	40c. brown-red, black and orange-brown	1·00	60
1015	40c. myrtle-green, black and claret	1·00	60
1016	80c. reddish brown, black and light grey-blue	2·50	1·90
1014/1016	Set of 3	4·00	2·75

Designs: No. 1014, T **244**; No. 1015, Seal of Solothurn; No. 1016, Old Town Hall, Stans.

245 Voltage Regulator from Jungfrau Railway's Power Station

246 C4/5 Class Steam Locomotive

(Des A. Flückiger (20c.), G. Rimensberger (40c.), K. Baumgartner (70c.), R. Hirter (1f.10). Photo Courvoisier)

1981 (3 Sept). Publicity Issue. T **245** and similar horiz designs. Multicoloured. P 11½.
1017	20c. Type **245**	65	50
1018	40c. Crossbow quality seal	1·00	60
1019	70c. Group of young people	1·80	1·40
1020	1f.10 Mosaic	2·75	2·40
1017/1020	Set of 4	5·50	4·50

Subjects: 20c. Opening of Technorama of Switzerland, Winterthur (museum of science and technology); 40c. 50th Anniversary of Organisation for Promotion of Swiss Products and Services; 70c. 50th Anniversary of Swiss Association of Youth Organisations; 1f.10 Restoration of St Peter's Cathedral, Geneva.

(Des C. Piatti. Photo Courvoisier)

1982 (18 Feb). Centenary of St Gotthard Railway. T **246** and similar horiz design. P 11½.
1021	40c. black and reddish purple	1·00	60
	a. Horiz strip. Nos. 1021/1022 plus label...	2·10	1·30
1022	40c. multicoloured	1·00	60

Designs: No. 1021, T **246**; No. 1022, Re 6/6 class electric locomotive. Nos. 1021/1022 were issued together in sheets of ten stamps, with *se-tenant* intervening labels showing a detail of the workers' memorial by Vincenzo Vela at Airolo station.

247 Hoteliers Association Emblem

248 Swearing Oath of Eternal Fealty, Rütli Meadow (detail of mural, Heinrich Danioth)

(Des P. Schiegg (20c.), K. Kaiser (40c.), A. Bovey (70c.), C. Kuhn-Klein (80c.), E. Hauri (110c.). Photo Courvoisier)

1982 (18 Feb). Publicity Issue. T **247** and similar horiz designs. Multicoloured. P 11½.
1023	20c. Type **247**	65	50
1024	40c. Flag formed from four Fs	1·00	60
1025	70c. Gas flame encircling emblem.....................	1·80	1·20
1026	80c. Lynx and scientific instruments	2·50	2·40
1027	110c. Retort	2·75	2·40
1023/1027	Set of 5	7·75	6·50

Subjects: 20c. Centenary of Swiss Hoteliers Association; 40c. 150th Anniversary of Swiss Gymnastic Society; 70c. 50th Anniversary of International Gas Union; 80c. 150th Anniversary of Natural History Museum, Berne; 110c. Centenary of Swiss Society of Chemical Industries.

(Des C. Piatti. Photo Courvoisier)

1982 (3 May). Europa. T **248** and similar horiz design. Multicoloured. P 11½.
1028	40c. Type **248**	1·50	60
1029	80c. Treaty of 1291 founding Swiss Confederation..	3·25	2·40

249 The Sun, Willisau

250 Aquarius and Old Berne

(Des A. Bovey. Photo Courvoisier)

1982 (27 May). Pro Patria. Inn Signs (1st series). Multicoloured. P 11½.
1030	20c. +10c. Type **249**	65	50
1031	40c. +20c. On the Wave, St Saphorin	1·90	60
1032	70c. +30c. The Three Kings, Rheinfelden.........	2·50	2·40
1033	80c. +40c. The Crown, Winterthur....................	3·75	3·50
1030/1033	Set of 4	8·00	6·25

See also Nos. 1056/1059.

(Des E. and M. Lenz. Eng K. Bickel, junior (1f.20, 1f.50, 1f.70, 1f.80, 4f., 4f.50), P. Schopfer (others). Recess and photo PTT, Bern)

1982 (23 Aug)–**86**. Signs of the Zodiac and Landscapes. T **250** and similar vert designs. P 11½.
1034	1f. multicoloured	2·50	35
1035	1f.10 brown, dull blue and dull violet-blue.....	2·75	35
1036	1f.20 myrtle green, cobalt and grey-brown ...	3·00	50
1036a	1f.40 multicoloured (11.2.86)............................	3·50	3·25
1037	1f.50 deep blue, azure and salmon..................	3·75	60
1038	1f.60 multicoloured	4·00	2·40
1039	1f.70 brown-ochre and deep turquoise-blue (17.2.83)	4·25	60
1040	1f.80 grey-brown, green and blackish green (17.2.83)..	4·50	2·40
1041	2f. cobalt, brown-ochre and deep blue (17.2.83)..	5·50	4·75
1042	2f. cobalt, brown-ochre and deep blue (24.11.83)..	5·00	60
1042a	2f.50 red, dull green and bronze green (19.2.85)..	6·25	1·80
1043	3f. Indian red, grey-green and greenish black (19.2.85)	7·50	60
1044	4f. bright yellow-green, violet and brown-purple (21.2.84)	10·00	1·20
1045	4f.50 brown-ochre, cobalt and chocolate (21.2.84)..	11·50	1·80
1034/1045	Set of 14	65·00	19·00

Designs: 1f. T **250**; 1f.10 Pisces and Nax, near Sion; 1f.20 Aries and the Graustock, Obwalden, 1f.40 Gemini and Bischofszell; 1f.50 Taurus and Basel Cathedral, 1f.60 Gemini and Schönengrund; 1f.70 Cancer and Wetterhorn; 1f.80 Leo and Areuse Gorge; 2f. (No. 1041), Virgo and Aletsch Glacier; 2f. (No. 1042), Virgo and Schwarzsee above Zermatt; 2f.50 Libra and Féchy; 3f. Scorpio and Corippo; 4f. Sagittarius and Glarus; 4f.50 Capricorn and Schuls.

251 Articulated Tram

252 Eurasian Perch

(Des K. Tanner (20c.), A. Koella (40c.), H. Schelbert (70c.), W. Mühlemann (80c.). Photo Courvoisier)

1982 (23 Aug). Publicity Issue. T **251** and similar horiz designs. Multicoloured. P 11½.
1046	20c. Type **251**	1·00	60
1047	40c. Salvation Army singer and guitarist	1·00	60
1048	70c. Dressage rider	1·80	1·70
1049	80c. Emblem...	2·00	1·90
1046/1049	Set of 4	5·25	4·25

Subjects: 20c. Centenary of Zürich trams; 40c. Centenary of Salvation Army in Switzerland; 70c. World Dressage Championship, Lausanne; 80c. 14th Congress of International Water Supply Association, Zürich.

(Des E. Witzig (20c.), E. and M. Lenz (40c.), R. Hirter (70c.), R.-V. Geiser (80c.). Photo Courvoisier)

1983 (17 Feb). Publicity Issue. T **252** and similar horiz designs. Multicoloured. P 11½.
1050	20c. Type **252**	1·30	50
1051	40c. University of Zürich	1·00	60
1052	70c. Teleprinter tape forming JP	1·80	1·70
1053	80c. Micrometer and cycloidal computer drawing	2·00	1·90
1050/1053	Set of 4	5·50	4·25

Subjects: 20c. Centenary of Swiss Fishing and Pisciculture Federation; 40c. 150th Anniversary of University of Zürich; 70c. Centenary of Swiss Journalists' Federation; 80c. Centenary of Swiss Machine Manufacturers' Association.

SWITZERLAND 1983

253 Jost Bürgi's Celestial Globe, 1594

254 Seal, 1832–1848

(Des H. Hartmann. Eng M. Müller. Recess and photo PTT, Bern)

1983 (3 May). Europa. T **253** and similar vert design. P 11½.
1054	40c. pale orange, rose-pink and purple-brown	1·30	60
1055	80c. yellowish green, azure and blue-black	3·25	1·80

Designs: 40c. T **253**; 80c. Niklaus Riggenbach's rack and pinion railway, 1871.

(Des B. Scarton. Photo Courvoisier)

1983 (26 May). Pro Patria. Inn Signs (2nd series). Horiz designs as T **249**. Multicoloured. P 11½.
1056	20c. +10c. The Lion, Heimiswil	1·20	85
1057	40c. +20c. The Cross, Sachsein	1·30	95
1058	70c. +30c. The Jug, Lenzburg Castle	3·25	2·40
1059	80c. +40c. The Cavalier, St George	3·75	3·50
1056/1059	Set of 4	8·50	7·00

(Des C. Piatti. Photo Courvoisier)

1983 (26 May). 150th Anniversary of Basel-Land Canton. P 11½.
1060	**254**	40c. multicoloured	1·00	60

255 Gallo-Roman Capital, Martigny

256 Pre-stamp Cover, 1839

(Des P. Ferret (20c.). Eleonore Schmid (40c.), W. Haettenschweiler (70c.). H.-J. Bolzhauser (80c.). Photo Courvoisier)

1983 (22 Aug). Publicity Issue. T **255** and similar horiz designs. P 11½.
1061	20c. pale orange and black	65	50
1062	40c. multicoloured	1·60	60
1063	70c. multicoloured	2·00	1·70
1064	80c. multicoloured	2·00	1·90
1061/1064	Set of 4	5·75	4·25

Designs: 20c. T **255** (Bimillenary of Octodurus/Martigny); 40c. Bernese Shepherd-dog and Schwyz Hunting Dog (Centenary of Swiss Kennel Club); 70c. Cyclists (Centenary of Swiss Cyclists and Motorcyclists Federation); 80c. Carrier Pigeon and world map (World Communications Year).

(Des H.-J. Bolzhauser (25c.), M. Dayer (50c.), L. Pizzotti (80c.). Photo Courvoisier)

1984 (21 Feb). Publicity Issue. T **256** and similar horiz designs. Multicoloured. P 11½.
1065	25c. Type **256**	1·30	45
1066	50c. Collegiate Church clock and buildings	1·30	50
1067	80c. Olympic rings and Lausanne	3·25	1·90
1065/1067	Set of 3	5·25	2·50

Subjects: 25c. National Stamp Exhibition, Zürich; 50c. 1100th Anniversary of Saint-Imier; 80c. Permanent headquarters of International Olympic Committee at Lausanne.

257 Bridge

258 Hexagonal Stove from Rosenburg Mansion, Stans

(Des J. Larrivière. Photo Courvoisier)

1984 (2 May). Europa. 25th Anniversary of European Posts and Telecommunications Conference. P 11½.
1068	**257**	50c. bright claret, deep carmine and crimson	1·90	1·20
1069		80c. dull ultramarine, deep bright blue and royal blue	3·25	1·90

(Des E. Witzig. Photo Courvoisier)

1984 (24 May). Pro Patria. Tiled Stoves. T **258** and similar vert designs. Multicoloured. P 11½.
1070	35c. +15c. Type **258**	1·30	1·20
1071	50c. +20c. Winterthur stove (by Hans Heinrich Pfau), Freuler Palace, Näfels	1·90	60
1072	70c. +30c. Box-stove (by Rudolf Stern) from Plaisance, Riaz	3·25	3·00
1073	80c. +40c. Frame-modelled stove (by Leonard Racle)	3·75	3·50
1070/1073	Set of 4	9·25	7·50

259 Bauschänzli, City Hall and Fraumunster

260 Burning Match

(Des K. Oberli. Photo Courvoisier)

1984 (24 May). Naba Züri 84 National Stamp Exhibition, Zürich. Sheet 145×70 mm containing T **259** and similar vert designs forming panorama of Zürich. Multicoloured. P 11½.
MS1074	50c. Type **259**; 50c. St Peter's; 50c. Town Hall, Helmhaus and Wasser Church; 50c. Cathedral (sold at 3f.)	7·50	7·25

(Des E. Hauri. Photo Courvoisier)

1984 (11 Sept). Fire Prevention. P 11½.
1075	**260**	50c. multicoloured	1·30	60

261 Railway Conductor's Equipment

262 Ernest Ansermet (orchestral conductor)

(Des U. Grünig (35c.), A. Wittmer (50c.), K. Wirth (70c.), E. Hauri (80c.). Photo Courvoisier)

1985 (19 Feb). Publicity Issue. T **261** and similar horiz designs. Multicoloured. P 11½.
1076	35c. Type **261** (centenary of Train Staff Association)	1·00	40
1077	50c. Stone with Latin inscription (2000 years of Rhaeto-Romanic culture)	1·30	50
1078	70c. Rescue of man (centenary of International Lake Geneva Rescue Society)	1·80	1·70
1079	80c. Grande Dixence dam (International Large Dams Congress, Lausanne)	2·50	1·90
1076/1079	Set of 4	6·00	4·00

(Des H. Erni. Photo Courvoisier)

1985 (7 May). Europa. Music Year. T **262** and similar vert design. Multicoloured. P 11½.
1080	50c. Type **262**	1·30	60
1081	80c. Frank Martin (composer)	2·50	1·80

263 Music Box, 1895

264 Baker

(Des K. Tanner. Photo Courvoisier)

1985 (28 May). Pro Patria. Musical Instruments. T **263** and similar horiz designs. Multicoloured. P 11½.
1082	25c. +10c. Type **263**	1·00	90
1083	35c. +15c. 18th-century box rattle	1·30	1·20

1985 SWITZERLAND

1084	50c. +20c. Emmental necked zither (by Peter Zaugg), 1828	1·90	60
1085	70c. +30c. Drum, 1571	3·75	3·00
1086	80c. +40c. 20th-century diatonic accordion	3·75	3·50
1082/1086	Set of 5	10·00	8·25

(Des A. Bovey (50c.), R.-V. Geiser (70c.). W. Wermelinger (80c.). Photo Courvoisier)

1985 (10 Sept). Publicity Issue. T **264** and similar horiz designs. Multicoloured. P 11½.

1087	50c. Type **264** (centenary of Swiss Master Bakers' and Confectioners' Federation)	1·30	60
1088	70c. Cross on abstract background (50th Anniversary of Swiss Radio International)	1·80	1·70
1089	80c. Geometric pattern and emblem (Postal, Telegraph and Telephone International World Congress, Interlaken)	2·00	1·90
1087/1089	Set of 3	4·50	3·75

FLUORESCENT PAPER. All stamps from No. 1090 were printed on fluorescent paper, *unless otherwise stated*.

265 Intertwined Ropes

266 Sportsmen

(Des R. Naef (35c.), H. Auchli (50c.), E. and M. Lenz (80c.), Harriet Höppner (90c.). F. Bauer (1f.10). Photo Courvoisier)

1986 (11 Feb). Publicity Issue. T **265** and similar horiz designs. P 11½.

1090	35c. multicoloured	90	85
1091	50c. deep brown, drab and dull vermilion	1·30	60
1092	80c. reddish orange, dull green and black	2·00	1·90
1093	90c. multicoloured	2·30	2·20
1094	1f.10 multicoloured	2·75	2·75
1090/1094	Set of 5	8·25	7·50

Designs: 35c. T **265** (50th Anniversary of Swiss Workers' Relief Organisation); 50c. Battle site on 1698 map (600th Anniversary of Battle of Sempach); 80c. Statuette of Mercury (2000th Anniversary of Roman Chur); 90c. Gallic head (Bimillenary of Vindonissa); 1f.10 Roman coin of Augustus (2000th Anniversary of Zürich).

(Des K. Wirth. Photo Courvoisier)

1986 (11 Feb). Pro Sport. P 11½.

1095	**266** 50c. +20c. multicoloured	1·80	1·20

267 Woman's Head

268 *Bridge in the Sun* (Giovanni Giacometti)

(Des H. Erni. Eng K. Bickel, junior. Recess and litho PTT, Bern)

1986 (27 May). Europa. T **267** and similar vert design. Multicoloured. P 13½.

1096	50c. Type **267**	1·90	60
1097	90c. Man's head	3·25	3·00

(Des H.-J. Bolzhauser. Photo Courvoisier)

1986 (27 May). Pro Patria. Paintings. T **268** and similar horiz designs. Multicoloured. P 11½.

1098	35c. +15c. Type **268**	1·30	1·20
1099	50c. +20c. *The Violet Hat* (Cuno Amiet)	1·90	60
1100	80c. +40c. *After the Funeral* (Max Buri)	3·75	3·50
1101	90c. +40c. *Still Life* (Félix Vallotton)	4·50	4·25
1098/1101	Set of 4	10·50	8·50

269 Franz Mail Van

270 Stylised Doves (International Peace Year)

(Des K. Oberli Eng P. Schopfer (5c., 45c. to 60c., 80c.), M. Müller (others). Recess and litho PTT, Bern)

1986 (9 Sept)–**89**. The Post Past and Present. T **269** and similar vert designs. P 13½×13.

1102	5c. yellow, deep reddish purple and deep carmine	65	15
1103	10c. deep bluish green, blue-green and salmon	65	15
1104	20c. dull orange, brown and pale blue (10.3.87)	65	30
1105	25c. deep turquoise-blue, greenish blue and yellow	1·00	60
1106	30c. greenish slate, black and lemon (10.3.87)	75	40
1107	35c. lake, rosine and lemon	1·30	70
1108	45c. pale blue, black and deep brown (10.3.87)	1·10	95
1109	50c. slate-violet, bright yellow-green and slate-purple (10.3.87)	1·30	60
	a. Perf 3 sides (8.9.88)	2·50	1·90
	ab. Booklet pane No. 1109a×10	26·00	
	b. Imperf (*horiz*) pair		
1110	60c. red-orange, lemon and reddish brown (10.3.87)	1·50	85
1111	75c. apple green, bronze green and carmine (7.3.89)	1·90	1·20
1112	80c. indigo, bright blue and brown	2·50	60
1113	90c. deep olive, yellow-brown and apple green	3·25	2·20
1102/1113	Set of 12	15·00	7·75

Designs: 5c. T **269**; 10c. Mechanised parcel sorting; 20c. Mule post; 25c. Letter cancelling machine; 30c. Stagecoach; 35c. Post Office counter clerk; 45c. Paddle-steamer *Stadt Luzern*, 1830s; 50c. Postman; 60c. Loading mail bags onto aeroplane; 75c. 17th-century mounted courier; 80c. Town postman, 1900s; 90c. Interior of railway sorting carriage.

The 5c., 10c., 25c., 35c., 80c. and 90c. were issued on both phosphorescent and fluorescent paper, the other values on fluorescent paper only.

The 25c., 35c., 80c. and 90c. were also issued in coils.

No. 1114 is vacant.

(Des Michèle Berri (35c.). A. Flückiger (50c.), P. Baur (80c.), P. Bataillard (90c.) Photo Courvoisier)

1986 (9 Sept). Publicity Issue. T **270** and similar horiz designs. Multicoloured. P 11½.

1115	35c. Type **270**	90	85
1116	50c. Sun behind snow-covered tree (50th Anniversary of Swiss Winter Relief Fund)	1·30	60
1117	80c. Symbols of literature and art (centenary of Berne Convention for protection of literary and artistic copyright)	2·30	2·20
1118	90c. Red Cross, Red Crescent and symbols of aggression (25th International Red Cross Conference meeting, Geneva)	2·30	2·20
1115/1118	Set of 4	6·00	5·25

271 Mobile Post Office

272 Scarabaeus (Bernhard Luginbühl)

(Des K. Tanner (35c.), P. Bataillard (50c.), S. Bundi (80c.), H. Hartmann (90c.). Michèle Berri (1f.10) Photo Courvoisier)

1987 (10 Mar). Publicity Issue. T **271** and similar horiz designs. Multicoloured. P 11½.

1119	35c. Type **271** (50th Anniversary of mobile post offices)	1·00	55
1120	50c. Lecturers of the seven faculties (450th Anniversary of Lausanne University)	1·30	50
1121	80c. Profile, Maple leaf and logarithmic spiral (150th Anniversary of Swiss Engineers' and Architects' Association)	2·30	1·80
1122	90c. Boeing 747-300/400 of Swissair and electric train (Geneva Airport rail link)	3·00	2·40
1123	1f.10 Symbolic figure and water (Bimillenary of Baden thermal springs)	3·25	3·00
1119/1123	Set of 5	9·75	7·50

(Des C. Piatti. Photo Courvoisier)

1987 (26 May). Europa. Sculpture. T **272** and similar horiz design. Multicolored. P 11½.

1124	50c. Type **272**	1·90	60
1125	90c. *Carnival Fountain*, Basel (Jean Tinguely)	3·75	3·00

SWITZERLAND 1987

273 Wall Cabinet, 1764   **274** Butcher cutting Chops

(Des E. and M. Lenz. Photo Courvoisier)

1987 (26 May). Pro Patria. Rustic Furniture. T **273** and similar horiz designs. Multicoloured. P 11½.
1126	35c. +15c. Type **273**	1·30	1·20
1127	50c. +20c. 16th-century chest	1·90	60
1128	80c. +40c. Cradle, 1782	3·75	3·50
1129	90c. +40c. Wardrobe, 1698	4·50	4·25
1126/1129 Set of 4		10·50	8·50

(Des K. Tanner (35c.), Lilian Perrin (50c.), A. Wittmer (90c.). Photo Courvoisier)

1987 (4 Sept). Publicity Issue. T **274** and similar horiz designs. Multicoloured. P 11½.
1130	35c. Type **274** (centenary of Swiss Master Butchers' Federation)	1·00	95
1131	50c. Profiles on stamps (50th Anniversary of Stamp Day)	1·50	60
1132	90c. Cheesemaker breaking up curds (centenary of Swiss Dairying Association)	3·25	3·00
1130/1132 Set of 3		5·25	4·00

275 Zug Clock Tower   **(276)**

(Des H. Schelbert. Photo Courvoisier)

1987 (4 Sept). Bicentenary of Tourism. T **275** and similar vert designs. Multicoloured. Phosphorescent paper (No. **MS**1137) or fluorescent paper (others). P 11½.
1133	50c. Type **275**	1·30	50
1134	80c. St Charles's Church, Negrentino, Prugiasco/Blenio valley	2·30	2·20
1135	90c. Witches Tower, Sion	3·25	3·00
1136	1f.40 Jörgenberg Castle, Waltens-burg/Vuorz, Surselva	4·00	3·75
1133/1136 Set of 4		9·75	8·50
MS1137 78×102 mm. Nos. 1133/1136		9·00	8·75

(Optd PTT, Bern)

1987 (7 Sept). Flood Victims Relief Fund. No. 1109 surch with T **276** in bright rose.
1138	50c. +50c. slate-violet, bright yellow-green and slate-purple	2·50	1·80

277 Society Emblem   **278** Junkers Ju 52/3m HB-HOT A702 of Swissair and Matterhorn

(Des Bernadette Baltis (25c.), V. Wyss (35c.), H. Paoli (50c.), A. Wittmer (80c.), H. Erni (90c.) Photo Courvoisier)

1988 (8 Mar). Publicity Issue. T **277** and similar horiz designs. Multicoloured. P 11½.
1139	25c. Type **277** (centenary of Swiss Women's Benevolent Society)	65	60
1140	35c. Brushing woman's hair (centenary of Swiss Master Hairdressers' Association)	90	85
1141	50c. St Fridolin banner and detail of Aegidius Tschudy's manuscript (600th Anniversary of Battle of Naefels)	1·50	60
1142	80c. Map and farming country seen from Beromünster radio tower (European Campaign for Rural Areas)	2·00	1·90
1143	90c. Girl playing shawm (50th Anniversary of Lucerne International Music Festival)	2·50	2·40
1139/1143 Set of 5		6·75	5·75

(Des H. Hartmann. Photo Courvoisier)

1988 (3 Mar). 50th Anniversary of Pro Aero Foundation. P 11½.
1144	**278** 140c. +60c. multicoloured	5·00	4·75

279 Rudolf von Neuenburg   **280** Arrows on Map of Europe

(Des E. and M. Lenz Photo Courvoisier)

1988 (24 May). Pro Patria. Minnesingers. T **279** and similar vert designs. Multicoloured. P 11½.
1145	35c. +15c. Type **279**	1·30	1·20
1146	50c. +20c. Rudolf von Rotenburg	1·90	60
1147	80c. +40c. Johannes Hadlaub	3·75	3·50
1148	90c. +40c. Hardegger	4·50	4·25
1145/1148 Set of 4		10·50	8·50

(Des S. Bundi. Photo Courvoisier)

1988 (24 May). Europa. Transport and Communications. T **280** and similar vert design. P 11½.
1149	50c. olive-bistre, bright emerald and blue-green	1·90	60
1150	90c. rose-lilac, light green and reddish violet	3·25	3·00

Designs: 50c. T **280**; 90c. Computer circuit on map of Europe.

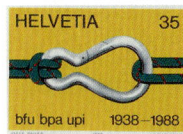

281 Snap Link

(Des J. Zwyer (35c.), E. and M. Lenz (50c.), B. la Roche (80c.), E. Kellenberger (90c.). Photo Courvoisier)

1988 (13 Sept). Publicity Issue. T **281** and similar horiz designs. Multicoloured. P 11½.
1151	35c. Type **281** (50th Anniversary of Swiss Accident Prevention Office)	90	85
1152	50c. Drilling letters (centenary of Swiss Metalworkers' and Watchmakers' Association)	1·30	60
1153	80c. Triangulation pyramid, theodolite and map (150th Anniversary of Swiss Federal Office of Topography)	2·00	1·90
1154	90c. International Red Cross Museum, Geneva (inauguration)	2·75	2·40
1151/1154 Set of 4		6·25	5·25

282 Meta (Jean Tinguely)

(Photo French Govt Ptg Wks)

1988 (25 Nov). Modern Art. P 13×12½.
1155	**282** 90c. multicoloured	5·75	5·50

A stamp of a similar design was issued by France.

283 Army Postman

284 King Friedrich II presenting Berne Town Charter (*Bendicht Tschachtlan Chronicle*)

(Des J. Ongaro (25c.), Bernadette Baltis (35c.), U. Stuber (50c.), H. Inderbitzi (80c.), J.-O. Bercher (90c.) Photo Courvoisier)

1989 (7 Mar). Publicity Issue. T **283** and similar horiz designs. Multicoloured. P 11½.

1156	25c. Type **283** (centenary of Swiss Army postal service)	1·30	60
1157	35c. Fontaine du Sauvage and Porte au Loup, Delémont (700th Anniversary of granting town charter)	1·30	1·20
1158	50c. Eye and composite wheel (centenary of Public Transport Association)	1·30	60
1159	80c. Diesel train on viaduct (centenary of Rhaetian railway)	3·25	3·00
1160	90c. St Bernard Dog and hospice (Bimillenary of Great St Bernard Pass)	3·25	2·40
1156/1160	Set of 5	9·25	7·00

(Des Lilian Perrin. Photo Courvoisier)

1989 (23 May). Pro Patria. Medieval Chronicles. T **284** and similar horiz designs. Multicoloured. P 11½.

1161	35c. +20c. Type **284**	1·50	1·20
1162	50c. +20c. Adrian von Bubenberg watching troops entering Murten (*Diebold Schilling's Berne Chronicle*)	2·00	60
1163	80c. +40c. Messenger presenting missive to Council of Zürich (*Gerold Edlibach Chronicle*)	3·75	3·50
1164	90c. +40c. Schilling presenting Chronicle to Council of Lucerne (*Diebold Schilling's Lucerne Chronicle*)	4·00	4·25
1161/1164	Set of 4	10·00	8·50

285 Hopscotch

(Des A. Bovey. Photo Courvoisier)

1989 (23 May). Europa. Children's Games. T **285** and similar vert design. Multicoloured. P 11½.

1165	50c. Type **285**	1·90	60
1166	90c. Blind-man's buff	3·25	3·00

286 Bricklayer

(Des W. Haettenschweiler. Eng P. Schopfer. Recess and litho PTT, Bern)

1989 (25 Aug)–**2001**. Occupations. T **286** and similar horiz designs. P 13×13½.

1168	2f.75 slate-purple, black and greenish yellow	7·00	3·50
1169	2f.80 orange-yellow, reddish brown and dull ultramarine (24.1.92)	7·00	4·75
1170	3f. bright blue, deep brown and light brown (5.7.94)	7·50	2·40
1171	3f.60 yellow-orange, purple-brown and purple (24.1.92)	9·00	6·00
1173	3f.75 bottle green, blue-green and bright green (6.3.90)	9·50	4·75
1174	4f. multicoloured (15.3.94)	10·00	4·50
1175	5f. deep ultramarine, yellow-ochre and bright blue (7.9.93)	12·50	3·50
	a. Paper with flourescent fibres (15.2.01)	31·00	12·00
1176	5f.50 grey, crimson and cerise	14·00	6·00
1168/1176	Set of 8 (*cheapest*)	70·00	31·00

Designs: 2f.75, T **286**; 2f.80, Cook; 3f. Carpenter; 3f.60 Pharmacist; 3f.75 Fisherman; 4f. Vine grower; 5f. Cheesemaker; 5f.50 Dressmaker.

Nos. 1177/1180 are vacant.

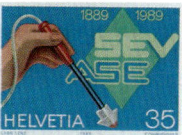

287 Testing Device **288** Exercises

(Des E. and M. Lenz (35c.). W. Weber (50c.), F. Bauer (80c.). R. Somazzi (90c.). R. Zoellig (1f.40). Photo Courvoisier)

1989 (25 Aug). Publicity Issue. T **287** and similar horiz designs. Multicoloured. P 11½.

1181	35c. Type **287** (centenary of Swiss Electrotechnical Association)	1·30	1·20
1182	50c. Family on Butterfly (50th Anniversary of Swiss Travel Fund)	1·30	60
1183	80c. *Wisdom* and *Science* (bronze statues) (centenary of Fribourg University)	2·00	1·90
1184	90c. Audio tape (1st Anniversary of National Sound Archives)	2·30	2·20
1185	140c. Bands of colour forming bridge (centenary of Interparliamentary Union)	3·50	3·25
1181/1185	Set of 5	9·25	8·25

(Des V. Wyss. Photo Courvoisier)

1989 (25 Aug). Pro Sport. P 11½.
1186	**288** 50c. +20c. multicoloured	1·80	1·20

289 1882 5c. and 50c. Stamps and Emblem

290 Cats

(Des B. Waltenspül (25c.), B. la Roche (35c.), Bernadette Baltis (50c.), R. Hirter (90c.). Photo Courvoisier)

1990 (6 Mar). Publicity Issue. T **289** and similar horiz designs. Multicoloured. P 11½.

1187	25c. Type **289** (centenary of Union of Swiss Philatelic Societies)	65	60
1188	35c. Locomotive and control car (inauguration of Zürich Rapid Transit System)	1·90	1·20
1189	50c. Mountain farmer (50th Anniversary of Assistance for Mountain Communities)	1·30	60
1190	90c. Ice hockey players (A-series World Ice Hockey Championships, Berne and Fribourg)	3·25	3·00
1187/1190	Set of 4	6·50	4·75

(Des C. Piatti. Eng M. Müller Recess and litho PTT, Bern)

1990 (6 Mar)–**95**. Animals. T **290** and similar vert designs. Multicoloured. P 13½×13.

1192	10c. Cow (24.1.92)	40	30
1193	50c. Type **290**	1·30	40
1194	70c. Rabbit (15.1.91)	1·80	60
	a. Perf 3 sides. Booklets (28.11.95)	3·75	3·50
	ab. Booklet pane. No. 1194a×10	39·00	
1195	80c. Barn Owls (15.1.91)	2·00	60
1196	100c. Horse and foal (16.3.93)	2·50	80
1197	110c. Geese (29.11.95)	2·75	1·20
1198	120c. Dog (16.3.93)	3·00	1·20
1199	140c. Sheep (29.11.95)	3·50	1·80
1200	150c. Goats (5.7.94)	3·75	1·20
1201	160c. Turkey (24.1.92)	4·00	3·50
1202	170c. Donkey (28.11.95)	4·50	1·80
1203	200c. Chickens (5.7.94)	5·00	1·70
1192/1203	Set of 12	31·00	13·50

The 70c. and 80c. were also issued in coils.

Nos. 1204 is vacant.

291 Flyswats and Starch Sprinklers Seller

292 Lucerne Post Office

(Des E. Witzig. Photo Courvoisier)

1990 (22 May). Pro Patria. Street Criers. T **291** and similar vert designs showing engravings by David Herrliberger. Multicoloured. P 11½.
1205	35c. +15c. Type **291**	1·30	1·20
1206	50c. +20c. Clock seller	1·90	60
1207	80c. +40c. Knife grinder	3·75	3·50
1208	90c. +40c. Couple selling Pinewood sticks	4·50	4·25
1205/1208	Set of 4	10·50	8·50

(Des K. Oberli. Eng M. Müller Recess and litho PTT, Bern)

1990 (22 May). Europa. Post Office Buildings. T **292** and similar horiz design. Multicoloured. P 13½.
1209	50c. Type **292**	1·90	60
1210	90c. Geneva Post Office	3·25	3·00

293 Conrad Ferdinand Meyer (writer)   **294** Anniversary Emblem and Crosses

(Des H. Erni. Eng P. Schopfer. Recess and litho PTT. Bern)

1990 (5 Sept). Celebrities. T **293** and similar vert designs. P 13½.
1211	35c. black and sage-green	1·30	1·20
1212	50c. black and blue	1·30	60
1213	80c. black and yellow	2·50	1·80
1214	90c. black and salmon-pink	3·25	2·40
1211/1214	Set of 4	7·50	5·50

Designs: 35c. T **293**; 50c. Angelika Kauffmann (painter): 80c. Blaise Cendrars (writer); 90c. Frank Buchser (painter).

(Des Rüttimann & Haas. Photo Courvoisier)

1990 (5 Sept). 700th Anniversary (1991) of Swiss Confederation (1st issue). T **294** and similar horiz design. P 11½.
1215	50c. Type **294**	1·30	60
1216	90c. Emblem and crosses (*different*)	3·75	3·00

See also Nos. 1219/1222 and 1224.

295 Geneva Cantonal Post Drivers' Brass Badge   **296** Figures on Jigsaw Pieces

(Des F. Bauer. Photo Courvoisier)

1990 (5 Sept). Helvetia Genève 90 National Stamp Exhibition. Sheet 102×78 mm containing T **295** and similar horiz designs. Multicoloured. P 11½.
MS1217 50c.+25c. Type **295**. 50c.+25c. Place du Bourg-de-Four, Geneva, 50c.+25c. Rousseau Island, Geneva, 50c.+25c. Geneva 1843 5+5c. stamp *on cover*	8·75 8·50

(Des H. Bürgin. Photo Courvoisier)

1990 (20 Nov). Population Census. P 11½.
1218	**296**	50c. multicoloured	1·30 60

297 700 JAHRE   **298** Alps and City Skyline

(Des A. Bovey. Photo Courvoisier)

1991 (22 Feb). 700th Anniversary of Swiss Confederation (2nd issue). T **297** and similar horiz designs, each showing a section of the Swiss cross. Multicoloured. P 11½.
1219	50c. Type **297**	1·60	60
	a. Block of 4 Nos. 1219/1222	6·75	
1220	50c. 700 ONNS	1·60	60
1221	50c. 700 ANS	1·60	60
1222	50c. 700 ANNI	1·60	60
1219/1222	Set of 4	5·75	2·20

Nos. 1219/1222 were issued together in *se-tenant* blocks of four within the sheet, each block having a composite design of the cross in the centre.

(Des F. Bauer. Photo Courvoisier)

1991 (22 Feb). 800th Anniversary of Berne. P 11½.
1223	**298**	80c. multicoloured	2·50 1·20

299 Federal Palace, Berne, and Capitol, Washington   **300** Jettison of Ariane Rocket Friction Protection Jacket

(Des H. Hartmann. Photo Courvoisier)

1991 (22 Feb). 700th Anniversary of Swiss Confederation (3rd issue). Swiss Emigration to USA. P 12.
1224	**299**	160c. multicoloured	5·00 3·25

A stamp of a simlar design was issued by USA.

(Des E. and M. Lenz. Photo Courvoisier)

1991 (14 May). Europa. Europe in Space. T **300** and similar horiz design. Multicoloured. P 11½.
1225	50c. Type **300**	1·90	60
1226	90c. Orbit of Halley's Comet, *Giotto* space probe and its trajectory	3·25	2·40

301 Abstract   **302** Stone Bridge, Lavertezzo

(Des W. Barth (50c.), H. Federle (70c.), M. Bosshart (80c.), W. Leuenberger (90c.) Photo Courvoisier)

1991 (14 May). Pro Patria. Modern Art. T **301** and similar horiz designs. Multicoloured. P 11½.
1227	50c. +20c. Type **301**	1·90	60
1228	70c. +30c. Artist's monogram	3·25	3·00
1229	80c. +40c. Labyrinth	3·75	3·50
1230	90c. +40c. Man and Beast	4·50	4·25
1227/1230	Set of 4	12·00	10·00

(Des P. Baur. Photo Courvoisier)

1991 (10 Sept). Bridges. T **302** and similar horiz designs. Multicoloured. P 11½.
1231	50c. Type **302**	1·50	60
1232	70c. Wooden Neubrügg, Bremgarten	2·30	1·40
1233	80c. Koblenz-Felsenau iron truss railway bridge	2·50	1·80
1234	90c. Garter concrete bridge, Simplon Pass	3·25	3·00
1231/1234	Set of 4	8·50	6·00

303 PTT Employees   **304** Lake Moesola

(Des R. Mühlemann. Photo Courvoisier)

1991 (10 Sept). Centenary of Swiss Postal, Telephone and Telegraph Officials' Union. P 11½.
1235	**303**	80c. multicoloured	2·00 1·90

(Des H. Schelbert. Litho PTT, Bern)

1991 (16 Dec). Mountain Lakes. T **304** and similar vert design. P 13½×13.
1236	50c. multicoloured	1·30	40
1237	80c. purple-brown, rose-red and claret	2·00	70

Designs: 50c. T **304**; 80c. Fishing boat moored at jetty on Melchsee. See also No. 1257.

1992 SWITZERLAND

305 Mouth of River Rhine and Caspian Tern

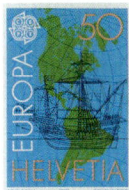
306 Map of Americas and *Santa Maria*

(Des A. Wittmer (50c.), W. Weber (80c.), B. Waltenspül (90c.). Photo Courvoisier)

1992 (24 Mar). Publicity Issue. T **305** and similar horiz designs. Multicoloured. P 11½.
1238	50c. Type **305** (centenary of Treaty for International Regulation of the Rhine)..	1·30	60
1239	80c. Family (50th Anniversary of Pro Familia)	2·00	1·60
1240	90c. Chemical formula and model of difluorobutane molecule (centenary of International Chemical Nomenclature Conference, Geneva)	2·30	2·20
1238/1240 Set of 3		5·00	4·00

Stamps of a similar design were issued by Austria.

(Des O. Galli. Photo Courvoisier)

1992 (24 Mar). Europa. 500th Anniversary of Discovery of America by Columbus. T **306** and similar vert design. Multicoloured. P 11½.
1241	50c. Type **306**	2·50	60
1242	90c. Route map of first voyage and sketch for statue of Columbus (Vincenzo Vela)	3·25	2·40

307 Skier

308 1780s, Earthenware Plate, Heimberg

(Des B. Cosendai (50c.), P. Chappuis (80c.), Y. Robellaz (90c.). Photo Courvoisier)

1992 (22 May). Sierre International Comics Festival. T **307** and similar horiz designs. Multicoloured. P 11½.
1243	50c. Type **307**	1·50	60
1244	80c. Mouse-artist drawing strip	2·50	1·20
1245	90c. Love-struck man holding bunch of stamp flowers behind back	3·00	2·40
1243/1245 Set of 3		6·25	3·75

(Des D. Traversi. Photo Courvoisier)

1992 (22 May). Pro Patria. Folk Art. T **308** and similar vert designs. Multicoloured. P 11½.
1246	50c. +20c. Type **308**	1·90	1·20
1247	70c. +30c. Paper cut-out by Johann Jakob Hauswirth	3·25	2·40
1248	80c. +40c. Maplewood cream spoon, Gruyères	3·75	3·50
1249	90c. +40c. Carnation from 1780 embroidered saddle cloth, Grisons	4·50	4·25
1246/1249 Set of 4		12·00	10·00

309 Flags and Alps

310 Clowns on Trapeze

(Des F. Dorner. Photo Courvoisier)

1992 (22 May). Alpine Protection Convention. P 12.
1250	**309** 90c. multicoloured	3·00	2·20

A stamp of a similar design was issued by Austria.

(Des R. Knie. Photo Courvoisier)

1992 (25 Aug). The Circus. T **310** and similar horiz designs. Multicoloured. P 11½.
1251	50c. Type **310**	1·50	60
1252	70c. Sea Lion with Auguste the clown	2·30	1·20
1253	80c. Chalky the clown and Elephant	2·75	1·80
1254	90c. Harlequin and Horse	3·00	2·40
1251/1254 Set of 4		8·50	5·50

311 Sport Pictograms

312 Train and Map

(Des J. Tinquely. Photo Courvoisier)

1992 (25 Aug). Pro Sport. P 11½×12.
1255	**311** 50c. +20c. black and bright greenish blue	1·80	1·20

(Des L. Pizzotti. Photo Courvoisier)

1992 (24 Nov). Centenary (1993) of Central Office for International Rail Carriage. P 11½.
1256	**312** 90c. multicoloured	3·25	2·20

313 A (first class) Mail

314 Zürich and Geneva 1843 Stamps

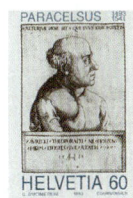
315 Paracelsus (after Augustin Hirschvogel) (500th birth anniversary)

(Des H. Schelbert. Eng M. Müller. Recess and litho PTT, Bern)

1993 (19 Jan). T **313** and similar vert design. P 13½×13.
1257	60c. deep blue, greenish yellow and new blue	1·90	60
1258	80c. dull vermilion, yellow-orange and scarlet	2·50	60

Designs: 60c. Lake Tanay; 80c. T **313**.

(Des H. Billharz. Photo Courvoisier)

1993 (16 Mar). 150th Anniversary of Swiss Postage Stamps. T **314** and similar vert designs. Multicoloured. P 11½.
1259	60c. Type **314**	1·50	60
1260	80c. Postal cancellation (stamps for postage)	2·00	1·60
1261	100c. Magnifying glass (stamp collecting)	2·50	2·40
1259/1261 Set of 3		5·50	4·25

(Des G. Ducimetiere (60c.), P. Scholl (80c.), J. Ongaro (180c.). Photo Courvoisier)

1993 (16 Mar). Publicity Issue. T **315** and similar designs. P 11½.
1262	60c. sepia, grey and blue	1·90	60
1263	80c. multicoloured	2·50	1·80
1264	180c. multicoloured	5·75	3·50
1262/1264 Set of 3		9·25	5·25

Designs: Vert—60c. T **315**; 80c. Discus thrower (from Greek vase) (inauguration of Olympic Museum, Lausanne). Horiz—180c. Worker's head (centenary of International Metalworkers' Federation).

316 *Hohentwiel* (lake paddle-steamer) and Flags

317 Interior of Media House, Villeurbanne, France

(Des A. Wittmer. Photo Courvoisier)

1993 (5 May). Lake Constance European Region. P 12.
1265	**316** 60c. multicoloured	1·90	1·10

Stamps of a similar design were issued by Austria and Germany.

SWITZERLAND 1993

(Des M. Botta. Eng P. Schopfer. Recess and litho PTT, Bern)

1993 (5 May). Europa. Contemporary Architecture. T **317** and similar vert design. P 13½.

1266	60c. ultramarine, black and turquoise-blue..	1·90	60
1267	80c. vermilion, black and slate	3·25	2·40

Designs: 60c. T **317**; 80c. House, Breganzona, Ticino.

318 Appenzell Dairyman's Earring

319 Work No. 095 (Emma Kunz)

(Des B. Scarton. Photo Courvoisier)

1993 (5 May). Pro Patria. Folk Art. T **318** and similar horiz designs. Multicoloured. P 11½.

1268	60c. +30c. Type **318**	2·50	1·80
1269	60c. +30c. Flühli enamelled glass bottle, 1738	2·50	1·80
1270	80c. +20c. Driving Cows to summer pasture (detail of mural, Sylvestre Pidoux)	3·75	3·50
1271	100c. +20c. Straw hat ornaments	4·50	4·25
1268/1271	Set of 4	12·00	10·00

(Des Bernadette Baltis. Photo Courvorsier)

1993 (7 Sept). Paintings by Swiss Women Artists. T **319** and similar square designs. Multicoloured. P 11½.

1272	60c. Type **319**	1·90	60
1273	80c. *Great Singer Lilas Goergens* (Aloïse) (33×33 *mm*)	2·50	1·20
1274	100c. *Under the Rain Cloud* (Meret Oppenheim) (33×33 *mm*)	3·25	2·40
1275	120c. *Four Spaces with Horizontal Bands* (Sophie Taeuber-Arp) (33×33 *mm*)	3·75	3·00
1272/1275	Set of 4	10·50	6·50

320 Kapell Bridge and Water Tower, Lucerne

321 Hieroglyphic, Cuneiform and Roman Scripts

(Des H. Hartmann. Litho PTT, Bern)

1993 (7 Sept). Kapell Bridge, Lucerne, Restoration Fund. P 13½×13.

1276	**320**	80c. +20c. deep carmine and orange-red	2·50	1·20

(Des F. Bauer. Photo Courvorsier)

1994 (15 Mar). Books and the Press Exhibition, Geneva. T **321** and similar horiz designs Multicoloured. P 11½.

1277	60c. Type **321**	1·90	60
1278	80c. Gothic letterpress script	2·00	1·80
1279	100c. Modern electronic fonts	2·50	2·40
1277/1279	Set of 3	5·75	4·25

322 Athletes

323 Footballers

(Des R. Hirter (60c.), B. Waltenspül (80c.), A. Wittmer (100c.), A. Bovey (180c.). Photo Courvoisier)

1994 (15 Mar). Publicity Issue. T **322** and similar horiz designs. Multicoloured. P 11½.

1280	60c. Type **322** (50th Anniversary of National Sports School, Magglingen)	1·90	60
1281	80c. Jakob Bernoulli (mathematician) (after Nicolas Bernoulli) and formula and diagram of the law of large numbers (International mathematicians Congress, Zürich)	2·00	1·70
1282	100c. Heads, Unisource emblem, globe and flags (collaboration of Swiss, Dutch and Swedish telecommunications companies)	2·50	2·40
1283	180c. Radar image, airliner and globe (50th Anniversary of International Civil Aviation Organisation)	5·00	4·25
1280/1283	Set of 4	10·50	8·00

(Des H. Schelbert. Photo Courvoisier)

1994 (15 Mar). World Cup Football Championship, USA, and Centenary (1995) of Swiss Football Association. P 11½.

1284	**323**	80c. multicoloured	3·25	1·80

324 Trieste (bathyscaphe)

325 Neuchâtel Weight-driven Clock (Jacques Matthey-Jonais)

(Des P. Baur. Photo Courvoisier)

1994 (17 May). Europa. Discoveries and Inventions. T **324** and similar vert design showing vehicles used by Auguste Piccard in deep-sea and stratospheric explorations. Multicoloured. P 12.

1285	60c. Type **324**	1·90	60
1286	100c. *FNRS* (stratosphere balloon)	3·75	3·00

(Des D. Traversi. Photo Courvoisier)

1994 (17 May). Pro Patria. Folk Art. T **325** and similar vert designs. Multicoloured. P 11½.

1287	60c. +30c. Type **325**	2·50	1·80
1288	60c. +30c. Embroidered pomegranate on linen	2·50	1·80
1289	80c. +40c. Mould for Kräfli pastry	3·75	3·50
1290	100c. +40c. Paper-bird cradle mobile	4·50	4·25
1287/1290	Set of 4	12·00	10·00

326 Symbolic Condom

327 Simenon and his Home, Echandens Castle, Lausanne

(Des N. de Saint Phalle. Photo Courvoisier)

1994 (15 Oct). Anti-AIDS Campaign. P 11½.

1291	**326**	60c. multicoloured	1·50	70

(Des P. Schopfer and D. Roegiest. Eng P. Schopfer. Recess and litho PTT, Bern)

1994 (15 Oct). Fifth Death Anniversary of Georges Simenon (novelist). P 13½.

1292	**327**	100c. multicoloured	3·25	2·40

Stamps of a similar design were issued by Belgium and France.

328 Swiss Electricity

329 Eurasian Beaver

(Des G. Staehelin (No. 1293), R. Mirer (No. 1294), P. Scholl (No. 1295), R. Zollig (No. 1296). Photo Courvoisier)

1995 (7 Mar). Publicity Issue. T **328** and similar designs. P 11½.

1293	60c. multicoloured	1·50	60
1294	60c. bright blue and black	1·50	60

1995 SWITZERLAND

1295	80c. multicoloured		2·00	1·20
1296	180c. multicoloured		4·50	4·25
1293/1296	Set of 4		8·50	6·00

Designs: Horiz—No. 1293, T **328** (centenary of Swiss Association of Electricity Producers and Distributors), No. 1295, 'sda ats)' (centenary of Swiss News Agency), No. 1296, 'ONU UNO' and emblem (50th Anniversary of United Nations Organisation). Vert—No. 1294, Wrestlers (centenary of Swiss Wrestling Association and National Wrestling and Alpine Herdsmen's Festival, Chur).

(Des Sibylle Erni. Photo Courvoisier)

1995 (7 Mar). Endangered Animals. T **329** and similar vert designs. Multicoloured. P 12.

1297	60c. Type **329**		1·90	60
1298	80c. Map Butterfly		2·50	1·90
1299	100c. Green Tree Frog		3·25	2·40
1300	120c. Little Owl		3·75	3·00
1297/1300	Set of 4		10·50	7·00

330 Cream Pail, 1776

331 Couple and Dove

(Des R. Hirter. Photo Courvoisier)

1995 (16 May). Pro Patria. Folk Art. T **330** and similar horiz designs. Multicoloured. P 11½.

1301	60c. +30c. Type **330**		2·50	1·80
1302	60c. +30c. Neuchâtel straw hat		2·50	1·80
1303	80c. +40c. Detail of chest lock, 1580		3·75	3·50
1304	100c. +40c. Langnau ceramic sugar bowl		4·50	4·25
1301/1304	Set of 4		12·00	10·00

(Des H. Erni. Recess, embossed and litho PTT, Bern)

1995 (16 May). Europa. Peace and Freedom. T **331** and similar horiz design. P 13½.

1305	60c. deep blue and cobalt		3·75	60
1306	100c. reddish brown and brown-ochre		6·25	3·00

Designs: 60c. T **331**; 100c. Europa with Zeus as Bull.

332 Basel (right-hand part)

333 Coloured Ribbons woven through River

(Des Bernadette Baltis. Photo Courvoisier)

1995 (16 May). Basler Taube 1995 Stamp Exhibition, Basel. Sheet 100×131 mm containing T **332** and similar vert designs. P 13×14.
MS1307 60c.+30c. black, deep violet-blue and new blue; 80c.+30c. multicoloured; 100c.+50c. black, deep violet-blue and new blue; 100c.+50c. black, deep violet-blue and new blue .... 14·00 13·00

Designs: 80c.+30c. Basel 2½r. Dove stamp (150th anniversary of issue); 60c.+30c., 100c.+50c. (2) Panorama of Basel by Matthäus Merian (composite design).

(Des Cornelia Eberle. Eng P. Schopfer. Recess and litho PTT, Bern)

1995 (5 Sept). Switzerland–Liechtenstein Co-operation. P 13½.

1308	**333**	60c. multicoloured	1·50	60

No. 1308 was valid for use in both Switzerland and Liechtenstein (see No. 1106 of Liechtenstein).

334 The Vocation of André Carrel (1925)

335 Ear, Eye and Mouth

(Des W. Jeker. Photo Courvoisier)

1995 (5 Sept). Centenary of Motion Pictures. T **334** and similar horiz designs. P 11½.

1309	60c. Type **334**		1·50	60
1310	80c. *Anna Göldin - The Last Witch*		2·00	1·80
1311	150c. *Pipilotti's Mistakes - Absolution*		3·75	3·50
1309/1311	Set of 3		6·50	5·25

(Des R. Bittel. Photo Courvoisier)

1995 (5 Sept). Telecom 95 International Telecommunications Exhibition, Geneva. P 11½.

1312	**335**	180c. multicoloured	4·50	4·25

336 A (first class) Mail

337 Emblem

(Des J.-B. Lévy. Litho PTT, Bern)

1995 (28 Nov). P 13½×13.

1313	**336**	90c. new blue, orange-vermilion and lemon	2·30	60
		a. Perf 3 sides. Booklets	3·25	3·00
		ab. Booklet pane. No. 1313a×10	34·00	

On 29 July 1999 this stamp was issued printed on paper which is bluish with glowing fibres when viewed under a UV lamp. It appears bright white under the lamp.
See also No. 1480.

(Des N. Lehr (No. 1314), W. Henkel (No. 1315), N. Troxler (No. 1316), Jenny Leibundgut (No. 1317), Sibylle von Fischer (No. 1318). Photo Courvoisier)

1996 (12 Mar). Publicity Issue. T **337** and similar horiz designs. Multicoloured. P 11½.

1314	70c. Type **337** (centenary of Touring Club of Switzerland)		1·80	85
1315	70c. Heart (50th anniversary of charity organisations)		1·80	85
1316	90c. Brass band (30th Federal Music Festival, Interlaken)		2·30	2·20
1317	90c. Young girls (centenary of Pro Filia (girls' aid society))		2·30	2·20
1318	180c. Jean Piaget (child psychologist, birth centenary)		4·50	4·25
1314/1318	Set of 5		11·50	9·25

338 Coloured Ribbons and Bern 96 Gymnastic Festival Emblem

339 Corinna Bille (writer)

(Des B. la Roche. Photo Courvoisier)

1996 (12 Mar). Pro Sport. P 11½.

1319	**338**	70c. +30c. multicoloured	2·50	2·40

(Des and Eng P. Schopfer. Recess and litho PTT, Bern)

1996 (14 May). Europa. Famous Women. T **339** and similar vert design. Multicoloured. P 13½.

1320	70c. Type **339**		1·80	60
1321	110c. Iris von Roten-Meyer (feminist writer)		2·75	2·75

340 Magdalena Chapel, Wolfenschiessen, and Cross

341 Olympic Rings

39

SWITZERLAND 1996

(Des H. Schelbert. Photo Courvoisier)

1996 (14 May). Pro Patria. Heritage. T **340** and similar vert designs. Multicoloured. P 11½.

1322	70c. +35c. Type **340**	3·25	1·80
1323	70c. +35c. Underground sawmill and workshop, Col-des-Roches	3·25	1·80
1324	90c. +40c. Baroque baths, Pfäfers	4·50	4·25
1325	110c. +50c. Roman road and milestone, Great St Bernhard	5·00	4·75
1322/1325	Set of 4	14·50	11·50

(Des A. Wittmer. Litho PTT, Bern)

1996 (14 May). Centenary of Modern Olympic Games. P 13½.

1326	**341**	180c. multicoloured	5·75	4·25

342 Representation of 1995 A Mail Stamp

343 Musical Movement and Mechanical Ring (Isaac-Daniel Piguet)

(Des J.-B. Lévy. Litho PTT, Bern)

1996 (27 June). Guinness World Record for Largest Living Postage Stamp (arrangement of people to represent stamp design). P 13½.

1327	**342**	90c. multicoloured	2·50	2·40

(Des B. Brüsch. Photo Courvoisier)

1996 (10 Sept). Bicentenary of Antoine Favre-Salomon's Invention of the Metal Teeth System for Music Boxes. T **343** and similar horiz designs. Multicoloured. P 11½.

1328	70c. Type **343**	1·90	85
1329	90c. Basso-piccolo mandolin cylinder music box (Eduard Jaccard)	2·50	2·40
1330	110c. Station automaton (Paillard & Co)	3·25	3·00
1331	180c. Kalliope disc music box	5·00	4·75
1328/1331	Set of 4	11·50	10·00

344 Pattern

345 The Golden Cow (Daniel Ammann)

(Des B. Müller-Meyer. Photo Heusser AG, Gümligen)

1996 (10 Sept). Greetings Stamps. Booklet stamps. T **344** and similar horiz designs. Multicoloured. Self-adhesive. Die-cut straight edge×wavy edge.

1332	90c. Type **344**	3·25	3·00
1333	90c. Mottled pattern	3·25	3·00
1334	90c. Coil pattern	3·25	3·00
1335	90c. Flower and leaf pattern	3·25	3·00
1332/1335	Set of 4	11·50	11·00

Nos. 1332/1335 are peeled directly from the cover of the booklet. It is not therefore possible to collect these as booklet panes.

(Photo Courvoisier)

1996 (26 Nov). Winning Entries in Stamp Design Competition. T **345** and similar vert designs. P 11½.

1336	70c. gold and bright blue	1·80	85
1337	90c. multicoloured	2·30	2·20
1338	110c. multicoloured	2·75	2·75
1339	180c. brown, black and new blue	4·50	4·25
1336/1339	Set of 4	10·00	9·00

Designs: 70c. T **345**; 90c. Wake with a Smile (Max Sprick); 110c. Leaves (Elena Emma-Pugliese); 180c. Dove (René Conscience).

346 Globi delivering Mail

(Des H. Schmid. Litho PTT, Berne)

1997 (11 Mar). Globi (cartoon character by Robert Lips). P 13½.

1340	**346**	70c. multicoloured	1·80	95

347 Venus of Octodurus

(Des B. Scarton. Photo Courvoisier)

1997 (11 Mar). Gallo-Romam Works of Art, T **347** and similar vert designs. Multicoloured. P 11½.

1341	70c. Type **347** (from Forum Claudii Vallensium (now Martigny))	1·80	1·20
1342	90c. Bust of Bacchus (from Augusta Raurica (now Augst))	2·30	2·40
1343	110c. Ceramic fragment showing Victory (from Iulio Magus (now Schleitheim))	2·75	3·00
1344	180c. Mosaic showing female theatrical mask (from Vallon)	4·50	4·75
1341/1344	Set of 4	10·00	10·00

Each stamp is inscribed with the name of the Foundation bearing responsibility for the preservation of the respective archaeological sites.

348 Class 460 Series 2000 Locomotive

349 Douglas DC-4 *Grand Old Lady* over Globe

(Des Michèle Berri. Photo Courvoisier)

1997 (11 Mar). 150th Anniversary of Zürich–Baden Rail link. T **348** and similar horiz designs. Multicoloured. P 11½.

1345	70c. Type **348**	2·30	1·20
1346	90c. Red Arrow railcar	3·00	2·40
1347	1f.40 Pullman coach	4·50	3·50
1348	1f.70 Limmat (first Swiss steam locomotive)	5·00	4·75
1345/1348	Set of 4	13·50	10·50

(Des A. Wittmer. Litho PTT, Bern)

1997 (11 Mar). 50th Anniversary of Swissair's North Atlantic Service. P 13½.

1349	**349**	180c. multicoloured	5·75	4·25

350 Farmland

351 *Devil and the Goat* (painting by Heinrich Danioth on rock face of Schöllenen Gorge)

(Des Rosmarie Tissi. Litho PTT, Bern)

1997 (13 May). Publicity Issue. T **350** and similar horiz design. Multicoloured. P 13½.

1350	70c. Type **350** (centenary of Swiss Farmers' Union)	1·80	70
1351	90c. Street plan (centenary of Swiss Municipalities' Union)	2·30	2·20

(Des P. Zimmermann. Eng H. Baldauf. Recess and litho PTT, Bern)

1997 (13 May). Europa. Tales and Legends. The Devil's Bridge. P 13½.

1352	**351**	90c. bright rose-red and blackish brown and yellow	2·50	2·40

1997 SWITZERLAND

352 St Valbert's Church, Soubey (Jura)   353 Clouds (Air)

(Des Bernadette Baltis. Photo Courvoisier)

1997 (13 May). Pro Patria. Heritage and Landscapes. T **350** and similar vert designs. Multicoloured. P 11½.
1353	70c. +35c. Type **352**	3·25	1·80
1354	70c. +35c. Culture mill, Lützelflüh (Berne)	3·25	1·80
1355	90c. +40c. Ittingen Charterhouse (Thurgau)	4·50	4·25
1356	110c. +50c. Casa Patriziale, Russo (Ticino)	5·00	4·75
1353/1356 Set of 4		14·50	11·50

(Des B. Oldani. Photo Courvoisier)

1997 (12 Sept). Energy 2000 (energy efficiency programme). The Elements. T **353** and similar horiz designs. Multicoloured. P 12×11½.
1357	70c. Type **353**	1·80	95
1358	90c. Burning wood (Fire)	2·30	2·40
1359	110c. Water droplets (Water)	2·75	3·00
1360	180c. Pile of soil (Earth)	4·50	4·75
1357/1360 Set of 4		10·00	10·00

354 King Rama V and President Adolf Deucher   355 Paul Karrer and Molecular Structure of Vitamin A

(Des R. Hirter. Litho PTT, Bern)

1997 (12 Sept). Centenary of Visit of King Rama V of Siam. Non-phosphorescent paper. P 13½.
1361	**354**	90c. multicoloured	2·30	2·20

A stamp of a similar design was issued by Thailand.

(Des C. Reuterswärd. Eng C. Slania. Recess and litho PTT, Bern)

1997 (13 Nov). The Nobel Prize. T **355** and similar horiz design. Non-phosphorescent paper. P 13½×13½.
1362	90c. black and grey	3·00	2·20
1363	110c. black and dull purple	3·50	2·75

Designs: 90c. T **355** (Chemistry Prize, 1937); 110c. Alfred Nobel (founder of Prize Fund).

Stamps of a similar design were issued by Sweden.

356 Woman and Boy (German)   357 Postal Service Emblem

(Des D. Rhyner. Litho PTT, Bern)

1997 (20 Nov). The Post keeps Us in Touch. T **356** and similar horiz designs. Non-phosphorescent paper. P 13½×13.
1364	70c. black, scarlet-vermilion and new blue	2·30	70
	a. Horiz strip of 4. Nos. 1364/1367	9·50	
1365	70c. black, lemon and new blue	2·30	70
1366	70c. black, lemon and bright green	2·30	70
1367	70c. black, bright green and scarlet-vermilion	2·30	70
1364/1367 Set of 4		8·25	2·50

Designs: No. 1364, T **356**; No. 1365, Boy wearing baseball cap with woman (French); No. 1366, Young couple (Italian); No. 1367, Girl and man (Romansch).

Nos. 1364/1367 were issued in horizontal se-tenant strips of four stamps within the sheet.

(Des K. Wälti and A. Frutiger (No. 1368), Wirú Identity, Zürich (No. 1369). Litho PTT, Bern)

1998 (7 Jan). Separation of Swiss Post and Swisscom (telecommunications). T **357** and similar horiz design. P 13½.
1368	90c. black, yellow and magenta	2·30	2·20
1369	90c. royal blue, new blue and vermilion	2·30	2·20

Designs: No. 1368, T **357**; No. 1369, Swisscom emblem.

358 Arrows   359 Winter Olympics, 2006

(Des Brigit Herrmann. Photo Courvoisier)

1998 (7 Jan). Bicentenary of Declaration of Helvetic Republic and 150th Anniversary of Swiss Federal State. T **358** and similar horiz designs. Multicoloured. P 11½.
1370	90c. Type **358**	2·50	2·40
	a. Block of 4. Nos. 1370/1373	10·50	
1371	90c. Face value at bottom right	2·50	2·40
1372	90c. Face value at top left	2·50	2·40
1373	90c. Face value at top right	2·50	2·40
1370/1373 Set of 4		9·00	8·75

Nos. 1370/1373 were issued together in se-tenant blocks of four stamps within the sheet.

(Des Candidacy Committee. Litho PTT, Bern)

1998 (12 Feb). Swiss Candidacy for Winter Olympic Games, 2006. P 13½.
1374	**359**	90c. multicoloured	2·50	2·40

360 Elderly Couple   361 On Top of the Simplon Pass

(Des Marianne Brügger (No. 1375), P. Scholl (No. 1376), J. Müller (No. 1377). Photo Courvoisier)

1998 (10 Mar). Publicity Issues. T **360** and similar horiz designs. Multicoloured. P 11½.
1375	70c. Type **360** (Old Age and Survivor's Insurance)	1·80	95
1376	70c. National Museum, Prangins Castle (centenary of Swiss National Museum, Zürich, and inauguration of Prangins branch)	1·80	95
1377	90c. Fingerprints (centenary of St Gallen University)	2·30	1·20
1375/1377 Set of 3		5·25	2·75

(Des Margret Schnyder. Litho PTT, Bern)

1998 (10 Mar-8 Sept). Paintings by Jean-Frédéric Schnyder. T **361** and similar horiz designs. Multicoloured. P 13×13½.
1378	10c. Type **361** (10.3.98)	40	25
1379	20c. Snowdrift near Neuthal (10.3.98)	65	40
1380	50c. Franches Montagnes (10.3.98)	1·50	60
1381	70c. Two Horses (10.3.98)	1·80	60
1382	90c. En Route (10.3.98)	2·30	65
1383	110c. Winter Morning by the Alpnachersee	2·75	1·10
1385	140c. Zug (8.9.98)	3·50	1·20
1386	170c. Olive Grove (8.9.98)	4·25	1·40
1387	180c. Near Reutigen (8.9.98)	4·50	2·20
1378/1387 Set of 9		19·00	7·50

362 St Gall, Rhine Valley   363 Lanterns

41

(Des M. Bucher. Photo Courvoisier)

1998 (12 May). Pro Patria. Heritage and Landscapes. T **362** and similar horiz designs. Multicoloured. P 11½.

1390	70c. +35c. Type **362**		3·25	2·40
1391	70c. +35c. Round church, Saas Balen		3·25	2·40
1392	90c. +40c. Forest, Bödmeren		3·75	3·50
1393	90c. +40c. The old refuge (museum), St Gotthard		4·50	3·50
1394	110c. +50c. Smithy, Corcelles		5·00	5·50
1390/1394	Set of 5		18·00	16·00

(Des W. Henkel. Litho PTT, Bern)

1998 (12 May). Europa. National Festivals. National Day. P 13×13½.

1395	**363**	90c. multicoloured	3·25	2·40

364 In-line Skating

365 Bridge 24, Slender West Lake, Yangzhou, China

(Des M. Eherhard. Photo Courvoisier)

1998 (8 Sept). Sports. Booklet stamps. T **364** and similar square designs. Multicoloured. Self-adhesive. Die-cut straight edge×wavy edge.

1396	70c. Type **364**	2·30	2·20
1397	70c. Snowboarding	2·30	2·20
1398	70c. Mountain biking	2·30	2·20
1399	70c. Basketball	2·30	2·20
1400	70c. Beach volleyball	2·30	2·20
1396/1400	Set of 5	10·50	10·00

Nos. 1396/1400 are peeled directly from the cover of the booklet and cannot therefore be collected as separate panes. The booklet also contains two labels giving the Post Office's website address.

(Des Xu Yan Bo (20c.), Bernadette Baltis (70c.), H. Anderegg (90c.). Eng P. Schopfer (20c.). Recess and litho (20c.) or litho (70c.). PTT Bern photo Courvoisier (90c.))

1998 (25 Nov). Lakes. T **365** and similar horiz design. Multicoloured. P 13½.

1401	**365**	20c. Type **365**	65	60
		a. Pair. Nos. 1401/1402	2·75	2·40
1402		70c. Chillon Castle, Lake Geneva	1·80	1·70
MS1403	96×70 mm. 90c. Chillon Castle and Bridge 24 (52×44 mm). P 11½		3·75	3·50

Nos. 1401/1402 were issued together in *se-tenant* pairs within the sheet.

In 1999 No. **MS**1403 was issued for the China 99 World Philatelic Exhibition. It was overprinted in gold China 1999 with emblem and with a gold/silver hologram and only occurs *cancelled on cover*.

Stamps of a similar design were issued by China.

366 Emblem and Face

367 Christmas Wrapping

(Des Esther Stingelin and B. Scarton. Litho PTT, Bern)

1998 (25 Nov). 50th Anniversary of Universal Declaration of Human Rights. P 13½.

1404	**366**	70c. multicoloured	1·80	1·20

(Des B. Brüsch. Litho PTT, Bern)

1998 (25 Nov). Christmas. P 13½.

1405	**367**	90c. multicoloured	2·30	2·40

368 Postman with Letter and Posthorn on Globe

369 Little Pingu carrying Parcel

(Des C. Sandoz. Photo Courvoisier)

1999 (21 Jan). 150th Anniversary of Swiss Postal Service. P 11½×12.

1406	**368**	90c. multicoloured	2·50	2·40

(Des O. Gutmann. Litho PTT, Bern)

1999 (9 Mar–6 Dec). Youth Stamps. Pingu (cartoon character). T **369** and similar horiz design. Multicoloured. P 13½.

1407	70c. Type **369**	1·80	1·20
	a. No strings on parcel (6.12.99)	1·80	1·20
	ab. Red circle on arm	£450	£425
1408	90c. Papa Pingu driving snowmobile	2·30	2·40
	a. No strings on parcel (6.12.99)	2·30	2·40

Nos. 1407/1408 were re-issued as Nos. 1407a/1408a on December 1999 with design altered.

370 Vieux Bois falls in Love at First Sight

371 Breitling *Orbiter 3*

(Des Suzanne Rivier. Litho Guhl & Scheibler, Aesch)

1999 (9 Mar). Birth Bicentenary of Rodolphe Töpffer (cartoonist). Booklet stamps. T **370** and similar horiz designs showing scenes from *The Love of Monsieur Vieux Bois*. Multicoloured. Self-adhesive. Die-cut straight edge×wavy edge.

1409	90c. Type **370**	3·00	2·75
1410	90c. Vieux Bois declares his love	3·00	2·75
1411	90c. Vieux Bois jumps in air from joy, knocking over furniture	3·00	2·75
1412	90c. Vieux Bois helping his love over wall	3·00	2·75
1413	90c. Wedding of Vieux Bois	3·00	2·75
1409/1413	Set of 5	13·50	12·50

Nos. 1409/1413 are peeled directly from the cover of the booklet. It is not therefore possible to collect these as booklet panes.

(Litho PTT, Bern)

1999 (24 Mar). First World Circumnavigation by Balloon (Bertrand Piccard and Brian Jones). P 13½.

1414	**371**	90c. multicoloured	3·25	2·20

372 Envelope Flap

(Des I. Moscatelli. Photo Courvoisier)

1999 (5 May). 125th Anniversary of Universal Postal Union. T **372** and another design. P 12.

1415	20c. Lemon and black	1·30	1·20
	a. Pair. Nos. 1415/1416	4·00	3·75
1416	70c. black, vermilion and lemon	2·50	2·40

Designs: 20c. T **372**. 55×29 mm—70c. UPU emblem on card in envelope.

Nos. 1415/1416 were issued together in *se-tenant* pairs within sheetlets of eight stamps, each pair forming a composite design.

373 Jester and Clown

374 Chestnuts from Malcantone

(Des R. Knie (No. 1417), J.-C. Maret and J.-P. Arlaud (No. 1418), J. Wandflüh (No. 1420); litho PTT Bern. Des A. Wittmer; photo Courvoisier (No. 1419))

1999 (5 May). Publicity Issue. T **373** and similar horiz designs. Phosphorescent paper (No. 1419) or paper with fluorescent fibres (others). P 11½ (No. 1419) or 13½ (others).

1417	70c. multicoloured	1·80	1·20
1418	90c. multicoloured	2·30	2·40

1419		90c. multicoloured	2·30	2·40
1420		1f.10 orange-vermilion and black	2·75	2·75
1417/1420		Set of 4	8·25	8·00

Designs: No. 1417, T **373** (50th Anniversary of SOS Children's Villages); No. 1418, Sketch of giant puppets (Wine-growers' Festival, Vevey); No. 1419, Flags of member countries and emblem (50th Anniversary of Council of Europe); No. 1420, Red Cross and emblem (50th Anniversary of Geneva Conventions).

(Des M. Bucher. Litho PTT, Bern)

1999 (5 May). Pro Patria. Heritage and Landscapes. T **374** and similar vert designs. Multicoloured. Paper with fluorescent fibres. P 13½.

1421		70c. +35c. Type **374**	3·25	2·40
1422		70c. +35c. La Sarraz Castle	3·25	2·40
1423		90c. +40c. *Uri* (lake steamer)	4·50	4·25
1424		110c. +50c. St Christopher carrying Baby Jesus (detail of fresco, St Paul's Chapel, Rhäzüns)	5·00	4·75
1421/1424		Set of 4	14·50	12·50

375 Ibex Horns (National Park, Engadine)

376 Roofs of Buildings

(Des N. Vital. Litho PTT, Bern)

1999 (5 May). Europa. Parks and Gardens. Paper with fluorescent fibres. P 13½.

1425	**375**	90c. black and ultramarine	3·25	2·40

(Des Susanne Huber and M. Schmid. Photo Courvoisier)

1999 (9 Sept). naba 2000 National Stamp Exhibition, St Gallen (1st issue). Sheet 66×85 mm containing T **376** and similar vert designs. Multicoloured. P 11½.

MS1426 20c.+10c. Type **376**; 70c.+30c. Spire of St Laurenzen's Church; 90c.+30c. Oriel window .... 11·50 10·00
See also No. **MS**1442.

377 Children holding Pictures

378 Schöllenen Gorge Monument, Suvorov and Soldiers

(Des Dinhard School (70c.), R. Hirter (90c.), Michéle Berri (1f.10). Litho PTT, Bern)

1999 (24 Sept). Publicity Issue. T **377** and similar horiz designs. Multicoloured. Paper with fluorescent fibres. P 13½.

1427		70c. Type **377** (Children's Rights)	1·80	1·20
1428		90c. Carl Lutz (Swiss diplomat in Budapest during Second World War, Commemoration)	2·50	2·40
1429		1f.10 Chemical model of ozone and globe (birth bicentenary of Christian Schönbein (chemist))	2·75	2·75
1430		180c. *Midday in the Alps* (death centenary of Giovanni Segantini (painter))	4·75	4·50
1427/1430		Set of 4	10·50	9·75

(Des B. Ilyukhin (No. 1431). Photo Courvoisier)

1999 (24 Sept). Bicentenary of General Aleksandr Suvorov's Crossing of the Alps. T **378** and similar horiz design. Multicoloured. P 12.

1431		70c. Type **378**	2·30	1·70
1432		110c. Suvorov vanguard (after engraving by L. Hess) passing Lake Klöntal	3·50	2·75

Stamps of a similar design were issued by Russia.

379 Christmas Bauble

380 2000 around Globe

(Des W. Henkel and Gigi Schmid. Litho PTT, Bern)

1999 (23 Nov). Christmas. P 13½.

1433	**379**	90c. multicoloured	2·30	2·20

(Des L. Marx. Photo Courvoisier)

1999 (23 Nov). Year 2000. P 11½.

1434	**380**	90c. multicoloured	2·30	2·20

381 Cyclist

382 Alphorn Player

(Des R. Hirter. Litho PTT Bern)

2000 (7 Mar). Centenary of International Cycling Union. P 13½.

1435	**381**	70c. multicoloured	2·30	1·20

(Des R. Bissig. Litho)

2000 (7 Mar). Snow Storms. T **382** and similar horiz designs. Multicoloured. P 13×13½.

1436		10c. Type **382**	30	15
1437		20c. Fondue	55	40
1438		30c. Jugs and Grapes on tray	90	70
1439		50c. Mountain Goat	1·30	1·20
1440		60c. Clock	1·50	1·40
1441		70c. St Bernard Dogs	1·80	1·10
1436/1441		Set of 6	5·75	4·50

The 50c. was also issued in coils.
See also No. 1479.

383 ON I

384 frau and Emblem

(Des Susanne Huber and M. Schmid. Photo Courvoisier)

2000 (10 May). naba 2000 National Stamp Exhibition, St Gallen (2nd issue). Sheet 65×85 mm containing T **383** and similar vert designs. Multicoloured. P 11½×12.

MS1442 20c.+10c. Type **383** (top right-hand corner); 20c.+10c. 5 (bottom left-hand corner); 70c.+35c. RAY (top left-hand corner); 90c.+45c. Rp (bottom right-hand corner) .... 12·00 11·50

The four stamps in No. **MS**1442 were issued together to form a composite design depicting a modern representation of a 1850 5r. Federal Administration stamp.

(Des Jenny Leibundgut. Litho PTT, Bern)

2000 (10 May). Centenary of National Council of Women. Paper with fluorescent fibres. P 13½.

1443	**384**	70c. multicoloured	1·80	1·20

385 Building Europe

386 Town Square, Nafels

(Des J.-P. Cousin. Litho PTT, Bern)

2000 (10 May). Europa. Paper with fluorescent fibres. P 13½.

1444	**385**	90c. multicoloured	2·50	2·40

(Des K. Oberli. Eng H. Baldauf. Recess and litho PTT, Bern)

2000 (10 May). Pro Patria. Townscapes 2000 (rejuvenation projects). T **386** and similar horiz designs. Multicoloured. Paper with fluorescent fibres. P 13½.

1445		70c. +35c. Type **386**	4·00	3·75
1446		70c. +35c. Main road, Tengia	4·00	3·75

SWITZERLAND 2000

1447	90c. +40c. Main road, Brugg...............		5·25	5·00
1448	90c. +40c. Marketplace, Carouge.........		5·25	5·00
1445/1448 Set of 4			17·00	16·00

387 Payerne Church and Violin

(Des Marina Ott. Litho PTT, Bern)

2000 (21 June)–**01**. Tourism. T **387** and similar horiz designs. Multicoloured. Paper with fluorescent fibres. P 13×13½.

1449	**387**	90c. multicoloured (20.9.01)	3·00	2·75
1450		100c. multicoloured (20.9.01)	3·25	3·00
1451		110c. deep blue, deep turquoise and vermilion (20.9.01)..................	3·50	3·25
1452		120c. multicoloured (21.6.00)	3·00	1·80
1453		130c. multicoloured (21.6.00)	3·25	1·90
1454		180c. multicoloured (21.6.00)	4·50	3·50
1455		200c. multicoloured (21.11.00)..........	5·00	3·50
1456		220c. multicoloured (13.3.01)	7·00	6·25
1457		300c. multicoloured (21.11.00)	7·50	4·75
1459		400c. multicoloured (13.3.01)	12·50	12·00
1449/1459 Set of 10			47·00	38·00

Designs: 90c. Willisan farm house and Horse; 100c. *La Suisse* (lake stream) and woman looking over Lake Geneva; 110c. Kleine Matterhorne glacier and skier; 120c. T **387**; 130c. St Saphorin Church and bottle of wine; 180c. National spring and bather, Vals; 200c. Landscape and walker; 220c. Bus and children; 300c. Stone bridge and mountain bike; 400c. Aeroplane fin and man with suitcase.

388 Embroidery

(Des P. Hostteller. Embroidered Bischoff Textil AG, St Gallen)

2000 (21 June). St Gallen Embroidery. Self-adhesive. Imperf.
1460	**388**	5f. cobalt and slate-blue	15·00	14·50
MS1461 158×132 mm. No. 1460×4.................			£375	£475

389 Emblem   **390** Alien from Outer Space (Yannick Kehrli)

(Des O. Galli. Litho PTT, Bern)

2000 (15 Sept). Population Census. Paper with fluorescent fibres. P 13½.
| 1462 | **389** | 70c. multicoloured .... | 1·80 | 1·20 |

(Litho Flexoprint Permapack, Rorschach)

2000 (15 Sept). Stampin the Future. Winning Entries in Children's International Painting Competition. Booklet stamps. T **390** and similar horiz designs. Multicoloured. Self-adhesive. Paper with fluorescent fibres. Die-cut straight edge×wavy edge.
1463		70c. Type **390**	3·75	3·50
1464		70c. Looks below the Sun (Charlotte Bättig)	3·75	3·50
1465		70c. The Perfect World (Sandra Dobler)	3·75	3·50
1466		70c. My Town (Stephanie Aerschmann)...........	3·75	3·50
1463/1466 Set of 4			13·50	12·50

Nos. 1463/1466 are peeled directly from the cover of the booklet. It is not therefore possible to collect these as booklet panes.

391 Swimming   **392** Cathedral and Horsemen

(Des B. Leuenberger. Photo Questa)

2000 (15 Sept). Olympic Games, Sydney. Booklet stamps. T **391** and similar circular designs. Multicoloured. Paper with fluorescent fibres. Self-adhesive. Die-cut straight edge.
1467		90c. Type **391**	3·75	3·50
1468		90c. Cycling	3·75	3·50
1469		90c. Running	3·75	3·50
1467/1469 Set of 3			10·00	9·50

Nos. 1467/1469 are peeled directly from the cover of the booklet. It is not therefore possible to collect these as booklet panes.

(Des M. Eberhard. Litho PTT, Bern)

2000 (21 Nov). Stamp Day. Paper with fluorescent fibres. P 13½.
| 1470 | **392** | 70c. multicoloured .... | 2·30 | 1·70 |

393 Dresden-style Tree Decoration   **394** Alice Rivaz

(Des Bernadette Baltis. Photo Courvoisier)

2000 (21 Nov). Christmas. Granite paper. P 11½.
| 1471 | **393** | 90c. multicoloured .... | 3·50 | 2·20 |

(Des P. Schopfer (70c.), R. Hirter (90c.), Y. Fidalgo (110c.), A. Wittmer (130c.). Litho PTT, Bern)

2001 (13 Mar). Anniversaries. T **394** and similar horiz designs. Paper with fluorescent fibres. P 13½.
1472		70c. multicoloured	1·80	1·20
1473		90c. multicoloured	3·00	2·40
1474		110c. vermilion, grey and black........	2·75	2·75
1475		130c. multicoloured	3·25	3·25
1472/1475 Set of 4			9·75	8·75

Designs: As T **394**—70c. T **394** (writer, birth centenary); 110c. CARITAS and jigsaw pieces (centenary of Caritas (Christian charity organisation)); 130c. Refugees (50th Anniversary of United Nations High Commissioner for Refugees). Size 39×30 mm—90c. Aeroplane (centenary of Aero-Club of Switzerland).

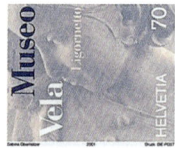

395 Flowers and Envelope   **396** Woman's Head

(Des M. Eberhard. Litho PTT, Bern)

2001 (13 Mar). Greetings Stamp. Paper with fluorescent fibres. P 13½.
| 1476 | **395** | 90c. multicoloured .... | 3·25 | 3·00 |

(Des Sabina Oberholzer (70c.), R. Schraivogel and Y. Netzhammer (90c.). Litho PTT, Bern (70c.), photo Courvoisier (90c.))

2001 (9 May). Anniversary and Event. T **396** and similar horiz design. Multicoloured. Paper with fluorescent fibres (70c.) or granite paper (90c.). P 13½ (70c.) or 11½ (90c.).
1477		70c. Type **396** (re-opening of Vela Museum, Ligornetto)...................................	2·30	2·20
1478		90c. Chocolate segment (centenary of Chocosuisse).................................	3·75	3·50

No. 1478 is printed in sheetlets of 15 stamps and is impregnated with the scent of chocolate.

2001 (9 May). Self-adhesive booklet stamps. Litho SNP Ausprint (70c.), Guhl & Scheibler, Aesch (90c.). Phosphorescent markings (70c.) or paper with fluorescent fibres (90c.). Die-cut wavy line×imperf (70c.) or imperf×die-cut wavy line (90c.).

1479	70c. multicoloured	2·30	2·20
1480	90c. new blue, orange vermilion and lemon	3·00	2·75

Designs: 70c. As No. 1441; 90c. T **336**.

Nos. 1479/1480 are peeled directly from the covers of the booklets. It is not therefore possible to collect these as booklet panes.

Nos. 1479/1480 were also available as coil stamps in rolls of 100 with the self-adhesive paper around each stamp removed.

The phosphorescent markings on No. 1479, which appear pink under UV light, form two short bars on the left and right-hand side of the stamp.

397 Italian Theatre, La Chaux-de-Fonds

398 Water

(Des V. Wyss. Litho PTT, Bern)

2001 (9 May). Pro Patria. Cultural Heritage. T **397** and similar horiz designs. Paper with fluorescent fibres. P 13½.

1481	70c. +35c.black, dull orange-red and red	3·50	3·25
1482	70c. +35c.black, grey-brown and light green	3·50	3·25
1483	90c. +40c.black, reddish brown and lemon	4·25	4·25
1484	90c. +40c.multicoloured	4·25	4·25
1481/1484	Set of 4	14·00	13·50

Designs: No. 1481, T **397**; No. 1482, Hauterive Monastery; No. 1483, Leuk Castle; No. 1484, Rorschach Granary.

(Des Jenny Leibundgut. Litho PTT, Bern)

2001 (9 May). Europa. Water Resources. Paper with fluorescent fibres. P 13½.

1485	**398**	90c. multicoloured	3·00	2·75

399 Blue Rainbow Fish

400 Straits Rhododendron (*Melastoma malabaricum*)

(Des M. Pfister. Photo Enschedé)

2001 (20 Sept). Illustrations from *Rainbow Fish* (book by Martin Pfister). T **399** and similar horiz design. Multicoloured. P 13×14.

1486	70c. Type **399**	2·30	2·20
1487	90c. Purple Rainbow Fish	3·00	2·75

(Des N. Loh and Suzanne Potterat. Litho Enschedé)

2001 (20 Sept). Switzerland–Singapore Joint Issue. Flowers. Sheet 98×68 mm containing T **400** and similar horiz designs. Multicoloured. P 13½×13.

MS1488 70c. Type **400**; 90c. *Saraca cauliflora*; 110c. Edelweiss (*Leontopodium alpinum*); 130c. Gentian (*Gentiana clusii*) .... 14·00 13·50

401 The Birth of Venus

402 Buildings (Beat Kehrli)

(Des T. Wetter. Litho PTT, Bern)

2001 (20 Sept). Death Centenary of Arnold Böcklin (artist). Paper with fluorescent fibres. P 13½.

1489	**401**	180c. multicoloured	5·50	5·25

(Litho PTT, Bern)

2001 (20 Nov). Stamp Day. Winning entry in stamp design competition. Paper with fluorescent fibres. P 13½.

1490	**402**	70c. multicoloured	2·30	2·20

403 Gablonz-style Christmas Tree Ornament

404 Ladder, Wall and Stars

(Des Bernadette Baltis. Litho Questa)

2001 (20 Nov). Christmas. Granite paper. P 11½.

1491	**403**	90c. multicoloured	3·00	2·75

(Des J. Wandflüh. Litho PTT, Bern)

2002 (12 Mar). Escalade (festival) (celebrating 400th Anniversary of defeat of Savoyard attack on the city), Geneva. Paper with fluorescent fibres. P 13½.

1492	**404**	70c. multicoloured	2·30	2·20

405 E and Towers, Biel

406 RABDe 500 InterCity Tilting Train (ICN)

(Des T. Steineman. Photo Questa)

2002 (12 Mar). Expo '02 National Exhibition, Biel, Murten, Neuchâtel and Yverdon-les-Bains (1st issue). T **405** and similar horiz designs, each featuring 'Arteplage' (exhibition platform) of each host town. Multicoloured. Granite paper. P 14×14½.

1493	70c. Type **405**	2·30	2·20
	a. Block of 4. Nos. 1493/1496	9·50	
1494	70c. Reversed 'P' and Monolith, Murten	2·30	2·20
1495	70c. O, pebble-shaped construction over water, Neuchâtel	2·30	2·20
1496	70c. 2 and artificial cloud, Yverdon-les-Bains	2·30	2·20
1493/1496	Set of 4	8·25	8·00

Nos. 1493/1496 were issued together in *se-tenant* blocks of four stamps.

See also No. **MS**1509.

(Des B. Kehrli. Photo Enschedé)

2002 (12 Mar). Centenary of Swiss Federal Railways (SBB) (national railway operator). T **406** and similar horiz designs. Multicoloured. P 13×14.

1497	70c. Type **406**	2·20	2·10
1498	90c. Inter-city 2000 double-deck train	3·00	2·75
1499	120c. Railcar, Lucerne–Lenzburg Seetal line	3·75	3·50
1500	130c. 119 Re 460 locomotive	4·25	4·00
1497/1500	Set of 4	12·00	11·00

407 Façade

408 Augusta A-109-K2 Helicopter and Hawker 800B Air Ambulance

(Des M. Gnehm. Litho PTT, Bern)

2002 (12 Mar). Centenary of Federal Parliament Building. Paper with fluorescent fibres. P 13½.

1501	**407**	90c. multicoloured	3·00	2·75

(Des R. Schenker. Litho and holography Cartor)

2002 (12 Mar). 50th Anniversary of Swiss Air Rescue (Rega). P 13×13½.

1502	**408**	180c. multicoloured	5·50	5·00

SWITZERLAND 2002

409 Clown

410 Bruzella, Ticino Canton

(Des H. Falk. Litho PTT, Bern)

2002 (15 May). Europa. Circus. T **409** and similar horiz design. Multicoloured. Paper with fluorescent fibres. P 13½.
1503	70c. Type **409**		2·20	2·10
1504	90c. Clown (*different*)		3·00	2·75

(Des T. Fluri. Litho Cartor)

2002 (15 May). Pro Patria. Water Mills Preservation. T **410** and similar horiz designs showing water mills. Multicoloured. P 13½.
1505	70c. +35c. Type **410**		3·00	2·75
1506	70c. +35c. Oberdorf, Basel Canton		3·00	2·75
1507	90c. +40c. Lussery-Villars, de Vaud Canton		3·75	3·50
1508	90c. +40c. Büren a. d. Aare, Berne Canton		3·75	3·50
1505/1508	Set of 4		12·00	11·50

411 X

412 Two Teddies (Switzerland, c. 1950)

(Des T. Steineman. Photo Questa)

2002 (15 May). Expo '02, Sixth National Exhibition, Biel, Murten, Neuchâtel and Yverdon-les-Bains (2nd issue). Sheet 95×70 mm. P 14×14½.
MS1509	**411** 90c. multicoloured		4·25	4·00

(Des U. Fueter and U. Hungerbühler. Litho Enschedé)

2002 (15 May). Centenary of the Teddy Bear. Booklet stamps. T **412** and similar multicoloured designs. Self-adhesive. Die-cut straight edge.
1510	90c. White Teddy with pink bow (France, 1925) (26×26 mm, round)		2·50	2·30
1511	90c. Type **412**		2·50	2·30
1512	90c. Teddy with grey-brown bow (Germany, 1904) (22×32 mm, oval)		2·50	2·30
1513	90c. Philibert, Swiss Post Teddy (Switzerland, 2002) (26×22 mm, rectangle)		2·50	2·30
1514	90c. Teddy with grey paws (England, c. 1920) (26×26 mm, round)		2·50	2·30
1510/1514	Set of 5		11·50	10·50

Nos. 1510/1514 are die-cut around the shape of the frame. The stamps peeled directly from the cover of the booklet. It is not therefore possible to collect these as booklet panes.

413 Emblem

414 Emperor Dragonfly (*Anax imperator*)

(Des R. Pfund. Litho Enschedé)

2002 (11 Sept). Membership of the United Nations. Ordinary paper. P 14×14½.
1515	**413** 90c. multicoloured		2·50	2·30

(Des Bernadette Baltis. Litho Enschedé)

2002 (17 Sept). Insects. T **414** and similar horiz designs. Multicoloured. Ordinary paper. P 14×14½.
1516	10c. Type **414**		55	50
1517	20c. Dark Green Fritillary (*Mesoacidalia aglaja*)		85	80
1518	50c. Alpine Longhorn Beetle (*Rosalia alpina*)		1·40	1·30
1519	100c. Striped bug (*Graphosoma lineatum*)		2·75	2·50
1516/1519	Set of 4		5·00	4·50

415 Printing Press (copper engraving, Abraham Bosse)

416 Ladybird on Leaf

(Des and Eng P. Schopfer. Recess and litho PTT, Bern)

2002 (17 Sept). Swiss Post Stamp Printers, Berne Commemoration. Paper with fluorescent fibres. P 13½.
1520	**415** 70c. multicoloured		2·20	2·10

No. 1520 was the last stamp printed by Swiss Post Stamp Printers.

(Des Bernadette Baltis. Litho Enschedé)

2002 (17 Sept). Greeting Stamp. Self-adhesive. Die-cut straight edge×p 12½.
1521	**416** 90c. multicoloured		2·75	2·50

No. 1521 was issued *se-tenant* with a label and was available both as a single stamp or in booklets of ten stamps plus ten *se-tenant* labels.

417 Quartz

418 Kingfisher and Jura Water Engineering System

(Des Schott Merz, Berne. Litho German State Ptg Wks, Berlin)

2002 (17 Sept)–**05**. Minerals. T **417** and similar horiz design. Multicoloured. Paper with fluorescent fibres. P 13½.
1522	200c. Type **417**		5·50	5·25
1523	300c. Rutilated quartz (9.9.03)		8·50	7·75
1524	400c. Fluorite (9.9.03)		11·00	10·50
1525	500c. Titanite		14·00	13·00
	a. Perf 13½×14 (10.5.05)		15·00	14·50

Nos. 1526/1534 are vacant.

(Des Michèle Berri. Litho Walsall Security Printers Ltd)

2002 (19 Nov). Stamp Day. Winning Entry in Stamp Design Competition. P 14.
1535	**418** 70c. multicoloured		2·00	1·80

419 Bohemian Cardboard Tree Decoration, c. 1900

420 Skier

(Des Bernadette Baltis. Photo Questa)

2002 (19 Nov). Christmas. Granite paper. P 11½.
1536	**419** 90c. multicoloured		2·50	2·30

(Des C. Spahr and E. Iseli. Litho Walsall Security Printers Ltd)

2002 (19 Nov). World Alpine Skiing Championship, St Moritz. P 14.
1537	**420** 90c. multicoloured		2·50	2·30

421 70

422 Hypericum (*Hypericum perforatum*)

(Des Sandra di Salvo. Litho and embossed Questa)

2003 (6 Mar). Centenary of Swiss National Association of the Blind and Library for the Blind and Visually Impaired. Paper with fluorescent fibres. P 14½.
| 1538 | **421** | 70c. orange-vermilion | 2·00 | 1·80 |

No. 1538 was embossed with 70 in Braille.

(Des Suzanne Potterat. Litho Walsall)

2003 (6 Mar)–**05**. Medicinal Plants. T **422** and similar vert designs. Multicoloured. P 14.
1539	70c. Type **422**	2·00	1·80
1540	90c. Periwinkle (*Vinca minor*)	2·50	2·30
1541	110c. Valerian (*Valeriana officinalis*)	3·00	2·75
1542	120c. *Arnica montana*	3·25	3·00
	a. Perf 14×14½ (1.9.05)	5·50	5·25
1543	130c. Centaury (*Centaurium minus*)	3·75	3·50
1544	180c. Mallow (*Malva sylvestris*)	5·00	4·75
	a. Perf 14×14½ (1.3.05)	6·25	5·75
1545	220c. Chamomile (*Matricaria chamomilla*)	6·25	5·75
	a. Perf 14×14½ (1.3.05)	7·75	7·25
1539/1545 Set of 7		23·00	21·00

423 Waterfall

424 Contour Lines, Compass and Runner

(Des R. Schenker. Litho Cartor)

2003 (6 Mar). International Year of Water. P 13×13½.
| 1546 | **423** | 90c. multicoloured | 2·50 | 2·30 |

A stamp of a similar design was issued by United Nations (Geneva).

(Des T. Dätwyler. Litho Cartor)

2003 (6 Mar). World Orienteering Championships, Rapperswil-Jona. P 13½.
| 1547 | **424** | 90c. multicoloured | 2·50 | 2·30 |

425 Horse's Head

426 Alinghi (yacht)

(Des L. Cocchi. Litho Cartor)

2003 (6 Mar). Centenary of Marché-Concours (Horse show and market), Saignelégier. P 13½.
| 1548 | **425** | 90c. multicoloured | 2·50 | 2·30 |

(Des R. Hirter. Litho Cartor)

2003 (7 Mar). Switzerland, America's Cup Winners, 2003. P 13×13½.
| 1549 | **426** | 90c. multicoloured | 3·50 | 3·25 |

427 Eagle

428 Laura Cake

(Des G. Regolini. Litho Questa)

2003 (8 May). Ticino 2003 International Stamp Exhibition, Locarno. Sheet 96×70 mm containing T **427** and similar vert design. Multicoloured. P 14½.
| MS1550 20c. Type **427**; 70c. Gentians | 3·25 | 3·00 |

(Des T. Tirabosco. Litho Questa)

2003 (8 May). 20th International Comics Festival, Sierre. Characters created by Tom Tirabosco. T **428** and similar horiz designs. Multicoloured. P 14½.
1551	70c. Type **428**	2·00	1·80
	a. Block of 4. Nos. 1551/1554	8·25	
1552	70c. Marco (heart)	2·00	1·80
1553	70c. Louis (black cloud)	2·00	1·80
1554	70c. Djema (music note)	2·00	1·80
1551/1554 Set of 4		7·25	6·50
MS1555 96×70 mm. 90c. Heidi (yellow Duck)	2·75	2·50

Nos. 1551/1554 were issued in *se-tenant* blocks of four within sheets of 16 stamps.

429 Innere Wynigen Bridge, Burgdorf, Berne Canton

430 Don't Forget the Discount Stamp (Donald Brun)

(Des T. Fluri and B. Breiter. Litho Cartor)

2003 (8 May). Pro Patria. Historic Bridges and Footbridges. T **429** and similar horiz designs showing bridges. Multicoloured. P 13½.
1556	70c. +35c. Type **429**	3·00	2·75
1557	70c. +35c. Salginatobel, Schiers, Grisons	3·00	2·75
1558	90c. +40c. Pont St-Jean, Saint Ursanne, Jura Canton	3·75	3·50
1559	90c. +40c. Reuss, Rottenschwil, Aargau Canton	3·75	3·50
1556/1559 Set of 4	12·00	11·50

(Litho Cartor)

2003 (8 May). Europa. Poster Art. P 13½×13.
| 1560 | **430** | 90c. multicoloured | 2·50 | 2·30 |

431 Diddl and Diddlina

432 Jungfrau-Aletsch-Bietschhorn Region

(T. Goletz. Litho Cartor)

2003 (9 Sept). Diddl (cartoon character created by Thomas Goletz) (1st series). T **431** and similar horiz design. Multicoloured. P 13½.
| 1561 | 70c. Type **431** | 2·00 | 1·80 |
| 1562 | 90c. Diddl chasing winged envelopes | 2·50 | 2·30 |

See also 1608/1609.

(Des B. Kehrli. German State Ptg Wks, Berlin)

2003 (9 Sept). UNESCO World Heritage Sites. T **432** and similar horiz designs. Multicoloured. P 12½×13.
1563	90c. Type **432**	2·50	2·30
1564	90c. Three Castles, Bellinzona	2·50	2·30
1565	90c. Berne Old City	2·50	2·30
1566	90c. St Gall Abbey Precinct	2·50	2·30
1567	90c. Müstair Convent	2·50	2·30
1563/1567 Set of 5	11·50	10·50

433 Onion Market, Berne

434 Wooden Horseman (Erzgebirge)

(Des Ursula Hirsbrunner. Litho Cartor)

2003 (19 Nov). Stamp Day. Winning Entry in Stamp Design Competition. P 13½.
| 1568 | **433** | 70c. multicoloured | 2·00 | 1·80 |

(Des Bernadette Baltis. Photo Questa)

2003 (19 Nov). Christmas. Regional Tree Decorations. T **434** and similar vert designs. Multicoloured. Granite paper. P 11½.
| 1569 | 70c. Type **434** | 2·00 | 1·80 |
| 1570 | 90c. Glass Father Christmas (Thuringa) | 2·50 | 2·30 |

SWITZERLAND 2003

435 Four-leafed Clover

436 Rex Potato Peeler (Alfred Neweczeral, 1947)

(Des Bernadette Baltis. Litho Enschedé)
2003 (19 Nov). Greetings Stamp. Self-adhesive. Die-cut straight edge×p 12½.
1571 435 130c. multicoloured .... 4·00 3·75
No. 1571 is die-cut around one leaf at foot outside the stamp design.
No. 1571 was issued with a *se-tenant* label and was available both as a single stamp or in booklets of ten stamps plus ten *se-tenant* labels.

(Des Susanne Perron and W. Mohrle. Litho Enschedé)
2003 (30 Dec)–**05**. Swiss Design Classics. T **436** and similar horiz designs. Multicoloured. Self-adhesive. Die-cut perf 12.

(a) Booklet stamps
1572		15c. Type **436**	55	50
1583		85c. Station clock (Hans Hilfiker, 1944)....	2·40	2·20
1584		100c. Armchair (Heidi Weber (1959) after Le Corbusier (1928)...........	6·00	5·50
1585		100c. Landi (chair) (Hans Coray, 1939) (31.3.04)...........	2·75	2·50
1586		220c. Fixpencil (Caran d'Ache, 1929) (10.5.05)	6·25	5·75

(b) Coil stamps
1587 50c. Riri (zip fastener) (7.9.04)............. 1·40 1·30
1572/1587 *Set of 6*... 17·00 16·00

Nos. 1584/1585 were each issued with a label inscribed 'Prioritaire' separated from the stamp by die-cutting. No. 1583/1586 were also available in business sheets of 50 stamps.
No. 1587 was issued in coils of 2000 stamps, single examples of which could be bought from the Philatelic Bureau.

Nos. 1588/1594 are vacant.

437 Titeuf and Nadia

438 Centenary Emblem

(Des Zep. Litho D.L.R.)
2004 (9 Mar). *Titeuf* (cartoon created by Philippe Chappuis (Zep)). T **437** and similar horiz designs. Multicoloured. P 14×13½.
1595 85c. Type **437** (Spring)............................. 2·40 2·20
1596 85c. Sitting in refrigerator (Summer)........ 2·40 2·20
1597 85c. Kicking leaves (Autumn)..................... 2·40 2·20
1598 85c. With snowman (Winter)...................... 2·40 2·20
1595/1598 *Set of 4*.. 8·75 8·00

(Des F. Trümpi. Litho Enschedé)
2004 (9 Mar). Centenary of FIFA (Fédération Internationale de Football Association). P 13½.
1599 438 1f. multicoloured .... 2·75 2·50

439 Family

440 Past and Present Players

(Des T. Dätwyler. Litho D.L.R.)
2004 (9 Mar). Cycling. Sheet 96×70 mm containing T **439** and similar horiz design. Multicoloured. P 13½.
MS1600 1f.×2, Type **439**; Two cyclist reading map .... 6·00 5·50

(Des W. Henkel. Litho Cartor)
2004 (9 Mar). 50th Anniversary of UEFA (Union of European Football Associations). P 13½.
1601 440 1f.30 multicoloured.......................... 3·75 3·50

441 Rays

442 Doorbell and 'Helvetia'

(Des C. Stuker and B. Trummer. Litho Cartor)
2004 (9 Mar). 50th Anniversary of CERN (European Organisation for Nuclear Research). P 14×13½.
1602 441 1f.80 gold, light blue and black.............. 5·00 4·75

(Des Emil Steinberger. Litho D.L.R.)
2004 (6 May). Humour. P 14½.
1603 442 85c. multicoloured .... 2·40 2·20

443 Bathing Pavilion, Gorgier

444 Diddl holding Pimboli

(Des T. Fluri. Litho Enschedé)
2004 (6 May). Pro Patria. Small Buildings Preservation. T **443** and similar horiz designs. Multicoloured. P 14×14½.
1604 85c. +40c. Type **443** .... 3·50 3·25
1605 85c. +40c. Granary, Oberramsern.................. 3·50 3·25
1606 1f. +50c. Seeburg landing stage, Lucerne.. 4·25 4·00
1607 1f. +50c. Ossuary, Gentilino .... 4·25 4·00
1604/1607 *Set of 4*.. 14·00 13·00

(T. Goletz. Litho Cartor)
2004 (6 May). Diddl (cartoon character created by Thomas Goletz) (2nd series). T **444** and similar horiz design. Multicoloured. P 13½.
1608 85c. Type **444** .... 2·00 1·80
1609 1f. Diddl holding flower .... 2·50 2·30

445 Olympic Rings, Stadium and Runner

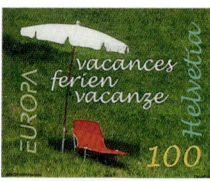
446 Sun Lounger and Parasol

(Des Karin Fanger-Schiesser. Litho Cartor)
2004 (6 May). Olympic Games, Athens. P 13½.
1610 445 1f. multicoloured .... 2·75 2·50

(Des Birgit Herrmann. Litho D.L.R.)
2004 (6 May). Europa. Holidays. P 14½.
1611 446 1f. multicoloured .... 2·75 2·50

447 Zeppelin NT Type Z No. 7

448 Boy leapfrogging Pumpkin

2004 SWITZERLAND

2004 (6 May). P 14½.
1612   **447**   1f.80 multicoloured .... 5·00   4·75

(Des Anita Hertig and Nicole Seliner. Litho Walsall)
2004 (7 Sept). Suisse Balance (healthy eating campaign). P 13½.
1613   **448**   85c. multicoloured .... 2·40   2·20

449 1854 10r. Stamp

450 Cat

(Des A. Witmer. Litho and embossed or litho)
2004 (7 Sept). 150th Anniversary of Strubeli (dishevelled) Stamps (first stamps showing seated Helvetia ('Mother of the Nation')). Sheet 96×70 mm containing T **449** and similar vert design. Multicoloured. P 13½.
MS1614   85c.×2, Type **449**; Coin showing Helvetia ....   5·25   5·00

(Des M. Roulin. Litho D.L.R.)
2004 (7 Sept). Swiss Animal Protection (SAP). T **450** and similar horiz designs. Multicoloured. P 14½.
1615   85c. Type **450** .... 2·40   2·20
1616   1f. Hedgehog .... 3·00   2·75
1617   1f.30 Pig .... 4·00   3·75
1615/1617 Set of 3 .... 8·50   7·75

451 Fossil and Mountains

452 Making Cheese

(Des B. Kehrli. Litho Enschedé)
2004 (7 Sept). UNESCO World Heritage Site. Mount San Giorgio. P 14×14½.
1618   **451**   1f. mauve and black .... 2·75   2·50

(Des J.-P. Zoller. Litho Walsall)
2004 (7 Sept). Traditional Foods. Cheese. T **452** and similar horiz design. Multicoloured. P 13½.
1619   1f. Type **452** .... 2·75   2·50
1620   1f. Cheeses and Grapes .... 3·75   3·50

453 Wood Grain

(Des T. Rathgreb. Screen printed)
2004 (7 Sept). Sustainable Wood Production. Self-adhesive. Straight edge.
1621   **453**   5f. ochre .... 14·00   13·00
No. 1621 was made from wood veneer which is peeled from the backing paper.

454 Hydroelectric Power

(Des Walter Pfenninger. Litho Cartor)
2004 (23 Nov). Stamp Day. Winning Entry in Stamp Design Competition. P 13½.
1622   **454**   85c. multicoloured .... 2·40   2·20

455 Star

457 Children Kissing

(Des Bernadette Baltis. Litho Enschedé)
2004 (23 Nov). Christmas. Tree Decorations. Sheet 160×56 mm containing T **455** and similar vert designs. Multicoloured. P 13½.
MS1623 85c. Type **455**; 85c. Church. 1f. Angel; 1f. Horse and rider; 1f. Father Christmas .... 13·50   12·50

No. 1624 and T **456** are vacant.

(Des R. Burri. Litho Enschedé)
2005 (3 Jan). Greetings Stamps. Booklet Stamps. T **457** and similar horiz designs. Self-adhesive. Die-cut perf 12.
1625   100c. black and scarlet vermilion .... 2·75   2·50
1626   100c. multicoloured .... 2·75   2·50
1627   100c. multicoloured .... 2·75   2·50
1628   100c. black and scarlet vermilion .... 2·75   2·50
1625/1628 Set of 4 .... 10·00   9·00
Designs: No. 1625, T **457**; No. 1626, Couple riding bicycle; No. 1627, Couple embracing; No. 1628, Couple in dodgem car Nos. 1625/1628, were each issued with a label inscribed 'Prioritaire' attached at foot.

458 Double Helix, Faces and Building Façade

459 Matterhorn superimposed on Inverted Map of Africa

(Des M. Trüeb. Litho Cartor)
2005 (8 Mar). 150th Anniversary of Federal Technology Institute, Zürich. P 13½.
1629   **458**   85c. multicoloured .... 2·40   2·20

(Des S. Eicher. Litho Cartor)
2005 (8 Mar). P 13½.
1630   **459**   85c. multicoloured .... 2·40   2·20

460 Cheeky Mouse typing Letter

461 Traditional Costume and Unspunnen Stone

(Des Uli Stein. Litho Cartor)
2005 (8 Mar). Cheeky Mouse (cartoon character created by Uli Stein). T **460** and similar horiz design. Multicoloured. P 13½.
1631   85c. Type **460** .... 2·40   2·20
1632   100c. Playing golf .... 2·75   2·50

(Des J. Horisberger. Litho Cartor)
2005 (8 Mar). Bicentenary of Folklore Festival, Unspunnen. P 14.
1633   **461**   100c. multicoloured .... 2·75   2·50

462 Coach-built Car   **463** Albert Einstein

(Des V. Noto. Litho Enschedé)

2005 (8 Mar). Centenary of Motor Show, Geneva. Sheet 96×70 mm containing T **462** and similar horiz design. Multicoloured. P 14.
MS1634 100c. Type **462**; 130c. Futuristic car .... 7·00   6·50

(Des J.-B. Lévy. Litho Cartor)

2005 (8 Mar). Centenary of Publication of *Special Theory of Relativity* by Albert Einstein. P 14.
1635   **463**   130c. multicoloured ....   3·75   3·50

464 Felix and Goats   **465** Rotach Houses, Wasserwerkstrasse, Zürich

(Litho Cartor)

2005 (10 May). *Letters from Felix* (children's book written by Annette Langen and illustrated by Constanza Droop). T **464** and similar horiz designs. Multicoloured. P 13×13½.
1636   85c. Type **464** ....   2·40   2·20
No. 1637 has been left for addition to this set.

(Des R. Bissig. Litho Cartor)

2005 (10 May). Pro Patria. T **465** and similar horiz designs. Multicoloured. P 13½.
1638   85c. +40c. Type **465** ....   3·50   3·25
1639   85c. +40c. Monte Carasso Abbey,
           Bellinzona, Ticino..   3·50   3·25
           a. Booklet pane. No. 1639×6 ....   22·00
1640   100c. +50c. St Katherinenthal Abbey,
           Diessenhofen ....   4·25   4·00
           a. Booklet pane. No. 1640×4 ....   18·00
1641   100c. +50c. Palais Wilson, Geneva ....   4·25   4·00
1638/1641 Set of 4..   14·00 13·00

466 Butterflies

(Des Sandra Schlapbach. Litho)

2005 (10 May). Greeting Stamp. Booklet Stamp. Self-adhesive. Die-cut perf 12.
1642   **466**   100c. multicoloured ....   2·75   2·50
No. 1642 was issued in booklets of ten stamps (2×2 and 3×2) and six labels.

467 Player

(Des P. Castella. Litho Enschedé)

2005 (10 May). Euro 2008. European Football Championships, Austria and Switzerland (1st issue). 13th European Visually Impaired Football Championships 2008, Austria and Switzerland. P 14×14½.
1643   **467**   100c. multicoloured ....   2·75   2·50
See also Nos. 1681, 1708, 1760 and 1761.

468 *Big-eared Clown* and *Monument in a Fertile Country*

(Des Claudia Bernet. Litho Enschedé)

2005 (10 May). Inauguration of Zentrum Paul Klee Exhibition Centre, Berne. P 13½×14.
1644   **468**   100c. multicoloured ....   2·75   2·50

469 Europe reflected in Dish Cover   **470** Subtractive Colours

(Des Annette Maiga. Litho Cartor)

2005 (10 May). Europa. Gastronomy. P 13½.
1645   **469**   100c. multicoloured ....   2·75   2·50

(Des Martine Chatagny. Litho Cartor)

2005 (6 Sept). My Stamp. Colour. T **470** and similar horiz design. Multicoloured. Self-adhesive. Die-cut perf 12½.
1646   50c. Type **470** ....   1·40   1·30
1647   100c. Additive colours ....   2·75   2·50

471 Skiers   **472** Horse's Head (Brigit Rohrbach)

(Des T. Dätwyler. Litho Austrian State Ptg Wks, Vienna)

2005 (6 Sept). Centenary of NaturFreunde Schweiz (conservation organisation). Sheet 110×90 mm containing T **471** and similar multicoloured designs. P 13½.
MS1648 85c. Type **471**; 100c. Chalet (*vert*); 110c. Hikers; 130c. Rock climber (*vert*) ....   12·50 11·50

(Litho Austrian State Ptg Wks, Vienna)

2005 (6 Sept). MMS (multimedia messaging). T **472** and similar vert designs. Multicoloured. P 14½×14.
1649   85c. Type **472** ....   2·40   2·20
1650   100c. Hiker (Peter Schumacher)..................   2·75   2·50
1651   130c. Sign post (Rémy Sager)......................   3·75   3·50
1652   180c. Footprint (Debora Ronchi)................   5·00   4·75
1649/1652 Set of 4..   12·50 11·50

473 Pocket Watch   **474** Globe and Landscape

(Des A. Furrer. Litho Cartor)

2005 (6 Sept). Watches. T **473** and similar horiz design. Multicoloured. P 13½×14.
1653   100c. Type **473** ....   2·75   2·50
1654   130c. Wristwatch..   3·75   3·50

2005 SWITZERLAND

(Des Dominque Hiestand. Litho Cartor)

2005 (22 Nov). Stamp Day. Winning Entry in Stamp Design Competition. P 13½.
| 1655 | **474** | 85c. multicoloured | 2·40 | 2·20 |

475 Mitre and Crosier   **476** Swiss Papal Guard

(Des Michèle Haas. Litho Cartor)

2005 (22 Nov). Christmas. T **475** and similar vert design. Multicoloured. P 13½.
| 1656 | 85c. Type **475** | 2·40 | 2·20 |
| 1657 | 100c. Gingerbread man | 2·75 | 2·50 |

(Des R. Mirer. Litho Austrian State Ptg Wks, Vienna)

2005 (22 Nov). 500th Anniversary of Swiss Papal Guard. T **476** and similar horiz design. Multicoloured. P 14½.
| 1658 | 85c. Type **476** | 2·40 | 2·20 |
| 1659 | 100c. Three guards facing left | 3·75 | 3·50 |

Stamps of a similar design were issued by Vatican City.

477 Curling   **478** Ibex

(Des Karin Schiesser. Litho Austrian State Ptg Wks, Vienna)

2005 (22 Nov). Winter Olympic Games, Turin. P 14.
| 1660 | **477** | 100c. multicoloured | 2·75 | 2·50 |

(Des R. Cavegn. Litho Cartor)

2006 (7 Mar). Centenary of Ibex Re-introduction Programme. P 13½×13.
| 1661 | **478** | 85c. multicoloured | 2·75 | 2·50 |

479 Simplon Tunnel between Rhone Valley and Val d'Ossola   **480** PostBus

(Des M. Weller. Litho Austrian State Ptg Wks, Vienna)

2006 (7 Mar). Railway Centenaries. T **479** and similar horiz design. Multicoloured. P 13½.
| 1662 | 85c. Type **479** | 2·75 | 2·50 |
| 1663 | 100c. Bern–Lötschberg–Simplon Railway (rapid train service) | 3·00 | 2·75 |

(Des Anja Goldi and D. Dreier. Litho)

2006 (7 Mar). Centenary of the PostBus Service. T **480** and similar horiz designs. Multicoloured. Self-adhesive. Die-cut perf 10½×11.
1664	85c. Type **480**	2·10	2·00
1665	100c. Double bus	2·50	2·30
1666	130c. School minibus	3·25	3·00
1664/1666	Set of 3	7·00	6·50

481 Fir   **482** Cuckoo

(Des Sutersager. Litho Austrian State Ptg Wks, Vienna)

2006 (7 Mar). Art Nouveau Exhibition, La Chaux-de-Fonds. T **481** and similar horiz design. Multicoloured. P 13½.
| 1667 | 100c. Type **481** | 2·50 | 2·30 |
| 1668 | 180c. Petals | 4·50 | 4·25 |

(Des Eva Weber. Photo Enschedé)

2006 (7 Mar)–09. Birds. T **482** and similar horiz designs. Multicoloured. Self-adhesive. Die-cut perf 12.
1669	85c. Chaffinch (*Fringilla coelebs*) (6.9.07)	2·20	2·10
	a. Booklet pane. No. 1669×10	23·00	
1670	100c. Great Tit (*Parus major*) (6.9.07)	2·50	2·40
	a. Booklet pane. No. 1670×10	26·00	
1671	110c. Wallcreeper (*Tichodroma muraria*) (6.9.07)	3·00	2·75
1672	120c. Grey-headed Woodpecker (*Picus canus*) (8.5.08)	2·75	2·75
1673	130c. Rufous-tailed Rock Thrush (*Monticola saxatilis*) (8.5.08)	3·25	3·00
	a. No label	3·25	3·00
1674	140c. Rock Partridge (*Alectoris graeca*) (1.4.09)	3·50	3·25
1675	180c. Tengmalm's Owl (*Aegolius funereus*) (6.9.07)	4·50	4·25
1676	190c. Red Kite (*Milvus milvus*) (1.4.09)	4·75	4·50
1677	220c. Great Crested Grebe (*Podiceps cristatus*) (8.5.08)	5·50	5·00
1678	240c. Type **482**	6·25	5·75
1669/1678	Set of 10	34·00	32·00

No. 1670 and 1673 have a label inscribed 'Prioritaire' attached at foot. Nos. 1676 and 1678 have the surplus self-adhesive paper around the stamp removed.

Nos. 1679/1680 are vacant.

483 Player   **484** Kasperli

(Des P. Castella. Litho Enschedé)

2006 (7 Mar). Euro 2008. European Football Championships, Austria and Switzerland (2nd issue).World Youth Football Championships. P 14×14½.
| 1681 | **483** | 85c. multicoloured | 2·75 | 2·50 |

(Des H. Steiger. Litho Austrian State Ptg Wks, Vienna)

2006 (9 May). Kasperli (children's book character written by Jorg Schneider and drawn by Heinz Steiger). P 14.
| 1682 | **484** | 85c. multicoloured | 2·75 | 2·50 |

485 Eiger   **486** Monastery Buildings

(Des Bernadette Baltis. Litho Enschedé)

2006 (9 May). Mountains. T **485** and similar multicoloured designs. P 14×14½.
1683	85c. Type **485**	2·75	2·50
	a. Horiz strip of 3. Nos. 1683/1685	8·50	
1684	85c. Monch (30×35 *mm*)	2·75	2·50
1685	85c. Jungfrau (39×35 *mm*)	2·75	2·50
1683/1685	Set of 3	7·50	6·75

Nos. 1683/1685 were issued in horizontal *se-tenant* strips of three stamps within the sheet, each strip forming a composite design of a panorama of the mountain range.

(Des M. Eberhard. Litho China State Ptg Wks, Beijing)

2006 (9 May). NABA National Stamp Exhibition, Baden. Wettingen Monastery. Sheet 105×70 mm containing T **486** and similar horiz designs. Multicoloured. P 13½×14.
MS1686 85c.+15c. Type **486**; 85c.+15c. Covered bridge; 100c.+50c. Building containing clock tower.   9·00   8·50

The stamps valued 85c.+15c have imperforate outside edges. The stamps and margins of No. **MS**1686 form a composite design of the monastery.

SWITZERLAND 2006

487 Schloss Heidegg, Gelfingen **488** Cow

(Des B. Leuenberger and J. Glauser. Litho Austrian State Ptg Wks, Vienna)

2006 (9 May). Pro Patria. T **487** and similar horiz designs. Multicoloured. P 14.
1687	85c. +40c. Type **487**	3·25	3·00
	a. Booklet pane. No. 1687×6	21·00	
1688	85c. +40c. Château de Prangins, Prangins	3·25	3·00
1689	100c. +50c. Villa Garbald, Castasegna	4·00	3·75
	a. Booklet pane. No. 1689×4	17·00	
1690	100c. +50c. Schloss Birseck, Arlesheim	4·00	3·75
1687/1690 Set of 4		13·00	12·00

(Litho Enschedé)

2006 (9 May). Switzerland through the Eyes of Foreign Artists. Patrice Killofer (France). T **488** and similar horiz designs. Multicoloured. P 14.
1691	85c. Type **488**	2·20	2·10
1692	100c. Brown Cow in water	2·50	2·40
1693	130c. Seated Cow losing its spots	3·25	3·00
1694	180c. Snow covered white Cow	4·50	4·25
1691/1694 Set of 4		11·00	10·50

489 Faces of Many Nations **490** Emblem

(Des Manuela Krebser. Litho Cartor)

2006 (9 May). Europa. Integration. P 13×13½.
1695	**489** 100c. multicoloured	2·50	2·50

(Litho Enschedé)

2006 (19 June). United Nations Human Rights Council, Geneva. P 14×14½.
1696	**490** 100c. multicoloured	2·75	2·50

491 Cocolino **492** Clown juggling Letters

(Litho Sprintpak)

2006 (7 Sept). Cocolino (cartoon character created by Oskar Weiss and Oskar Marti). Booklet stamp. Self-adhesive. Die-cut perf 11.
1697	**491** 85c. multicoloured	2·40	2·20

No. 1697 was issued in booklets of ten stamps.

(Des Dimtri Verscio. Litho Cartor)

2006 (7 Sept). Dimtri the Clown. P 13½×13.
1698	**492** 100c. multicoloured	2·50	2·40

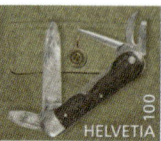

493 Clock Face **494** First Knife

(Des M. Eberhard. Litho China State Ptg Wks, Beijing)

2006 (7 Sept). Baden City Tower. Sheet 105×70 mm containing T **493** and similar vert design. Multicoloured. P 14½×14×imperf.
MS1699 100c.+50c.×2, Type **493**; Base of tower and fountain		9·25	8·50

The stamps and margins of No. **MS**1699 form a composite design.

(Des N. and P. Spalinger. Litho Austrian State Ptg Wks, Vienna)

2006 (7 Sept). Victorinox Swiss Officer's Knife. T **494** and similar horiz design. Multicoloured. . P 14.
1700	100c. Type **494**	3·00	2·75
1701	130c. Modern knife	4·00	3·75

495 Gelterkinder Cherries **496** Boy wearing Conductor's Cap

(Des Flavia Travaglini. Photo Enschedé)

2006 (7 Sept). ProSpecieRara (rare breeds association) (1st issue). T **495** and similar horiz design. Multicoloured. Self-adhesive. Die-cut perf 12.
1702	200c. Type **495**	5·75	5·25
1703	300c. Spätlauber Apple	8·50	8·00

See also Nos. 1707 and 1782.

(Des Bruno Castellani. Litho Cartor)

2006 (21 Nov). Stamp Day. Winning Entry in Stamp Design Competition. 150th Anniversary of Olten, the Railway Town. P 14×13½.
1704	**496** 85c. multicoloured	2·50	2·40

497 Star Singers **498** Player

(Des Michèle Haas. Photo Cartor)

2006 (21 Nov). Christmas Customs. T **497** and similar vert design. Multicoloured. P 14×13½.
1705	85c. Type **497**	2·50	2·40
1706	100c. Candles on Advent wreath	3·00	2·75

(Des Flavia Travaglini. Photo Enschedé)

2006 (21 Nov). ProSpecieRara (rare breeds association) (2nd issue). Horiz design as T **495**. Multicoloured. Self-adhesive. Die-cut perf 12.
1707	400c. Hauszwetschge Plums	11·50	10·50

(Des Pierre Castella. Litho Cartor)

2007 (6 Mar). Euro 2008. European Football Championship, Switzerland and Austria (3rd issue). Women's Football. P 13½×14.
1708	**498** 85c. multicoloured	2·50	2·40

499 Bernese Mountain Dog **500** Town Hall

(Des Bea Artico. Litho)

2007 (6 Mar). Centenary of Swiss Club for Bernese Mountain Dogs. Self-adhesive. Die-cut perf 11.
1709	**499** 85c. multicoloured	2·50	2·40

(Des Beat Kehrli. Litho Austrian State Ptg Wks, Vienna)

2007 (6 Mar). Stein am Rhein Millenary. T **500** and similar multicoloured designs. P 14.
1710	85c. Type **500**	2·50	2·40
	a. Horiz strip of 3. Nos. 1710/1712	7·75	

2007 SWITZERLAND

1711	85c. Painted houses (41×36 *mm*)	2·50	2·40
1712	85c. Municipal (market) fountain and Zur Meise (guildhall) (34×36 *mm*)	2·50	2·40
1710/1712	Set of 3	6·75	6·50

Nos. 1710/1712 were issued in horizontal *se-tenant* strips of three stamps in sheets of 15 (3×5), each strip forming a composite design.

501 Security Features

(Des Jörg Zintzmeyer. Litho)

2007 (6 Mar). Centenary of National Bank. T **501** and similar horiz design. Multicoloured. Self-adhesive. Die-cut perf 11.

| 1713 | 85c. Type **501** | 2·50 | 2·40 |
| 1714 | 100c. Banknote | 3·00 | 2·75 |

502 Cup, Jewel and Snake (Legend of Charlemagne and the Snake)   **503** Leonhard Euler

(Des Reinhard Fluri. Litho Enschedé)

2007 (6 Mar). Legends and Stories. T **502** and similar vert designs. Multicoloured. P 11.

1715	85c. Type **502**	2·50	2·40
1716	100c. Girl and Water Lilies (Fenetta, the Island Maiden)	3·00	2·75
1717	130c. Horse and rider (The Judge of Bellinzona)	4·00	3·75
1718	180c. Woman flying over lake and mountains (Margaretha)	5·50	5·00
1715/1718	Set of 4	13·50	12·50

(Des Angelo Boog. Litho Cartor)

2007 (6 Mar). 300th Birth Anniversary of Leonhard Euler (mathematician and scientist). P 13½×14.

| 1719 | **503** | 130c. multicoloured | 4·00 | 3·75 |

503a Roger Federer and Trophy   **504** Coloured Balls

(Des Roland Hirter. Litho Enschedé)

2007 (27 Apr). Roger Federer. Tennis World Champion. P 14×14½.

| 1720 | **503a** | 100c. multicoloured | 3·00 | 2·75 |

(Des Sandra di Salvo. Litho Cartor)

2007 (27 Apr). Centenary of Swiss Association of Day Care Centres. P 13½.

| 1721 | **504** | 85c. multicoloured | 2·50 | 2·40 |

505 Three Adults and Two Children

506 Via Jacobi   **508** Scouts

(Des Müller Lütolf. Lenticular)

2007 (27 Apr). Centenary of Museum of Communication, Berne. T **505** and similar horiz design. Multicoloured. Self-adhesive. Die-cut.

| 1722 | 85c. Type **505** | 2·50 | 2·40 |
| 1723 | 100c. Five adults | 3·00 | 2·75 |

Nos. 1722/1723 were die-cut around to simulate perforations and were printed by lenticular process, producing 3-D animated images.

(Des Vito Noto. Litho Bagel Security Print, Düsseldorf)

2007 (27 Apr). Pro Patria. Traditional Routes. T **506** and similar horiz designs. Multicoloured. P 13½.

1724	85c. +40c. Type **506**	3·75	3·50
	a. Booklet pane. No. 1724×6	24·00	
1725	85c. +40c. Via Jura	3·75	3·50
1726	100c. +50c. Via Cook	4·50	4·25
	a. Booklet pane. No. 1726×4	19·00	
1727	100c. +50c. Via Gottardo	4·50	4·25
1724/1727	Set of 4	15·00	14·00

T **507** is vacant.

(Des Marc Weller. Litho Austrian State Ptg Wks, Vienna)

2007 (27 Apr). Europa. Centenary of Scouting. P 14.

| 1728 | **508** | 100c. multicoloured | 3·00 | 2·75 |
| | | a. Tête-bêche pair. No. 1728×2 | 6·25 | 5·75 |

509 Skt. Adolf Thron-Flühe-Blume (Adolf Wölfli)   **510** Schellen-Ursli on Bridge

(Litho Enschedé)

2007 (27 Apr). Outsider Art. T **509** and similar vert design. Multicoloured. P 14½×14.

| 1729 | 100c. Type **509** | 3·00 | 2·75 |
| 1730 | 180c. Untitled (Carlo Zinelli) | 5·50 | 5·00 |

(Des Sandra di Salvo. Litho)

2007 (6 Sept). Schellen-Ursli (children's book character created by Selina Chonz and illustrated by Alois Carigiet.) Booklet Stamp. Self-adhesive. Die-cut perf 10½×11.

| 1731 | **510** | 85c. multicoloured | 2·50 | 2·40 |
| | | a. Smaller name at foot 9·5 mm | 3·00 | 2·75 |

No. 1731 was issued in booklets of ten stamps.
The name at footnote the normal stamp measures 12 mm.

511 The Dancer   **512** Family and Hearts

(Des Nina Corti. Litho Austrian State Ptg Wks, Vienna)

2007 (6 Sept). Nina Corti (flamenco dancer). P 13½.

| 1732 | **511** | 85c. multicoloured | 2·50 | 2·40 |

(Des Victoria Leonard. Litho)

2007 (6 Sept). Greetings Stamps. Congratulations. T **512** and similar horiz designs. Multicoloured. Self-adhesive. Die-cut perf 11.

1733	85c. Type **512**	2·50	2·40
1734	100c. Boy and stars	3·00	2·75
1735	130c. Woman and flowers	4·00	3·75
1733/1735	Set of 3	8·50	8·00

513 Mönch (*Frankenstein* (Mary Shelley))

514 Skiers and Bee Tag

(Litho Cartor)

2007 (6 Sept). Switzerland through the Eyes of Foreign Artists. Swiss Landscape and English Literature. Photographs by James Peel (British artist). T **513** and similar multicoloured designs. P 13½.

1736	85c. Type **513**	2·50	2·40
1737	100c. Lauterbrunnen (*At Staubbach Falls* (William Wordsworth)) (*vert*)	3·00	2·75
1738	130c. Lac Léman (*The Prisoner of Chillon* (Lord Byron)) (*vert*)	4·00	3·75
1739	180c. Reichenbach Fall (*The Final Problem* (Sir Arthur Conan Doyle))	5·50	5·00
1736/1739	Set of 4	13·50	12·50

2007 (31 Oct). Internet Stamp. Self-adhesive. Die-cut perf 11.
| 1740 | **514** | 100c. multicoloured | 3·00 | 2·75 |

No. 1740 contains a Bee Tag (a two dimensional code which, when used with the appropriate software, connects a mobile telephone to the internet). The code gives entry to a competition to win Swiss Tourism prize.

515 Monastery   **516** Nativity

(Des Christian Kitmüller. Litho Enschedé)

2007 (20 Nov). Einsiedeln. Sheet 105×70 mm. P 13½×13½.
MS1741 **515** 85c. multicoloured .... 11·00 10·00

The stamps and margins of No. **MS**1741 form a composite design. No. **MS**1741 was for sale at Philatelic outlets from 13 November 2007, and only on sale at Post Offices in the Einsiedeln area.

(Des Michèle Haas. Litho Cartor)

2007 (20 Nov). Christmas. T **516** and similar vert designs. Multicoloured. P 14×13½.

1742	85c. Type **516**	2·50	2·40
1743	100c. Decorated tree	3·00	2·75
1744	130c. Presents	4·00	3·75
1742/1744	Set of 3	8·50	8·00

517 Heart-shaped Silhouette   **518** Potato

(Des Christian Schwizgebel (85c.), Pia Arm (100c.), Christianne and Jaqueline Saugy (130c.) or Verena Kühni (180c.))

2007 (20 Nov). Silhouettes. T **517** and similar vert designs. Self-adhesive. Die-cut perf 11.
1745	85c. black and carmine-vermilion	2·50	2·40
1746	100c. black and emerald	3·00	2·75
1747	130c. black and blue	4·00	3·75
1748	180c. black and orange	5·50	5·00
1745/1748	Set of 4	13·50	12·50

Designs: 85c. T **517**; 100c. Tree shaped in circle; 130c. Tree with family cycling below; 180c. Symmetrical tree of Peacock feathers with dancers below.

Nos. 1745/1748 were on sale at Philatelic outlets from 13 November 2007. The following stamps were on sale from Philatelic outlets on 26 February 2008.

(Des Hans Tanner. Litho Cartor)

2008 (4 Mar). International Year of the Potato. P 13½.
| 1749 | **518** | 85c. multicoloured | 2·50 | 2·40 |

519 Lars   **520** Albrecht von Haller

2008 (4 Mar). *The Little Polar Bear Lars* (created by Hans de Beer). Booklet Stamp. Self-adhesive. Die-cut 11×11½.
| 1750 | **519** | 85c. multicoloured | 2·50 | 2·40 |

(Des Marco Trüeb. Litho Cartor)

2008 (4 Mar). 300th Birth Anniversary of Albrecht von Haller (physician, botanist and poet). P 13½.
| 1751 | **520** | 85c. multicoloured | 2·50 | 2·40 |

521 Horses   **522** Violin

(Des Dominique Rossier. Litho Enschedé)

2008 (4 Mar). 50th Anniversary of Horse Foundation (refuge), Jura. T **521** and similar horiz designs. Multicoloured. P 13½.

1752	85c. Type **521**	2·50	2·40
	a. Horiz strip of 3. Nos. 1752/1754	7·75	
1753	85c. Track and four Horses	2·50	2·40
1754	85c. Two Horses and building	2·50	2·40
1752/1754	Set of 3	6·75	6·50

Nos. 1752/1754 were issued in horizontal *se-tenant* strips of three stamps within the sheet, each strip forming a composite design.

(Des Beat Kehrli. Litho Bagel, Düsseldorf)

2008 (4 Mar). Musical Instruments. T **522** and similar vert designs. Multicoloured. P 13×14.
1755	85c. Type **522**	2·50	2·40
1756	100c. Accordian	3·00	2·75
1757	130c. Electric guitar	4·00	3·75
1758	180c. Saxophone	5·50	5·00
1755/1758	Set of 4	13·50	12·50

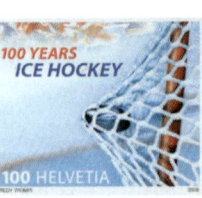 

523 Puck in Net   **524** Player

(Des Fredy Trümpi. Litho)

2008 (4 Mar). Centenary of Swiss Ice Hockey Association. P 13½.
| 1759 | **523** | 100c. multicoloured | 3·00 | 2·75 |

(Des Pierre Castella. Litho Enschedé)

2008 (4 Mar). Euro 2008. European Football Championship, Austria and Switzerland (4th issue). Local Football. P 13½×14.
| 1760 | **524** | 100c. multicoloured | 3·00 | 2·75 |

Nos. 1643, 1681, 1708 and 1760 together form a composite design of a football enclosing players.

2008 SWITZERLAND

525 Pitch

527 Birds in Flight forming Envelope

(Des Mxomedia. Photo Enschedé)

2008 (4 Mar). Euro 2008. European Football Championship, Austria and Switzerland (5th issue). Self-adhesive. Die-cut perf 12×13.
1761   **525**   100c. emerald .... 3·00   2·75

The following stamps were on sale from Philatelic outlets on 24 April 2008.

No. 1762 and T **526** have been left for Euro 2008, issued on 8 May 2008, not yet received.

(Des Paul Bühler. Litho Cartor)

2008 (8 May). Europa. The Letter. P 13×13½.
1763   **527**   100c. multicoloured .... 3·00   2·75

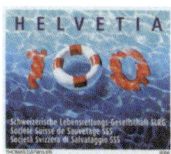

528 '100'   **529** Mountain Biking

(Des Thomas Dätwyler. Litho Cartor)

2008 (8 May). Centenary of Swiss Life Saving Society. P 13½.
1764   **528**   100c. multicoloured .... 3·00   2·75

(Des Silvio Galbucci. Litho Enschedé)

2008 (8 May). Olympic Games, Beijing. T **529** and similar horiz design. Multicoloured. P 14×14½.
1765   100c. Type **529** .... 3·00   2·75

530 Via Sbrinz and Schitzturm Tower, Stansstad   **532** Wheat

(Des Vito Noto. Litho Bagel Security Print, Düsseldorf)

2008 (8 May). Pro Patria. Traditional Routes. T **530** and similar horiz designs. Multicoloured. P 13½.
1767   85c. +40c. Type **530** .... 3·75   3·50
         a. Booklet pane. No. 1767×6 .... 24·00
1768   85c. +40c. East Gate, Avenches and Columns, Nyon .... 3·75   3·50
1769   100c. +50c. Via Valtellina, Cavaglia and Dürrboden restaurant .... 4·50   4·25
1770   100c. +50c. Via Stockalper, Engi and Old Hospice .... 4·50   4·25
         a. Booklet pane. No. 1770×4 .... 19·00
1767/1770 Set of 4 .... 15·00   14·00

No. 1771 is vacant.

The following stamps were all on sale from 28 August 2008 from Philatelic outlets and from 4 September 2008 at Post Offices.

(Des Beatrice Wurgler. Litho Enschedé)

2008 (4 Sept). Cereals. T **532** and similar horiz designs. Multicoloured. Self-adhesive. Die-cut perf 12.
1772   10c. Type **532** 35   30
1773   15c. Barley 45   45
1774   20c. Rye 60   55
1775   50c. Oats .... 1·50   1·40
1772/1775 Set of 4 .... 2·50   2·40

Nos. 1772/1775 were issued with the surplus paper around each stamp removed and the designs alternating within the sheet.

533 Cheese

534 Old Bridge, Bad Säckingen–Stein/Aargau

(Des Laura Mangiavacchi (Italy). Litho Bagel Security Print, Düsseldorf)

2008 (4 Sept). Switzerland through the Eyes of Foreign Artists. T **533** and similar horiz designs. Multicoloured. P 14.
1776   85c. Type **533** .... 2·50   2·40
1777   100c. Chocolate .... 3·00   2·75
1778   130c. Clock .... 4·00   3·75
1779   180c. Tools (Swiss army pocket knives) ...... 5·50   5·00
1776/1779 Set of 4 .... 13·50   12·50

The following stamps were on sale on 28 August 2008 from Philatelic outlets and Post Offices on 4 September 2008.

(Des Bernadette Baltis. Litho German State Ptg Wks, Berlin)

2008 (4 Sept). Bridges. P 14.
1780   **534**   100c. multicoloured .... 3·00   2·75
A stamp of a similar design was issued by Germany.

535 Stylised Figures

(Des Fredi Murer. Photo Cartor)

2008 (4 Sept). Fredi Murer (film maker). P 13×13 ½.
1781   **535**   100c. multicoloured .... 3·00   2·75

(Des Flavia Travaglini. Photo Enschedé)

2008 (4 Sept). ProSpecieRara (rare breeds association) (3rd issue). Horiz design as T **495**. Multicoloured. Self-adhesive. Die-cut perf 12.
1782   500c. Catillac Pear .... 15·00   14·00

The following stamps were on sale from 14 November 2008 from Philatelic outlets and from 21 November 2008 at Post Offices.

536 Local Food

(Des Vito Noto. Litho Enschedé)

2008 (21 Nov). Stamp Day, Bellinzona. Sheet 105×70 mm. P 14.
MS1783 **536** 85c. multicoloured .... 3·25   3·00

537 Bauble

(Des Jenny Leibundgut. Litho and die-stamped Cartor)

2008 (21 Nov). Christmas Baubles. T **537** and similar vert design. Multicoloured. P 13½.
1784   85c. Type **537** .... 3·00   2·75
1785   100c. Star shaped bauble .... 3·50   3·25
1786   130c. Bell shaped bauble .... 4·75   4·25
1784/1786 Set of 3 .... 10·00   9·25

55

538 *Rotes Quadrat* (Max Bill)   **539** Brown Bear

(Litho Cartor)

2008 (21 Nov). Art. T **538** and similar design. Each black and bright scarlet. P 13½.
1787	100c. Type **538**	3·50	3·25
1788	130c. *Eier im Spiegel* (eggs in a mirror) (Hans Finsler) (30×42 mm)	4·75	4·25

The following stamps were on sale at Philatelic outlets from 21 February 2009 and at Post Offices from 5 March 2009.

(Des Michèle Berri. Litho Cartor)

2009 (5 Mar). Centenary of Pro Natura (conservation organisation). P 14×13½.
1789	**539** 85c. multicoloured	3·00	2·75

540 Rigi (steam ship)   **541** Boot

(Des Rene Sager. Litho Bagel Security Print)

2009 (5 Mar). 50th Anniversary of Verkehrshaus Transport Museum. T **540** and similar horiz designs. Multicoloured. P 13×13½.
1790	85c. Type **540**	3·00	2·75
1791	100c. Dufaux race car	3·50	3·25
1792	130c. Lockheed Orion 9C Special aircraft	4·75	4·25
1790/1792	Set of 3	10·00	9·25

(Des Susanne Krieg. Litho Enschedé)

2009 (5 Mar). International Ice Hockey Federation World Championships, Berne and Zürich–Kloten. Self-adhesive gum. Die-cut perf 13½×14.
1793	**541** 100c. multicoloured	3·50	3·25

542 Vadret da Morteratsch   **543** John Calvin

(Des Thomas Kissling. Litho and serigraphy Enschedé)

2009 (5 Mar). Glacial Shrinkage. P 14×13½.
1794	**542** 100c. multicoloured	3·50	3·25

The printing method allows No. 1794 to show the glacier as it is now, or as it was in 1850 when the stamp is tilted.

(Des Laurent Donner. Litho Cartor)

2009 (5 Mar). 500th Birth Anniversary of John Calvin (theologian). P 13½×14.
1795	**543** 100c. multicoloured	3·50	3·25

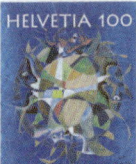 

544 The Human Mind   **545** Hans Ulrich Grubenmann

(Hans Erni. Litho Enschedé)

2009 (5 Mar). Birth Centenary of Hans Erni (stamp designer). T **544** and similar vert design. Multicoloured. P 14.
1796	100c. Type **544**	3·50	3·25
1797	130c. *Human Hands*	4·75	4·25

(Des Bernard Schulp. Litho Cartor)

2009 (5 Mar). 300th Birth Anniversary of Hans Ulrich Grubenmann (engineer). P 13½.
1798	**545** 85c. multicoloured	3·25	3·00

The following stamps were on sale at Philatelic outlets from 22 April 2009 and at Post Offices from 8 May 2009.

546 Kittens   **547** Birch

(Des André Seiffert. Litho Enschedé)

2009 (8 May). European Wild Cat (*Felis silvestris*). Self-adhesive. Die-cut perf 13½×14.
1799	**546** 85c. multicoloured	3·25	3·00

(Des Reinhard Fluri. Litho Enschedé)

2009 (8 May). Ancient Trees. T **547** and similar vert designs. Multicoloured. Self-adhesive. Die-cut perf 13½.
1800	85c. Type **547**	3·25	3·00
1801	100c. Oak	3·75	3·50
1802	130c. Willow	5·00	4·75
1800/1802	Set of 3	11·00	10·00

548 Via Francigena and Great St Bernhard Hospice   **549** '@' and Type

(Des Vito Noto. Litho Bagel Security Print, Düsseldorf)

2009 (8 May). Pro Patria. Traditional Routes. T **548** and similar horiz designs. Multicoloured. P 13½.
1803	85c. +40c. Type **548**	5·00	4·50
	a. Booklet pane. No. 1803×6	31·00	
1804	85c. +40c. Via Salina, track and Berne Gate, Murten	5·00	4·50
1805	100c. +50c. Via Spluga, Viamala, Zillis-Reischen and Albertini House, Splügen	5·75	5·25
1806	100c. +50c. Via Rhenana, Basel Old Town and salt drilling towers, Rheinfelden	5·75	5·25
	a. Booklet pane. No. 1806×4	24·00	
1803/1806	Set of 4	19·00	18·00
MS1807	105×70 mm. 100c.+50c. Illuminated roads (centenary of Pro Patria organisation)	6·25	5·50

(Des Meike Kollmann. Litho Bagel Security Print, Düsseldorf)

2009 (8 May). Graphics. From Guttenberg to the Internet. P 13½×14.
1808	**549** 100c. multicoloured	3·75	3·50

550 Planets and *Helvetia* Asteroid

(Des Markus Griesser. Litho Austrian State Ptg Wks, Vienna)

2009 (8 May). Europa. Astronomy. Phosphor markings. P 13×13½.
1809	**550** 100c. multicoloured	3·75	3·50

Phosphor ink was applied to the orbital rings and bodies.

2009 SWITZERLAND

551 Stiva da Morts (Place of Mourning, Vrin)   **552** Princess Lillifee

(Des Daniel Dreier. Litho Bagel Security Print, Düsseldorf)

2009 (8 May). Architecture. T **551** and similar horiz design. Multicoloured. P 13½.
1810	100c. Type **551**		3·75	3·50
1811	180c. Pentorama Community Centre, Amriswil		7·00	6·50

The following stamps were on sale at Philatelic outlets from 27 August 2009 and at Post Offices from 3 September 2009.

(Des Monika Finsterbusch. Litho and serigraphy Enschedé)

2009 (3 Sept). Princess Lillifee (character created by Monika Finsterbusch). Booklet stamps. Self-adhesive. Die-cut perf 12.
1812	**552**	85c. multicoloured	3·25	3·00

No. 1812 is printed with glitter applied to parts of the design.

553 Goats and Lead Cows   **554** 'Den Zwang abwrft' (independence)

(Des Albert Manser. Litho Cartor)

2009 (3 Sept). Alpaufahrt (moving animals to and from alpine pastures), Appenzell. T **553** and similar multicoloured designs. P 13½.
1813	85c. Type **553**		3·25	3·00
	a. Strip of 3. Nos. 1813/1815		10·00	
1814	85c. Cows and calves (32×37 mm)		3·25	3·00
1815	85c. Bull and Horse drawn cart (34×37 mm)		3·25	3·00
1813/1815 Set of 3			8·75	8·00

Nos. 1813/1815 were printed, *se-tenant*, in horizontal strips of three stamps within the sheet, each strip forming a composite design of the procession.

(Des Ktja Dengel and Kuno Ebert (Germany). Litho Bagel Security Print, Düsseldorf)

2009 (3 Sept). Switzerland through the Eyes of Foreign Artists. T **554** and similar multicoloured designs showing red flowers with a central white cross and parts of a poem by Friedrich Schiller describing Swiss virtues. P 14×13.
1816	85c. Type **554**		3·25	3·00
1817	100c. 'Sich selbst genug' (self-sufficiency) (vert)		3·75	3·50
1818	130c. 'die Menschlichkeit noch ehrt' (humanity) (vert)		5·00	4·75
1819	180c. 'sich bescheidet' (modesty)		7·00	6·50
1816/1819 Set of 4			17·00	16·00

555 Design as 1903 Stamp (T **18**)   **556** Refugees and Red Cross

(Des Matine Dietrich-Chatagny. Litho Cartor)

2009 (3 Sept). Centenary of Swiss Stamp Dealers' Association. P 13½.
1820	**555**	100c. light bright green and bright yellowish green	3·75	3·50

No. 1820 has a stamp size label attached at either left or right showing SSDA emblem.

(Des Paul Bühler. Litho Bagel Security Print, Düsseldorf)

2009 (3 Sept). 60th Anniversary of Geneva Conventions. P 14×13.
1821	**556**	100c. multicoloured	3·75	3·50

557 Wedding   **558** Crane (emblem of Gruyères)

(Des Sabina Oberholzer and Renato Tagli. Litho Enschedé)

2009 (3 Sept). Greetings Stamps. T **557** and similar horiz designs. Multicoloured. Self-adhesive. Die-cut perf 14×14½.
1822	100c. Type **557**		3·75	3·50
1823	100c. Birth		3·75	3·50
1824	100c. Anniversary		3·75	3·50
1822/1824 Set of 3			10·00	9·50

The following stamps were on sale at Philatelic outlets from 13 November 2009 and at Post Offices from 20 November 2009.

(Des Dominique Rossier. Litho Enschedé)

2009 (20 Nov). Stamp Day. Gruyères. Sheet 70×105 mm. Die-cut perf 14½×14.
MS1825	**558**	85c. multicoloured	3·75	3·50

559 Santa Hat   **560** Alpine Skier

(Des Jenny Leibundgut. Litho and die-stamped Cartor)

2009 (20 Nov). Christmas. T **559** and similar vert designs. Multicoloured. P 13½.
1826	85c. Type **559**		3·25	3·00
1827	100c. Tree		3·75	3·50
1828	130c. Parcel		5·00	4·75
1826/1828 Set of 3			11·00	10·00

(Des Trummer and Stuker. Litho Cartor)

2009 (20 Nov). Winter Olympic Games and Paralympic Games, Vancouver. T **560** and similar horiz design. Multicoloured. P 13½.
1829	130c. Type **560**		5·00	4·75

561 Procession   **562** Emblem

(Des Andreas Daniel Vetsch. Litho Cartor)

2010 (12 Jan). Centenary of Basel Carnival. T **561** and similar multicoloured designs showing procession. P 14×13½.
1830	100c. Type **561**		3·75	3·50
	a. Strip of 3. Nos. 1830/1832		12·00	
1831	100c. Four figures and float (44×37 mm)		3·75	3·50
1832	100c. Band		3·75	3·50
1830/1832 Set of 3			10·00	9·50

No. 1833 is vacant.

(Des Urs Lieber and Enzo Granella. Litho Bagel Security Print, Düsseldorf)

2010 (4 Mar). 550th Anniversary of Basel University. P 14×13.
1834	**562**	85c. deep turquoise-green, orange-red and black	3·25	3·00

SWITZERLAND 2010

563 Peacock Goats   **564** Grandjean Monoplane and Ernest Failloubaz

(Des Corinne Bromundt. Litho Enschedé)

2010 (4 Mar). International Year of Biodiversity. Self-adhesive. Die-cut perf 14½×14.
| 1835 | **563** | 85c. multicoloured | 3·25 | 3·00 |

(Des Fredy Trümpi. Litho Cartor)

2010 (4 Mar). Centenary of Swiss Aviation. T **564** and similar horiz designs. Multicoloured. P 13½.
1836	85c. Type **564** (1st flight of Swiss aircraft by Swiss pilot)	3·25	3·00
1837	100c. Airbus A340 (modern civil aviation)	3·75	3·50
1838	130c. Geo Chavez flying Blériot XI monoplane (first flight over Alps)	5·00	4·75
1839	180c. Acrobatic aeroplane, glider and air balloon (aviation sport)	7·00	6·50
1836/1839	Set of 4	17·00	16·00

565 Script   **566** Dancers and Headdress (Federal Costume Festival, Schwyz)

(Des Marco Trüeb. Litho Bagel Security Print, Düsseldorf)

2010 (4 Mar). Centenary of Swiss Cancer League. P 14×13.
| 1840 | **565** | 100c. multicoloured | 3·75 | 3·50 |

(Des Müller Lütolf. Litho and embossed (Nos. 1841/1842), litho and varnish (No. 1843) or litho (No. 1844) Enschedé)

2010 (4 Mar). Traditional Swiss Customs. T **566** and similar horiz designs. Multicoloured. P 14×14½.
1841	100c. Type **566**	3·75	3·50
1842	100c. Alphorn and yodellers (centenary of Swiss Yodelling Association)	3·75	3·50
1843	100c. Drum (Federal Drumming and Piping Festival, Interlaken)	3·75	3·50
1844	100c. Marksman and target (Federal Marksmen's Festival, Aarau)	3·75	3·50
1841/1844	Set of 4	13·50	12·50

Nos. 1841/1842 have the headdress and alphorn respectively, embossed, No. 1843 has varnish applied to the drum and No. 1844 is additionally perforated with a die-cut hole in the centre of the target.

567 Neissen Funicular Railway   **568** School Boy

(Des Marc Weller. Litho Enschedé)

2010 (6 May). Centenary of Bernina Railway. T **567** and similar multicoloured design. P 14½×14 (vert) or 14×14½ (horiz).
| 1845 | 85c. Type **567** | 3·25 | 3·00 |
| 1846 | 100c. Bernina railway line (*horiz*) | 3·75 | 3·50 |

(Des Suzanne Potterat. Litho Bagel Security Print, Düsseldorf)

2010 (6 May). Death Centenary of Albert Anker (artist). P 13½×13.
| 1847 | **568** | 85c. multicoloured | 3·25 | 3·00 |

569 Johann Hebel and Basel   **570** Charles the Bold in Flight

(Des Christian Kitmüller. Litho Cartor)

2010 (6 May). 250th Birth Anniversary of Johann Peter Hebel (theologian and writer). P 13½.
| 1848 | **569** | 85c. multicoloured | 3·25 | 3·00 |

(Des Daniel Dreier and Maya Arber. Litho Bagel Security Print, Düsseldorf)

2010 (6 May). Pro Patria. *Battle of Murten* Panorama by Louis Braun. Multicoloured. P 13½.
1849	85c. +40c. Type **570**	5·00	4·50
	a. Booklet pane. No. 1849×6	31·00	
1850	85c. +40c. Archers and Duke of Somerset and mount dead by his tent	5·00	4·50
1851	100c. +50c. Burgundian cavalry under attack	5·75	5·25
1852	100c. +50c. Confederate troops with flags and halberds	5·75	5·25
	a. Booklet pane. No. 1852×4	24·00	
1849/1852	Set of 4	19·00	18·00

571 Equilibres (Peter Fischli and David Weiss)   **572** Figures

(Litho Enschedé)

2010 (6 May). Centenary of Kunsthaus (musuem of fine arts), Zürich. Self-adhesive. Die-cut perf 14×14½.
| 1853 | **571** | 100c. multicoloured | 3·75 | 3·50 |

(Des Simon Hauser and David Schwarz. Litho Cartor)

2010 (6 May). Bicentenary of Public Welfare Society. P 13½.
| 1854 | **572** | 100c. new blue and pale grey | 3·75 | 3·50 |

573 Heidi and Goats (*Heidi* by Johanna Spyri)   **574** Big Top from Below

(Des Karin Widmer. Litho Cartor)

2010 (6 May). Europa. Children's Books. P 13½×13.
| 1855 | **573** | 100c. multicoloured | 3·75 | 3·50 |

(Des Werner Jeker. Litho Cartor)

2010 (6 May). World Circus 2010, Geneva. P 13½.
| 1856 | **574** | 140c. multicoloured | 5·50 | 5·00 |

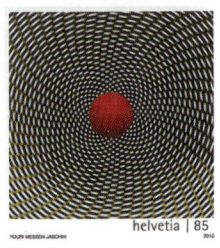

575 Jimmy Flitz   **576** Sphere

(Des Viviane Dommann. Litho Enschedé)

2010 (3 Sept). Jimmy Flitz (cartoon character created by Roland Zoss). Booklet Stamp. Self-adhesive. Die-cut perf 12.
| 1857 | 575 | 85c. multicoloured | 3·25 | 3·00 |

(Litho)

2010 (3 Sept). Optical Art. Designs by Youri Messen-Jaschin (artist). T **576** and similar square designs. Multicoloured. Self-adhesive. Die-cut perf 14×13½.
1858		85c. Type **576**	3·25	3·00
1859		100c. Blue, black and red squares	3·75	3·50
1860		140c. Circles within a lined square	5·50	5·00
1858/1860	Set of 3		11·50	10·50

Nos. 1858/1860 were perforated through the backing paper. The backing paper of Nos. 1858/1860 was slit to facilitate removal.

577 Therapod   578 Words

(Des Angelo Boog. Litho Cartor)

2010 (3 Sept). Swiss Paleontology. Saurians. T **577** and similar horiz designs. Multicoloured. P 13½×14.
1861		85c. Type **577**	3·25	3·00
1862		100c. Ichthyosaur	3·75	3·50
1863		140c. Raeticodactylus filisurensis	5·50	5·00
1861/1863	Set of 3		11·50	10·50

(Des Franz Hohler. Litho)

2010 (3 Sept). Franz Hohler (writer). P 13×13½.
| 1864 | 578 | 100c. bright yellowish, green lemon and black | 3·75 | 3·50 |

579 Jeanne Hersch   580 Rolf Liebermann

(Des Tessa Gerster. Litho Gutenberg AG, Liechtenstein)

2010 (3 Sept). Birth Centenary of Jeanne Hersch (philosopher). P 13½.
| 1865 | 579 | 100c. multicoloured | 3·75 | 3·50 |

(Des Roberto Renfer. Litho Bagel Security Print, Germany)

2010 (3 Sept). Swiss Composers Birth Centenaries. T **580** and similar horiz design. P 13½.
| 1866 | | 100c. Type **580** | 3·75 | 3·50 |
| 1867 | | 140c. Heinrich Sutermeister | 5·50 | 5·00 |

581 'TA' and 'EFT'   582 Gustave Moynier and Henry Dunant

(Des Demian Conrad. Litho Giesecke & Devrient, Germany)

2010 (3 Sept). 50th Anniversary of European Free Trade Association. P 14.
| 1868 | 581 | 140c. greenish yellow and black | 5·50 | 5·00 |

(Des Martin Eberhard. Litho Gutenberg AG, Liechtenstein)

2010 (3 Sept). Death Centenaries of Henry Dunant and Gustave Moynier (founders of precursor of Red Cross). P 13½×14.
| 1869 | 582 | 190c. multicoloured | 7·25 | 6·75 |

583 Zahringer Fountain and Zytglogge Medieval Clock Tower, Berne   584 Candle and Star

(Des Reinhard Fluri. Litho Enschedé)

2010 (4 Nov). Stamp Day. Sheet 70×105 mm. P 14×13½.
| MS1870 | 583 | 85c. multicoloured | 3·75 | 3·25 |

(Des Jenny Leibundgut. Litho and die-stamp silver foil Giesecke & Devrient, Germany)

2010 (4 Nov). Christmas. T **584** and similar vert designs. Multicoloured. 13½.
1871		85c. Type **584**	3·25	3·00
1872		100c. Snowflake	3·75	3·50
1873		140c. Angel and star	5·50	5·00
1871/1873	Set of 3		11·50	10·50

585 Lace-making Bobbins   586 Findus, Chicken, Mouse and Cheese

(Des Beat Kehrli. Litho Enschedé)

2010 (4 Nov). Traditional Swiss Handicrafts. T **585** and similar horiz design. Multicoloured. Self-adhesive. Die-cut perf 12.
| 1874 | | 200c. Type **585** | 7·75 | 7·00 |
| 1875 | | 300c. Hands holding tools and carving of Fox | 11·50 | 10·50 |

Nos. 1874/1875 were printed with the surplus paper around the stamps removed.
See also Nos. 1895/1896.

(Des Sven Nordqvist. Litho Enschedé)

2011 (3 Mar). Pettersson and Findus (Pettson och Findus) (created by Sven Nordqvist). Self-adhesive. Die-cut perf 12.
| 1876 | 586 | 85c. multicoloured | 3·75 | 3·25 |

No. 1876 was issued in sheets with the surplus paper around the stamp removed and also issued in booklets of ten stamps with the surplus paper retained.

 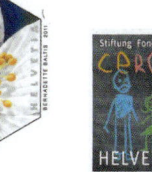

587 Bee and Flower   588 Able-bodied and Disabled Children

(Des Bernadette Baltis. Gutenberg AG, Liechtenstein)

2011 (3 Mar). Bees. P 12 (with one circular hole at each of six corners).
| 1877 | 587 | 85c. multicoloured | 3·75 | 3·25 |

(Des Urs Lieber and Enzo Granella. Litho Cartor)

2011 (3 Mar). 50th Anniversary of Cerebral Foundation. P 13½.
| 1878 | 588 | 85c. multicoloured | 3·75 | 3·25 |

SWITZERLAND 2011

589 Gymnasts

590 *Cucurbita pepo* (Courgette flower)

(Des Dominique Rossier. Litho CDS Testpack Company, Germany)

2011 (3 Mar). World Gymnaestrada, Lausanne. P 13½.
1879   **589**   85c. multicoloured ....   3·75   3·25

(Des Reinhsrd Fluri. Litho Enschedé)

2011 (3 Mar). Vegetable Flowers. T **590** and similar horiz designs. Multicoloured. Self-adhesive. Die-cut perf 12.
1880   85c. Type **590** ....   3·75   3·25
1881   100c. *Pisum sativum* (Snow Pea) ....   4·50   4·00
1882   110c. *Allium ursinum* (Wild Garlic) ....   5·00   4·50
1883   260c. *Cynara scolymus* (Artichoke) ....   11·50   10·50
1880/1883 *Set of 4* ....   22·00   20·00

Nos. 1880/1881 were printed both in booklets of ten stamps, with the surplus paper around the stamps retained, and in sheet with the surplus paper removed.

No. 1881 was printed, *se-tenant*, with a label at foot inscribed 'A-PRIORITY- PRIORITAIRE'.

Nos. 1882/1883 were only printed in sheets with the surplus paper removed.

591 Maison de Halles

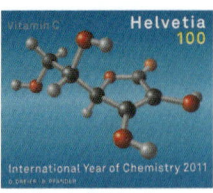
592 Panda

(Des Dominique Rossier. Litho Cartor)

2011 (3 Mar). Neuchâtel Millenary. 13½.
1884   **591**   100c. multicoloured ....   4·50   4·00

(Des Pierre Aerni. Lithp Gutenberg AG, Liechtenstein)

2011 (3 Mar). 50th Anniversary of World Wide Fund for Nature (WWF).
1885   **592**   100c. multicoloured ....   4·50   4·00

593 Max Frisch   **594** Vitamin C Molecule Construct

(Des Simon Hauser and David Schwarz. Litho Giesecke & Devrient, Germany)

2011 (3 Mar). Birth Centenary of Max Frisch (writer). P 13½.
1886   **593**   100c. black ....   4·50   4·00

(Des Daniel Dreier and Barbara Pfander. Litho and embossed Cartor)

2011 (3 Mar). International Year of Chemistry. P 13½.
1887   **594**   100c. multicoloured ....   4·50   4·00

595 Mountains and Valley (Urnerboden)

(Des Emanuel Hengartner and Irène Elber. Litho Cartor)

2011 (5 May). 50th Anniversary of National Anthem. Sheet 105×70 mm containing T **595** and similar horiz designs. Multicoloured. P 13½.
MS1888 25c.×4, Type **595**; Lake and mountains
         (Urnersee bei Flüelen); Tree on hillock (Urigen);
         Sunset over mountains (Schächentaler Windgällen)..   4·75   4·50

The stamps of No. MS1888 each contain a different translation of the first verse of the Anthem, using each of the four languages spoken in Switzerland, only visible when viewed under ultraviolet light.

596 Sunlight through Trees

597 'ART IS RESISTANCE'

(Des Bea Würgler. Litho Giesecke & Devrient)

2011 (5 May). Europa. Forests. P 13½.
1889   **596**   100c. multicoloured ....   4·50   4·00

(Des Thomas Hirschhorn. Litho Enschedé)

2011 (5 May). Art. Venice Biennale. P 14×14½.
1890   **597**   100c. multicoloured ....   4·50   4·00

598 PS *Piemonte*

599 Muggestutz

(Des Sandra di Salvo. Litho Cartor)

2011 (6 May). Pro Patria. Steam Navigation in Switzerland. T **598** and similar horiz designs. Multicoloured. P 13½.
1891   85c. +40c. Type **598** ....   5·50   5·00
             a. Booklet pane. Nos. 1891×6 ....   34·00
1892   85c. +40c. PS *Gallia* ....   5·50   5·00
1893   100c. +50c. PS *Blümlisalp* ....   6·75   6·00
             a. Booklet pane. No. 1893×4 ....   28·00
1894   100c. +50c. PS *La Suisse* ....   6·75   6·00
1891/1894 *Set of 4* ....   22·00   20·00

Nos. 1891 and 1893 were produced both in sheets and, 1891×6, and 1893×4, in booklets of ten stamps.

(Des Beat Kehrli. Litho Enschedé)

2011 (5 May). Traditional Swiss Handicrafts. Coil Stamps. Horiz designs as T **585**. Multicoloured. Self-adhesive. Die-cut perf 12.
1895   400c. Potter 'throwing' pot on wheel ....   18·00   16·00
1896   500c. Blacksmith working at anvil ....   22·00   20·00

Nos. 1888/1889 were printed in coils with the surplus paper around the stamps removed.

(Des Susanna Schmid-Germann)

2011 (9 Sept). *Muggestutz* (written and drawn by Susanna Schmid-Germann). Booklet Stamp. Self-adhesive. Die-cut perf 12½.
1897   **599**   85c. multicoloured ....   4·25   4·00

600 Paul Burkhard

601 *Frucht 07*

(Des Roberto Renfer. Litho Giesecke & Devrient, Germany)

2011 (9 Sept). Birth Centenary of Paul Burkhard (composer). P 13½.
1898   **600**   100c. multicoloured ....   5·00   4·75

(Des Shirana Shahbazi. Litho Gutenberg AG, Liechtenstein)

2011 (9 Sept). Art. P 13½.
1899   **601**   100c. multicoloured ....   5·00   4·75

A stamp of a similar design was issued by Liechtenstein.

 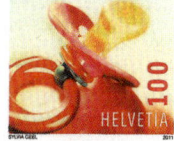

602 Terraces and Erosion Prevention Walls   **603** Baby's Dummy

(Des Bernard Völlmy. Litho CDS Testpack Company, Germany)

2011 (9 Sept). World Heritage Site. Lavaux Vineyard Terraces. T **602** and similar multicoloured designs. P 14×13½.
1900	100c. Type **602**	5·00	4·75
	a. Strip of 3. Nos. 1900/1902	16·00	
1901	100c. Terraces, Saint-Saphorin and Lake Geneva (41×36 *mm*)	5·00	4·75
1902	100c. Lake Geneva, Le Grammont and gateway (37×36 *mm*)	5·00	4·75
1900/1902	Set of 3	13·50	13·00

Nos. 1900/1902 were printed, *se-tenant*, in horizontal strips of three stamps within the sheet, each strip forming a composite design.

(Des Sylvia Geel. Litho Cartor)

2011 (9 Sept). Greetings Stamps. T **603** and similar horiz designs. Multicoloured. Self-adhesive. Die-cut perf 13½.
1903	100c. Type **603**	5·00	4·75
1904	100c. Heart	5·00	4·75
1905	100c. Two glasses of champagne	5·00	4·75
1906	100c. Two rings	5·00	4·75
1903/1906	Set of 4	18·00	17·00

604 Dungarees (Bajram Mahmuti)   **605** Chapel

(Litho Gutenberg AG, Liechtenstein)

2011 (9 Sept). Art. Disabled Artists. T **604** and similar multicoloured designs. P 13½.
1907	85c. Type **604**	4·25	4·00
1908	100c. Emmental (Claudia Aebi-Torre) (*horiz*)	5·00	4·75
1909	140c. Mond (Christian Oppliger) (*horiz*)	7·00	6·75
1910	190c. Untitled (Flavia Trachsel)	9·50	9·00
1907/1910	Set of 4	23·00	22·00

(Des Raphael Volery. Litho Cartor)

2011 (24 Nov). Christmas. T **605** and similar horiz designs. Multicoloured. Self-adhesive. Die-cut perf 13½.
1911	85c. Type **605**	4·25	4·00
1912	100c. Sleigh carrying presents and decorated tree	5·00	4·75
1913	140c. Chalet, wreath, presents and tree	7·00	6·75
1911/1913	Set of 3	14·50	14·00

 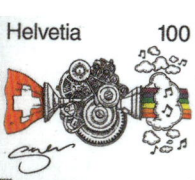

606 Château de Villa, Sierre   **607** Flag in Music out

(Des Christian Hutter. Litho Gutenberg AG, Liechtenstein)

2011 (24 Nov). Stamp Day. Philasierre 2011 Stamp Exhibition. Sheet 70×105 mm. P 13½.
MS1914	**606** 85c. multicoloured	4·50	4·25

(Des Stress. Litho Giesecke & Devrient, Germany)

2011 (24 Nov). Stress (Andres Andrekson) (rapper). P 13½.
1915	607 100c. multicoloured	5·00	4·75

608 Locomotive   **609** Emblem

(Des Raphael Schenker. Litho CDS Testpack Company, Germany)

2012 (8 Mar). Centenary of Jungfrau Railway. P 13½.
1916	608 100c. multicoloured	5·00	4·75

(Des Manuela Pfrunder. Litho and gold foil die-stamped Enschedé)

2012 (8 Mar). 150th Anniversary of Swiss Brass Band Association. P 14½×14.
1917	609 100c. multicoloured	5·00	4·75

610 Beaver   **611** Abstract from Civil Code

(Des Flavia Travaglini. Litho CDS Testpack Company, Germany)

2012 (8 Mar). Fauna. P 13½.
1918	610 100c. multicoloured	5·00	4·75

(Des Demian Conrad. Litho Giesecke & Devrient, Germany)

2012 (8 Mar). Centenary of Swiss Civil Code. P 13½.
1919	611 100c. multicoloured	5·00	4·75

612 St Gallus   **613** Little Tiger, Little Bear and Tigerduck

(Des Massimo Milano. Litho CDS Testpack Company, Germany)

2012 (8 Mar). 1400th Birth Anniversary of St Gallus. P 13½.
1920	612 100c. multicoloured	5·00	4·75

(Des Janosch. Litho Enschedé)

2012 (8 Mar). 80th Birth Anniversary of Janosch (Horst Eckert) (chidren's writer and illustrator). Booklet Stamp. Self-adhesive. Die-cut perf 12.
1921	613 100c. Multicoloured	5·00	4·75

614 Elm Village   **615** *Lycopersicion lycopersicum* (Tomato)

(Des Peider C. Jenny. Litho Cartor)

2012 (8 Mar). World Heritage Site. Martinsloch 'Window' (hole (21 metres high by 18 metres wide) in mountains of Tectonic Areana Sardona). T **614** and similar multicoloured designs. P 14×13½.
1922	100c. Type **614**	5·00	4·75
	a. Horiz strip of 3. Nos. 1922/1924	16·00	

SWITZERLAND 2012

1923	100c. Sunlight through 'window' on 13/14 March or 30 September–1 October (41×36 *mm*)		5·00	4·75
1924	100c. Sunlight through 'window' shining on church tower, Elm (37×36 *mm*)		5·00	4·75
1922/1924 *Set of 3*			13·50	13·00

Nos. 1922/1924 were printed, *se-tenant*, in horizontal strips of three stamps within the sheet, each strip forming a composite design.

(Des Reinhard Fluri. Litho Enschedé)

2012 (8 Mar). Vegetable Flowers. T **615** and similar horiz designs. Multicoloured. Self-adhesive. Die-cut perf 12.

1925	140c. Type **615**	7·00	6·75
1926	180c. *Phaseolus coccineus* (Runner Bean)	9·00	8·50
1927	190c. *Allium cepa* (Onion)	9·50	9·00
1925/1927 *Set of 3*		23·00	22·00

Nos. 1925/1927 were printed in sheets with the surplus paper around the stamps removed.

616 Station Clock (Hans Hilfiker, 1944) and Station Clock Tidied Up

(Des Ursus Wehrli. Litho Giesecke & Devrient, Germany)

2012 (9 May). Art. Tidying up Art, Ursus Wehrli. P 13½.
| 1928 | **616** | 100c. multicoloured | 5·00 | 4·75 |

617 Blood Droplet as Balloon   **618** Mother-in-Law's Visit

(Des Oscar Ribes. Litho Cartor)

2012 (9 May). Blood Donation Campaign. P 13½.
| 1929 | **617** | 100c. multicoloured | 5·00 | 4·75 |

(Des Max Spring. Litho Giesecke & Devrient)

2012 (9 May). Europa. Visit. P 13½.
| 1930 | **618** | 100c. multicoloured | 5·00 | 4·75 |

619 Cabrio Cable Car   **620** Survey

(Des Fredy Trümpi. Litho CDS Testpack Company, Germany)

2012 (9 May). Opening of Staserhorn Cabrio Cable Car. P 13½.
| 1931 | **619** | 100c. multicoloured | 5·00 | 4·75 |

(Des Ricco Meierhofer. Litho Enschedé)

2012 (9 May). Centenary of Cadastral (Official) Surveying. P 14×14½.
| 1932 | **620** | 100c. multicoloured | 5·00 | 4·75 |

621 William Tell with Crossbow   **622** Löwenbrunnen Fountain, Utendorf

(Des Roland Hirter. Litho CDS Testpack Company, Germany)

2012 (9 May). Anniversaries of the *William Tell* Plays at Altdorf and Interlaken. T **621** and similar horiz design. Multicoloured. Self-adhesive. Die-cut perf 13.
| 1933 | 100c. Type **621** (500th Anniversary) | 5·00 | 4·75 |
| 1934 | 100c. Outdoor production of *William Tell* at Interlaken (centenary) | 5·00 | 4·75 |

(Des Bernadette Baltis. Litho)

2012 (9 May). Pro Patria. Small Buildings. T **622** and similar vert designs. Multicoloured. P 13½.

1935	85c. +40c. Type **622**	6·25	6·00
	a. Booklet pane. Nos. 1935×6	39·00	
1936	85c. +40c. Fermes des Troncs' building, Mézières, Vaud	6·25	6·00
1937	100c. +50c. Villa Abendstern Summer House, Wädenswil	7·50	7·25
1938	100c. +50c. Crotti (cold store), Brusio, Poschiavo'	7·50	7·25
	a. Booklet pane. No. 1938×4	31·00	
1935/1938 *Set of 4*		25·00	24·00

623 Butterbur   **624** Hands on Steer Wheel (James Bond)

(Litho Enschedé)

2012 (6 Sept). Franz Gertsch. T **623** and similar vert designs. Multicoloured. P 13.
1939	85c. Type **623**	4·25	4·00
1940	100c. Grasses	5·00	4·75
1941	140c. Cima del Mar	7·00	6·75
1939/1941 *Set of 3*		14·50	14·50

(Litho Cartor)

2012 (6 Sept). Pop Art by Peter Stampfli. T **624** and similar square designs. Multicoloured. P 14×13.
1942	85c. Type **624**	4·25	4·00
1943	100c. Bowler hat (Bond Street)	5·00	4·75
1944	200c. Jelly and cream (Pudding)	10·00	9·50
1942/1944 *Set of 3*		17·00	16·00

625 Brown Long-eared Bat (*Illustration reduced, actual size* 105×70 *mm*)

(Des A. Boog. Litho Gutenberg AG, Liechtenstein)

2012 (6 Sept). Endangered Fauna. Sheet 105×70 mm. P 13½.
| MS1945 | **625** | 100c. multicoloured | 14·00 | 13·50 |

626 Zürich

(Litho Cartor)
2012 (6 Sept). Cities of Switzerland. T **626** and similar horiz designs. Multicoloured. P 13×13½.
1946	100c. Type **626**	3·00	4·75
1947	100c. Geneva	5·00	4·75
1948	100c. Basel	5·00	4·75
1946/1948	Set of 3	13·50	13·00

627 Building on Village Square

(Des Beat Kehrli. Litho Cartor)
2012 (6 Sept). National Stamp Exhibition (NABA), Stans. Sheet 105×70 mm containing T **627** and similar vert design. Multicoloured. P 13.
MS1949 85c.+45c. Type **627**; 85c.+45c. Building on village square (*different*); 100c+55c. Fountain and monument (37×70 *mm*); 100c+55c. Motor glider (67×28 *mm*) .... 24·00 23·00

The stamps of No. **MS**1949 'bleed' to the edge of the sheet, are imperforate on one or two sides depending on position, and together form a composite design.

Nos. 1950/1951 are vacant.

628 Altstätten   **629** Tree-shaped Christmas Lights

(Des Christine Suter and Naima Schalcher. Litho Gutenberg AG, Liechtenstein)
2012 (22 Nov). Stamp Day. Rhine Valley Stamp Exhibition. Sheet 105×70 mm. P 13½×14.
MS1952 **628** 85c. multicoloured .... 4·50 4·25

(Des Paul Bühler. Litho Cartor)
2011 (24 Nov). Christmas. T **629** and similar vert designs (background colour given). Multicoloured. Self-adhesive. Die-cut perf 13½.
1953	85c. Type **629**	4·25	4·00
1954	100c. Star-shaped Christmas lights (green)	5·00	4·75
1955	140c. Arched Christmas lights (blue)	7·00	6·75
1953/1955	Set of 3	14·50	14·00

630 Yakari and Butterfly   **631** Safety Helmets

(Des Derib. Litho Enschedé)
2012 (22 Nov). Yakari (cartoon character created by Derib & Job (Claude de Ribaupierre and André Jobin)). T **630** and similar horiz design. Self-adhesive. Die-cut perf 12.
| 1956 | 100c. Type **630** | 5·00 | 4·75 |
| 1957 | 100c. Yakari riding Little Thunder | 5·00 | 4·75 |

Nos. 1956/1957 were issued both in coils, with the surplus paper around the stamps removed and the designs alternating along the coil, and, each×5, in booklets of ten stamps with the paper around the stamp retained.

(Des Urs Lieber. Litho Cartor)
2013 (7 Mar). 50th Anniversary of Swiss Protection and Support Service. P 13½.
1958 **631** 85c. multicoloured .... 4·25 4·00

632 Legs and 'bfu'   **633** Mountains

(Des René Sager. Litho Cartor)
2013 (7 Mar). 75th Anniversary of Swiss Council for Accident Protection (bfu). P 13½.
1959 **632** 85c. rose-red and new blue .... 4·25 4·00

(Des Fredy Trümpi. Litho Gutenberg AG, Schaan, Liechtenstein)
2013 (7 Mar). 150th Anniversary of Swiss Alpine Club. Sheet 105×70 mm containing T **633** and similar multicoloured designs. P 12×imperf.
MS1960 85c. Type **633**; 100c. Climber (28×70 *mm*); 140c. Hikers (78×28 *mm*); 190c. Doldenhorn mountain hut (28×42 *mm*) .... 21·00 20·00

The stamps of No. **MS**1960 'bleed' to the edge of the sheet, are imperforate on one or two sides depending on position, and together form a composite design.

634 Train on Viaduct   **635** Gottlieb Duttweiler

(Des Marc Weller. Litho Cartor)
2013 (7 Mar). Centenary of Lötschberg Railway. P 13½.
1961 **634** 100c. multicoloured .... 5·00 4·75

(Des Christian Kitzmüller. Litho Giesecke & Devrient, Germany)
2013 (7 Mar). 125th Birth Anniversary of Gottlieb Duttweiler (pioneer grocer). P 13½.
1962 **635** 100c. multicoloured .... 5·00 4·75

636 Saanen Goat Kid and Swiss Mountain Dog Puppy

(Des Brigitte Schärer. Litho Giesecke & Devrient, Germany)
2013 (7 Mar). 500th Anniversary of Integration of Appenzell Ausserrhoden and Appenzell Innerrhoden into Swiss Confederation. P 13½.
1963 **636** 100c. multicoloured .... 5·00 4·75

637 Faces   **638** *Autumn Migration*

(Des Martine Dietrich. Litho Gutenberg AG, Schaan, Luxembourg)

2013 (7 Mar). Faces Switzerland. Photographs of Winners of On-line Competition. P 12.
1964	**637** 100c. multicoloured	5·00	4·75

(Des Martine Dietrich-Chatagny after Ernst Kreidolf. Litho Enschedé)

2013 (7 Mar). 150th Birth Anniversary of Ernst Kreidolf (writer and illustrator). Booklet Stamps. T **638** and similar horiz design. Multicoloured. Self-adhesive. Die-cut 13½.
1965	100c. Type **638**	5·00	4·75
1966	100c. With the Pansies	5·00	4·75

The stamps are peeled directly from the booklet cover.

639 Straw Hat, Strohmuseum, Wohlen   **640** Tribelhorn Electric Three-wheeled Delivery Van

(Des Vito Noto. Litho)

2013 (7 May). Pro Patria. Small Museums. T **639** and similar vert designs. Multicoloured. P 13½.
1967	85c. +40c. Type **639**	6·25	6·00
	a. Booklet pane. Nos. 1967×6	39·00	
1968	85c. +40c. Wax Toad, Museum Fram, Einsiedeln	6·25	6·00
1969	100c. +50c. Wooden Cow with 'Gort' markings, Toggenburger Museum, Lichtensteig	7·50	7·25
1970	100c. +50c. Carpenter's plane, Bagnes Museum, Villette	7·50	7·25
	a. Booklet pane. No. 1970×4	31·00	
1967/1970	Set of 4	25·00	24·00

(Des Peter Hummel. Litho Gutenberg AG, Schaan, Liechtenstein)

2013 (7 May). Europa. Postal Vehicles. T **640** and similar horiz design. Multicoloured. P 13½.
1971	100c. Type **640**	5·00	4·75
1972	100c. Kyburz DXP electric three-wheeled scooter	5·00	4·75

641 White Stork   **642** *They I you he we*

(Des Corinne Oesch and Daniel Hug. Litho Enschedé)

2013 (7 May). White Stork. Action Plan for the White Stork Initiative. Self-adhesive. Die-cut perf 14½×14.
1973	**641** 100c. multicoloured	5·00	4·75

(Des Valentin Carron. Litho Giesecke & Devrient, Germany)

2013 (7 May). Art. Venice Biennale. P 13½.
1974	**642** 100c. multicoloured	5·00	4·75

643 *Capsicum annuum* (Bell Pepper flower)   **644** Team Members

(Des Reinhard Fluri. Litho Enschedé)

2013 (7 May). Vegetable Flowers. T **643** and similar horiz designs. Multicoloured. Self-adhesive. Die-cut perf 12.
1975	130c. Type **643**	6·50	6·25
1976	220c. *Allium porrum* (Leek flowers)	11·00	10·50

Nos. 1975/1976 were printed in sheets with the surplus paper around the stamps removed.

(Des Beat Leuenberger and Jürg Glauser. Gutenberg AG, Schaan, Liechtenstein)

2013 (31 May). Switzerland. Silver Medallists, World Ice Hockey Championships, Stockholm and Helsinki. P 13½.
1977	**644** 100c. multicoloured	5·00	4·75

645 Chicks   **646** The Kiss

(Des Judith Brennwald. Litho Enschedé)

2013 (5 Sept). Farm Animals. T **645** and similar horiz designs. Multicoloured. P 14.
1978	85c. Type **645**	4·25	4·00
1979	100c. Calves	5·00	4·75
1980	140c. Lambs	7·00	6·75
1981	190c. Piglets	9·50	9·00
1978/1981	Set of 4	23·00	22·00

(Des Peyo. Litho Enschedé)

2013 (5 Sept). Comics. *The Smurfs* (characters created by Peyo (Pierre Culliford)). Booklet Stamps. T **646** and similar multicoloured design. Self-adhesive. Die-cut perf 12.
1982	100c. Type **646**	5·00	4·75
1983	100c. Papa Smurf	5·00	4·75

647 Berne   **648** Butterfly and Waterway

(Des Eveline Maio (No. 1984), Lorena Falivene (No. 1985) or Selina Locher (No. 1986). Litho Enschedé)

2013 (5 Sept). Cities of Switzerland. Winning Entries in Design-a-Stamp Competition. T **647** and similar horiz designs. Multicoloured. Self-adhesive. Die-cut perf 14.
1984	100c. Type **647**	5·00	4·75
1985	100c. Buildings on hillside, Lausanne	5·00	4·75
1986	100c. Machinery, technology and leaf outlines against buildings, Winterthur	5·00	4·75
1984/1986	Set of 3	13·50	13·00

(Des Fanchon Cartier and Simon Moser. Litho Gutenberg AG, Liechtenstein)

2013 (5 Sept). Restoration and Rehabilitation of Waterways. T **648** and similar vert designs. Multicoloured. P 13½×14.
1987	100c. Type **648**	5·00	4·75
	a. Strip of 3. Nos. 1987/1989	16·00	
1988	100c. Bird on rock	5·00	4·75
1989	100c. Trout leaping	5·00	4·75
1987/1989	Set of 3	13·50	13·00

Nos. 1987/1989 were printed, *se-tenant*, in horizontal strips of three stamps within the sheet, each strip forming a composite design.

649 Goldvreneli

(Des Martine Dietrich. Litho and gold-foil embossed Cartor)
2013 (5 Sept). Goldvreneli. Sheet 105×70 mm. P 13½.
MS1990 **649** 600c. multicoloured .... 29·00 28·00
No. **MS**1990 was issued, cancelled, as a gift to subscribers, enclosed in a folder.

650 Bell

651 Fox

(Des Martin Eberhard. Litho and embossed Gutenberg AG, Schaan, Liechtenstein)
2013 (14 Nov). Stamp Day. Aarau. Sheet 105×70 mm. P 14.
MS1991 **650** 85c. multicoloured .... 4·50 4·25

(Des Steffy Merz. Litho Enschedé)
2013 (14 Nov). Christmas. T **651** and similar horiz designs. Multicoloured. Self-adhesive. Die-cut perf 14×14½.
1992   85c. Type **651** .... 4·25 4·00
1993   100c. Deer and lantern .... 5·00 4·75
1994   140c. Owl and bauble .... 7·00 6·75
1995   190c. Squirrel and lantern .... 9·50 9·00
1992/1995 Set of 4 .... 23·00 22·00

652 Guitar as Swan

653 Snow-covered Buildings

(Des Polo Hofer. Litho Giesecke & Devrient, Germany)
2013 (14 Nov). Polo Hofer (Urs Hofer) (rock singer). P 13½.
1996   **652** 100c. multicoloured .... 5·00 4·75

(Des Leander Wenger. Litho Enschedé)
2013 (14 Nov). Matter Valley. Sheet 105×70 mm. P 13½×14.
MS1997 **653** 200c. multicoloured .... 9·50 9·00

654 Mount Fuji, Japan

655 Cantharellus cibarius

(Des Stefanie Haberli-Bachmann. Litho Cartor)
2014 (6 Feb). 150th Anniversary of Switzerland–Japan Diplomatic Relations. T **654** and similar vert design. Multicoloured. P 13.
1998   100c. Type **654** .... 5·00 4·75
          a. Pair. Nos. 1998/1999 .... 15·00 14·50
1999   190c. Spring in Swiss mountains .... 9·50 9·00
Nos. 1998/1999 were printed, *se-tenant*, in horizontal pairs within the sheet.

(Des Karin Hänni. Litho Enschedé)
2014 (6 Mar). Fungi. T **655** and similar horiz designs. Multicoloured. P 12.
2000   10c. Type **655** 50 50
          a. Block of 4. Nos. 2000/2003 .... 5·00
2001   15c. *Lactarius lignyotus* 80 75
2002   20c. *Hydnellum caerulcum* .... 1·00 95
2003   50c. *Strobilomyces strobilaceus* .... 2·50 2·50
2000/2003 Set of 4 .... 4·25 4·25
Nos. 2000/2003 were printed in *se-tenant* blocks of four stamps within the sheet, with surplus paper around the stamps removed.

656 Epidote

657 Envelope

(Des Daniel Dreier. Litho and foil die-stamped Cartor)
2014 (6 Mar). International Year of Crystallography. T **656** and similar vert design. Multicoloured. P 13.
2004   85c. Type **656** .... 4·25 4·00
2005   100c. Amethyst .... 5·00 4·75

(Des Barbara Ehrbar. Litho Giesecke & Devrient, Germany)
2014 (6 Mar). 125th Anniversary of Swiss Army Post. P 13½.
2006   **657** 100c. multicoloured .... 5·00 4·75

658 On the Beach

659 Tree Stump, Hiker and Mountains

(Des Beat Sigel. Litho Enschedé)
2014 (6 Mar). Comics. *Fred and Fun* (cartoon created by Beat Sigel). T **658** and similar multicoloured design. Self-adhesive. Die-cut perf 12 (No. 2008) or die-cut (No. 2007).
2007   100c. Type **658** .... 5·00 4·75
2008   100c. Fred (30×25 *mm*) .... 5·00 4·75
Nos. 2007/2008 were issued both in coils, with the surplus paper around the stamps removed and the designs alternating along the coil, and in booklets of nine stamps, No. 2007 and No. 2008×8 with the paper around the stamp retained.

SWITZERLAND 2014

(Des Andreas Panzer. Litho Gutenberg AG, Liechtenstein)

2014 (6 Mar). Centenary of Swiss National Park. T **659** and similar multicoloured designs. P 13½×14.

2009	100c. Type **659**	5·00	4·75
	a. Strip of 3. Nos. 2009/2011	16·00	
2010	100c. Raptor in flight and Piz Nair (32×34 mm)	5·00	4·75
2011	100c. Conifer and cloud-shrouded mountains (35×34 mm)	5·00	4·75
2009/2011	Set of 3	13·50	13·00

Nos. 2009/2011 were printed, *se-tenant*, in horizontal strips of three stamps within the sheet, each strip forming a composite design.

660 McDonnell Douglas F/A-18 Hornet

661 Basel Larval Clown Mask, Ortsmuseum, Binningen

(Des Fredy Trümpi. Litho Giesecke & Devrient, Germany)

2014 (6 Mar). Centenary of Swiss Airforce. T **660** and similar horiz design. Multicoloured. P 13½.

2012	100c. Type **660**	5·00	4·75
2013	140c. Northrop F-5 Tiger	7·00	6·75

(Des Vito Noto. Litho)

2014 (8 May). Pro Patria. Small Museums. T **661** and similar vert designs. Multicoloured. P 14×14½.

2014	85c. +40c. Type **661**	6·25	6·00
	a. Booklet pane. Nos. 2014×6	39·00	
2015	85c. +40c. Marseille roof tile, Museo del Malcantone, Curio	6·25	6·00
2016	100c. +50c. Apprentice watch, Mueum Hôtel-Dieu, Porrentruy	7·50	7·25
	a. Booklet pane. No. 2016×4	31·00	
2017	100c. +50c. Reconstructed medieval hurdy gurdy, Musical Instrument Collection, Willisau	7·50	7·25
2014/2017	Set of 4	25·00	24·00

Nos. 2014 and 2016 were produced both in sheets and, 2014×6, and 2016×4, in booklets of ten stamps.

662 Symbols of Renewable Energy

663 Carriage

(Des Ricco Meierhofer. Litho Giesecke & Devrient, Germany)

2014 (8 May). Renewable Energy. P 13½.
2018 **662** 100c. multicoloured .... 5·00 4·75

(Des Susanne Perron. Litho Bagel Security Print, Düsseldorf)

2014 (8 May). 125th Birth Anniversary of Pilatus Cogwheel Railway. P 13×14.
2019 **663** 100c. multicoloured .... 5·00 4·75

664 Florian Klauser, Basketball Player

665 Dulcimer

(Des Jenny Leibundgut. Litho Cartor)

2014 (8 May). Special Olympics National Games. P 13½.
2020 **664** 100c. multicoloured .... 5·00 4·75

(Des Marc Weller. Litho Giesecke & Devrient, Germany)

2014 (8 May). Europa. Musical Instruments. T **665** and similar horiz design. Multicoloured. P 13½.

2021	100c. Type **665**	5·00	4·75
	a. Pair. Nos. 2021/2022	10·50	9·75
2022	100c. Alphorn	5·00	4·75

Nos. 2021/2022 were printed, *se-tenant*, in horizontal pairs within the sheet.

666 St Gallen

667 Zytglogge, Bern

(Des Shana Messerli (No. 2023), Jaira Peyer (No. 2024) or Amaru Eslava (No. 2025). Litho Cartor)

2014 (8 May). Cities of Switzerland. Winning Entries in Design-a-Stamp Competition. T **666** and similar horiz designs. Multicoloured. Self-adhesive. Die-cut perf 13½.

2023	100c. Type **666**	5·00	4·75
2024	100c. Selfie, Lucerne	5·00	4·75
2025	100c. Mountain, diver and boat, Lugano	5·00	4·75
2023/2025	Set of 3	13·50	13·00

(Des Kaspar Eigensatz. Enschedé)

2014 (21 May). Tower Clocks. Bicentenary of Switzerland–Russia Diplomatic Relations. T **667** and similar square design. Multicoloured. P 13×13½.

2026	100c. Type **667**	5·00	4·75
2027	140c. Kazansky Station Clock, Moscow	7·00	6·75

Stamps of a similar design were issued by Russia.

668 Weasel

669 Symbols of Painting and Plastering

(Des Naomi Giewald. Litho Cartor)

2014 (4 Sept). Fauna. T **668** and similar horiz designs. Multicoloured. P 13½.

2028	85c. Type **668**	4·25	4·00
2029	100c. Marmot	5·00	4·75
2030	140c. Spotted Nutcracker	7·00	6·75
2031	190c. Red Deer	9·50	9·00
2028/2031	Set of 4	23·00	22·00

(Des Urs Lieber. Litho Giesecke & Devrient, Germany)

2014 (4 Sept). Swiss Skills Bern 2014 Design-a-Stamp Competition. Swiss Association of Painters and Plasterers. P 13½.
2032 **669** 100c. multicoloured .... 5·00 4·75

670 Garfield eating Chocolate

671 Coach and Route

(Litho Enschedé)

2014 (4 Sept). Comics. *Garfield* (cartoon created by Jim Davis). Booklet Stamps. T **670** and similar multicoloured design. Self-adhesive. Die-cut perf 12.

2033	100c. Type **670**	5·00	4·75
2034	100c. Garfiled and Odie eating fondue	5·00	4·75

Nos. 2033/2034 were issued in booklets of ten stamps.

(Des Beat Leuenberger. Litho Cartor)
2014 (4 Sept). Lindau via Fussach to Milan Courier. P 13½.
2035 **671** 140c. multicoloured .... 7·00 6·75

672 Record

673 Alpine Chalet

(Des Thomas Rathgeb. Litho Enschedé)
2014 (4 Sept). Swiss Music. Sheet 168×137 mm. Self-adhesive. Die-cut rouletting.
MS2036 **672** 500c. multicoloured .... 25·00 24·00
No. **MS**2036 was printed on wood-free cardboard, cut around in the shape of a record player and, the stamp when removed, would play Swiss brass band music on an appropriate turntable.

(Des Daniel Fuchs. Litho Gutenberg AG,
Schaan, Liechtenstein)
2014 (6 Nov). Swiss Landscapes. Emmental. Sheet 105×70 mm. P 12.
MS2037 **673** 200c. multicoloured .... 10·50 10·00

674 Nativity Crib and Decorations

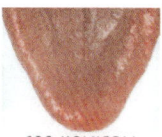
675 Tongues

(Des Dominique Rossier. Litho Cartor)
2014 (13 Nov). Christmas. T **674** and similar horiz designs. Multicoloured. Self-adhesive. Die-cut perf 13½.
2038 85c. Type **674** .... 4·25 4·00
2039 100c. Santa and stockings .... 5·00 4·75
2040 140c. Candles and dining table .... 7·00 6·75
2041 190c. Cookies and food cooking in kitchen .... 9·50 9·00
2038/2041 Set of 4 .... 23·00 22·00

(Des Pipilotti Rist. Litho Cartor)
2014 (13 Nov). The Senses. Taste. P 12½×13.
2042 **675** 100c. multicoloured .... 5·00 4·75

676 Horse Stud

(Des Beatrice Zehnder. Litho Gutenberg AG,
Schaan, Liechtenstein)
2014 (13 Nov). Stamp Day. Saignelégier. Sheet 105×70 mm. P 14×13½.
MS2043 **676** 100c.+50c. multicoloured .... 8·00 7·50

677 Ammonite (*Illustration reduced, actual size 105×70 mm*)

(Des Christian Kitzmüller. Litho and embossed Gutenberg
AG, Schaan, Liechtenstein)
2015 (5 Mar). Ammonite. Sheet 105×70 mm. P 14.
MS2044 **677** 200c. multicoloured .... 10·50 10·00

678 Dalmatian Dog

(Des André Seiffert. Litho Enschedé)
2015 (5 Mar). Pets. T **678** and similar horiz designs. Multicoloured. Self-adhesive. Die-cut perf 14.
2045 85c. Type **678** .... 4·25 4·00
2046 100c. Cat .... 5·00 4·75
2047 140c. Rabbit .... 7·00 6·75
2048 190c. Hamster .... 9·50 9·00
2045/2048 Set of 4 .... 23·00 22·00

679 Martinsberg Community Centre Stairs, Baden and Roof Vault Murals Convent of St John, Müstair

680 Symbols of Finance

(Des Stephanie Häberli-Bachmann. Litho Cartor)
2015 (5 Mar). Centenary of Swiss Federal Commission for Monument Preservation (FCMP). P 13½.
2049 **679** 100c. multicoloured .... 5·00 4·75

(Des Stephan Kuhn. Litho Cartor)
2015 (5 Mar). Centenary of the Swiss Federal Tax Administration (FTA). P 13½.
2050 **680** 100c. multicoloured .... 5·00 4·75

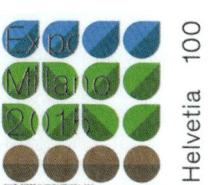
681 Emblem

2015 (5 Mar). Expo Milan. Feeding the Planet, Energy for Life. P 13.
2051 **681** 100c. multicoloured .... 5·00 4·75

SWITZERLAND 2015

682 Marksmen at Morgarten Shooting Championships
683 Rhine Falls

(Des Rudolf Mirer. Litho Cartor)

2015 (5 Mar). Historical Events. T **682** and similar horiz design. Multicoloured. P 13½.
2052	100c. Type **682**	5·00	4·75
2053	100c. Bataille de Marignan, 16th-century tableau	5·00	4·75

(Des Robert Bösch. Litho Cartor)

2015 (5 Mar). Swiss Landscapes. Rhine Falls. T **683** and similar multicoloured designs. P 14.
2054	100c. Type **683**	5·00	4·75
	a. Horiz strip of 3. Nos. 2054/2056	16·00	
2055	100c. Rhine Falls (centre) (35×36 mm)	5·00	4·75
2056	100c. Rhine Falls (right) (32×36 mm)	5·00	4·75
2054/2056 *Set of 3*		13·50	13·00

Nos. 2054/2056 were printed, *se-tenant*, in horizontal strips of three stamps, each strip forming a composite design of the falls.

 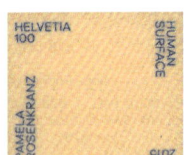

684 Ruins
685 Skin

(Des Christian Stuker. Litho Cartor)

2015 (5 Mar). 1500th Anniversary of Abbey of Saint-Maurice. T **684** and similar square designs. Multicoloured. P 13½.
2057	100c. Type **684**	5·00	4·75
	a. Pair. Nos. 2057/2058	10·50	9·75
2058	100c. Reliquary	5·00	4·75
2059	100c. Manuscript	5·00	4·75
	a. Pair. Nos. 2059/2060	10·50	9·75
2060	100c. Stained glass window	5·00	4·75
2057/2060 *Set of 4*		18·00	17·00

Nos. 2057/2058 and 2059/2060, respectively, were printed, *se-tenant*, in horizontal pairs.

(Des Pamela Rosenkranz. Litho Cartor)

2015 (7 May). Art. Venice Biennale. Flocked paper. P 13½.
2061	**685**	100c. multicoloured	5·00	4·75

The surface of No. 2061 is textured to represent human skin. It is reported that variations of this design exist.

686 Families and Mountains
687 Trike

(Des Theresia Nuber. Litho Gutenberg AG, Schaan, Liechtenstein)

2015 (7 May). 75th Anniversary of Swiss Sponsorship for Mountain Communities. P 13½.
2062	**686**	100c. multicoloured	5·00	4·75

(Des Manuela Weisskopf. Litho Gutenberg AG, Schaan, Liechtenstein)

2015 (7 May). Europa. Old Toys. T **687** and similar horiz design. Multicoloured. P 13½.
2063	100c. Type **687**	5·00	4·75
	a. Pair. Nos. 2063/2064	10·50	9·75
2064	100c. Duck-shaped rocking chair	5·00	4·75

688 Geneva
689 Tobacco Pouch with Brass Embellishments, Appenzell

(Des Tessa Gerster. Litho Cartor)

2015 (7 May). Bicentenary of Geneva, Neuchâtel and Valais joining Swiss Confederation. T **688** and similar horiz designs showing canton emblems. Multicoloured. P 13½.
2065	100c. Type **688**	5·00	4·75
2066	100c. Neuchâtel	5·00	4·75
2067	100c. Valais	5·00	4·75
2065/2067 *Set of 3*		13·50	13·00

(Des Vito Noto. Litho Enschedé)

2015 (7 May). Pro Patria. Small Museums. T **689** and similar horiz designs. Multicoloured. P 14×14½.
2068	85c. +40c Type **689**	6·25	6·00
2069	85c. +40c Wine barrel, Vine and Wine Museum, Aigle	6·25	6·00
	a. Booklet pane. Nos. 2069×6	39·00	
2070	100c. +50c Disc brooch with glass and filigree ornamentation, Frauenfeld	7·50	7·25
	a. Booklet pane. Nos. 2070×4	31·00	
2071	100c. +50c 18th-century carved butter board, Saanen Museum of the Countryside	7·50	7·25
2068/2071 *Set of 4*		25·00	24·00

Nos. 2069 and 2070 were produced both in sheets and, 2069×6, and 2070×4, in booklets of ten stamps.

690 Pic Pic, 1906
691 Rose

(Des Vito Noto. Litho Enschedé)

2015 (3 Sept). Historic Swiss Cars. T **690** and similar horiz designs showing early vehicles. Multicoloured. Self-adhesive. Die-cut perf 13½.
2072	85c. Type **690**	4·25	4·00
2073	100c. Martini, 1897	5·00	4·75
2074	140c. Tribelhorn, 1902	7·00	6·75
2075	190c. Fischer, 1908	9·50	9·00
2072/2075 *Set of 4*		23·00	22·00

(Des Julia Reichle and Martina Pelosi. Litho Enschedé)

2015 (3 Sept). Greetings Stamps. Winning designs in Design-a-Stamp Competition. T **691** and similar horiz designs showing symbols of greetings. Multicoloured. Self-adhesive. Die-cut perf 12.
2076	85c. Type **691**	4·25	4·00
2077	85c. Snail shell	4·25	4·00
2078	100c. Ladybird	5·00	4·75
2079	100c. Quill pen	5·00	4·75
2076/2079 *Set of 4*		17·00	16·00

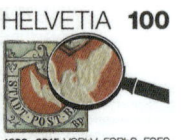 

692 Stamp and Magnifier
693 Marsupilami

(Des Kaspar Eigensatz. Litho Cartor)

2015 (3 Sept). 125th Anniversary of Union of Swiss Philatelic Societies (USPS). Multicoloured. P 13½.
2080	**692**	100c. multicoloured	5·00	4·75

(Litho Enschedé)

2015 (3 Sept). Comics. *Marsupilami* (cartoon created by Dargaud and Lombard). Booklet Stamps. T **693** and similar design. Multicoloured. Self-adhesive. Die-cut perf 13.
2081	100c. Type **693**	5·00	4·75

2015 SWITZERLAND

| 2082 | 100c. Marsupilami, sticking his tongue out..... | 5·00 | 4·75 |

Nos. 2081/2082, each×5 were issued in booklets of ten stamps.

694 Bundle of franked envelopes

695 Circular Viking design scarf buckle (Åland)

(Des Müller Lütolf. Litho Cartor)

2015 (3 Sept). 175th Anniversary of First Postage Stamp (Penny Black). Horiz design showing first stamp. P 13½.
| 2083 | **694** | 100c. Multicoloured... | 5·00 | 4·75 |

(Des Celia Mattsson. Litho and embossed Cartor)

2015 (3 Sept). Traditional Silver Jewellery. T **695** and similar design. Multicoloured. P 13.
| 2084 | | 100c. Type **695** .... | 5·00 | 4·75 |
| 2085 | | 140c. Bernese flower-shaped brooch (Switzerland) .... | 7·00 | 6·75 |

Stamps of a similar design were issued by Åland Islands.

696 DivertMento

(Des Kaspar Eisensatz. Litho Cartor)

2015 (12 Nov). DivertiMento (Comedians Jonny Fischer and Manu Burkart). P 14.
| 2086 | **696** | 50c. multicoloured... | 2·50 | 2·40 |

No. 2086 was printed, *se-tenant*, in blocks of four stamps within the sheet, each block forming a composite design.
No. 2086 was perforated in a semi-circle contained within an outer, perforated, diamond-shape.

697 Highway Viaduct over Lake Gruyère   **698** Presents

(Des Michèle Berri. Litho Gutenberg AG, Schaan, Liechtenstein)

2015 (12 Nov). Stamp Day. Bulle. Sheet 125×70 mm containing T **697** and similar multicoloured design. P 14.
| MS2087 | 50c.+25c.×2, Type **697**; Gibloux Radio Tower (36×40 *mm*)... | 7·75 | 7·50 |

(Des Bea Würgler. Litho Cartor)

2015 (12 Nov). Christmas. T **698** and similar vert designs showing snow globes. Multicoloured. Self-adhesive. Die-cut perf 13½.
2088		85c. Type **698**	4·25	4·00
2089		100c. Penguin and Christmas tree...................	5·00	4·75
2090		140c. Baubles and star....................................	7·00	6·75
2091		190c. Candles and Holly	9·50	9·00
2088/2091		Set of 4...	23·00	22·00

699 Lavaux   **700** Marie Heim-Vögtlin

(Des Marco Trüeb. Litho Cartor)

2016 (3 Mar). 75th Anniversary of Swiss Merchant Fleet. T **699** and similar horiz designs showing ships. Multicoloured. P 13½.
2092		85c. Type **699**	4·25	4·00
2093		100c. *Lugano*..	5·00	4·75
2094		150c. *Lausanne*	7·50	7·25
2095		200c. *Stockhorn*	10·00	9·50
2092/2095		Set of 4	24·00	23·00

(Des Daniel Steffen. Litho Cartor)

2016 (3 Mar). Death Centenary of Marie Heim-Vögtlin (first female Swiss physician with her own practice). P 13½.
| 2096 | **700** | 100c. multicoloured... | 5·00 | 4·75 |

701 Henri Nestlé   **702** Mother panicking

(Des Christian Stuker. Litho Enschedé)

2016 (3 Mar). 150th Anniversary of Nestlé Company. Henri Nestlé Commemoration. Self-adhesive. Die-cut perf 14×14½.
| 2097 | **701** | 100c. grey-black and greenish yellow....... | 5·00 | 4·75 |

(Des Wili Spirig. Litho Bagel Security Print)

2016 (3 Mar). 50th Anniversary of Tox Info Suisse 145 (24 hour poison information). P 14×13.
| 2098 | **702** | 100c. multicoloured... | 5·00 | 4·75 |

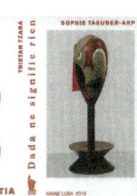

703 People   **704** Medical Personnel and Patients

(Des Tom Künzli. Litho Enschedé)

2016 (3 Mar). Centenary of Organisation of Swiss Living Abroad (ASO). P 13½.
| 2099 | **703** | 100c. multicoloured... | 5·00 | 4·75 |

(Des Unikum Graphic Design. Litho Cartor)

2016 (3 Mar). 150th Anniversary of Swiss Red Cross. P 13½.
| 2100 | **704** | 100c. multicoloured... | 5·00 | 4·75 |

705 Molly Monster   **706** Portrait of Jean Arp (Sophie Taeuber-Arp)

(Des Derib. Litho Enschedé)

2016 (3 Mar). Comics. Molly Monster (cartoon character created by Ted Sieger). T **705** and similar horiz designs. Multicoloured. Self-adhesive. Die-cut perf 12.
| 2101 | | 100c. Type **705** .... | 5·00 | 4·75 |
| 2102 | | 100c. Molly Moster riding in cable car............. | 5·00 | 4·75 |

Nos. 2101/2102 were issued, each×5, in booklets of ten stamps.

(Des Marie Lusa. Litho Cartor)

2016 (3 Mar). Centenary of the DADA Movement in Art. T **706** and similar vert design. Multicoloured. P 13½.
| 2103 | | 100c. Type **706** .... | 5·00 | 4·75 |
| 2104 | | 100c. *Hugo Ball in Cubist Costume* (Hugo Ball) | 5·00 | 4·75 |

707 Waterfowl and Swans, Säntis and Romanshorn **708** Tawny Owl

(Des Wemako Kommunikation. Litho Cartor)

2016 (12 May). Lake Constance. T **707** and similar square designs. Multicoloured. P 14½.
2105	85c. Type **707**		4·25	4·00
	a. Strip of 3. Nos. 2105/2107		13·50	
2106	85c. Feet on jetty, Obersee		4·25	4·00
2107	85c. Reeds and lakeside houses, Untersee and Ermatingen		4·25	4·00
2105/2107 Set of 3			11·50	11·00

Nos. 2105/2107 were printed, *se-tenant*, in horizontal strips of three stamps within the sheet, each strip forming a composite design of Lake Constance.

(Des Sonja Burger. Litho and varnish Cartor)

2016 (12 May). Fauna. Nocturnal Animals. T **708** and similar horiz designs. Multicoloured. P 13½.
2108	85c. Type **708**	4·25	4·00
2109	100c. Dormouse	5·00	4·75
2110	150c. Glowworm	7·50	7·25
2111	200c. Hedgehog	10·00	9·50
2108/2111 Set of 4		24·00	23·00

709 Burg Zug **710** Wrestlers

(Des Angelo Boog. Litho Cartor)

2016 (12 May). Pro Patria. Fortresses and Castles of Switzerland. T **709** and similar horiz designs. Multicoloured. P 13½.
2112	85c. +40c. Type **709**	6·25	6·00
	a. Booklet pane. No. 2112×4 and 2113×6	75·00	
2113	100c. +50c. Schloss Neu-Bechburg	7·50	7·25

No. 2112 was issued both in sheets and in booklets of ten stamps (with No. 2113).

(Des Beat Leuenberger and Jürg Glauser. Litho Enschedé)

2016 (12 May). Swiss Wrestling and Alpine Games Festival, Estavayer-le-Lac. P 13½.
2114	**710**	100c. multicoloured	5·00	4·75

711 Mountains **712** Roller painting Contaminated Landscape Green

(Des Vaudeville Studio. Litho, varnish and powdered stone Cartor)

2016 (12 May). Opening of the Gotthard Railway Tunnel. T **711** and similar square design. Multicoloured. P 14.
2115	100c. Type **711**	5·00	4·75
	a. Pair. Nos. 2115/2116, plus label	10·50	9·75
2116	100c. Sunshine on snowy valley	5·00	4·75

Nos. 2115/2116 were printed, *se-tenant*, in horizontal strips of two stamps surrounding a central illustrated label the whole forming a composite design of mountain range. The strip, No. 2115a, was printed using real Gotthard rock ground into dust.

(Des Doxia Sergidou (No. 2117) or Nicola Carpi and Dina Christ (No. 2118). Litho Giesecke & Devrient GmbH, Security Ptg, Leipzig)

2016 (12 May). Europa. Think Green. T **712** and similar horiz design. Multicoloured. P 13½.
2117		100c. Type **712**	5·00	4·75
		a. Pair. Nos. 2117/2118	10·50	9·75
2118		100c. Head of leaves ('Think Green')	5·00	4·75

Nos. 2117/2118 were printed, *se-tenant*, in horizontal pairs within the sheet.

713 Solar Impulse

(Des Beat Leuenberger and Jürg Glauser)

2016 (26 July). *Solar Impulse* (long-range experimental solar-powered aircraft). P 13×13½.
2119	**713**	100c. multicoloured	5·00	4·75

714 Brig Railway Station **715** Aerogramme and Aircraft

(Des Marc Weller. Litho Enschedé)

2016 (8 Sept). Railway Stations. T **714** and similar horiz designs. Multicoloured. Self-adhesive. Die-cut perf 12.
2120	85c. Type **714**	4·25	4·00
	a. Block of 4. Nos. 2120/2123	28·00	
2121	100c. Lucerne	5·00	4·75
2122	150c. Bellinzona	7·50	7·25
2123	200c. Geneva	10·00	9·50
2120/2123 Set of 4		24·00	23·00

Nos. 2120/2123 were printed in blocks of four within the sheet, with the surplus paper around the stamp removed.
Nos. 2120/2121, respectively, were also printed in booklets of ten stamps with the surplus paper retained.
No. 2121 was printed with a label inscribed 'PRIORITY' attached at foot.

(Des Fredy Trümpi. Litho Gutenberg AG, Schaan, Liechtenstein)

2016 (8 Sept). Aerophilately Day. P 13½.
2124	**715**	100c. multicoloured	5·00	4·75

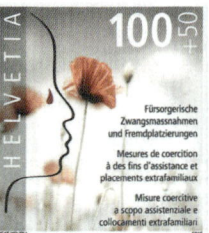

716 Flower **717** Symbols of Victims

(Des Martine Dietrich. Litho and laser cutting Enschedé)

2016 (8 Sept). Summer. Sheet 105×70 mm containing T **716** and similar multicoloured design. P 13½.
MS2125	100c.×2, Type **716**; Butterfly (78×44 *mm*)	10·50 9·75

The stamps of No. **MS**2125 were laser cut throughout the designs.

(Des Beat Kehrli. Litho Cartor)

2016 (8 Sept). Compulsory Social Measures and Forced Fostering Victims Awareness Campaign. P 13×13½.
2126	**717**	100c. +50c. multicoloured	7·50	7·25

2016 SWITZERLAND

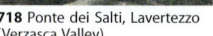

718 Ponte dei Salti, Lavertezzo (Verzasca Valley)
719 Oberaargau

(Des Kaspar Eigensatz. Litho Enschedé)

2016 (8 Sept). Tourism. Sheet 105×70 mm. P 13½×14.
MS2127 **718** 200c. multicoloured .... 10·50   9·75

(Litho Enschedé)

2016 (17 Nov). Stamp Day. Oberaargau. Sheet 125×70 mm containing T **719** and similar design. Multicoloured. P 14.
MS2128 50c.+25c.×2, Type **719**; Water meadow flowers .... 7·75   7·50

720 Christmas Tree   **721** Yello

(Des Ludek Martschini. Litho Cartor)

2016 (17 Nov). Christmas. T **720** and similar horiz designs. Self-adhesive. Die-cut perf 13½.
2129	85c. emerald and azure	4·25	4·00
	a. Block of 4. Nos. 2129/2132	28·00	
2130	100c. new blue and azure	5·00	4·75
2131	150c. carmine and azure	7·50	7·25
2132	200c. yellow-brown and azure	10·00	9·50
2129/2132 Set of 4		24·00	23·00

Designs: 85c. T **720**; 100c. Snowman; 150c. Angel; 200c. Sledge. Nos. 2129/2132 were printed with the surplus paper around the stamps removed.

(Des Yello. Litho Cartor)

2016 (17 Nov). Yello (Dieter Meier and Boris Blank) (electronic music band). P 13½.
2133 **721** 100c. multicoloured .... 5·00   4·75

722 Swiss Mountains (Lacs de Fenêtre)   **723** Basel Railway Station

(Des Brigit Herrmann and Michel Roggo (No. 2134) or Brigit Herrmann (No. 2135). Litho Gutenberg AG, Schaan)

2016 (17 Nov). Switzerland–Dominican Republic Friendship. Landscapes. T **722** and similar horiz design. Multicoloured. P 13½.
2134	100c. Type **722**	5·00	4·75
	a. Pair. Nos. 2134/2135	10·50	9·75
2135	100c. Beach, Dominican Republic (Playa Bavaro)	5·00	4·75

Nos. 2134/2135 were printed, *se-tenant*, in horizontal pairs within the sheet.

(Des Marc Weller. Litho Cartor)

2016 (17 Nov). Railway Stations. Self-adhesive. Die-cut perf 12.
2136 **723** 530c. multicoloured .... 27·00 25·00

No. 2136 was printed with the surplus paper around the stamp removed.

724 Emblem   **725** Young Otter

(Des Jenny Leibundgut. Litho Enschedé)

2017 (2 Mar). 50th Anniversary of Swiss Heart Foundation. P 13½.
2137 **724** 85c. multicoloured .... 4·25   4·00

(Des Simon Hofer. Litho Cartor)

2017 (2 Mar). Young Animals. T **725** and similar horiz designs. Multicoloured. Self-adhesive. Die-cut perf 13½.
2138	85c. Type **725**	4·25	4·00
2139	100c. Lynx kitten	5·00	4·75
2140	150c. Wolf cub	7·50	7·25
2141	200c. Bear cub	10·00	9·50
2138/2141 Set of 4		24·00	23·00

726 Niklaus von Flüe   **727** Making 'Anna' Glass

(Des Markus Bucher. Litho Cartor)

2017 (2 Mar). 600th Birth Anniversary of Niklaus von Flüe (Brother Klaus) (farmer, councillor, judge, mystic and patron saint of Switzerland). P 13½.
2142 **726** 100c. multicoloured .... 5·00   4·75

(Des Simon Hauser and David Schwarz. Litho and varnish Enschedé)

2017 (2 Mar). Bicentenary of Hergiswil Glass Craftsmanship. P 13½.
2143 **727** 100c. multicoloured .... 5·00   4·75

728 Early Bicycle (the Draisine)   **729** Cable Car

(Des Vaudeville Studios. Litho Cartor)

2017 (2 Mar). Bicentenary of the Bicycle. T **728** and similar horiz design. Black. P 13½×14.
2144	100c. Type **728**	5·00	4·75
2145	100c. Modern drop-handlebars cycle	5·00	4·75

(Des Unikum Graphic Design. Litho Enschedé)

2017 (2 Mar). 50th Anniversary of Schilthorn (Piz Gloria) Cable Car and Revolving Restaurant. T **729** and similar horiz design. Multicoloured. P 14×14½.
2146	100c. Type **729**	5·00	4·75
2147	100c. Revolving restaurant	5·00	4·75

730 Selun and Frümsel Mountain Peaks   **731** Visconteo Castle

(Des Bernadette Baltis)

2017 (11 May). Churfirsten Mountain Range. T **730** and similar horiz designs. Multicoloured. P 13½.
2148	85c. Type **730**	4·25	4·00
	a. Strip of 4. Nos. 2148/2151	18·00	
2149	85c. Brisi and Zuestoll peaks	4·25	4·00
2150	85c. Schibenstoll and Hindrrugg peaks	4·25	4·00
2151	85c. Chäserrugg	4·25	4·00
2148/2151 *Set of 4*		15·00	14·50

Nos. 2148/2151 were printed, *se-tenant*, in horizontal strips of four stamps within the sheet, each strip forming a composite design.

(Des Angelo Boog. Litho Cartor)

2017 (11 May). Pro Patria. Fortresses and Castles of Switzerland. T **731** and similar horiz designs. Multicoloured. P 13½.
2152	85c. +40c. Type **731**	6·25	6·00
	a. Booklet pane. No. 2152×4 and No. 2153×6	75·00	
2153	100c. +50c. Schloss Oberhofen	7·50	7·25

No. 2152 was issued both in sheets and in booklets of ten stamps (with No. 2153).

732 Leopard   **733** Swiss Locomotive and Machine Works Engine Number 5 (1891–1892)

(Des Jannuzzi Smith. Litho Cartor)

2017 (11 May). 70th Anniversary of Festival del Film, Locarno. P 13½.
2154	**732** 100c. multicoloured	5·00	4·75

(Des Arnold & Braun Grafik Design. Litho Enschedé)

2017 (11 May). 125th Anniversary of Brienz Rothorn Railway. P 14×13½.
2155	**733** 100c. multicoloured	5·00	4·75

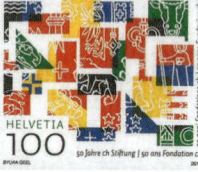 

734 Symbols of Swiss Cantons   **735** Old and Young Communicating

(Des Sylvia Geel. Litho Cartor)

2017 (11 May). 50th Anniversary of 'CH' Foundation for Federal Co-operation. P 13½.
2156	**734** 100c. multicoloured	5·00	4·75

(Des Team Dänzer. Litho Bagel Security Print)

2017 (11 May). Centenary of Pro Senectute Foundation (supporting elderly people). P 13½.
2157	**735** 100c. +50c. multicoloured	7·50	7·25

736 Symbols of Festival   **737** Sasso Corbaro and Montebello Castles

(Des Mansing Tang. Litho Cartor)

2017 (11 May). Unspunnen (traditional celebration of Swiss mountain life). P 13½.
2158	**736** 100c. multicoloured	5·00	4·75

(Des Bernadette Baltis. Litho Gutenberg AG)

2017 (11 May). Europa. Castles. T **712** and similar horiz design. Multicoloured. P 13½.
2159	100c. Type **737**	5·00	4·75
	a. Pair. Nos. 2159/2160	10·50	9·75
2160	100c. Castelgrande	5·00	4·75

Nos. 2159/2160 were printed, *se-tenant*, in horizontal pairs within the sheet.

738 10-centime Zweisimmen Postal Stationery Envelope cancelled on the First Issue Date

(Des Raphael Schenke. Litho Cartor)

2017 (7 Sept). 150th Anniversary of Tübli Letters. Sheet 105×70 mm. P 14.
MS2161	**738** 85c. multicoloured	4·50	4·25

739 Emoji   **740** Selfie

(Des Kaspar Eigensatz. Litho Enschede)

2017 (7 Sept). Emoji. Booklet Stamps. T **739** and similar horiz design. Multicoloured. Self-adhesive. Die-cut perf 12.
2162	85c. Type **739**	4·25	4·00
2163	100c. Sense of Cool Emoji	5·00	4·75

(Des Nicole Jara Vizcardo. Litho and silver foil Cartor)

2017 (7 Sept). Letters v Email. The Selfie Stamp. P 13½.
2164	**740** 100c. multicoloured	5·00	4·75

No. 2160 has a reflective surface, which acts as mirror.

741 Creux de Van

(Des Thal Graphics (from a photograph by Roland Gerth). Litho Cartor)

2017 (7 Sept). Creux du Van (rock formation). Sheet 105×70 mm. P 13½.
MS2165	**741** 100c. multicoloured	5·25	5·00

742 Saint Sebastian (Roman soldier and Christian martyr)   **743** Postcard arriving in Swiss Mountains

(Des Raphael Volery. Litho Cartor)

2017 (7 Sept). 500th Anniversary of Bern Cathedral Vaulted Ceiling. T **742** and similar horiz design. Multicoloured. P 13½.
2166	100c. Type **742**	5·00	4·75
2167	100c. Centre of the reticulated vaulted ceiling, with Bern's Coat of Arms	5·00	4·75

(Des Max Spring. Litho Giesecke & Devrient GmbH, Leipzig)

2017 (7 Sept). Postcrossing (people from many countries sending each other traditional postcards). T **743** and similar horiz designs. Multicoloured. P 13½.

2168	100c. Type **743**		5·00	4·75
2169	150c. Postcard with Swiss Cow arriving in Europe		7·50	7·25
2170	200c. Postcard with Swiss Alpenhorn arriving in Asia		10·00	9·50
2168/2170 Set of 3			20·00	19·00

744 Appenzell

(Des Marc Weller. Litho Cartor)

2017 (7 Sept). Railway Stations. T **744** and similar horiz designs. Multicoloured. Self-adhesive. Die-cut perf 12.

2171	110c. Type **744**		5·50	5·25
	a. Block of 4. Nos. 2171/2174			
2172	130c. Zug		6·50	6·25
2173	140c. Interlaken Ost		7·00	6·75
2174	180c. Scuol-Tarasp (Rhaetian Railway Station)		9·00	8·75
2171/2174 Set of 4			25·00	24·00

Nos. 2171/2174 were printed with the surplus paper around the stamp removed.

745 Smelling a Quince Fruit

(Des Jwan Reber. Litho Gutenberg AG)

2017 (7 Sept). The Scent of Quince. Swiss Fruit of the Year. Sheet 105×70 mm. P 12.

MS2175 **745** 200c. multicoloured			10·50	9·75

The stamp of No. **MS**2175 is impregnated with the scent of Quince which is released when the stamp is rubbed.

746 Sainte-Croix and Lake Neuchâtel **747** Snowman and Sledge (*Silent Night*)

(Des Tessa Gerster. Litho Cartor)

2017 (16 Nov). Stamp Day. Sainte-Croix. Sheet 125×35 mm containing T **746** and similar horiz design. Multicoloured. P 14×14½.

MS2176 50c.+25c.×2, Type **746**; Music box mechanism			7·75	7·50

(Des Boris Pilleri. Litho Enschedé)

2017 (16 Nov). Christmas. T **747** and similar horiz designs illustrating Christmas carols. Multicoloured. Self-adhesive. Die-cut perf 11.

2177	85c. Type **747**		4·25	4·00
2178	100c. Bells and bauble showing world map (*Jingle Bells*)		5·00	4·75
2179	150c. Santa making phone call (*We wish you a Merry Christmas*)		7·50	7·25
2180	200c. Snow covered traffic lights (*Snow falls softly at Night*)		10·00	9·50
2177/2180 Set of 4			24·00	23·00

Nos. 2177/2180 were printed with the surplus paper around the stamp removed.

748 Heart **749** Simmental Cow

(Des Benel Kallen. Litho and silver foil Enschedé)

2017 (16 Nov). Love. P 13½×14.

2181	**748** 100c. multicoloured		5·00	4·75

No. 2181 was printed both in sheets of 20, and in small sheets of six stamps cut around in the shape of a heart.

(Des Lisa Behmel. Litho Gutenberg AG, Schaan, Liechtenstein)

2017 (16 Nov). Swiss Cows. Simmental. P 13½.

2182	**749** 100c. multicoloured		5·00	4·75

750 Zürich Station **751** Celebration

(Des Marc Weller. Litho Enschedé)

2017 (16 Nov). Railway Stations. Self-adhesive. Die-cut perf 12.

2183	**750** 400c. multicoloured		20·00	19·00

No. 2183 was printed with the surplus paper around the stamp removed.

(Des Dominique Wittwer. Litho Enschedé)

2018 (29 Jan). Swiss Olympic 2018. Winter Olympic Games, Pyeongchang. P 14.

2184	**751** 100c. multicoloured		5·00	4·75

752 Emblem **753** Neolithic Pot

(Des Claudine Etter. Litho Cartor)

2018 (22 Feb). 60th Anniversary of Swiss League against Rheumatism. P 13½.

2185	**752** 85c. multicoloured		4·25	4·00

(Des Franziska Schott and Marco Schibig. Litho Cartor)

2018 (1 Mar). Year of Cultural Heritage. T **753** and similar vert design. P 13½.

2186	85c. Type **753**		4·25	4·00
2187	100c. Sogn Benedetg chapel (Peter Zumthor), 1989		5·00	4·75

754 Great Spotted Woodpecker **755** Symbols of Aid

(Des Sonja Burger. Litho Enschedé)

2018 (1 Mar). Animals of the Forest. T **754** and similar horiz designs. Multicoloured. Self-adhesive. Die-cut perf 12.

2188	85c. Type **754**		4·25	4·00
	a. Block of 4. Nos. 2188/2191		28·00	
2189	100c. Red Squirrel		5·00	4·75

SWITZERLAND 2018

2190	150c. Roe Deer		7·50	7·25
2191	200c. Badger		10·00	9·50
2188/2191	Set of 4		24·00	23·00

Nos. 2188/2191 were printed both in sheets, and together in blocks of four stamps with the surplus paper around the stamps removed.

(Des Barbara Seiler. Litho Cartor)

2018 (1 Mar). 75th Anniversary of Swiss Mountain Aid. P 13½.
2192	**755**	100c. multicoloured	5·00	4·75

756 Anniversary Emblem   **757** Heritage Steam Locomotive

(Des Max Henschel. Litho Gutenberg AG, Schaan)

2018 (1 Mar). Centenary of SUVA (Swiss National Accident Fund). P 13½.
2193	**756**	100c. multicoloured	5·00	4·75

(Des Fabienne Bertschinger. Litho Enschedé)

2018 (1 Mar). Railways. 125th Anniversary of Schynige Platte Railway and Wengernalp Railway. T **757** and similar horiz design. Multicoloured. P 14.
2194	100c. Type **757**	5·00	4·75
2195	100c. Modern electric locomotive	5·00	4·75

758 1843 4r. and 6r. Stamps (As Types **C1** and **C2**)   **759** Rüschlikon

(Des Fabienne Angehrn. Litho Gutenberg AG, Schaan)

2018 (1 Mar). 175th Anniversary of Swiss Stamps. P 13½.
2196	**758**	100c. +50c. multicoloured	7·50	7·25

(Des Pierre-Abraham Rochat. Litho Cartor)

1918 (9 May). 50th Anniversary of Ballenburg Open Air Museum. T **759** and similar horiz designs showing houses. Multicoloured. P 13½.
2197	85c. Type **759**	4·25	4·00
2198	85c. Vals	4·25	4·00
2199	100c. Cugnasco	5·00	4·75
2200	100c. Lancy	5·00	4·75
2197/2200	Set of 4	17·00	16·00

760 Hagenwil Water Castle   **761** Player

(Des Angelo Boog. Litho Cartor)

2018 (17 May). Pro Patria. Fortresses and Castles of Switzerland. T **760** and similar horiz design. Multicoloured. P 13½.
2201	85c. +40c. Type **760**	6·25	6·00
	a. Booklet pane. No. 2201×4	26·00	
2202	100c. +50c. Romont Castle	7·50	7·25
	a. Booklet pane. No. 2202×6	46·00	

(Des Bettina Häfliger. Litho Enschedé)

2018 (17 May). Traditional Swiss Sports. Hornussen. P 13½.
2203	**761**	100c. multicoloured	5·00	4·75

762 Pharmacist   **763** Competitors

(Des Julia Reichle and Martina Pelosi. Litho Bagel Security Print, Düsseldorf)

2018 (17 May). 175th Anniversary of Swiss Pharmacists' Association. P 13½.
2204	**762**	100c. multicoloured	5·00	4·75

(Des Moritz Adler and Mathias Zimmermann. Litho Bagel Security Print, Düsseldorf)

2018 (17 May). Union Cycliste Internationale (UCI) Mountain Bike (MTB) World Championships 2018, Lenzerheide. P 13½.
2205	**763**	100c. multicoloured	5·00	4·75

764 Funicular Railway Car   **765** Spreuer Bridge, Lucerne

(Des Diego Balli. Litho Enschedé)

2018 (17 May). Railways. 125th Anniversary of Stanserhorn Railway. P 14½×14.
2206	**764**	100c. multicoloured	5·00	4·75

(Des René Sager. Litho Gutenberg AG, Schaan)

2018 (17 May). Europa. Bridges. T **765** and similar horiz design. Multicoloured. P 13½.
2207	100c. Type **765**	5·00	4·75
2208	100c. Trift Bridge, Gadmental	5·00	4·75

766 Stamp Display   **767** Pope Francis

(Des Fabienne Angehrn. Litho Gutenberg AG, Schaan)

2018 (17 May). National Stamp Exhibition (NABA), Stans. P 13½.
2209	**766**	100c. +50c. multicoloured	7·50	7·25

(Litho)

2018 (21 June). Pope Francis' Visit to Switzerland. P 14.
2209a	**767**	100c. multicoloured	5·00	4·75

768 Zweisimmen   **769** Four-leaved Clover

(Des Marc Weller. Litho Enschedé)

2018 (6 Sept). Railway Stations. T **768** and similar horiz designs. Multicoloured. Self-adhesive. Die-cut perf 12.
2210	10c. Type **768**	50	50
	a. Block of 4. Nos. 2210/2213	6·00	
2211	15c. Huttwil	75	70
2212	20c. Alp Grüm	1·00	95
2213	50c. Fleurier	2·50	2·40
2210/2213	Set of 4	4·25	4·00

Nos. 2210/2213 were printed with the surplus paper around the stamp removed.

(Des Claudine Etter. Litho Enschedé)

2018 (6 Sept). Greetings Stamps. T **769** and similar horiz designs showing symbols of greetings. Multicoloured. Self-adhesive. Die-cut perf 12.

2214	85c. Type **769**	4·25	4·00
	a. Block of 4. Nos. 2214/2217		
2215	85c. Bird carrying envelope	4·25	4·00
2216	100c. Ladybird	5·00	4·75
2217	100c. Envelope containing Olive branch	5·00	4·75
2214/2217	Set of 4	17·00	16·00

770 Alpenstein

(Des Steve Hadorn. Litho)

2018 (6 Sept). Mountains. Alpstein. Sheet 107×70 mm. P 13½.
MS2218 **770** 100c. multicoloured .... 5·25 5·00

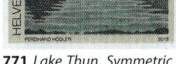

771 Lake Thun, Symmetric Reflection

772 Fairy, Frog King, the Town Musicians of Bremen, and the Witch from Hansel and Gretel

(Des Daniel Steffen. Litho)

2018 (6 Sept). Death Centenary of Ferdinand Hodler (artist). P 13½.
2219 **771** 100c. multicoloured .... 5·00 4·75

(Des Viviane Dommann. Litho)

2018 (6 Sept). Fairy Tales. T **772** and similar horiz design. Multicoloured. P 13½.

2220	100c. Type **772**	5·00	4·75
2221	100c. Puss in Boots, Wolf and the Kids, Mother Hulda and Rapunzel	5·00	4·75

773 Queen of Hearts

774 Bottmingen Water Castle

(Des Jens Riedweg. Litho)

2018 (6 Sept). Card Games. Swiss Jass. T **773** and similar vert designs. Multicoloured. P 13½.

2222	100c. Type **773**	5·00	4·75
	a. Strip of 4. Nos. 2222/2225	21·00	
2223	100c. King of Clubs	5·00	4·75
2224	100c. Jack of Bells	5·00	4·75
2225	100c. King of Acorns	5·00	4·75
2222/2225	Set of 4	18·00	17·00

Nos. 2222/2225 were printed, *se-tenant*, in horizontal strips of four stamps within the sheet.

(Des Martin Mägli. Litho Enschedé)

2018 (15 Nov). Christmas. T **774** and similar horiz designs. Multicoloured. Self-adhesive. Die-cut perf 12.

2226	85c. Type **774**	4·25	4·00
	a. Block of 4. Nos. 2226/2229	28·00	
2227	100c. Kandersteg Church	5·00	4·75
2228	150c. Bedretto Village	7·50	7·25
2229	200c. Saint-Ursanne Bridge	10·00	9·50
2226/2229	Set of 4	24·00	23·00

Nos. 2226/2229 were printed with the surplus paper around the stamp removed.

775 Fondue **776** *Auricula muris*

(Des Francisco Rojas. Litho Enschedé)

2018 (15 Nov). Fondue. T **775** and similar square design. Multicoloured. P 13½.

2230	100c. Type **775**	5·00	4·75
2231	100c. Cheese	5·00	4·75

(Des Fanny Hartman)

2018 (15 Nov). Flora. Medicinal Plants. Sheet 149×45 mm containing T **776** and similar square designs. Multicoloured. P 14½.
MS2232 100c.×4, Type **776**; *Aconitum*; *Tithymalus paralius*; *Scolymus non aculeatus* .... 21·00 20·00

777 Allschwil Street **778** Bern

(Des Kevin Hill. Litho)

2018 (17 Nov). Stamp Day. Allschwil. Sheet 125×45 mm. P 13½.
MS2233 **777** 100c.+50c. multicoloured .... 7·75 7·50

(Des Marc Weller. Litho Enschedé)

2018 (15 Nov). Railway Stations. Self-adhesive. Die-cut perf 12.
2234 **778** 360c. multicoloured .... 18·00 17·00

No. 2234 was printed with the surplus paper around the stamp removed.

779 Carnival **780** Brig–Domodossola Route

(Des Domo Löw. Litho Gutenberg AG, Schaan)

2019 (24 Jan). Basel Carnival. Intangible Cultural Heritage of Humanity. P 13½.
2235 **779** 100c. multicoloured .... 5·00 4·75

(Des Judith Kurmann. Litho Cartor)

2019 (7 Mar). Centenary of PostBus. T **780** and similar horiz design. Multicoloured. P 13½.

2236	85c. Chur–Laax in Graubünden route	4·25	4·00
2237	100c. Type **780**	5·00	4·75

781 Dog   **782** Pig

(Des Christian Kitzmüller. Litho Enschedé)

2019 (7 Mar). Animals Friends. T **781** and similar vert designs. Self-adhesive. Die-cut perf 12.
2238	85c. Type **781**	4·25	4·00
	a. Block of 4. Nos. 2238/2241	28·00	
2239	100c. Cat	5·00	4·75
2240	150c. Rabbit	7·50	7·25
2241	200c. Pony	10·00	9·50
2238/2241	Set of 4	24·00	23·00

Nos. 2238/2241 were printed both in sheets, and together in blocks of four stamps with the surplus paper around the stamps removed.

(Des Janine Wiget. Litho Enschedé)

2019 (7 Mar). Greetings Stamps. Flocked paper. Self-adhesive. Die-cut.
2242	**782** 100c. multicoloured	5·00	4·75

No. 2242 was cut around in the shape of a pig.

783 Häfeli DH-3 Biplane   **784** Alfred Escher

(Des Beat Felber. Litho Enschedé)

2019 (7 Mar). Centenary of Swiss Air Transport. P 13.
2243	**783** 100c. multicoloured	5·00	4·75

(Des Jürg Glauser. Litho Cartor)

2019 (7 Mar). Birth Bicentenary of Johann Heinrich Alfred Escher vom Glas (Alfred Escher) (politician, business leader and railways pioneer). P 13½.
2244	**784** 100c. multicoloured	5·00	4·75

785 Clown   **786** Helvetia, where is that

(Des Christine Burkhard. Litho Gutenberg AG, Schaan)

2019 (7 Mar). Centenary of Swiss National Circus Knie. T **785** and similar vert design. Multicoloured. P 13½.
2245	100c. Type **785**	5·00	4·75
	a. Pair. Nos. 2245/2246	10·50	9·75
2246	100c. Winged Horse	5·00	4·75

Nos. 2245/2246 were printed, *se-tenant*, in horizontal pairs within the sheet.

(Des Arnaud Tosi. Litho Enschedé)

2019 (7 Mar). Fumetto Comic Festival. Winning Design in Festival Competition. T **786** and similar vert designs. Multicoloured. P 13½.
2247	100c. Type **786**	5·00	4·75
	a. Strip of 3. Nos. 2247/2249	16·00	
2248	100c. Helvetia? to a mountain, Svizzera? to a Cow, Schweiz? to a Swan	5·00	4·75
2249	100c. Swiss chocolate, Swiss penknife, Swiss watch	5·00	4·75
2247/2249	Set of 3	13·50	13·00

Nos. 2247/2249 were printed, *se-tenant*, in horizontal strips of three stamps within the sheet.

POSTCARD STAMPS

P **1** Tourism Emblem

(Des Martine Chatagny. Litho Enschedé)

2002 (19 Nov). Self-adhesive gum. No value expressed. Imperf×die-cut perf 13½.
P1	P **1**	(1f.30) multicoloured	3·75	3·50
P2		(1f.80) multicoloured	5·00	4·75

No. P1 was for use only on postcards sent to countries within Europe and No. P2 to overseas countries. They were not valid for use on other mail or in combination with other stamps.

MACHINE LABELS

A

1976 (9 Aug). Designs as T **A**. Background design shows posthorn pattern. Face values 5c. to 9995c. in 5c. steps.
Fixed values: 9.8.76   40c., 70c., 80c. (with codes)
                   26.6.78   40c., 70c., 80c. (without codes)

At first only four machines were installed and these dispensed labels as T **A** but with an additional number and letter in the bottom frame, indicating the issuing machine;
A1, Zürich main railway station
A2, Bern
A3, Grindelwald
A4, Geneva
In June 1978 these code letters and numbers were removed and many more machines were installed throughout Switzerland.

Five different types of label without code letters have been identified:
A. As illustration T **A**, with narrow letters about 4 mm high, value printed in bright purple on granite paper (26.6.78)
B. As illustration T **A**, with broader letters about 3½ mm high, value printed in bright purple on granite paper (26.2.79)
C. As illustration T **A**, printed in deep carmine on granite paper (15.6.81)
D. As illustration T **A**, printed in bright purple on fibre-less paper (20.7.81)
E. As illustration T **A**, printed in deep carmine on fibre-less paper (20.7.81)

1990 (5 Nov). Design as T **A** but background design shows yellow crosses. Face values 5c. to 9995c. in 5c. steps.
Fixed values: 9.11.90   35c., 50c., 80c., 90c.
                   14.10.91   50c., 70c., 80c., 90c.
                   1.1.96   70c., 90c., 110c., 180c.
                   1.7.00   70c., 90c., 120c., 130c.
                   1.1.04   85c., 100c., 120c., 130c.

1993 (2 Nov). Design as T **A** but background design shows outline map of Switzerland. Face values 5c. to 9995c. in 5c. steps.
Fixed values: 2.11.93

B

1995 (17 June). Design as T **B**. Inscribed BASLER TAUBE 95. Face values 5c. to 9995c. in 5c. steps.
Fixed values: 17.6.95   60c., 80c., 100c.
Withdrawn from sale 31 December 1995.

SWITZERLAND / Machine Labels / Stamp Booklets

C Summer

1996 (14 May). The Four Seasons. Horiz designs as T **C** showing the four seasons. Multicoloured. Fluorescent paper. Face values 10c. to 9990c. in 10c. steps.

Fixed values: 14.5.96 70c., 90c., 110c., 180c.
1.7.00 70c., 90c., 120c., 130c.
1.1.04 85c., 100c., 120c., 130c.

Designs: Summer, Grisons (T **C**); Spring, Jura (Daisies in foreground); Autumn, Tessin (multicoloured trees and shrubs in foreground); Winter, Alps (snow covered mountains).

From September 2003 the fixed values were available in face values 5c. to 9995c. in 5c. steps.

D Aeroplane

2001 (20 Sept). Transport. Horiz designs as T **D** showing different forms of transport. Multicoloured. Face values 10c. to 9990c. in 10c. steps.

Fixed values: 20.9.01 70c., 90c., 120c., 130c.
1.1.04 85c., 100c., 120c., 130c.

Designs: Lorry; Car; Train; Aeroplane (T **D**).

E National Flag

2005 (6 Sept). National Flag. Horiz designs as T **E** showing the Swiss flag. Multicoloured. Face values 5c. to 9995c. in 5c. steps.

Fixed values: 6.9.05 85c., 100c., 120c., 130c.

Designs: Flag (T **E**); Flag (*different*).

STAMP BOOKLETS

The following checklist covers, in simplified form, booklets issued by Switzerland. It is intended that it should be used in conjunction with the main listings and details of stamps and panes listed there are not repeated.

Nos. SB19/SB25 were sold at 5c. over face value. Booklets prepared for use in automatic machines have the suffix S.

Some booklets exist in more than one version, differing in advertisements on the cover; such differences are not covered by this list.

Booklets containing the 1986, 1989 and 1992 Pro Sport stamps were privately produced by the Swiss Sports Federation.

Booklets containing Pro Patria stamps are listed at the end of this section; those containing Pro Juventute stamps are listed after that section.

Prices are for complete booklets

Booklet No.	Date	Contents and Cover Price	Price
SB1	1904	Cross and Numeral (Type **9**). W **8** 4 panes, No. 129×6 (1f.20)	£1400
SB2	1904	Cross and Numeral (Type **9**). W **8** 4 panes, No. 130B×6 (2f.40)	£3500
SB3	1905	Cross and Numeral (Type **9**). W **13** 4 panes, No. 196×6 (1f.50)	£3000
SB4	1905	Cross and Numeral (Type **9**). W **13** 4 panes, No. 197×6 (2f.40)	£1900
SB5	1907	Tell's Son (Type **15**). 4 panes, No. 227×6 (1f.20)	£900
SB6	1907	Helvetia (Type **16**). 4 panes, No. 228×6 (2f.40)	£650
SB7	1909	Sitting Helvetia (Type **17**). 4 panes, No. 233×6 (3f.)	£600
SB8	1909	Tell's Son (Type **18**). 5 panes, No. 247×6 (60c.)	£375
SB9	1909	Tell's Son (Type **18**). 5 panes, No. 249×6 (1f.50)	£1900
SB10	1909	Helvetia (Type **19**). 5 panes, No. 250×6 (3f.)	£650
SB11	1910	Tell's Son (Type **18a**). 5 panes, No. 257×6 (1f.50)	£7500
SB12	1911	Tell's Son (Type **18b**). 5 panes, No. 260×6 (60c.)	£750
SB13	1911	Tell's Son (Type **18b**). 5 panes, No. 263×6 (1f.50)	£350
SB14	1915	Tell's Son (Type **18a**). 5 panes, No. 254×6 (90c.)	£325
SB15	1915	Tell (Type **21**). 5 panes, No. 279×6 (3f.)	£275
SB16	1917	Tell's Son (Type **18a**). 5 panes, No. 255×6 (90c.)	£275
SB17	1917	Tell's Son (Type **18b**) and Tell (Type **21**). 4 panes, No. 263×6, 3 panes, No. 279×6 (3f.)	£300
SB18	1918	Tell's Son (Type **18a**) and Tell (Type **21**). 1 pane, No. 258×6; 1 pane, No. 279×6; 1 pane, No. 2796, 2 panes, No. 285×6 (3f.50)	£300
SB19	1921	Tell's Son (Type **18a**) and Tell (Type **21**). 1 pane, No. 310×6; 1 pane, No. 279×6; 1 pane, No. 279b; 2 panes, No. 314×6 (3f.95+5c.)	£225
SB20	1921	Tell's Son (Type **18b**) and Tell (Type **21**). 1 pane, No. 264a; 2 panes, No. 280×6; 2 panes, No. 287×6 (3f.95+5c.)	£300
SB21	1924	Tell's Son (Type **18b**) and Tell (Type **21**). 1 pane, No. 265a; 2 panes, No. 280×6; 2 panes, No. 288×6 (3f.95+5c.)	£300
SB22	1925	Tell's Son (Type **18b**) and Tell (Type **21**). 1 pane, No. 265a; 2 panes, No. 280×6; 2 panes, No. 289×6 (3f.95+5c.)	£350
SB23	1927	Tell's Son (Type **18b**) and Tell (Type **21**). 1 pane, No. 266a; 2 panes, No. 280×6; 2 panes, No. 289×6 (3f.95+5c.)	£350
SB24	1928	Tell's Son (Type **18b**) and Tell (Type **21**). 1 pane, No. 266b; 2 panes, No. 281×6; 2 panes, No. 289×6 (3f.95+5c.)	£350
SB25	1930–1933	Tell's Son (Type **18b**) and Tell (Type **21**). 1 pane, No. 267a; 2 panes, No. 282×6; 2 panes, No. 289×6 (3f.95+5c.)	£350
		a. Grilled gum Nos. 267ba, 282b and 289b (1933)	£1300
SB26	1935	Landscapes (as Type **48**). 1 pane, No. 351×6; 1 pane, No. 352×6; 1 pane, No. 353×6, 1 pane, No. 354×6 (3f.)	£350
SB27	1936	Landscapes (as Type **48**). 2 panes, No. 351×6; 2 panes, No. 352×6; 1 pane, No. 354×6 (3f.)	£350
SB28	1936	Landscapes (as Type **48**). 1 pane, No. 351×6; 3 panes, No. 352×6, 2 panes, No. 354×6 (4f.50)	£350
SB29	1936	Landscapes (as Type **52**). 1 pane, No. 369A×10 (50c.)	£425
SB30	1936	Landscapes (as Types **48** and **52**). 2 panes, No. 369B×6; 2 panes, No. 352×6; 1 pane, No. 354×6 (3f.)	£475
SB31	1937	Landscapes (as Type **52**). 2 panes, No. 369A×6, 2 panes, No. 370A×6, 1 pane, No. 374A×6 (3f.)	£325
		a. Grilled gum. Nos. 369B, 370B and 374Bd	£550
SB32	1937	Landscapes (as Type **52**). 1 pane, No. 369A×6, 3 panes, No. 370A×6, 2 panes, No. 374A×6 (4f.50)	£550
		a. Grilled gum. Nos. 369B, 370B and 374Bd	£650
SB33	1937–1939	Landscapes (as Type **52**). 2 panes, No. 369A×6, 2 panes, No. 370Ad×6, 1 pane, No. 375A×6 (1939) (3f.)	£225

SWITZERLAND / Stamp Booklets

		a. Grilled gum. Nos. 369B, 370Bd and 375B (1937) (3f.)	£2750
		b. Mixed gum. Nos. 369A, 370Bd and 375A (1939)	£600
SB34S	1939	National Exhibition, Zürich (Type **64**). 1 pane, No. 394Ba×10 (50c.)	£250
SB35	1939	Landscapes (as Type **52**). 1 pane, No. 369A×6; 3 panes, No. 370Ad×6, 2 panes, No. 375A×6 (4f.50)	£300
		a. Grilled gum. Nos. 3696, 370Bd and 375B	£375
SB36	1942	Landscapes (as Type **52**). 2 panes, No. 369A×6, 2 panes, No. 371A×6; 1 pane, No. 375A×6 (3f.)	£250
SB37	1942	Landscapes (as Type **52**). 1 pane, No. 369A×6; 3 panes, No. 371A×6; 2 panes, No. 375A×6 (4f.50)	£275
SB38	1943	Landscapes (as Type **52**). 2 panes, No. 369A×6, 2 panes, No. 372A×6; 1 pane, No. 375A×6 (3f.)	£170
SB39	1943	Landscapes (as Type **52**). 1 pane, No. 369A×6; 3 panes, No. 372A×6, 2 panes, No. 375A×6 (4f.50)	£275
SB40	1948	Landscapes (as Type **52**). 2 panes, No. 489×6; 2 panes, No. 490×6; 1 pane, No. 491×6 (3f.)	£250
SB41	1948	Landscapes (as Type **52**). 1 pane, No. 489×6; 3 panes, No. 490×6; 2 panes, No. 491×6 (4f.50)	£300
SB42S	1948	Landscapes (as Type **52**). 1 pane, No. 489×10 (50c.)	£300
SB43S	1949	Technology (Type **107**). 1 pane, No. 511×10 (50c.)	£200
SB44	1950	Technology (as Types **106/107**). 1 pane, No. 511×4; 3 panes, No. 512×4; 2 panes, No. 514a×4 (3f.)	£225
SB45	1950	Technology (as Types **106/107**). 3 panes, No. 511×4; 5 panes, No. 512×4; 3 panes, No. 514a×4 (5f.)	£225
SB46S	1960	Postal History 1 pane, No. 614×10 (50c.)	55·00
SB47	1960–1966	Postal History 1 pane, No. 614×4; 3 panes, No. 615×4; 2 panes, No. 617×4 (3f.)	65·00
		a. Phosphor. Nos. 614p, 615p and 617p (1966)	75·00
SB48	1960–1966	Postal History and Monuments 2 panes, No. 614×4; 3 panes, No. 615×4; 3 panes, No. 617×4; 1 pane, No. 622×4 (6f.)	80·00
		a. As above but containing Nos. 614p, 615p, 617p and 622 (1966)	£100
		b. As above containing No. 614, 615p, 617p and 622 (1966)	65·00
SB49	1962–1966	Postal History 2 panes, No. 614×4; 2 panes, No. 615×4; 1 pane, No. 617×4 (2f.)	40·00
		a. Phosphor. Nos. 614p, 615p and 617p (1966)	65·00
SB50	1962–1967	Postal History 3 panes, No. 614×4; 5 panes, No. 615×4, 3 panes, No. 617×4 (5f.)	50·00
		a. Phosphor. Nos. 614p, 615p and 617p (1967)	45·00
		b. Mixed. 3 panes, No. 614p×4; 3 panes, No. 615×4; 2 panes, No. 615p×4; 3 panes, No. 617×4 (1967)	45·00
SB51S	1967	Postal History 1 pane, No. 615×10 (1f.)	55·00
SB52	1968	Postal History and Monuments 2 panes, No. 615p×4; 1 pane, 2 panes, No. 615pb; 2 panes, No. 617p×4; No. 619p×4 (5f.)	65·00
SB53S	1970	Monuments (2nd series) 1 pane, No. 699×10 (1f.)	55·00
SB54	1970	Monuments (2nd series) 2 panes, No. 699×4; 1 pane, No. 699b; 2 panes, No. 701×4; 2 panes, No. 702×4 (5f.)	32·00
SB55	1973	Monuments (2nd series) 2 panes, No. 699×4; 1 pane, No 700×4; 3 panes, No. 702×4 (5f.)	32·00
SB56	5.1.76–1978	Monuments (1st and 2nd series) 1 pane, No. 699b; 2 panes, No. 701×4; 2 panes, No. 621p×4 (5f.) Green cover. Contents on front overprinted	32·00
		a. Orange cover. Contents on front overprinted (1976)	45·00
		b. Green cover. Correct contents printed on front and PTT posthorn emblem (1976)	37·00
		c. Green cover. New PTT emblem (cross over PTT) (1978)	37·00
SB57	5.1.79–1983	Folk Customs 1 pane, No. 940ab; 2 panes, No. 941ab, 2 panes, No. 943ab (5f.) Couple dancing on front. Orange cover	21·00
		a. As above but blue cover (1980)	32·00
		b. As above but green cover (1981)	45·00
		c. Couple with whips on front. Grey cover (1.4.82)	60·00
		d. As c. but blue cover (18.4.83)	75·00
SB58	1.2.84–1985	Folk Customs 1 pane, No. 939ab; 1 pane, No. 940ac; 1 pane, No. 942ab; 1 pane, No. 944ab, 1 pane, No. 944ac (5f.) Yellow cover	35·00
		a. Orange cover (2.9.85)	£130
SB59	2.9.85	Folk Customs 1 pane, No. 939ab; 1 pane, No. 940ac; 1 pane, No. 942ab; 4 panes, No. 944ab (10f.)	45·00
SB60	8.9.88	The Post Past and Present 1 pane, No. 1109ab (5f.)	27·00
SB61	22.2.91	700th Anniversary of Swiss Confederation 1 pane, No. 1219a×2 (4f.)	20·00
SB62	19.1.93	Lake Taney 1 pane, No. 1257×10 (6f.)	35·00
SB63	30.6.94	A Mail (Type **313**). 1 pane, No. 1258×10 (8f.)	26·00
SB64	28.11.94	Rabbit 1 pane, No. 1194ab (7f.)	40·00
SB65	28.11.94	A Mail (Type **336**) 1 pane, No. 1313ab (9f.)	35·00
SB66	12.3.96	Pro Sport (Type **338**) 1 pane, No. 1319×10 (10f.)	26·00
SB67	10.9.96	Greetings Stamps. Self-adhesive Nos. 1332/1335, each×2 (7f.20)	27·00
SB68	8.9.98	Sports Self-adhesive Nos. 1396/1400, each×2 (7f.)	24·00
SB69	9.3.99	Rodolphe Topffer Self-adhesive Nos. 1409/1413, each×2 plus 4 labels (9f.)	31·00
SB70	29.7.00	Publicity Issue 1 pane, No. 1418×10 (9f.)	24·00
SB71	15.9.00	Stampin the Future Nos. 1463/1466, each×2 (5f.60)	31·00
SB72	15.9.00	Olympic Games, Sydney Nos. 1467/1469, (2f.70)	12·00
SB73	9.5.01	St Barnard. Self-adhesive No. 1479×12 (8f.40)	29·00
SB74	9.5.01	A Mail (Type **336**). Self-adhesive No. 1480×12 (10f.80)	37·00
SB75	15.5.02	Centenary of the Teddy Bear. Self-adhesive Nos. 1510/1514, each×2 (9f.)	26·00
SB76	17.9.02	Greeting stamp. Self-adhesive No. 1521×10, plus 10 labels (9f.)	29·00
SB77	17.9.03	Greeting Stamp. Self-adhesive No. 1571×10, plus 10 labels	41·00
SB78	30.12.03	Design Classics. Self-adhesive No. 1572×10	5·75
SB79	30.12.03	Design Classics. Self-adhesive No. 1583×10	25·00
SB80	30.12.03	Design Classics. Self-adhesive No. 1584×10	65·00
SB81	3.1.05	Greeting Stamp. Self-adhesive Nos. 1625/1628, each×2	23·00
SB82	10.5.05	Greeting Stamp. Self-adhesive No. 1642×10	29·00
SB83	10.5.05	Design Classics. Self-adhesive No. 1585×10	29·00
SB84	7.9.06	Cocolino. Self-adhesive No. 1697×10	25·00
SB85	6.9.07	Chaffinch. Self-adhesive No. 1669a	24·00
SB86	6.9.07	Great Tit. Self-adhesive No. 1670a	27·00
SB87	6.9.07	Schellen-Ursli. Self-adhesive No. 1731×10	26·00
SB88	4.3.08	*Little Polar Bear Lars*. Self-adhesive No. 1750×10	26·00
SB89	3.3.10	Princess Lillifee No. 1812×10 (8f.50)	34·00
SB90	3.9.10	Jimmy Flitz No. 1857×10 (8f.50)	34·00
SB91	3.3.11	Pettersson and Findus No. 1876×10 (8f.50)	39·00
SB92	3.3.11	Vegetable Flowers No. 1880×10 (8f.50)	39·00

SWITZERLAND / Stamp Booklets / 'Pro Juventute' Charity Stamps

SB93	3.3.11	Vegetable Flowers No. 1881×10 (10f.)	46·00
SB94	9.9.11	Muggestutz No. 1897×10 (8f.50)	44·00
SB95	8.3.12	80th Birth Anniversary of Janosch (Horst Eckert) No. 1921×10 (10f.)	55·00
SB96	22.11.12	Yakari Nos. 1936/1937, each×5 (10f.)	75·00
SB97	7.3.13	150th Birth Anniversary of Ernst Kreidolf Nos. 1965/1966, each×5 (10f.)	55·00
SB98	5.9.13	The Smurfs Nos. 1982/1983, each×5 (10f.)	55·00
SB99	6.3.14	Fred and Fun No. 2007 and No. 2008×8 (9f.)	46·00
SB100	4.9.14	Garfield Nos. 2033/2034, each×5 (10f.)	55·00
SB101	3.9.15	Marsupilami Nos. 2081/2082, each×5 (10f.)	55·00
SB102	3.3.16	Molly Monster Nos. 2101/2102, each×5 (10f.)	55·00
SB103	8.9.16	Railway Stations No. 2120×10 (8f.50)	44·00
SB104	8.9.16	Railway Stations No. 2121×10 (10f.)	55·00
SB105	7.9.17	Emoji Nos. 2162/2163, each×5 (9f.25)	47·00

PRO PATRIA STAMP BOOKLETS

The premium on the stamps was for the benefit of the Swiss National Day Fund. The booklets were sold at a further premium above face value to defray the cost of making them up. In 1990 and 1991 this premium was 50c.; from 1992 it was 80c.

In 1989 a booklet containing No. 1162×10 was produced by the National Day Committee as an experiment and sold in selected localities by schoolchildren; it cannot therefore be considered a Post Office issue.

Booklet No.	Date	Contents	Price
PSB1	1990	1 pane, No. 1206×10	20·00
PSB2	1991	1 pane, No. 1227×10	20·00
PSB3	1992	1 pane, No. 1246×10	20·00
PSB4	1993	1 pane, No. 1268×10	26·00
PSB5	1994	1 pane, No. 1289×10	39·00
PSB6	1995	1 pane, No. 1303×10	39·00
PSB7	1996	1 pane, No. 1324×10	46·00
PSB8	1997	1 pane, No. 1355×10	46·00
PSB9	1998	1 pane, No. 1392×10	39·00
PSB10	1999	1 pane, No. 1423×10	46·00
PSB11	2000	1 pane, No. 1448×10	60·00
PSB12	2001	1 pane, No. 1483×10	44·00
PSB13	2002	1 pane, No. 1508×10	39·00
PSB14	2003	1 pane, No. 1556×10	31·00
PSB15	2004	2 panes, No. 1604×6 and No. 1606×4	40·00
PSB16	2005	2 panes, No. 1639a and No. 1640a	41·00
PSB17	2006	2 panes, No. 1687a and No. 1689a	39·00
PSB18	2007	2 panes, No. 1724a and No. 1726a	44·00
PSB19	2008	2 panes, No. 1767a and No. 1770a	44·00
PSB20	2009	2 panes, No. 1803a and No. 1806a (14f.50)	60·00
PSB21	2010	2 panes, No. 1849a and No. 1852a (14f.50)	60·00
PSB22	2011	2 panes, No. 1891a and No. 1893a (13f.50)	65·00
PSB23	2012	2 panes, No. 1935a and No. 1938a (13f.50)	75·00
PSB24	2013	No. 1967a and No. 1970a (13f.50)	75·00
PSB25	2014	No. 2014a and No. 2016a (13f.50)	75·00
PSB26	2015	No. 2069a and No. 2070a (13f.50)	75·00
PSB27	2016	No. 2112a (13f.50)	80·00
PSB28	2017	No. 2152a (13f.50)	80·00
PSB29	2018	No. 2201a and No. 2202a (14f.)	75·00

'PRO JUVENTUTE' CHARITY STAMPS

As a special exception these have not been included in chronological order in the general list as to do so effectively would entail renumbering so many stamps.

PREMIUMS. All 'Pro Juventute' stamps are sold at an additional premium which goes to Benevolent Societies. Until 1937 these premiums were not shown on the stamps, but were as follows:
2c. for all 3c. franking values, 5c. for all 5c., 7½c., 10c., 15c. and 20c. values; and 10c. for all 30c. and 40c. values.
From 1937, when the premium first appeared on the designs, we show it in the catalogue listing.

PRINTING PROCESSES AND DESIGNS. The issues from 1913 to 1926 are typographed at the Mint and the designs show the costumes or Arms of the cantons named. Thenceforward printing processes and designs varied as described below.

INSCRIPTIONS. All the following are inscribed 'PRO JUVENTUTE' and the year of issue, except Nos. J1a/J8 which are undated.

C **1** Helvetia and Matterhorn   C **2** Appenzell   C **4**   C **6**

(Des A. Grasset)

1913 (1 Dec). W **13**. P 12×11½.
J1	C **1**	5c. green	5·00	14·00

(Des W. Balmer. Eng J. Sprenger)

1915 (1 Dec). T C **2** and similar type. Buff paper. W **13**. P 11½.
J1a		5c. green (Type C **2**)	5·00	18·00
		b. Tête-bêche (pair)	£150	£1600
J2		10c. red (Girl from Lucerne)	£160	£130

(Des W. Balmer. Eng J. Sprenger)

1916 (1 Dec). T C **4** and similar portraits. Buff paper. W **13**. P 11½.
J3		3c. violet (Freiburg)	10·00	65·00
J4		5c. green (Bern)	22·00	17·00
J5		10c. red (Vaud)	90·00	£120
J3/J5 Set of 3			£110	£180

(Des W. Balmer. Eng J. Sprenger)

1917 (1 Dec). T C **6** and similar types. Buff paper. W **13**. P 11½.
J6		3c. violet (Valais)	5·25	90·00
J7		5c. green (Unterwalden)	13·00	8·25
J8		10c. red (Ticino)	33·00	43·00
J6/J8 Set of 3			46·00	£130

C **9** Uri   C **11** Nidwalden   C **14** Schwyz

(This and the following issues to 1926 were designed by R. Munger. The shield is in all cases outlined in black.)

1918 (1 Dec). T C **9** and similar type. Buff paper. W **13**. P 11½.
J9		10c. red, yellow and black (Type C **9**)	14·50	43·00
J10		15c. violet, red, yellow and black (Geneva)	18·00	22·00

1919 (1 Dec). T C **11** and similar types. Cream paper. W **13**. P 11½.
J11		7½c. red, grey and black (Type C **11**)	5·00	22·00
J12		10c. green, red and black (Vaud)	5·00	22·00
J13		15c. red, violet and black (Obwalden)	9·25	12·00
J11/J13 Set of 3			17·00	50·00

1920 (1 Dec). T C **14** and similar types. Cream paper. W **13**. P 11½.
J14		7½c. red, grey and black (Type C **14**)	6·25	26·00
J15		10c. blue, red and black (Zürich)	10·00	28·00
J16		15c. red, blue, violet and black (Ticino)	6·25	12·50
J14/J16 Set of 3			20·00	60·00

SWITZERLAND / 'Pro Juventute' Charity Stamps

C **17** Valais   C **20** Zug   C **24** Basel

1921 (1 Dec). T C **17** and similar types. Cream paper. W **13**. P 11½.
J17	10c. red, black and green (Type C **17**)	95	5·25
J18	20c. black, orange, red and violet (Bern)	3·75	7·75
J19	40c. red and blue (Switzerland)	16·00	95·00
J17/J19 *Set of 3*		19·00	95·00

1922 (1 Dec). T C **20** and similar types. Cream paper. W **13**. P 11½.
J20	5c. brown-orange, pale blue and black	95	10·00
J21	10c. sage-green and black	95	4·25
J22	20c. violet, pale blue and black	2·00	4·25
J23	40c. blue, scarlet and black	18·00	£110
J20/J23 *Set of 4*		20·00	£120

Arms: 5c. T C **20**; 10c. Freiburg; 20c. Lucerne; 40c. Switzerland.

1923 (1 Dec). T C **24** and similar types. Cream paper. W **13**. P 11½.
J24	5c. brown-orange and black	55	8·25
J25	10c. sage-green, red, black and yellow	55	4·50
J26	20c. violet, green, red and black	1·10	4·50
J27	40c. blue, red and black	13·00	85·00
J24/J27 *Set of 4*		13·50	90·00

Arms: 5c. T C **24**; 10c. Glarus; 20c. Neuchâtel; 40c. Switzerland.

C **28** Appenzell   C **32** St Gall   C **36** Thurgau

1924 (1 Dec). T C **28** and similar types. Cream paper. W **13**. P 11½.
J28	5c. black and lilac	50	3·00
J29	10c. red, green and black	95	1·70
J30	20c. black, yellow and carmine	95	2·20
J31	30c. red, blue and black	3·25	24·00
J28/J31 *Set of 4*		5·00	28·00

Arms: 5c. T C **28**; 10c. Solothurn; 20c. Schaffhausen; 30c. Switzerland.

1925 (1 Dec). T C **32** and similar types. Cream paper. W **13**. P 11½.
J32	5c. green, black and violet	50	2·50
J33	10c. black and green	50	1·70
J34	20c. black, blue, yellow and red	70	1·70
J35	30c. red, blue and black	1·80	17·00
J32/J35 *Set of 4*		3·25	21·00

Arms: 5c. T C **32**; 10c. Appenzell–Ausser–Rhoden; 20c. Graubunden; 30c. Switzerland.

1926 (1 Dec). T C **36** and similar types. Cream paper. W **13**. P 11½.
J36	5c. purple, green, bistre and black	50	2·10
J37	10c. green, black and carmine	50	2·10
J38	20c. carmine, black and blue	70	2·50
J39	30c. blue, carmine and black	1·80	20·00
J36/J39 *Set of 4*		3·25	24·00

Arms: 5c. T C **36**; 10c. Basel; 20c. Aargau; 30c. Switzerland and Lion of Lucerne.

C **40** Forsaken Orphan   C **42** J. H. Pestalozzi   C **43** J. H. Pestalozzi

(Des K. Bickel (20c.), E. G. Rüegg (others). 5c., 10c. typo, Mint. 20c. recess, Survey Dept. 30c. photo, at Leiden (Holland))

1927 (1 Dec). T C **40** (and similar type), T C **42** and T C **43**. P 11½.

*(a) Granite paper. W **13***
J40	5c. maroon and yellow/*greyish*	50	4·25
J41	10c. green and rose/*greenish*	50	85
J42	20c. scarlet	70	85

(b) Plain paper. No wmk.
J43	30c. blue and black	1·80	14·00
J40/J43 *Set of 4*		3·25	18·00

Designs: 5c. T C **40**; 10c. Orphan at Pestalozzi School; 20c. T C **42**; 30c. T C **43**.

C **44** Lausanne   C **47** J. H. Dunant

(Des F. Pauli. Photo at Leiden, Holland (30c.). Others Des R. Münger. Typo Mint (others))

1928 (1 Dec). T C **44** (similar types) and T C **47**. P 11½.

*(a) Buff granite paper. W **13***
J44	5c. vermilion, purple and black	50	3·50
J45	10c. vermilion, blue-green and black	50	1·60
J46	20c. black, yellow and carmine	45	1·60

(b) Plain paper. No wmk
J47	30c. blue and scarlet	2·00	12·50
J44/J47 *Set of 4*		3·00	17·00

Arms: 5c. T C **44**; 10c. Winterthur; 20c. St Gall; 30c. T C **47**.

C **48** Mount San Salvatore Lake Lugano   C **49** Nicholas de Flüe

(Des F. Gos (5c.), E. Boss (10c., 20c.), A. Stockmann (30c.). Photo Enschedé, Haarlem)

1929 (1 Dec). T C **48** (similar types) and T C **49**. Plain paper. No wmk. P 11×11½.
J48	5c. vermilion and violet	50	2·20
J49	10c. grey-blue and bistre-brown	50	2·20
J50	20c. blue and carmine	50	2·20
J51	30c. indigo	2·10	22·00
J48/J51 *Set of 4*		3·25	26·00

Designs: 5c. T C **48**; 10c. Mount Titlis, Lake Engstlen; 20c. Mount Lyskamm from Riffelberg; 30c. T C **49**.

C **50** Freiburg   C **51** A. Bitzius (Jeremias Gotthelf)

(30c. Des F. Pauli. Recess Survey Dept. Others des P. Boesch. Typo Mint)

1930 (1 Dec). T C **50** (similar types) and T C **51**. Granite paper. W **13**. P 11½.
J52	5c. ultramarine, black and green/*buff*	50	2·10
J53	10c. yellow, vermilion, black and violet/*buff*	50	1·30
J54	20c. yellow, green, black and carmine/*buff*	50	1·30
J55	30c. slate-blue	2·00	9·00
J52/J55 *Set of 4*		3·25	12·50

Designs: 5c. T C **50**; 10c. Arms of Altdorf; 20c. Arms of Schaffhausen; 30c. T C **51**.

C **52** St Moritz and Silvaplana Lakes   C **53** Alexandre Vinet

(30c. Des G. Matter. Recess Survey Dept. Others des E. Jordi. Photo Courvoisier)

1931 (1 Dec). T C **52** (similar views) and T C **53**. Granite paper. P 11½.

(a) No wmk
J56	5c. green (Type C **52**)	75	2·50
J57	10c. violet (Wetterhorn)	50	1·30
J58	20c. brown-lake (Lac Léman)	1·20	1·90

*(b) W **13***
J59	30c. ultramarine (Type C **53**)	7·50	30·00
J56/J59 *Set of 4*		9·00	32·00

SWITZERLAND / 'Pro Juventute' Charity Stamps

C **54** Flag Waver   C **55** Eugen Huber

(30c. Des and eng K. Bickel. Recess Orell Füssli.
Others des H. B. Wieland. Typo PTT, Bern)

1932 (1 Dec). T C **54** (similar types) and T C **55**. Granite paper. P 11½.

(a) No wmk

J60	5c. scarlet and green (Type C **54**)		60	3·00
J61	10c. orange (Putting the Weight)		75	3·50
J62	20c. scarlet (Wrestlers)		95	3·00

(b) W **13**

J63	30c. ultramarine (Type C **55**)		3·50	13·50
J60/J63 Set of 4			5·25	21·00

> **PRINTERS.** All Swiss Girl types from 1933 to 1936 were designed by Jules Courvoisier, Nos. J82/J83, J85, J87, J93/J95, J97/J99 and J101/J103 by C. Liner and Nos. J86 and J89/J91 by H. Zaugg. They were all printed in photogravure by L. Courvoisier, La Chaux-de-Fonds. Types C **57**, C **59**, C **61**, C **62**, C **64** (and No. J81), C **67**, C **69**, C **71** and C **73**/C **74** were designed and engraved by K. Bickel and all recess-printed by Orell Füssli, Zürich, except Types C **64** (and No. J81), C **67**, C **69**, C **71** and C **73**/C **74** which were recess printed at the PTT Printing Bureau, Bern.

C **56** Vaud   C **57** P. Gregoire Girard   C **59** A. von Haller

1933 (1 Dec). T C **56** (similar types) and T C **57**. Granite paper. P 11½. 30c. W **13**, others unwmkd.

J64	5c. green and buff (Type C **56**)		60	2·75
J65	10c. violet and buff (Bern)		60	2·50
J66	20c. scarlet and buff (Ticino)		75	3·50
	a. Buff background inverted		£1100	£2250
J67	30c. blue (Type C **57**)		3·75	14·00
J64/J67 Set of 4			5·25	20·00

1934 (1 Dec). T C **59** and designs as T C **56**. Granite paper (Nos. J68/J70 with grilled gum). P 11½. 30c. W **13**, others unwmkd.

J68	5c. green and buff (Appenzell)		50	2·50
J69	10c. violet and buff (Valais)		70	1·70
J70	20c. scarlet and buff (Graubunden)		75	2·50
J71	30c. blue (Type C **59**)		3·75	13·50
J68/J71 Set of 4			5·25	18·00

C **61** Stefano Franscini   C **62** H. G. Nägeli

1935 (1 Dec). T C **61** and designs as T C **56**. Granite paper (Nos. J72/J75 with grilled gum). P 11½. 30c. W **13**, others unwmkd.

J72	5c. green and buff (Basel)		50	3·00
J73	10c. violet and buff (Lucerne)		70	1·70
J74	20c. scarlet and buff (Geneva)		75	5·00
J75	30c. blue (Type C **61**)		3·75	17·00
J72/J75 Set of 4			5·25	24·00

1936 (1 Dec). T C **62** and similar designs as T C **56**. Granite paper (Nos. J77/J79 with grilled gum). P 11½. 5c. W **13**, others unwmkd.

J76	5c. green (Type C **62**)		50	1·30
J77	10c. bright purple and buff (Neuchâtel)		95	1·30
J78	20c. vermilion and buff (Schwyz)		55	3·25
J79	30c. bright blue and buff (Zürich)		6·25	55·00
J76/J79 Set of 4			7·50	55·00

C **64** General Henri Dufour   C **66** Youth

1937 (1 Dec). Types C **64** and C **66** and similar types. No wmk. P 11½.

(a) Plain paper

J80	5c. +5c. blue-green		50	90
J81	10c. +5c. bright purple		50	90

(b) Granite paper

J82	20c. +5c. vermilion, buff and silver		75	90
J83	30c. +10c. ultramarine, buff and silver		2·10	9·50
J80/J83 Set of 4			3·50	11·00

Designs: 5c. T C **64**. As T C **64**—10c. Nicholas de Flüe; 20c. T C **66**; 30c. as T C **66**, but with girl's head facing reverse direction.

1937 (20 Dec). 25th Anniversary of 'Pro Juventute' Stamp Issues. Sheet 105×55 mm. As Nos. J82/J83. Imperf.

MSJ83*a* 20c.+5c. red and silver; 30c.+10c. ultramarine and silver .... 10·50 90·00

Designs: 20c.+5c. T C **66**; 30c.+10c. Girl.

C **67** Salomon Gessner   C **69** General Herzog   C **71** Gottfried Keller

1938 (1 Dec). T C **67** and similar designs as T C **56**. P 11½.

(a) Plain paper

J84	5c. +5c. emerald-green (Type C **67**)		50	90

(b) Granite paper

J85	10c. +5c. violet and buff (St Gall)		50	90
J86	20c. +5c. scarlet and buff (Uri)		70	90
J87	30c. +10c. blue and buff (Aargau)		2·75	10·50
J84/J87 Set of 4			4·00	12·00

1939 (1 Dec). T C **69** and similar designs as T C **56**. P 11½.

(a) Plain paper

J88	5c. +5c. emerald-green (Type C **69**)		50	90

(b) Granite paper

J89	10c. +5c. violet and buff (Freiburg)		50	90
J90	20c. +5c. scarlet and buff (Nidwalden)		50	2·50
J91	30c. +10c. blue and buff (Basel)		2·75	24·00
J88/J91 Set of 4			3·75	25·00

1940 (30 Nov). T C **71** and similar designs as T C **56**. P 11½.

(a) Plain paper

J92	5c. +5c. green (Type C **71**)		50	90
	a. Error "1918" in margin		£2500	£4500

(b) Granite paper

J93	10c. +5c. brown and buff (Thurgau)		50	90
J94	20c. +5c. scarlet and buff (Solothurn)		60	90
J95	30c. +10c. blue and buff (Zug)		2·40	14·50
J92/J95 Set of 4			3·50	15·00

First printing of No. J92 was inscribed '1818–1890' instead of '1819'. This was corrected before issue but previously distributed examples of the error exist.

C **73** Johann Kasper Lavater   C **74** Niklaus Riggenbach (rack railway pioneer)

1941 (1 Dec). Bicentenaries (a) of Birth of Lavater (philosopher) and (b) of Death of Richard (clockmaker). T C **73** and similar designs as T C **56**. P 11½.

J96	5c. +5c. green		50	50
J97	10c. +5c. brown and buff		50	60
J98	20c. +5c. scarlet and buff		75	60

SWITZERLAND / 'Pro Juventute' Charity Stamps

J99	30c. +10c. blue	1·80	11·50
J96/J99 Set of 4		3·25	12·00
MSJ99a 75×70 mm. Nos. J97/J98. Imperf.		£140	£550

Designs: 5c. T C **73**; 10c. and 20c. Girls in the National Costumes of Schaffhausen and Obwalden; 30c. Daniel Jean Richard.

(Nos. J100 and J103. Des and eng K. Bickel. Recess Plain paper. Mint, Bern. Nos. J102/J103. Des C. Liner. Photo Granite paper. Courvoisier, La Chaux-de-Fonds)

1942 (1 Dec). T C **74** and similar designs as T C **56**. P 11½.

J100	5c. +5c. green	50	90
J101	10c. +5c. brown and buff	50	90
J102	20c. +5c. scarlet and buff	50	90
J103	30c. +10c. blue	2·40	7·75
J100/J103 Set of 4		3·50	9·50

Designs: 5c. T C **74**; 10c., 20c. Girls in the National Costumes of Appenzell Ausser–Rhoden and Glarus; 30c. Conrad Escher von der Linth (statesman).

> **PRINTERS.** All Alpine flowers designs from 1943 to 1949 were designed by H. Fischer and printed in photogravure by Courvoisier on granite paper. Types C **75**, C **77**/C **82** and No. J113 were designed and engraved by K. Bickel and recess-printed at the PTT Printing Bureau, Bern on plain paper.

C **75** Emanuel von Fellenberg C **76** Silver Thistle C **77** Numa Droz

1943 (1 Dec). Death Centenary of Philip Emanuel von Fellenberg (economist). T C **75** and alpine flower designs as T C **76**. P 11½.

J104	5c. +5c. green	50	90
J105	10c. +5c. blackish olive, buff and grey	50	90
J106	20c. +5c. lake, yellow and pink	50	90
J107	30c. +10c. blue, pale blue and black	1·90	14·50
J104/J107 Set of 4		3·00	15·00

Designs: 5c. T C **75**; 10c. T C **76**; 20c. Ladies' Slipper; 30c. Gentian.

1944 (1 Dec). Birth Centenary of Numa Droz (statesman). T C **77** and alpine flower designs as T C **76**. P 11½.

J108	5c. +5c. green	50	85
J109	10c. +5c. olive, yellow and green	50	85
J110	20c. +5c. red, yellow and grey	50	85
J111	30c. +10c. blue, grey and light blue	2·00	15·00
J108/J111 Set of 4		3·25	16·00

Designs: 5c. T C **77**; 10c. Edelweiss; 20c. Martagon Lily; 30c. *Aquilegia alpina*.

C **78** Ludwig Forrer C **79** Rudolf Töpffer C **80** Jacob Burckhardt (historian)

1945 (1 Dec). Birth Centenaries of Ludwig Forrer (statesman) and Susanna Orelli (social reformer). T C **78** and similar portrait type and alpine flower designs as T C **76**. P 11½.

J112	5c. +5c. green	65	90
J113	10c. +10c. red-brown	65	90
J114	20c. +10c. rose-red, pink and yellow	75	90
J115	30c. +10c. blue, mauve and grey	3·00	16·00
J112/J115 Set of 4		4·50	17·00

Designs: 5c. T C **78**; 10c. Susanna Orelli; 20c. *Rosa alpina* (Alpine Dog Rose); 30c. *Crocus albiflorus* (Spring Crocus).

1946 (30 Nov). Death Centenary of Rudolf Töpffer (author and painter). T C **79** and alpine flower designs as T C **76**. P 11½.

J116	5c. +5c. green	95	90
J117	10c. +10c. green, grey and orange	95	90
J118	20c. +10c. lake, grey and yellow	1·00	1·30
J119	30c. +10c. blue, mauve and grey	5·25	13·00
J116/J119 Set of 4		7·25	14·50

Designs: 5c. T C **79**; 10c. Narcissus; 20c. Houseleek; 30c. Blue Thistle.

1947 (1 Dec). T C **80** and alpine flower designs as T C **76**. P 11½.

J120	5c. +5c. green	90	90
J121	10c. +10c. grey-black, yellow and grey	90	90
J122	20c. +10c. red-brown orange and grey	1·10	90
J123	30c. +10c. blue, pink and grey	4·25	14·00
J120/J123 Set of 4		6·50	15·00

Designs: 5c. T C **80**; 10c. Alpine Primrose; 20c. Orange Lily; 30c. Cyclamen.

C **81** General U. Wille C **82** Nicholas Wengi

1948 (1 Dec). T C **81** and alpine flower designs as T C **76**. P 11½.

J124	5c. +5c. purple	95	85
J125	10c. +10c. green, yellow and grey	1·20	85
J126	20c. +10c. brown, carmine and buff	1·50	85
J127	40c. +10c. blue, yellow and grey	5·75	14·00
J124/J127 Set of 4		8·50	15·00

Designs: 5c. T C **81**; 10c. Foxglove; 20c. Rust-leaved Alpine Rose; 40c. Lily of Paradise.

1949 (1 Dec). T C **82** and alpine flower designs as T C **76**. P 11½.

J128	5c. +5c. brown-lake	95	90
J129	10c. +10c. blue-green, grey and yellow	95	90
J130	20c. +10c. brown, light blue and buff	95	90
J131	40c. +10c. blue, mauve and yellow	5·75	13·00
J128/J131 Set of 4		7·75	14·00

Designs: 5c. T C **82**; 10c. *Pulsatilla alpina*; 20c. Alpine Clematis; 40c. Superb Pink.

C **83** General Theophil Sprecher von Bernegg C **84** Red Admiral Butterfly C **85** Johanna Spyri (authoress)

(No. J132 Des and Eng Karl Bickel. Recess PTT, Bern. Nos. J133/J136 des Niklaus Stoecklin. Photo Granite paper. Courvoisier)

1950 (1 Dec). T C **83** and insect designs as T C **84**. P 11½.

J132	C **83**	5c. +5c. purple-brown	95	55
J133	C **84**	10c. +10c. brown, vermilion, black and turquoise	95	95
J134	–	20c. +10c. black, violet-blue and red-orange	1·50	1·40
J135	–	30c. +10c. brown, grey and magenta	7·25	26·00
J136	–	40c. +10c. yellow, blackish brown and light blue	7·25	22·00
J132/J136 Set of 5			16·00	46·00

Designs: 20c Clifton's Nonpareil (Moth); 30c. Honey Bee; 40c. Moorland Clouded Yellow (Butterfly).

(No. J137 Des and Eng K. Bickel. Recess PTT, Bern. Nos. J138/J141 des H. Fischer. Photo Granite paper. Courvoisier)

1951 (1 Dec). T C **85** and insect designs as T C **84**. P 11½.

J137	5c. +5c. claret	1·00	50
J138	10c. +10c. deep blue and light green	1·00	85
J139	20c. +10c. black, cream and magenta	1·60	85
J140	30c. +10c. black, orange and olive	4·75	12·00
J141	40c. +10c. brown, red and light ultramarine	6·50	12·00
J137/J141 Set of 5		13·50	24·00

Designs: 5c. T C **85**; 10c. Banded Agrion (Dragonfly); 20c. Scarce Swallowtail (Butterfly); 30c. Orange-tip (Butterfly); 40c. Viennese Emperor Moth.

C **86** Portrait of a Boy (Anker) C **87** Portrait of a Girl (Anker) C **88** Jeremias Gotthelf (novelist) (Albert Bitzius)

(No. J142 Des and Eng K. Bickel. Recess PTT. Bern. Nos. J143/J146 des N. Stoecklin. Photo Granite paper. Courvoisier)

1952 (1 Dec). T C **86** and insect designs as T C **84**. P 11½.

J142	5c. +5c. lake	1·00	50

SWITZERLAND / 'Pro Juventute' Charity Stamps

J143	10c. +10c. red-orange, black and pale blue-green		1·00	85
J144	20c. +10c. cream, black and mauve		1·00	1·40
J145	30c. +10c. light blue, black and bistre-brown		4·75	12·00
J146	40c. +10c. buff, brown and pale violet-blue		4·75	12·00
J142/J146 Set of 5			11·50	24·00

Designs: 5c. T C **86**; 10c. Seven-spotted Ladybird; 20c. Marbled White (Butterfly); 30c. Chalk-hill Blue (Butterfly); 40c. Oak Eggar Moth.

(Nos. J147, J151 Des and Eng K. Bickel. Recess PTT, Bern. Nos. J148/J150 des H. Fischer. Photo Granite paper. Courvoisier)

1953 (1 Dec). T C **87** and similar portrait and insect designs as T C **84**. P 11½.

J147	5c. +5c. lake		90	45
J148	10c. +10c. rose, sepia and pale blue-green		1·00	90
J149	20c. +10c. black, buff and rose-magenta		1·20	1·30
	a. Booklet pane. Nos. J149×4 and J150×2		£110	
J150	30c. +10c. black, scarlet and yellow-olive		5·00	12·00
J151	40c. +10c. blue		6·75	12·00
J147/J151 Set of 5			13·50	24·00

Designs: 5c. T C **87**; 10c. Black Arches Moth; 20c. Camberwell Beauty (Butterfly); 30c. *Purpureus kaehleri* (Longhorn Beetle); 40c. F. Hodler (self-portrait).

Nos. J149/J150 were also issued together in sheets comprising 16 of the 20c. and eight of the 30c. and sold at 8f. The composition of the sheet produces horizontal and vertical *se-tenant* pairs and also horizontal *tête-bêche* pairs of the two values. (*Price per sheet un*, £650).

(No. J152 Eng K. Bickel (after Dietler). Recess PTT, Bern. Nos. J153/J156 des N. Stoecklin. Photo Granite paper. Courvoisier)

1954 (1 Dec). T C **88** and insect designs as T C **84**. P 11½.

J152	5c. +5c. purple-brown		95	50
J153	10c. +10c. multicoloured		95	75
J154	20c. +10c. multicoloured		1·90	90
J155	30c. +10c. multicoloured		6·00	12·00
J156	40c. +10c. black, yellow, red and pale blue		6·00	12·00
J152/J156 Set of 5			14·00	24·00

Designs: 5c. T C **88**; 10c. Garden Tiger Moth; 20c. Buff-tailed Bumble Bee; 30c. *Ascalaphus libelluloides* (Owl-fly); 40c. Swallowtail (Butterfly).

C **89** C. Pictet de-Rochemont   C **90** Carlo Maderno (architect)   C **91** Leonhard Euler von Basel (mathematician)

(No. J157. Eng K. Bickel. Recess PTT, Bern. Nos. J158/J161 des H. Fischer. Photo Granite paper. Courvoisier)

1955 (1 Dec). T C **89** and insect designs as T C **84**. P 11½.

J157	5c. +5c. brown-purple		1·00	50
J158	10c. +10c. brown-purple, sepia, yellow, blue and yellow-green		1·00	90
J159	20c. +10c. black, deep blue, yellow and red		1·40	90
J160	30c. +10c. black, red, cream and yellow-brown		6·00	8·50
J161	40c. +10c. black, carmine and pale blue		6·50	9·50
J157/J161 Set of 5			14·50	18·00

Designs: 5c. T C **89**; 10c. Peacock (Butterfly); 20c. Great Horntail; 30c. Yellow Tiger Moth; 40c. Apollo (Butterfly).

(No. J162. Eng K. Bickel. Recess PTT, Bern. Nos. J163/J166 des N. Stoecklin. Photo Granite paper. Courvoisier)

1956 (1 Dec). T C **90** and insect designs as T C **84**. P 11½.

J162	5c. +5c. brown-purple		95	50
J163	10c. +10c. deep green, carmine-red and green		95	85
J164	20c. +10c. violet, sepia, yellow and rose-carmine		95	85
J165	30c. +10c. blue, indigo and olive-yellow		3·75	7·75
J166	40c. +10c. pale yellow, sepia and cobalt		4·50	8·25
J162/J166 Set of 5			10·00	16·00

Designs: 5c. T C **90**; 10c. Common Burnet (Moth); 20c. Lesser Purple Emperor (Butterfly); 30c. Blue Ground Beetle; 40c. Large White (Butterfly).

(No. J167. Eng K. Bickel, after painting by E. Handmann. Recess PTT, Bern. Nos. J168, J171 des N. Stoecklin. Nos. J169/J170 des H. Fischer. Photo Granite paper. Courvoisier)

1957 (30 Nov). T C **91** and insect designs as T C **84**. P 11½.

J167	5c. +5c. claret		1·00	50
J168	10c. +10c. yellow-orange, brown, greenish yellow and olive		1·00	90
J169	20c. +10c. yellow, deep brown and magenta		1·00	90
J170	30c. +10c. emerald, deep blue-green and light brown-purple		4·00	7·00
J171	40c. +10c. brown, red, sepia and cobalt		3·25	5·75
J167/J171 Set of 5			9·25	13·50

Designs: 5c. T C **91**; 10c. Clouded Yellow (Butterfly); 20c. Magpie Moth; 30c. Rose Chafer (Beetle); 40c. Rosy Underwing (Moth).

C **92** Albrecht von Haller (naturalist)   C **93** Pansy   C **94** Karl Hilty (lawyer)

(No. J172 Eng K. Bickel, after painting by S. Freudenberger. Recess PTT, Berne. Nos. J173/J176 des H. Schwarzenbach. Photo Granite paper. Courvoisier)

1958 (1 Dec). T C **92** and wild flowers as T C **93**. P 11½.

J172	5c. +5c. claret		95	50
J173	10c. +10c. yellow, brown and green		95	85
J174	20c. +10c. yellow, cerise, green and carmine-lake		95	85
J175	30c. +10c. yellow, blue, green and bistre-brown		2·50	4·50
J176	40c. +10c. yellow, grey, green and deep blue		2·50	4·50
J172/J176 Set of 5			7·00	10·00

Designs: 5c. T C **92**; 10c. T C **93**; 20c. Chinese Aster; 30c. Morning Glory; 40c. Christmas Rose.

(No. J177. Eng K. Bickel, after photo in Swiss National Library, Bern. Recess PTT, Bern. Nos. J178/J181 des H. Schwarzenbach. Photo Granite paper. Courvoisier)

1959 (1 Dec). T C **94** and wild flower types as T C **93**. P 11½.

J177	5c. +5c. claret		50	45
J178	10c. +10c. yellow, light brown, green and blue-green		50	45
J179	20c. +10c. scarlet, green and purple		50	45
J180	30c. +10c. yellow, orange, green and olive		3·00	4·50
J181	50c. +10c. magenta, yellow, green, grey and ultramarine		3·00	4·00
J177/J181 Set of 5			6·75	8·75

Designs: 5c. T C **94**; 10c. Marsh Marigold; 20c. Poppy; 30c. Nasturtium; 50c. Sweet Pea.

C **95** A. Calame (painter)   C **96** J. Furrer (First President of Swiss Confederation)

(No. J182. Eng K. Bickel, after lithograph by J. Hébert. Recess PTT, Bern. Nos. J183/J186 des H. Schwarzenbach. Photo Granite paper. Courvoisier)

1960 (1 Dec). T C **95** and wild flowers as T C **93**. P 11½.

J182	5c. +5c. greenish blue		50	50
J183	10c. +10c. yellow, yellow-green, drab and deep green		50	50
J184	20c. +10c. yellow-green, sepia and magenta		50	50
J185	30c. +10c. yellow-green, blue and orange-brown		3·25	6·00
J186	50c. +10c. greenish yellow, yellow-green and ultramarine		3·25	6·50
J182/J186 Set of 5			7·25	12·50

Designs: 5c. T C **95**; 10c. Dandelion; 20c. Phlox; 30c. Larkspur; 50c. Thorn Apple.

(No. J187. Eng K. Bickel, after lithograph by J. Hasler. Recess PTT, Bern. Nos. J188/J191 des H. Schwarzenbach. Photo Granite paper. Courvoisier)

1961 (1 Dec). T C **96** and wild flowers as T C **93**. P 11½.

J187	5c. +5c. deep blue		50	45
J188	10c. +10c. yellow, red, yellow-green and deep green		50	45
J189	20c. +10c. yellow, grey, green and red		50	45
J190	30c. +10c. violet, yellow, green and purple		2·10	3·50
J191	50c. +10c. yellow, green, brown and blue		2·40	4·00
J187/J191 Set of 5			5·50	8·00

Designs: 5c. T C **96**; 10c. Sunflower; 20c. Lily-of-the-Valley; 30c. Iris; 50c. Silverweed.

SWITZERLAND / 'Pro Juventute' Charity Stamps

C **97** Child's World   C **98** Mother and Child

C **98a** Mother and Child (*Illustration reduced, actual size 82×62 mm*)

(Des P. Roshardt (5c., 50c.), H. Steiner (10c., 30c.), F. Iselin (20c.), E. Renggli (100c.). Photo Granite paper. Courvoisier)

1962 (1 Dec). 50th Anniversary of Pro Juventute Foundation. T C **97** and similar designs inscr 'PRO JUVENTUTE 1912–1962' and Types C **98**/C **98a**. P 11½ or imperf. (No. **MS**J196*a*).

J192	5c. +5c. rose, green, yellow and slate-violet	50	45
J193	10c. +10c. carmine-red and green	50	45
J194	20c. +10c. light green, sepia, pink and orange-red	50	90
J195	30c. +10c. red, magenta and yellow	1·40	1·90
J196	50c. +10c. yellow, brown and blue	2·00	1·90
J192/J196 Set of 5		4·50	5·00
MSJ196*a* 82×62 mm. 100c.+20c. multicoloured (×2) (sold at 3f.)		9·00	7·25

Designs: Horiz as T C **97**—5c. Apple blossom; 10c. T C **97**; 30c. Child's World (child in meadow); 50c. Forsythia. Vert—20c. T C **98**. Vert as T C **98a**—100c.+20c.

PHOSPHORESCENT PAPER. All stamps from No. J197 to J248 are printed on phosphorescent paper with violet fibres, *unless otherwise stated*. See note below T **143**.

C **99** Portrait of a Boy (Anker)   C **100** Portrait of a Girl (Anker)   C **101** West European Hedgehogs

(5c. Des and Eng K. Bickel. Recess PTT, Bern. Others des W. Weiskönig. Photo Courvoisier)

1963 (30 Nov). T C **99** and wild flowers as T C **93**. P 11½.

J197	5c. +5c. greenish blue	65	55
	a. Ordinary white paper	3·00	3·50
J198	10c. +10c. yellow, yellow-brown, light blue and green	95	4·50
	a. Ordinary granite paper	2·10	1·40
J199	20c. +10c. orange-red, yellow-green and carmine	2·10	8·75
	a. Ordinary granite paper	2·10	1·40
J200	30c. +10c. rose, light blue, yellow-green and brown	2·50	2·75
J201	50c. +10c. bright purple, yellow green and blue	2·50	2·75
J197/J201 Set of 5 (cheapest)		7·75	8·00

Designs: 5c. T C **99**; 10c. Ox-eye Daisy; 20c. Geranium; 30c. Cornflower; 50c. Carnation.

(5c. Des and Eng K. Bickel. Recess. Plain paper. PTT, Bern. Others des W. Weiskönig. Photo Courvoisier)

1964 (1 Dec). T C **100** and wild flowers as T C **93**. P 11½.

J202	5c. +5c. turquoise-blue	50	45
J203	10c. +10c. orange, yellow and green	50	45
J204	20c. +10c. rose-red, green and carmine	60	45
J205	30c. +10c. bright purple, green and brown	1·10	85
J206	50c. +10c. red, yellow, grey-brown, green and blue	1·40	1·30
J202/J206 Set of 5		3·75	3·25

Designs: 5c. T C **100**; 10c. Daffodil; 20c. Rose; 30c. Red Clover; 50c. White Water Lily.

(Des H. Erni. Photo Courvoisier)

1965 (1 Dec). T C **101** and similar vert animal designs. P 11½.

J207	5c. +5c. ochre, chocolate and red	50	45
J208	10c. +10c. ochre, brown, black and greenish blue	50	45
J209	20c. +10c. grey-blue, brown and orange-brown	55	45
J210	30c. +10c. deep blue, black and yellow	95	85
J211	50c. +10c. black, brown and bright blue	1·20	85
J207/J211 Set of 5		3·25	2·75

Animals: 5c. T C **101**; 10c. Alpine Marmots; 20c. Red Deer; 30c. Eurasian Badgers; 50c. Arctic Hares.

(Des H. Erni. Photo Courvoisier)

1966 (1 Dec). Vert animal designs as T C **101**. Multicoloured. P 11½.

J212	5c. +5c. Stoat	50	45
J213	10c. +10c. Eurasian Red Squirrel	50	45
J214	20c. +10c. Red Fox	55	45
J215	30c. +10c. Brown Hare	95	85
J216	50c. +10c. Chamois	1·20	85
J212/J216 Set of 5		3·25	2·75

C **102** Roe Deer   C **103** Capercaeillie   C **104** McGredy's Sunset Rose

(Des C. Piatti. Photo Courvoisier)

1967 (1 Dec). Vert animal designs as T C **102**. Multicoloured. P 11½.

J217	10c. +10c. Type C**102**	50	35
J218	20c. +10c. Pine Marten	65	45
J219	30c. +10c. Ibex	95	45
J220	50c. +20c. European Otter	1·40	90
J217/J220 Set of 4		3·25	1·90

(Des W. Wehinger. Photo Courvoisier)

1968 (28 Nov). T C **103** and similar vert bird designs, Multicoloured. P 11½.

J221	10c. +10c. Type C **103**	50	35
J222	20c. +10c. Northern Bullfinch	65	45
J223	30c. +10c. Woodchat Shrike	95	45
J224	50c. +20c. Firecrest	1·40	90
J221/J224 Set of 4		3·25	1·90

(Des W. Wehinger. Photo Courvoisier)

1969 (1 Dec). Vert bird designs as T C **103**. Multicoloured. P 11½.

J225	10c. +10c. Eurasian Goldfinch	50	35
J226	20c. +10c. Golden Oriole	60	45
J227	30c. +10c. Wallcreeper	95	45
J228	50c. +20c. Jay	1·40	90
J225/J228 Set of 4		3·00	1·90

(Des R. Gerbig. Photo Courvoisier)

1970 (1 Dec). Vert bird designs as T C **103**. Multicoloured. P 11½.

J229	10c. +10c. Blue Tits	50	35
J230	20c. +10c. Hoopoe	60	45
J231	30c. +10c. Great Spotted Woodpecker	95	45
J232	50c. +20c. Great Crested Grebes	1·40	90
J229/J232 Set of 4		3·00	1·90

(Des R. Gerbig. Photo Courvoisier)

1971 (1 Dec). Vert bird designs as T C **103**. Multicoloured. P 11½.

J233	10c. +10c. Common Redstarts	50	20
J234	20c. +10c. Bluethroats	65	30
J235	30c. +10c. Peregrine Falcon	1·00	45
J236	40c. +20c. Mallards	2·20	1·90
J233/J236 Set of 4		4·00	2·50

(Des A. M. Trechslin. Photo Courvoisier)

1972 (1 Dec). Vert Rose designs as T C **104**. Multicoloured. P 11½.

J237	10c. +10c. Type C **104**	50	20
J238	20c. +10c. Miracle	60	30
J239	30c. +10c. Papa Meilland	95	45
J240	40c. +20c. Madame Dimitriu	2·20	1·90
J237/J240 Set of 4		3·75	2·50

SWITZERLAND / 'Pro Juventute' Charity Stamps

C **105** Chestnut   C **106** Arms of Aarburg   C **107** Letter Balance

(Des K. Baumgartner. Photo Courvoisier)

1973 (29 Nov). Fruits of the Forest. T C **105** and similar vert designs. Multicoloured. P 11½.

J241	15c. +5c. Type C **105**	50	30
J242	30c. +10c. Cherries	60	35
J243	40c. +20c. Blackberries	1·40	1·00
J244	60c. +25c. Bilberries	2·40	2·10
J241/J244	Set of 4	4·50	3·50

(Des H. Schwarzenbach. Photo Courvoisier)

1974 (29 Nov). Fruits of the Forest. Vert designs as T C **105**. Multicoloured. P 11½.

J245	15c. +10c. Daphne	65	30
J246	30c. +20c. Belladonna	95	40
J247	50c. +20c. Laburnum	1·60	1·30
J248	60c. +25c. Mistletoe	2·00	1·50
J245/J248	Set of 4	4·75	3·25

Nos. J245 and J247 were issued on fibre-less paper.

PHOSPHORESCENT PAPER. All stamps from No. J249 are printed on phosphorescent, fibre-less paper, *unless otherwise stated*.

(Des Courvoisier (10c.), K. Baumgartner (15c, 30c., 50c.). V. Wyss-Fischer (60c.). Photo Courvoisier)

1975 (27 Nov). Vert designs as T C **105**. Multicoloured. P 11½.

J249	10c. +5c. Post-Brent (postman's hamper)	60	55
J250	15c. +10c. Hepatica	50	40
J251	30c. +20c. Rowan	95	45
J252	50c. +20c. Yellow Deadnettle	1·50	1·20
J253	60c. +25c. Sycamore	2·00	1·70
J249/J253	Set of 5	5·00	3·75

(Des V. Wyss-Fischer (20c., 80c.). H. Schwarzenbach (40c.). Photo Courvoisier)

1976 (29 Nov). Fruits of the Forest. Vert designs as T C **105**. Multicoloured. P 11½.

J254	20c. +10c. Barberry	55	30
J255	40c. +20c. Black Elder	1·20	40
J256	40c. +20c. Lime	1·20	45
J257	80c. +40c. Lungwort	2·30	2·20
J254/J257	Set of 4	4·75	3·00

(Des A. M. Trechslin. Photo Courvoisier)

1977 (28 Nov). Roses. Vert designs as T C **104**. Multicoloured. P 11½.

J258	20c. +10c. *Rosa foetida bicolor*	60	35
J259	40c. +20c. Parfum de l' Hay	1·20	45
J260	70c. +30c. *R. foetida persiana*	2·00	1·80
J261	80c. +40c. *R. centifolia muscosa*	2·50	2·30
J258/J261	Set of 4	5·75	4·50

(Des G. Cambin. Photo Courvoisier)

1978 (28 Nov). Arms of the Communes. T C **106** and similar vert designs. Multicoloured. P 11½.

J262	20c. +10c. Type C **106**	60	35
J263	40c. +20c. Gruyères	1·10	45
J264	70c. +30c. Castasegna	2·00	1·50
J265	80c. +40c. Wangen	3·00	2·20
J262/J265	Set of 4	6·00	4·00

(Des G. Cambin. Photo Courvoisier)

1979 (28 Nov). Arms of the Communes. Vert designs as T C **106**. Multicoloured. P 11½.

J266	20c. +10c. Cadro	65	40
J267	40c. +20c. Rüte	1·10	45
J268	70c. +30c. Schwamendingen	2·00	1·70
J269	80c. +40c. Perroy	3·00	2·30
J266/J269	Set of 4	6·00	4·25

(Des G. Cambin. Photo Courvoisier)

1980 (26 Nov). Arms of the Communes. Vert designs as T C **106**. Multicoloured. P 11½.

J270	20c. +10c. Cortaillod	60	40
J271	40c. +20c. Sierre	1·30	45
J272	70c. +30c. Scuol	2·00	1·80
J273	80c. +40c. Wolfenschiessen	3·00	2·20
J270/J273	Set of 4	6·25	4·25

(Des G. Cambin. Photo Courvoisier)

1981 (26 Nov). Arms of the Communes. Vert designs as T C **106**. Multicoloured. P 11½.

J274	20c. +10c. Uffikon	60	40
J275	40c. +20c. Torre	1·20	45
J276	70c. +30c. Benken	2·00	1·80
J277	80c. +40c. Préverenges	3·00	2·20
J274/J277	Set of 4	6·00	4·25

(Des E. Witzig (10c.), Anne Marie Trechslin (others). Photo Courvoisier)

1982 (25 Nov). T C **107** and vert Rose designs as T C **104**. Multicoloured. P 11½.

J278	10c. +10c. Type C **107**	1·00	30
J279	20c. +10c. La Belle Portugaise	55	30
J280	40c. +20c. Hugh Dickson	1·20	45
J281	70c. +30c. Mermaid	2·00	1·70
J282	80c. +40c. Madame Caroline Testout	3·00	2·30
J278/J282	Set of 5	7·00	4·50

C **108** Kitchen Stove, c. 1850   C **109** Heidi and Goat (Johanna Spyri)

(Des G. Rimensberger. Photo Courvoisier)

1983 (24 Nov). Children's Toys. T C **108** and similar horiz designs. Multicoloured. P 11½.

J283	20c. +10c. Type C **108**	1·10	50
J284	40c. +20c. Rocking Horse, 1826	1·70	50
J285	70c. +30c. Doll, c. 1870	2·20	2·00
J286	80c. +40c. Steam locomotive, c. 1900	3·25	2·50
J283/J286	Set of 4	7·50	5·00

(Des G. Rimensberger. Photo Courvoisier)

1984 (26 Nov). Characters from Children's Books. T C **109** and similar horiz designs. Multicoloured. P 11½.

J287	35c. +15c. Type C **109**	1·10	1·00
J288	50c. +20c. Pinocchio and kite (Carlo Callodi)	1·50	70
J289	70c. +30c. Pippi Longstocking (Astrid Lindgren)	3·25	2·75
J290	80c. +40c. Max and Moritz on roof (Wilhelm Busch)	3·75	3·25
J287/J290	Set of 4	8·75	7·00

(Des G. Rimensberger. Photo Courvoisier)

1985 (26 Nov). Characters from Children's Books. Horiz designs as T C **109**. Multicoloured. P 11½.

J291	35c. +15c. Hansel, Gretel and Witch	1·10	1·00
J292	50c. +20c. Snow White and the seven dwarves	1·50	70
J293	80c. +40c. Red Riding Hood and Wolf	3·25	2·75
J294	90c. +40c. Cinderella and Prince Charming	3·75	3·25
J291/J294	Set of 4	8·75	7·00

C **110** Teddy Bear   C **111** Girl carrying Pine Branch and Candle

(Des E. Witzig. Photo Courvoisier)

1986 (25 Nov). Children's Toys. T C **110** and similar vert designs. Multicoloured. P 11½.

J295	35c. +15c. Type C **110**	1·10	1·00
J296	50c. +20c. Spinning top	1·90	50
J297	80c. +40c. Steamroller	3·50	3·25
J298	90c. +40c. Doll	4·00	3·75
J295/J298	Set of 4	9·50	7·75

(Des Eleonore Schmid. Photo Courvoisier)

1987 (24 Nov). Child Development Pre-school Age. T C **111** and similar vert designs. Multicoloured. P 11½.

J299	25c. +10c. Type C **111**	95	85
J300	35c. +15c. Mother breastfeeding baby	1·60	1·30

SWITZERLAND / 'Pro Juventute' Charity Stamps

J301	50c. +20c. Toddler playing with bricks	1·50	70
J302	80c. +40c. Children playing in sand	2·75	2·50
J303	90c. +40c. Father with child on his shoulders	3·25	3·00
J299/J303 Set of 5		9·00	7·50

C **112** Learning to Read   C **113** Community Work

(Des Harriet Höppner. Photo Courvoisier)

1988 (25 Nov). Child Development School Age. T C **112** and similar vert designs. Multicoloured. P 11½.

J304	35c. +15c. Type C **112**	1·10	1·00
J305	50c. +20c. Playing triangle	1·70	60
J306	80c. +40c. Learning arithmetic	3·25	3·00
J307	90c. +40c. Drawing	4·00	3·75
J304/J307 Set of 4		9·00	7·50

(Des R. Mühlemann. Photo Courvoisier)

1989 (24 Nov). Child Development Adolescence. T C **113** and similar vert designs. Multicoloured. P 11½.

J308	35c. +15c. Type C **113**	1·10	1·00
J309	50c. +20c. Young couple (friendship)	1·70	60
J310	80c. +40c. Boy at computer screen (vocational training)	3·25	3·00
J311	90c. +40c. Girl in laboratory (higher education and research)	4·00	3·75
J308/J311 Set of 4		9·00	7·50

C **114** Building Model Ship (hobbies)   C **115** Ramsons

(Des F. Bauer. Photo Courvoisier)

1990 (20 Nov). Child Development. Leisure Activities. T C **114** and similar horiz designs. Multicoloured. P 11½.

J312	35c. +15c. Type C **114**	1·50	1·20
J313	60c. +20c. Youth group	1·70	70
J314	80c. +40c. Sport	3·25	3·00
J315	90c. +40c. Music	4·00	3·75
J312/J315 Set of 4		9·50	7·75

(Des V. Wyss-Fischer. Photo Courvoisier)

1991 (26 Nov). Woodland Flowers. T C **115** and similar vert designs. Multicoloured. P 11½.

J316	50c. +25c. Type C **115**	1·80	1·20
J317	70c. +30c. Wood Cranesbill	2·20	2·00
J318	80c. +40c. Nettle-leaved Bellflower	3·25	3·00
J319	90c. +40c. Few-leaved Hawkweed	3·50	3·25
J316/J319 Set of 4		9·75	8·50

C **116** Melchior (wooden puppet)   C **117** Christmas Wreath

(Des Bernadette Baltis. Photo Courvoisier)

1992 (24 Nov). Christmas (No. J320) and Trees (others). T C **116** and similar horiz designs showing silhouette of tree and close-up of its leaves and fruit. Multicoloured. P 11½.

J320	50c. +25c. Type C **116**	2·00	1·00
J321	50c. +25c. Beech	2·00	1·00
J322	70c. +30c. Norway Maple	3·00	2·00
J323	80c. +40c. Pedunculate Oak	3·25	2·50
J324	90c. +40c. Norway Spruce	3·75	3·50
J320/J324 Set of 5		12·50	9·00

(Des Bernadette Baltis. Photo Courvoisier)

1993 (23 Nov). Christmas (No. J325) and Woodland Plants (others). T C **117** and similar vert designs. Multicoloured. P 11½.

J325	60c. +30c. Type C **117**	2·50	1·60
J326	60c. +30c. Male Fern	2·50	1·60
J327	80c. +40c. Guelder Rose	3·25	3·00
J328	100c. +50c. *Mnium punctatum*	4·25	3·25
J325/J328 Set of 4		11·50	8·50

C **118** Candles   C **119** Detail of The Annunciation (after Bartolomé Murillo)

(Des B. Brüsch. Photo Courvoisier)

1994 (28 Nov). Christmas (No. J329) and Fungi (others). T C **118** and similar horiz designs. Multicoloured. P 11½.

J329	60c. +30c. Type C **118**	2·40	1·60
J330	60c. +30c. Wood Blewit (*Lepista nuda*)	2·40	1·60
J331	80c. +40c. Red Boletus (*Leccinum* sp.)	3·50	3·00
J332	100c. +50c. Shaggy Pholiota (*Pholiota squarrosa*)	4·25	3·25
J329/J332 Set of 4		11·50	8·50

(Des G. Forster. Photo Courvoisier)

1995 (28 Nov). Christmas (No. J333) and Wildlife (others). T C **119** and similar horiz designs. Multicoloured. P 11½.

J333	60c. +30c. Type C **119**	2·50	1·50
J334	60c. +30c. Brown Trout	2·50	1·50
J335	80c. +40c. Grey Wagtail	3·50	3·00
J336	100c. +50c. Spotted Salamander	4·25	3·50
J333/J336 Set of 4		11·50	8·50

C **120** Shooting Star and Constellations   C **121** Mistletoe

(Des B. Struchen. Photo Courvoisier)

1996 (26 Nov). Christmas (No. J337) and Wildlife (others). T C **120** and similar horiz designs. Multicoloured. P 11½.

J337	70c. +35c. Type C **120**	3·00	2·20
J338	70c. +35c. European Grayling	3·00	2·20
J339	90c. +45c. Crayfish	3·75	3·50
J340	110c. +55c. European Otter	4·75	4·25
J337/J340 Set of 4		13·00	11·00

(Des Eleonore Schimd. Photo Courvoisier)

1997 (20 Nov). Christmas (No. J341) and Wildlife (others). T C **121** and similar horiz designs. Multicoloured. P 11½.

J341	70c. +35c. Type C **121**	3·25	2·20
J342	70c. +35c. Three-spined Stickleback	3·25	2·20
J343	90c. +45c. Yellow-bellied Toad	4·00	3·50
J344	110c. +55c. Ruff	4·50	4·25
J341/J344 Set of 4		13·50	11·00

C **122** Christmas Bell   C **123** Children and Snowman (Margaret Strub)

(Des B. Struchen. Photo Courvoisier)

1998 (8 Nov). Christmas (No. J345) and Wildlife (others). T C **122** and similar horiz designs. Multicoloured. P 11½.

J345	70c. +35c. Type C **122**	3·25	2·00

J346	70c. +35c. Ramshorn Snail	3·25	2·00
J347	90c. +45c. Great Crested Grebe	3·75	3·50
J348	110c. +55c. Pike	4·75	4·25
J345/J348	Set of 4	13·50	10·50

(Litho PTT, Bern)

1999 (23 Nov). Christmas (No. J349) and Illustrations from *Nicolo the Clown* (picture book by Verena Pavoni) (others). T C **123** and similar vert designs. Multicoloured. P 13½.

J349	70c. +35c. Type C **123**	3·25	2·20
J350	70c. +35c. Nicolo holding guitar	3·25	2·20
J351	90c. +45c. Nicolo with his father	3·75	3·25
J352	110c. +55c. Nicolo with Donkey	4·25	4·00
J349/J352	Set of 4	13·00	10·50

C **124** Santa Claus   C **125** Santa Claus and Cat

(Litho PTT, Bern)

2000 (21 Nov). Christmas. Illustrations from *Little Albert* (book) by Albert Manser. T C **124** and similar horiz designs. Multicoloured. Paper with fluorescent fibres. P 13½.

J353	70c. +35c. Type C **124**	3·50	3·00
J354	70c. +35c. Boys sitting on fence and girl	3·50	3·00
J355	90c. +45c. Little Albert with umbrella	4·50	4·00
J356	90c. +45c. Children sledging	4·50	4·00
J353/J356	Set of 4	14·50	12·50

(Des Gabi Fluck (No. J357) and Stephan Brülhart (others) Litho PTT, Bern)

2001 (20 Nov). Illustrations from Children's Books. T C **125** and similar vert designs. Multicoloured. Paper with fluorescent fibres. P 13½.

J357	70c. +35c. Type C **125** (*What's Santa Claus Doing?* (text Karin von Oldersausen, illustrations Gabi Fluck))	3·50	3·00
J358	70c. +35c. Leopold the Leopard in tree (*Leopold and the Sun* by Stephan Brülhart)	3·50	3·00
J359	90c. +45c. Bear on scooter (*Honey Bear* by S. Brülhart)	4·50	4·00
J360	90c. +45c. Tom the Monkey in tree (*Leopold and the Sun*)	4·50	4·00
J357/J360	Set of 4	14·50	12·50

C **126** Christmas Rose   C **127** Playing with Christmas Toys

(Des Anne Marie Trechslin. Litho Enschedé)

2002 (19 Nov). Roses. T C **126** and similar vert designs. Multicoloured. P 13½.

J361	70c. +35c. Type C **126**	3·50	3·00
J362	70c. +35c. Ingrid Bergman	3·50	3·00
J363	90c. +45c. Belle Vaudoise	4·50	4·00
J364	90c. +45c. Charmian	4·50	4·00
J365	130c. +65c. Frühlingsgold	6·50	6·00
J361/J365	Set of 5	20·00	18·00

No. J361 is impregnated with the fragrance of Cinnamon and Cloves and Nos. J362/J365 with the perfume of Roses.

(Des Anne Marie Trechslin. Litho Banknote Corporation of America Inc, Browns Summit, North Carolina)

2003 (19 Nov). Children's Rights. The Right to Play. T C **127** and similar horiz designs. Multicoloured. Self-adhesive gum. Die-cut perf 10½×11.

J366	70c. +35c. Type C **127**	3·50	3·25
J367	85c. +35c. Playing shop	4·00	3·75
J368	90c. +45c. Skateboarding	4·50	4·00
J369	100c. +45c. Playing music	4·75	4·25
J366/J369	Set of 4	15·00	13·50

C **128** Family and Giraffe   C **129** Children enclosed in Lifebuoy

(Des Patricia Brunner. Litho Banknote Corporation of America Inc, Browns Summit, North Carolina)

2004 (23 Nov). Children's Rights. Right to Education. T C **128** and similar horiz designs. Multicoloured. Self-adhesive gum. Die-cut perf 10½×11.

J370	85c. +40c. Type C **128**	4·50	4·25
J371	85c. +40c. Playing cards	4·50	4·25
J372	100c. +50c. Listening to older person read	5·25	5·00
J373	100c. +50c. Teacher and pupils	5·25	5·00
J370/J373	Set of 4	18·00	17·00

(Des A. Boog. Litho)

2005 (22 Nov). Children's Rights. Right to Leisure and Play. T C **129** and similar horiz designs. Multicoloured. Self-adhesive gum. Die-cut perf 10½×11.

J374	85c. +40c. Type C **129**	4·50	4·25
J375	85c. +40c. Boy and girl catching Cherries in mouth	4·50	4·25
J376	100c. +50c. Children and laptop computer	5·25	5·00
J377	100c. +50c. Boy wishing	5·25	5·00
J374/J377	Set of 4	18·00	17·00

C **130** Singer (Veronica Jesus Garcia Pinto)   C **131** Camping (Christine Fischer)

(Des T. Scapa (No. J381). Litho Tesa Bandfix AG)

2006 (22 Nov). Winning Designs in Children's Painting Competition My Dream Profession. T C **130** and similar horiz designs. Multicoloured. Self-adhesive gum. Die-cut perf 11.

J378	85c. +40c. Type C **130**	4·50	4·25
J379	85c. +40c. Workshop (garage owner) (Stéphane Arada)	4·50	4·25
J380	100c. +50c. Dog with bandaged leg (vert) (Lea Mayer)	5·25	5·00
J381	100c. +50c. Angel	5·25	5·00
J378/J381	Set of 4	18·00	17·00

Nos. J378/J381 were issued in sheets with the surplus paper around the stamp removed.

Nos. J379/J380, each×6, were also issued in booklets of 12 stamps with the paper retained.

(Des Ted Scapa (No. J385) Litho Tesa Bandfix Ag)

2007 (20 Nov). Winning Designs in Children's Design a Stamp Competition. Holiday Fun. T C **131** and similar horiz designs. Multicoloured. Die-cut perf 11.

J382	85c. +40c. Type C **131**	4·50	4·25
J383	85c. +40c. Mountains (Jonathon Balest)	4·50	4·25
J384	100c. +50c. Sunshine (Morena Rufatti)	5·25	5·00
J385	100c. +50c. Angels carrying heart	5·25	5·00
J382/J385	Set of 4	18·00	17·00

Nos. J382/J385 were issued in sheets with the surplus paper around the stamp removed.

Nos. J382 and J384, each×6, were also issued in booklets of 12 stamps with the paper retained.

C **132** Friendship unites (Andrea Andreazzi)   C **133** Letters to Parents

(Des Ted Scapa (No. J389). Litho Tesa Bandfix AG)

2008 (21 Nov). Winning Designs in Children's Design a Stamp Competition. Friendship. T C **132** and similar horiz designs. Multicoloured. Die-cut perf 11.

J386	85c. +40c. Type C **132**	4·50	4·25

SWITZERLAND / 'Pro Juventute' Charity Stamps

J387	85c. +40c. Friendship provides support (Manon Peng)		4·50	4·25
J388	100c. +50c. Friendship is a source of happiness (Delia Candolo)		5·25	5·00
J389	100c. +50c. Friendship is uplifting		5·25	5·00
J386/J389 Set of 4			18·00	17·00

Nos. J386/J389 were issued in sheets with the surplus paper around the stamp removed.
Nos. J386 and J388, each×6, were also issued in booklets of 12 stamps with the paper retained.

(Des Theresia Nuber. Litho Enschedé)

2009 (20 Nov). Pro Juventute Foundation. T C **133** and similar horiz designs. Multicoloured. Self-adhesive. Die-cut perf 12.

J390	85c. +40c. Type C **133**		4·50	4·25
J391	85c. +40c. Tree branches and children (holiday pass scheme)		4·50	4·25
J392	100c. +50c. Parents back to back (Tel. 147 advice line)		5·25	5·00
J393	100c. +50c. Children and stamps (stamp sales)		5·25	5·00
J390/J393 Set of 4			18·00	17·00

Nos. J390/J393 were issued in sheets with the surplus paper around the stamp removed.
Nos. J392 and J393, each×6, were also issued in booklets of 12 stamps with the paper retained.

C **134** Child and Toy Pig   C **135** Baby

(Des Tessa Gerster. Litho Enschedé)

2010 (4 Nov). Children and Money. T C **134** and similar horiz designs. Multicoloured. Self-adhesive. Die-cut perf 12.

J394	85c. +40c. Type C **134**		4·50	4·25
J395	85c. +40c. Child thinking of teddy bear		4·50	4·25
J396	100c. +40c. Child with toy pig and teddy bear		5·25	5·00
J397	100c. +50c. Child with toy pig carrying present		5·25	5·00
J394/J397 Set of 4			18·00	17·00

Nos. J395 and J397 were printed both in large sheets and, each×6, in booklets of 12 stamps.
Nos. J394 and J396 were printed in sheets.

(Des Martina Pelosi and Julia Reichle. Litho Enschedé)

2011 (24 Nov). Security, Friendship, Trust and Confidence. T C **135** and similar horiz designs. Multicoloured. Self-adhesive. Die-cut perf 12.

J398	85c. +40c. Type C **135**		4·50	4·25
J399	85c. +40c. Teenager		4·50	4·25
J400	100c. +50c. Girl		5·25	5·00
J401	100c. +50c. Boy		5·25	5·00
J398/J401 Set of 4			18·00	17·00

Nos. J398/J401 were printed both in large sheets and, each×3, in booklets of 12 stamps.

C **136** Children swinging   C **137** Children playing, 1959

(Des Nadine Colin. Litho Enschedé)

2012 (8 Mar). Centenary of Projuventute Foundation. Self-adhesive. Die-cut perf 12.

J402	C **136** 100c. +50c. multicoloured		5·25	5·00

(Des Margrethe Guttchen-Lipps (No. J403), Celestino Piatti (No. J404) or Victor Rutz (No. J405). Litho Enschedé)

2012 (22 Nov). Centenary of Pro Juventute Foundation. Posters. T C **137** and similar vert designs. Multicoloured. Self-adhesive. Die-cut perf 12.

J403	85c. +40c. Type C **137**		4·50	4·25
J404	100c. +50c. Child in High Chair, 1955		5·25	5·00
J405	100c. +50c. Infant with doll, 1952		5·25	5·00
J403/J405 Set of 3			13·50	13·00

C **138** SBB Rae 2/4 Roter Pfeil (Red Arrow) Light Railcar   C **139** Children with Lanterns

(Des Laszlo Horvath. Litho Enschedé)

2013 (14 Nov). Model Railways. T C **138** and similar horiz designs showing children's faces and model trains. Multicoloured. Self-adhesive. Die-cut perf 12.

J406	85c. +40c. Type C **138**		4·50	4·25
J407	100c. +50c. SBB Ce6/8 Krokodil electric locomotive		5·25	5·00
J408	100c. +50c. SBB Ae 6/6 locomotive		5·25	5·00
J406/J408 Set of 3			13·50	13·00

Nos. J406/J408 were printed both in large sheets and, each×4, in booklets of 12 stamps.

(Des Nicolas d'Aujourd'hui. Litho Enschedé)

2014 (13 Nov). Family Rituals. T C **139** and similar horiz designs showing children. Multicoloured. Self-adhesive. Die-cut perf 12.

J409	85c. +40c. Type C **139**		4·50	4·25
J410	100c. +50c. Story telling		5·25	5·00
J411	100c. +50c. Christmas baking		5·25	5·00
J409/J411 Set of 3			13·50	13·00

Nos. J409/J411 were printed both in sheets of ten with the surplus paper around the stamp removed, and, each×4, in booklets of 12 stamps with the surplus paper retained.

C **140** Eating Lunch   C **141** Playing Hopscotch

(Des Nicolas d'Aujourd'hui. Litho Enschedé)

2015 (13 Nov). Family Rituals. T C **140** and similar horiz designs showing families. Multicoloured. Self-adhesive. Die-cut perf 12.

J412	85c. +40c. Type C **140**		4·50	4·25
J413	100c. +50c. Around the Christmas tree		5·25	5·00
J414	100c. +50c. Making homemade toys		5·25	5·00
J412/J414 Set of 3			13·50	13·00

Nos. J412/J414 were printed both in sheets of ten with the surplus paper around the stamp removed, and, each×4, in booklets of 12 stamps with the surplus paper retained.

(Des Christian Kitzmüller. Litho Enschedé)

2016 (13 Nov). School Days. T C **141** and similar horiz design. Multicoloured. Self-adhesive. Die-cut perf 12.

J415	85c. +40c. Type C **141**		4·50	4·25
J416	100c. +50c. Children and teacher at blackboard		5·25	5·00

Nos. J415/J416 were printed both in sheets of ten with the surplus paper around the stamp removed, and, each×6, in booklets of 12 stamps with the surplus paper retained.

C **142** Children   C **143** Boy and Building Bricks

(Des Christian Kitzmüller)

2017 (16 Nov). School Days. T C **142** and similar horiz design. Multicoloured. Self-adhesive. Die-cut perf 12.

J417	85c. +40c. Type C **142**		4·50	4·25
J418	100c. +50c. Childrens choir		5·25	5·00

Nos. J417/J418 were printed both in sheets of ten with the surplus paper around the stamp removed, and, each×6, in booklets of 12 stamps with the surplus paper retained.

(Des Mark Baumgartner. Litho Enschedé)
2018 (15 Nov). Happy Childhood. T C **143** and similar horiz design. Multicoloured. Self-adhesive. Die-cut perf 12.

J419	85c. +40c. Type C	4·50	4·25
J420	100c. +50c. Girl blowing bubbles	5·25	5·00

Nos. J419/J420 were printed both in sheets of ten with the surplus paper around the stamp removed, and, each×6, in booklets of 12 stamps with the surplus paper retained.

'PRO JUVENTUTE' STAMP BOOKLETS

The following checklist covers booklets containing 'Pro Juventute' stamps. It is intended that it should be used in conjunction with the main listings so that details of stamps and panes listed there are not repeated.

With the exception of No. JSB1, all these booklets were sold at above face value, the premium being used to defray the costs of making up the booklets. From 1953–1966 inclusive this premium was 20c.; from 1967–1972, 40c.; from 1973–1989, 60c.; and from 1990 onwards, 1f.

Prices are for complete booklets

Booklet No.	Date	Contents and Cover Price	Price
JSB1	1915	5 panes, No. J1a×6	£2500
JSB2	1953	1 pane, No. J147×6; 1 pane, J148×6; 1 pane, J149a. Text On Cover in French	£300
JSB3	1953	As No. JSB2, but text On Cover in German	£150
JSB4	1954	3 panes, No. J152×4; 3 panes, J153×4; 1 pane, J154×4	£120
JSB5	1955	3 panes, No. J157×4; 3 panes, J158×4; 1 pane, J159×4	90·00
JSB6	1956	3 panes, No. J162×4; 3 panes, J163×4; 1 pane, J164×4	65·00
JSB7	1957	3 panes, No. J167×4; 3 panes, J168×4; 1 pane, J169×4	£225
JSB8	1958	3 panes, No. J172×4; 3 panes, J173×4; 1 pane, J174×4	70·00
JSB9	1959	3 panes, No. J177×4; 3 panes, J178×4; 1 pane, J179×4	37·00
JSB10	1960	3 panes, No. J182×4; 3 panes, J183×4; 1 pane, J184×4	37·00
JSB11	1961	3 panes, No. J187×4; 3 panes, J188×4; 1 pane, J189×4	37·00
JSB12	1962	4 panes, No. J192×4; 4 panes, J193×4	37·00
JSB13	1963	3 panes, No. J197×4; 3 panes, J198×4; 1 pane, J199×4	42·00
JSB14	1964	3 panes, No. J202×4; 3 panes, J203×4; 1 pane, J204×4	25·00
JSB15	1965	3 panes, No. J207×4; 3 panes, J208×4; 1 pane, J209×4	17·00
JSB16	1966	3 panes, No. J212×4; 3 panes, J213×4; 1 pane, J214×4	17·00
JSB17	1967	2 panes, No. J217×4; 2 panes, J218×4; 1 pane, J219×4	15·00
JSB18	1968	2 panes, No. J221×4; 2 panes, J222×4; 1 pane, J223×4	13·50
JSB19	1969	2 panes, No. J225×4; 2 panes, J226×4; 1 pane, J227×4	13·00
JSB20	1970	2 panes, No. J229×4; 2 panes, J230×4; 1 pane, J231×4	13·00
JSB21	1971	2 panes, No. J233×4; 2 panes, J234×4; 1 pane, J235×4	13·50
JSB22	1972	2 panes, No. J237×4; 2 panes, J238×4; 1 pane, J239×4	13·00
JSB23	1973	3 panes, No. J241×4; 1 pane, J242×4; 1 pane, J243×4	15·00
JSB24	1974	2 panes, No. J245×4, 2 panes, J246×4	13·50
JSB25	1975	2 panes, No. J249×4; 1 pane, J250×4, 2 panes, J251×4	15·00
JSB26	1976	2 panes, No. J254×4; 1 pane, J255×4; 1 pane, J256×4	14·50
JSB27	1977	2 panes, No. J258×4; 2 panes, J259×4	15·00
JSB28	1978	2 panes, No. J262×4; 2 panes, J263×4	14·00
JSB29	1979	2 panes, No. J266×4; 2 panes, J267×4	14·50
JSB30	1980	2 panes, No. J270×4; 2 panes, J271×4	16·00
JSB31	1981	2 panes, No. J274×4; 2 panes, J275×4	15·00
JSB32	1982	2 panes, No. J279×4; 2 panes, J280×4	14·50
JSB33	1983	2 panes, No. J283×4; 2 panes, J284×4	23·00
JSB34	1984	1 pane, No. J287×4; 3 panes, J288×4	23·00
JSB35	1985	3 panes, No. J292×4	19·00
JSB36	1986	3 panes, No. J296×4	24·00
JSB37	1987	2 panes, No. J299×4, 2 panes, J301×4	21·00
JSB38	1988	3 panes, No. J306×4	40·00
JSB39	1989	3 panes, No. J309×4	21·00
JSB40	1990	1 pane, No. J313×10	18·00
JSB41	1991	1 pane, No. J316×10	19·00
JSB42	1992	1 pane, No. J321×10	21·00
JSB43	1993	1 pane, No. J326×10	26·00
JSB44	1994	1 pane, No. J330×10	25·00
JSB45	1995	1 pane, No. J334×10	26·00
JSB46	1996	1 pane, No. J338×10	31·00
JSB47	1997	1 pane, No. J342×10	34·00
JSB48	1998	1 pane, No. J345×6; 1 pane, J347×4	36·00
JSB49	1999	1 pane, No. J350×6; 1 pane, J351×4	36·00
JSB50	2000	1 pane, No. J354×6; 1 pane, 355×4	40·00
JSB51	2001	1 pane, No. J358×6; 1 pane, J359×4	40·00
JSB52	2002	1 pane, No. 362×6; 1 pane, 363×4	40·00
JSB53	2003	1 pane, No. J367×6; 1 pane No. J369×6	60·00
JSB54	2004	1 pane, No. J371×6; 1 pane No. J373×6	65·00
JSB55	2005	1 pane, No. J374×6; 1 pane No. J376×6	65·00
JSB56	2006	1 pane, No. J379×6; 1 pane No. J380×6	65·00
JSB57	2007	1 pane, No. J382×6; 1 pane No. J384×6	65·00
JSB58	2008	1 pane, No. J386×6; 1 pane No. J388×6	65·00
JSB59	2009	1 pane, Nos. J390 and J393, each×6	65·00
JSB60	2010	1 pane, Nos. J395 and J397, each×6	65·00
JSB61	2011	1 pane, Nos. J398/J400, each×3	50·00
JSB62	2012	1 pane, No. J403/J405, each×4	65·00
JSB63	2013	Model Railways 1 pane, Nos. J406/J408, each×4	65·00
JSB64	2014	Family Ritual 1 pane, Nos. J409/J411, each×4 (17f.)	65·00
JSB65	2015	Family Ritual 1 pane, Nos. J415/J416, each×6 (16f.50)	65·00
JSB66	2016	School Days 1 pane, Nos. J415/J416, each×6 (17f.)	65·00
JSB67	2017	School Days 1 pane, Nos. J417/J418, each×6 (16f.50)	65·00
JSB68	2018	Happy Childhood 1 pane, Nos. J419/J420, each×6 (16f.50)	65·00

POSTCARD STAMP BOOKLETS

PCSB1	19.11.02	Tourism Emblem (Type P **1**) No. P1×6 (7f.20)	24·00
PCSB2	19.11.02	Tourism Emblem No. P2×6 (10f.)	31·00

SWITZERLAND / Design Index

DESIGN INDEX

This index provides in a condensed form a key to designs and subjects of Swiss stamps. In all sections, where the same design, or subject, appears more than once in a set only the first number is given.

Portraits are listed under surnames only; those without surnames (e.g. rulers and some saints) are under forenames. Works of art and inventions are indexed under the artist's, or inventors, name, where this appears on the stamp. Other issues appear under the main subject or part of the inscription. The Pro Juventute stamp designs are also included in this index.

100 ... 1764
700 Anni ... 1222
700 Ans ... 1221
700 Jahre ... 1219
700 Onns ... 1220
7.9.87 (overprint) ... 1138
1291–1991 ... 1215, 1224
1903 Stamp ... 1820

A

A ... 1258, 1313, 1327, 1480
Aarburg ... J262
Aargau ... J87
Abbey of Saint-Maurice ... 2057
Able-bodied and Disabled children ... 1878
Academia ... 1120
Accordian ... 1086
Aerogramme and Aeroplane ... 2124
Aerophilately Day ... 2124
Aeroplane ... 317, 349, 362, 415, 441, 466, 472, 499, 546, 570, 597, 613, 681, 758, 771, 828, 923, 974, 1006, 1110, 1122, 1144, 1349, 1473, 2012
Agence Telegraphique Suisse ... 786
AHV ... 1375
Aide aux pays de developpement ... 644
Aigle ... 932
Airport ... 974
Airship ... 897
Aloise ... 1273
Alpenstein ... **MS**2218
Alphirtenfest ... 560
Alphorn ... 2022
Alpine Chalet ... **MS**2037
Alpine Games Festival ... 2114
Alpine Skier ... 1829
Altstatten ... 941c, **MS**1952
Altstoffe sammeln ... 427
Amethyst ... 2005
Ammann ... 971
Ammonite ... **MS**2044
Angel ... J333, 2131
Animals ... 2138, 2188, 2238
Anker ... 1004, 1847
Annee de l'Enfant ... 982
Annee de l'Handicape ... 1003
Annee de la femme ... 895
Annee de la Nature ... 800
Annee Intern de la Paix ... 1115
Annee Mondiale des Communications ... 1064
Annee Mondiale du Refugie ... 612
Anni per la Gioventu ... **MS**196*a*
Ansermet ... 1080
Appenzell ... 700, J101
Architectural heritage ... 907
Architecture ... 1810
Ariane (rocket) ... 984, 1225
Armee du Salut *see* Salvation Army
Arms ... 724, J262, J266, J270, J274
Army Postman ... 1156
Art ... 1729, 1787, 1890, 1899, 1928, 1974, 2061
Art Nouveau ... 1667
ASSO ... 689
Astronomical clock ... 866*b*
Astronomy ... 1809
Automatic telephone service ... 647

B

Baby ... J398
Baby's dummy ... 1903
Baden ... 1123, **MS**1699
Badgers ... J210, 2191
Bahnstation ... 661
Baker ... 1087
Ballenberg ... 1002
Ballenberg Open Air Museum ... 2197
Banting ... 823
Barramini ... 783
Barrel ... J249
Basel ... 579, 622, 732, 770, 807, **MS**810, **MS**879, 946, 985, 1060, 1948, 2136, J91
Basel Carnival ... 1830, 2235
Basel University ... 611, 1834
Basel-Mulhouse Airport ... 974
Basketball ... 1399, 2020
Bat ... **MS**1945
Bather ... 1451
Battle of Murten ... 1849
Beach Volleyball ... 1400
Bear ... 2141
Beaver ... 1297, 1918
Bee and flower ... 1877
Bees ... J134, J154, 1877
Beetles ... J150, J165, J170
Bell ... J345, **MS**1991
Bellinzona ... 624, 918, 2122
Benken ... J276
Bergdorf ... 956
Bergün ... 939
Bern ... 426, 550, 623, 645, 672, 690, **MS**718, 790, 827, 885, 929, 954, 1026, 1223, 1984, 2026, 2234
Bern Cathedral ... 2166
Bern Convention ... 1117
Bernegg ... J132
Bernese Mountain Dog ... 1709
Bernina Railway ... 1845
Berries ... J243
BFU ... 1151
Bicycle ... 1457, 2144
Bider ... 923
Bienne ... 620
Big Top ... 1856
Biplane ... 2243
Birds ... 341, 343, 731, 1200, 1238, 1339, 1671, J193, J221, J225, J229, J233, J335, J344, J347
Blacksmith ... 1896
Blair ... 884
Blind ... 743
Blind-man's bluff ... 1166
Blood droplet ... 1929
Blue Cross ... 927
Bodmer ... 691
Boot ... 1793
Borel ... 882
Borromini ... 783
Bottmingen Water Castle ... 2226
Bovet ... 959
Boy and Pumpkin ... 1613
Boy holding crossbow ... 257, 292, 325b
Boy with guitar ... J350
Boy with umbrella ... J355
Brandver Hutung ... 1075
Breastfeeding ... J300
Breitling Orbiter ... 1414
Brick wall ... 644
Bricklayer ... 1168
Bridges ... 1231, 1556, 1731, 1780, **MS**2127, 2207
Brienz Rothorn Railway ... 2155
Brig ... 953, 2120
Brown Bear ... 1789
Brown Long-eared Bat ... **MS**1945
Buchser ... 1214
Burckhardt ... J120
Burkhard ... 1898
Bus ... 380, 471, 502, 549, 996, 1454
Butcher ... 1130
Butterflies ... 938, 1298, 1642, J133, J136, J139, J144, J149, J156, J158, J161, J164, J168
Butterfly and Waterway ... 1987
Buxhundpresse ... 1277

C

Cable car ... 1931, 2146
Cabrio Cable car ... 1931
Cadre ... J266
Calame ... J182
Calven ... 403
Calves ... 1979
Calvin ... 1795
Campagne europeene pour le monde rural ... 1142
Cancer ... 610
Candle and star ... 1871
Candles ... J329, 2091
Capital ... 860, 937
Card Games ... 2222
Carnival ... 2235
Carpenter ... 1170
Carriage ... 2019
Cars ... 988
Carving ... 986
Castasegna ... J264
Castle ... 2151, 2159, 2201
Cat ... 2046, 2239
Cats ... 1193, 1615
Celebrations ... 2184
Cendrars ... 1213
Centenadium ... 430
Cereals ... 1772
Cerebral Foundation ... 1878
CERN ... 733, 1602
Cervin ... 726
Champagne glasses ... 1905
Chapel ... 1911
Château and Sun ... **MS**1914
Cheeky Mouse (cartoon character) ... 1631
Cheese ... 1776, 2231
Cheesemaker ... 1132, 1175, 1619
Chef ... 1169
Chemins de fer *see* Railways
Cherries ... J242
Chess ... 757
Chestnut ... J241
Chickens ... 1203
Chicks ... 1978
Child ... 911, J40, J142, J147, J193, J197, J202
Child and branches ... J82
Child and toy pig ... J394
Child in field ... J195
Child playing with bricks ... J301
Children ... 1427, J354
Children and money ... J398
Children crossing road ... 569, 779
Children on swing ... J402
Children playing ... J403
Children playing in sand ... J302
Children's book characters ... J287, J291
Children's Books ... 1855
Children's paintings ... 1463, J378, J382, J386
Children's Rights ... J366, J370, J374
Chillon ... 958
Chimney ... J290
Chine-Suisse ... 1401
Chocolate ... 1478
Christmas ... 1569, **MS**1623, 1656, 1705, 1743, 1784, 1822, 1871, 1911, 1953, 1992, 2038, 2088, 2129, 2177, 2226
Christmas decoration ... 1433, 1569, **MS**1623, 1784
Christmas tree ... 2089, 2129
Christmas wreath ... J325
Churfirsten Mountains ... 2148
Cinderella ... J294
Cinquieme Suisse ... 739
Cities ... 1946
Clock ... 1287
Clocks ... 1928
Clowns ... 1251, J351, 2245
Club de Femmes Alpinistes ... 755
CNA ... 964
Coach ... 380, 502, 547, 567, 597, 1119
Coach and horses ... 501, 2035
Cocolino (cartoon character) ... 1697
Cogwheel ... 751
Coins ... 664, 692, 981, 1094, 2050
Coloured balls ... 1721
Colours ... 1646
Comedians ... 2086
Comic strips ... 1243, 1251, 1340, 1551, 2007, 2033, 2081, 2101, 2247
Composers' ... 1866
Comptoir ... 769
Computer ... J310
Confoederatio ... 424, 428, 431, 437, 461, 467, 473, 495, 506, 522, 527, 536, 541
Constitution federale ... 891
Corbusier ... 841
Cortaillod ... J270
Corti ... 1732
Counting ... J306
Courgette flower ... 1880
Cow ... 1192, 1336, 1691, 2182
Crayfish ... J339
Creux de Van ... **MS**2165
Crossbow ... 589, 1018
Crystallography ... 2005
CSAJ ... 1019
Cuckoo ... 1669
Curling ... 1660
Cycling ... 1063, 1398, 1435, 1468, **MS**1600
Cyclists ... 2205

D

DADA Art Movement ... 2103
Dalmatian ... 2045
Dancer ... 1732
Dancers ... 1841
Dancing ... 1008
Davos ... 730, 922
Deer ... 919, J209, J217, 1993
Delemont ... 1157
Delivery van ... 1971
Desarmement ... 343, 349
Developpement ... 808
Diablerets ... 817
Diddl (cartoon characters) ... 1561, 1608
Dimitri the Clown ... 1698

SWITZERLAND / Design Index

Dinosaurs....1861
Disabled Artists....1907
Discus thrower....1263
Dish aerial....844
Dogs....1062, 1160, 1198, 2238
Doll....J285, J298
Donkey....1202, J352
Doorbell....1603
Doorways....859
Dormouse....2109
Double helix....1629
Dove....1139
Dragonfly....J138
Drawing....J307
Dressage....1048
Dressmaker....1176
Drilling....1152
Droz....J108
Druckerei PTT....997
Drum....1085
Dufaux....925
Dufour....J80
Dulcimer....2021
Dunant....960, J47, 1869
Dungarees....1907
Duttweiler....1962

E

Eagle....**MS**1550
Economise energy....921
EFTA....744
Eiger....1683
Einsiedeln....631
Einstein....842, 1635
Elderly faces....2157
Electric locomotive....2195
Elephant....1253
Elm Village....1922
Emblem....1834, 1917, 2051, 2185
Embroidery....1460, **MS**1461
Emojis....2161
Endangered Fauna....**MS**1945
Energie 2000....1357
Engelberg....713
Envelope....2006
Envelopes....2083
Epidote....2004
Erni....1796
Escher....353, 2244
Esperanto....973
Esposizione Nationale *see* Exposition Nationale
ETV....1024
Euler....396, 1719, J167
Euro 2008 European Football Championship....1760, 1761
Europa....585, 606, 642, 653, 668, 682, 696, 727, 740, 745, 756, 772, 791, 811, 829, 867, 880, 898, 913, 930, 953, 975, 989, 1008, 1028, 1054, 1068, 1080, 1096, 1124, 1149, 1165, 1209, 1225, 1241, 1266, 1285, 1305, 1320, 1352, 1395, 1425, 1444, 1485, 1560, 1611, 1645, 1695, 1763, 1809, 1855, 1889, 1930, 1971, 2021, 2063, 2117, 2159, 2207
European Football Championship....1681, 1708
European Free Trade Association....1868
European Wild Cat....1799
Expo Milan....2051
Exposition Nationale....394
Eye....1158

F

Fabrikgesetz....936
Faces....1964
Fairy Tales....2220
Family....1733
Farm Animals....1978
Father with child on shoulders....J303
Fauna....1918, 2028, 2108
Favre....352
Federal Technology Institute....1629
Federer....734, 1720
Fellenberg....J104
Fern....J326
Fetes des Vignerons....1418
FHDSCF....716
FIFA....1599
Figures....1854
Film Festival....2154
Finsteraarhorn....742
Fireman....787
Fischer....908
Fish....599, 1050, J334, J338, J342, J348
Fisherman....1173
Flag and Music....1915
Flags....744, 1250, J60
Flora....**MS**2232
Florentini....719
Flowers....J105, J109, J114, J117, J121, J125, J129, J173, J178, J183, J188, J192, J198, J203, J237, J250, J258, J279, J316, 1560, 1975, **MS**2125
Flue....J51, J81
Folklore Festival....1633
Fondation Pierre Glanadda....1341
Fondue....2230
Fonoteca nazionale Lugano....1184
Font....866*a*
Food....**MS**1783
Football....552, 797, J314, 1643, 1760, 1761
Fore I....820
Forests....1889
Formula....1240
Forrer, J.....413
Forrer, L.....J112
Fortresses and Castles....2112
Fossils....605, 638, 650
Four-leaf Clover....1571, 2214
Fox....J214, 1992
Franscini....J75
Frau....1443
Frauenfeld....709
Fribourg....628, 951, 1014, J89
Fribourg University....1183
Frisch....1886
Frog....1299
Frucht 07 (painting)....1899
Fruit....910, J242, J254
Fumetto Comic Festival....2247
Fungi....J330, 2000
Funicular....1845, 2206
Furrer....J187
Fürstentum Leichtenstein....1308

G

Gais....702
Garfield....2033
Gargoyle....864
Geese....1197
Gemeinnutziger....1139
Geneva....399, 428, 561, 596, 621, 646, 690, 724, 733, 896, 943, 950, 988, 1020, 1118, 1122, 1154, **MS**1217, 1947, 2065, 2123
Geneva Airport....758
Geneva Convention....1821
Geneva University....600
Geneve *see* Geneva
Gertsch....1939
Gessner....J84
Giacometti....839
Giornico....402
Giotto (space probe)....1226
Girard....J67
Girl carrying candle....J299
Glacier....1794
Glarus....J102
Glider....681
Globe....1655
Glowworm....2110
Goat....1200, J287, 1835
Goat and puppy....1963
Goats and Cows....1813
Gold coin....**MS**1990
Gonin....821
Gotthard Railway Tunnel....2115
Gotthelf....J55, J152
Grand-St-Bernard....687, 1160
Grandson....916
Graphic....576
Great Spotted Woodpecker....2188
Greetings Stamps....1571, 1625, 1822, 1903, 2076, 2214, 2242
Grubenmann....1798
Gruyeres....J263
Guelder Rose....J327
Guinness record....1327
Guisan....782
Guitar....1996
Gun....878
Gymnastics....804, 877
Gymnasts....1879

H

Hagenwil....955
Hagenwil Water Castle....2201
Hairdressing....1140
Haller....J71, J172
Hallwil....935
Hamster....2048
Handicrafts....1874, 1895
Hands on steering wheel....1942
Hansel and Gretel....J291, 2220
Harbour....518
Hares....599, J211, J215
Hasler....990
Hat....559, 1302
Heart....1315, 1904, 2137, 2181
Hebel....1848
Hedgehogs....J207, 2111
Heer....676
Heidi....J287
Heidi and Goats....1855
Heim-Vogtlin....2096
Heimatwerk....986
Helicopter....837
Helmet....763, 1958
Helvetia....487
Herisau....941
Hersch....1865
Herzog....J88
Hesse....969
Hilty....J177
Historical Events....2052
Hockey stick....646
Hodler....J151
Hofer....1996
Honegger....843
Hopscotch....1165
Hornussen....2203
Horse....1196, 1254, 1752
Horsemen....1470
Horses....**MS**2043
Hot-air balloon....924, 973
Hoteliers Society....1023
Hour-glass....752
Houses....2197
Huber....J63
Hunger....673
Hurdling....877
Hydroelectric power station....516, 1622

I

Ibex....1661
Ice hockey....483, 1190, 1977
IGO....1025
INSA1....965
Insects....J133, J138, J143, J148, J153, J158, J163, J168
Interlaken....560, 1089
Internaba....**MS**879
International Ice Hockey Federation....1793
International Year of Biodiversity....1835
International Year of Chemistry....1887
Internationale Rheinregulierung....1238
Interparliamentary Union....1185
Interpol....846
Ioannes *see* John, St
ITU....717, 728

J

Jack of Bells....2224
Jahrder Frau....895
Jenatsch....411
Jigsaw pieces....1218, 1474
Jimmy Flitz (cartoon character)....1857
John, St....658
JP....1052
Jung....961
Jungfrau....415
Jungfrau Railway....1916
Jungfraujoch....661
Juphilex 1977....929
Jura....966

K

Karrer....1362
Kasperli (children's character)....1682
Kauffman....1212
Keller....J92
Kern....989
King....J320
King of Acorns....2225
King of Clubs....2223
Kingfisher....731
Kite....J288
Kittens....1799, 2139
Klee....968
Koch....822
Kocher....746
Kreidolf....1965
Kreuzberge....778
Kulturguterschutz....937
Kunsthaus (Museum of Fine Arts)....1853
Kunz....1272
Kussnacht....943*c*
Kyburg....915

L

La Poste....1368
Lace-making....1874
Ladybird....1515, 2078, J143
Lake....515, 1236, 1257
Lake Constance....2105

SWITZERLAND / Design Index

Lake Steamer 1265
Lambs 1980
Landesausstellung 394
Landestopographie 1153
Landscapes 355, 371, 415, 847, 1034
Laupen 398, 944
Lausanne 434, 558, 576, 617, 646, 683, 769, 886, 948, 1048, 1067, 1079, 1985
Lausanne University 1120
Lavater J96
Lavaux Vineyard terraces 1900
Leaves 1338
Legends 1715
Legs 1959
Lemanex 78 948, **MS**952
Lenzburg 698
Leopard 2154
Leprosy 911
Les Diablerets 817
Les Rangiers 401
Letter balance J278
Letter box 995
Letter cancelling 1105
Letter sorting 1113
Letters from Felix (children's book) 1636
Letters to parents J390
Leuk 844
Libre 1279
Liebermann 1866
Liestal 711
Lighted match 1075
Link 1151
Linth J103
Little Tiger, Little Bear and Tigerduck 1921
Livre 1278
Lizard J336
Logs J308
Loisurles fabriques 936
Lotschberg 672
Lotschberg Railway 1961
Lotschenta I. 947
Love 2181
Lowenbrunnen Fountain 1935
Lucas *see* Luke, St
Lucerne 549, 625, 660, 768, 897, 949, 972, 1143, 1276, 2024, 2121
Lugano 757, 1184, 2025
Luke, St 657
Lutz 1428
Luzern *see* Lucerne

M

Maderno J162
Making glass 2143
Malaria 662
Mammals 599, 919, 1252, J207, J212, J217
Mann 970
Manuscript 2059
Maps...551, 765, 999, 1091, 1142, 1149, 1241, 1256
Marcus *see* Mark, St
Mark, St 656
Market 1884
Marksmen 2052
Marmot 2029
Martigny 1061
Martin 1081
Mathematica 1281
Matter Valley **MS**1997
Matterhorn 725, 1630
Matthaeus *see* Matthew, St
Matthew, St 655
Medallion 862
Medical personnel 2100
Medicinal plants **MS**2232
Melchior J320
Men linking hands 300
Mendrisio 945
Menschenrechte 1404
Merchant ships 2092
Messenger 614
Meta 1155
Meteorology 999
Metres convention 894
Meyer 1211
Microscope J311
Minerals 602, 636, 649
Mistletoe J341
Mitte Iho Izer 926
Mobile phone 1649
Mobile Post Office 380, 471, 547, 1119
Molecular diagram 1240
Molecule 1887
Monastery **MS**1741
Monoplane 1836
Montreaux 1005
Morse key 983
Mosaic 1020
Moscow 2027
Mother and child J194, **MS**J196*a*, 2098
Moths J134, J141, J146, J148, J153, J160, J163, J169, J171
Motor Show **MS**1634
Mount Fuji 1998
Mountain biking 1765, 2205
Mountains 284, 298, 338, 342, 355, 371, 489, 1236, 1257, 1683, **MS**1960, 2062, 2115, 2134, 2148, **MS**2218J48, J56
Mountains and Valley **MS**1888
Mouse 1244
Muggestutz 1897
Mule driver 616
Mule post 1104
Multi-media messaging 1649
Murer 1781
Murten 917
Museum of Communication 1722
Museums 1967, 2014
Music 1117, J315
Musical instruments 1755, 2021
Musikfest 1316
Musse Internationale d'Horlogerie 873

N

NABA **MS**1686
NABA 2012 1949
Naba Zuri '84 **MS**1074
Nabag **MS**600*a*
Nabra **MS**718, **MS**810
Nafels 699, 1141
Nageli J76
National Anthem **MS**1888
National Bank 1713
National Stamp Exhibition 2209
Nature protection 838
Nestle 2097
Neuchatel 486, 703, 724, 1884
Nidwalden J90
Nobel 1363
Nocturnal Animals 2108
Nomenclatutre Chimique 1240
Numeral 801, 397
Numeral within circle of stars D105
Numismatic Society 981
Nursing 14
Nyon 587

O

Oberaargau **MS**2128
Obwalden J98
OCTI 754
Offenbach 944*b*
Old Cars 2072
Old Toys 2063
Olympic Games 434, 481, 1067, 1326, 1374, 1610, 1765
Oppenheim 1274
Optical Art 1858
Orelli J113
Organisation de' Aviation 1283
Organisation International du Travail 780
Oriel 865
Oron 977
Otter J220, J340, 2138
Outline of head 2126
Owls 599, 640, **MS**641, 1195, 1200, 1300, 1994, 2108

P

Painting 1974, 2219
Paleonotology 1861
Panda 1885
Paracelsus 1262
Paralympic Games, Vancouver 1829
Parcel bow 1405
Parcel sorting 1103
Paris 675
Parrainage pour communes de montagne 1189
Patrimoine architectural *see* Architectural heritage
Paul Klee Exhibition Centre 1644
Pax 302, 447, 460
Payerne 706
Peacock Goat 1835
Pedestrian crossing 569
Pegasus 768
Penny Black 2083
People 2099
'Per registere raccogliete la roba vecchia' 427
Pestalozzi 465
Pets 2045
Pettersson and Findus 1876
Pfyffer 410
Pharmacist 1171, 2204
Photography 951
Piaget 1318
Piccard 962
Pictet-de-Rochemont J157
Pig 2242
Piglet 1981
Pilatus Cogwheel railway 2019
Pilot wearing goggles 319
Pingu 1407
Pinocchio J288
Pistol 878
Piz Palu 799
Planets 1809
Plants J245, J254
Player 2203
Ploughing 414
Pocket watch 1653
Pompiers *see* Fire Service
Pony 2241
Pop Art 1942
Pope Francis 2209*a*
Population census 798
Porrentury 708, 979
Post 1364, 1406
Post box 995, J289
Post Office Counter 1107
Post van 471, 1102
Postal stationery **MS**2161
Postal vehicles 1971
Postcards 2168
Postcrossing 2168
Postbus 567, 1664, 2236
Posters J403
Posthorn 500, 893
Postman 617, 1109
Potatoes 1749
Pot 2186
Potter 1895
'Pour tenir recuperez les matieres usagees' 427
Prangins Museum 1376
Pratteln 933
Presents 2088
Preverenges J277
Prince J294
Princess Lillifee 1812
Pro Aero ... 423, 433, 466, 499, 681, 828, 1007, 1144
Pro Aqua 688, 1049
Pro Augusta 1342
Pro Familia 1239
Pro Fauna 599
Pro Filia 1317
Pro Infirmis 788
Pro lvliomayo 1343
Pro Natura 731
Pro Patria 537, 542, 553, 562, 571, 580, 591, 601, 636, **MS**641, 648, 663, 676, 691, 719, 734, 746, 759, 774, 793, 813, 831, 869, 887, 901, 915, 932, 955, 977, 991, 1010, 1030, 1049, 1056, 1070, 1082, 1098, 1126, 1145, 1161, 1205, 1227, 1246, 1268, 1287, 1301, 1322, 1390, 1421, 1445, 1481, 1556, 1604, 1638, 1687
Pro Sport 1095, 1186, 1255, 1319
Pro Vallon 1344
Procession 1830
ProSpecieRara (rare breeds association) 1702
Prospect 1085
Protect the Alps 1250
Protection civile 578, 835
PS Piemonte 1891
PTT Union 1235
Public Welfare Office 1854
Puss in Boots 2221
Putting the Shot 523, 1009, J61
Pylons 510

Q

Queen of Hearts 222
Quill pen 845, 2079
Qunice **MS**2175

R

Rabbit 1194, 2047, 2240
Radio 818, 826, 1088
Railway bridge 480
Railway Stations 2136, 2171, 2183, 2210
Railways 477, 512, 577, 597, 659, 672, 825, 1021, 1046, 1122, 1159, 1188, 1256, J286, 1345, 1662, 2120, 2194, 2206, 2234
Ramuz 840
Rapperswil 980
Reading J304
Recor **MS**2036
Red Cross 460, 674, **MS**675*a*, 1118, 1420, 1869
Red Cross Museum 1154
Red Deer 2031
Red flower 1816
Red Riding Hood J293
Red Squirrel 2189

SWITZERLAND / Design Index

Refugees and Red Cross 1821
Reka 1182
Renewable Energy 2018
Restaurant 2147
Ret-Romania 1077
Reynold 412
RhB 1159
Rheinreguilerung 1238
Rheinschiffahrt 551
Rheinschiffahrtsakte 766
Rhine Falls 2054
Richard J99
Rifle-shooting 526
Riggenbach J100
Rigi (steam ship) 1790
Rilke 967
Rings 1906
Riva San Vitale 705
Rivaz 1472
Road 517
Rocking chair 2064
Rocking horse J284
Roe Deer 2190
Roller Painting 2117
Romisch-Chur 1092
Ropes 1090
Rose 2076
Roses 806, 1476, J237, J258, J278
Rousseau 663
Ruins 2057
Running 525, 805, 1007, 1469, 1610
Rüte J267

S

SAC 671
Safety helmets 1264, 1958
Saffa 588
Saint-Imier 1066
Sainte-Croix **MS**2176
SAJV 1019
Salut *see* Salvation Army
Salvation Army 590, 1047
Samedan 701
San Bernardino 753
San Gottardo *see* St Gotthard
Santa hat 1826
Sargans 934
Satellite 983
SATUS 877
SBRV 1087
SCF 716
Schaffhausen 627, J97
Schoeck 784
Schonbein 1429
School Boy (painting) 1847
Schwamendingen J268
Schwyz 630
Schynige Railway 2194
Scissors 571
SCMV 1140
Scooter 1972
Scouts 670, 1728
Script 1840
Sculpture 1853
Scuol J272
Seal 1014, 1060
Sea Lion 1252
Security, Trust and Confidence J398
Seedorf Uri 710
Segantini 1430
Selfie 2164
Semaine Suisse *see* Swiss Week
Sempach 401, 1091
Senses 2042
SEV 181
Snow White and the Seven Dwarfs J292
SFG 1024
SFV 1050
SGB 1000
SGCI 1027
Sheep 1199
Shield, flowers and mountains D274, F268
Shield over mountains 332
Shields J9, J11, J14, J17, J24, J28, J32, J36, J44, J52
Ships 597, 1078, 1108, 1241, J312
SIA 1121
Sierre J271
Sign 861
Silhouettes 1745
Silver Jewelry 2084
Simenon 1292
Simplon 568
SISL 1078
SJH 878
Skating 730, 922, 1396
Skiing 484, 874, 1243, **MS**1648, 1740
Skin 2061
SKV 845
Sledging J356, 2132
Sleigh J353
Small Buildings 1935
Small Museums 2014, 2068
SMUV 1152
SMV 1132
Snail J346
Snail Shell 2077
Snake 1715
Snow-covered buildings **MS**1997
Snowboarding 1397
Snowman J349, 2130, 2177
Snowplough 513
Snowstorms 1436, 1479
Societe d'Histoire de l'Art 987
Societe d'Utilite Publique des Femmes 1139
Solar panels 2018
Solar-powered Aircraft 2119
Soldiers 689
Solothurn 629, 941*b*, 1015, J94
Spannorter 836
Special Olympics 2020
Spelterini 924
Sphere 1858
Spiez 978
Spinning top J296
Sport 1280
Spotted Nutcracker 2030
Sprick 1337
Spyri J137
Squirrels J213, 1995
SRB 1063
SSIO 1027
St Bernard 1160
St Bernard tunnel 687
St Gall 598, **MS**600*a*, 626, J85, 2023
St Gallen *see* St Gall
St Gallen University 1377
St Gallus 1920
St Gotthard 352, 577, 920, 1001
St Moritz 481, 874
St Peters Cathedral 1020
St Pierre-de-Clages Church 707
Stael 785
Stagecoach 1106
Stained glass windows 774, 813, 2060
Stairs and hallway 2049
Stamp and Magnifier 2080
Stamp Day 1568, 1704, **MS**1783, **MS**1870, **MS**1914, **MS**1952, **MS**1991, **MS**2043, **MS**2087, **MS**2128, **MS**2176, **MS**2233
Stamp display 2209
Stamp printing press 997
Stamps 715, 764, 807, 1131, 1187, 1259, **MS**1614
Stans 1016
Stars 532, J337, 2090
Steam Navigation 1891
Steam Roller J297
Steam train 2155, 2194
Stein am Rhein 1710
Stephan 883
Stop Aids 1291
Stove J283
Straw hat 1967
Summer **MS**2125
Sun 752, 861
Sunlight through trees 1889
Sursee 942
Survey 1932
Survey mark 521
Suspension railway 519
SUVA 763, 963
Suvorov 1431
Swimming 1467
Swiss Air Transport 2243
Swiss Airforce 2012
Swiss Alpine Club **MS**1960
Swiss Army Post 2006
Swiss Association of Painters and Plasterers 2032
Swiss Aviation 1850
Swiss Brass Band Association 1917
Swiss Cancer League 1840
Swiss Cars 2072
Swiss Civil Code 1919
Swiss Council for Accident Protection 1959
Swiss Cows 2182
Swiss Customs 1841
Swiss design classics 1572, 1585
Swiss Electricity 1293
Swiss Federal Commission for Monument Preservation 2049
Swiss Federal Tax Administration 2050
Swiss Heart Foundation 2137
Swiss Ice Hockey Association 1759
Swiss Landscape 1736, **MS**2037, 2054
Swiss League against Rheumatism 2185
Swiss Living Abroad Association 2099
Swiss Mountain Aid 2192
Swiss Music **MS**2036
Swiss National Accident Fund 2193
Swiss National Circus 2245
Swiss National Parks 2009
Swiss Papal Guard 1658
Swiss Pharmacists Association 2204
Swiss Philatelic Societies 2080
Swiss Protection and Support Service 1958
Swiss Red Cross 2100
Swiss Sponsorship for Mountain Communities 2062
Swiss Sports Federation 892
Swiss Stamp Dealers' Association 1820
Swiss Stamps 2196
Swiss week 751
Swissair 1006
Swisscore 1369
Switzerland–Japan Diplomatic Relations 1998
Symbol 445
Symbols 2032, 2156, 2158, 2192

T

Taeuber-Arp 1275
Tarasp 957
Taste 2042
TCS 1314
Techorama 1017
Teddy Bear J295
Telecom 95 1312
Telecommunications 809, 818
Telephone 906, 912, 998
Tell 295
Tents 767
Terre des Hommes 875, 398
The Little Polar Bear Lars (book) 1750
The Smurfs (comic) 1982
Therapod 1861
Think Green 2117
Thun 878
Thurgau J93
Tinguely 1155
Titeuf (cartoon character) 1595
Toad J343
Tobacco pouch 2068
Toepffer J116, 1409
Tomato flower 1925
Tongues 2042
Topography 1153
Torre J275
Tourism 1133, **MS**1137, **MS**2127
Tourisme pedestre 938
Tower Clocks 2026
Tox Info Suisse 2098
Toys J283, J295
Traditional Routes 1724, 1767, 1803
Trains J286, 477, 659, 672, 1021, 1159, 1188, 1256, 1961
Transport 597, 1122, 1256
Transports publics 1158
Tree and scroll 488
Tree-shaped lights 1953
Trees 612, 827, 909, 985, 1116, 1800, J321
Triangle (instrument) J305
Trike 2063
Tubli Letters **MS**2161
Tunnel S. Bernardino 753
Turkey 1203
Typeface 1808

U

UEFA 1601
Uffikon J274
UIT *see* ITU
UNESCO World Heritage Sites 1563, 1618
UNICEF 982
Union 1350
Union Interparlementaire 1185
Unisource 1295
United Nations Human Rights Council 1696
UNO 789
Unspunnen 2148
UPU 336, 503, 790, 885, 1415
UPU Congress 1771
Uri J86
USKA 983

V

Valais 724
Vegetable flowers 1880, 1925, 1975
Vegetables 910
Vela Museum 1477
Venice Biennale 1890, 2061
Vevey 559, 928
Viaducts 511, 1961, **MS**2087

Victorinox	1700
Viellesse	752
Ville de Lucerne (airship)	897
Vindonissa	1093
Vine grower	1174
Vinet	J59
Violin	1449, 1755
Visconteo Castle	2148
Visite	1361
Visits	1930
von Flue	2142
von Haller	1751
VSJ	1052
VSM	1053, 1130

W

Walker	1453
Wanderwege	938
Wangen	J265
Warning triangle	824
Waterfalls	493
Waterfowl	2105
Weasel	2028
Weathervane	866
Wedding	1822
Welti	354
Wengi	J128
Wettstein	485
Wheat	673, 1772
Wheelchair	905
White Stork	1973
Wille	J124
William Tell	1933
Window	858
Wine	1450
Wing	788
Winged envelope	339
Winged figure	323
Winged horse	2246
Winter Olympic Games	1660, 2184
Winterhilfe	1116
Winterthur	1017, 1986
Witch	J291
Wolf	2140
Wolfenschiessen	704, J273
Woman and mountains	286
Women in traditional costumes	J64, J68, J72, J77
Wood grain	1621
Worker	780
World Circus	1856
World Cup 94	1284
World Gymnaestrada	1879
World Heritage Sites	1900, 1922
World Wide Fund for Nature	1885
Wrench	824
Wrestlers	2114
Wrestling	524, J62, 2114

Y

Yakari (cartoon character)	1956
Year 2000	1434
Year of Cultural Heritage	2186
Yello	2133
Yersin	819
Young couple	J309
Youths	J313

Z

Zahringer Fountain	**MS**1870
Zeppelin (airship)	1612
Zodiac signs	1034
ZPV	1076
Zug	712, J95
Zum Durchhalten Zürich	391, 588, 619, 940, 1046, 1065, 1094
Zürich	1946, 2183
Zürich Airport	546
Zürich University	1051
Zurigo *see* Zürich	
Zwingli	781, 399

International Organisations situated in Switzerland

The stamps listed under this heading were issued by the Swiss Post Office primarily for the use of officials of the Organisations named.

PRICES FOR UNUSED STAMPS. Prior to 1 February 1944 the stamps listed were not available unused to collectors but only postally used. On that date the stamps then in use were made available to collectors in unused condition. We therefore quote unused prices only for those issues which have been on sale to the public, although others do exist unused.

A. LEAGUE OF NATIONS

(LN **1**)   (LN **2**)

Various issues optd with T LN **1**

1922–44.

(I) Types 17, 20 to 24, 41 and 43.

LN1	**18b**	2½c. bistre/*buff* (1928)	—	1·30
LN2	**18a**	3c. ultramarine/*buff* (1930)	—	17·00
		a. Grilled gum (1933)	—	19·00
LN3	**18b**	5c. orange/*buff*	—	8·50
LN4		5c. violet-grey/*buff* (1925)	—	7·00
LN5		5c. deep claret/*buff* (1927)	—	4·00
LN5a		5c. deep green/*buff* (1931)	—	42·00
		ab. Grilled gum (1933)	—	36·00
LN6	**18a**	7½c. green/*buff* (1927)	—	1·30
LN7	**21**	10c. green/*buff*	—	1·30
LN8		10c. blue/green/*buff* (1928)	—	2·75
LN8a		10c. reddish violet/*buff* (1931)	—	6·25
LN9		15c. brown-lake/*buff* (1927)	—	2·75
LN10		20c. purple/*buff*	—	14·00
LN11		20c. scarlet/*buff* (1925)	—	5·25
LN12		25c. orange-red/*buff*	—	18·00
LN13		25c. scarlet/*buff*	—	2·50
LN14		25c. yellow-brown/*buff* (1928)	—	34·00
LN15	**17**	30c. pale green and yellow-brown	—	23·00
LN16	**21**	30c. blue/*buff* (1924)	—	12·00
		a. Grilled gum (1932)	—	£700
LN17	**17**	35c. yellow and green	—	15·00
LN18		40c. blue	—	2·75
LN19		40c. yellow-green and deep magenta (1925)	—	32·00
LN20		50c. yellow-green and deep green	—	18·00
		a. Chalk-surfaced paper. Grilled gum (1935)	1·60	3·75
LN21		60c. orange-brown	50·00	2·50
		a. Chalk-surfaced paper. Grilled gum (1944)	39·00	£400
LN22		70c. buff and violet (1924)	—	55·00
		a. Chalk-surfaced paper. Grilled gum (1936)	2·50	4·25
LN23		80c. buff and olive-grey	—	8·50
		a. Chalk-surfaced paper. Grilled gum (1942)	4·00	5·00
LN24	**41**	90c. scarlet, deep green and green (1924)	—	26·00
		a. Chalk-surfaced paper. Grilled gum (1936)	—	8·00
LN25	**17**	1f. pale green and claret	—	10·50
		a. Chalk-surfaced paper. Grilled gum (1942)	—	9·00
LN26	**41**	1f.20 scarlet, brown-lake and salmon-pink (1924)	—	12·50
		a. 'HFLVETIA'	—	£450
		b. Chalk-surfaced paper. Grilled gum (1936)	4·00	6·50
LN27		1f.50 scarlet, blue and greenish blue (1924)	—	26·00
		a. Chalk-surfaced paper. Grilled gum (1935)	4·25	7·75
LN28		2f. scarlet, black and olive-grey (1924)	—	25·00
		a. Chalk-surfaced paper. Grilled gum (1936)	4·50	8·50
LN29	**22**	3f. rose-carmine	—	55·00
LN29a	**43**	3f. red-brown (1937)	—	£275
		as. Opt 'SPECIMEN'	£350	
LN30	**23**	5f. deep ultramarine	—	£120
LN31		5f. deep blue (No. 336) (1928)	—	£140
LN32	**24**	10f. deep mauve	—	£225
LN33		10f. deep grey-green (1928)	—	£225

1932.

(II) International Disarmament Conference.

LN34	**44**	5c. blue-green	—	29·00
LN35		10c. bright orange	—	2·75
LN36		20c. magenta	—	2·75
LN37		30c. bright blue	—	85·00
LN38		60c. bistre-brown	—	22·00
LN39	**45**	1f. olive-grey and blue	—	20·00
LN34/LN39 Set of 6			—	£150

1934–35.

*(III) As T **48** (Landscape types. Typo).*

LN40		3c. yellow-olive	—	80
LN41		5c. blue-green (1935)	—	95
LN42		15c. orange (1935)	—	2·10
LN43		25c. orange-brown	—	31·00
LN44		30c. ultramarine	—	2·75
LN40/LN44 Set of 5			—	34·00
LN40s/LN41s and LN43s/LN44s Optd 'SPECIMEN' Set of 4			£750	

1937–43.

*(IV) As T **52** (Landscape types. Recess).*
A. Smooth white non-granite paper

LN45A		3c. yellow-olive	30	90
LN46A		5c. blue-green	30	90
LN47A		10c. bright purple (I) (No. 370)	—	30·00
		c. Type (II) (No. 370d)	—	1·70
LN48A		10c. red-brown (1942)	—	1·70
LN49A		10c. chestnut (1943)	70	1·70
LN50A		15c. orange	65	95
LN51A		20c. scarlet (II) (No. 374Ad)	—	3·25
LN51Ac		20c. scarlet (II) (No. 375) (1942)	95	2·50
LN52A		25c. yellow-brown	85	1·70
LN53A		30c. dull ultramarine	85	1·60
LN54A		35c. bright green	85	1·60
LN55A		40c. grey	1·20	1·80
LN45A/LN55A Set of 12 (cheapest)			—	18·00

B. Non-granite paper with grilled gum

LN45B		3c. yellow-olive	—	90
LN46B		5c. blue-green	—	95
LN47B		10c. bright purple (I) (No. 370)	—	24·00
		c. Type (II) (No. 370d)	—	10·00
LN50B		15c. orange	—	1·30
LN51B		20c. scarlet (II) (No. 3745Bd)	—	5·75
LN52B		25c. yellow-brown	—	2·40
LN53B		30c. dull ultramarine	—	2·00
LN54B		35c. bright green	—	9·50
LN55B		40c. grey	—	9·50
LN45As/LN46As, LN48As/LN49As, LN51As/LN51Acs, LN47Bs, LN50Bs, LN52Bs/LN55Bs Optd 'SPECIMEN' Set of 12			£1200	

1938.

(V) Nos. 382/385.
*(a) Optd with T LN **1***

LN56		20c. red and buff	—	2·75
LN57		30c. blue and pale blue	—	5·00
LN58		60c. brown and buff	—	9·00
LN59		1f. black and buff	—	15·00
LN56/LN59 Set of 4			—	29·00
LN56s/LN59s Optd 'SPECIMEN' Set of 4			£500	

*(b) Optd with T LN **2***

LN60		20c. red and buff	—	3·50
LN61		30c. blue and pale blue	—	6·50
LN62		60c. brown and buff	—	11·00
LN63		1f. black and buff (R.)	—	19·00
LN60/LN63 Set of 4			—	36·00
LN60s/LN63s Optd 'SPECIMEN' Set of 4			£500	

1939.

(VI) Nos. 388B/390B.

LN64		3f. red-brown	5·00	16·00
LN65		5f. slate-blue	7·50	26·00
LN66		10f. green	18·00	50·00
LN64/LN66 Set of 3			27·00	85·00
LN64s/LN66s Optd 'SPECIMEN' Set of 3			£200	

COURRIER DE LA
SOCIÉTÉ
DES NATIONS

(LN **3**)

SWITZERLAND / International Organisations

1944. Optd as T LN **3**; as shown on Nos. LN67/LN75, larger type on Nos. LN76/LN84, or in two lines (still larger type) on LN85/LN87.

*(a) As T **52** (Landscape types. Recess. Smooth white paper)*

LN67		3c. yellow-olive	45	65
LN68		5c. blue-green	45	65
LN69		10c. chestnut	1·10	70
LN70		15c. orange	45	80
		a. Grilled gum	£2750	£4000
LN71		20c. scarlet (No. 375)	60	1·40
		a. Grilled gum	£2750	£4000
LN72		25c. yellow-brown	70	1·60
		a. Grilled gum	£2750	£4000
LN73		30c. dull ultramarine	80	1·70
LN74		35c. bright green	85	1·70
LN75		40c. grey	90	3·25
		a. Grilled gum	£2750	£4000

(b) Nos. 405 to 413

LN76		50c. deep violet-blue/*blue-green*	1·80	3·75
LN77		60c. reddish brown/*cinnamon*	2·10	5·25
LN78		70c. deep reddish purple/*mauve*	2·10	5·25
LN79		80c. black/*olive-grey*	1·80	4·00
LN80		90c. scarlet/*pink*	1·80	4·00
LN81		1f. myrtle green/*blue-green*	1·90	4·25
LN82		1f.20 plum/*olive-grey*	2·75	6·00
LN83		1f.50 indigo/*buff*	3·25	6·50
LN84		2f. brown-lake/*pink*	4·00	8·50

(c) Nos. 388B/390B

LN85		3f. red-brown	7·25	16·00
LN86		5f. slate-blue	12·00	26·00
LN87		10f. green	20·00	50·00
LN67/LN87	Set of 21		60·00	£140

B. INTERNATIONAL LABOUR OFFICE

S.d.N. Bureau international du Travail (LB **1**)

(LB **2**)

*Various issues optd with T LB **1***

1923–44.

*(I) Types **17**, **20** to **24**, **41** and **43**.*

LB1	**18b**	2½c. bistre/*buff* (1927)	—	80
LB2	**18a**	3c. ultramarine/*buff* (1930)	—	2·50
LB3	**18b**	5c. orange/*buff*	—	95
LB4		5c. deep claret/*buff* (1927)	—	75
LB5	**18a**	7½c. green/*buff* (1927)	—	80
LB6	**21**	10c. green/*buff*	—	95
LB7		10c. blue-green/*buff* (1928)	—	1·60
LB8		15c. brown-lake/*buff* (1928)	—	2·50
LB9		20c. purple/*buff*	—	26·00
LB10		20c. scarlet/*buff* (1927)	—	6·50
LB11		25c. scarlet/*buff*	—	1·70
LB12		25c. yellow-brown/*buff* (1928)	—	4·75
LB13	**17**	30c. pale green and yellow-brown	—	£110
LB14	**21**	30c. blue/*buff* (1925)	—	4·00
LB15	**17**	35c. yellow and green	—	17·00
LB16		40c. blue	—	1·70
LB17		40c. yellow-green and deep magenta (1928)	—	33·00
LB18		50c. yellow-green and deep green	—	7·75
		a. Chalk-surfaced paper. Grilled gum (1942)	2·75	3·50
LB19		60c. orange-brown	2·75	2·75
LB20		70c. buff and violet (1924)	—	39·00
		a. Chalk-surfaced paper. Grilled gum (1937)	2·40	3·75
LB21		80c. buff and olive-grey	21·00	3·50
		a. Chalk-surfaced paper. Grilled gum (1944)	40·00	£325
LB22	**41**	90c. scarlet, deep green and green (1925)	—	6·50
		a. Chalk-surfaced paper. Grilled gum (1942)	—	15·00
LB23	**17**	1f. pale green and claret	—	4·25
		a. Chalk-surfaced paper. Grilled gum (1942)	—	5·25
LB24	**41**	1f.20 scarlet, brown-lake and salmon-pink (1925)	—	7·25
		a. 'HFLVETIA'	—	£1200
		b. Chalk-surfaced paper. Grilled gum (1942)	21·00	6·00
LB25		1f.50 scarlet, blue and greenish blue (1925)	—	22·00
		a. Chalk-surfaced paper. Grilled gum (1937)	4·00	4·75
LB26		2f. scarlet, black and olive-grey (1925)	—	45·00
		a. Chalk-surfaced paper. Grilled gum (1936)	4·75	8·50
LB27	**22**	3f. rose-carmine	—	33·00
LB27a	**43**	3f. red-brown (1937)	—	£275
		as. Opt 'SPECIMEN'	£350	
LB28	**23**	5f. deep ultramarine	—	55·00
LB29		5f. deep blue (No. 336) (1928)	—	£120
LB30	**24**	10f. deep mauve	—	£250
LB31		10f. deep grey-green (1930)	—	£225

1932.

(II) International Disarmament Conference.

LB32	**44**	5c. blue-green	—	2·00
LB33		10c. bright orange	—	1·90
LB34		20c. magenta	—	2·00
LB35		30c. bright blue	—	12·50
LB36		60c. bistre-brown	—	12·50
LB37	**45**	1f. olive-grey and blue	—	16·00
LB32/LB37	Set of 6		—	42·00

1936.

*(III) T **48** (Landscape type. Typo).*

LB38	**48**	3c. yellow-olive	—	8·50

1937–43.

*(IV) As T **52** (Landscape types. Recess).*

A. Smooth white non-granite paper

LB39A	3c. yellow-olive	45	1·20
LB40A	5c. blue-green	45	1·20
LB41A	10c. bright purple (I) (No. 370)	—	4·75
	c. Type II (No. 370d)	—	8·50
LB41Ad	10c. red-brown (1942)	—	1·70
LB41Ae	10c. chestnut (1943)	80	1·70
LB42A	15c. orange	60	2·10
LB43A	20c. scarlet (III) (No. 374d)	—	4·00
LB43Ac	20c. scarlet (No. 375) (1942)	95	1·70
LB44A	25c. yellow-brown	70	2·75
LB45A	30c. dull ultramarine	70	2·20
LB46A	35c. bright green	80	3·00
LB47A	40c. grey	1·30	3·75
LB39A/LB47A	Set of 12 (cheapest)	—	27·00

B. Non-granite paper with grilled gum

LB39B	3c. yellow-olive	—	2·00
LB40B	5c. blue-green	—	2·00
LB41B	10c. bright purple (I) (No. 370)	—	3·25
LB42B	15c. orange	—	3·75
LB43B	20c. scarlet (III) (No. 374d)	—	4·00
LB44B	25c. yellow-brown	—	6·00
LB45B	30c. dull ultramarine	—	5·50
LB46B	35c. bright green	—	6·75
LB47B	40c. grey	—	6·50

LB40As, LB41Ads/LB42As, LB43Acs/LB46s, LB39Bs, LB41Bs, LB43Bs and LB47Bs Optd 'SPECIMEN' Set of 12 .... £1200

1938.

(V) Nos. 382/385.

*(a) Optd with T LB **1***

LB48	20c. red and buff	—	2·75
LB49	30c. blue and pale blue	—	5·00
LB50	60c. brown and buff	—	8·75
LB51	1f. black and buff	—	13·00
LB48/LB51	Set of 4	—	27·00
LB48s/LB51s	Optd 'SPECIMEN' Set of 4	£500	

*(b) Optd with T LB **2***

LB52	20c. red and buff	—	5·75
LB53	30c. blue and pale blue	—	5·25
LB54	60c. brown and buff	—	10·50
LB55	1f. black and buff (R.)	—	10·50
LB52/LB55	Set of 4	—	29·00
LB52s/LB55s	Optd 'SPECIMEN' Set of 4	£500	

1939.

(VI) Nos. 388B/390B.

LB56	3f. red-brown	6·50	12·50
LB57	5f. slate-blue	7·75	26·00
LB58	10f. green	12·50	45·00
LB56/LB58	Set of 3	24·00	75·00
LB56s/LB58s	Optd 'SPECIMEN' Set of 3	£200	

1944. Various issues optd 'COURRIER DU BUREAU INTERNATIONAL DU TRAVAIL,' as T LN **3**; in three lines on Nos. LB59/LB76 or in two lines on Nos. LB77/LB79.

*(a) As T **52** (Landscape types. Recess. Smooth white paper)*

LB59	3c. yellow-olive	45	65
LB60	5c. blue-green	45	65
LB61	10c. chestnut	45	65
LB62	15c. orange	80	95
LB63	20c. scarlet (No. 375)	65	95

SWITZERLAND / International Organisations

LB64	25c. yellow-brown		80	1·20
LB65	30c. dull ultramarine		90	2·20
LB66	35c. bright green		1·10	2·50
LB67	40c. grey		1·20	2·75

(b) Nos. 405/413

LB68	50c. deep violet-blue/*blue-green*		2·50	12·50
LB69	60c. reddish brown/*cinnamon*		2·50	12·50
LB70	70c. deep reddish purple/*mauve*		2·75	12·50
LB71	80c. black/*olive-grey*		80	2·10
LB72	90c. scarlet/*pink*		80	2·10
LB73	1f. myrtle green/*blue-green*		80	2·10
LB74	1f.20 plum/*olive-grey*		1·20	2·75
LB75	1f.50 Indigo/*buff*		1·60	3·75
LB76	2f. brown-lake/*pink*		2·00	4·75

(c) Nos. 388B/390B

LB77	3f. red-brown		5·00	9·75
LB78	5f. slate-blue		7·25	17·00
LB79	10f. green		16·00	38·00
LB59/LB79 Set of 21			45·00	£120

BUREAU INTERNATIONAL DU TRAVAIL
(LB **3**)

LB **4** Miners (bas-relief)

Visite du Pape Paul VI Genève 10 juin 1969
(LB **5**)

1950 (1 Feb). Nos. 511/521 optd with T LB **3**.

LB80	5c. orange		9·00	9·00
LB81	10c. yellow-green		9·00	9·00
LB82	15c. turquoise		13·00	15·00
LB83	20c. maroon (II)		13·00	15·00
LB84	25c. scarlet		15·00	15·00
LB85	30c. olive		15·00	15·00
LB86	35c. brown		15·00	15·00
LB87	40c. blue		15·00	15·00
LB88	50c. bluish grey		23·00	15·00
LB89	60c. blue-green		24·00	24·00
LB90	70c. violet		29·00	34·00
LB80/LB90 Set of 11			£160	£160

(Des H. Thöni. Eng K. Bickel. Recess PTT, Bern)

1956 (22 Oct)–**60**. T LB **4** and similar design inscr 'BUREAU INTERNATIONAL DU TRAVAIL'. P 11½.

LB91	LB **4**	5c. slate-purple	45	35
LB92	–	10c. green	45	35
LB93	–	20c. scarlet	3·50	3·50
LB94	–	20c. carmine (24.10.60)	45	45
LB95	–	30c. orange (24.10.60)	65	65
LB96	LB **4**	40c. blue	4·00	4·00
LB97	–	50c. blue (24.10.60)	90	90
LB98	–	60c. brown	80	80
LB99	–	2f. reddish purple	2·40	2·40
LB91/LB99 Set of 9			12·00	12·00

Design: Horiz—20c. (2), 30c., 60c., 2f. Globe, flywheel and factory chimney.

1969 (10 June). Visit of Pope Paul VI to Geneva. No. LB95 optd with T LB **5**.

LB100	30c. orange		55	55

LB **6** New Headquarters Building

LB **7** Man at Lathe

(Photo Courvoisier)

1974 (30 May). Inauguration of New ILO Headquarters, Geneva. Phosphorescent granite paper. P 11½.

LB101	LB **6**	80c. multicoloured	1·10	1·10

(Des H. Ernie. Photo Courvoisier)

1975 (15 Feb)–**88**. T LB **7** and similar horiz designs. Granite paper (30c., 60c., 100c.). Phosphorescent paper. P 11½.

LB102	30c. lake-brown		45	45
LB103	60c. deep ultramarine		70	70
LB104	90c. red-brown, dull vermilion and dull green (13.9.88)		1·80	1·80
LB105	100c. green		1·20	1·20
LB106	120c. ochre and reddish brown (22.8.83)		1·60	1·60

LB102/LB106 Set of 5			5·25	5·25

Designs: 30c. T LB **7**; 60c. Woman at drilling machine; 90c. Welder and laboratory assistant; 100c. Surveyor with theodolite; 120c. Apprentice and instructor with slide gauge.

LB **8** Keys

(Des M. Pastore. Litho PTT, Bern)

1994 (17 May). 75th Anniversary of International Labour Organisation. Phosphorescent paper. P 13½.

LB107	LB **8**	180c. multicoloured	4·00	4·00

C. INTERNATIONAL BUREAU OF EDUCATION

(Des M. Pastore. Litho PTT, Bern)

1944 (15 May). Various issues optd 'COURRIER DU BUREAU INTERNATIONAL D'EDUCATION', as T LN **3**, in black, in three lines on Nos. LE1/LE18, or in two lines on Nos. LE19/LE21.

*(a) As T **52** (Landscape types. Recess. Smooth white paper)*

LE1	3c. yellow-olive		70	1·70
LE2	5c. blue-green		80	2·50
LE3	10c. chestnut		80	2·50
LE4	15c. orange		80	2·50
LE5	20c. scarlet (No. 375)		80	2·50
LE6	25c. yellow-brown		80	2·50
LE7	30c. dull ultramarine		1·40	3·75
LE8	35c. bright green		1·40	3·75
LE9	40c. grey		1·50	4·00

(b) Nos. 405/413

LE10	50c. deep violet-blue/*blue-green*		7·75	25·00
LE11	60c. reddish brown/*cinnamon*		7·75	25·00
LE12	70c. deep reddish purple/*mauve*		7·75	25·00
LE13	80c. black/*olive-grey*		80	2·75
LE14	90c. scarlet/*pink*		1·10	3·75
LE15	1f. myrtle green/*blue-green*		1·50	4·00
LE16	1f.20 plum/*olive-grey*		1·60	5·25
LE17	1f.50 indigo/*buff*		1·90	6·00
LE18	2f. brown-lake/*pink*		2·30	6·25

(c) Nos. 388B/390B

LE19	3f. red-brown		9·50	27·00
LE20	5f. slate-blue		15·00	45·00
LE21	10f. green		22·00	70·00
LE1/LE21 Set of 21			80·00	£250

B I É
BUREAU INTERNATIONAL D'ÉDUCATION
(LE **1**)

(LE **2**)

LE **3** Globe on Books

1946 (12 Jan). No. 465 optd with T LE **1**.

LE22	**86**	10c. purple (R.)	90	90

1948 (1 Oct). Nos. 489/494 optd with T LE **2**.

LE23	5c. reddish brown		5·50	5·50
LE24	10c. green		5·50	5·50
LE25	20c. chestnut		5·50	5·50
LE26	25c. scarlet		5·50	5·50
LE27	30c. deep turquoise-blue		6·00	6·00
LE28	40c. deep blue		6·00	6·00
LE23/LE28 Set of 6			31·00	31·00

1950 (1 Feb). Nos. 511/521 optd with T LE **2**.

LE29	5c. orange		2·10	2·50
LE30	10c. yellow-green		2·10	3·25
LE31	15c. turquoise		2·10	3·25
LE32	20c. maroon (II)		5·25	12·50
LE33	25c. scarlet		15·00	25·00
LE34	30c. olive		15·00	25·00
LE35	35c. brown		10·00	16·00
LE36	40c. blue		10·00	17·00
LE37	50c. bluish grey		13·00	18·00

SWITZERLAND / International Organisations

LE38		60c. blue-green	15·00	22·00
LE39		70c. violet	15·00	26·00
LE29/LE39 Set of 11			95·00	£150

(Des D. Brun. Eng K. Lieven (T LE **3**). Des H. Hartmann. Eng K. Bickel (others). Recess PTT, Bern)

1958 (22 Sept)–**60**. T LE **3** and similar vert design inscr 'BUREAU INTERNATIONAL D'EDUCATION'. P 11½.

LE40	LE **3**	5c. slate-purple	20	20
LE41		10c. green	30	30
LE42	–	20c. scarlet	3·75	3·75
LE43	–	20c. carmine (24.10.60)	55	55
LE44	–	30c. orange (24.10.60)	65	65
LE45	LE **3**	40c. blue	4·75	4·75
LE46		50c. blue (24.10.60)	75	75
LE47	–	60c. brown	90	90
LE48		2f. purple	2·75	2·75
LE40/LE48 Set of 9			13·00	13·00

Design: 20c. (2), 30c., 60c., 2f. Pestalozzi Monument, Yverdon.

D. WORLD HEALTH ORGANISATION

ORGANISATION MONDIALE DE LA SANTÉ

(LH **1**)

1948 (24 June). Nos. 489/492 and 494 optd with T LH **1**.

LH1	5c. reddish brown	6·50	5·25
LH2	10c. green	6·50	6·50
LH3	20c. chestnut	6·50	6·50
LH4	25c. scarlet	6·50	8·00
LH5	40c. deep blue	6·50	9·00
LH1/LH5 Set of 5		29·00	32·00

1948 (24 June)–**50**. Various issues optd as T LH **1** but larger.

(a) Nos. 511/521

LH6	5c. orange	2·00	1·70
LH7	10c. yellow-green	2·75	2·75
LH8	15c. turquoise	3·00	3·50
LH9	20c. maroon (II)	6·75	9·75
LH10	25c. scarlet	6·75	9·75
LH11	30c. olive	5·50	8·00
LH12	35c. brown	6·00	12·00
LH13	40c. blue	5·50	6·25
LH14	50c. bluish grey	6·50	10·00
LH15	60c. blue-green	7·25	16·00
LH16	70c. violet	8·50	16·00

(b) Nos. 408/413 and 388B/390B

LH17	80c. black/*olive-grey*	6·50	6·00
LH18	90c. scarlet/*pink*	13·00	15·00
LH19	1f. myrtle green/*blue-green*	8·75	6·75
LH20	1f.20 plum/*olive-grey*	16·00	23·00
LH21	1f.50 indigo/*buff*	33·00	23·00
LH22	2f. brown-lake/*pink*	12·00	10·50
LH23	3f. red-brown	65·00	55·00
LH24	5f. slate-blue	26·00	19·00
LH25	10f. green	£140	£110
LH6/LH25 Set of 20		£350	£325

Dates of issue: The 80c., 1f., 2f. and 5f. were issued on 24.6.48 and the remainder on 1.2.50.

LH **2** Staff of Aesculapius

ERADICATION DU PALUDISME

(LH **3**)

(Des H. Thöni. Eng A. Yersin. Recess PTT, Bern)

1957 (16 Sept)–**60**. P 11½.

LH26	LH **2**	5c. slate-purple	20	20
LH27		10c. green	30	30
LH28		20c. scarlet	3·50	3·50
LH29		20c. carmine (24.10.60)	55	55
LH30		30c. orange (24.10.60)	70	70
LH31		40c. blue	4·75	4·75
LH32		50c. blue (24.10.60)	85	85
LH33		60c. brown	90	90
LH34		2f. reddish purple	2·75	2·75
LH26/LH34 Set of 9			13·00	13·00

1962 (19 Mar). Malaria Eradication. No. LH32 optd with T LH **3**.

LH35	LH **2**	50c. blue	1·30	1·30

LH **4** Staff of Aesculapius

(Des H. Thöni. Litho (140c.) or typo (others) PTT, Bern)

1975 (15 Feb)–**86**. Phosphorescent granite paper (30c. to 100c.). P 11½.

LH36	LH **4**	30c. pale yellowish green, brown-purple and rose	55	55
LH37		60c. lemon, blue and pale blue	95	95
LH38		90c. greenish yellow, violet and bright reddish violet	1·40	1·40
LH39		100c. pale blue, red-brown and orange	1·60	1·60
LH40		140c. light green, turquoise and rosine (27.5 86)	2·00	2·00
LH36/LH40 Set of 5			5·75	5·75

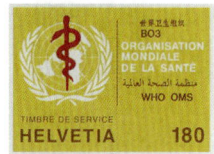

LH **5** Staff of Aesculapius

(Litho PTT, Bern)

1995 (28 Nov). Phosphorescent paper. P 13.

LH41	LH **5**	180c. olive-yellow, yellow-brown and rosine	4·00	4·00

E. INTERNATIONAL REFUGEES ORGANISATION

ORGANISATION INTERNATIONALE POUR LES RÉFUGIÉS

(LR **1**)

(Litho PTT, Bern)

1950 (1 Feb). Various issues optd with T LR **1**.

(a) Nos. 511/512, 514/515 and 518

LR1	5c. orange	38·00	27·00
LR2	10c. yellow-green	38·00	27·00
LR3	20c. maroon (II)	38·00	27·00
LR4	25c. scarlet	38·00	27·00
LR5	40c. blue	38·00	27·00

(b) Nos. 408, 410 and 413

LR6	80c. black/*olive-grey*	38·00	70·00
LR7	1f. myrtle green/*blue-green*	38·00	20·00
LR8	2f. brown-lake/*pink*	38·00	20·00
LR1/LR8 Set of 8		£275	£225

F. WORLD METEOROLOGICAL ORGANISATION

LM **1** The Elements   LM **2** WMO Emblem

(Des D. Brun (T LM **1**), E. Poncy (20c., 60c., 2f.). Eng A. Yersin. Recess PTT Bern)

1956 (22 Oct)–**60**. T LM **1** and similar design inscr 'ORGANISATION METEOROLOGIQUE MONDIALE'. P 11½.

LM1	LM **1**	5c. slate-purple	20	20
LM2		10c. green	30	30
LM3	–	20c. scarlet	3·50	3·50
LM4	–	20c. carmine (24.10.60)	55	55
LM5	–	30c. orange (24.10.60)	65	65
LM6	LM **1**	40c. blue	4·75	4·75
LM7		50c. blue (24.10.60)	80	80

LM8		60c. brown	95	95
LM9		2f. reddish purple	4·00	4·00
LM1/LM9	Set of 9		14·00	14·00

Design: Horiz—20c. (2), 30c., 60c., 2f. Weathervane.

(Des H. Hartmann. Eng K. Bickel-Courtin. (T LM **2**).
Photo Courvoisier (80c.) or recess PTT, Bern (others))

1973 (30 Aug). Centenary of World Meteorological Organisation. T LM **2** and similar horiz design inscr 'OMI OMM 1873 1973'. Granite paper. P 11½.

LM10	LM **2**	30c. rose-carmine	55	55
LM11	–	40c. new blue	70	70
LM12	–	80c. violet and gold	1·20	1·20
LM13	LM **2**	1f. yellow-brown	1·50	1·50
LM10/LM13	Set of 4		3·50	3·50

G. UNIVERSAL POSTAL UNION

LP **1** UPU Monument Bern   LP **2** Letter Post

(Des H. Thorn (5c., 40c., 2f.); E. Poncy (others).
Eng K. Bickel. Recess PTT, Bern)

1957 (16 Sept)–**60**. T LP **1** and similar horiz design inscr 'UNION POSTALE UNIVERSELLE'. P 11½.

LP1	LP **1**	5c. slate-purple	20	20
LP2	–	10c. green	30	30
LP3	–	20c. scarlet	4·00	4·00
LP4	–	20c. carmine (24.10.60)	55	55
LP5	–	30c. orange (24.10.60)	70	70
LP6	LP **1**	40c. blue	4·75	4·75
LP7	–	50c. blue (24.10.60)	80	80
LP8	–	60c. brown	95	95
LP9	LP **1**	2f. reddish purple	2·75	2·75
LP1/LP9	Set of 9		13·50	13·50

Design: 10c., 20c. (2), 30c., 60c. Pegasus (sculpture).

(Des B. Waltenspül. Photo Courvoisier)

1976 (16 Sept)–**89**. T LP **2** and similar horiz designs. Phosphorescent paper. P 11½.

LP10		40c. deep reddish purple, greenish blue and claret	70	70
LP11		80c. multicoloured	1·10	1·10
LP12		90c. multicoloured	1·40	1·40
LP13		100c. multicoloured	1·50	1·50
LP14		120c. multicoloured (22.8.83)	2·00	2·00
LP15		140c. slate, royal blue and vermilion (7.3.89)	2·75	2·75
LP10/LP15	Set of 6		8·50	8·50

Designs: 40c. T LP **2**; 80c. Parcel Post; 90c. Financial Services; 100c. Technical Co-operation; 120c. Carrier Pigeon, international reply coupon and postal money order; 140c. Express Mall Service.
The 120c. and 140c. are additionally inscribed 'TIMBRE DE SERVICE'.

LP **3** Computer, Mail Sacks and Globe   LP **4** Hand reaching for Rainbow

(Des B. Waltenspül. Litho PTT, Bern)

1995 (28 Nov). Phosphorescent paper. P 13½.

LP16	LP **3**	180c. multicoloured	3·50	3·50

(Des J.-M. Folon. Litho PTT, Bern)

1999 (9 Mar). 125th Anniversary of Universal Postal Union. T LP **4** and similar horiz design. Multicoloured. P 13½.

LP17		20c. Type LP **4**	45	45
		a. Block. Nos. 1416/1417 plus 2 labels	2·00	2·00
LP18		70c. Hand holding rainbow	1·40	1·40

Nos. LP17/LP18 were issued together in sheets containing two blocks, each consisting of the two values arranged in chessboard fashion with two labels, one showing the UPU emblem and the other giving the anniversary dates.

LP **5** 'Q' and Letter   LP **6** Symbols of Communication (Nasir Tahir)

(Des D. Dreier. Litho Enschedé)

2003 (9 Sept). P 14×14½.

LP19	LP **5**	90c. multicoloured	2·10	2·10

(Des D. Lienhard. Litho Enschedé)

2005 (6 Sept). P 14×14½.

LP20	LP **6**	100c. multicoloured	1·90	1·90

LP **7** Flying Postman and Hands   LP **8** Centre International de Conférences Genève (conference venue)

(Des Rorie Katz. Litho Cartor)

2007 (6 Sept). P 13½×14.

LP21	LP **7**	180c. multicoloured	3·50	3·50

Stamps of a similar design were issued by United Nations in New York, Geneva and Vienna.

(Des Andre Sandman. Litho Bagel Security Print, Düsseldorf)

2008 (23 July). 24th UPU Congress, Geneva. P 13½.

LP22	LP **8**	130c. multicoloured	3·75	3·75

LP **9** Rene de Saint-Marceaux (sculptor and creator of statue used as emblem of Universal Postal Union) and UPU Monument   LP **10** Dove

(Des Silvia Brüllhardt. Eng Elsa Catelin. Recess and litho)

2009 (9 Oct). Centenary of UPU Monument. Rene de Saint-Marceaux (sculptor and creator of statue used as emblem of Universal Postal Union) Commemoration. P 13½.

LP23	LP **8**	180c. multicoloured	4·25	4·25

A stamp of a similar design was issued by France.

(Des Daniel Dreier and Maya Arber. Litho Gutenberg AG, Liechtenstein)

2012 (9 Oct). 25th Universal Postal Congress, Doha. P 13½.

LP24	LP **10**	190c. multicoloured	4·50	4·50

H. UNITED NATIONS

NATIONS UNIES
OFFICE EUROPÉEN

(LU **1**)

1950 (1 Feb). Various issues optd with T LU **1**.

(a) Nos. 511/521

LU1		5c. orange	1·20	4·00
LU2		10c. yellow-green	1·30	4·00
LU3		15c. turquoise	2·20	5·25
LU4		20c. maroon (II)	2·75	7·50
LU5		25c. scarlet	4·50	12·50
LU6		30c. olive	4·50	12·50
LU7		35c. brown	4·50	12·50
LU8		40c. blue	6·50	15·00
LU9		50c. bluish grey	7·75	20·00
LU10		60c. blue-green	10·00	21·00
LU11		70c. violet	13·00	20·00

(b) Nos. 408/413 and 388B/390B

LU12		80c. black/*olive-grey*	15·00	17·00
LU13		90c. scarlet/*pink*	19·00	20·00
LU14		1f. myrtle green/*blue-green*	19·00	20·00
LU15		1f.20 plum/*olive-grey*	24·00	24·00
LU16		1f.50 indigo/*buff*	24·00	24·00
LU17		2f. brown-lake/*pink*	24·00	24·00
LU18		3f. red-brown	£180	£225
LU19		5f. slate-blue	£180	£225
LU20		10f. green	£225	£275
LU1/LU20 Set of 20			£700	£900

LU **2**   LU **3**   LU **4**

(Des H. Thöni. Photo Courvoisier)

1955 (24 Oct). Tenth Anniversary of UN. P 11½.

LU21	LU **2**	40c. blue and yellow	5·25	6·50

(Des H. Thöni. Eng A. Yersin (T LU **3**), K. Bickel (T LU **4**).
Recess, PTT Bern)

1955 (24 Oct)–**59**. P 11½.

LU22	LU **3**	5c. slate-purple	30	30
LU23		10c. green	45	45
LU24	LU **4**	20c. vermilion	7·50	7·50
LU25		20c. carmine (24.10.59)	55	55
LU26		30c. orange (24.10.59)	70	70
LU27	LU **3**	40c. blue	8·50	8·50
LU28		50c. blue (24.10.59)	80	80
LU29	LU **4**	60c. brown	95	95
LU30		2f. purple	3·50	3·50
LU22/LU30 Set of 9			21·00	21·00

ANNÉE MONDIALE DU RÉFUGIÉ

1959   1960

(LU **5**)   LU **6** Palace of Nations, Geneva

1960 (7 Apr). World Refugee Year Nos. LU25 and LU28 optd as T LU **5**.

LU31	LU **4**	20c. carmine	55	55
LU32	LU **3**	50c. blue (R.)	80	80

(Des H. Hartmann. Eng A. Yersin. Recess PTT, Bern)

1960 (24 Oct). 15th Anniversary of UN Granite paper. P 11½.

LU33	LU **6**	5f. greenish blue	7·75	7·75

LU **7**   LU **8** UNCSAT Emblem

(Des H. Them. Eng A. Yersin (10c., 50c.), K. Bickel (others).
Recess PTT, Bern)

1962 (24 Oct). Opening of UN Philatelic Museum. Geneva. T LU **7** and similar design. P 11½.

LU34	LU **7**	10c. green and red	30	30
LU35	–	30c. orange and blue	55	55
LU36	LU **7**	50c. blue and red	80	80
LU37	–	60c. brown and green	1·10	1·10
LU34/LU37 Set of 4			2·50	2·50

Designs: Horiz—30c., 60c. As T LU **4** but inscr 'ONU MUSEE PHILATELIQUE'.

(Des H. Them. Eng A. Yersin (50c.), K. Bickel (2f.).
Recess; emblem typo PTT, Bern)

1963 (4 Feb). UN Scientific and Technological Conference, Geneva (UNCSAT). T LU **8** and similar design. P 11½.

LU38		50c. carmine and blue	80	80
LU39		2f. yellow-green and purple	3·25	3·25

Designs: Vert—50c. T LU **8**. Horiz—2f. As T LU **4** but with emblem.

Under the terms of a postal agreement between the Swiss Post Office and the United Nations the Swiss issues for the Palais des Nations at Geneva were withdrawn on 4 October 1969 and replaced by United Nations issues with face value in Swiss currency. These are listed in this volume under United Nations, Geneva Headquarters.

I. INTERNATIONAL TELECOMMUNICATION UNION

LT **1** Transmitting Aerial   LT **2** New Headquarters Building

(Des D. Brun. Eng H. Heusser (T LT **1**). Des H. Thöni.
Eng A. Yersin (others). Recess PTT, Bern)

1958 (22 Sept)–**60**. T LT **1** and similar vert design inscr 'UNION INTERNATIONALE DES TELECOMMUNICATIONS'. P 11½.

LT1	LT **1**	5c. slate-purple	20	20
LT2		10c. green	30	30
LT3	–	20c. scarlet	4·00	4·00
LT4		20c. carmine (24.10.60)	55	55
LT5		30c. orange (24.10.60)	70	70
LT6	LT **1**	40c. blue	4·50	4·50
LT7		50c. blue (24.10.60)	80	80
LT8	–	60c. brown	95	95
LT9		2f. purple	2·75	2·75
LT1/LT9 Set of 9			13·50	13·50

Design: 20c., (2), 30c., 60c., 2f. Receiving aerials.

(Des A. Cserno and J.-J. Chevalley. Photo Courvoisier)

1973 (30 Aug). Inauguration of New ITU Headquarters, Geneva. P 11½.

LT10	LT **2**	80c. black and light blue	1·30	1·30

LT **3** Boeing 747 and Ocean-liner   LT **4** Optical Fibre Cables

(Des A. Cserno and J.-J. Chevalley. Eng H. Heusser.
Recess and photo PTT, Bern)

1976 (12 Feb). World Telecommunications Network. T LT **3** and similar horiz designs. Phosphorescent granite paper. P 11½.

LT11		40c. deep ultramarine and orange-red	70	70
LT12		90c. violet, cobalt and lemon	1·40	1·40
LT13		1f. brown-red, blue-green and orange-yellow	1·60	1·60
LT11/LT13 Set of 3			3·25	3·25

Designs: 40c. Sound waves; 90c. T LT **3**; 1f. Face and microphone in television screen.

(Des J.-J. Chevalley and P. Langlois. Litho PTT, Bern)

1988 (13 Sept). P 11½.

LT14	LT **4**	1f.40 multicoloured	2·20	2·20

LT **5** Emblem emitting Radio Signals   LT **6** a b c and X-ray of Bone Joint (Tele-education)

(Des J.-J. Chevalley. Litho PTT, Bern)

1994 (17 May). One Hundred Years of Radio. Phosphorescent paper. P 13½.

LT15	LT **5**	1f.80, multicoloured	3·25	3·25

SWITZERLAND / International Organisations

(Des A. Baldinger. Photo Courvoisier)
1999 (9 Mar). T LT **6** and similar horiz design. Multicoloured. P 11½.
LT16	10c. Type LT **6**	45	45
LT17	100c. Arrow and x-ray of bone joint (Telemedicine)..............................	1·80	1·80

LT **7** Stylised Face

(Des D. Dreier. Litho Enschedé)
2003 (9 Sept). P 14×14½.
LT18	LT **7** 90c. multicoloured....................	2·75	2·75

J. WORLD INTELLECTUAL PROPERTY ORGANISATION

LV **1** WIPO Seal

(Des R. Hirter. Litho PTT, Bern)
1982 (27 May)–**85**. T LV **1** and similar horiz designs. Multicoloured. P 11½.
LV1	40c. Type LV **1**	65	65
LV2	50c. Face and symbolic representation of intellect (10.9.85).................	95	95
LV3	80c. WIPO building, Geneva	1·10	1·10
LV4	100c. Hand pressing buttons, retort and cogwheel (industrial property).....	1·60	1·60
LV5	120c. Head, ballet dancer, cello and book (Copyright).............................	1·90	1·90
LV1/LV5	Set of 5..	5·50	5·50

K. INTERNATIONAL OLYMPIC COMMITTEE

LW **1** Olympic Rings   LW **2** Olympic Rings, Stadium and Runner

(Des J. Folon. Photo)
2000 (15 Sept). Olympic Games, Sydney. Self-adhesive booklet stamps. Die-cut.
LW1	LW **1**	20c. multicoloured........................	1·50	1·50
LW2		70c. multicoloured........................	2·30	2·30

(Des Karin Fanger-Schiesser. Litho Cartor)
2004 (6 May). Olympic Games, Athens. P 13½.
LW3	LW **2**	1f. multicoloured.........................	3·00	3·00

LW **3** Sportsmen   LW **4** Ice Hockey

(Des R. Hirter. Litho Cartor)
2004 (23 Nov). International Year of Sport and Physical Education (2005). P 13½.
LW4	LW **3**	180c. multicoloured.....................	5·50	5·50

This stamp was also sold by United Nations (Geneva).

(Des Karin Schiesser. Litho Bagel Security-Print, Mönchengladbach)
2005 (22 Nov). Winter Olympic Games, Turin. P 13½×13.
LW5	LW **4**	130c. multicoloured.....................	3·50	3·50

LW **5** BMX Cyclist   LW **6** Bobsleigh

(Des Silvio Galbucci. Litho Enschedé)
2008 (8 May). Olympic Games, Beijing. P 13½.
LW6	LW **5**	180c. multicoloured.....................	4·00	4·00

(Des Trummer and Ttuker. Litho Cartor)
2009 (20 Nov). Winter Olympic Games, Vancouver. P 14×14¼.
LW7	LW **6**	100c. multicoloured.....................	2·75	2·50

STAMP BOOKLETS

LWSB1	15.9.00 Olympic Games, Sydney Nos. LW1/LW2 (90c.).................	4·00

Liechtenstein

Austrian stamps were valid in Liechtenstein up to 31 January 1921

1912. 100 Heller = 1 Krone
1921. 100 Rappen = 1 Franc (Swiss)

The principality of Liechtenstein, founded in 1719, achieved sovereignty in 1806 and became fully independent in 1866.

I. ISSUES OF THE AUSTRIAN POST OFFICE

Prince John II
12 November 1858–11 February 1929

The first post office in Liechtenstein was opened at Balzers in 1818. Austria took responsibility for the postal service in the principality and from 1850, when postage stamps were first issued in Austria, unoverprinted stamps of Austria were sold for use there. Even after the introduction of special stamps for Liechtenstein in 1912, Austrian stamps continued to be used until 1921 either alone or in conjunction with those stamps.

Such usage can only be identified by the cancellation. During the period of the Austrian postal administration only the following post offices operated in Liechtenstein: Balzers. Vaduz (opened 1845). Nendeln (1864–1912). Schaan (1872), Triesen (1890) and Eschen (transferred from Nendeln in 1912). Early single-line cancellers for Vaduz were inscribed 'VADUTZ'.

The Austrian administration ended in February 1920.

1 Prince John II   **2**   **3**

(Des K. Moser. Die eng F. Shirnböck. Typo Austrian Govt Wks, Vienna)

1912–16. P 12½×13.

(a) Thick surfaced paper (2.2.12)

1	1	5h. green	60.00	26.00
2		10h. rose	£120	26.00
3		25h. blue	£120	85.00
1/3 Set of 3			£275	£120

(b) Thin unsurfaced paper 1916

4	1	5h. green	18.00	31.00
5		10h. red	£130	44.00
6		25h. blue	£900	£275
		a. Ultramarine (1.16)	£550	£600
4/6 Set of 3 (cheapest)			£650	£325

Nos. 1/3 with a circular cancellation inscribed 'VADUZ' and the letter 'b' and dated during February 1912 were supplied cancelled-to-order by the Philatelic Bureau in Vienna. At the end of February the canceller was sent to Vaduz for normal use.

A 15h. red was prepared in 1917 but was not issued.
Nos. 1/12 imperforate were sold only in Vienna.

(Des K. Moser. Die eng F. Shirnböck. Typo Austrian Govt Wks, Vienna)

1917 (15 June)–**18.** P 12½×13.

7	2	3h. violet	3.25	3.00
8		5h. yellow-green	3.25	3.00
9	3	10h. claret	3.25	3.00
10		15h. red-brown	3.25	3.00
11		20h. deep green (11.18)	3.25	3.00
12		25h. blue	3.25	3.00
7/12 Set of 6			18.00	16.00

See note under No. 6.

1918 (12 Nov). 60th Anniversary of Prince John's Accession. As T **3** but dated 1858–1918 in upper corners. P 12½×13.

13	3	20h. deep green	1.80	4.25

(4)

1920 (3 Mar).

*(a) Optd with T **4***

14	2	5h. yellow-green	4.50	12.00
		a. Opt double	23.00	£130
15	3	10h. claret	4.50	13.00
		a. Opt double	23.00	£170
16		25h. blue	4.50	13.00
		a. Opt double	23.00	£170

(5)   (6)

*(b) Surch as T **5** or T **6***

17	2	40h. on 3h. violet	4.50	13.00
18	3	1kr. on 15h. red-brown	4.50	13.00
19		2½kr. on 20h. deep green	4.50	13.00
14/19 Set of 6			24.00	70.00

II. ISSUES OF PRINCIPALITY OF LIECHTENSTEIN

The constitution was adopted on 5 October 1921.

7   **8** Castle of Vaduz

(Types **7** to **11** and T D **11**. Des L. Kasimir. Recess Paulussen & Co. Vienna)

1920 (from May). Imperf.

20	7	5h. olive-bistre	60	8.75
21		10h. orange	60	8.75
22		15h. indigo	60	8.75
23		20h. brown	60	8.75
24		25h. olive-green	60	8.75
25		30h. slate-grey	60	8.75
26		40h. carmine	60	8.75
27	8	1k. blue	60	8.75
20/27 Set of 8			4.25	65.00

9 Prince John I   **10** Arms   D **11**

1920 (July). P 12½.

28	7	5h. olive-bistre	55	95
29		10h. orange	55	95
30		15h. indigo	55	95
31		20h. red-brown	55	95
32	–	25h. olive-green	55	95
33	7	30h. slate-grey	55	95
34	–	40h. claret	55	95
35	–	50h. apple-green	55	95
36	–	60h. red-brown	55	95
37	–	80h. bright rose	55	95
38	8	1k. lilac	1.10	1.40
39	–	2k. light blue	1.10	2.30
40	9	5k. grey-black	1.10	4.00
41		7½k. slate	1.10	4.00
42	10	10k. ochre	1.10	6.75
28/42 Set of 15			12.00	28.00

Designs: As T **8**—25h. Chapel of St Mamertus; 40h. Gutenberg Castle; 50h. Courtyard of Vaduz Castle; 60h. Red House, Vaduz; 80h. Church Tower at Schaan; 2k. Bendern. As T **9**—7½k. Prince John II.

1920 (July). POSTAGE DUE. P 12½.

D43	D **11**	5h. red	45	65
D44		10h. red	45	65

1920 LIECHTENSTEIN

D45		15h. red.............	45	65
D46		20h. red.............	45	65
D47		25h. red.............	45	65
D48		30h. red.............	45	65
D49		40h. red.............	45	65
D50		50h. red.............	45	65
D51		80h. red.............	45	65
D52		1k. blue.............	65	2·00
D53		2k. blue.............	65	2·40
D54		5k. blue.............	65	3·00
D43/D54 Set of 12			5·50	12·00

11 Madonna

(12) 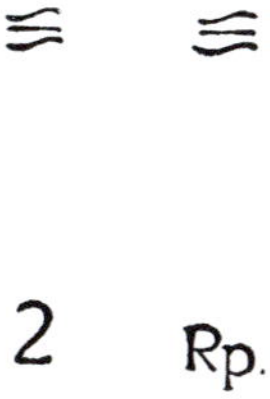 (13)

(Des T. and L. Kasimir. Recess Paulussen & Co, Vienna)

1920 (5 Oct). Prince John's 80th Birthday.

A. P 12½

43A	11	50h. olive-green.............	1·30	3·00
44A		80h. rose-red.............	1·30	3·00
45A		2k. blue.............	1·30	4·25
43A/45A Set of 3			4·00	9·25

B. Imperf

43B	11	50h. olive-green.............	6·50	£1400
44B		80h. rose-red.............	6·50	£1400
45B		2k. blue.............	6·50	£1400

1921. No. 21 surch in Swiss currency, in violet.

46	12	2r. on 10h. orange (1.2.21)	2·30	60·00
		a. Opt inverted	£130	£250
		b. Opt double	£150	£225
		c. Opt double, one inverted	£150	£275
47	13	2r. on 10h. orange (27.2.21)	1·30	42·00
		a. Opt inverted	£110	£225
		b. Opt double	£110	£225
		c. Opt double, one inverted	£140	£300

14 Arms

15 St Mamertus Chapel

16 Vaduz

(Des L. Kasimir. Recess Paulussen & Co, Vienna)

1921 (Feb–Nov). Swiss Currency.

A. P 12½

48A		2½r. black-brown.............	2·30	20·00
49A		3r. orange.............	2·30	20·00
50A		5r. olive.............	20·00	3·00
51A		7½r. indigo.............	9·50	50·00
52A		10r. yellow-green.............	42·00	20·00
53A		13r. red-brown.............	12·50	£120
		a. Perf 12½×9½	£225	
54A		15r. deep violet.............	29·00	90·00
48A/54A Set of 7			£110	£300

B. P 9½

47aB	14	2r. olive-yellow.............	2·30	19·00
48B		2½r. black-brown.............	2·30	£100
49B		3r. orange.............	£180	£7000
50B		5r. olive.............	£100	33·00
51B		7½r. indigo.............	£350	£1500
52B		10r. yellow-green.............	38·00	20·00
53B		13r. red-brown.............	£140	£3500
54B		15r. deep violet.............	38·00	36·00

1921. P 12½.

55	15	20r. black and violet.............	£100	3·25
56	–	25r. black and rose-red.............	5·00	6·50
		a. Black and brown-red.............	50·00	£200

57	–	30r. black and deep green.............	£110	29·00
58	–	35r. black and brown.............	9·75	24·00
59	–	40r. black and blue.............	14·50	9·00
60	–	50r. black and deep green.............	25·00	12·50
61	–	80r. black and grey.............	45·00	£110
62	16	1f. black and lake.............	75·00	75·00
55/62 Set of 8			£350	£250

Designs: As T **15**—25r. Vaduz Castle; 30r. Bendern; 35r. Prince John II; 40r. Church Tower at Schaan; 50r. Gutenberg Castle; 80r. Red House, Vaduz.

All designs are also known to exist imperforate.
See also Nos. 65/66.

10
(18)

1924 (Mar–Apr). Nos. 51 and 53 surch as T **18**, in red.

A. P 12½

63A	14	5r. on 7½r. indigo.............	2·30	5·00
64A		10r. red-brown.............	29·00	80·00

B. P 9½

63B	14	5r. on 7½r. indigo.............	26·00	24·00
64B		10r. red-brown.............	2·50	4·75

(Recess Mint Berne)

1924–25. Granite paper. Wmk Cross (T **13** of Switzerland). P 11½.

65	14	10r. yellow-green (6.24).............	31·00	4·25
66		30r. black and blue (1925).............	23·00	4·25

Design: 30r. Bendern (as No. 57).

19 Vine-dresser

20 Castle of Vaduz

21 Government Bldg and Church, Vaduz

(Des E. Verling. Eng K. Sprenger. T **19**, typo, Mint, Berne; T **20**, recess, Landestopographie, Berne; T **21** recess, Mint, Berne)

1924–27. Granite Paper. Wmk Cross. P 11½.

67	19	2½r. magenta and sage green (20.12.27).............	2·10	10·00
68		5r. blue and brown (9.24).............	4·25	1·60
69		7½r. brown and green (20.12.27).............	3·25	10·00
70	20	10r. green (4.25).............	17·00	1·60
71	19	15r. blue-green and maroon (20.12.27).............	16·00	60·00
72	20	1r. red (3.26).............	65·00	2·00
73	21	1½f. blue (4.25).............	£120	£170
67/73 Set of 7			£200	£225

The 10r. and 20r. were each issued both in sheets and in coils (from 1930).

22 Prince John II

23

(Des E. Verling. Eng K. Sprenger. Recess Landestopographie, Berne)

1925 (5 Oct). 85th Birthday of Prince John. Granite paper. Wmk Cross. P 11½.

74	22	10r. +5r. green.............	60·00	36·00
75		20r. +5r. carmine-red.............	35·00	36·00
76		30r. +5r. blue.............	10·50	10·00
74/76 Set of 3			95·00	75·00

(Des by E. Verling. Typo Mint, Berne)

1927 (5 Oct). 87th Birthday of Prince John. Granite paper. Wmk Cross. P 11½.

77	23	10r. +5r. green.............	14·00	36·00
78		20r. +5r. maroon.............	14·00	36·00
79		30r. +5r. blue.............	10·00	31·00
77/79 Set of 3			34·00	95·00

The Arms are in black, yellow, red, green and pale blue in each case.

LIECHTENSTEIN 1928

24 Salvage Work by Austrian Soldiers   **D 25**

(Des E. Verling. Litho Orell Füssli, Zürich)

1928 (6 Feb). Flood Relief. T **24** (and similar types). P 11½.
80	5r. +5r. brown and plum	22·00	36·00
81	10r. +10r. brown and green	31·00	48·00
82	20r. +10r. brown and scarlet	31·00	48·00
83	30r. +10r. brown and blue	26·00	48·00
80/83	Set of 4	£100	£160

Designs: 5r. Railway bridge between Buchs and Schaan; 10r. Village of Ruggell; 20r. T **24**; 30r. Salvage work by Swiss soldiers.

(Des E. Verling. Typo Mint, Berne)

1928 (2 Apr). POSTAGE DUE. Granite paper. Wmk Cross. P 12.
D84	D **25**	5r. vermilion and violet	2·00	4·75
D85		10r. vermilion and violet	2·00	4·75
D86		15r. vermilion and violet	3·00	22·00
D87		20r. vermilion and violet	3·00	4·75
D88		25r. vermilion and violet	3·00	14·50
D89		30r. vermilion and violet	10·00	22·00
D90		40r. vermilion and violet	12·50	24·00
D91		50r. vermilion and violet	15·00	29·00
D84/D91	Set of 8		45·00	£110

25 Prince John II   **26** Prince John II, 1858–1928

(Des E. Verling. T **25**, Typo, Mint, Berne; T **26**, Recess Orell Füssli, Zürich)

1928 (12 Nov). 70th Anniversary of the Accession of Prince John II. P 11½.

(a) Wmk Cross. Granite paper
84	25	10r. olive and red-brown	9·50	9·50
85		20r. olive and vermilion	13·00	19·00
86		30r. olive and dull blue	44·00	33·00
87		60r. olive and magenta	90·00	£130

(b) No wmk. Thick white paper
88	26	1f.20 deep ultramarine	75·00	£150
89		1f.50 sepia	£130	£350
90		2f. carmine	£130	£350
91		5f. green	£130	£400
84/91	Set of 8		£550	£1300

Prince Francis I
11 February 1929–25 July 1938

27 Prince Francis I as a boy   **28** Prince Francis I

(Des H. C. Kosel. Photo Wiener Kunstdruck, Vienna)

1929 (2 Dec). Accession of Prince Francis I. Types **27** and **28** (and similar types). P 11½.
92	10r. green	1·00	6·00
93	20r. scarlet	1·30	9·50
94	30r. blue	2·30	36·00
95	70r. brown	35·00	£200
92/95	Set of 4	36·00	£225

Designs: 10r. T **27**; 20r. T **28**; 30r. Princess Elsa; 70r. Prince Francis and Princess Elsa.

31 Girl Vintager   **32** Prince Francis I and Princess Elsa

(Des H. C. Kosel. Photo Rosenbaum Bros. Vienna)

1930. T **31** and similar designs.

A. Perf 10½
96A	3r. lake (1.7.30)	1·60	4·25
97A	5r. deep green (12.8.30)	4·50	10·00
98A	10r. deep reddish lilac (12.8.30)	3·25	10·00
99A	20r. scarlet (12.8.30)	60·00	10·00
100A	25r. slate-green (10.9.30)	11·50	60·00
101A	30r. blue (12.8.30)	11·50	16·00
105A	60r. blackish green (12.8.30)	£150	60·00
106A	90r. maroon (12.8.30)	£150	£500
107A	1f.20 sepia (10.9.30)	£180	£500
108A	1f.50 deep violet-blue (10.9.30)	95·00	£110
109A	2f. red-brown and deep bluish green (10.9.30)	£110	£200

B. Perf 11½
97B	5r. deep green (12.8.30)	5·00	4·25
98B	10r. deep reddish lilac (12.8.30)	4·75	4·25
99B	20r. scarlet (12.8.30)	39·00	5·25
100B	25r. slate-green (10.9.30)	£150	£500
101B	30r. blue (12.8.30)	10·50	6·50
102B	35r. grey-green (10.9.30)	£13000	£22000
104B	50r. brownish black (12.8.30)	£225	£325
105B	60r. blackish-green (12.8.30)	£150	48·00
106B	90r. maroon (12.8.30)	£160	£200
107B	1f.20 sepia (10.9.30)	£225	£375
108B	1f.50 deep violet-blue (10.9.30)	75·00	£100
109B	2f. red-brown and deep bluish green (10.9.30)	£120	£200

C. Perf 11½×10½
98C	10r. deep reddish lilac (12.8.30)	15·00	£180
101C	30r. blue (12.8.30)	£1500	£3500
102C	35r. grey-green (10.9.30)	15·00	31·00
103C	40r. brown (12.8.30)	15·00	13·00
104C	50r. brownish black (12.8.30)	£150	28·00
107C	1f.20 sepia (10.9.30)	£13000	£22000
109C	2f. red-brown and deep bluish green (10.9.30)	£5500	£11000

D. Perf compound of 10½ and 11½*
98D	10r. deep reddish lilac (12.8.30)	75·00	£275
99D	20r. scarlet (12.8.30)	£160	£550
101D	30r. blue (12.8.30)	£250	£600
105D	60r. blackish green (12.8.30)	£325	£950
109D	2f. red-brown and deep bluish green (10.9.30)	£750	£2750

Designs: Vert—3r. T **31**; 5r. Mountain Three Sisters–Edelweiss; 10r. Alpine Cattle–Alpine Roses; 20r. Courtyard of Vaduz Castle; 25r. Mountain Naafkopf; 30r. Valley of Samina; 35r. Rofenberg Chapel; 40r. St Mamertus' Chapel; 50r. Kurhaus at Malbun; 60r. Gutenberg Castle; 90r. Schellenberg Monastery; 1f.20, Vaduz Castle; 1f.50, Pfälzer club hut. Horiz—2f. T **32**.

* The stamps with compound perfs have three sides 10½, and one side 11½, or three sides 11½ and one side 10½. The 10r. also exists perf 10½×11½ and 10½×11½×11½×10½ (same prices as No. 98D).

34 Monoplane over Vaduz Castle and Rhine Valley   **35** Airship LZ-127 *Graf Zeppelin* over Alps

(Des H. C. Kosel. Photo Rosenbaum Bros, Vienna)

1930 (12 Aug). AIR. T **34** (and similar types). Backgrounds of grey wavy lines. P 10½×11½ (1f.) or 10½ (others).
110	15r. sepia	16·00	26·00
111	20r. deep blue-green	36·00	35·00
112	25r. brown	21·00	65·00
113	35r. blue	33·00	60·00
114	45r. deep green	65·00	£130

1931 LIECHTENSTEIN

115	1f. claret		75·00	95·00
110/115	Set of 6		£225	£375

Designs: Vert—15r., 20r. Biplane over snowy mountain peak. Horiz—25r., 35r. Biplane over Vaduz Castle; 45r., 1f. T **34**.

(Des H. C. Kosel. Photo Wiener Kunstdruck, Vienna)

1931 (10 June). AIR. T **35** (and similar type). P 11½.

116		1f. blackish green	£100	£190
117		2f. deep slate-blue	£200	£550
116s/117s	H/S 'MUSTER' in red Set of 2		£150	

Designs: 1f. T **35**; 2f. Different view of LZ-127 *Graf Zeppelin* over Alps.

REGIERUNGS
DIENSTSACHE
(O 36)   36   37 Princess Elsa

1932 (1 Apr). OFFICIAL. Nos. 97, etc. optd with T O **36**.

A. Perf 10½

O118A	5r. (Blk.)	21·00	80·00
O119A	10r. (R.)	£130	60·00
O120A	20r. (B.)	£325	£120
O121A	30r. (R.)	30·00	£100
O124A	60r. (R.)	20·00	70·00
O125A	1f.20 (G.)	£225	£700

B. Perf 11½

O118B	5r. (Blk.)	17·00	22·00
O119B	10r. (R.)	£100	22·00
O120B	20r. (B.)	£110	22·00
O121B	30r. (R.)	25·00	29·00
O122B	35r. (Blk.)	£12000	£17000
O123B	50r. (B.)	£180	£425
O124B	60r. (R.)	20·00	70·00
O125B	1f.20 (G.)	£200	£550

C. Perf 11½×10½

O119C	10r. (R.)	£1100	£2750
O122C	35r. (Blk.)	18·00	48·00
O123C	50r. (B.)	£100	31·00
O119C/O123C	Set of 3	£1100	£2500

D. Perf compound*

O119D	10r. (R.)	£375	£1200
O123D	50r. (B.)	£450	£1200

O119As, O118Bs, O120Bs/O121Bs, O123Bs/O125Bs
and O122Cs H/S 'MUSTER' in violet Set of 8 .... £400

* No. O119D has three sides perf 10½. and one side 11½. No. O123D three sides 11½ and one side 10½.

(Des H. C. Kosel. Photo Chwala, Vienna)

1932 (19 Dec). Youth Charities. Types **36** and **37** (different medallion portraits). P 11½.

118		10r. +5r. deep green (Type **36**)	30·00	60·00
119		20r. +5r. rose-scarlet (Type **37**)	30·00	60·00
120		30r. +10r. blue (Prince Francis)	38·00	85·00
118/120	Set of 3		90·00	£180

38 Mountain   (O 39)   39 Prince Francis I
Naafkopf

(Des H. C. Kosel. Photo Elbemühl, Vienna)

1933 (23 Jan). T **38** and similar designs. P 14½.

121		25r. bright orange	£325	£130
122		90r. deep green	16·00	£150
123		1f.20 red-brown	£150	£450
121/123	Set of 3		£450	£650

Designs: 25r. T **38**; 90r. Gutenberg Castle; 1f.20, Vaduz Castle.

1933 (24 Jan). OFFICIAL. Nos. 121 and 123 optd with T O **39**.

O126		25r. bright orange	60·00	80·00
O127		1f.20 red-brown	£130	£500
		a. Opt double		£550

(Des H. C. Kosel. Photo Courvoisier)

1933 (28 Aug). Prince Francis's 80th Birthday, Granite paper. P 11.

124	**39**	10r. bright violet	35·00	65·00

125		20r. scarlet	35·00	65·00
126		30r. bright blue	35·00	65·00
124/126	Set of 3		95·00	£180

40   41 Three   42 Vaduz Castle
      Sisters

 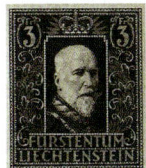

43 Pfälzer Hut, Bettlerjoch   44 Prince Francis I

45 Arms of Liechtenstein   46 Golden Eagle

> **GRILLED GUM.** A gum breaker was used on some of the paper between 1933 and 1942, to prevent curling. The machinery impressed a grill into the gum with enough force to transfer the pattern to the paper and we therefore quote prices for both unused and used examples.

(3r. to 1f.50 des H. C. Kosel and H. Sieger, photo Courvoisier. 2f. des H. C. Kosel, 3f., 5f. des R. Junk; eng F. Lorber; recess Govt Ptg Wks, Vienna)

1933–35. Types **40/45** and similar designs. Granite paper (3r. to 1f.50). Grilled gum (15r., 30r., 40r., 1f.50). P 12½ (2f. to 5f.) or 11½ (others).

127	3r. brown-red (17.12.34)	55	1·20
128	5r. emerald (17.12.34)	7·75	3·00
	a. Grilled gum	6·25	16·00
129	10r. reddish violet (17.12.34)	4·25	2·00
	a. Grilled gum	1·00	12·00
130	15r. reddish orange (9.12.35)	55	2·00
131	20r. red (1.1.35)	1·00	2·00
132	25r. yellow-brown (1.1.35)	38·00	95·00
133	30r. blue (9.12.35)	7·75	3·00
134	35r. bronze green (9.12.35)	8·00	26·00
135	40r. sepia (9.12.35)	2·50	10·00
136	50r. brown (18.6.34)	35·00	31·00
137	60r. dull purple (18.6.34)	3·25	12·00
138	90r. deep green (18.6.34)	12·50	43·00
139	1f.20 deep blue (18.6.34)	4·50	43·00
140	1f.50 red-brown (9.12.35)	5·75	50·00
141	2f. red-brown (19.8.35)	£120	£325
142	3f. blue (15.12.33)	£180	£325
143	5f. dull purple (6.5.35)	£550	£1700

Designs: 3r. T **40**; As T **41**—5r. T **41**; 10r. Schaan Church; 15r. Bendern am Rhein; 20r. Town Hall, Vaduz; 25r. Saminatal. As T **42**—30r. Saminatal (*different*); 35r. Schellenberg ruins; 40r. Government Building, Vaduz; 50r. T **42**; 60r. Vaduz Castle (*different*); 90r. Gutenberg Castle. As T **43**—1f.20 T **43**; 1f.50, Valüna. As T **44**—2f. Princess Elsa; 3f. T **44**; 5f. T **45**.

The 10r. and 20r. were each issued both in sheets and in coils.

See also Nos. **MS**144, **MS**153, 174 and 225/226.

1934 (29 Sept). Vaduz First Liechtenstein Philatelic Exhibition. Sheet 105×125 mm. Granite paper. P 12.

MS144	**45**	5f. chocolate	£2500	£3750

(Des L. Hesshaimer. Photo Courvoisier)

1934–36. AIR. T **46** and similar vert designs. Granite paper. P 11½.

145		10r. bright reddish violet (1.4.35)	16·00	70·00
		a. Grilled gum (1.3.36)	9·75	40·00
146		15r. red-orange (1.4.35)	39·00	80·00
		a. Grilled gum (10.4.36)	29·00	80·00

LIECHTENSTEIN 1934

147	20r. scarlet (1.4.35)		39·00	85·00
	a. Grilled gum (10.4.36)		34·00	85·00
148	30r. greenish blue (1.4.35)		39·00	80·00
	a. Grilled gum (10.4.36)		34·00	80·00
149	50r. emerald (17.12.34)		23·00	70·00
	a. Grilled gum (1.5.36)		26·00	65·00
145/149 Set of 5 (cheapest)			£110	£325

Designs: 10r. T **46**; 15r. to 20r. Golden Eagles in flight; 30r. Ospreys in nest; 50r. Golden Eagle on rock.

1934–35. OFFICIAL.

(a) Nos. 128/132 optd with T O **39**

O150	5r. emerald (R.) (1.4.35)		3·00	4·75
O151	10r. reddish violet (1.4.35)		6·25	4·75
O152	15r. reddish orange (V.) (9.12.35)		1·00	4·75
O153	20r. red (1.4.35)		1·50	4·75
O154	25r. yellow-brown (R.) (3.1.35)		55·00	£140
O155	25r. yellow-brown (Blk.) (17.12.35)		5·00	26·00

(b) Nos. 133, 136, 138, 140 optd as T O **39**, *but 17 mm in diameter*

O156	30r. blue (R.) (9.12.35)		7·50	14·50
O157	50r. brown (V.) (17.12.34)		2·00	7·75
O158	90r. deep green (1.4.35)		12·50	80·00
O159	1f.50 red-brown (B.) (9.12.35)		65·00	£350
O150/O159 Set of 10			£140	£575

60 Rp (48)

49 Airship LZ-129 *Hindenburg* and Schaan Church

1935 (24 June). AIR. Surch with T **48**.

150	**34**	60r. on 1f. claret (No. 115)	55·00	90·00

(Des L. Hesshaimer. Photo Courvoisier)

1936 (1 May). AIR. T **49** and similar horiz design. Granite paper. Grilled gum. P 11½.

151	1f. carmine	75·00	£160
152	2f. bright violet	49·00	£160

Designs: 1f. T **49**; 2f. Airship LZ-127 *Graf Zeppelin* over Schaan Airport.

1936 (24 Oct). Second Liechtenstein Philatelic Exhibition and Opening of Postal Museum, Vaduz. Sheet 165×119 mm containing two each of Nos. 131 and 133. Imperf.

MS153 Sold at 2 fr.		25·00	80·00

51 Masescha am Triesenberg

52 Schellenberg Castle

(Des M. Schiestl. Photo Courvoisier)

1937–38. Types **51**/**52** and similar designs Granite paper. Grilled gum (3r. to 50r., 1f.). P 11½.

154	3r. red-brown (24.7.37)	55	95
155	5r. emerald-green and buff (15.9.37)	55	55
156	10r. violet and buff (15.6.37)	55	55
157	15r. black and buff (15.11.37)	55	95
158	20r. red and buff (4.10.37)	55	95
159	25r. brown and buff (15.10.37)	1·00	5·25
160	30r. bright blue and buff (2.12.37)	5·75	2·00
161	40r. dull green and buff (13.8.37)	3·75	4·25
162	50r. brown and buff (15.6.37)	4·50	9·50
163	60r. buff (1.2.38)	4·00	4·75
164	90r. slate-violet (1.2.38)	26·00	60·00
165	1f. deep claret and buff (13.8.37)	3·75	24·00
166	1f.20 purple-brown and buff (1.4.38)	13·50	43·00
167	1f.50 bluish slate and buff (15.2.38)	5·75	43·00
154/167 Set of 14		65·00	£180

Designs: As T **51**—3r. Schalun ruins; 5r. T **51**; 10r. Knight and Vaduz Castle; 15r. Upper Saminatal; 20r. Church and bridge at Bendern; 25r. Steg Chapel and girl. As T **52**—30r. Farmer and orchard, Triesenberg; 40r. T **52**; 50r. Knight and Gutenberg Castle; 60r. Baron von Brandis and Vaduz Castle; 90r. Three Sisters mountain; 1f. Boundary-stone on Luzienssteig; 1f.20 Minstrel and Gutenberg Castle; 1f.50 Lawena (Schwarzhorn).

53 Roadmakers at Triesenberg

54 Josef Rheinberger

(Des H. Raebiger. Photo Courvoisier)

1937 (30 June). Workers' Issue. T **53** and similar horiz designs. Granite paper. Grilled gum. P 11½.

168	10r. mauve	2·50	3·00
169	20r. scarlet	2·50	4·25
170	30r. blue	2·50	5·25
171	50r. brown	2·50	6·00
168/171 Set of 4		9·00	17·00

Designs: 10r. Bridge at Malbun; 20r. T **53**; 30r. Binnen Canal Junction; 50r. Francis Bridge near Planken.

No. 172 is vacant.

1937–41. OFFICIAL. Nos. 155/156, 158/160, 162, 165 and 167 optd as T O **39**, but 17 mm in diameter.

O173	5r. emerald-green and buff (29.9.37)	50	95
O174	10r. violet and buff (R.) (17.7.37)	1·00	3·00
O175	20r. red and buff (V.) (6.10.37)	2·00	3·75
O176	20r. red and buff (Blk.) (6.7.41)	2·00	3·75
O177	25r. brown and buff (26.11.37)	1·00	3·75
O178	30r. bright blue and buff (Blk.) (6.12.37)	3·00	4·00
O179	50r. brown and buff (R.) (17.7.37)	1·50	3·00
O180	1f. deep claret and buff (20.8.37)	1·60	16·00
O181	1f.50 bluish slate and buff (P.) (16.2.38)	4·50	24·00
O173/O181 Set of 9		15·00	55·00

1938 (30 July). Third Liechtenstein Philatelic Exhibition, Vaduz. Sheet 100×135 mm containing stamps as No. 175 in different colour in a block of four. P 12.

MS173	**54**	50r.×4 slate-blue	39·00	39·00

Prince Francis Joseph II

25 July 1938–13 November 1989

(Des R. Junk. Eng F. Lorber. Recess Govt Ptg Wks, Vienna)

1938 (15 Aug). Death of Prince Francis I. P 12½.

174	**44**	3f. black/*yellow*	19·00	£160

(Des W. Dachauer. Eng F. Lorber. Recess Govt Ptg Wks, Vienna)

1939 (17 Mar). Birth Centenary of Josef Gabriel Rheinberger (composer). P 12½.

175	**54**	50r. greenish slate	1·60	8·50

See No. **MS**173.

55 Black-headed Gulls

56 Offering Homage to First Prince

(Des L. Hesshaimer. Photo Courvoisier)

1939 (3 Apr). AIR. T **55** and similar horiz designs. Granite paper. Grilled gum. P 11½.

176	10r. reddish violet (Barn Swallows)	1·80	2·00
	a. Smooth gum	1·00	9·00
177	15r. red-orange (Type **55**)	1·00	5·25
178	20r. brown-red (Herring Gulls)	4·00	2·00
179	30r. blue (Common Buzzard)	2·10	4·25
180	50r. emerald (Northern Goshawk)	5·50	7·00
181	1f. carmine (Lammergeier)	3·75	31·00
182	2f. reddish violet (Lammergeier)	3·75	31·00
176/182 Set of 7 (cheapest)		19·00	75·00

(Des and eng E. Zotow. Recess Govt Ptg Wks, Vienna)

1939 (29 May). Homage to Francis Joseph II. P 12.

183	**56**	20r. lake	2·10	4·25
184		30r. lake	2·10	3·75
185		50r. blue-green	2·10	4·25
183/185 Set of 3			5·75	11·00

57 Francis Joseph II   D **58**

(Des J. Troyer. Eng F. Lorber. Recess Govt Ptg Wks, Vienna)

1939. As T **57** (various types). P. 12.
186	2f. blue-green/*cream* (18.12.39)	13·50	70·00
187	3f. deep violet/*cream* (18.12.39)	9·00	70·00
188	5f. brown/*cream* (29.5.39)	27·00	45·00
186/188	Set of 3	45·00	£170

Designs: 2f. Cantonal Arms; 3f. Arms of the Principality; 5f. T **57**. No. 188 was issued in sheetlets of four stamps.

(Des J. Troyer. Eng A. Yersin. Design recess; value typo. PTT Bureau, Berne)

1940 (1 July). POSTAGE DUE. P 11½.
D189	D **58**	5r. carmine and blue	2·30	6·50
D190		10r. carmine and blue	1·00	1·90
D191		15r. carmine and blue	1·60	9·00
D192		20r. carmine and blue	1·30	3·00
D193		25r. carmine and blue	2·50	6·00
D194		30r. carmine and blue	5·50	10·00
D195		40r. carmine and blue	5·50	9·50
D196		50r. carmine and blue	7·00	10·00
D189/D196	Set of 8		24·00	50·00

Postage Due stamps were no longer used after 31 December 1958.

58 Prince John when a Child   **59** Prince John II

(Des K. Gessner (3f.), J. Troyer (others). Photo Courvoisier)

1940 (10 Aug–5 Oct). Birth Centenary of Prince John II. T **58** and similar horiz designs and T **59**. Granite paper. Grilled gum. P 11½.
189	20r. brown-red	1·00	4·25
190	30r. indigo	1·00	6·00
191	50r. slate-green	2·10	20·00
192	1f. brown-violet	15·00	£120
193	1f.50 violet-black	19·00	£110
194	3f. brown (5.10.40)	7·50	42·00
189/194	Set of 6	41·00	£275

Designs: Portraits as a child (20r.); in early manhood (30r.), in middle age (50r.), and in later life (1f. and T **59**). Memorial tablet (1f.50).

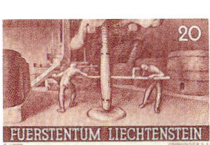

60 Wine Press   **61** Madonna and Child

(Des C. Liner. Photo Courvoisier)

1941 (7 Apr). Agricultural Propaganda. T **60** and similar horiz designs. Granite paper. Grilled gum. P 11½.
195	10r. brown	1·60	2·00
196	20r. claret	2·75	3·00
197	30r. blue	2·75	5·25
198	50r. myrtle-green	4·50	31·00
199	90r. violet	5·00	36·00
195/199	Set of 5	15·00	70·00

Designs: 10r. Harvesting Maize; 20r. T **60**; 30r. Sharpening scythe; 50r. Milkmaid and Cow; 90r. Girl wearing traditional headdress.

(Des J. Troyer. Eng E. Zotow. Recess PTT Bureau, Berne)

1941 (7 July). Granite paper. P 11½.
200	**61**	10f. brown-purple/*yellow-ochre*	75·00	£190

Issued in sheetlets of four stamps.

62 Prince Hans Adam   **63** St Lucius preaching

(Des J. Troyer. Photo Courvoisier)

1941 (18 Dec). T **62** and similar horiz designs. Granite paper. Grilled gum. P 11½.
201	20r. brown-red	1·00	3·00
202	30r. red	1·00	5·25
203	1f. violet-grey	4·00	31·00
204	1f.50 green	4·00	34·00
201/204	Set of 4	9·00	65·00

Portraits: 20r. T **62**; 30r. Prince Wenzel; 1f. Prince Anton Florian; 1f.50, Prince Joseph.

(Des and eng E. Zotow. Recess PTT Bureau, Berne)

1942 (22 Apr). 600th Anniversary of Separation from Estate at Montfort. T **63** and similar horiz designs. Granite paper. P 11½.
205	20r. brown-red/*flesh*	2·10	2·00
206	30r. blue/*flesh*	1·60	5·25
207	50r. olive-green/*flesh*	4·00	12·00
208	1f. sepia/*flesh*	6·00	26·00
209	2f. dull violet/*flesh*	6·00	26·00
205/209	Set of 5	18·00	65·00

Designs: 20r. T **63**; 30r. Count of Montfort replanning Vaduz; 50r. Counts of Montfort-Werdenberg and Sargans signing treaty; 1f. Battle of Gutenberg; 2f. Homage to Prince of Liechtenstein.

64 Prince John Charles   **65** Princess Georgina

(Des J. Troyer. Photo Courvoisier)

1942 (5 Oct). T **64** and similar vert designs. Granite paper. Grilled gum. P 11½.
210	20r. rose (Type **64**)	1·00	2·00
211	30r. blue (Francis Joseph I)	1·00	4·25
212	1f. purple (Alois I)	3·75	28·00
213	1f.50 brown (John I)	3·75	29·00
210/213	Set of 4	8·50	55·00

(Des J. Troyer. Photo Courvoisier)

1943 (5 Mar). Marriage of Prince Francis Joseph II and Countess Georgina von Wildczek. As T **65** (various portraits). P. 11½.
214	10r. purple	1·00	2·75
215	20r. brown-red	1·00	2·75
216	30r. slate-blue	1·00	2·75
214/216	Set of 3	2·75	7·50

Portraits: Vert—10r. Francis Joseph II; 20r. T **65**. Horiz (44×25 *mm*)—30r. Prince and Princess.

66 Alois II   **67** Marsh Land

(Des J. Troyer. Photo Courvoisier)

1943 (5 July). As T **66** (portraits of Princes). P 11½.
217	20r. red-brown (Type **66**)	1·00	2·00
218	30r. ultramarine (John II)	2·10	3·00
219	1f. blackish brown (Francis I)	2·75	16·00
220	1f.50 slate-green (Francis Joseph II)	2·75	16·00
217/220	Set of 4	7·75	33·00

(Des E. Zotow (centres), J. Troyer (frames). Photo Courvoisier)

1943 (6 Sept). Completion of Irrigation Canal. Various designs as T **67**. P 11½.
221	10r. blackish violet	60	1·10
222	30r. blue	95	4·25
223	50r. blue-green	2·50	18·00

LIECHTENSTEIN 1943

224		2f. olive-brown	4·75	29·00
221/224	*Set of 4*		8·00	47·00

Designs: 10r. T **67**; 30r. Draining the canal; 50r. Ploughing reclaimed land; 2f. Harvesting crops.

(Des M. Schiestl and J. Troyer. Photo Courvoisier)

1943 (27 Dec). New designs as T **41**. P 11½.
225	10r. violet-grey (Vaduz Castle)	80	95
226	20r. red-brown (Gutenberg Castle)	1·20	2·00

Each issued both in sheets and in coils.

69 Planken   **70** Prince Francis Joseph II

(Des J. Troyer. Photo Courvoisier)

1944 (17 Apr)–**49**. Views as T **69**. Buff backgrounds. P 11½.
227	3r. brown (Planken)	55	50
228	5r. green (Bendern)	55	50
228*a*	5r. brown (Bendern) (1.12.49)	55·00	2·75
229	10r. violet-grey (Triesen) (11.9.44)	55	50
230	15r. blue-grey (Ruggell) (11.9.44)	70	1·60
231	20r. brown-red (Vaduz)	70	95
232	25r. violet-brown (Triesenberg)	70	2·00
233	30r. blue (Schaan)	75	95
234	40r. brown (Balzers) (11.9.44)	1·00	2·50
235	50r. slate-blue (Mauren)	1·30	4·25
236	60r. light green (Schellenberg) (11.9.44)	7·75	10·00
237	90r. olive-green (Eschen) (11.9.44)	7·75	11·50
238	1f. claret (Vaduz Castle) (11.9.44)	4·75	11·50
239	1f.20 red brown (Valuna Valley) (16.11.44)	4·75	12·00
240	1f.50 blue (Lawena) (16.11.44)	4·75	12·00
227/240	*Set of 15*	80·00	65·00

(Des F. Lorber. Photo Courvoisier)

1944 (22 Dec). Buff backgrounds. P 11½.
241	**70**	2f. brown	11·50	36·00
242	–	3f. green (Princess Georgina)	7·00	26·00

See also Nos. 302/303.

72   **73**

(Des J. Troyer. Photo Courvoisier)

1945 (9 April). Birth of Crown Prince Johann Adam Pius (now known as Prince Hans Adam). P 11½.
243	**72**	20r. lake, yellow and gold	1·80	95
244		30r. blue yellow and gold	1·80	3·00
245		100r. grey, yellow and gold	4·75	11·50
243/245	*Set of 3*		7·50	14·00

(Des J. Troyer. Eng K. Bickel. Recess PTT Bureau, Berne)

1945 (3 Sept)–**47**. P 11½.
246	**73**	5f. grey-blue/*buff*	36·00	60·00
247		5f. red-brown/*buff* (20.3.47)	55·00	85·00

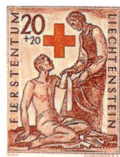 

74 First Aid   **75** St Lucius

(Des J. Seger. Photo Courvoisier)

1945 (27 Nov). Red Cross. As T **74** and similar vert designs. Cross in red. Buff backgrounds. P 11½.
248	10r. +10r. purple (Mother and children)	2·20	4·50
249	20r. +20r. claret (Type **74**)	2·20	6·25
250	1f. +1f.40 blue (Nurse and invalid)	11·50	44·00
248/250	*Set of 3*	14·00	49·00

(Des J. Troyer. Eng K. Bickel. Recess PTT Bureau, Berne)

1946 (14 Mar). P 11½.
251	**75**	10f. grey/*buff*	90·00	65·00

Issued in sheetlets of four stamps.

(Des E. Verling. Photo Courvoisier)

1946 (10 Aug). Fourth Liechtenstein Philatelic Exhibition, Vaduz and 25th Anniversary of Postal Agreement with Switzerland. Sheet 84×60 mm. P 11½.
MS251*a* 10r. (×2) Old Postal Coach (*horiz*), violet, brown and buff (*sold at* 3f.)	80·00	90·00

76 Red Deer Stag   (O **77**)

(Des J. Seger. Photo Courvoisier)

1946 (10 Dec). As T **76** (various designs). P 11½.
252	20r. brown-red (Type **76**)	6·75	5·75
253	30r. greenish blue (Arctic Hare)	8·00	7·50
254	1f.50 brown-olive (Capercaillie)	11·50	25·00
252/254	*Set of 3*	24·00	34·00

1947 (3 July). OFFICIAL. Nos. 228, etc optd with T O **77**.
O255	5r. green (Bendern)	3·25	2·00
O256	10r. violet-grey (Triesen)	3·25	2·00
O257	20r. brown-red (Vaduz)	4·00	2·00
O258	30r. blue (Schaan)	5·25	3·00
O259	50r. slate-blue (Mauren)	5·25	6·25
O260	1f. claret (Vaduz Castle)	20·00	20·00
O261	1f.50 blue (Lawena)	20·00	21·00
O255/O261	*Set of 7*	55·00	50·00

77 Chamois   **78** Princess Elsa

(Des J. Seger. Photo Courvoisier)

1947 (15 Oct). As T **77** (various designs). P 11½.
255	20r. brown-lake (Type **77**)	11·00	8·75
256	30r. greenish blue (Alpine Marmot)	13·50	10·00
257	1f.50 sepia (Golden Eagle)	11·50	35·00
255/257	*Set of 3*	32·00	48·00

See also Nos. 283/285.

(Des H. C. Kosel. Eng F. Lorber. Recess State Printing Wks, Vienna)

1947 (15 Dec). Death of Princess Elsa. P 14½.
258	**78**	2f. black/*yellow*	9·50	28·00

79 Wilbur Wright   **80** *Ginevra de Benci* (da Vinci)   (**81**)

(Des J. Troyer. Photo Courvoisier)

1948. AIR. Pioneers of Flight. As T **79** (various portraits). P 11½.
259	10r. blue-green (6.4.48)	1·60	65
260	15r. violet (6.4.48)	1·60	2·50
261	20r. red-brown (6.4.48)	2·20	1·30
	a. Orange-brown	£225	8·25
262	25r. brown-lake (6.4.48)	3·25	4·00
263	40r. violet-blue (15.7.48)	3·75	4·00

1949 LIECHTENSTEIN

264	50r. greenish blue (15.7.48)	4·25	4·00
265	1f. brown-purple (15.7.48)	7·00	8·25
266	2f. claret (15.7.48)	10·50	10·00
267	5f. olive-green (6.4.48)	14·00	13·00
268	10f. black (12.10.48)	85·00	41·00
259/268	*Set of 10*	£120	80·00

Portraits: 10r. Leonardo da Vinci; 15r. Joseph Montgolfier; 20r. Jakob Degen; 25r. Wilhelm Kress; 40r. Etienne Robertson; 50r. William Henson; 1f. Otto Lilienthal; 2f. Salomon Andrée; 5f. T **79**; 10f. Icarus.

(Des J. Troyer. Photo Courvoisier)

1949. As T **80** (paintings). P 11½.
269	10r. green (15.3.49)	2·00	80
270	20r. brown-red (15.3.49)	3·00	1·70
271	30r. sepia (23.5.49)	6·00	2·10
272	40r. light blue (23.5.49)	16·00	2·10
273	50r. violet (15.3.49)	12·50	14·50
274	60r. grey (23.5.49)	32·00	13·50
275	80r. orange-brown (15.3.49)	6·00	9·00
276	90r. olive (23.5.49)	28·00	12·50
277	120r. magenta (15.3.49)	6·00	11·50
269/277	*Set of 9*	£100	60·00

Designs: 10r. T **80**; 20r. *Portrait of a Young Girl* (Rubens); 30r. *Self-portrait of Rembrandt in plumed hat*; 40r. *Stephan Gardiner, Bishop of Winchester* (Quentin Massys); 50r. *Madonna and Child* (Hans Memling); 60r. *Franz Meister in 1456* (Jehan Fouquet); 80r. *Lute Player* (Orazio Gentileschi); 90r. *Portrait of a Man* (Bernhardin Strigel); 120r. *Portrait of a Man (Duke of Urbino)* (Raphael).
See also No. **MS**279a.

1949 (14 Apr). No 227 surch with T **81**.
278	**69**	5r. on 3r. brown and buff (Br.)	1·50	1·20
		a. Full point after 'p' touching (pos. 16)	£1100	£1300

82 Posthorn and Map of World

83 Rossauer Castle

(Des P. Châtillon. Photo Courvoisier)

1949 (23 May). 75th Anniversary of Universal Postal Union. P 11½.
279	**82**	40r. blue	8·00	9·00

1949 (6 Aug). Fifth Liechtenstein Philatelic Exhibition, Vaduz. Sheet 122×70 mm containing paintings as 1949 issue in new colours. Imperf.
MS279a 10r. blue-green (as 10r.); 20r. magenta (as 80r.); 40r. blue (as 120r.). Sold at 3f. £225 £225

(Des J. Seger. Eng H. Ranzoni (1f.50), F. Lorber (others). Recess Govt Ptg Wks, Vienna)

1949 (15 Nov). 250th Anniversary of Acquisition of Domain of Schellenberg. T **83** and similar designs. P 14½.
280	20r. purple	5·25	4·75
281	40r. deep blue	18·00	13·00
282	1r.50 brown-red	23·00	21·00
280/282	*Set of 3*	42·00	35·00

Designs: Horiz—20r. T **83**; 40r. Bendern Church. Vert—1f.50, Prince Johann Adam I.

84 Roebuck

(**85**)

(Des J. Seger. Photo Courvoisier)

1950 (7 Mar). As T **84** (animals). P 11½.
283	20r. brown-lake (Type 84)	25·00	9·50
284	30r. blue-green (Black Grouse)	21·00	14·50
285	80r. sepia (Eurasian Badger)	75·00	95·00
283/285	*Set of 3*	£110	£110

1950 (7 Nov). No 279 surch with T **85**.
286	**82**	100r. on 40r. blue	65·00	£100

O **86**

86 Boy cutting Loaf

(Des K. Bickel. Design recess, value typo PTT Bureau, Berne)

1950 (7 Nov)–**68**. OFFICIAL. Buff paper. Yellow gum. P 11½.
O287	O **86**	5r. bright purple and grey	50	45
O288		10r. green and magenta	50	45
O289		20r. brown and blue	50	45
O290		30r. brown-purple and scarlet	65	60
O291		40r. blue and red-brown	90	80
O292		55r. grey-green and scarlet	1·60	1·50
		a. White granite paper	80·00	£225
O293		60r. blue-grey and magenta	1·60	1·50
		a. White granite paper (5.68)	10·00	38·00
O294		80r. red-orange and grey	1·80	1·60
O295		90r. sepia and blue	1·90	1·80
O296		1f.20 turquoise and orange	2·50	2·50
		a. 'Q' for 'O' in face value	28·00	30·00
O287/O296	*Set of 10*		11·00	10·50

Nos. O287/O296 also come with white gum (*price £70, unused*).
See also Nos. O495/O506.

(Des M. Hausle. Photo Courvoisier)

1951 (3 May). Designs as T **86**. P 11½.
287	5r. magenta	1·00	55
288	10r. green	1·00	95
289	15r. chestnut	12·00	11·00
290	20r. sepia	2·40	1·50
291	25r. claret	12·50	11·50
292	30r. grey-green	7·50	1·40
293	40r. turquoise-blue	22·00	14·00
294	50r. brown-purple	16·00	7·25
295	60r. brown	16·00	7·00
296	80r. red-brown	21·00	14·50
297	90r. yellow-olive	44·00	14·50
298	1f. violet-blue	£130	15·00
287/298	*Set of 12*	£250	90·00

Designs: 5r. T **86**; 10r. Man whetting scythe; 15r. Mowing; 20r. Girl with Sweetcorn; 25r. Haywain; 30r. Gathering Grapes; 40r. Man with scythe, 50r. Herdsman with Cows; 60r. Ploughing; 80r. Girl carrying basket of fruit; 90r. Women gleaning; 1f. Tractor hauling load.

The 10r. and 20r. were each issued both in sheets and in coils.

87 Lock on the Canal (Aelbert Cuyp)

88 Willem von Heythuysen, Burgomaster of Haarlem (Frans Hals)

(Frames des A. Frommelt. Photo Courvoisier)

1951 (24 July). Paintings. Types **87/88** and similar design. P 11½.
299	**87**	10r. +10r. olive-green	20·00	16·00
300	**88**	20r. +10r. blackish brown	20·00	25·00
301	–	40r. +10r. blue	20·00	19·00
299/301	*Set of 3*		55·00	55·00

Design: As T **87**—40r. *Landscape* (Jacob van Ruysdael).

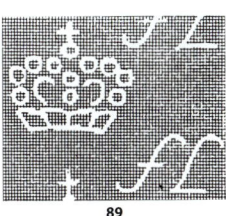
89

90 Vaduz Castle

LIECHTENSTEIN 1951

(Des and eng F. Lorber. Recess State Ptg Works, Vienna)

1951 (20 Nov)–**52**. As Nos. 241/242 but redrawn and T **90**. Buff granite paper. W **89** (sideways).

A. P 12½×12
302A	**70**	2f. deep blue	35·00	65·00
303A	–	3f. lake-brown	£350	£225

B. Perf 14½
302B	**70**	2f. deep blue	£1900	£325
303B	–	3f. lake-brown	£225	£375
304	**90**	5f. bronze-green (25.9.52)	£375	£325

Design: 3f. Princess Georgina.

91 *Portrait* (Giovanni Savoldo)   **92** *Madonna and Child* (Sandro Botticelli)

(Frames des A. Frommelt. Photo Courvoisier)

1952 (27 Mar). Paintings. Types **91/92** and similar design. P 11½.
305	**91**	20r. plum	95·00	6·00
306	**92**	30r. brown-olive	65·00	16·00
307	–	40r. deep blue	31·00	13·00
305/307 Set of 3			£170	32·00

Design: As T **91**—40r. *St John* (Andrea del Sarto).

(93)

1952 (25 Sept). No. 281 surch with T **93**, in carmine.
308		1f.20 on 40r. deep blue	50·00	£120

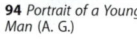

94 *Portrait of a Young Man* (A. G.)   **95** *St Nicholas* (Bartholomäus Zeitblom)

(Frames des A. Frommelt. Photo Courvoisier)

1953 (5 Feb). Paintings from Prince's Collection. Types **94/95** and similar designs. P 11½.
309	**94**	10r. bronze-green	5·25	2·00
310	**95**	20r. bistre-brown	39·00	5·25
311	–	30r. chocolate	70·00	17·00
312	–	40r. deep Prussian blue	80·00	£100
309/312 Set of 4			£170	£110

Designs: As T **95**—30r. *St Christopher* (Lucas Cranach, the elder). As T **94**—40r. *Leonhard, Count of Hag* (Hans von Kulmbach).

96 Lord Baden-Powell

(Des A. Frommelt. Recess Waterlow & Sons)

1953 (4 Aug). 14th International Scout Conference. P 13½.
313	**96**	10r. green	5·25	2·00
314		20r. deep brown	29·00	5·00
315		25r. scarlet	26·00	37·00
316		40r. deep blue	25·00	12·50
313/316 Set of 4			75·00	50·00

97 Alemannic Ornamental Disc (*c.* AD 600)   **98** Prehistoric Walled Settlement, Borscht

(Des A. Hild. Photo Courvoisier)

1953 (26 Nov). Opening of National Museum, Vaduz. T **97** and similar vert design and T **98**. P 11½.
317	**97**	10r. deep orange-brown	22·00	25·00
318	**98**	20r. bronze-green	22·00	25·00
319	–	1f.20 indigo	£110	65·00
317/319 Set of 3			£140	£100

Design: 1f.20, Rössen jug (*c.* 3000 BC).

99 Footballers

(Des J. Seger. Photo Courvoisier)

1954 (18 May). Football. T **99** and similar horiz designs. P 11½.
320		10r. red-brown and pale rose-red	5·75	2·00
321		20r. bronze-green and sage-green	17·00	3·00
322		25r. deep brown and yellow-brown	36·00	60·00
323		40r. blackish violet and grey	34·00	20·00
320/323 Set of 4			85·00	75·00

Designs: 10r. T **99**; 20r. Footballer kicking ball; 25r. Goalkeeper; 40r. Two footballers.

For similar sporting designs see Nos. 332/335, 340/343, 351/354, 363/366.

(99a)

1954 (28 Sept). Nos. 299/301 surch as T **99a**.
324		35r. on 10r.+10r. olive-green (G.)	7·75	5·00
325		60r. on 20r.+10r. blackish brown (Br.)	39·00	21·00
326		65r. on 40r.+10r. blue (B.)	12·00	15·00
324/326 Set of 3			55·00	37·00

100 Madonna and Child   **101** Princess Georgina

(Des and eng K. Bickel. Recess PTT Bureau, Berne)

1954 (16 Dec). Termination of Marian Year. P 11½.
327	**100**	20r. chestnut	6·75	5·50
328		40r. greenish black	39·00	33·00
329		1f. sepia	39·00	38·00
327/329 Set of 3			75·00	70·00

(Des H. Schütz (2f.), L. Pfeffer (3f.). Eng H. T. Schimek. Recess State Ptg Works, Vienna)

1955 (5 Apr). T **101** and similar vert portrait. Buff paper. P 14½.
330		2f. deep brown (Prince Francis Joseph II)	£170	£100
331		3f. blackish green (Type **101**)	£170	£100

(Des J. Seger. Photo Courvoisier)

1955 (14 June). Mountain Sports. Horiz designs as T **99**. P 11½.
332		10r. plum and turquoise-blue	5·25	2·00
333		20r. myrtle-green and olive-bistre	14·00	2·00
334		25r. blackish brown and cobalt	36·00	36·00

335	40r. blackish olive and pale brown-red		36·00	14·50
332/335	Set of 4		80·00	49·00

Designs: 10r. Slalom racer; 20r. Mountaineer hammering in piton; 25r. Skier; 40r. Mountaineer resting on summit.

102 Crown Prince John Adam Pius   **103**

(Des A. Frommelt. Photo Courvoisier)

1955 (14 Dec). Tenth Anniversary of Liechtenstein Red Cross. T **102** and similar vert portraits inscr '1945 1955'. Cross in red. P 11½.

336	10r. blackish violet (Type **102**)		5·75	1·50
337	20r. slate-green (Prince Philip)		12·00	3·50
338	40r. bistre-brown (Prince Nicholas)		14·00	14·50
339	60r. brown-lake (Princess Nora)		14·00	8·50
336/339	Set of 4		41·00	25·00

See also No. 350.

(Des J. Seger. Photo Courvoisier)

1956 (21 June). Athletics. Horiz designs as T **99**. P 11½.

340	10r. bronze-green and pale red-brown		4·25	1·50
341	20r. deep purple and pale olive-green		8·00	1·50
342	40r. chocolate and pale blue		11·00	8·25
343	1f. deep olive-brown and pale vermilion		26·00	32·00
340/343	Set of 4		44·00	39·00

Designs: 10r. Throwing the javelin; 20r. Hurdling; 40r. Pole vaulting; 1f. Running.

(Des A. Frommelt. Photo Courvoisier)

1956 (21 Aug). 150th Anniversary of Sovereignty of Liechtenstein. P 11½.

344	**103**	10r. deep dull purple and gold	5·50	2·00
345		1f.20 blackish blue and gold	23·00	8·75

104 Prince Francis Joseph II   **105** Norway Spruce

(Des from painting by Max Poebing-Mylot. Photo Courvoisier)

1956 (21 Aug). 50th Birthday of Prince Francis Joseph II. P 11½.

346	**104**	10r. green	3·75	1·00
347		15r. deep ultramarine	7·25	6·25
348		25r. deep purple	7·25	6·25
349		60r. deep brown	17·00	5·50
346/349	Set of 4		32·00	17·00

1956 (21 Aug). Sixth Philatelic Exhibition, Vaduz. As T **102** but inscr '6 BRIEFMARKEN-AUSSTELLUNG'. Photo. P 11½.

350		20r. deep olive-green	6·50	1·50

(Des J. Seger. Photo Courvoisier)

1957 (14 May). Gymnastics. Horiz designs as T **99**. P 11½.

351		10r. bronze-green and rose-pink	5·25	2·00
352		15r. plum and pale bluish green	11·00	12·00
353		25r. deep bluish green and pale drab	14·00	14·00
354		1f.50 sepia and bistre-yellow	46·00	40·00
351/354	Set of 4		70·00	60·00

Designs showing Gymnast: 10r. Somersaulting; 15r. Vaulting; 25r. Exercising with rings; 1f.50, Somersaulting on parallel bars.

(Des A. Frommelt. Photo Courvoisier)

1957 (10 Sept). Liechtenstein Trees and Bushes. T **105** and similar vert designs. P 11½.

355		10r. deep slate-purple (Type **105**)	9·00	4·50
356		20r. brown-lake (Wild Rose bush)	9·00	2·00
357		1f. green (Silver Birch)	15·00	15·00
355/357	Set of 3		30·00	19·00

For similar designs see Nos. 369/371, 375/377 and 401/403.

106 Lord Baden-Powell   **107** St Mamertus Chapel

(Des A. Frommelt. Photo Courvoisier)

1957 (10 Sept). 50th Anniversary of Boy Scout Movement and Birth Centenary of Lord Baden-Powell (founder). T **106** and similar vert design. P 11½.

358		10r. deep violet blue	3·00	3·00
		a. Pair. Nos. 358/359	6·25	6·25
359		20r. deep brown	3·00	3·00

Designs: 10r. Torchlight procession; 20r. T **106**.

Nos. 358/359 were issued together in *se-tenant* pairs within sheets of 12 stamps.

(Des A. Frommelt. Photo Courvoisier)

1957 (16 Dec). Christmas. Vert designs as T **107**. P 11½.

360		10r. sepia	3·00	1·00
361		40r. deep blue	7·00	14·00
362		1f.50 brown-purple	25·00	24·00
360/362	Set of 3		32·00	35·00

Designs: 10r. T **107**; (From St Mamertus Chapel)—40r. Altar shrine; 1f.50, *Pietà* (sculpture).

For similar designs see Nos. 372/374 and 392/394.

(Des J. Seger. Photo Courvoisier)

1958 (18 Mar). Sports. Horiz designs as T **99**. P 11½.

363		15r. reddish violet and light blue	2·10	3·00
364		30r. deep olive and pale reddish purple	12·00	16·00
365		40r. blackish green and salmon	20·00	17·00
366		90r. sepia and light yellow-green	5·25	8·75
363/366	Set of 4		35·00	40·00

Designs: 15r. Swimmer; 30r. Fencers; 40r. Tennis player; 90r. Racing cyclists.

108 Relief Map of Liechtenstein   **109**

(Des J. Seger. Photo Courvoisier)

1958 (18 Mar). Brussels International Exhibition. P 11½.

367	**108**	25r. slate-purple, yellow-ochre and vermilion	1·80	1·50
368		40r. slate-purple, greenish blue and vermilion	2·75	1·50

(Des A. Frommelt. Photo Courvoisier)

1958 (12 Aug). Liechtenstein Trees and Bushes. Vert designs as T **105**. P 11½.

369		20r. sepia (Sycamore)	7·75	2·30
370		50r. deep olive (Holly)	25·00	11·00
371		90r. blackish violet (Yew)	7·75	7·00
369/371	Set of 3		36·00	18·00

(Des A. Frommelt. Photo Courvoisier)

1958 (4 Dec). Christmas. Vert designs as T **107**. P 11.

372		20r. slate-green	5·75	5·00
373		35r. blackish violet	5·75	6·75
374		80r. sepia	7·25	4·75
372/374	Set of 3		17·00	15·00

Designs: 20r. St Maurice and St Agatha; 35r. St Peter; 80r. St Peter's Chapel, Mals-Balzers.

(Des M. Frommelt. Photo Courvoisier)

1959 (15 Apr). Liechtenstein Trees and Bushes. Vert designs as T **105**. P 11½.

375		20r. deep lilac (Red-berried Larch)	14·50	5·50

LIECHTENSTEIN 1959

376		50r. brown-red (Red-berried Elder)		11·00	6·50
377		90r. deep myrtle green (Linden)		7·75	8·00
375/377 Set of 3				30·00	18·00

(Des M. Frommelt. Photo Courvoisier)

1959 (15 Apr). Pope Pius XII Mourning. P 11½.
378	109	30r. purple and gold	2·20	2·10

110 Flags of Vaduz Castle and Rhine Valley

111 Harvester

(Des J. Seger (5r. to 60r.), A. Ender (75r. to 1f.50). Photo Courvoisier)

1959 (23 July)–**64**. Various horiz views as T **110** and scenes as T **111**. P 11½.
379	5r. olive-brown (30.5.61)	55	55
380	10r. deep slate-purple	65	65
381	20r. deep magenta	65	65
382	30r. brown-red	80	65
383	40r. bronze-green (30.5.61)	1·30	85
384	50r. deep blue	1·10	1·00
385	60r. turquoise-blue	1·40	1·20
386	75r. yellow-brown (19.9.60)	2·20	2·30
387	80r. olive-green (3.10.61)	1·80	1·60
388	90r. purple (3.10 61)	1·90	1·60
389	1f. brown (3.10.61)	2·50	1·80
390	1f.20 deep orange-red (7.4.60)	3·00	2·30
390a	1f.30 bluish green (15.4.64)	2·75	2·20
391	1f.50 greenish blue (7.4.60)	3·75	2·40
379/391 Set of 14		22·00	18·00

Designs: Horiz—5r. Bendern Church; 10r. T **110**; 20r. Rhine Dam; 30r. Gutenberg Castle; 40r. View from Schellenberg; 50r. Vaduz Castle; 60r. Naafkopf-Falknis Mountains (view from the Bettlerjoch); 1f.20, Harvesting Apples; 1f.30, Farmer and wife; 1f.50, Saying grace at table. Vert—75r. T **111**; 80r. Alpine haymaker; 90r. Girl in vineyard; 1f. Mother in kitchen.

(Des M. Frommelt. Photo Courvoisier)

1959 (2 Dec). Christmas. Various vert designs similar to T **107**. P 11½.
392	5r. deep myrtle-green	1·10	55
393	60r. olive-brown	12·50	9·50
394	1f. brown-purple	11·00	6·50
392/394 Set of 3		22·00	15·00

Designs: 5r. Bendern Church belfry; 60r. Relief on bell of St Theodul's Church; 1f. Sculpture on tower of St Lucius's Church.

112 Bell 47J Ranger Helicopter

(**113**)

(Des M. Frommelt. Photo Courvoisier)

1960 (7 Apr). AIR. 30th Anniversary of First Liechtenstein Airmail Stamps. T **112** and similar horiz designs. P 11½.
395	30r. orange-red	5·25	6·00
396	40r. deep blue	8·75	6·00
397	50r. brown-purple	21·00	10·50
398	75r. olive-green	4·25	6·00
395/398 Set of 4		35·00	26·00

Designs: 30r. T **112**; 40r. Boeing 707 jetliner; 50r. Convair 990A Coronado; 75r. Douglas DC-8.

1960 (7 Apr). World Refugee Year. Nos 367/368 surch as T **113**.
399	108	30r. +10r. on 40r.	2·30	2·30
400		50r. +10r. on 25r.	3·75	3·75

(Des M. Frommelt. Photo Courvoisier)

1960 (19 Sept). Liechtenstein Trees and Bushes. Vert designs as T **105**. P 11½.
401	20r. yellow-brown	12·50	9·75
402	30r. reddish purple	12·50	21·00
403	50r. deep bluish green	40·00	32·00
401/403 Set of 3		60·00	55·00

Designs: 20r. Beech tree; 30r. Juniper; 50r. Mountain Pines.

114 Europa Honeycomb

115 Princess Gina

(Des L. Jäger. Photo Harrison & Sons)

1960 (19 Sept). Europa. P 14.
404	114	50r. multicoloured	£130	70·00

(Des J. Seger. Eng H. Ranzoni. Recess State Printing Works, Vienna)

1960 (6 Dec)–**64**. T **115** and similar portraits. P 14.
404a	1f.70 violet (15.4.64)	3·00	2·00
405	2f. deep blue	4·50	3·50
406	3f. deep brown	5·25	4·00
404a/406 Set of 3		11·50	8·50

Portraits: 1f.70, Crown Prince Hans Adam; 2f. T **115**; 3f. Prince Francis Joseph II.

116 Heinrich von Frauenberg

117 Power Transmission

(Photo Courvoisier)

1961 (30 May). Minnesingers (1st issue). Vert designs as T **116**. P 11½.
407	15r. multicoloured	80	90
408	25r. multicoloured	1·00	1·00
409	35r. multicoloured	1·40	1·40
410	1f. multicoloured	3·25	3·00
411	1f.50 multicoloured	13·50	20·00
407/411 Set of 5		18·00	24·00

Designs (reproductions from the Manessian Manuscript of Songs): 15r. T **116**; 25r. Ulrich von Liechtenstein; 35r. Ulrich von Gutenberg; 1f. Konrad von Altstätten; 1f.50 Walther von der Vogelweide.

See also Nos. 415/418, 428/431 and **MS**525.

(Des L. Jäger. Photo Harrison)

1961 (3 Oct). Europa. P 13½.
412	117	50r. multicoloured	75	70

117a Prince John II

118 Clasped Hands

(Des J. Seger, Photo Courvoisier)

1962 (2 Aug). 50th Anniversary of First Liechtenstein Postage Stamps. Sheet 133×118 mm. T **117a** and similar horiz designs. P 11½.
MS412a	5r. myrtle-green; 10r. rose-carmine; 25r. grey-blue (sold at 3f.)	12·00	8·00

Designs: 5r. T **117a**; 10r. Prince Francis I; 25r. Prince Francis Joseph II.

(Des M. Frommelt. Photo Courvoisier)

1962 (2 Aug). Europa. P 11½.
413	118	50r. red and indigo	1·00	1·00

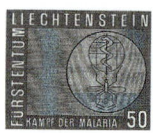
119 Campaign Emblem

120 Pietà

112

1962 LIECHTENSTEIN

(Des L. Jäger. Eng K. Bickel, Jr. Recess PTT Bureau, Berne)

1962 (2 Aug). Malaria Eradication. P 11½.
414 **119** 50r. deep turquoise-blue............ 1·30 1·00

(Photo Courvoisier)

1962 (6 Dec). Minnesingers (2nd issue). Multicoloured designs as T **116**. P 11½.
415   20r. King Konradin .... 1·00 1·00
416   30r. Kraft von Toggenburg .... 1·50 1·40
417   40r. Heinrich von Veldig .... 1·50 1·40
418   2f. *The Tannhäuser* .... 2·10 2·10
415/418 *Set of 4* .... 5·50 5·25

(Des M. Frommelt. Photo Courvoisier)

1962 (6 Dec). Christmas. Vert designs as T **120**. P 11½.
419   30r. deep magenta 90 90
420   50r. orange-red .... 1·10 1·10
421   1f.20 deep blue .... 2·20 2·10
419/421 *Set of 3* .... 3·75 3·75
Designs: 30r. T **120**; 50r. Fresco with Angel; 1f.20, View of Mauren.
See also Nos. 438/440.

121 Prince Francis Joseph II

122 Milk and Bread

(Des J. Seger. Eng H. Ranzoni. Recess State Ptg Wks, Vienna)

1963 (3 Apr). 25th Anniversary of Reign of Prince Francis Joseph II. P 13½×14.
422 **121** 5f. deep grey-green .... 9·00 6·25

(Des G. Malin. Photo Courvoisier)

1963 (26 Aug). Freedom from Hunger. P 11½.
423 **122** 50r. brown, purple and carmine-red ..... 1·30 1·10

123 Angel of Annunciation

124 Europa

(Des L. Jäger. Photo Courvoisier)

1963 (26 Aug). Red Cross Centenary. T **123** and similar vert designs. Cross in red; background pale grey. P 11½.
424   20r. olive-yellow and emerald-green 65 65
425   80r. reddish violet and pale mauve .... 1·10 1·10
426   1f. grey-blue and ultramarine .... 1·80 1·60
424/426 *Set of 3* .... 3·25 3·00
Designs: 20r. T **123**; 80r. The Epiphany; 1f. Family.

(Des G. Malin. Photo Courvoisier)

1963 (26 Aug). Europa. P 11½.
427 **124** 50r. multicoloured .... 1·80 1·30

(Photo Courvoisier)

1963 (5 Dec). Minnesingers (3rd issue). Multicoloured designs as T **116**. P 11½.
428   25r. Heinrich von Sax 75 65
429   30r. Kristen von Hamle 95 85
430   75r. Werner von Teufen .... 1·20 1·10
431   1f.70 Hartmann von Aue .... 2·30 2·10
428/431 *Set of 4* .... 4·75 4·25

125 Olympic Rings and Flags

126 Arms of Counts of Werdenberg, Vaduz

(Des J. Seger. Photo Courvoisier)

1964 (15 Apr). Olympic Games, Tokyo. P 11½.
432 **125** 50r. red, black and greenish blue .... 1·10 1·00

(Photo Courvoisier)

1964 (1 Sept). Arms (1st issue). T **126** and similar vert designs. Multicoloured. P 11½.
433   20r. Type **126** 45 40
434   30r. Barons of Brandis 50 45
435   80r. Counts of Sulz .... 1·00 90
436   1f.50 Counts of Hohenems .... 2·00 1·80
433/436 *Set of 4* .... 3·50 3·25
See also Nos. 443/446.

127 Roman Castle, Schaan

128 Peter Kaiser

(Des G. Malin. Photo Enschedé)

1964 (1 Sept). Europa. P 13×14.
437 **127** 50r. multicoloured .... 1·80 1·30
   a. Missing brown £2750

(Photo Courvoisier)

1964 (9 Dec). Christmas. Vert designs as T **120**. P 11½.
438   10r. deep slate-purple 45 40
439   40r. deep blue 55 50
440   1f.30 reddish purple .... 2·00 1·80
438/440 *Set of 3* .... 2·75 2·40
Designs: 10r. Masescha Chapel; 40r. Mary Magdalene (altar painting); 1f.30, St Sebastian, Madonna and Child, and St Rochus (altar painting).

(Des and eng K. Bickel. Recess PTT Bureau, Berne)

1964 (9 Dec). Death Centenary of Peter Kaiser (historian). P 11½.
441 **128** 1f. bluish green/*cream* .... 1·70 1·60

129 Madonna (wood sculpture, c. 1700)

130 Europa Links (ancient belt-buckle)

(Des and eng K. Bickel. Recess PTT Bureau, Berne)

1965 (22 Apr). P 11½.
442 **129** 10f. vermilion .... 16·00 9·50
Issued in sheetlets of four stamps.

1965 (31 Aug). Arms (2nd issue). As T **126** (vert designs). Multicoloured. P 11½.
443   20r. von Schellenberg 45 45
444   30r. von Hamle 55 50
445   80r. von Frauenberg .... 1·20 1·10
446   1f. von Ramschwag .... 1·40 1·30
443/446 *Set of 4* .... 3·25 3·00

(Des G. Malin. Photo Courvoisier)

1965 (31 Aug). Europa. P 11½.
447 **130** 50r. chocolate, pale grey and ultramarine .... 1·10 95

131 Jesus in the Temple

LIECHTENSTEIN 1965

(Des L. Jäger, after painting by Nigg. Photo Courvoisier)

1965 (7 Dec). Birth Centenary of Ferdinand Nigg (painter). T **131** and similar designs. P 11½.
448	10r. bronze-green and yellow-green	40	35
449	30r. lake-brown and orange	50	45
450	1f.20 deep bluish green and bright blue	1·40	1·30
448/450 Set of 3		2·10	1·90

Designs: Vert—10r. The Annunciation; 30r. The Magi. Horiz—1f.20, T **131**.

132 Princess Gina and Prince Franz (after painting by Pedro Leitao)

(Photo Courvoisier)

1965 (7 Dec). Special Issue. P 11½.
451	**132**	75r. black, flesh, gold and light grey	1·20	1·00

See also No. 457.

133 Telecommunications Symbols   **134** Tree (Wholesome Earth)

(Des G. Malin. Photo Courvoisier)

1965 (7 Dec). Centenary of International Telecommunications Union. P 11½.
452	**133**	25r. multicoloured	60	45

(Des L. Jäger. Photo Courvoisier)

1966 (26 Apr). Nature Protection. T **134** and similar horiz designs. P 11½.
453	10r. myrtle-green and greenish yellow	40	35
454	20r. Prussian blue and light blue	45	40
455	30r. ultramarine and blue-green	50	45
456	1f.50 red and yellow	1·90	1·70
453/456 Set of 4		3·00	2·50

Designs: 10r. T **134**; 20r. Bird (Pure Air); 30r. Fish (Clean Water); 1f.50, Sun (Protection of Nature).

(Photo by Atelier Dita Herein, Vaduz. Photo Courvoisier)

1966 (26 Apr). Prince Franz Joseph II's 60th Birthday. As T **132** but with portrait of Prince Franz and inscr '1906–1966'. P 11½.
457	1f. agate, light brown, gold and light grey	1·60	1·40

135 Arms of Herren von Richenstein   **136** Europa Ship

(Des L. Jäger. Photo Courvoisier)

1966 (6 Sept). Arms of Triesen Families. T **135** and similar vert designs. Multicoloured. P 11½.
458	20r. Type **135**	40	40
459	30r. Jinker Vaistli	55	50
460	60r. Edle von Trisun	90	80
461	1f.20 Die von Schiel	1·60	1·40
458/461 Set of 4		3·00	2·75

(Des G. and J. Bender, and G. Malin. Autotype process (photo) Enschedé)

1966 (6 Sept). Europa. P 14½×13½.
462	**136**	50r. multicoloured	1·10	95

137 Vaduz Parish Church   **138** Cogwheels

(Des J. Seger. Photo Courvoisier)

1966 (6 Dec). Restoration of Vaduz Parish Church. T **137** and similar vert designs. P 11½.
463	5r. light yellow-green and orange-red	20	20
464	20r. purple and light bistre	40	40
465	30r. Prussian blue and pale brown-red	55	50
466	1f.70 lake-brown and pale green	2·50	2·20
463/466 Set of 4		3·25	3·00

Designs: 5r. T **137**; 20r. St Florin; 30r. Madonna; 1f.70, God the Father.

(Des O. Bonnevalle. Photo Courvoisier)

1967 (20 Apr). Europa. P 11½.
467	**138**	50r. multicoloured	95	90

139 The Man from Malanser   **140** Crown Prince Hans Adam

(Des L. Jäger. Photo Courvoisier)

1967 (20 Apr). Liechtenstein Sagas (1st issue). T **139** and similar horiz designs. Multicoloured. P 11½.
468	20r. Type **139**	35	35
469	30r. The Treasure of Gutenberg	60	55
470	1f.20 The Giant of Guflina	2·00	1·70
468/470 Set of 3		2·75	2·30

See also Nos. 492/494 and 516/518.

(Des A. Pilch. Eng A. Nefe and R. Toth. Recess State Ptg Wks, Vienna)

1967 (29 June). Royal Wedding. Sheet (86×95 *mm*) comprising T **140** and similar vert design. P 14×13½.
MS471	1f.50 indigo and light blue (Type **140**); 1f.50, red-brown and light red-brown (Princess Marie)	5·50	5·00

141 Alpha and Omega   **142** Father J. B. Büchel

(Des G. Malin. Photo Courvoisier)

1967 (25 Sept). Christian Symbols. T **141** and similar vert designs. Multicoloured. P 11½.
472	20r. Type **141**	35	35
473	30r. Tropaion (Cross as victory symbol)	50	45
474	70r. Christ's monogram	1·10	1·00
472/474 Set of 3		1·80	1·60

(Des and eng H. Heüsser. Recess and photo PTT, Berne)

1967 (25 Sept). J. B. Büchel Commemoration (educator, historian and poet). Phosphorescent paper. P 11½.
475	**142**	1f. lake and pale green	1·80	1·40

1967 LIECHTENSTEIN

143 'EFTA'

144 Peter and Paul, Mauren

(Des J. Seger. Photo Courvoisier)

1967 (25 Sept). European Free Trade Association. P 11½.
476	**143**	50r. multicoloured	90	85

(Des G. Malin. Photo Courvoisier)

1967–71. T **144** and similar vert designs showing Patrons of the Church. Multicoloured. P 11½.
477		5r. St Joseph, Planken (29.8.68)	20	15
478		10r. St Lawrence, Schaan (25.4.68)	35	35
479		20r. Type **144** (7.12.67)	40	40
480		30r. St Nicholas, Balzers (7.12.67)	55	45
480a		40r. St Sebastian, Nendeln (11.6.71)	70	55
481		50r. St George, Schellenberg (25.4.68)	90	60
482		60r. St Martin, Eschen (25.4.68)	1·00	70
483		70r. St Fridolin, Ruggell (7.12.67)	1·20	85
484		80r. St Gallus, Triesen (25.4.68)	1·40	95
485		1f. St Theodolus, Triesenberg (25.4.68)	1·80	1·50
486		1f.20 St Anna, Vaduz Castle (7.12.67)	2·00	1·80
487		1f.50 St Marie, Bendern-Camprin (29.8.68)	2·50	1·90
488		2f. St Lucius (patron saint of Liechtenstein) (5.12.68)	3·75	2·40
477/488 Set of 13			15·00	11·50

The 10r. and 20r. were each issued both in sheets and in coils.

145 Campaign Emblem

146 Europa Key

(Des J. Seger. Photo Courvoisier)

1967 (7 Dec). Technical Assistance. P 11½.
489	**145**	50r. +20r. multicoloured	1·20	1·10

(Des H. Schwarzenbach and J. Schädler. Photo Courvoiser)

1968 (25 Apr). Europa. P 11½.
490	**146**	50r. gold, black, ultramarine and bright red	90	85

147 Arms of Liechtenstein and Wilczek

148 Sir Rowland Hill

(Des L. Jäger. Photo Courvoisier)

1968 (29 Aug). Silver Wedding Anniversary of Prince Francis Joseph II and Princess Gina. P 11½.
491	**147**	75r. multicoloured	1·40	1·10

(Des L. Jäger. Photo Courvoisier)

1968 (29 Aug). Liechtenstein Sagas (2nd issue). Horiz designs as T **139**. Multicoloured. P 11½.
492		30r. The Treasure of St Mamerten	50	40
493		50r. The Hobgoblin in the Bergerwald	70	60
494		80r. The Three Sisters	1·40	1·00
492/494 Set of 3			2·30	1·80

(Des K. Bickel. Design recess, value typo PTT Bureau, Berne)

1968 (29 Aug)–**69**. OFFICIAL. As Nos. O287/O296. Colours changed and new values. White granite paper. P 11½.
O495	O **86**	5r. olive-brown and orange	25	20
O496		10r. violet and red	35	25
O497		20r. red and emerald	40	40
O498		30r. green and red	50	45
O499		50r. deep blue and red	85	75
O500		60r. orange and blue	1·00	95
O501		70r. deep claret and emerald	1·10	1·00
O502		80r. grey-green and red	1·30	1·20
O503		95r. slate-green and red (24.4.69)	1·40	1·30
O504		1f. reddish purple and turquoise	1·70	1·70
O505		1f.20 chestnut and turquoise	2·30	2·20
O506		2f. agate and orange (24.4.69)	3·00	2·75
O495/O506 Set of 12			13·00	12·00

(Des A. Pilch. Eng A. Nefe. Recess State Ptg Wks, Vienna)

1968 (5 Dec). Pioneers of Philately (1st issue). T **148** and similar vert designs. P 14×13½.
495		20r. bronze-green (Type **148**)	40	40
496		30r. red-brown (Philippe de Ferrary)	50	45
497		1f. black (Maurice Burrus)	1·70	1·40
495/497 Set of 3			2·30	2·00

See also Nos. 504/505 and 554/556.

150 Arms of Liechtenstein

151 Colonnade

(Des A. Pilch. Eng A. Fischer. Recess State Ptg Wks, Vienna)

1969 (24 Apr). P 14×13½.
498	**150**	3f.50 blackish brown	5·50	3·50

(Des L. Gasbarra, G. Belli and J. Seger. Photo Harrison)

1969 (24 Apr). Europa. P 14½.
499	**151**	50r. multicoloured	90	75

152 Biology

153 Arms of St Luzi Monastery

(Des H. Erni. Photo Courvoisier)

1969 (28 Aug). 250th Anniversary of Liechtenstein. T **152** and similar horiz designs. Multicoloured. P 11½.
500		10r. Type **152**	40	40
501		30r. Physics	55	45
502		50r. Astronomy	90	75
503		80r. Art	1·50	1·20
500/503 Set of 4			3·00	2·50

(Des A. Pilch. Eng A. Nefe. Recess State Ptg Wks, Vienna)

1969 (28 Aug). Pioneers of Philately (2nd issue). Vert portraits as T **148**. P 14×13½.
504		80r. blackish brown (Carl Lindenberg)	1·50	1·10
505		1f.20 deep blue (Theodore Champion)	2·20	1·70

(Des L. Jäger. Photo Courvoisier)

1969–71. Arms of Church Patrons. T **153** and similar vert designs showing Arms. Multicoloured. P 11½.
506		20r. St Johann's Abbey (3.12.70)	35	35
507		30r. Type **153** (4.12.69)	55	40
508		30r. Ladies' Priory, Schänis (3.12.70)	55	40
509		30r. Knights Hospitalers, Feldkirch (2.9.71)	55	40
510		50r. Pfäfers Abbey (4.12.69)	90	65
511		50r. Weingarten Abbey (2.9.71)	90	65
512		75r. St Gallen Abbey (3.12.70)	1·40	90
513		1f.20 Ottobeuren Abbey (2.9.71)	2·20	1·70
514		1f.50 Chur Episcopate (4.12.69)	2·75	1·90
506/514 Set of 9			9·25	6·50

LIECHTENSTEIN 1969

154 Symbolic T   **155** Orange Lily

(Des J. Seger. Photo State Ptg Wks, Vienna)

1969 (4 Dec). Centenary of Liechtenstein Telegraph System. P 13½.
515 **154** 30r. multicoloured 55 40

(Des L. Jäger. Photo Courvoisier)

1969 (4 Dec). Liechtenstein Sagas (3rd issue). Horiz designs as T **139**. Multicoloured. P 11½.
516   20r. The Cheated Devil 40 35
517   50r. The Fiery Red Goat 85 55
518   60r. The Grafenberg Treasure .... 1·00 80
516/518 Set of 3 .... 2·00 1·50

(Des G. Malin. Photo Courvoisier)

1970 (30 Apr). Nature Conservation Year. Liechtenstein Flowers (1st issue). T **155** and similar vert floral designs. Multicoloured. P 11½.
519   20r. Type **155** 40 35
520   30r. Wild Orchid 70 50
521   50r. Ranunculus 95 90
522   1f.20 Bog Bean .... 2·20 1·90
519/522 Set of 4 .... 3·75 3·25
See also Nos. 532/535 and 548/551.

156 Flaming Sun   **157** Prince Wenzel

(Des L. le Brocquy and J. Schädler. Litho State Ptg Wks, Berlin)

1970 (30 Apr). Europa. P 14.
523 **156** 50r. yellow, deep blue and light green   95 75

(Des from photo by W. Wachter. Photo Courvoisier)

1970 (30 Apr). 25th Anniversary of Liechtenstein Red Cross. P 11½.
524 **157** 1f. multicoloured .... 1·90 1·40

(Photo Courvoisier)

1970 (27 Aug). 800th Anniversary of Wolfram von Eschenbach. Sheet 73×96 mm containing vert designs similar to T **116** from the *Codex Manesse*. Multicoloured. P 11½.
MS525 30r. Wolfram von Eschenbach; 50r. Reinmar the Fiddler; 80r. Hartmann von Starkenberg; 1f.20 Friedrich von Hausen. *Sold for 3f.* .... 5·75 5·50

158 Prince Francis Joseph II   **159** *Mother and Child* (sculpture, R. Schädler)

(Des A. Pilch. Eng A. Nefe (2f.50, 3f.). Des W. Wachter. Eng W. Pfeiler (1f.70,). Recess State Ptg Wks, Vienna)

1970–74. T **158** and similar vert portraits. P 14×13½.
526   1f.70 bottle green (5.12.74) .... 3·25 2·10
526a   2f.50 deep ultramarine (11.6.71) .... 5·00 3·50
527   3f. black (3.12.70) .... 5·75 3·75
526/527 Set of 3 .... 12·50 8·50
Designs: 1f.70, Prince Hans Adam, 2f.50, Princess Gina; 3f. T **158**.

(Photo Courvoisier)

1970 (3 Dec). Christmas. P 11½.
528 **159** 30r. multicoloured 55 45

160 Bronze Boar (La Tène period)   **161** Europa Chain

(Des L. Jäger. Photo Courvoisier)

1971 (11 Mar). Inauguration of National Museum. T **160** and similar horiz designs. P 11½.
529   25r. black, dull violet-blue and ultramarine .   45 40
530   30r. bright green and sepia 50 45
531   75r. multicoloured .... 1·30 95
529/531 Set of 3 .... 2·00 1·60
Designs: 25r. T **160**; 30r. Ornamental Peacock (Roman, 2nd-century); 75r. Engraved bowl (13th-century).

(Des G. Malin. Photo Courvoisier)

1971 (11 Mar). Liechtenstein Flowers (2nd issue). Vert designs similar to T **155**. Multicoloured. P 11½.
532   10r. Cyclamen 45 40
533   20r. Moonwort 50 45
534   50r. Superb Pink 95 85
535   1f.50 Alpine Columbine .... 2·50 2·20
532/535 Set of 4 .... 4·00 3·50

(Des H. Haflidason, adapted J. Schädler. Litho State Ptg Wks, Vienna)

1971 (11 June). Europa. P 13½.
536   **161** 50r. yellow, light blue and black 95 85

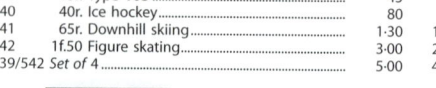

162 Part of Text   **163** Cross-country Skiing

(Des L. Jäger. Photo Courvoisier)

1971 (2 Sept). 50th Anniversary of 1921 Constitution. T **162** and similar square design. Multicoloured. P 11½.
537   70r. Type **162** .... 1·30 1·20
538   80r. Princely crown .... 1·50 1·30

(Des H. Erni. Photo Courvoisier)

1971 (9 Dec). Winter Olympic Games, Sapporo, Japan (1972). T **163** and similar vert designs. Multicoloured. P 11½.
539   15r. Type **163** 45 45
540   40r. Ice hockey 80 75
541   65r. Downhill skiing .... 1·30 1·00
542   1f.50 Figure skating .... 3·00 2·50
539/542 Set of 4 .... 5·00 4·25

164 *Madonna and Child* (sculpture, Andrea della Robbia)   **165** Gymnastics

(Photo Courvoisier)

1971 (9 Dec). Christmas. P 11½.
543   **164** 30r. multicoloured 70 50

(Des H. Erni. Photo Courvoisier)

1972 (16 Mar). Olympic Games, Munich. T **165** and similar horiz designs. Multicoloured. P 11½.
544   10r. Type **165** 30 25
545   20r. High jumping 50 45
546   40r. Running 70 65
547   60r. Throwing the discus .... 1·00 90
544/547 Set of 4 .... 2·30 2·00

1972 LIECHTENSTEIN

(Des G. Malin. Photo Courvoisier)

1972 (16 Mar). Liechtenstein Flowers (3rd issue). Vert designs similar to T **155**. Multicoloured. P 11½.

548	20r. Sulphur Anemone		50	40
549	30r. Turk's-cap Lily		55	50
550	60r. Alpine Centaury		1·30	95
551	1f.20 Reed-mace		2·40	1·80
548/551	Set of 4		4·25	3·25

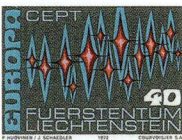 

166 Communications   **167** Bendern

(Des P. Huovinen, adapted J. Schädler. Photo Courvoisier)

1972 (16 Mar). Europa. P 11½.

552	**166**	40r. multicoloured	1·00	85

(Des J. Seger. Eng H. Ranzoni. Recess State Ptg Wks, Vienna)

1972 (8 June). Liba '72 Stamp Exhibition, Vaduz. Sheet 101×65 mm containing T **167** and similar horiz design. P 13½.

MS553	1f. slate-violet; 2f. rose-red	5·75	5·50

Designs: 1f. T **167**; 2f. Vaduz castle.

(Des A. Pilch. Eng A. Nefe. Recess State Ptg Wks, Vienna)

1972 (7 Sept). Pioneers of Philately (3rd series). Vert portraits as T **148**. P 14×13½.

554	30r. slate-green		55	50
555	40r. maroon		80	70
556	1f.30 deep ultramarine		2·40	1·90
554/556	Set of 3		3·50	2·75

Portraits: 30r. Emilio Diena; 40r. Andre de Cock; 1f.30, Theodore E. Steinway.

168 Faun   **169** Madonna with Angels (F. Nigg)

(Des R. Schädler. Photo Courvoisier)

1972 (7 Sept). Natural Art. Motifs fashioned from roots and branches. T **168** and similar vert designs. Multicoloured. P 11½.

557	20r. Type **168**		40	35
558	30r. Dancer		55	45
559	1f.10 Owl		2·10	1·50
557/559	Set of 3		2·75	2·10

(Photo Courvoisier)

1972 (7 Dec). Christmas. P 11½.

560	**169**	30r. multicoloured	70	55

170 Lawena Springs   **171** Europa Posthorn

(Des L. Jäger Eng H. Heüsser. Recess PTT Bureau, Berne)

1972 (7 Dec)–73. Landscapes. T **170** and similar horiz designs. Phosphorescent paper. P 11½.

561	5r. purple and pale yellow (6.12.73)		20	15
562	10r. slate green and pale sage-green		30	30
563	15r. chestnut and pale yellow-olive		40	35
564	25r. plum and pale blue (6.12.73)		45	40
565	30r. plum and pale ochre (8.3.73)		55	45
566	40r. plum and pale cinnamon (6.12.73)		70	60
567	50r. deep blue and pale lilac (7.6.73)		1·00	65
568	60r. myrtle-green and pale greenish yellow (7.6.73)		1·10	80
569	70r. deep blue and pale cobalt (7.6.73)		1·30	95
570	80r. deep bluish green and pale sage-green		1·50	1·10
571	1f. red-brown and pale apple-green		2·10	1·40
572	1f.30 deep blue and pale apple-green (8.3.73)		2·40	1·80
573	1f.50 sepia and light blue		2·75	2·00
574	1f.80 bistre-brown and pale brown (8.3.73)		3·25	2·40
575	2f. sepia and pale turquoise-blue (6.12.73)		3·75	2·75
561/575	Set of 15		20·00	14·50

Designs: 5r. Silum; 10r. T **170**; 15r. Ruggeller Reed; 25r. Steg, Kirchlispitz; 30r. Feld Schellenberg; 40r. Rennhof Mauren; 50r. Tidrüfe; 60r. Eschner Riet; 70r. Mittagspitz; 80r. Schaan Forest; 1f. St Peter's Chapel, Mals; 1f.30, Frommenhaus; 1f.50, Ochsenkopf; 1f.80, Hehlawangspitz; 2f. Saminaschlucht.

The 50r. was issued both in sheets and in coils.

(Des J. Schädler, after L. F. Anisdahl. Photo Courvoisier)

1973 (8 Mar). Europa. P 11½.

576	**171**	30r. multicoloured	55	45
577		40r. multicoloured	70	65

172 Chambered Nautilus Goblet   **173** Arms of Liechtenstein

(Des W. Wachter. Photo Courvoisier)

1973 (7 June). Treasures from Prince's Collection (1st series). Drinking Vessels. T **172** and similar vert designs. Multicoloured. P 11½.

578	30r. Type **172**		55	45
579	70r. Ivory tankard		1·30	95
580	1f.10 Silver cup		2·10	1·70
578/580	Set of 3		3·50	2·75

See also Nos. 589/592.

(Des A. Pilch. Eng W. Seidel. Recess and photo State Ptg Works, Vienna)

1973 (6 Sept). P 14.

581	**173**	5f. multicoloured	9·50	6·50

174 False Ringlet   **175** Madonna (Bartolomeo di Tommaso da Foligno)

(Des L. Jäger. Photo Courvoisier)

1973 (6 Dec). Small Fauna of Liechtenstein (1st series). T **174** and similar horiz designs. Multicoloured. P 11½.

582	30r. Type **174**		55	45
583	40r. Curlew		70	65
584	60r. Edible Frog		1·10	90
585	80r. Grass Snake		1·60	1·10
582/585	Set of 4		3·50	2·75

See also Nos. 596/599.

(Des K. Gessner. Eng A. Nefe. Recess and photo State Ptg Wks, Vienna)

1973 (6 Dec). Christmas. P 13½.

586	**175**	30r. multicoloured	70	50

LIECHTENSTEIN 1974

176 *Shouting Horseman* (sculpture, Andrea Riccio)

177 Footballers

(Des W. Wachter. Photo Courvoisier)

1974 (21 Mar). Europa. T **176** and similar vert design. Multicoloured. P 11½.
587		30r. Type **176**	60	50
588		40r. *Squatting Aphrodite* (sculpture, Antonio Susini)	80	70

(Des W. Wachter. Photo Courvoisier)

1974 (21 Mar). Treasures from Prince's Collection (2nd series). Chinese Porcelain. Vert designs, similar to T **172**, but dated 1974. Multicoloured. P 11½.
589		30r. Vase, 19th-century	55	45
590		50r. Vase, 1740	90	70
591		60r. Vase, 1830	1·10	90
592		1f. Vase, *circa* 1700	2·00	1·50
589/592 Set of 4			4·00	3·25

(Des B. Kaufmann. Photo Courvoisier)

1974 (21 Mar). World Cup Football Championship, West Germany. P 11½.
593	**177**	80r. multicoloured	1·60	1·30

178 Posthorn and UPU Emblem

179 Bishop Marxer

(Des B. Kaufmann. Photo State Ptg Wks, Vienna)

1974 (6 June). Centenary of Universal Postal Union. P 13½.
594	**178**	40r. black, bright green and gold	80	70
595		60r. black, vermilion and gold	1·30	1·00

(Des L. Jäger. Photo Courvoisier)

1974 (6 June). Small Fauna of Liechtenstein (2nd series). Horiz designs as T **174**. Multicoloured. P 11½.
596		15r. Mountain Newt	40	35
597		25r. Adder	50	40
598		70r. Cynthia's Fritillary (Butterfly)	1·60	1·20
599		1f.10 Three-toed Woodpecker	2·10	1·80
596/599 Set of 4			4·25	3·50

(Des A. Pilch. Eng A. Fischer. Recess and photo State Ptg Wks, Vienna)

1974 (6 June). Death Bicentenary of Bishop Franz Marxer. P 13½.
600	**179**	1f. multicoloured	2·10	1·80

180 Prince Francis Joseph II and Princess Gina

181 St Florian

(Des K. Gessner. Eng W. Pfeiler. Recess and photo State Ptg Wks Vienna)

1974 (5 Sept). P 13½×14.
601	**180**	10f. agate and gold	14·00	11·00

No. 601 was issued in sheetlets of four stamps.

(Des W. Wachter. Photo Courvoisier)

1974 (5 Dec). Christmas. Glass Paintings. T **181** and similar vert designs. Multicoloured. P 11½.
602		30r. Type **181**	55	45
603		50r. St Wendelin	90	75
604		60r. St Mary, Anna and Joachim	1·10	90
605		70r. Jesus in Manger	1·20	1·00
602/605 Set of 4			3·50	2·75

182 Prince Constantin

183 *Cold Sun* (M. Frommelt)

(Des L. Jäger. Photo Courvoisier)

1975 (13 Mar). Liechtenstein Princes. T **182** and similar horiz designs. P 11½.
606		70r. myrtle-green and gold	1·40	1·10
607		80r. brown-purple and gold	1·80	1·30
608		1f.20 deep violet-blue and gold	2·30	1·90
606/608 Set of 3			5·00	3·75

Designs: 70r. T **182**; 80r. Prince Maximilian; 1f.20, Prince Alois.

(Photo Courvoisier)

1975 (13 Mar). Europa. Paintings. T **183** and similar horiz design. Multicoloured. P 11½.
609		30r. Type **183**	55	45
610		60r. *Village* (L. Jäger)	1·10	90

184 Imperial Cross

185 Red Cross

(Des O. Zeiller. Eng W. Seidel (30r., 2f.), A. Fischer (60r., 1f., 1f.30.). Recess and photo Ptg Wks, Vienna)

1975 (5 June–4 Sept). Imperial Insignia (1st series). T **184** and similar multicoloured designs. P 14.
611		30r. Type **184**	55	45
612		60r. Imperial Sword	1·40	1·00
613		1f. Imperial Orb	1·80	1·50
614		1f.30 Imperial Robe (50×32 *mm*) (4.9.75)	3·75	3·25
615		2f. Imperial Crown	4·50	3·50
611/615 Set of 5			11·00	8·75

No. 614 was issued in sheets of eight.
See also Nos. 670/673.

(Des Regina Marxer. Photo Courvoisier)

1975 (5 June). 30th Anniversary of Liechtenstein Red Cross. P 11½.
616	**185**	60r. multicoloured	1·30	90

186 St Mamerten, Triesen

187 Speed Skating

(Des G. Malin. Photo Courvoisier)

1975 (4 Sept). European Architectural Heritage Year. T **186** and similar horiz designs. Multicoloured. P 11½.
617		40r. Type **186**	1·00	90
618		50r. Red House, Vaduz	1·10	1·00
619		70r. Prebendary buildings, Eschen	1·60	1·20
620		1f. Gutenberg Castle, Balzers	2·10	1·90
617/620 Set of 4			5·25	4·50

(Des B. Kaufmann. Photo Courvoisier)

1975 (4 Dec). Winter Olympic Games, Innsbruck. T **187** and similar horiz designs. Multicoloured. P 11½.
621		20r. Type **187**	50	45
622		25r. Ice hockey	65	55
623		70r. Skiing (downhill)	1·60	1·40
624		1f.20 Skiing (slalom)	2·10	1·70
621/624 Set of 4			4·25	3·75

1975 LIECHTENSTEIN

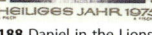
188 Daniel in the Lions' Den

189 *Mouflon*

194 *Singing Angels*

195 *Pisces*

(Des A. Pilch. Recess and photo State Ptg Wks, Vienna)

1975 (4 Dec). Christmas and Holy Year. Capitals in Chur Cathedral. T **188** and similar vert designs. P 13½.

625	30r. deep reddish violet and gold	55	45
626	60r. deep green and gold	1·30	90
627	90r. brown-lake and gold	1·90	1·30
625/627 Set of 3		3·50	2·40

Designs: 30r. T **188**; 60r. Madonna; 90r. St Peter.

(Des W. Wachter. Photo Courvoisier)

1976 (11 Mar). Europa. Ceramics by Prince Hans von Liechtenstein. T **189** and similar vert design. Multicoloured. P 11½.

| 628 | 40r. Type **189** | 1·00 | 90 |
| 629 | 80r. Ring-necked Pheasant and Brood | 1·80 | 1·20 |

190 Crayfish

191 Roman Fibula

(Des L. Jäger. Photo Courvoisier)

1976 (11 Mar). World Wildlife Fund. T **190** and similar vert designs. Multicoloured. P 11½.

630	25r. Type **190**	65	55
631	40r. Turtle	1·00	90
632	70r. European Otter	2·00	1·10
633	80r. Lapwing	2·40	1·40
630/633 Set of 4		5·50	3·50

(Des G. Malin. Photo Courvoisier)

1976 (11 Mar). 75th Anniversary of National Historical Society. P 11½.

| 634 | **191** | 90r. multicoloured | 2·10 | 1·40 |

192 Obverse of 50f. Coin depicting portrait of Prince

193 Judo

(Des L. Jäger, Photo Courvoisier)

1976 (10 June). 70th Birthday of Prince Francis Joseph II. Sheet 102×65 mm containing T **192** and similar horiz design. Multicoloured. Imperf.

| **MS**635 1f. Type **192**; 1f. Reverse of 50f. coin depicting Arms of Liechtenstein | 4·50 | 3·75 |

(Des L. Jäger. Photo Courvoisier)

1976 (10 June). Olympic Games, Montréal. T **193** and similar vert designs. Multicoloured. P 11½.

636	35r. Type **193**	60	50
637	50r. Volleyball	1·00	90
638	80r. Relay	1·60	1·40
639	1f.10 Long jumping	2·10	1·90
636/639 Set of 4		4·75	4·25

(Des K. Gessner. Eng W. Seidel (50r., 70r.), A. Fischer (1f.). Recess and photo State Ptg Wks, Vienna)

1976 (9 Sept). 400th Birth Anniversary (1977) of Peter Paul Rubens (painter). T **194** and similar multicoloured designs. P 14 (1f.) or 13½×14 (others).

640	50r. Type **194**	1·10	95
641	70r. *Sons of the Artist*	1·50	1·30
642	1f. *The Daughters of Cecrops* (49×39 mm)	5·50	4·75
640/642 Set of 3		7·25	6·25

(Des M. Hunziker. Photo Courvoisier)

1976 (9 Sept). Signs of the Zodiac (1st series). T **195** and similar vert designs. Multicoloured. P 11½.

643	20r. Type **195**	50	45
644	40r. Aries	75	65
645	80r. Taurus	1·50	1·30
646	90r. Gemini	1·60	1·40
643/646 Set of 4		4·00	3·50

See also Nos. 666/669 and 710/713.

196 Child Jesus of Prague

197 Sarcophagus Statue, Chur Cathedral

(Des and photo Courvoisier)

1976 (9 Dec). Christmas. Monastic Wax Sculptures. T **196** and similar multicoloured designs. P 11½.

647	20r. Type **196**	40	35
648	50r. The Flight into Egypt (*vert*)	1·00	90
649	80r. Holy Trinity (*vert*)	1·50	1·30
650	1f.50 Holy Family	2·50	2·20
647/650 Set of 4		4·75	4·25

(Des A. Pilch. Eng W. Seidel. Recess and photo State Ptg Wks, Vienna)

1976 (9 Dec). Bishop Ortlieb von Brandis of Chur Commemoration. P 13½×14.

| 651 | **197** | 1f.10 chestnut and gold | 2·00 | 1·80 |

O 198 Government Building, Vaduz

199 Map of Liechtenstein, 1721 (J. Heber)

(Des O. Zeiller. Eng A. Fischer. Recess and typo State Ptg Wks, Vienna)

1976 (9 Dec)–89. OFFICIAL. P 13½×14.

O652	O **198**	10r. brown and bluish violet	20	15
O653		20r. carmine and greenish blue	25	20
O654		35r. deep blue and vermilion	45	40
O655		40r. reddish violet and emerald	65	55
O656		50r. slate-green and cerise	75	65

LIECHTENSTEIN 1977

O657	70r. brown-purple and blue-green..	1·10	95
O658	80r. blue-green and bright purple...	1·20	1·10
O659	90r. bluish violet and turquoise-blue	1·50	1·30
O660	1f. olive-grey and bright purple.....	1·60	1·40
O661	1f.10 chocolate and bright blue.......	1·80	1·50
O662	1f.50 myrtle green and scarlet............	2·50	2·00
O663	2f. red-orange and greenish blue ..	3·25	2·50
O664	5f. reddish purple and yellow-orange (4.9.89)	20·00	18·00
O652/O664 Set of 13		28·00	25·00

(Des and photo Courvoisier)

1977 (10 Mar). Europa. T **199** and similar horiz design. Multicoloured. P 12½×12.

664	40r. Type **199**	90	75
665	80r. View of Vaduz, 1815 (F. Bachmann)	1·40	1·20

(Des M. Hunziker. Photo Courvoisier)

1977 (10 Mar). Signs of the Zodiac (2nd series). Vert designs as T **195**. Multicoloured. P 11½.

666	40r. Cancer	85	75
667	70r. Leo	1·30	1·20
668	80r. Virgo	1·50	1·30
669	1f.10 Libra	2·10	1·90
666/669 Set of 4		5·25	4·75

(Des O. Zeiller. Eng W. Seidel (40r., 80r.), A. Fischer (50r., 90r.) Recess and photo State Ptg Wks, Vienna)

1977 (8 June). Imperial Insignia (2nd series). Vert designs as T **184**. Multicoloured. P 14.

670	40r. Holy Lance and Reliquary with Particle of the Cross	75	65
671	50r. St Matthew (Imperial Book of Gospels)	80	70
672	80r. St Stephen's Purse	1·40	1·20
673	90r. Tabard of Imperial Herald	1·60	1·40
670/673 Set of 4		4·00	3·50

200 Coin of Emperor Constantine II

201 Frauenthal Castle, Styria

(Des L. Jäger, Photo Courvoisier)

1977 (8 June). Coins (1st series). T **200** and similar vert designs. Multicoloured. P 11½.

674	35r. Type **200**	70	65
675	70r. Lindau Brakteat	1·40	1·20
676	80r. Coin of Ortlieb von Brandis	1·60	1·40
674/676 Set of 3		3·25	3·00

See also Nos. 707/709.

(Des O. Stefferl. Eng W. Seidel (20r., 80r.), A. Fischer (50r., 90r.) Recess and photo State Ptg Wks, Vienna)

1977 (8 Sept). Castles. T **201** and similar horiz designs. P 13½×14.

677	20r. bronze-green and gold	45	40
678	50r. crimson and gold	1·00	90
679	80r. blackish lilac and gold	1·80	1·50
680	90r. indigo and gold	2·00	1·80
677/680 Set of 4		4·75	4·25

Designs: 20r. T **201**; 50r. Gross-Ullersdorf, Moravia; 80r. Liechtenstein Castle, near Mödling, Austria; 90r. Palais Liechtenstein, Alserbachstrasse, Vienna.

202 Children in Costume

203 Princess Tatjana

(Des A. Pilch. Photo Courvoisier)

1977 (8 Sept). National Costumes. T **202** and similar vert designs. Multicoloured. P 11½.

681	40r. Type **202**	65	55
682	70r. Two girls in traditional costume	1·50	1·30
683	1f. Woman in festive costume	2·00	1·80
681/683 Set of 3		3·75	3·25

(Des L. Jäger. Photo Courvoisier)

1977 (7 Dec). Princess Tatjana. P 11½.

684	**203** 1f.10 yellowish brown, reddish brown and gold	2·30	2·00

204 Angel

205 Palais Liechtenstein, Bankgasse, Vienna

(Des J. Seger. Photo Courvoisier)

1977 (7 Dec). Christmas Sculptures by Erasmus Kern. T **204** and similar vert designs. Multicoloured. P 11½.

685	20r. Type **204**	45	40
686	50r. *St Rochus*	80	70
687	80r. *Madonna*	1·50	1·30
688	1f.50 *God the Father*	2·75	2·40
685/688 Set of 4		5·00	4·25

(Des O. Stefferl. Eng W. Seidel (40r.). A. Fischer (80r.). Recess and photo State Ptg Wks, Vienna)

1978 (2 March). Europa. T **205** and similar horiz design. P 14.

689	40r. Prussian blue and gold	90	75
690	80r. brown-lake and gold	1·50	1·30

Designs: 40r. T **205**; 80r. Feldsberg Castle.

206 Farmhouse, Triesen

207 Vaduz Castle

(Des G. Malin. Photo Courvoisier)

1978 (2 March–1 June). Buildings. T **206** and similar vert designs. Multicoloured. P 12×11½.

691	10r. Type **206** (1.6.78)	25	20
692	20r. Upper village of Triesen (1.6.78)	45	40
693	35r. Barns, Balzers (1.6.78)	65	55
694	40r. Monastery building, Bendern (1.6.78)	75	65
695	50r. Rectory tower, Balzers-Mäls	95	85
696	70r. Rectory, Mauren	1·30	1·20
697	80r. Farmhouse, Schellenberg	1·40	1·30
698	90r. Rectory, Balzers	1·60	1·40
699	1f. Rheinberger House, Vaduz	1·80	1·50
700	1f.10 Vaduz Mitteldorf	1·90	1·70
701	1f.50 Town Hall, Triesenberg (1.6.78)	2·75	2·30
702	2f. National Museum and Administrator's residence, Vaduz (1.6.78)	3·50	3·00
691/702 Set of 12		16·00	13·50

(Des O. Stefferl. Eng W. Seidel (40r., 70r.), A. Fischer (50r., 80r.). Recess and photo State Ptg Wks, Vienna)

1978 (1 June). 40th Anniversary of Prince Francis Joseph II's Accession. T **207** and similar horiz designs. Multicoloured. P 13½×14.

703	40r. Type **207**	85	75
704	50r. Courtyard	95	85
705	70r. Hall	1·40	1·20
706	80r. High altar, Castle chapel	1·60	1·40
703/706 Set of 4		4·25	3·75

1978 LIECHTENSTEIN

208 Coin of Prince Charles

209 *Portrait of a Piebald* (J. G. von Hamilton and A. Faistenberger)

210 Adoration of the Shepherds

(Des L. Jäger. Photo Courvoisier)

1978 (7 Sept). Coins (2nd series). T **208** and similar vert designs. Multicoloured. P 11½.

707	40r. Type **208**	65	60
708	50r. Coin of Prince John Adam	80	70
709	80r. Coin of Prince Joseph Wenzel	1·50	1·30
707/709	*Set of 3*	2·75	2·30

(Des M. Hunziker. Photo Courvoisier)

1978 (7 Sept). Signs of the Zodiac (3rd series). Vert designs as T **195**. Multicoloured. P 11½.

710	40r. Scorpio	70	60
711	50r. Sagittarius	95	85
712	80r. Capricorn	1·50	1·30
713	1f.50 Aquarius	3·00	2·50
710/713	*Set of 4*	5·50	4·75

(Des A. Böcskör. Eng A. Fischer (1f.10), W. Seidel (others). Recess and photo State Ptg Wks, Vienna)

1978 (7 Dec). Paintings. T **209** and similar designs. Multicoloured. P 12 (1f.10) or 13½ (others).

714	70r. Type **209**	1·30	1·10
715	80r. *Portrait of a Blackish-brown Stallion* (J. G. von Hamilton)	1·50	1·30
716	1f.10 *Golden Carriage of Prince Joseph Wenzel* (Martin von Meytens) (48½×38 *mm*)	1·80	1·50
714/716	*Set of 3*	4·25	3·50

(Des and photo Courvoisier)

1978 (7 Dec). Christmas. Church Windows of Triesenberg. T **210** and similar vert designs. Multicoloured. P 11½.

717	20r. Type **210**	50	45
718	50r. Enthroned Madonna with St Joseph	90	75
719	80r. Adoration of the Magi	1·50	1·30
717/719	*Set of 3*	2·50	2·30

211 Comte AC-8 Mail Plane *St Gallen* over Schaan

(Des O. Stefferl. Photo Courvoisier)

1979 (8 Mar). Europa. T **211** and similar horiz design. Multicoloured. P 11½.

720	40r. Type **211**	90	75
721	80r. Airship *Graf Zeppelin* over Vaduz Castle	1·70	1·50

212 Child Drinking

(Des R. Altmann. Photo Courvoisier)

1979 (8 Mar). International Year of the Child. T **212** and similar vert designs. Multicoloured. P 11½.

722	80r. Type **212**	1·40	1·30
723	90r. Child eating	1·70	1·50
724	1f.10 Child reading	1·90	1·70
722/724	*Set of 3*	4·50	4·00

213 Ordered Wavefield

214 Abstract Composition

(Des J. Schädler. Photo Courvoisier)

1979 (7 June). 50th Anniversary of International Radio Consultative Committee (CCIR). P 11½.

725	**213**	50r. blue and black	90	75

(Des L. Jäger. Photo Courvoisier)

1979 (7 June). Liechtenstein's Entry into Council of Europe. P 11½.

726	**214**	80r. multicoloured	1·40	1·30

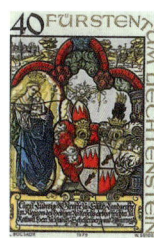

215 Sun rising over Continents

216 Arms of Carl Ludwig von Sulz

(Des H. P. Gassner. Photo Courvoisier)

1979 (7 June). Development Aid. P 11½.

727	**215**	1f. multicoloured	1·70	1·50

(Des A. Böcskör. Eng A. Fischer (70r.), W. Seidel (others). Recess and photo State Ptg Wks, Vienna)

1979 (7 June). Heraldic Windows in Liechtenstein National Museum. T **216** and similar vert designs. Multicoloured. P 13½.

728	40r. Type **216**	90	75
729	70r. Arms of Barbara von Sulz	1·30	1·20
730	1f.10 Arms of Ulrich von Ramschwag and Barbara von Hallwil	2·10	1·90
728/730	*Set of 3*	3·75	3·50

217 Saints Lucius and Florian (fresco, Waltensberg-Vuorz Church)

218 Base of Ski-slope, Valüna

(Des A. Pilch. Eng A. Fischer. Recess and photo State Ptg Wks, Vienna)

1979 (6 Sept). Patron Saints. P 13½×12½.

731	**217**	20f. multicoloured	27·00	24·00

Issued in sheets of four.

(Des B. Kaufmann. Photo Courvoisier)

1979 (6 Dec). Winter Olympics, Lake Placid. T **218** and similar horiz designs. Multicoloured. P 11½.

732	40r. Type **218**	90	75

LIECHTENSTEIN 1979

733	70r. Malbun and Ochsenkopf		1·20	1·10
734	1f.50 Ski-lift, Sareis		2·40	2·10
732/734	Set of 3		4·00	3·50

219 The Annunciation

220 Maria Leopoldine von Esterhazy (bust by Canova)

(Des A. Böcskör. Eng W. Seidel (80r.), A. Fischer (others).
Recess and photo State Ptg Wks, Vienna)

1979 (6 Dec). Christmas. T **219** and similar horiz designs showing embroideries by F. Nigg. Multicoloured. P 13½.

735	20r. Type **219**		50	45
736	50r. Christmas		95	90
737	80r. Blessed are the Peacemakers		1·60	1·40
735/737	Set of 3		2·75	2·50

(Des L. Jäger. Photo Courvoisier)

1980 (10 Mar). Europa. T **220** and similar vert design. P 11½.

738	40r. dull yellow-green, deep blue-green and gold		65	55
739	80r. brown, deep carmine-red and gold		1·40	1·20

Designs: 40r. T **220**; 80r. Maria Theresia von Liechtenstein (after Martin von Meytens).

221 Arms of Andreas Büchel, 1690

222 3r. Stamp of 1930

(Des H. P. Gassner. Photo Courvoisier)

1980 (10 Mar). Arms of Bailiffs (1st series). T **221** and similar horiz designs. Multicoloured. P 11½.

740	40r. Type **221**		70	60
741	70r. Georg Marxer, 1745		1·30	1·20
742	80r. Luzius Frick, 1503		1·50	1·40
743	1f.10 Adam Oehri, 1634		2·00	1·90
740/743	Set of 4		5·00	4·50

See also Nos. 763/766 and 788/791.

A set of three stamps, 40r., 70r., 1f.10, for Olympic Games, Moscow, was prepared but not issued.

(Des H. P. Gassner. Photo Courvoisier)

1980 (8 Sept). 50th Anniversary of Postal Museum. P 11½.

744	**222**	80r. brown-lake, deep bluish green and grey	1·60	1·40

223 Milking Pail

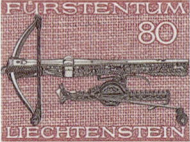

224 Crossbow

(Des G. Malin. Photo Courvoisier)

1980 (8 Sept). Alpine Dairy Farming Implements. T **223** and similar vert designs. Multicoloured. P 11½.

745	20r. Type **223**	45	40

746	50r. Wooden heart dairy herd descent marker		90	80
747	80r. Butter churn		1·60	1·50
745/747	Set of 3		2·75	2·40

The 20r. and 50r. were each issued both in sheets and in coils.

(Des A. Pilch. Eng W. Seidel (80r.), A. Fischer (others).
Recess and photo State Ptg Wks, Vienna)

1980 (8 Sept). Hunting Weapons. T **224** and similar horiz designs. P 13½×14.

748	80r. blackish brown and brown-lilac		1·60	1·50
749	90r. black and blue-green		1·80	1·60
750	1f.10 brownish black and deep yellow-ochre		2·00	1·80
748/750	Set of 3		4·75	4·50

Designs: 80r. T **224**; 90r. Spear and knife; 1f.10, Rifle and powder horn.

225 Triesenberg Costumes

226 Beech Trees, Matrula (spring)

(Des A. Pilch. Photo Courvoisier)

1980 (8 Sept). Costumes. T **225** and similar horiz designs. Multicoloured. P 11½.

751	40r. Type **225**		75	70
752	70r. Dancers, Schellenberg		1·50	1·40
753	80r. Brass band, Mauren		1·60	1·50
751/753	Set of 3		3·50	3·25

(Des W. Wachter. Eng W. Seidel (40r., 1f.50), A. Fischer (others).
Recess and photo State Ptg Wks, Vienna)

1980 (9 Dec). The Forest through the Four Seasons. T **226** and similar vert designs. Multicoloured. P 13½.

754	40r. Type **226**		75	70
755	50r. Firs in the Valorsch (summer)		1·00	90
756	80r. Beech trees, Schaan (autumn)		1·60	1·40
757	1f.50 Edge of forest, Oberplanken (winter)		2·75	2·40
754/757	Set of 4		5·50	4·75

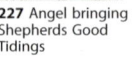

227 Angel bringing Shepherds Good Tidings

228 National Day Procession

(Des G. Malin. Photo Courvoisier)

1980 (9 Dec). Christmas. T **227** and similar vert designs. Multicoloured. P 11½.

758	20r. Type **227**		45	40
759	50r. Crib		90	80
760	80r. Epiphany		1·60	1·50
758/760	Set of 3		2·75	2·40

(Des Regina Marxer. Photo Courvoisier)

1981 (9 Mar). Europa. T **228** and similar vert design. Multicoloured. P 12×12½.

761	40r. Fireworks at Vaduz Castle		80	70
762	80r. Type **228**		1·60	1·40

(Des H. P. Gassner. Photo Courvoisier)

1981 (9 Mar). Arms of Bailiffs (2nd series). Horiz designs as T **221**. Multicoloured. P 11½.

763	40r. Anton Meier, 1748		80	75
764	70r. Kaspar Kindle, 1534		1·40	1·20
765	80r. Hans Adam Negele, 1600		1·60	1·50
766	1f.10 Peter Matt, 1693		2·30	2·10
763/766	Set of 4		5·50	5·00

1981 LIECHTENSTEIN

229 Prince Alois and Princess Elisabeth with Francis Joseph

230 Scout Emblems

(Des H. P. Gassner. Photo Courvoisier)

1981 (9 June). 75th Birthday of Prince Francis Joseph II. Sheet 120×87 mm containing T **229** and similar vert designs. Multicoloured. P 11½.
MS767 70r. Type **229**; 80r. Princes Alois and Francis Joseph; 150r. Prince Francis Joseph II .... 6·00 5·50

(Des L. Jäger. Photo Courvoisier)

1981 (9 June). 50th Anniversary of Liechtenstein Boy Scout and Girl Guide Movements. P 11½.
768 **230** 20r. multicoloured 60 55

231 Symbols of Disability

232 St Theodul (sculpture)

(Des G. Malin. Photo Courvoisier)

1981 (9 June). International Year of Disabled Persons. P 11½.
769 **231** 40r. multicoloured 75 70

(Des B. Kaufmann. Photo Courvoisier)

1981 (9 June). 1600th Birth Anniversary of St Theodul. P 11½.
770 **232** 80r. multicoloured .... 1·50 1·40

233 Xanthoria parietina

234 Gutenberg Castle

(Des L. Jäger. Eng W. Seidel. Recess and photo State Ptg Wks, Vienna)

1981 (7 Sept). Mosses and Lichens. T **233** and similar vert designs. Multicoloured. P 14×13½.
771 40r. Type **233** 75 70
772 50r. Parmelia physodes 90 80
773 70r. Sphagnum palustre .... 1·30 1·20
774 80r. Amblystegium serpens .... 1·80 1·60
771/774 Set of 4 .... 4·25 3·75

(Des O. Zeiller. Eng W. Seidel (20r., 40r.), A Fischer (others) Recess and photo State Ptg Wks, Vienna)

1981 (7 Sept). Gutenberg Castle. T **234** and similar horiz designs. Multicoloured. P 13½.
775 **234** 20r. Type **234** 70 65
776 40r. Courtyard .... 1·30 1·20
777 50r. Parlour .... 1·40 1·30
778 1f.10 Great Hall .... 2·75 2·50
775/778 Set of 4 .... 5·50 5·00

235 Cardinal Karl Borromäus von Mailand

236 St Nicholas blessing Children

(Des A. Böcskör. Eng Maria Laurent (40r., 1f.), W. Seidel (others). Recess and photo State Ptg Wks, Vienna)

1981 (7 Dec). Famous Visitors to Liechtenstein (1st series). T **235** and similar square designs. Multicoloured. P 14.
779 40r. Type **235** 75 70
780 70r. Johann Wolfgang von Goethe (writer).. 1·30 1·20
781 80r. Alexandre Dumas, the younger (writer) 1·40 1·30
782 1f. Hermann Hesse (writer) .... 1·90 1·70
779/782 Set of 4 .... 4·75 4·50
See also Nos. 804/807 and 832/835.

(Des B. Kaufmann. Photo Courvoisier)

1981 (7 Dec). Christmas. T **236** and similar vert designs. Multicoloured. P 11½.
783 20r. Type **236** 45 40
784 50r. Adoration of the Kings 90 80
785 80r. Holy Family .... 1·60 1·50
783/785 Set of 3 .... 2·75 2·40

237 Peasant Revolt, 1525

238 Triesenberg Sports Ground

(Des A. Pilch. Photo Courvoisier)

1982 (8 Mar). Europa. T **237** and similar horiz design. Multicoloured. P 11½.
786 40r. Type **237** 75 70
787 80r. King Wenceslaus with Counts (Imperial direct rule, 1396) .... 1·60 1·50

(Des H. P. Gassner. Photo Courvoisier)

1982 (8 Mar). Arms of Bailiffs (3rd series). Horiz designs as T **221**. Multicoloured. P 11½.
788 40r. Johann Kaiser, 1664 .... 90 80
789 70r. Joseph Anton Kaufmann, 1748 .... 1·40 1·30
790 80r. Christoph Walser, 1690 .... 1·70 1·60
791 1f.10 Stephan Banzer, 1658 .... 2·30 2·10
788/791 Set of 4 .... 5·75 5·25

(Des B. Kaufmann. Photo Courvoisier)

1982 (7 June). World Cup Football Championship, Spain. T **238** and similar horiz designs. Multicoloured. P 11½.
792 15r. Type **238** 30 30
793 25r. Eschen/Mauren playing fields 50 45
794 1f.80 Rheinau playing fields, Balzers .... 3·25 3·00
792/794 Set of 3 .... 3·75 3·50

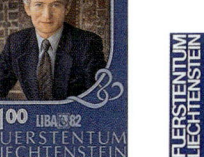 

239 Crown Prince Hans Adam

240 Tractor (agriculture)

(Des D. Constantine and Cornelia Eberle. Photo Courvoisier)

1982 (7 June). Liba 82 Stamp Exhibition. T **239** and similar vert design. Multicoloured. P 11½.
795 1f. Type **239** .... 1·80 1·70
796 1f. Princess Marie Aglaë .... 1·80 1·70

123

(Des H. P. Gassner. Photo Courvoisier)

1982 (20 Sept). Rural Industries T **240** and similar horiz designs. Multicoloured. P 11½.

797	30r. Type **240**	65	60
798	50r. Cutting flowers (horticulture)	90	80
799	70r. Worker and logs (forestry)	1·40	1·30
800	150r. Worker and milk (dairy farming)	3·00	2·75
797/800	Set of 4	5·25	5·00

241 Neu Schellenberg

242 Angelika Kauffmann (artist, self-portrait)

(Des and eng W. Seidel. Recess and photo State Ptg Wks, Vienna)

1982 (20 Sept). 150th Birth Anniversary of Moritz Menzinger (artist). T **241** and similar horiz designs. Multicoloured. P 13½×14.

801	40r. Type **241**	90	80
802	50r. Vaduz	1·10	1·00
803	100r. Bendern	2·10	2·00
801/803	Set of 3	3·75	3·50

(Des A. Böcskör. Eng W. Seidel (40r., 70r.), M. Laurent (others). Recess and photo State Ptg Wks, Vienna)

1982 (6 Dec). Famous Visitors to Liechtenstein (2nd series). T **242** and similar square designs. Multicoloured. P 14.

804	40r. Emperor Maximilian I (after Bernhard Strigel)	90	80
805	70r. Georg Jenatsch (liberator of Grisons)	1·50	1·20
806	80r. Type **242**	1·80	1·60
807	1f. St Fidelis of Sigmaringen	2·10	2·00
804/807	Set of 4	5·75	5·00

243 Angel playing Lute

244 Notker Balbulus of St Gall

(Des H. P. Gassner. Photo Courvoisier)

1982 (6 Dec). Christmas. T **243** and similar vert designs showing details from Chur Cathedral High Altar by Jakob Russ. Multicoloured. P 11½.

808	20r. Type **243**	45	40
809	50r. Madonna and child	90	80
810	80r. Angel playing organ	1·60	1·50
808/810	Set of 3	2·75	2·40

(Des G. Gloser. Photo Courvoisier)

1983 (7 Mar). Europa. T **244** and similar vert design. Multicoloured. P 11½.

811	40r. Type **244**	75	70
812	80r. Hildegard of Bingen	1·60	1·50

245 Shrove Thursday

246 River Bank

(Des Regina Marxer. Eng W. Seidel. Recess and photo State Ptg Wks, Vienna)

1983 (7 Mar). Shrovetide and Lent Customs. T **245** and similar vert designs. Multicoloured. P 14.

813	40r. Type **245**	80	70
814	70r. Shrovetide carnival	1·50	1·40
815	1f.80 Lent Sunday bonfire	3·75	3·50
813/815	Set of 3	5·50	5·00

(Des H. P. Gassner. Photo Courvoisier)

1983 (6 June). Anniversaries and Events. T **246** and similar square designs. Multicoloured. P 11½.

816	20r. Type **246** (Council of Europe river and coasts protection campaign)	50	45
817	40r. Montgolfier Brothers' balloon (bicentenary of manned flight)	70	65
818	50r. Airmail envelope (World Communications Year)	90	80
819	80r. Plant and hands holding spade (overseas aid)	1·50	1·40
816/819	Set of 4	3·25	3·00

247 Schaan

248 Princess Gina

(Photo Courvoisier)

1983 (6 June). Landscape Paintings by Anton Ender. T **247** and similar square designs. Multicoloured. P 11.

820	40r. Type **247**	90	80
821	50r. Gutenberg Castle	1·00	90
822	200r. Steg Reservoir	4·25	3·75
820/822	Set of 3	5·50	5·00

(Des W. Wachter. Photo Courvoisier)

1983 (5 Sept). T **248** and similar vert design. Multicoloured. P 11½.

823	2f.50 Type **248**	4·50	4·00
824	3f. Prince Francis Joseph II	5·25	5·00

249 Pope John Paul II

250 Snowflake and Stripes

(Des J. A. Slominski (Slomi). Photo Courvoisier)

1983 (5 Sept). Holy Year. P 11½.

825	**249** 80r. multicoloured	1·50	1·40

(Des H. Leupin. Photo Courvoisier)

1983 (5 Dec). Winter Olympic Games, Sarajevo. T **250** and similar vert designs. Multicoloured. P 11½.

826	40r. Type **250**	90	80
827	80r. Snowflake	1·60	1·40
828	1f.80 Snowflake and rays	3·75	3·25
826/828	Set of 3	5·75	5·00

251 Seeking Shelter

252 Aleksandr Vassilievich Suvorov (Russian general)

(Des H. P Gassner. Photo Courvoisier)

1983 (5 Dec). Christmas. T **251** and similar horiz designs. Multicoloured. P 11½.

829	20r. Type **251**	45	40
830	50r. Infant Jesus	1·00	90
831	80r. Three Kings	1·60	1·50
829/831	Set of 3	2·75	2·50

1984 LIECHTENSTEIN

(Des A. Böcskör. Eng M. Laurent (40r., 80r.), W. Seidel (others).
Recess and photo State Ptg Wks, Vienna)

1984 (12 Mar). Famous Visitors to Liechtenstein (3rd series). T **252** and similar square designs. Multicoloured. P 14.
832	40r. Type **252**	90	80
833	70r. Karl Rudolf von Buol-Schauenstein, Bishop of Chur	1·40	1·30
834	80r. Carl Zuckmayer (dramatist)	1·60	1·50
835	1f. Curt Goetz (actor)	2·10	2·00
832/835	Set of 4	5·50	5·00

253 Bridge

254 The Warning Messenger

(Des J. Larrivière and E. Frick. Photo Courvoisier)

1984 (12 Mar). Europa. 25th Anniversary of European Posts and Telecommunications Conference. P 11½.
836	**253**	50r. greenish blue and deep new blue	90	80
837		80r. rose and lake-brown	1·50	1·40

(Des B. Gassner. Eng W. Seidel. Recess and photo State Ptg Wks, Vienna)

1984 (12 June). Liechtenstein Legends. *The Destruction of Trisona*. T **254** and similar vert designs, each sepia, olive-grey and new blue. P 14.
838	35r. Type **254**	70	65
839	50r. The buried town	1·00	90
840	80r. The spared family	1·50	1·40
838/840	Set of 3	3·00	2·75

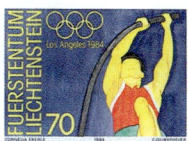
255 Pole Vaulting

(Des Cornelia Eberle. Photo Courvoisier)

1984 (12 June). Olympic Games, Los Angeles. T **255** and similar horiz designs. Multicoloured. P 11½.
841	70r. Type **255**	1·40	1·30
842	80r. Throwing the discus	1·50	1·40
843	1f. Putting the shot	1·80	1·60
841/843	Set of 3	4·25	3·75

256 Currency (trade and banking)

(Des H. P. Gassner. Photo Courvoisier)

1984 (10 Sept). Occupations T **256** and similar horiz designs. Multicoloured. P 11½.
844	5r. Type **256**	20	15
845	10r. Plumber adjusting pipe (building trade)	25	25
846	20r. Operating machinery (industry–production)	40	35
847	35r. Draughtswoman (building trade–planning)	70	65
848	45r. Office worker and world map (industry–sales)	95	85
849	50r. Cook (tourism)	1·00	90
850	60r. Carpenter (building trade–interior decoration)	1·30	1·20
851	70r. Doctor injecting patient (medical services)	1·50	1·40
852	80r. Scientist (industrial research)	1·60	1·50
853	100r. Bricklayer (building trade)	1·80	1·60
854	120r. Flow chart (industry–administration)	2·20	2·00
855	150r. Handstamping covers (post and communications)	3·00	2·75
844/855	Set of 12	13·50	12·00

257 Princess Marie

258 Annunciation

(Des W. Wachter. Eng W. Seidel. Recess and photo State Ptg Wks, Vienna)

1984 (10 Dec). T **257** and similar vert design. Multicoloured. P 14.
856	1f.70 Type **257**	3·25	2·20
857	2f. Crown Prince Hans Adam	3·75	2·75

(Des Helga Hilti. Photo Courvoisier)

1984 (10 Dec). Christmas T **258** and similar vert designs. Multicoloured. P 11½.
858	35r. Type **258**	50	45
859	50r. Holy Family	1·00	90
860	80r. The three kings	1·70	1·60
858/860	Set of 3	3·00	2·75

259 Apollo and the Muses playing Music

260 St Elisabeth Convent, Schaan

(Des Cornelia Eberle. Photo Courvoisier)

1985 (11 Mar). Europa. Music Year. T **259** and similar horiz designs showing details from 18th-century harpsichord lid. Multicoloured. P 11½.
861	50r. Type **259**	1·00	90
862	80r. Apollo and the Muses playing music (*different*)	1·50	1·40

(Des O. Zeiller. Eng M. Laurent (1f.), W. Seidel (others). Recess and photo State Ptg Wks, Vienna)

1985 (11 Mar). Monasteries. T **260** and similar horiz designs. Multicoloured. P 13½×14.
863	50r. Type **260**	90	80
864	1f. Schellenberg Convent	1·80	1·70
865	1f.70 Gutenberg Mission, Balzers	3·25	3·00
863/865	Set of 3	5·25	5·00

261 Princess Gina and handing out of Rations

262 Justice

(Des Cornelia Eberle. Photo Courvoisier)

1985 (10 June). 40th Anniversary of Liechtenstein Red Cross. T **261** and similar horiz designs. Multicoloured. P 11½.
866	20r. Type **261**	50	45
867	50r. Princess Gina and Red Cross ambulance	1·30	1·10
868	120r. Princess Gina with refugee children	2·50	2·30
866/868	Set of 3	3·75	3·50

(Des G. Gloser. Photo Courvoisier)

1985 (10 June). Cardinal Virtues. T **262** and similar vert designs. Multicoloured. P 11½.
869	35r. Type **262**	65	60
870	50r. Temperance	90	80
871	70r. Prudence	1·30	1·20
872	1f. Fortitude	1·90	1·70
869/872	Set of 4	4·25	3·75

263 Papal Arms **264** Portrait of a Canon (Quentin Massys)

(Des G. Malin. Photo Courvoisier)

1985 (2 Sept). Papal Visit. Sheet 100×67 mm containing T **263** and similar vert designs. Multicoloured. P 11½.
MS873 50r. Type **263**; 80r. St Maria zum Trost Chapel; 170r. Our Lady of Liechtenstein (statue) (29×43 mm) .... 6·00 5·50

(Des Cornelia Eberle. Eng M. Laurent (1f.), W Seidel (others). Recess and photo State Ptg Wks, Vienna)

1985 (2 Sept). Paintings in Metropolitan Museum, New York. T **264** and similar vert designs. Multicoloured. P 13½×14.
874	50r. Type **264**	1·30	1·20
875	1f. *Clara Serena Rubens* (Rubens)	2·10	2·00
876	1f.20 *Duke of Urbino* (Raphael)	2·50	2·30
874/876	Set of 3	5·25	5·00

265 Halberd used by Charles I's Bodyguard **266** Frankincense

(Des O. Zeiller. Eng W. Seidel. Recess and photo State Ptg Wks, Vienna)

1985 (9 Dec). Guards' Weapons and Armour. T **265** and similar horiz designs. Multicoloured. P 13½×14.
877	35r. Type **265**	65	60
878	50r. Morion used by Charles I's bodyguard	1·00	90
879	80r. Halberd used by Carl Eusebius's bodyguard	1·50	1·40
877/879	Set of 3	2·75	2·50

(Des J. Schädler. Photo Courvoisier)

1985 (9 Dec). Christmas. T **266** and similar vert designs. Multicoloured. P 11½.
880	35r. Type **266**	70	65
881	50r. Gold	1·00	90
882	80r. Myrrh	1·50	1·40
880/882	Set of 3	3·00	2·75

267 Puppets performing Tragedy **268** Courtyard

(Des P. Flora. Eng W. Seidel. Recess and photo State Ptg Wks, Vienna)

1985 (9 Dec). Theatre. T **267** and similar horiz designs. Multicoloured. P 14.
883	50r. Type **267**	1·00	90
884	80r. Puppets performing comedy	1·60	1·50
885	1f.50 Opera	3·00	2·75
883/885	Set of 3	5·00	4·75

(Des G. Malin. Photo Courvoisier)

1986 (10 Mar)–89. Vaduz Castle. T **268** and similar vert designs. Multicoloured. P 11½.
886	20r. Type **268**	45	40
887	25r. Keep (6.3.89)	50	45
888	50r. Castle	90	80
889	90r. Inner gate (9.3.87)	1·60	1·50
890	1f.10 Castle from gardens	1·80	1·60
891	1f.40 Courtyard (*different*) (9.3.87)	2·75	2·50
886/891	Set of 6	7·25	6·50

The 20r. and 50r. were each issued both in sheets and in coils.

269 Barn Swallows **270** Offerings

(Des L. Jäger. Photo Courvoisier)

1986 (10 Mar). Europa. Birds. T **269** and similar vert design. Multicoloured. P 11½.
892	50r. Type **269**	1·10	1·00
893	90r. European Robin	1·80	1·70

(Des F. Gehr. Photo Courvoisier)

1986 (10 Mar). Lenten Fast. P 11½.
894	**270** 1f.40 multicoloured	3·00	2·75

271 Palm Sunday **272** Karl Freiherr Haus von Hausen

(Des Regina Marxer. Eng W. Seidel. Recess and photo State Ptg Wks, Vienna)

1986 (9 June). Religious Festivals. T **271** and similar vert designs. Multicoloured. P 14.
895	35r. Type **271**	70	65
896	50r. Wedding	90	80
897	70r. Rogation Day procession	1·40	1·30
895/897	Set of 3	2·75	2·50

(Des E. Frick. Photo Courvoisier)

1986 (9 June). 125th Anniversary of Liechtenstein Land Bank. P 11½.
898	**272** 50r. deep chocolate. brown-ochre and buff	1·00	90

273 Francis Joseph II **274** Roebuck in Ruggeller Riet

(Des O. Zeiller. Eng W. Seidel. Recess and photo State Ptg Wks, Vienna)

1986 (9 June). 80th Birthday of Prince Francis Joseph II. P 13½.
899	**273** 3f.50 multicoloured	6·50	5·75

(Des W. Oehry. Eng W. Seidel. Recess and photo State Ptg Wks, Vienna)

1986 (9 Sept). Hunting. T **274** and similar vert designs. Multicoloured. P 13×13½.
900	35r. Type **274**	70	65
901	50r. Chamois at Rappenstein	1·00	90
902	1f.70 Stag in Lawena	3·50	3·25
900/902	Set of 3	4·75	4·25

1986 LIECHTENSTEIN

   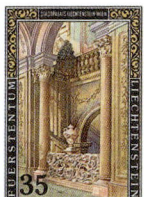

275 Cabbage and Beetroot
276 Archangel Michael
282 Prince Alois (frame as in first stamps)
283 Staircase

(Des P. Kindle. Photo Courvoisier)

1986 (9 Sept). Field Crops. T **275** and similar horiz designs. Multicoloured. P 11½.
903	50r. Type **275**		1·00	90
904	80r. Red Cabbages		1·60	1·50
905	90r. Potatoes, Onions and Garlic		1·80	1·70
903/905	Set of 3		4·00	3·75

(Des L. Schnüriger. Photo Courvoisier)

1986 (9 Dec). Christmas. T **276** and similar vert designs. Multicoloured. P 11½.
906	35r. Type **276**		75	70
907	50r. Archangel Gabriel		1·10	1·00
908	90r. Archangel Raphael		2·00	1·80
906/908	Set of 3		3·50	3·25

(Des O. Zeiller and K. Moser. Eng W. Seidel. Recess and photo State Ptg Wks, Vienna)

1987 (9 June). 75th Anniversary of First Liechtenstein Stamps. P 14.
918	**282**	2f. multicoloured	4·50	4·00

(Des O. Zeiller. Photo Courvoisier)

1987 (7 Sept). Liechtenstein City Palace, Vienna. T **283** and similar vert designs. Multicoloured. P 11½.
919	35r. Type **283**		75	70
920	50r. Minoritenplatz doorway		1·00	90
921	90r. Staircase (*different*)		1·90	1·70
919/921	Set of 3		3·25	3·00

277 Silver Fir
278 Gamprin Primary School
284 Arms
285 Constitution Charter, 1862

(Des L. Jäger. Photo Courvoisier)

1986 (9 Dec). Tree Bark. T **277** and similar vert designs. Multicoloured. P 11½.
909	25r. Type **277**		55	50
910	90r. Norway Spruce		2·00	1·80
911	1f.40 Pedunculate Oak		3·00	2·75
909/911	Set of 3		5·00	4·50

(Des H. P. Gassner. Photo Courvoisier)

1987 (9 Mar). Europa. T **278** and similar vert design. Multicoloured. P 11½.
912	50r. Type **278**		1·10	1·00
913	90r. Schellenberg parish church		1·90	1·70

(Des G. Malin. Photo Courvoisier)

1987 (7 Sept). 275th Anniversary of Transfer of County of Vaduz to House of Liechtenstein. P 11½.
922	**284**	1f.40 multicoloured	3·00	2·75

(Des E. Frick. Photo Courvoisier)

1987 (7 Sept). 125th Anniversary of Liechtenstein Parliament. P 11½.
923	**285**	1f.70 multicoloured	3·50	3·25

280 Niklaus von Flüe
281 Miller's Thumb (*Cottus gobio*)
286 St Matthew
287 The Toil of the Cross-Country Skier

(Des G. Gloser. Photo Courvoisier)

1987 (9 Mar). 500th Death Anniversary of Niklaus von Flüe (martyr). P 11½.
914	**280**	1f.10 multicoloured	2·10	2·00

(Des L. Jäger. Photo Courvoisier)

1987 (9 June). Fish (1st series). T **281** and similar horiz designs. Multicoloured. P 11½.
915	50r. Type **281**		1·00	90
916	90r. Brook Trout (*Salmo trutta fario*)		2·00	1·80
917	1f.10 European Grayling (*Thymallus thymallus*)		2·50	2·30
915/917	Set of 3		5·00	4·50
See also Nos. 959/961.				

(Des Cornelia Eberle. Eng W. Seidel. Recess and photo State Ptg Wks, Vienna)

1987 (7 Dec). Christmas. T **286** and similar vert designs showing illuminations from *Golden Book of Pfäfers*. Multicoloured. P 14.
924	35r. Type **286**		85	75
925	50r. St Mark		1·10	1·00
926	60r. St Luke		1·40	1·30
927	90r. St John		2·00	1·80
924/927	Set of 4		4·75	4·25

(Des P. Flora. Eng W. Seidel. Recess and photo State Ptg Wks, Vienna)

1987 (7 Dec). Winter Olympic Games, Calgary (1988). T **287** and similar horiz designs. Multicoloured. P 14×13½.
928	25r. Type **287**		65	55
929	90r. The Courageous Pioneers of Skiing		2·10	1·90
930	1f.10 As Our Grandfathers used to Ride on a Bobsled		2·75	2·40
928/930	Set of 3		5·00	4·25

LIECHTENSTEIN 1988

288 Dish Aerial   **289** Agriculture

(Des H. P. Gassner. Photo Courvoisier)

1988 (7 Mar). Europa. Transport and Communications. T **288** and similar vert design. Multicoloured. P 11½.
931	50r. Type **288**	1·10	1·00
932	90r. Maglev monorail	2·00	1·80

(Des L. Jäger. Photo Courvoisier)

1988 (7 Mar). European Campaign for Rural Areas. T **289** and similar horiz designs. Multicoloured. P 11½.
933	80r. Type **289**	2·00	1·80
934	90r. Village centre	2·20	2·00
935	1f.70 Road	3·25	3·00
933/935	Set of 3	6·75	6·00

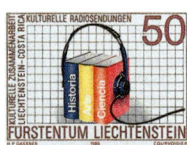

290 Headphones on Books (radio broadcasts)   **291** Crown Prince Hans Adam

(Des H. P. Gassner (50c.), E. J. Hidalgo (1f.40). Photo Courvoisier)

1988 (6 June). Costa Rica–Liechtenstein Cultural Co-operation. T **290** and similar horiz design. P 11½.
936	50r. multicoloured	1·40	1·30
937	1f.40 carmine-red, brown ochre and myrtle green	4·25	3·75

Designs: 50r. T **290**; 1f.40, Man with pen and radio (adult education).

Stamps of a similar design were issued by Costa Rica.

(Des O. Zeiller. Eng W. Seidel. Recess and photo State Ptg Wks Vienna)

1988 (6 June). 50th Anniversary of Accession of Prince Francis Joseph II. Sheet 100×68 mm containing T **291** and similar vert designs. Multicoloured. P 14×13½.
MS938	50r. Type **291**; 50r. Prince Alois; 2f. Prince Francis Joseph II	9·00	8·25

292 St Barbara's Shrine, Balzers   **293** Cycling

(Des G. Gloser. Photo Courvoisier)

1988 (5 Sept). Wayside Shrines. T **292** and similar vert designs. Multicoloured. P 11½.
939	25r. Type **292**	65	55
940	35r. Shrine containing statues of Christ, St Peter and St Paul at Oberdorf, Vaduz	85	75
941	50r. St Anthony of Egypt's shrine, Fallagass, Ruggel	1·40	1·30
939/941	Set of 3	2·50	2·30

(Des P. Flora. Eng W. Seidel. Recess and photo State Ptg Wks, Vienna)

1988 (5 Sept). Olympic Games, Seoul. T **293** and similar horiz designs. Multicoloured. P 14×13½.
942	50r. Type **293**	1·10	1·00
943	80r. Gymnastics	2·00	1·80
944	90r. Running	2·20	2·00
945	1f.40 Equestrian event	3·75	3·25
942/945	Set of 4	8·25	7·25

294 Joseph and Mary   **295** Letter beside Footstool (detail)

(Des G. Gloser. Photo Courvoisier)

1988 (5 Dec). Christmas. T **294** and similar vert designs. Multicoloured.
946	35r. Type **294**	75	70
947	50r. Infant Jesus	1·10	1·00
948	90r. Wise Men presenting gifts to Jesus	1·80	1·60
946/948	Set of 3	3·25	3·00

(Des Cornelia Eberle. Eng W. Seidel. Recess and photo State Ptg Wks, Vienna)

1988 (5 Dec). *The Letter* (portrait of Marie-Thérèse, Princesse de Lamballe by Anton Hickel). T **295** and similar vert designs. Multicoloured. P 13×13½.
949	50r. Type **295**	1·40	1·30
950	90r. Desk and writing materials (detail)	2·20	2·00
951	2f. *The Letter* (complete painting)	4·50	4·00
949/951	Set of 3	7·25	6·50

296 Cat and Mouse   **298** Rheinberger and Score

(Des E. Bermann. Photo Courvoisier)

1989 (6 Mar). Europa. Children's Games. T **296** and similar vert design. Multicoloured. P 11½.
952	50r. Type **296**	1·40	1·30
953	90r. Hide and Seek	2·20	2·00

(Des H. P. Gassner. Eng W. Seidel. Recess and photo State Ptg Wks, Vienna)

1989 (6 Mar). 150th Birth Anniversary of Josef Gabriel Rheinberger (composer). P 14×13½.
954	**298** 2f.90 black, chalky blue and bright purple	6·00	5·25

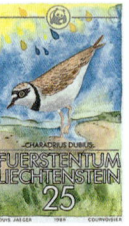

299 Little Ringed Plover (*Charadrius dubius*)   **300** Northern Pike (*Esox lucius*)

(Des L. Jäger. Photo Courvoisier)

1989 (5 June). Endangered Animals. T **299** and similar vert designs. Multicoloured. P 11½.
955	25r. Type **299**	65	55
956	35r. Green Tree Frog (*Hyla arborea*)	90	80
957	50r. Lacewing *Libelloides coccajus*	1·50	1·40
958	90r. Polecat (*Putorius putorius*)	3·00	2·75
955/958	Set of 4	5·50	5·00

1989 LIECHTENSTEIN

(Des L. Jäger. Photo Courvoisier)

1989 (5 June). Fish (2nd series). T **300** and similar horiz designs. Multicoloured. P 11½.

959	50r. Type **300**	90	80
960	1f.10 Lake Trout (*Salmo trutta lacustris*)	2·40	2·10
961	1f.40 Stone Loach (*Noemacheilus barbatulus*)	3·25	3·00
959/961 Set of 3		6·00	5·25

301 Return of Cattle from Alpine Pastures

302 Falknis

(Des Regina Marxer. Eng W. Seidel. Recess and photo State Ptg Wks, Vienna)

1989 (4 Sept). Autumn Customs. T **301** and similar vert designs. Multicoloured. P 14.

962	35r. Type **301**	75	70
963	50r. Peeling Corn cobs	1·10	1·00
964	80r. Cattle market	1·80	1·60
962/964 Set of 3		3·25	3·00

(Photo Courvoisier)

1989 (4 Sept)–**93**. Mountains. T **302** and similar horiz designs showing watercolours by Josef Schädler. P 11½.

965	5r. multicoloured (5.6.90)	15	15
966	10r. multicoloured (3.9.90)	20	20
967	35r. multicoloured (3.9.90)	70	65
968	40r. multicoloured (3.6.91)	85	75
969	45r. multicoloured (5.6.90)	90	80
970	50r. multicoloured	1·00	90
971	60r. multicoloured (3.9.90)	1·10	1·00
972	70r. multicoloured (5.6.90)	1·30	1·10
973	75r. multicoloured	1·40	1·30
974	80r. bluish violet, cinnamon and black	1·70	1·50
975	1f. multicoloured (5.6.90)	2·20	2·00
976	1f.20 multicoloured (3.9.90)	2·50	2·30
977	1f.50 multicoloured	3·00	2·75
978	1f.60 multicoloured (2.3.92)	3·75	3·25
979	2f. multicoloured (1.3.93)	4·50	4·00
965/979 Set of 15		23·00	20·00

Designs: 5r. Augstenberg; 10r. Hahnenspiel; 35r. Nospitz; 40r. Ochsenkopf; 45r. Three Sisters; 50r. T **302**; 60r. Kuhgrat; 70r. Galinakopf; 75r. Plassteikopf; 80r. Naafkopf; 1f. Schönberg; 1f.20, Bleikaturm; 1f.50, Garsellitürm; 1f.60, Schwarzhorn; 2f. Scheienkopf.

No. 980 is vacant.

Prince Hans Adam II
13 November 1989

303 Melchior and Balthasar

304 Mace Quartz

(Des Cornelia Eberle. Eng W. Seidel. Recess and photo State Ptg Wks, Vienna)

1989 (4 Dec). Christmas. T **303** and similar multicoloured designs showing details of triptych by Hugo van der Goes. P 13½ (50r.) or 13½×14 (others).

981	35r. Type **303**	75	70
982	50r. Kaspar and Holy Family (27×34 mm)	1·10	95
983	90r. St Stephen	2·00	1·80
981/983 Set of 3		3·50	3·00

(Des Ursula Kühne. Eng W. Seidel. Recess and photo State Ptg Wks, Vienna)

1989 (4 Dec). Minerals. T **304** and similar horiz designs. Multicoloured. P 13½×13.

984	50r. Type **304**	1·20	1·10
985	1f.10 Globe pyrite	2·40	2·10
986	1f.50 Calcite	3·25	3·00
984/986 Set of 3		6·25	5·50

305 Nendeln Forwarding Agency, 1864

306 Penny Black

(Des H. P. Gassner. Photo Courvoisier)

1990 (5 Mar). Europa. Post Office Buildings. T **305** and similar vert design. Multicoloured. P 11½.

987	50r. Type **305**	1·10	95
988	90r. Vaduz post office, 1976	2·00	1·80

(Des H. P. Gassner. Photo Courvoisier)

1990 (5 Mar). 150th Anniversary of the Penny Black. P 11½.

989	**306**	1f.50 multicoloured	3·75	3·25

307 Footballers

308 Tureen, Oranges and Grapes

(Des R. Sprenger. Photo Courvoisier)

1990 (5 Mar). World Cup Football Championship, Italy. P 12×11½.

990	**307**	2f. multicoloured	4·75	4·25

(Des Cornelia Eberle. Eng W. Seidel. Recess and photo State Ptg Wks, Vienna)

1990 (5 June). Ninth Death Anniversary of Benjamin Steck (painter). T **308** and similar square designs. Multicoloured. P 14.

991	50r. Type **308**	1·30	1·10
992	80r. Apples and pewter bowl	1·80	1·60
993	1f.50 Basket, Apples, Cherries and pewter jug	3·75	3·25
991/993 Set of 3		6·25	5·25

309 Princess Gina

310 Ring-necked Pheasant

(Des H. P. Gassner. Photo Courvoisier)

1990 (5 June). Prince Francis Joseph II and Princess Gina Commemoration. T **309** and similar horiz design. Multicoloured. P 11½.

994	2f. Type **309**	3·75	3·50
995	3f. Prince Francis Joseph II	6·00	5·25

(Des W. Oehry. Eng W. Seidel. Recess and photo State Ptg Wks, Vienna)

1990 (3 Sept). Game Birds. T **310** and similar vert designs. Multicoloured. P 13×13½.

996	25r. Type **310**	70	65
997	50r. Black Grouse	1·10	1·00
998	2f. Mallard	4·75	4·25
996/998 Set of 3		6·00	5·25

LIECHTENSTEIN 1990

311 Annunciation   **312** St Nicholas

(Photo Courvoisier)

1990 (3 Dec). Christmas. T **311** and similar vert designs. Multicoloured. P 12.
999	35r. Type **311**		90	80
1000	50r. Nativity		1·10	95
1001	90r. Adoration of the Magi		1·80	1·60
999/1001	Set of 3		3·50	3·00

(Des Regina Marxer. Eng W. Seidel. Recess and photo State Ptg Wks, Vienna)

1990 (3 Dec). Winter Customs. T **312** and similar vert designs. Multicoloured. P 14.
1002	35r. Type **312**		85	75
1003	50r. Awakening on New Year's Eve		1·10	95
1004	1f.50 Giving New Year greetings		3·50	3·25
1002/1004	Set of 3		5·00	4·50

313 Mounted Courier   **314** Olympus 1 Satellite

(Des P. Flora. Eng W. Seidel. Recess and photo State Ptg Wks, Vienna)

1990 (3 Dec). 500th Anniversary of Regular European Postal Services. P 13½×14.
1005	**313**	90r. multicoloured	2·20	2·00

(Des H. P. Gassner. Photo Courvoisier)

1991 (4 Mar). Europa. Europe in Space. T **314** and similar vert design. Multicoloured. P 11½.
1006	50r. Type **314**		1·10	95
1007	90r. Meteosat satellite		2·00	1·80

315 St Ignatius de Loyola (founder of Society of Jesus)   **316** UN Emblem and Dove

(Des Martha Griebler. Photo Courvoisier)

1991 (4 Mar). Anniversaries. T **315** and similar horiz design. Multicoloured. P 11½.
1008	80r. Type **315** (500th birth anniversary)		1·80	1·60
1009	90r. Wolfgang Amadeus Mozart (composer, death bicentenary)		2·00	1·80

(Des Cornelia Eberle. Photo Courvoisier)

1991 (4 Mar). Admission to United Nations Membership (1990). P 11½.
1010	**316**	2f.50 multicoloured	5·50	4·75

317 Non-Commissioned Officer and Private   **318** Near Maloja (Giovanni Giacometti)

(Des P. Flora, eng W. Seidel (70r.). Des and eng W. Seidel (others). Recess and photo State Ptg Wks, Vienna)

1991 (3 June). 125th Anniversary of Last Mobilisation of Liechtenstein's Military Contingent (to the Tyrol). T **317** and similar horiz designs. Multicoloured. P 13½×14.
1011	50r. Type **317**		1·10	95
1012	70r. Tunic, chest and portrait		1·60	1·40
1013	1f. Officer and private		2·00	1·80
1011/1013	Set of 3		4·25	3·75

(Des Ursula Kühne. Photo Courvoisier)

1991 (3 June). 700th Anniversary of Swiss Confederation. T **318** and similar vert designs, showing paintings by Swiss artists. Multicoloured. P 11½.
1014	50r. Type **318**		1·10	95
1015	80r. Rhine Valley (Ferdinand Gehr)		1·60	1·40
1016	90r. Bergell (Augusto Giacometti)		1·90	1·70
1017	1f.10 Hoher Kasten (Hedwig Scherrer)		2·40	2·10
1014/1017	Set of 4		6·25	5·50

319 Stampless and Modern Covers   **320** Princess Marie

(Des E. Frick. Photo Courvoisier)

1991 (2 Sept). Liba 92 National Stamp Exhibition, Vaduz. P 11½.
1018	**319**	90r. multicoloured	2·10	1·90

(Des H. P. Gassner. Eng W. Seidel. Recess and photo State Ptg Wks, Vienna)

1991 (2 Sept). T **320** and similar vert design. Multicoloured. P 13×13½.
1019	3f. Type **320**		5·25	4·75
1020	3f.40 Prince Hans Adam II		6·25	5·75

 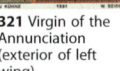 

321 Virgin of the Annunciation (exterior of left wing)   **322** Cross-country Skiers and Testing for Drug Abuse

(Des Ursula Kühne. Eng W. Seidel. Recess and photo State Ptg Wks, Vienna)

1991 (3 Dec). Christmas. T **321** and similar vert designs showing details of the altar from St Mamertus Chapel, Triesen. Multicoloured. P 13½×14.
1021	50r. Type **321**		1·10	95
1022	80r. Madonna and Child (wood-carving attr. Jörg Syrlin, inner shrine)		1·60	1·40
1023	90r. Angel Gabriel (exterior of right wing)		2·00	1·80
1021/1023	Set of 3		4·25	3·75

1991 LIECHTENSTEIN

(Des H. Anderegg. Photo Courvoisier)

1991 (3 Dec). Winter Olympic Games, Albertville. T **322** and similar vert designs. Multicoloured. P 11½.
1024	70r. Type **322**	1·70	1·50
1025	80r. Ice hockey player tackling opponent and helping him after fall	1·90	1·70
1026	1f.60 Downhill skier and fallen skier caught in safety net	3·00	2·75
1024/1026	Set of 3	6·00	5·25

323 Relay Race, Drugs and Shattered Medal

324 Aztecs

(Des H. Anderegg. Photo Courvoisier)

1992 (2 Mar). Olympic Games. Barcelona. T **323** and similar vert designs. Multicoloured. P 11½.
1027	50r. Type **323**	1·10	95
1028	70r. Cycling road race	1·80	1·60
1029	2f.50 Judo	5·75	5·25
1027/1029	Set of 3	7·75	7·00

(Des H. von Vogelsang. Photo Courvoisier)

1992 (2 Mar). Europa. 500th Anniversary of Discovery of America by Columbus. T **324** and similar horiz design. Multicoloured. P 12.
| 1030 | 80r. Type **324** | 1·90 | 1·70 |
| 1031 | 90r. Statue of Liberty and New York skyline | 2·00 | 1·80 |

325 Clown in Envelope (Good Luck)

326 Arms of Liechtenstein–Kinsky Alliance

(Des Martha Griebler; photo Courvoisier (Nos. 1032/1033). Des P. Flora, eng W. Seidel; recess and photo State Ptg Wks, Vienna (Nos. 1034/1035).)

1992 (1 June). Greetings Stamps. T **325** and similar horiz designs. Multicoloured. P 12½ (Nos. 1032/1034) or 14×13½ (Nos. 1034/1035).
1032	50r. Type **325**	1·10	95
1033	50r. Wedding rings in envelope and harlequin violinist	1·10	95
1034	50r. Postman blowing horn (31×21 *mm*)	1·10	95
1035	50r. Flying postman carrying letter sealed with heart (31×21 *mm*)	1·10	95
1032/1035	Set of 4	4·00	3·50

(Photo Courvoisier)

1992 (1 June). Liba '92 National Stamp Exhibition. Silver Wedding Anniversary of Prince Hans Adam and Princess Marie. Sheet 100×67 mm containing T **326** and similar vert design. Multicoloured. P 11½.
MS1036 2f. Type **326**; 2f.50, Royal couple (photo by Anthony Buckley) ... 10·50 10·00

327 Blechnum spicant

328 Reading Edict

(Des Cornelia Eberle. Eng W. Seidel. Recess and photo State Ptg Wks, Vienna)

1992 (7 Sept). Ferns. T **327** and similar square designs. Multicoloured. P 14.
1037	40r. Type **327**	85	75
1038	50r. Maidenhair Spleenwort (*Asplenium trichomanes*)	1·10	95
1039	70r. Hart's-tongue (*Phyllitis scolopendrium*)	1·50	1·40
1040	2f.50 *Asplenium ruta-muraria*	5·50	5·00
1037/1040	Set of 4	8·00	7·25

(Des P. Flora. Eng W. Seidel. Recess and photo State Ptg Wks, Vienna)

1992 (7 Sept). 650th Anniversary of County of Vaduz. P 13½×14.
| 1041 | **328** 1f.60 multicoloured | 4·25 | 3·75 |

329 Chapel of St Mamertus, Triesen

330 Crown Prince Alois

(Des G. Gloser. Photo Courvoisier)

1992 (7 Dec). Christmas. T **329** and similar vert designs. Multicoloured. P 11½.
1042	50r. Type **329**	90	80
1043	90r. Crib, St Gallus's Church, Triesen	1·80	1·60
1044	1f.60 St Mary's Chapel, Triesen	3·25	3·00
1042/1044	Set of 3	5·25	4·75

(Des H. P. Gassner. Eng W. Seidel. Recess and photo State Ptg Wks, Vienna)

1992 (7 Dec). P 13×13½.
| 1045 | **330** 2f.50 multicoloured | 5·50 | 5·00 |

331 Nafkopf and Huts, Steg

332 910805 (Bruno Kaufmann)

(Des Ursula Kühne. Photo Courvoisier)

1993 (1 Mar). 140th Birth Anniversary of Hans Gantner (painter). T **331** and similar horiz designs. Multicoloured. P 11½.
1046	50r. Type **331**	1·10	95
1047	60r. Hunting Lodge, Sass	1·30	1·10
1048	1f.80 Red House, Vaduz	3·75	3·50
1046/1048	Set of 3	5·50	5·00

(Des S. Bockmühl. Photo Courvoisier)

1993 (1 Mar). Europa. Contemporary Art. T **332** and similar vert design. Multicoloured. P 11½.
| 1049 | 80r. Type **332** | 1·90 | 1·70 |
| 1050 | 1f. *The little Blue* (Evi Kliemand) | 2·30 | 2·10 |

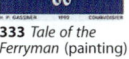
333 *Tale of the Ferryman* (painting)

334 Tree of Life

(Des H. P. Gassner. Photo Courvoisier)

1993 (7 June). Tibetan Collection in the National Museum. T **333** and similar vert designs. Multicoloured. P 11½.
| 1051 | 60r. Type **333** | 1·30 | 1·10 |

1052	80r. Religious dance mask	1·80	1·60
1053	1f. *Tale of the Fish* (painting)	2·20	2·00
1051/1053 Set of 3		4·75	4·25

(Des Cornelia Eberle. Photo Courvoisier)

1993 (7 June). Missionary Work. P 11½.
1054	**334**	1f.80 multicoloured	4·00	3·50

335 *The Black Hatter* (F. Hundertwasser)
336 Crown Prince Alois and Duchess Sophie of Bavaria

(Eng W. Seidel. Recess and photo State Ptg Wks, Vienna)

1993 (7 June). Homage to Liechtenstein. P 14×13½.
1055	**335**	2f.80 multicoloured	6·25	5·75

(Des H. P. Gassner (from photograph by Klaus Schädler). Photo Courvoisier)

1993 (7 June). Royal Wedding. Sheet 100×67 mm. P 11½.
MS1056	**336**	4f. multicoloured	10·50	10·00

337 Origanum
338 Eurasian Badger
339 Now that the Quiet Days are Coming... (Rainer Maria Rilke)

(Des Cornelia Eberle. Eng W. Seidel. Recess and photo State Ptg Wks, Vienna)

1993 (6 Sept). Flowers. T **337** and similar vert designs showing illustrations from *Hortus Botanicus Liechtensteinensis*. Multicoloured. P 13×13½.
1057	50r. Type **337**	1·30	1·10
1058	60r. Meadow Sage	1·40	1·30
1059	1f. *Seseli annuum*	2·20	2·00
1060	2f.50 Large Self-heal	5·25	4·75
1057/1060 Set of 4		9·25	8·25

(Des W. Dehry. Eng W. Seidel. Recess and photo State Ptg Wks, Vienna)

1993 (6 Sept). Animals. T **338** and similar vert designs. Multicoloured. P 13×13½.
1061	60r. Type **338**	1·30	1·20
1062	80r. Beech Marten	2·00	1·80
1063	1f. Red Fox	2·50	2·30
1061/1063 Set of 3		5·25	4·75

(Des F. Neugebauer and Ursula Kühne. Photo Courvoisier)

1993 (6 Dec). Christmas T **339** and similar vert designs. Multicoloured. P 11½.
1064	60r. Type **339**	1·30	1·10
1065	80r. Can You See the Light... (Th. Friedrich)	1·90	1·70
1066	1f. Christmas, Christmas... (R. A. Schröder)	2·20	2·00
1064/1066 Set of 3		4·75	4·25

340 Ski Jump
341 Seal and Title Page

(Des H. Anderegg. Photo Courvoisier)

1993 (6 Dec). Winter Olympic Games, Lillehammer, Norway (1994). T **340** and similar vert designs. Multicoloured. P 11½.
1067	60r. Type **340**	1·30	1·10
1068	80r. Slalom	1·80	1·60
1069	2f.40 Bobsleighing	5·50	5·00
1067/1069 Set of 3		7·75	7·00

(Des Cornelia Eberle (60r.), Ursula Kühne (1f.80). Photo Courvoisier)

1994 (7 Mar). Anniversaries. T **341** and similar horiz design. Multicoloured. P 11½.
1070	60r. Type **341** (275th Anniversary of Principality)	1·30	1·20
1071	1f.80 State, Prince's and Olympic flags (centenary of International Olympic Committee)	4·00	3·50

342 Andean Condor (*Vultur gryphus*)
343 Football Pitch and Hopi Indians playing Kickball

(Des H. P. Gassner. Eng W. Seidel. Recess and photo State Ptg Wks, Vienna)

1994 (7 Mar). Europa. Discoveries of Alexander von Humboldt. T **342** and similar vert design. Multicoloured. P 13×13½.
1072	80r. Type **342**	1·80	1·60
1073	1f. *Rhexia cardinalis* (plant)	2·40	2·10

(Des E. Frick, Photo Courvoisier)

1994 (7 Mar). World Cup Football Championship, USA. P 11½.
1074	**343**	2f.80 multicoloured	5·50	5·00

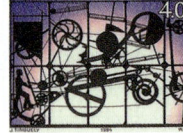

344 Elephant with Letter
345 Eulogy of Madness (mobile, Jean Tinguely)

(Des Regina Marxer. Photo Courvoisier)

1994 (6 June). Greetings Stamps. T **344** and similar horiz designs. Multicoloured. P 12½.
1075	60r. Type **344**	1·50	1·40
1076	60r. Cherub with flower and hearts	1·50	1·40
1077	60r. Pig with four-leaf Clover	1·50	1·40
1078	60r. Dog holding bunch of Tulips	1·50	1·40
1075/1078 Set of 4		5·50	5·00

(Eng W. Seidel. Recess and photo State Ptg Wks, Vienna)

1994 (6 June). Homage to Liechtenstein. P 13½×14.
1079	**345**	4f. black, rose and reddish violet	9·50	8·75

346 Spring
347 Strontium

(Des Martha Griebler. Photo Courvoisier)

1994 (5 Sept). Seasons of the Vine. T **346** and similar horiz designs. Multicoloured. P 11½.
1080	60r. Type **346**	1·50	1·40
	a. Block of 4. Nos. 1080/1083	6·25	
1081	60r. Vine leaves (Summer)	1·50	1·40
1082	60r. Trunk in snowy landscape (Winter)	1·50	1·40
1083	60r. Grapes (Autumn)	1·50	1·40
1080/1083 Set of 4		5·50	5·00

Nos. 1080/1083 were issued together in *se-tenant* blocks of four stamps within the sheet, each block forming a composite design.

1994 LIECHTENSTEIN

(Des Ursula Kühne. Eng W. Seidel. Recess and photo State Ptg Wks, Vienna)

1994 (5 Sept). Minerals. T **347** and similar horiz designs. Multicoloured. P 13½×13.
1084	60r. Type **347**		1·50	1·40
1085	80r. Quartz		2·00	1·80
1086	3f.50 Iron dolomite		7·25	6·50
1084/1086 Set of 3			9·75	8·75

348 The True Light

349 Earth

(Des Anne Frommelt. Photo Courvoisier)

1994 (5 Dec). Christmas. T **348** and similar vert designs. Multicoloured. P 11½.
1087	60r. Type **348**		1·30	1·20
1088	80r. Peace on Earth		2·00	1·80
1089	1f. Behold, the House of God		2·50	2·30
1087/1089 Set of 3			5·25	4·75

(Des E. Steiner. Eng W. Seidel. Recess and photo State Ptg Wks, Vienna)

1994 (5 Dec). The Four Elements. T **349** and similar square designs. Multicoloured. P 14.
1090	60r. Type **349**		1·30	1·20
1091	80r. Water		2·00	1·80
1092	1f. Fire		2·30	2·10
1093	2f.50 Air		5·50	5·00
1090/1093 Set of 4			10·00	9·00

350 The Theme of all our Affairs must be Peace

351 UN Flag and Bouquet of Flowers

(Des Cornelia Eberle. Photo Courvoisier)

1995 (6 Mar). Europa. Peace and Freedom. T **350** and similar horiz design, showing quotations of Franz Josef II. Multicoloured. P 11½.
1094	80r. Type **350**		2·00	1·80
1095	1f. Through Unity comes Strength and the Bearing of Sorrows		2·50	2·30

(Des Ursula Kühne (60r.), Regina Marxer (1f.80), L. Jäger (3f.50). Photo Courvoisier)

1995 (6 Mar). Anniversaries and Event. T **351** and similar multicoloured designs. P 11½.
1096	60r. Princess Marie with children (50th Anniversary of Liechtenstein Red Cross) (horiz)		1·50	1·40
1097	1f.80 Type **351** (50th Anniversary of United Nations Organisation)		3·50	3·25
1098	3f.50 Alps (European Nature Conservation Year)		8·00	7·25
1096/1098 Set of 3			11·50	10·50

352 Falknis Mountains

353 One Heart and One Soul

(Des M. Frommelt. Photo Courvoisier)

1995 (6 June). Birth Centenary of Anton Frommelt (painter). T **352** and similar horiz designs. Multicoloured. P 11½.
1099	60r. Type **352**		1·70	1·50
1100	80r. Three Oaks		2·30	2·10
1101	4f.10 The Rhine		9·00	8·25
1099/1101 Set of 3			11·50	10·50

(Des Nico. Photo Courvoisier)

1995 (6 June). Greetings Stamps. T **353** and similar horiz designs. Multicoloured. P 12½.
1102	60r. Type **353**		1·40	1·30
	a. Vert strip of 4. Nos. 1102/1105		5·75	
1103	60r. Bandage round Sunflower (Get Well)		1·40	1·30
1104	60r. Baby arriving over rainbow (Hurrah! Here I am)		1·40	1·30
1105	60r. Delivering letter by hot-air balloon (Write again)		1·40	1·30
1102/1105 Set of 4			5·00	4·75

Nos. 1102/1105 were issued in vertical *se-tenant* strips of four stamps within the sheet.

354 Coloured Ribbons woven through River

355 Arnica (*Arnica montana*)

(Des Cornelia Eberle. Eng P. Schopfer. Recess and litho PTT, Berne)

1995 (5 Sept). Liechtenstein–Switzerland Co-operation. P 13½.
1106	**354**	60r. multicoloured	1·80	1·60

No. 1106 was valid for use in both Liechtenstein and Switzerland (see No. 1308 of Switzerland).

(Des Cornelia Eberle. Eng W. Seidel. Recess and litho State Ptg Wks, Vienna)

1995 (5 Sept). Medicinal Plants. T **355** and similar vert designs. Multicoloured. P 13×13½.
1107	60r. Type **355**		1·80	1·60
1108	80r. Giant Nettle (*Urica dioica*)		2·10	1·90
1109	1f.80 Common Valerian (*Valeriana* sp.)		4·25	4·00
1110	3f.50 Fig-wort (*Ranunculus* sp.)		8·00	7·25
1107/1110 Set of 4			14·50	13·50

356 Angel (detail of painting)

357 Lady with Lapdog (Paul Wunderlich)

(Des Marianne Siegl. Eng W. Seidel. Recess and photo State Ptg Wks, Vienna)

1995 (4 Dec). Christmas T **356** and similar vert designs showing painting by Lorenzo Monaco. Multicoloured. P 14×13½.
1111	60r. Type **356**		1·30	1·10
1112	80r. *Virgin Mary with Infant and Two Angels*		1·90	1·70
1113	1f. *Angel facing left* (detail of painting)		2·50	2·30
1111/1113 Set of 3			5·25	4·50

(Des and eng W. Seidel. Recess and photo State Ptg Wks, Vienna)

1995 (4 Dec). Homage to Liechtenstein. P 14×13½.
1114	**357**	4f. multicoloured	9·50	8·50

358 Eschen

LIECHTENSTEIN 1996

(Des O. Zeiller (10r.), O. Zeiller and Marianne Siegl (others). Photo Courvoisier)

1996 (4 Mar)–**2001**. Tourism. T **358** and similar horiz design. Multicoloured. P 11½.

1115	10r. Type **358**	30	25
1116	20r. Planken (3.3.97)	50	45
1117	50r. Ruggell (6.3.00)	1·30	1·10
1117a	60r. Balzers (6.3.00)	1·50	1·40
1117b	70r. Schellenburg (5.6.01)	1·70	1·50
1118	80r. Ruggell (1.3.99)	1·80	1·60
1119	1f. Nendeln (1.3.99)	2·20	2·00
1120	1f.10 Eschen (6.3.00)	2·50	2·30
1121	1f.20 Triesen (1.3.99)	2·75	2·40
1122	1f.30 Triesen (3.3.97)	3·00	2·75
1123	1f.40 Mauren (6.3.00)	3·25	3·00
1124	1f.70 Schaanwald (3.3.97)	3·75	3·50
1125	1f.80 Malbun (5.6.01)	4·00	3·50
1125a	1f.90 Schaan (6.3.00)	4·25	3·75
1126	2f. Gamprin (2.6.98)	4·50	4·00
1126a	2f.20 Balzers (5.6.01)	4·75	4·25
1127	4f. Triesenburg (2.6.98)	9·00	8·00
1128	4f.50 Bendern (5.6.01)	10·00	9·25
1129	5f. Vaduz Castle (4.3.01)	11·00	10·00
1115/1129 Set of 19		65·00	60·00

359 Crucible

360 Kinsky and Diary Extract, 7 March 1917

(Des L. Jäger. Photo Courvoisier)

1996 (4 Mar). Bronze Age in Europe. P 11½.
1130 **359** 90r. multicoloured .... 2·75 2·50

(Des H. P. Gassner. Photo Courvoisier)

1996 (4 Mar). Europa. Famous Women. Nora, Countess Kinsky (mother of Princess Gina of Liechtenstein). T **360** and similar horiz design. P 11½.

1131	90r. brownish grey, deep reddish purple and deep turquoise-blue	2·75	2·50
1132	1f.10 brownish grey, deep turquoise-blue and deep reddish purple	3·25	3·00

Designs: 90r. T **360**; 1f.10, Kinsky and diary extract for 28 February 1917.

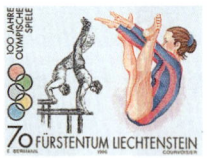

361 Gymnastics

(Des E. Bermann. Photo Courvoisier)

1996 (3 June). Centenary of Modern Olympic Games. T **361** and similar horiz designs. Multicoloured. P 11½.

1133	70r. Type **361**	1·90	1·80
1134	90r. Hurdling	2·40	2·30
1135	1f.10 Cycling	2·75	2·50
1133/1135 Set of 3		6·25	6·00

362 Primroses

(Des Ursula Kühne. Photo Courvoisier)

1996 (3 June). Birth Centenary of Ferdinand Gehr (painter). T **362** and similar horiz designs. Multicoloured. P 11½.

1136	70r. Type **362**	1·90	1·80
1137	90r. Daisies	2·40	2·30
1138	1f.10 Poppy	2·75	2·50
1139	1f.80 Buttercups (33×23 mm)	4·75	4·75
1136/1139 Set of 4		10·50	10·00

363 State Arms

(Des Cornelia Eberle. Eng W. Seidel. Recess photo and embossed)

1996 (2 Sept). P 14.
1140 **363** 10f. multicoloured .... 21·00 20·00

364 Veldkirch, 1550   **365** Poltava

(Des and eng W. Seidel. Recess and photo State Ptg Wks, Vienna)

1996 (2 Sept). Millenary of Austria. P 13½.
1141 **364** 90r. multicoloured .... 2·30 2·20

(Des Cornelia Eberle. Eng W. Seidel. Recess and photo State Ptg Wks, Vienna)

1996 (2 Dec). Eugen Zotow (painter) Commemoration. T **365** and similar square designs. Multicoloured. P 14.

1142	70r. Type **365**	1·90	1·80
1143	1f.10 Three Brothers in a Berlin Park	3·00	3·00
1144	1f.40 Vaduz	3·75	3·50
1142/1144 Set of 3		7·75	7·50

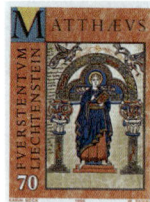 

366 St Matthew   **367** Franz Schubert

(Des Karin Beck. Eng W. Seidel. Recess and photo State Ptg Wks, Vienna)

1996 (2 Dec). Christmas. T **366** and similar vert designs showing illustrations from illuminated manuscript *Liber Viventium Fabariensis*. Multicoloured. P 14.

1145	70r. Type **366**	1·90	1·80
1146	90r. Emblems of St Mark	2·30	2·20
1147	1f.10 Emblems of St Luke	2·75	2·50
1148	1f.80 Emblems of St John	4·75	4·50
1145/1148 Set of 4		10·50	10·00

(Des Martha Griebler. Eng W. Seidel. Recess and photo State Ptg Wks, Vienna)

1997 (3 Mar). Birth Bicentenary of Franz Schubert (composer). P 13½.
1149 **367** 70r. multicoloured .... 2·00 1·90

368 The Wild Gnomes   **369** Madonna and Child with St Lucius and St Florinus (Gabriel Dreher)

1997 LIECHTENSTEIN

(Des Regina Marxer. Photo Courvoisier)
1997 (3 Mar). Europa. Tales and Legends. T **368** and similar square design. Multicoloured. P 12×11½.
1150	90r. Type **368**	2·20	2·10
1151	1f.10 Man, Pumpkin and Rabbit (The Foal of Planken)	3·00	2·75

(Des Marianne Siegl. Eng W. Seidel. Recess and photo State Ptg Wks, Vienna)
1997 (2 June). National Patron Saints. P 13½×13.
1152	**369**	20f. multicoloured	48·00	46·00

370 Phaeolepiota aurea
371 Steam Train, Schaanwald Halt

(Des Iris Heeb. Eng W. Seidel. Recess and photo State Ptg Wks, Vienna)
1997 (22 Aug). Fungi. T **370** and similar square designs. Multicoloured. P 14.
1153	70r. Type **370**	1·90	1·80
1154	90r. *Helvella silvicola*	2·30	2·20
1155	1f.10 Orange Peel Fungus (*Aleuria aurantia*)..	3·00	2·75
1153/1155	Set of 3	6·50	6·00

See also Nos. 1238/1240.

(Des J. Schädler. Photo Courvoisier)
1997 (22 Aug). 125th Anniversary of Liechtenstein Railways. T **371** and similar horiz designs. Multicoloured. P 11½.
1156	70r. Type **371**	1·90	1·80
1157	90r. Diesel-electric train, Nendeln station	2·50	2·40
1158	1f.80 Electric train, Shaan-Vaduz station	4·75	4·50
1156/1158	Set of 3	8·25	7·75

372 Girl with Flower (Enrico Baj)
373 Basket of Roses

(Des W. Seidel. Photo Courvoisier)
1997 (22 Aug). Homage to Liechtenstein. P 11½.
1159	**372**	70r. multicoloured	1·90	1·80

(Des H. Preute. Eng W. Seidel. Recess and photo Austrian State Ptg Wks, Vienna)
1997 (1 Dec). Christmas. Glass Tree Decorations. T **373** and similar square designs. Multicoloured. P 14.
1160	70r. Type **373**	1·90	1·80
1161	90r. Bell	2·30	2·20
1162	1f.10 Bauble	3·00	2·75
1160/1162	Set of 3	6·50	6·00

374 Cross-country
375 *Verano* (The Summer)

(Des P. Sinawehl. Photo Courvoisier)
1997 (1 Dec). Winter Olympic Games, Nagano, Japan (1998). Skiing. T **374** and similar horiz designs. Multicoloured. P 12½.
1163		70r. Type **374**	1·90	1·80
1164		90r. Slalom	2·50	2·40
1165		1f.80 Downhill	4·75	4·50
1163/1165	Set of 3		8·25	7·75

(Photo Courvoisier)
1998 (2 Mar). Homage to Liechtenstein. Paintings by Heinz Mack. T **375** and similar vert designs. Multicoloured. P 11½.
1166	70r. Type **375**	1·90	1·80
	a. Vert strip of block of 4. Nos. 1166/1169	7·75	
1167	70r. Homage to Liechtenstein	1·90	1·80
1168	70r. Between Day and Dream	1·90	1·80
1169	70r. Salute Cirico!	1·90	1·80
1166/1169	Set of 4	6·75	6·50

Nos. 1166/1169 were issued together in *se-tenant* blocks of four stamps plus one vertical *se-tenant* strip within sheets of 20.

376 Prince's Festival Procession, Vaduz
377 National Flags on Bridge

(Des Evelyne Bermann. Photo Courvoisier)
1998 (2 Mar). Europa. National Festivals. T **376** and similar horiz design. Multicoloured. P 11½.
1170	90r. Type **376**	2·30	2·20
1171	1f.10 Music Societies Festival, Gutenberg Castle, Balzers	3·00	2·75

(Des H. P. Gassner. Photo Courvoisier)
1998 (2 Mar). 75th Anniversary of Liechtenstein–Switzerland Customs Treaty. P 11½.
1172	**377**	1f.70 multicoloured	4·25	4·00

378 Goalkeeper
379 Clown with Queen of Hearts

(Des L. Jäger. Photo Courvoisier)
1998 (2 Mar). World Cup Football Championship, France. P 12.
1173	**378**	1f.80 multicoloured	4·75	4·50

(Des P. Flora. Recess and photo State Ptg Wks, Vienna)
1998 (2 June). Greeting Stamps. Clowns. T **379** and similar horiz designs. Multicoloured. P 14½×14.
1174	70r. Type **379**	1·90	1·80
	a. Vert strip of 4. Nos. 1174/1177	7·75	
1175	70r. Clown holding four-leaf Clovers	1·90	1·80
1176	70r. Clown raising hat	1·90	1·80
1177	70r. Clown holding heart	1·90	1·80
1174/1177	Set of 4	6·75	6·50

Nos. 1174/1147 were issued together in vertical *se-tenant* strips of four stamps within the sheet.

380 Wooden Milk Vat
381 Expelling of Johann Langer from Liechtenstein

(Des J. Schädler. Photo Couvoisier)
1998 (7 Sept). Traditional Crafts (1st series). T **380** and similar square designs. Multicoloured. P 11½.
1178	90r. Type **380**	2·20	2·10
1179	2f.20 Clog	5·50	5·25
1180	3f.50 Wheel	8·75	8·25
1178/1180	Set of 3	15·00	14·00

See also Nos. 1257/1259.

(Des Regina Marxer. Photo Courvoisier)
1998 (7 Sept). 150th Anniversary of 1848 Revolutions in Europe. P 11½.
1181 381 1f.80 multicoloured .... 5·25 5·00

382 Virgin Mary
383 Zum Löwen Guest House

(Des Marianne Siegl. Recess and photo Austrian State Ptg Wks, Vienna)
1998 (7 Dec). Christmas. T **382** and similar multicoloured designs. P 14.
1182 70r. Type **382** .... 1·90 1·80
1183 90r. The Nativity (35×26 *mm*) .... 2·30 2·20
1184 1f.10 Joseph .... 3·00 2·75
1182/1184 Set of 3 .... 6·50 6·00

Nos. 1182 and 1184 show details of the complete relief depicted on No. 1183.

(Des G. Malin. Photo Courvoisier)
1998 (7 Dec). Preservation of Historical Environment (1st series). Hinterschellenberg. T **383** and similar multicoloured designs. P 11½.
1185 90r. Type **383** .... 2·40 2·30
1186 1f.70 St George's Chapel (*vert*) .... 4·25 4·00
1187 1f.80 Houses .... 4·50 4·25
1185/1187 Set of 3 .... 10·00 9·50

See also Nos. 1250/1252, 1274/1275, 1292/1293, 1358/1359, 1386/1387, 1428/1429, 1462/1463 and 1498.

384 Automatic and Manual Switchboards
385 Eschen

(Des Karin Beck. Photo Courvoisier)
1998 (7 Dec). Centenary of Telephone in Liechtenstein. P 11½.
1188 384 2f.80 multicoloured .... 7·25 7·00

(Des L. Jäger. Photo Courvoisier)
1999 (1 Mar). 300th Anniversary of Purchase of the Unterland by Prince Johann Adam. Sheet 107×68 mm containing T **385** and similar horiz designs. Multicoloured. P 11½.
MS1189 90r.×5 plus label, Composite design of the Unterland showing the villages of Eschen, Gamprin, Mauren, Ruggell and Schellenberg .... 14·50 14·00

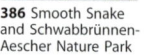

386 Smooth Snake and Schwabbrünnen-Aescher Nature Park
387 Council Anniversary Emblem and Silhouettes

(Des Cornelia Eberle. Photo Courvoisier)
1999 (1 Mar). Europa. Parks and Gardens. T **386** and similar vert design. Multicoloured. P 11½.
1190 90r. Type **386** .... 3·00 2·75
1191 1f.10 Corncrake and Ruggell marsh .... 3·50 3·50

(Des Rapallo. Photo Courvoisier)
1999 (25 May). Anniversaries and Events. T **387** and similar vert designs. Multicoloured. P 12×11½.
1192 70r. Type **387** (50th Anniversary of Council of Europe and European Convention on Human Rights) .... 1·90 1·80
1193 70r. Bird with envelope in beak (125th Anniversary of Universal Postal Union) .... 1·90 1·80
1194 70r. Heart in hand (75th Anniversary of Caritas Liechtenstein (welfare organisation)) .... 1·90 1·80
1192/1194 Set of 3 .... 5·25 4·75

388 Judo
389 *Herrengasse*

(Des P. Sinawehl (Nos. 1200/1203), A. Tuma (others). Photo Courvoisier)
1999 (25 May). Eighth European Small States Games, Liechtenstein. T **388** and similar horiz designs. Multicoloured. P 11½.
1195 70r. Type **388** .... 2·10 1·90
1196 70r. Swimming .... 2·10 1·90
1197 70r. Throwing the Javelin .... 2·10 1·90
1198 90r. Cycling .... 2·50 2·30
1199 90r. Shooting .... 2·50 2·30
1200 90r. Tennis .... 2·50 2·30
1201 90r. Squash .... 2·50 2·30
1202 90r. Table tennis .... 2·50 2·30
1203 90r. Volleyball .... 2·50 2·30
1195/1203 Set of 9 .... 19·00 18·00

(Des and eng W. Seidel. Recess and photo Austrian State Ptg Wks, Vienna)
1999 (9 Sept). Paintings by Eugen Verling. T **389** and similar horiz designs. P 14.
1204 70r. Type **389** .... 2·10 2·00
1205 2f. Old Vaduz with Castle .... 5·50 5·00
1206 4f. House in Fürst-Franz-Josef Street, Vaduz .... 10·50 10·00
1204/1206 Set of 3 .... 16·00 15·00

390 Scene from *Faust*, Act I

(Des Martha Griebler. Eng W. Seidel. Recess and photo Austrian State Ptg Wks, Vienna)
1999 (9 Sept). 250th Birth Anniversary of Johann Wolfgang Goethe (poet and playwright). T **390** and similar horiz design. Multicoloured. P 14.
1207 1f.40 Type **390** .... 4·00 3·75
1208 1f.70 Faust and the Devil sealing wager ...... 5·25 4·75

391 *The Annunciation*

(Des Ursula Kühne. Eng W. Seidel. Recess and photo Austrian State Ptg Wks, Vienna)
1999 (6 Dec). Christmas. Paintings by Joseph Walser from Chapel of Our Lady of Comfort, Dux. T **391** and similar horiz designs. Multicoloured. P 13½×14.
1209 70r. Type **391** .... 2·10 1·90
1210 90r. *Nativity* .... 2·75 2·50
1211 1f.10 *Adoration* .... 3·25 3·00
1209/1211 Set of 3 .... 7·25 6·75

1999 LIECHTENSTEIN

392 Identification Mark on Door, Übersaxen

393 Johannes Gutenberg

(Des H. Fritsch. Photo Courvoisier)

1999 (6 Dec). Walser Identification Marks. T **392** and similar vert designs. Multicoloured. P 11½.
1212	70r. Type **392**	2·10	1·90
1213	90r. Mark on mural	2·75	2·50
1214	1f.80 Mark on axe	4·75	4·50
1212/1214	Set of 3	8·75	8·00

(Des Martha Griebler. Eng W. Seidel. Recess and photo Austrian State Ptg Wks, Vienna)

1999 (6 Dec). 600th Birth Anniversary of Johannes Gutenberg (inventor of printing press). P 13½.
1215	**393**	3f.60 multicoloured	11·00	10·00

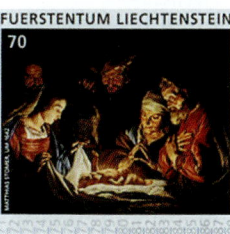

394 *The Adoration of the Shepherds* (Matthias Stomer)

395 Emblem

(Des Karin Beck. Photo Courvoisier)

2000 (1 Jan). Bimillenary of Christianity. Sheet 108×68 mm containing T **394** and similar square design. Multicoloured. P 12.
MS1216 70r. Type **394**; 1f.10, *Three Kings* (Ferdinand Gehr) ... 6·50 6·25

(Des H. P. Gassner. Photo Courvoisier)

2000 (1 Jan). Provision of Postal Services by Liechtenstein Post in Partnership with Swiss Post. P 11½.
1217	**395**	90r. multicoloured	3·00	2·75

396 *Mars and Rhea Silvia* (Peter Paul Rubens)

397 *Fragrance of Humus*

(Des Cornelia Eberle. Eng W. Seidel. Recess and photo Austrian State Ptg Wks, Vienna)

2000 (6 Mar). Paintings. T **396** and similar horiz design. Multicoloured. P 13½×13.
1218	70r. Type **396**	2·10	1·90
1219	1f.80 *Cupid with Soap-Bubble* (Rembrandt)	4·75	4·50

(Eng W. Seidel. Recess and photo Austrian State Ptg Wks, Vienna)

2000 (9 May). EXPO 2000 World's Fair, Hanover, Germany. T **397** and similar vert designs showing paintings by Friedensreich Hundertwasser. Multicoloured. P 14×13½.
1220	70r. Type **397**	2·50	2·40
1221	90r. *Do Not Wait Houses-Move*	3·00	3·00
1222	1f.10 *The Car: a Drive Towards Nature and Creation*	4·00	3·75
1220/1222	Set of 3	8·50	8·25

398 Building Europe

399 *Dove of Peace* (Antonio Martini)

(Des J.-P. Cousin. Photo Courvoisier)

2000 (9 May). Europa. P 11½×12.
1223	**398**	1f.10 multicoloured	4·00	3·75

(Des Marianne Siegl. Photo Courvoisier)

2000 (9 May). Peace 2000. T **399** and similar horiz designs showing paintings by members of Association of Mouth and Foot Painting Artists. Multicoloured. P 12×11½.
1224	1f.40 Type **399**	4·25	4·00
1225	1f.70 *World Peace* (Alberto Alvarez)	4·75	4·50
1226	2f.20 *Rainbow* (Eiichi Minami)	6·00	5·75
1224/1226	Set of 3	13·50	13·00

400 Koalas on Rings (Gymnastics)

401 *The Dreaming Bee* (Joan Miró)

(Des Rapello. Photo Courvoisier)

2000 (4 Sept). Olympic Games Sydney. T **400** and similar horiz designs. Multicoloured. P 12.
1227	80r. Type **400**	2·20	2·10
1228	1f. Joey leaping over crossbar (High jump)	2·75	2·75
1229	1f.30 Emus approaching finish line (Athletics)	3·50	3·25
1230	1f.80 Duckbill Platypuses in swimming race	5·25	5·00
1227/1230	Set of 4	12·00	12·00

(Des Cornelia Eberle. Eng W. Seidel (2f.). Recess. State Ptg Wks, Vienna (2f.) or photo Courvoisier (others))

2000 (4 Sept). Inauguration of Art Museum. T **401** and similar vert designs. Multicoloured. P 14×13½ (2f.) or 12 (others).
1231	80r. Type **401**	2·50	2·50
1232	1f.20 *Cube* (Sol LeWitt)	4·25	4·00
1233	2f. *Bouquet of Flowers* (Roelant Savery) (31×46 mm)	6·50	6·25
1231/1233	Set of 3	12·00	11·50

402 Peace Doves

403 Root Crib

(Des H. P. Gassner. Photo Courvoisier)

2000 (4 Sept). 25th Anniversary of Organisation for Security and Co-operation in Europe. P 12×11½.
1234	**402**	1f.30 multicoloured	3·75	3·50

(Des Ursula Kühne. Eng W. Seidel. Recess and photo State Ptg Wks, Vienna)

2000 (4 Dec). Christmas. Cribs. T **403** and similar horiz designs. Multicoloured. P 14.
1235	80r. Type **403**	2·10	2·10
1236	1f.30 Oriental crib	3·50	3·50
1237	1f.80 Crib with cloth figures	5·25	5·00
1235/1237	Set of 3	9·75	9·50

(Des Iris Heeb. Eng. W. Seidel. Recess and photo State Ptg Wks, Vienna)

2000 (4 Dec). Fungi. Square designs as T **370**. Multicoloured. P 14.
1238	90r. *Mycena adonis*	2·50	2·50
1239	1f.10 *Chalciporus amarellus*	3·00	3·00
1240	2f. Pink Waxcap (*Hygrocybe calyptriformis*)	5·50	5·25
1238/1240 Set of 3		10·00	9·75

404 Postman delivering Parcel   **405** Silver Easter Egg

(Des Rapallo. Photo Courvoisier)

2001 (5 Mar). Greetings Stamps. T **404** and similar horiz design. Multicoloured. Granite paper. P 12×11½.
1241	70r. Type **404**	2·10	2·00
1242	70r. Postman delivering flowers	2·10	2·00

The prices for Nos. 1241/1242 are for the stamps with the parcel (No. 1241) and flowers (No. 1242) intact. The parcel and flowers can be scratched away to reveal a greetings message.

(Des Silvia Ruppen. Eng W.Seidel. Recess and photo State Ptg Wks, Vienna)

2001 (5 Mar). Decorated Easter Eggs. T **405** and similar vert designs. Multicoloured. P 13½×14.
1243	1f.20 Type **405**	3·75	3·50
1244	1f.80 Cloissonné egg	5·00	4·75
1245	2f. Porcelain egg	5·25	5·00
1243/1245 Set of 3		12·50	12·00

406 Mountain Spring   **407** Emblem

(Des J. Schädler. Photo Courvoisier)

2001 (5 Mar). Europa. Water Resources. Granite paper. P 11½×12.
1246	**406** 1f.30 multicoloured	3·50	3·25

(Des H. P. Gassner. Photo Courvoisier)

2001 (5 Mar). Liechtenstein Presidency of Council of Europe. Granite paper. P 11½×11½.
1247	**407** 1f.80 multicoloured	4·75	4·50

408 Carolingian Cruciform Fibula   **409** St Theresa's Chapel, Schaanwald

(Des G. Malin. Photo Courvoisier)

2001 (5 June). Centenary of Historical Association. T **408** and similar vert designs. Multicoloured. Granite paper. P 11½×12.
1248	70r. Type **408**	2·10	2·00
1249	70r. *Mars of Gutenberg* (statue)	2·10	2·00

(Des G. Malin. Photo Courvoisier)

2001 (3 Sept). Preservation of Historical Environment (2nd series). T **409** and similar vert designs. Multicoloured. P 11½.
1250	70r. Type **409**	2·10	2·00
1251	90r. St Johann's Torkel (wine press), Mauren	2·50	2·40
1252	1f.10 Pirsch Transformer Station, Schaanwald	3·25	3·00
1250/1252 Set of 3		7·00	6·75

410 Mary and kneeling Votant (Chapel of Our Lady, Dux, Schann)   **411** Rheinberger and Scene from *Zauberwort* (song cycle)

(Des Marianne Siegl. Eng W. Seidel. Recess and photo State Ptg Wks, Vienna)

2001 (3 Sept). Votive Paintings. T **410** and similar vert designs. Multicoloured. P 13½.
1253	70r. Type **410**	2·10	2·00
1254	1f.20 Mary and Jesus, St George among other Saints, and text of vow (St George's Chapel, Schellenberg)	3·50	3·25
1255	1f.30 Mary, St Joseph of Arimathea, St Christopher, Johann Christoph Walser (votant) and text of vow (Chapel of Our Lady, Dux, Schann)	3·75	3·50
1253/1255 Set of 3		8·50	8·00

(Des Martha Griebler. Eng W. Seidel Recess and photo State Ptg Wks, Vienna)

2001 (3 Sept). Death Centenary of Josef Gabriel Rheinberger (composer). P 14.
1256	**411** 3f.50 multicoloured	10·50	10·00

(Des J. Schädler. Photo Courvoisier)

2001 (3 Dec). Traditional Crafts (2nd series). Square designs as T **380**. Multicoloured. P 12.
1257	70r. Agricultural implements and horseshoe	2·10	2·00
1258	90r. Rake	2·75	2·50
1259	1f.20 Harness	3·50	3·25
1257/1259 Set of 3		7·50	7·00

412 Annunciation   **413** Square

(Photo Courvoisier)

2001 (3 Dec). Christmas. T **412** and similar vert designs showing medallions from The Joyful, Sorrowful and Glorious Rosary Cycle. Multicoloured. P 12.
1260	70r. Type **412**	2·10	2·00
1261	90r. Nativity	2·75	2·50
1262	1f.30 Presentation of Jesus at the Temple	3·75	3·50
1260/1262 Set of 3		7·75	7·25

(Photo Courvoisier)

2001 (3 Dec). Paintings by Gottfried Honeggar. T **413** and similar vert design. Multicoloured. P 11½.
1263	1f.80 Type **413**	5·50	5·25
1264	2f.20 Circle	6·50	6·00

414 Mountains and River   **415** Schellenberg

(Des L. Jäger. Photo State Ptg Wks, Vienna)

2002 (4 Mar). International Year of Mountains and 50th Anniversary of the International Commission of Alpine Protection. T **414** and similar vert design. Multicoloured. P 14×13½.
1265	70r. Type **414**		2·00	1·90
1266	1f.20 Stylised mountains		3·50	3·25

(Des Marianne Siegl. Photo State Ptg Wks, Vienna)

2002 (4 Mar). 30th Death Anniversary of Friedrich Kaufmann (artist). T **415** and similar horiz designs. Multicoloured. P 13½×14.
1267	70r. Type **415**		2·10	2·00
1268	1f.30 *Schaan*		3·50	3·25
1269	1f.80 *Steg*		5·25	5·00
1267/1269	Set of 3		9·75	9·25

 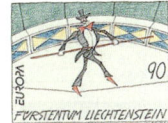

416 Space Shuttle and Bee   **417** Man on Tightrope

(Des Silvia Ruppen. Photo State Ptg Wks, Vienna)

2002 (4 Mar). Liechtenstein's participation in NASA Space Technology and Research Students Project. P 13½×14.
1270	**416** 90r. multicoloured		2·75	2·50

The project submitted by the Liechtenstein Gymnasium concerned the study of the effects of space on Carpenter Bees.

(Des P. Flora. Eng W. Seidel. Recess and photo State Ptg Wks, Vienna)

2002 (4 Mar). Europa. Circus. T **417** and similar horiz design. Multicoloured. P 14½×14.
1271	90r. Type **417**		2·50	2·40
1272	1f.30 Juggler		3·75	3·50

418 Emblem   **419** Houses, Popers

(Des Cornelia Eberle. Photo State Ptg Wks, Vienna)

2002 (4 Mar). Liba '02 National Stamp Exhibition, Vaduz (1st issue). P 14×13½.
1273	**418** 1f.20 multicoloured		3·50	3·25

See also Nos. 1282/1283 and 1318/1320.

(Des G. Malin. Photo State Ptg Wks, Vienna)

2002 (3 June). Preservation of Historical Environment (3rd series). T **419** and similar horiz design. Multicoloured. P 14×13½.
1274	70r. Type **419**		2·10	2·00
1275	1f.20 House, Weiherring		3·50	3·25

420 Footballers   **421** Princess Marie

(Des S. Bockmühl. Photo State Ptg Wks, Vienna)

2002 (3 June). World Cup Football Championship, Japan and South Korea. P 13½×14.
1276	**420** 1f.80 multicoloured		5·50	5·25

(Des Marianne Siegl. Photo State Ptg Wks, Vienna)

2002 (3 June). The Royal Couple. T **421** and similar horiz design. Multicoloured. P 13½.
1277	3f. Type **421**		9·00	8·50
1278	3f.50 Prince Hans-Adam II		10·50	10·00

422 Ghost Orchid (*Epipogium aphyllum*)   **423** Stamps and Emblem

(Des Regina Marxer. Photo State Ptg Wks, Vienna)

2002 (8 Aug). Orchids. T **422** and similar vert designs. Multicoloured. P 13½.
1279	70r. Type **422**		2·10	2·00
1280	1f.20 Fly Orchid (*Ophrys insectifera*)		3·50	3·25
1281	1f.30 Black Vanilla Orchid (*Nigritella nigra*)		3·75	3·50
1279/1281	Set of 3		8·50	8·00

(Des Cornelia Eberle. Photo State Ptg Wks, Vienna)

2002 (8 Aug). Liba 02 National Stamp Exhibition, Vaduz (2nd issue). 90th Anniversary of First Liechtenstein Stamps. T **423** and similar vert design. Multicoloured. P 13½.
1282	90r. Type **423**		2·75	2·50
1283	1f.30 Stamps showing royal family		3·75	3·50

424 Princess Sophie   **425** Mary and Joseph

(Des Marianne Siegl. Photo State Ptg Wks, Vienna)

2002 (8 Aug). Prince Alois and Princess Sophie. T **424** and similar horiz design. Multicoloured. P 13½.
1284	2f. Type **424**		5·75	5·50
1285	2f.50 Prince Alois		7·25	7·00

(Des Regina Hassler. Photo State Ptg Wks, Vienna)

2002 (25 Nov). Christmas. Batik. T **425** and similar vert designs. Multicoloured. P 14×13½.
1286	70r. Type **425**		2·10	2·00
1287	1f.20 Nativity		3·50	3·25
1288	1f.80 Flight into Egypt		5·00	4·75
1286/1288	Set of 3		9·50	9·00

426 The Eagle, Vaduz   **427** St Fridolin Parish Church

(Des S. Scherrer. Eng W. Seidel Recess and photo State Ptg Wks, Vienna)

2002 (25 Nov). Inn Signs. T **426** and similar horiz designs. Multicoloured. P 13½×14.
1289	1f.20 Type **426**		3·50	3·25
1290	1f.80 The Angel, Balzers		5·00	4·75
1291	3f. The Eagle, Bendern		8·50	8·25
1289/1291	Set of 3		15·00	14·50

(Des G. Malin. State Ptg Wks, Vienna)

2003 (3 Mar). Preservation of Historical Environment (4th series). T **427** and similar multicoloured design. P 13½.
1292	70r. Type **427**		2·10	2·00
1293	2f.50 House, Spidach (*horiz*)		7·00	6·75

LIECHTENSTEIN 2003

428 Postal Emblem

429 Pruning Vines

(Des Karin Beck. Litho State Ptg Wks, Vienna)
2003 (3 Mar). Europa. Poster Art. P 13½×13.
| 1294 | **428** | 1f.20 multicoloured | 3·50 | 3·25 |

(Des Martha Griebler. Litho State Ptg Wks, Vienna)
2003 (3 Mar). Viticulture (1st issue). T **429** and similar square designs. Multicoloured. P 14.
1295	1f.30 Type **429**	4·00	3·75
1296	1f.80 Tying up vines	5·50	5·25
1297	2f.20 Hoeing	7·25	7·00
1295/1297 Set of 3		15·00	14·50

See also Nos. 1301/1303, 1304/1306 and 1312/1314.

430 Bridge

(Des Marianne Siegl. Photo State Ptg Wks, Vienna)
2003 (2 June). 50th Anniversary of Liechtenstein Association for the Disabled. P 14.
| 1298 | **430** | 70r. multicoloured | 2·30 | 2·10 |

431 Renovated Buildings and Ammonite

(Des Marianne Siegl. Photo State Ptg Wks, Vienna)
2003 (2 June). Renovation of National Museum. T **431** and similar horiz design. Multicoloured. P 14.
| 1299 | 1f.20 Type **431** | 3·50 | 3·25 |
| 1300 | 1f.30 Verweserhaus building and bailiff's shield | 3·75 | 3·75 |

(Des Martha Griebler. Photo State Ptg Wks, Vienna)
2003 (2 June). Viticulture (2nd issue). Square designs as T **429**. Multicoloured. P 14.
1301	1f.20 Looping the tendrils	3·50	3·25
1302	1f.80 Removing leaves from around Grapes	5·50	5·25
1303	3f.50 Reducing top growth	10·50	10·00
1301/1303 Set of 3	18·00	17·00

(Des Martha Griebler. Photo State Ptg Wks, Vienna)
2003 (1 Sept). Viticulture (3rd issue). Square designs as T **429**. Multicoloured. P 14.
1304	70r. Thinning out	2·50	2·40
1305	90r. Harvesting	3·00	2·75
1306	1f.10 Pressing the Grapes	4·00	3·75
1304/1306 Set of 3	8·50	8·00

432 St George

433 Parents and Young on Nest

(Des and eng W. Seidel. Recess and Photo State Ptg Wks, Vienna)
2003 (1 Sept). Saints (1st series). T **432** and similar vert designs. Multicoloured. P 13½.
1307	1f.20 Type **432**	3·50	3·25
1308	1f.20 St Blaise	3·50	3·25
1309	1f.30 St Vitus	3·75	3·50
1310	1f.30 St Erasmus	3·75	3·50
1307/1310 Set of 4	13·00	12·00

See also Nos. 1323/1328 and 1367/1370.

(Des A. Tuma. Eng W. Seidel. Recess and Photo State Ptg Wks, Vienna)
2003 (1 Sept). Conservation of White Storks in Rhine Valley. P 13×13½.
| 1311 | **433** | 2f.20 multicoloured | 7·25 | 6·50 |

(Des Martha Griebler. Photo State Ptg Wks, Vienna)
2003 (24 Nov). Viticulture (4th issue). Square designs as T **429**. Multicoloured. P 14.
1312	70r. Tasting	2·10	2·00
1313	90r. Harvesting ice-wine Grapes	2·50	2·40
1314	1f.20 Bottling	3·50	3·50
1312/1314 Set of 3	7·25	7·00

434 Archangel Gabriel appearing to Mary

435 Cow (Laura Beck)

(Des Ursula Spoerry. Photo State Ptg Wks, Vienna)
2003 (24 Nov). Christmas. T **434** and similar vert designs. Multicoloured. P 14½×13½.
1315	70r. Type **434**	2·10	2·00
1316	90r. Nativity	2·50	2·40
1317	1f.30 Three Kings	3·75	3·50
1315/1317 Set of 3	7·50	7·00

(Photo State Ptg Wks, Vienna)
2003 (24 Nov). Liba 02 National Stamp Exhibition, Vaduz (3rd issue). Children's Drawing Competition Winners. T **435** and similar multicoloured designs. P 14½×13½ (horiz) or 13½×14½ (vert).
1318	70r. Type **435**	2·20	2·10
1319	1f.80 Bee (Laura Lingg)	5·50	5·25
1320	1f.80 Apple tree (Patrick Marxer) (*vert*)	5·50	5·25
1318/1320 Set of 3	12·00	11·50

436 Hands enclosing Leaves

437 Hot Air Balloon

(Des Sabine Bockmühl. Photo State Ptg Wks, Vienna)
2004 (3 Jan). 50th Anniversary of AHV (retirement insurance). P 14.
| 1321 | **436** | 85r. multicoloured | 2·40 | 2·30 |

(Des Corina Marxer. Photo State Ptg Wks, Vienna)
2004 (1 Mar). Europa. Holidays. P 14½×13½.
| 1322 | **437** | 1f.30 multicoloured | 4·50 | 4·25 |

(Des and eng W. Seidel. Recess and Photo State Ptg Wks, Vienna)
2004 (1 Mar). Saints (2nd series). Vert designs as T **432**. Multicoloured. P 13½.
1323	1f. St Achatius	2·75	2·75
1324	1f. St Margaret	2·75	2·75
1325	1f.20 St Christopher	3·50	3·25
1326	1f.20 St Pantaleon	3·50	3·25
1327	2f.50 St Cyriacus	6·50	6·25
1328	2f.50 St Aegidius	6·50	6·25
1323/1328 Set of 6	23·00	22·00

2004 LIECHTENSTEIN

438 Bendern   **439** Olympic Torch

(Photo State Ptg Wks, Vienna)

2004 (1 June)–06. Tourism. T **438** and similar horiz designs showing aerial views of Liechtenstein. Multicoloured. P 14.

1329		15r. Type **438**	45	40
1330		85r. Gross-Teg	2·40	2·30
1331		1f. Tuass	2·75	2·50
1332		1f.50 Oberland (21.11.05)	4·25	4·00
1333		1f.60 Ruggeller Riet (21.11.05)	4·50	4·25
1334		2f.50 Canal (6.3.06)	6·50	6·25
1335		3f. Naafkopf (21.11.05)	7·75	7·50
1336		3f.50 Rhine Valley (6.3.06)	9·50	9·00
1337		6f. Gutenberg	15·00	14·50
1329/1337	Set of 9		48·00	46·00

Nos. 1338/1349 are vacant.

(Des P. Sinewal. Photo State Ptg Wks, Vienna)

2004 (1 June). Olympic Games, Athens 2004. P 14.
1350	**439**	85r. multicoloured	2·75	2·50

440 Bee Orchid   **441** Mathematical
(*Ophrys apifera*)   Symbols

(Des Regina Marxer. Photo State Ptg Wks, Vienna)

2004 (1 June). Orchids. T **440** and similar vert designs. Multicoloured. P 13½.

1351		85r. Type **440**	2·40	2·30
1352		1f. *Orchis ustulata*	2·75	2·50
1353		1f.20 *Epipactis purpurata*	3·50	3·25
1351/1353	Set of 3		7·75	7·25

(Des B. Kaufman. Photo State Ptg Wks, Vienna)

2004 (6 Sept). Science. T **441** and similar vert designs. P 14.

1354		85r. Type **441**	2·40	2·30
1355		1f. Atomic diagram (physics)	2·75	2·50
1356		1f.30 Molecular structure (chemistry)	3·50	3·25
1357		1f.80 Star map and Saturn (astronomy)	4·75	4·50
1354/1357	Set of 4		12·00	11·50

442 Two-storied House on   **443** The Annunciation
Unterdorfstrasse (street)

(Des G. Malin. Photo State Ptg Wks, Vienna)

2004 (6 Sept). Preservation of Historical Environment (5th series). T **442** and similar multicoloured design. P 13½.
1358		2f.20 Type **442**	5·00	4·75
1359		2f.50 Unterdorfstrasse (street)	5·75	5·50

(Des Marianne Siegl. Photo State Ptg Wks, Vienna)

2004 (22 Nov). Christmas. T **443** and similar vert designs. Multicoloured. Elongated perf 7.
1360		85r. Type **443**	3·00	2·75
1361		1f. Nativity	4·50	4·00
1362		1f.80 Adoration of the Magi	6·25	5·75
1360/1362	Set of 3		12·50	11·50

The images of Nos. 1360/1362 are surrounded by three equidistant rows of punched holes, the centre row is triangular, the second row circular and the third row is of smaller circles.

444 Ammonite   **445** Map of Europe as
                    Manuscript (emblem of
                    Rinascimento Virtuale)

(Des H. Preute. Eng W. Seidel. Recess and photo State Ptg Wks, Vienna)

2004 (22 Nov). Fossils. T **444** and similar square designs. Multicoloured. P 14.
1363		1f.20 Type **444**	3·50	3·25
1364		1f.30 Sea Urchin	3·75	3·50
1365		2f.20 Shark's tooth	7·25	6·75
1363/1365	Set of 3		13·00	12·00

(Eng W. Seidel. Recess and photo)

2004 (22 Nov). Rinascimento Virtuale (Europe-wide co-operation in digital palimpset (old manuscripts) research). P 14.
1366	**445**	2f.50 multicoloured	7·75	7·25

(Des and eng W. Seidel. Recess and Photo State Ptg Wks, Vienna)

2005 (7 Mar). Saints (3rd issue). Vert designs as T **432**. Multicoloured. P 13½.
1367		85r. St Eustachius	2·50	2·40
1368		85r. St Dionysius	2·50	2·40
1369		1f.80 St Barbara	5·00	4·75
1370		1f.80 St Katharina	5·00	4·75
1367/1370	Set of 4		13·50	13·00

446 Female Customer, Waiters   **447** *Venus in Front of the*
and Chef   *Mirror* (Peter Paul Rubens)

(Des O. Weiss. Photo State Ptg Wks, Vienna)

2005 (7 Mar). Europa. Gastronomy. P 13½.
1371	**446**	1f.30 multicoloured	4·50	4·25

(Des and eng W. Seidel. Recess and photo State Ptg Wks, Vienna)

2005 (7 Mar). Liechtenstein Museum, Garden Palace, Vienna. P 14.
1372	**447**	2f.20 multicoloured	7·25	6·75

A stamp of the same design was issued by Austria.

448 Triesenberg   **449** *Flower Vase*
                  in a Window Niche
                  (Ambrosius Bosschaert)

(Des S. Bockmühl. Photo State Ptg Wks, Vienna)

2005 (7 Mar). Tourism. P 13½.
1373 **448** 3f.60 multicoloured .... 11·50 10·50

(Photo State Ptg Wks, Vienna)

2005 (18 May). Paintings. T **449** and similar vert designs. Multicoloured. P 14.
1374 85r. Type **449** .... 3·25 3·00
1375 85r. *Magnolias* (Chen Hongshou) .... 3·25 3·00

Stamps of a similar design were issued by People's Republic of China.

450 Rossle, Schaan   **451** Herman Sieger (founder)

(Des S. Scherrer. Eng W. Seidel Recess and photo State Ptg Wks, Vienna)

2005 (6 June). Inn Signs. T **450** and similar vert designs. Multicoloured. P 14.
1376 1f. Type **450** .... 3·00 2·75
1377 1f.40 Edelweiss, Triesenberg .... 4·00 3·75
1378 2f.50 Lowen, Bendern .... 7·25 6·75
1376/1378 Set of 3 .... 13·00 12·00

(Des Cornelia Eberle. Photo State Ptg Wks, Vienna)

2005 (6 June). 75th Anniversary of Postal Museum. T **451** and similar horiz designs. Multicoloured. P 13½×14.
1379 1f.10 Type **451** .... 3·25 3·00
1380 1f.30 Stamps .... 3·75 3·50
1381 1f.80 Postcard sent by Zeppelin mail .... 5·50 5·00
1379/1381 Set of 3 .... 11·50 10·50

452 Bargalla   **453** Oberbendern

(Des J. Schadler. Photo State Ptg Wks, Vienna)

2005 (5 Sept). Alpine Pastures. T **452** and similar horiz designs. Multicoloured. P 13½×14.
1382 85r. Type **452** .... 2·50 2·30
1383 1f. Pradamee .... 2·75 2·75
1384 1f.30 Gritsch .... 3·75 3·50
1385 1f.80 Valuna .... 5·00 4·75
1382/1385 Set of 4 .... 12·50 12·00

See also Nos. 1410/1412, 1448/1450 and 1470/1471.

(Des G. Malin. Photo State Ptg Wks, Vienna)

2005 (5 Sept). Preservation of Historical Environment (6th series). T **453** and similar vert design. Multicoloured. P 13½×14.
1386 85r. Type **453** .... 2·50 2·30
1387 2f.50 Schwurplatz .... 6·00 5·75

454 *Plecotus auritus*   **455** Virgin and Child

(Des L. Jäger. Photo State Ptg Wks, Vienna)

2005 (5 Sept). Bats. T **454** and similar square design. Multicoloured. P 14½.
1388 1f.80 Type **454** .... 5·50 5·00
1389 2f. *Myotis myotis* .... 6·00 5·50

(Photo State Ptg Wks, Vienna)

2005 (21 Nov). Christmas. Wood Carvings by Toni Gstohl. T **455** and similar vert designs. Multicoloured. P 14½×13½.
1390 85r. Type **455** .... 2·75 2·50
1391 1f. Holy family .... 3·25 3·00
1392 1f.30 Three Kings .... 4·25 4·00
1390/1392 Set of 3 .... 9·25 8·50

456 Skier and Angel   **457** Peat Cutters

(Des Corina Marxer. Photo State Ptg Wks, Vienna)

2005 (21 Nov). Winter Olympic Games, Turin. T **456** and similar square designs. Multicoloured. P 14½.
1393 1f.20 Type **456** .... 3·50 3·25
1394 1f.30 Cross country skier and Wild Boar .... 3·75 3·50
1395 1f.40 Slalom skier .... 4·25 4·00
1393/1395 Set of 3 .... 10·50 9·75

(Photo State Ptg Wks, Vienna)

2006 (6 Mar). Eugen Wilhelm Schüepp (artist) Commemoration. T **457** and similar horiz design showing paintings. Multicoloured. P 14×14½.
1396 1f. Type **457** .... 3·75 3·50
1397 1f.80 *Neugut, Schaan* .... 6·75 6·25

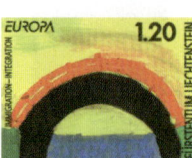 

458 Bridge (Nadja Beck)   **459** *Lost in her Dreams* (Friedrich von Amerling)

(Photo State Ptg Wks, Vienna)

2006 (6 Mar). Europa. Integration. Winning Entries in Children's Painting Competition. T **458** and similar horiz design. Multicoloured. P 14×14½.
1398 1f.20 Type **458** .... 4·25 4·00
1399 1f.30 Face (Elisabeth Müssner) .... 4·50 4·25

(Des and eng W. Seidel. Recess and photo)

2006 (6 Mar). Liechtenstein Museum, Garden Palace, Vienna. P 14.
1400 **459** 2f.20 multicoloured .... 8·50 7·75

A stamp of the same design was issued by Austria.

460 Prince Johann I   **461** Woman holding Base Clef (culture)

(Des G. Malin. Eng W. Seidel. Recess and photo State Ptg Wks, Vienna)

2006 (6 June). Bicentenary of Sovereignty. T **460** and similar vert designs. Multicoloured. P 14.
1401 85r. Type **460** .... 3·00 2·75
1402 1f. National Colours .... 3·75 3·50
1403 1f.20 Ruling House Colours .... 4·50 4·25
1404 1f.80 State Arms .... 6·25 5·75
1401/1404 Set of 4 .... 16·00 14·50

(Des Karin Negele. Photo State Ptg Wks, Vienna)

2006 (6 June). Tourism. T **461** and similar vert designs. Multicoloured. P 14.
1405	85r. Type **461**		3·00	2·75
1406	1f. Hiker (summer)		3·75	3·50
1407	1f.20 Diner (hospitality)		4·50	4·25
1408	1f.80 Skier (winter)		6·25	5·75
1405/1408 Set of 4			16·00	14·50

462 Players on Field

(Des Sabine Bockmühl. Photo State Ptg Wks, Vienna)

2006 (6 June). World Cup Football Championship, Germany. P 14.
1409	**462**	3f.30 multicoloured	11·00	10·00

(Des J. Schadler. Photo State Ptg Wks, Vienna)

2006 (4 Sept). Alpine Pastures. Horiz designs as T **452**. Multicoloured. P 13½×14.
1410	85r. Lawena		3·00	2·75
1411	1f.30 Gapfahl		3·75	3·50
1412	2f.40 Gafadura		6·75	6·25
1410/1412 Set of 3			12·00	11·50

463 The Magic Flute
(Wolfgang Amadeus Mozart)

(Des O. Weiss. Photo State Ptg Wks, Vienna)

2006 (4 Sept). Composers and Works. T **463** and similar horiz designs. Multicoloured. P 14×13½.
1413	1f. Type **463**		3·50	3·25
	a. Sheetlet of 8. Nos. 1413/1420		29·00	
1414	1f. *Radetzky March* (Johann Strauss Sr)		3·50	3·25
1415	1f. *Rhapsody in Blue* (George Gershwin)		3·50	3·25
1416	1f. *Water Music* (George Frideric Handel)		3·50	3·25
1417	1f. *Pastoral Symphony* (Ludwig van Beethoven)		3·50	3·25
1418	1f. *Waltz of the Flowers* (Pytor Ilyich Tchaikovsky)		3·50	3·25
1419	1f. *The Swan* (Camille Saint-Saëns)		3·50	3·25
1420	1f. *Midsummer Night's Dream* (Felix Mendelssohn)		3·50	3·25
1413/1420 Set of 8			25·00	23·00

Nos. 1413/1420 were issued in *se-tenant* sheets of eight stamps with enlarged inscribed margins.

464 Mozart   **465** The Annunciation

(Des Martha Griebler. Photo State Ptg Wks, Vienna)

2006 (4 Sept). 250th Birth Anniversary of Wolfgang Amadeus Mozart. P 14×13½.
1421	**464**	1f.20 multicoloured	4·50	4·25

(Des Marianne Siegl. Eng Wolfgang Siegl. Recess and photo State Ptg Wks, Vienna)

2006 (20 Sept). Christmas. Paintings from Chapel of St Mary, Dux. T **465** and similar vert designs. Multicoloured. P 13½×14.
1422	85r. Type **465**		3·00	2·75
1423	1f. The Nativity		3·75	3·50
1424	1f.30 Presentation of Jesus		4·50	4·25
1422/1424 Set of 3			10·00	9·50

466 Curta Calculator   **467** Governor's Residence and Liechtenstein Institute

(Des Hans Peter Gassner. Photo State Ptg Wks, Vienna)

2006 (20 Nov). Technical Innovations. T **466** and similar square designs. Multicoloured. P 14.
1425	1f.30 Type **466**		5·00	4·50
1426	1f.40 Carrana narrow film camera		5·25	4·75
1427	2f.40 PVA sliding calliper		7·75	7·25
1425/1427 Set of 3			16·00	15·00

See also Nos. 1451/1453 and 1495/1497.

(Des Georg Malin. Photo State Ptg Wks, Vienna)

2006 (20 Nov). Preservation of Historical Environment (7th series). T **467** and similar multicoloured design. P 13½×14.
1428	1f.80 Type **467**		5·00	4·75
1429	3f.50 Bühl, Gamprin		10·00	9·50

468 Violinist (Allegro)   **469** Trail Sign (This Way)

(Des Oskar Weiss. Photo State Ptg Wks, Vienna)

2007 (5 Mar). Music. Tempo and Temperament. T **468** and similar horiz designs. Multicoloured. P 14×13½.
1430	85r. Type **468**		3·00	2·75
1431	1f.80 Gramophone and flying music sheets (Capriccio)		5·50	5·00
1432	2f. Brass players (Crescendo)		6·25	5·75
1433	3f.50 Pianist and flaming piano (Con fuoco)		11·00	10·50
1430/1433 Set of 4			23·00	22·00

(Des Ewald Frick. Photo State Ptg Wks, Vienna)

2007 (5 Mar). Europa. Centenary of Scouting. P 14×13½.
1434	**469**	1f.30 multicoloured	4·25	4·00

470 Portrait of a Lady (Bernardino Zaganelli da Cottignola)   **472** Castle and Vaduz

471 Letter Post

(Des Wolfgang Seidel. Recess and photo)

2007 (5 Mar). Liechtenstein Museum, Garden Palace, Vienna. P 14.
1435	**470**	2f.40 multicoloured	7·75	7·25

A stamp of a similar design was issued by Austria.

(Des Marianne Siegel. Photo State Ptg Wks, Vienna)

2007 (4 June). Greetings Cards. T **471** and similar horiz designs. Multicoloured. Elongated perf 7.
1436		85r. Type **471**	3·00	2·75
1437		1f. Boys carrying bier containing envelope (courier post)	3·50	3·25
1438		1f.30 Swallow holding envelope (airmail)	4·50	4·25
1436/1438 *Set of 3*			10·00	9·25

The images of Nos. 1436/1438 are surrounded by three equidistant rows of punched holes, the centre row is triangular, the second row circular and the third row is of smaller circles.

(Des and eng Wolfgang Siegl. Recess and litho State Ptg Wks, Vienna)

2007 (4 June). Tourism. The Rhine. T **472** and similar horiz designs showing paintings by Johann Ludwig Bleuler. Multicoloured. P 13½×14½.
1439		1f. Type **472**	3·25	3·00
1440		1f.30 Ratikon Mountains	4·25	4·00
1441		2f.40 Confluence of Ill and Rhine	7·00	6·50
1439/1441 *Set of 3*			13·00	12·00

473 Nendeln

(Des Sabine Bockmühl. Photo State Ptg Wks, Vienna)

2007 (4 June). Tourism. Liechtenstein from the Air. T **473** and similar horiz designs showing paintings by Johann Ludwig Bleuler. Multicoloured. P 13½×14½.
1442		1f.10 Type **473**	3·50	3·25
1443		1f.80 Malbun	5·50	5·00
1444		2f.60 Arable land	7·75	7·25
1442/1444 *Set of 3*			15·00	14·00

474 *Trichodes apiarius* (Bee Beetle)

(Des Ingrid Berney. Litho and varnish State Ptg Wks, Vienna)

2007 (3 Sept). Insects. T **474** and similar horiz designs. Multicoloured. P 14.
1445		85r. Type **474**	3·00	2·75
1446		1f. *Cetonia aurata* (Rose Chafer)	3·75	3·50
1447		1f.30 *Dytiscus marginalis* (Great Diving Beetle)	5·00	4·50
1445/1447 *Set of 3*			10·50	9·75

The insects shown in Nos. 1445/1447 have a high gloss finish.

(Des Josef Schädler. Photo State Ptg Wks, Vienna)

2007 (3 Sept). Alpine Pastures. Horiz designs as T **452**. Multicoloured. P 13½×14½.
1448		1f. Hintervalorsch	3·25	3·00
1449		1f.40 Sucka	4·25	4·00
1450		2f.20 Guschfiel	6·75	6·25
1448/1450 *Set of 3*			13·00	12·00

(Des Hans Peter Gassner. Photo State Ptg Wks, Vienna)

2007 (3 Sept). Technical Innovations. Square designs as T **466**. Multicoloured. P 14.
1451		1f.30 Hilti hammer and drill	4·25	4·00
1452		1f.80 Kaiser walking excavator	5·50	5·00
1453		2f.40 aluFer heating surface	7·00	6·50
1451/1453 *Set of 3*			15·00	14·00

475 Liechtenstein from the Air

(Litho State Ptg Wks, Vienna)

2007 (1 Oct). SEPAC (small European mail services). P 14.
1454	**475**	1f.30 multicoloured	5·00	4·50

476 St Mary Chapel, Gamprin-Oberbühl

477 Rainbow over Three Sisters Massif

(Des Hermi Geissmann. Photo State Ptg Wks, Vienna)

2007 (19 Nov). Christmas. T **476** and similar horiz designs. Multicoloured. P 13½×14½.
1455		85r. Type **476**	3·00	2·75
1456		1f. Büel Chapel, Eschen	3·75	3·50
1457		1f.30 St Wolfgang Chapel, Triesen	5·00	4·50
1455/1457 *Set of 3*			10·50	9·75

(Litho State Ptg Wks, Vienna)

2007 (19 Nov). Natural Phenomena. T **477** and similar square designs. Multicoloured. P 14½.
1458		85r. Type **477**	3·00	2·75
1459		1f. Lightning over Bendern	3·75	3·50
1460		1f.80 Halo over Malbun	6·75	6·25
1458/1460 *Set of 3*			12·00	11·50

478 Landtagsgebäude (designed by Hansjörg Göritz)

479 St Martin's Church

(Des Hans Peter Gassner. Photo State Ptg Wks, Vienna)

2007 (19 Nov). Architecture. New Parliament Building, Vaduz. P 14.
1461	**478**	1f.30 multicoloured	5·00	4·50

(Des Georg Malin. Photo State Ptg Wks, Vienna)

2007 (19 Nov). Preservation of Historical Environment (8th series). T **479** and similar multicoloured design. P 13½×14 (vert) or 14×13½ (horiz).
1462		2f. Type **479**	6·75	6·25
1463		2f.70 Eschen Mill, St Martinsring (*horiz*)	9·00	8·50

480 Industrial Buildings, Spoerry-Areal, Vaduz (industry)

481 Firefighters

(Des Hans Peter Gassner. Litho Austrian State Ptg Wks, Vienna)

2008 (3 Mar). National Identity. Liechtenstein as Brand (1st series). T **480** and similar horiz designs. Multicoloured. P 14.
1464		85r. Type **480**	3·00	2·75
1465		1f. St Mamertus Chapel, Triesen (homeland)	3·75	3·50
1466		1f.30 Vaduz Castle (monarchy)	5·00	4·50
1464/1466 *Set of 3*			10·50	9·75

See also Nos. 1527/1529 and 1570/1572.

(Des Evelyne Bermann. Litho Austrian State Ptg Wks, Vienna)

2008 (3 Mar). Volunteer Civil Protection (1st issue). Volunteer Fire Service. P 14.
1467	**481**	1f. multicoloured	3·75	3·50

See also Nos. 1502, 1539/1540 and 1637/1638.

2008 LIECHTENSTEIN

482 *Princess Marie Franziska von Liechtenstein* (Friedrich von Amerling) **483** *Script*

(Des Wolfgang Seidel. Recess and photo Austrian State Ptg Wks, Vienna)

2008 (3 Mar). Liechtenstein Museum, Garden Palace, Vienna P 14.
| 1468 | **482** | 2f.40 multicoloured | 8·50 | 7·75 |

A stamp of a similar design was issued by Austria.

(Des Cornelia Eberle. Litho Austrian State Ptg Wks, Vienna)

2008 (3 Mar). Europa. The Letter. P 14.
| 1469 | **483** | 1f.30 multicoloured | 5·00 | 4·50 |

(Des Josef Schädler. Photo Austrian State Ptg Wks, Vienna)

2008 (3 Mar). Alpine Pastures. Horiz designs as T **452**. Multicoloured. P 13½×14½.
| 1470 | 2f.60 Schaan, Guschg | 7·75 | 7·25 |
| 1471 | 3f. Balzers, Güschgle | 9·00 | 8·50 |

484 *Huanhuan and Jingjing (martial arts)* **485** *Osmia brevicornis*

(Des Xiao Hong. Litho Austrian State Ptg Wks, Vienna)

2008 (2 June). Olympic Games, Beijing. T **484** and similar vert design showing games' mascots. Multicoloured. P 14½×13½.
| 1472 | 85c. Type **484** | 2·50 | 2·40 |
| 1473 | 1f. Huanhuan and Yingying (football and table tennis) | 3·25 | 3·00 |

(Des Silvia Ruppen. Litho Austrian State Ptg Wks, Vienna)

2008 (2 June). Endangered Insects. T **485** and similar square designs. Multicoloured. P 14½.
1474	85c. Type **485**	2·75	2·50
1475	1f. *Epeoloides coecutiens*	3·25	3·00
1476	1f.30 *Odynerus spinipes*	4·25	3·75
1474/1476	Set of 3	9·25	8·25

486 *Marathon* **487** *St Stephen's Cathedral (Austria)*

(Des Johannes Joos. Litho Austrian State Ptg Wks, Vienna)

2008 (2 June). Paralympics, Beijing. T **486** and similar horiz design showing stylised athletes. Multicoloured. P 13½×14½.
| 1477 | 1f.30 Type **486** | 4·25 | 4·00 |
| 1478 | 1f.80 Table tennis | 6·75 | 6·25 |

(Des Corina Marxer. Litho Austrian State Ptg Wks, Vienna)

2008 (2 June). EURO 2008 Football Championships. T **487** and similar horiz designs. Multicoloured. P 14.
1479	1f.30 Type **487**	4·25	4·00
1480	1f.30 Flag, dancer and musician (Liechtenstein)	4·25	4·00
1481	1f.30 Alphorn and Matterhorn (Switzerland)	4·25	4·00
1479/1481	Set of 3	11·50	11·00

488 *Mother and Queen of the Precious Blood* **489** *Schoolmaster Lämpel*

(Des Karin Beck and Heinz Schadler. Litho Austrian State Ptg Wks, Vienna)

2008 (2 June). 150th Anniversary of Schellenberg Convent. P 14.
| 1482 | **488** | 2f.20 multicoloured | 6·75 | 6·25 |

(Des Leone Ming and Christine Böhmwalder. Litho Austrian State Ptg Wks, Vienna)

2008 (1 Sept). Death Centenary of Heinrich Christian William Busch (writer and cartoonist). T **489** and similar horiz designs. Multicoloured. P 14.
1483	1f.30 Type **489**	4·25	4·00
	a. Sheetlet of 8. Nos. 1483/1490	35·00	
1484	1f.30 *Hans Huckebein*	4·25	4·00
1485	1f.30 *Max and Moritz*	4·25	4·00
1486	1f.30 *Widow Bolte*	4·25	4·00
1487	1f.30 *Pious Helen*	4·25	4·00
1488	1f.30 *Fips the Monkey*	4·25	4·00
1489	1f.30 *Tailor Bock*	4·25	4·00
1490	1f.30 *Balduin Bählamm*	4·25	4·00
1483/1490	Set of 8	31·00	29·00

Nos. 1483/1490 were issued in *se-tenant* sheetlets of eight stamps.

490 *Karl I of Liechtenstein* **491** *Candle Wreath*

(Des Adolf Tuma. Eng Wolfgang Seidel. Recess and photo Austrian State Ptg Wks, Vienna)

2008 (1 Sept). 400th Anniversary of Princes of Liechtenstein. Sheet 58×77 mm. P 14.
| MS1491 | **490** | 5f. multicoloured | 16·00 | 15·00 |
| | a. Imperf | £750 | £750 |

The stamp and margin of No. **MS**1491 form a composite design of painting.

(Des Stefan Erne. Litho Enschedé)

2008 (17 Nov). Christmas. T **491** and similar multicoloured designs. P 14½.
1492	85r. Type **491**	3·00	2·75
1493	1f. Children carrying Holly (*horiz*)	3·75	3·50
1494	1f.30 Decorated tree	5·00	4·50
1492/1494	Set of 3	10·50	9·75

(Des Hans Peter Gassner. Photo Austrian State Ptg Wks, Vienna)

2008 (17 Nov). Technical Innovations. Square designs as T **466**. Multicoloured. P 14.
1495	1f.20 Neutrik XLR cable connector NC3MX	4·50	4·25
1496	1f.40 Ivoclar Vivadent blue phase polymerisation unit	5·00	4·75
1497	2f.20 ThyssenKrupp Presta DeltaValve control	7·75	7·25
1495/1497	Set of 3	16·00	14·50

492 Schädler Ceramics Building, Nendeln

493 Postworker accepting Parcel

(Des Georg Malin. Photo Austrian State Ptg Wks, Vienna)
2008 (17 Nov). Preservation of Historical Environment (9th series). P 14.
1498　**492**　3f.80 multicoloured........................... 13·50　12·50

(Des Cornelia Eberle. Litho Austrian State Ptg Wks, Vienna)
2009 (2 Mar). Postal Service. T **493** and similar vert designs. Multicoloured. P 14.
1499　　85c. Type **493**.................................... 3·00　2·75
1500　　1f. Delivering..................................... 3·75　3·50
1501　　1f.30 Sorting..................................... 4·50　4·25
1499/1501 Set of 3... 10·00　9·50

494 First Aid

495 Unfolding (woman and Butterfly)

(Des Evelyne Bermann. Litho Austrian State Ptg Wks, Vienna)
2009 (2 Mar). Volunteer Civil protection (2nd series). Association of Liechtenstein Samaritan Volunteers. P 14.
1502　**494**　1f. multicoloured............................ 3·75　3·50

(Litho Enschedé)
2009 (2 Mar). The Printer's Art (1st series). Linocuts by Stephan Sude. T **495** and similar vert designs. P 14.
1503　　1f. black and rose-pink...................... 3·75　3·50
1504　　1f.30 black and grey-olive................... 5·00　4·50
1505　　2f.70 black and pale blue.................... 9·75　9·00
1503/1505 Set of 3... 17·00　15·00
Designs: 1f. T **495**; 1f.30 Awareness (man crying); 2f.70 Fulfilment (elderly man and mountains).
See also Nos. 1627/1628 and 1693/1694.

496 Super Nova (Leta Krahenbuhl)

497 Land Register

(Litho and holography. Austrian State Ptg Wks, Vienna)
2009 (2 Mar). Europa. Astronomy. P 14½.
1506　**496**　1f.30 multicoloured.......................... 5·00　4·50

(Des Heinz Schädler. Litho Enschedé)
2009 (2 Mar). Bicentenary of Land Register. P 14.
1507　**497**　3f.30 multicoloured.......................... 12·00　11·00

498 Ants and Forest

499 Summit Cross, Kuegrat

(Des Ewald Frick. Litho Austrian State Ptg Wks, Vienna)
2009 (8 June). Forest. T **498** and similar vert designs. Multicoloured. P 14.
1508　　85c. Type **498**.................................... 3·00　2·75
1509　　1f. Path through woods.................... 3·75　3·50
1510　　1f.40 Tree and rock............................. 5·00　4·75
1511　　1f.60 Mountain, lake and log pile...... 6·00　5·50
1508/1511 Set of 4... 16·00　15·00

(Des Marco Nescher. Litho Enschedé)
2009 (8 June). Centenary of Alpine Association. T **499** and similar multicoloured designs showing summit crosses. P 14.
1512　　1f. Type **499**...................................... 3·75　3·50
1513　　1f.30 Langspitz (vert)............................ 5·00　4·50
1514　　2f.20 Rappastein (vert).......................... 7·75　7·25
1515　　2f.40 Jahn-Turm und Wolan................. 8·50　7·75
1512/1515 Set of 4... 23·00　21·00

500 Vaduz Castle in Spring　　**501** *Pieris rapae*

(Des Jaques Sonderer. Photo Austrian State Ptg Wks, Vienna)
2009 (8 June). Vaduz Castle through the Seasons. T **500** and similar horiz design. Multicoloured. P 14.
1516　　1f.30 Type **500**................................... 5·00　4·50
1517　　1f.80 In summer.................................. 6·75　6·25
See also Nos. 1562/1563.

(Des Stefan Erne. Litho Gutenberg AG)
2009 (7 Sept). Butterflies. T **501** and similar horiz designs. Multicoloured. P 12½.
1518　　85c. Type **501**.................................... 3·00　2·75
1519　　1f. *Parnassius apollo*......................... 3·75　3·50
1520　　1f.30 *Melanargia galathea*.................. 5·00　4·50
1521　　2f. *Vanessa atlanta*............................. 7·00　6·50
1518/1521 Set of 4... 17·00　16·00

502 Emblem

503 Badminton Cabinet (detail)

(Des Sabine Bockmühl. Litho Enschedé)
2009 (7 Sept). 75th Anniversary of Liechtenstein Philatelic Society. P 13.
1522　**502**　1f.30 multicoloured.......................... 5·00　4·50
No. 1522 is pierced around the central design.

(Des Adolf Tuma. Eng Wolfgang Seidel. Recess and photo Austrian State Ptg Wks, Vienna)
2009 (7 Sept). Liechtenstein Museum, Garden Palace, Vienna. T **503** and similar multicoloured designs showing details of Badminton Cabinet. P 14.
1523　　1f.30 Type **503**................................... 5·00　4·50
1524　　2f. Three birds and bouquet (detail centre) (34×49 mm)......................... 7·00　6·50
1525　　4f. Red-capped bird and Lilies (detail left).... 14·00　13·00
1523/1525 Set of 3... 23·00　22·00

504 Chapel of St Mamerta, Trisien

(Litho Austrian State Ptg Wks, Vienna)
2009 (16 Sept). SEPAC (small European mail services). P 14.
1526 **504** 1f.30 multicoloured .... 5·00 4·50

505 Lifestyle Museum, Schellenberg

506 Annunciation

(Des Hans Peter Gassner. Litho Gutenberg AG)
2009 (16 Nov). National Identity. Liechtenstein as Brand (2nd series). T **505** and similar square designs. Multicoloured. P 12½.
1527	20r. Type **505** (community)	90	85
1528	50r. Former Customs House, Vaduz (finance)	1·80	1·70
1529	60r. Parish House, Bendern (dialogue)	2·20	2·10
1527/1529	Set of 3	4·50	4·25

(Des Stephanie Keiser. Litho Enschedé)
2009 (16 Nov). Christmas. Advent Windows created by Pupils of Primary School, Gamprin. T **506** and similar vert designs. Multicoloured. P 13½×14.
1530	85r. Type **506**	3·00	2·75
1531	1f. Journey to Bethlehem	3·75	3·50
1532	1f.30 The Nativity	5·00	4·50
1533	1f.80 The Three Magi	6·75	6·25
1530/1533	Set of 4	17·00	15·00

507 University of Applied Sciences (Karl+Probst), Vaduz

508 Alpine Skier

(Des Bruno Kopfli. Litho Austrian State Ptg Wks, Vienna)
2009 (16 Nov). Modern Architecture (1st issue). T **507** and similar horiz designs. Multicoloured. P 14.
1534	85r. Type **505**	3·00	2·75
1535	2f.60 Art Museum (Morger, Degelo and Kerez), Vaduz	9·75	9·00
1536	3f.50 Ruggell–Nofels Border Crossing between Liechtenstein and Austria (EFFEFF)	13·50	12·50
1534/1536	Set of 3	24·00	22·00
See also Nos. 1545/1546.

(Des Mark Heine. Litho Enschedé)
2010 (2 Feb). Winter Olympic Games, Vancouver. T **508** and similar multicoloured design. P 14.
| 1537 | 1f. Type **508** | 3·75 | 3·50 |
| 1538 | 1f.80 Nordic skier | 6·75 | 6·25 |

509 Mountain Rescue (Liechtenstein Mountain Rescue (founded by Liechtenstein Alpine Association))

510 Hillside Farming

(Des Evelyne Bermann. Litho Austrian State Ptg Wks, Vienna)
2010 (1 Mar). Volunteer Civil Protection (3rd series). Volunteer Rescue Services. T **508** and similar horiz design. Multicoloured. P 14.
| 1539 | 85r. Type **509** | 3·00 | 2·75 |
| 1540 | 1f.30 Water rescue (founded by Bubbles diving club) | 5·00 | 4·50 |

(Des Silvia Ruppen. Litho Enschedé)
2010 (1 Mar). Agriculture. T **510** and similar vert designs. Multicoloured. P 14×13½.
1541	85r. Type **510**	3·00	2·75
1542	1f. Agriculture and the environment	3·75	3·50
1543	1f.10 Technology in farming	4·25	4·00
1544	1f.30 Farm animals	5·00	4·50
1541/1544	Set of 4	14·50	13·50

511 Natural Gas Filling Station (EFFEFF), Vaduz

(Des Bruno Köpfli. Litho Austrian State Ptg Wks, Vienna)
2010 (1 Mar). Modern Architecture (2nd issue). T **511** and similar horiz designs. Multicoloured. P 13½×14.
| 1545 | 2f.60 Type **511** | 9·75 | 9·00 |
| 1546 | 3f.60 Liechtenstein Electric Power Authority Transformer Station (Marcel Ferrier) | 13·50 | 12·50 |

512 Vaduz

513 Ariadne giving Theseus the Thread

(Des Leone Ming. Recess and photo Austrian State Ptg Wks, Vienna)
2010 (1 May). Expo 2010, Shanghai. Sheet 102×136 mm containing T **512** and similar multicoloured design. P 14.
| MS1547 | 1f.60 Type **512**; 1f.90 Tidal bore on Qiantang river (32×60 mm) | 13·50 | 12·50 |
| | a. Imperf | 13·50 | 12·50 |

(Des Adolf Tuma. Eng Wolfgang Seidel. Recess and photo Austrian State Ptg Wks, Vienna)
2010 (7 June). Liechtenstein Museum, Garden Palace, Vienna. T **513** and similar multicoloured designs showing ceiling frescoes by Johann Michael Rottmayr. P 14.
| 1548 | 1f. Type **513** | 3·75 | 3·50 |
| 1549 | 1f.40 Surrender of Golden Fleece to Jason | 5·00 | 4·75 |

514 Figures supporting Roof

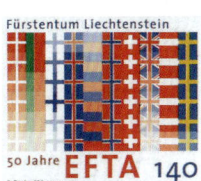
515 Flags of Members

516 Finger Print

(Des Vanessa Rupf (1f.), Sabine Bockmühl (1f.40) or René Wolfinger (1f.90). Litho Enschedé or Gutenberg AG)
2011 (7 June). 50th Anniversaries. P 14×13½ (1f.), 12×12½ (1f.40) or 12½ (1f.90).
| 1550 | **514** | 1f. olive-bistre and black (Disability Insurance) | 3·75 | 3·50 |

LIECHTENSTEIN 2010

1551	515	1f.40 multicoloured (EFTA)	5·00	4·75
1552	516	1f.90 pale yellow-olive and slate grey (Interpol in Vaduz)	6·75	6·25
1550/1552		Set of 3	14·00	13·00

517 *Coenonympha oedippus* (False Ringlet)

(Des Stefan Erne. Litho Gutenberg AG)

2010 (7 June). Butterflies. T **517** and similar horiz designs. Multicoloured. Self-adhesive. Die-cut perf 12×12½.

1553	1f.40 Type **517**	5·00	4·75
1554	1f.60 *Gonepteryx rhamni* (Brimstone)	6·00	5·50
1555	2f.60 *Papilio machaon* (Old World Swallowtail)	9·75	9·00
1553/1555	Set of 3	19·00	17·00

518 Roadway and Eschnerberg

(Des Josef Heeb. Litho Enschedé)

2010 (6 Sept). Liechtenstein Panorama. Valley Landscape. T **518** and similar horiz design. P 14½×14.

1556	1f. Type **518**	3·75	3·50
	a. Pair. Nos. 1556/1557	7·75	7·25
1557	1f. Field and Alvier mountains	3·75	3·50

Nos. 1556/1557 were printed, *se-tenant*, in horizontal pairs within sheets of ten stamps with enlarged illustrated upper margin, each pair forming a composite design.

519 Hydropower

520 Children and Symbols of Magic and Fantasy

(Des Vito Noto. Litho and photo)

2010 (6 Sept). Renewable Energy. T **519** and similar horiz designs. Multicoloured. P 13×14.

1558	1f. Type **519**	3·75	3·50
1559	1f.40 Wood	5·00	4·75
1560	2f.80 Near-surface geothermal power	10·50	9·75
1558/1560	Set of 3	17·00	16·00

Nos. 1558/1560 are treated with heat sensitive ink which when pressed reveals pictogram of the energy illustrated.

(Des Mariagrazia Orlandini. Litho Austrian State Ptg Wks, Vienna)

2010 (6 Sept). Europa. Children's Books. P 14.
| 1561 | **520** | 1f.40 multicoloured | 5·00 | 4·75 |

521 Autumn

522 Annunciation

(Des Jaques Sonderer. Litho Austrian State Ptg Wks, Vienna)

2010 (6 Sept). Vaduz Castle through the Seasons. T **521** and similar vert design. Multicoloured. P 14.

| 1562 | 1f.40 Type **521** | 5·00 | 4·75 |
| 1563 | 1f.90 Winter | 6·75 | 6·25 |

(Des C. Eberle)

2010 (15 Nov). Christmas. Maria Hilf Ceiling Frescos. T **522** and similar horiz designs. Multicoloured. P 14.

1564	85r. Type **522**	3·00	2·75
1565	1f. Visitation of the Blessed Virgin Mary	3·75	3·50
1566	1f.40 Candlemas	5·00	4·75
1564/1566	Set of 3	10·50	10·00

523 *Normale e anormale* (Alighiero Boetti)

524 Schaan-Vaduz Rail Station (industry)

2010 (15 Nov). Liechtenstein Museum of Art. Arte Povera. T **523** and similar horiz designs. Multicoloured. P 14.

1567	100r. Type **523**	3·75	3·50
1568	220r. *Testa* (sculpture) (Marisa Merz)	7·75	7·25
1569	360r. Untitled (sculpture) (Jannis Kounellis)	13·50	12·50
1567/1569	Set of 3	237·00	21·00

(Des Hans Peter Gassner)

2010 (15 Nov). Buildings. Liechtenstein as Brand (3rd series). T **524** and similar square designs. Multicoloured. P 12½.

1570	1f.10 Type **524**	3·00	2·75
1571	1f.30 Red House, Vaduz (homeland)	3·75	3·50
1572	1f.80 Parish church, Triesenberg (community)	5·00	4·75
1570/1572	Set of 3	10·50	10·00

525 Athletics, Volleyball and Cycling

526 Quick Response Code

(Des René Michlig. Litho Austrian State Ptg Wks, Vienna)

2011 (14 Mar). Small European States' Games 2011, Liechtenstein. T **525** and similar horiz designs. P 13½.

1573	85r. bronze and black	3·00	2·75
1574	1f. silver and black	3·75	3·50
1575	1f.40 gold and black	5·00	4·75
1573/1575	Set of 3	10·50	10·00

(Des Ewald Frick (No. 1576) and Melanie Schaper (No. 1577). Litho Gutenberg AG)

2011 (14 Mar). Anniversaries. T **526** and similar design. Self-adhesive. Die-cut perf 12½.

| 1576 | 1f. multicoloured | 3·75 | 3·50 |
| 1577 | 1f. black and gold (31×37 *mm*) | 3·75 | 3·50 |

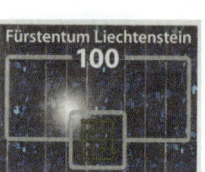

527 Photovoltaic Cells

528 Cloisonné Enamelled Egg from Moscow Workshop and Solemn Early Mass at Easter in St Isaac's Cathedral, St Petersburg (etching by Vasily Ivanovich Navozov)

(Des Vito Noto. Litho and photo Austrian State Ptg Wks, Vienna)

2011 (14 Mar). Renewable Energy. T **527** and similar horiz designs. Multicoloured. P 14.
1578	1f. Type **527**		3·75	3·50
1579	1f.10 Solar energy		4·25	4·00
1580	2f.90 Wind energy		10·50	9·75
1578/1580 Set of 3			17·00	16·00

Nos. 1578/1590 are treated with heat sensitive ink which when pressed reveals pictogram of the energy illustrated.

(Des Silvia Ruppen and Inge R. Madlé. Litho Enschedé)

2011 (14 Mar). Decorated Easter Eggs, collected by Adulf Peter Goop. T **528** and similar multicoloured designs. P 14.
1581	1f. Type **528**		3·75	3·50
1582	1f.40 Faberge egg with Apple blossom and Anichkov Palace on Nevsky Prospekt in St Petersburg (47×32 mm)		5·00	4·75
1583	2f.60 Egg with Swan motif made by Pavel Akimovich Ovchinnikov and Red Square with St Basil's Cathedral		9·75	9·00
1581/1583 Set of 3			17·00	16·00

529 Prince Nikolaus   **530** Tree as Ecosystem

(Des Adolf Tuma from portraits by Ludmila d'Oultremont. Eng Adolf Tuma. Recess, litho and gold foil die-stamped Austrian State Ptg Wks, Vienna)

2011 (6 June). Children of Hereditary Prince and Princess. T **529** and similar vert designs. Multicoloured. P 13½.
1583*a*	1f. Type **529**		3·75	3·50
1583*b*	1f.80 Prince Georg		6·75	6·25
1583*c*	2f. Princess Marie Caroline		7·00	6·50
1583*d*	2f.60 Prince Joseph Wenzel		9·75	9·00
1583*a*/1583*d* Set of 4			25·00	23·00
MS1584 82×110 mm. As Nos. 1583*a*/1583*d*			28·00	26·00

(Des Louis Jäger. Litho Gutenberg AG)

2011 (6 June). Europa. Forests. P 12½.
1585	**530**	1f.40 multicoloured	5·00	4·75

531 *Inachis* io (Peacock)   **532** *Fruit* (Shirana Shahbazi)

(Des Stefan Erne. Litho Gutenberg AG)

2011 (6 June). Butterflies. T **531** and similar horiz design. Multicoloured. Self-adhesive. Die-cut perf 12½.
1586	2f.20 Type **531**	7·75	7·25
1587	5f. *Anthocharis cardamines* (Orange Tip)	18·00	17·00

(Litho Gutenberg AG)

2011 (9 Sept). Art. P 13½×14.
1588	**532**	1f. multicoloured	3·75	3·50

A stamp of a similar design was issued by Switzerland.

533 *Falco subbuteo* (Hobby)

(Des Jacques Sonderer. Litho Gutenberg AG)

2011 (9 Sept). Engangered Bird Species. 50th Anniversary of WWF. Sheet 146×208 mm containing T **533** and similar hexagonal designs. Multicoloured. Self-adhesive. Die-cut perf 12½.
MS1589 1f.×8, Type **533**; *Glaucidium passerinum* (Pygmy Owl); *Jynx torquilla* (Wryneck); *Oriolus oriolus* (Oriole); *Luscinia megarhynchos* (Nightingale); *Phoenicurus phoenicurus* (Redstart); *Lanius collurio* (Red-backed Shrike); *Saxicola rubetra* (Whinchat)	36·00	34·00

534 Alpine Rhine

(Litho Enschedé)

2011 (9 Sept). 24 Hours in Liechtenstein. Paintings by Xiao Hui Wang. T **534** and similar horiz design. Multicoloured. P 13½×14.
1590	1f.30 Type **534**	5·25	5·00
1591	3f.70 Water Reflections, Gutenberg Castle, Balzers	14·50	13·50

535 Ruggell Marsh

(Des Marco Nescher. Litho Austrian State Ptg Wks, Vienna)

2011 (28 Sept). SEPAC (small European mail services). P 14.
1592	**535**	1f.40 multicoloured	5·50	5·00

536 Crib, Parish Church of St Gallus, Triesen

(Des Stéphanie Keiser. Litho Gutenberg AG)

2011 (14 Nov). Christmas. Cribs. T **536** and similar multicoloured designs. Self-adhesive. Die-cut perf 12½.
1593	85r. Type **536**	3·25	3·00
1594	1f. St Florin Parish Church, Vaduz (38×32 mm)	4·00	3·75
1595	1f.40 Parish Church of the Assumption Bendern (32×38 mm)	5·50	5·00
1593/1595 Set of 3		11·50	10·50

537 Gutenberg Castle, Balzers

(Des Adolf Tuma. Eng Adolf Tuma. Recess and litho Austrian State Ptg Wks, Vienna)

2011 (14 Nov). Castles in Liechtenstein. T **537** and similar horiz designs. Multicoloured. P 13½×14.
1596	1f. Type **537**	4·00	3·75
1597	1f.40 Schellenberg ruins	5·50	5·00
1598	2f. Schalun ruins	7·50	7·00
1599	2f.60 Vaduz Castle from north	10·50	9·75
1596/1599 Set of 4		25·00	23·00

LIECHTENSTEIN 2011

538 Dragons

(Des Stefan Erne. Litho Gutenberg AG)

2011 (14 Nov). Chinese New Year. Year of the Dragon. Sheet 146×208 mm. Scarlet and gold. Self-adhesive. Die-cut perf 13×12½.
MS1600 1f.90×4, Type **538**×4 .... 33·00   31·00
The design of T **538** is laser cut through the backing paper.

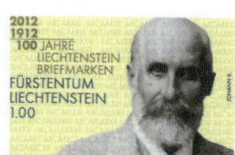

539 Franz I

(Des H P Gasner. Litho Enschedé)

2012 (1 Feb). Centenary of Liechtenstein Stamps. T **539** and similar horiz designs. Multicoloured. P 13½.
1601	1f. Type **539**	4·00	3·75
1602	1f.40 Franz I	5·50	5·00
1603	2f.20 Franz Josef II	8·25	7·75
1604	2f.80 Hans-Adam II	11·50	10·50
1601/1604	Set of 4	26·00	24·00
MS1605	142×100 mm. As Nos. 1601/1604. Imperf	29·00	27·00

540 Constitutional Charter signed by Prince Johann II

(Des Cornelia Eberle. Litho and embossed Cartor)

2012 (5 Mar). 150th Anniversary of Parliament and Constitution. T **540** and similar horiz design. Multicoloured. P 13½.
1606	1f. Type **540**	4·00	3·75
1607	1f.40 Authorisation for Governor Karl Haus von Hausen to formally open Parliament	5·50	5·00

541 Cattle returning from Alpine Pastures   **542** Dahlia

(Des Julia Kubik. Litho Enschedé)

2012 (5 Mar). Europa. Visit Liechtenstein. P 14.
1608	**541**	1f.40 multicoloured	5·50	5·00

(Des Stefan Erne. Litho Druckerei Gutenberg AG, Schaan)

2012 (14 June). Flowers. T **542** and similar vert designs. Self-adhesive. Die-cut perf 13½.
1609	85c. Type **542**	3·25	3·00
1610	1f.40 Peony	5·50	5·00
1611	5f. Zinnia	20·00	18·00
1609/1611	Set of 3	26·00	23·00

Nos. 1612/1613 and T **543** are left for Panorama issued on 14 June 2012, not yet received.

544 Swimming

(Des Marc Weymann. Litho Enschedé)

2012 (14 June). LOSV 2012 in London (Liechtenstein Olympic Sports Association). T **544** and similar horiz design. Multicoloured. P 13½.
1614	1f. Type **544**	4·00	3·75
1615	1f.40 Tennis	5·50	5·00

545 Pfälzerhütte and Buildings   **546** Planken and Schaan

(Des Corinna Rogger)

2012 (14 June). Pfälzerhütte (mountain hut and inn), Liechtenstein. P 14.
1616	**545**	1f.40 multicoloured	5·50	5·00

A stamp of a similar design was issued by Germany.

(Des Louis Jäger. Litho Enschedé)

2012 (14 June). 300th Anniversary of Purchase of Oberland by Prince Johann Adam. Sheet 100×45 mm containing T **546** and similar vert designs showing stylised flags of the six Oberland communities. Multicoloured. Imperf×P 14.
MS1617 1f. Type **546**; 1f.40 Vaduz and Triesenberg; 2f.60 Triesen and Balzers .... 20·00   18·00

547 Guschg Herdsmen's Doll (N. Schwarz)   **548** Brasier, 1908

(Litho Gutenberg AG)

2012 (16 Aug). LIBA 2012 National Stamp Exhibition. Winning Designs in Children's Drawing Competition. Sheet 100×55 mm containing T **547** and similar vert designs. Multicoloured. P 13½.
MS1618 1f. Type **547**; 1f.40 Giant of Guflina (R. Graf); 3f.60 The Three Sisters (G. Rodrigues-Margreiter) ...... 23·00   21·00

(Des Mark Heine. Litho and gold foil die-stamped Cartor)

2012 (3 Sept). Collections in Liechtenstein. Classic Cars. T **548** and similar horiz designs. Multicoloured. P 13½.
1619	85c. Type **548**	3·25	3·00
1620	1f. Stanley Steamer, 2011	4·00	3·75
1621	1f.40 Ford Model T Speedster, 1915	5·50	5·00
1622	1f.90 Hinstin, 1920	7·25	6·75
1619/1622	Set of 4	18·00	17·00

549 Till Eulenspiegel

(Des Oskar Weiss. Litho Enschedé)

2012 (3 Sept). Famous Figures from Literature. Sheet 146×208 mm containing T **549** and similar horiz designs. Multicoloured. P 14.
MS1623 1f.×8, Type **549**; Sherlock Holmes; Don Quixote; Hamlet; Robin Hood; Robinson Crusoe; Baron Münchhausen; Quasimodo .... 33·00 31·00

(Des Stefan Erne. Litho Gutenberg AG)

2012 (4 Oct). No. 1587 surch as T **550**. Self-adhesive. Die-cut perf 12½.
1624   600f. on 500f. multicoloured .... 20·00 18·00

 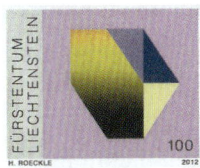

551 Christ's Descent from the Cross   **552** Geometric Shape (from Tilings)

(Des Adolf Tuma. Recess and litho Austrian State Printing House, Vienna)

2012 (12 Nov). Princely Treasures. Reliefs by Massimiliano Soldani-Benzi. T **551** and similar vert design. Multicoloured. P 14.
1625   1f. Type **551** .... 4·00 3·75
1626   1f.40 Christ on the Mount of Olives .... 5·50 5·00

(Des Hanna Roeckle. Litho Enschedé)

2012 (12 Nov). The Printer's Art (2nd series). Art Print. Screen Printing. T **552** and similar horiz design. Multicoloured. P 13½×14.
1627   1f. Type **552** .... 4·00 3·75
1628   1f.40 Geometric shape (pink) .... 5·50 5·00

553 Raphael   **554** Snake

(Des Stéphanie Keiser. Litho Gutenberg AG)

2012 (12 Nov). Christmas. Archangels. T **553** and similar horiz designs. Each gold. Self-adhesive. Die-cut perf 12×12½.
1629   85c. Type **553** .... 3·25 3·00
1630   1f. Michael .... 4·00 3·75
1631   1f.40 Gabriel .... 5·50 5·00
1632   1f.90 Uriel .... 7·25 6·75
1629/1632 Set of 4 .... 18·00 17·00

(Des Stefan Erne. Litho and gold foil die-stamped Gutenberg AG)

2012 (12 Nov). Chinese New Year. Year of the Snake. Sheet 208×148 mm. Scarlet and gold. Self-adhesive. Die-cut perf 12½.
MS1633 1f.90×4, Type **554**×4 .... 33·00 31·00
The design of T **554** is laser cut through the backing paper.

555 Fibonacci Squence

(Des Hans Peter Gassner. Litho and silver foil die-stamped Cartor)

2013 (4 Mar). Mathematics and Nature. T **555** and similar horiz designs. Multicoloured. P 13½.
1634   1f. Type **555** .... 4·00 3·75
1635   2f.60 Quotients of adjacent Fibonacci numbers .... 10·50 9·75
1636   4f. Golden Ratio .... 15·00 14·00
1634/1636 Set of 3 .... 27·00 25·00

556 Avalanche Rescue Dogs and Handlers   **557** Vehicle Wheels

(Des Evelyne Bermann. Litho Austrian State Printing House, Vienna)

2013 (4 Mar). Volunteer Civil Protection (4th series). T **556** and similar horiz design. Multicoloured. P 13½×14.
1637   1f. Type **556** .... 4·00 3·75
1638   1f.40 Civil protection .... 5·50 5·00

(Des Mirjam Büchel. Litho Cartor)

2013 (4 Mar). Europa. Postal Vehicles. Winning Entry in Design-a-Stamp Competition. P 14½.
1639   **557**   1f.40 multicoloured .... 5·50 5·00

558 Switzerland

(Des Stefan Erne. Litho Cartor)

2013 (4 Mar). 90th Anniversary of Liechtenstein–Switzerland Customs Treaty. T **558** and similar horiz design. Multicoloured. P 13½.
1640   2f. Type **558** .... 7·50 7·00
   a. Pair. Nos. 1640/1641 .... 16·00 14·50
1641   2f. Liechtenstein .... 7·50 7·00
Nos. 1640/1641 were printed, *se-tenant*, in horizontal pairs within the sheet, each pair forming a panoramic composite design.

559 Old Rhine Bridge, Vaduz–Sevelan   **560** Young Ibex

(Des Bruno Köpfli. Litho Enschedé)

2013 (3 June). Bridges between Liechtenstein and Switzerland (1st issue). T **559** and similar multicoloured designs. P 14×13½.
1642   85c. Type **559** .... 3·25 3·00
   a. Pair. Nos. 1642/1643 .... 7·50 7·00
1643   1f. Old Rhine Bridge side view (covered wooden bridge) (60×30 mm) .... 4·00 3·75
1644   1f.40 Railway bridge, Schaan-Buchs .... 5·50 5·00
   a. Pair. Nos. 1644/1645 .... 13·50 12·50
1645   1f.90 Railway bridge, side view (60×30 mm) .. 7·25 6·75
1642/1645 Set of 4 .... 18·00 17·00
Nos. 1642/1643 and 1644/1645, respectively, were printed, *se-tenant*, in horizontal pairs within the sheet.
See also Nos. 1672/1675.

(Des Erich Beck. Litho Gutenberg AG)

2013 (3 June). Young Alpine Animals. T **560** and similar horiz designs. Multicoloured. Self-adhesive. Die-cut perf 12×12½.
1646   85c. Type **560** .... 3·25 3·00
1647   1f. Chamois .... 4·00 3·75
1648   1f.40 Marmot .... 5·50 5·00
1649   1f.90 Alpine Hare .... 7·25 6·75
1646/1649 Set of 4 .... 18·00 17·00

LIECHTENSTEIN 2013

561 View of Vaduz   **562** *Gentiana rhaetica*

(Des Heinz Schädler. Recess and litho Cartor)

2013 (3 June). Painters from Liechtenstein. Hans Kliemand Commemoration. T **561** and similar horiz design showing pen and ink drawings. Buff paper. P 13.

1650	1f. black and carmine	4·00	3·75
1651	1f.90 black and blue	7·25	6·75

Designs: 1f. T **561**; 1f.90 View into Rhine Valley.

(Des Stefan Erne. Litho Gutenberg AG, Schaan)

2013 (3 June). Flora. Alpine Flowers. T **562** and similar vert designs. Self-adhesive. Die-cut perf 12½.

1652	1f. Type **562**	4·00	3·75
1653	1f.90 *Myosotis alpestris*	7·25	6·75
1654	4f. *Rhododendron hirsutum*	15·00	14·00
1652/1654	Set of 3	24·00	22·00

563 Aston Martin DB 2/4   **564** Ballerina (dance)

(Des Mark Heine. Litho and gold foil die-stamped Cartor)

2013 (2 Sept). Collections in Liechtenstein. Sports and Touring Cars. T **563** and similar horiz designs. Multicoloured. P 14½×13.

1655	85c. Type **563**	3·25	3·00
1656	1f. Ferrari 250 GT PF	4·00	3·75
1657	1f.40 Jaguar XK 140	5·50	5·00
1658	1f.90 Mercedes 300 SL	7·25	6·75
1655/1658	Set of 4	18·00	17·00

(Des Stéphanie Keise. Litho Gutenberg AG)

2013 (2 Sept). Performing Arts in Liechtenstein. T **564** and similar horiz designs. Multicoloured. Self-adhesive. Die-cut perf 12½.

1659	1f. Type **564**	4·00	3·75
1660	1f.40 Actors (theatre)	5·50	5·00
1661	2f. Dancers (musical theatre)	7·50	7·00
1662	4f. Magician (cabaret)	15·00	14·00
1659/1662	Set of 4	29·00	27·00

565 Voyage of the Argonauts   **566** Annunciation

(Litho Cartor)

2013 (2 Sept). Art. Ivan Masoyedov (Eugen Zotow) Commemoration. T **565** and similar horiz design. Multicoloured. P 14.

1663	1f.40 Type **565**	5·50	5·00
	a. Pair. Nos.1663/1664	17·00	16·00
1664	2f.60 *Silium*	10·50	9·75

Nos. 1663/1664 were printed, *se-tenant*, in horizontal and vertical pairs of stamps and two stamp-size labels in sheets of 12. Stamps of similar designs were issued by Russia.

(Des Louis Jäger. Litho and silver foil die-stamped Gutenberg AG)

2013 (10 Nov). Christmas. Themes from the Christmas Story. T **566** and similar vert designs. Self-adhesive. Die-cut perf 12½.

1665	85c. Type **566**	3·25	3·00
1666	1f. The Nativity	4·00	3·75
1667	1f.40 Angel appearing to shepherds	5·50	5·00
1668	1f.90 Three Kings	7·25	6·75
1665/1668	Set of 4	18·00	17·00

567 Silk-faced Wallcovering

(Des Hans Peter Gassner. Litho, gold foil die-stamped and embossed Cartor)

2012 (12 Nov). Princely Treasures. Silk Wallcovering from Liechtenstein Museum, Vienna. Sheet 120×85 mm containing T **567** and similar vert designs. Multicoloured. Silk-faced paper. P 14½.

MS1669 1f. Type **567**; 1f.40 Wallcovering, emblem lower; 3f.60 Wallcovering, emblem higher .... 24·00   22·00

(Des Stefan Erne. Litho and gold foil die-stamped Gutenberg AG)

2013 (13 Nov). Chinese New Year. Year of the Horse. Sheet 208×148 mm containing square designs as T **554**. Each scarlet and gold. Self-adhesive. Die-cut perf 12½.

MS1670 1f.90×4, Horse ....

The designs of No. **MS**1670 are laser cut through the backing paper. T **568** is unavailable.

569 Mountains   **570** Foot and Cycle Bridge

(Des Alexander Doll and Nathalia Brovko. Litho, thermography and silver foil die-stamped Cartor)

2013 (10 Nov). Winter Olympic Games, Sochi. P 13½.
1671   **569**   2f.60 multicoloured .... 10·50   9·75

A stone originating from Sochi was ground up, mixed with paint and applied to the stamp by thermography, which can be felt when rubbed.

(Des Bruno Köpfli. Litho Enschedé)

2014 (10 Mar). Bridges between Liechtenstein and Switzerland (2nd issue). T **570** and similar multicoloured designs. P 14×13½.

1672	85c. Type **570**	3·25	3·00
	a. Pair. Nos. 1672/1673	7·50	7·00
1673	1f. Buchs–Schaan bridge (60×30 *mm*)	4·00	3·75
1674	1f.40 Rhine bridge (roadway)	5·50	5·00
	a. Pair. Nos. 1674/1675	13·50	12·50
1675	1f.90 Bendern–Haag bridge bridge, side view (60×30 *mm*)	7·25	6·75
1672/1675	Set of 4	18·00	17·00

Nos. 1672/1673 and 1674/1675, respectively, were printed, *se-tenant*, in horizontal pairs within the sheet.

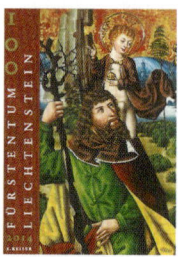 

571 St Christopher carrying Christ Child   **572** J. G. Rheinberger

(Des Stéphanie Keiser. Litho Cartor)

2014 (10 Mar). Winged Altar (Gothic triptych altar donated to National Museum). Sheet 208×118 mm containing T **571** and similar multicoloured designs. P 14 (1f. and 2f.) or 13½ (6f.).
MS1676 1f. Type **571**; 2f. St Sebastian; 6f. St Anne, Virgin and Child (84×44 mm) .... 36·00 34·00

No. **MS**1676 was issued with an integral front cover containing 'windows' to view the stamps, with the whole altar displayed when opened.

(Des Cornelia Eberle. Litho Enschedé)

2014 (10 Mar). 175th Birth Anniversary of Josef Gabriel Rheinberger (composer). P 13½.
1677   **572**   1f.40 multicoloured................................ 5·50 5·00

573 Drum   **574** Pope John Paul II

(Des Armin Hoop. Litho Gutenberg AG, Schaan)

2014 (10 Mar). Europa. Musical Instruments. P 12½.
1678   **573**   1f.40 multicoloured................................ 5·50 5·00

(Des Cornelia Eberle. Litho and gold foil die-stamped Enschedé)

2014 (28 Apr). Canonisation of Pope John Paul II. Sheet 58×77 mm. P 14½×14.
MS1679 1f.40 Type **574** multicoloured........................ 5·75 5·25

575 Denar   **576** Yellow-bellied Toad

(Des Sven Beham. Litho, embossed and foil die-stamped Cartor)

2014 (2 June). Archaeological Finds in Liechtenstein. Coins. T **575** and similar horiz designs. Multicoloured. P 13½.
1680   85r. Type **575** .... 3·25 3·00
1681   1f. Gulden .... 4·00 3·75
1682   1f.40 Pfennig .... 5·25 5·00
1680/1682 Set of 3 .... 11·50 10·50

(Des Silvia Ruppen. Litho Gutenberg AG, Schaan)

2014 (2 June). Amphibians. T **576** and similar square designs. Multicoloured. Self-adhesive. Die-cut perf 12½.
1683   85c. Type **576** .... 3·25 3·00
1684   2f.90 Crested Newt .... 11·50 10·50
1685   3f.70 Alpine Salamander .... 14·50 13·50
1683/1685 Set of 3 .... 26·00 24·00

577 Iris sibirica   **578** Rolls Royce Phantom II

(Des Stefan Erne. Litho Gutenberg AG, Schaan)

2014 (2 June). Bog Flowers. T **577** and similar vert designs. Self-adhesive. Die-cut perf 12½.
1686   1f. Type **577** .... 4·00 3·75
1687   2f.80 *Parnassia palustris* .... 11·50 10·50
1688   3f.60 *Menyanthes trifoliata* .... 14·50 13·50
1686/1688 Set of 3 .... 27·00 25·00

(Des Mark Heine. Litho and gold foil die-stamped Cartor)

2014 (1 Sept). Collections in Liechtenstein. Saloon Cars. T **578** and similar horiz designs. Multicoloured. P 14½×13.
1689   85c. Type **578** .... 3·25 3·00
1690   1f. Pierce Arrow Type 133 .... 4·00 3·75
1691   1f.40 Studebaker Big Six .... 5·50 5·00
1692   1f.90 Jaguar Mark IV .... 7·25 6·75
1689/1692 Set of 4 .... 18·00 17·00

See also No. 1698.

579 Dust Image A   **580** Metamorphosis Sequence 1

(Des Brigitte Hasler. Litho and foil die-stamped Enschedé)

2014 (1 Sept). The Printer's Art (3rd series). Art Print. Etching. T **579** and similar square design. Multicoloured. P 13½.
1693   1f. Type **579** .... 4·00 3·75
1694   1f.40 Dust Image B .... 5·50 5·00

(Des Hans Peter Gassner. Litho and embossed Cartor)

2014 (1 Sept). International Year of Crystallography. T **580** and similar horiz design. Multicoloured. P 13½.
1695   1f. Type **580** .... 4·00 3·75
1696   2f. Metamorphosis Sequence 2 .... 7·50 7·00

581 Wheel, Boat and Donkey

(Des Hans Peter Gassner. Litho Enschedé)

2014 (1 Sept). Lindau to Milan Courier (Lindau Messenger). P 14×13½.
1697   **581**   1f.40 multicoloured................................ 5·50 5·00

(Des Mark Heine. Litho and gold foil die-stamped Cartor)

2014 (10 Nov). Collections in Liechtenstein. Saloon Cars. Horiz design as T **578**. Multicoloured. P 14½×13.
1698   85c. As Type **578** .... 3·25 3·00

A typographical error was found in the issue Rolls-Royce Phantom II, it was printed without a hyphen. As Rolls-Royce is a brand name, it was reissued with the correct spelling.

582 Friedenskapelle Malbun   **583** Famille Rose Teller

(Des Erich Beck. Litho and silver foil die-stamped Gutenberg AG)

2014 (10 Nov). Christmas. Mountain Chapels. T **582** and similar horiz designs. Multicoloured. Self-adhesive. Die-cut perf 12½.
1699   85c. Type **582** .... 3·25 3·00
1700   1f. St Wendelinskapelle Steg .... 4·00 3·75
1701   1f.40 St Theodulskapelle Masescha .... 5·50 5·00
1699/1701 Set of 3 .... 11·50 10·50

(Des Silvia Ruppen. Litho and gold foil die-stamped Enschedé)

2014 (10 Nov). Princely Treasures. Porcelain from China. T **583** and similar vert designs. Multicoloured. P 13½ (1f. and 3f.60) or 11½ (others).
1702   1f. Type **583** .... 4·00 3·75
1703   1f.90 Kraak-Kendi jug with silver mounts (27×43 mm) .... 7·25 6·75
1704   2f.80 Imari baluster vase with lid (27×43 mm) .... 11·50 10·50
1705   3f.60 Imari plate with Lotus blossoms .... 14·50 13·50
1702/1705 Set of 4 .... 34·00 31·00

LIECHTENSTEIN 2014

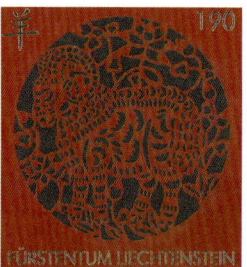

584 Sheep

589 As 1912 Stamp of Liechtenstein   **590** Polar Bear

(Des Stefan Erne. Litho and gold foil die-stamped Gutenberg AG)

2014 (10 Nov). Chinese New Year. Year of the Sheep. Sheet 146×161 mm. Scarlet and gold. Self-adhesive. Die-cut perf 12½.
MS1706   1f.90×4, Type **584**×4 .... 33·00   31·00
The design of T **584** is laser cut through the backing paper.
No. MS1706 is cut around in the shape of a Sheep

(Des Stefan Erne. Litho Enschedé)

2015 (2 Mar). 175th Anniversary of World's First Stamp (Penny Black). Self-adhesive. Die-cut perf 13×12.
1714   **589**   1f.40 bright blue and silver .... 5·50   5·00

(Des Brigitte Lampert. Litho Cartor)

2015 (2 Mar). Europa. Old Toys. T **590** and similar vert design showing figurines. Multicoloured. P 13½.
1715   1f.40 Type **590** .... 5·25   5·00
1716   1f.40 Goat on Lemon .... 5·25   5·00

585 Geometric (Singapore)

591 Anniversary Emblem   **592** Play of Light

(Des Hong Sek-Chern (Liechtenstein) or Jens W. Beyrich (Singapore). Litho Cartor)

2014 (10 Nov). Liechtenstein and Singapore. T **585** and similar horiz design. P 13×13½.
1707   1f.90 scarlet, grey and silver .... 7·25   6·75
1708   1f.90 multicoloured .... 7·25   6·75
Designs: 1f.90×2, T **585**; Cityscape (Liechtenstein).
Stamps of a similar design were issued by Singapore.

(Des Sabine Bockmühl. Litho Enschedé)

2015 (2 Mar). 25th Anniversary of United Nations Membership. P 13½×13.
1717   **591**   1f.90 multicoloured .... 7·25   6·75

(Des Leone Ming. Litho Enschedé)

2015 (2 Mar). International Year of Light. Fluorescent coated paper. P 14×13½.
1718   **592**   1f.90 multicoloured .... 7·25   6·75
No. 1718 is perforated through the sphere.
The pink colour turns to violet in ultraviolet light.

586 Prince Hans-Adam II

(Des Hans Peter Gassner. Eng Inge Madlé. Recess and litho Enschedé)

2014 (10 Nov). 25th Anniversary of Accession of Prince Hans-Adam II. P 13½×14.
1709   **586**   2f. multicoloured .... 7·50   7·00

(Des Hans Peter Gassner. Eng Inge Madlé. Recess and litho Enschedé)

2015 (14 Feb). 70th Birth Anniversary of Prince Hans-Adam II. Sheet 120×100 mm containing horiz designs as T **586**. Multicoloured, colour of background and inscription given. P 13½×14.
MS1710 1f. As Type **586** (green); 2f. As Type **586** (orange-brown), each×2 .... 24·00   22·00

No. 1711 is vacant.

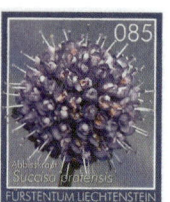

593 Succisa pratensis

(Des Stefan Erne. Litho Gutenberg AG)

2015 (1 June). Flora. Meadow Flowers. T **593** and similar vert designs. Self-adhesive. Die-cut perf 12½×12.
1719   85c. Type **593** .... 3·25   3·00
1720   1f. *Astrantia major* .... 4·00   3·75
1721   1f.30 *Leucanthemum vulgare* .... 5·25   5·00
1719/1721 Set of 3 .... 11·50 10·50

587 Hat   **588** Emblem

594 Pond

(Des Stéphanie Keiser. Litho Gutenberg AG)

2015 (2 Mar). 50th Anniversary of Liechtenstein Traditional Costume Association. Self-adhesive. Die-cut perf 12×13.
1712   **587**   85c. multicoloured .... 3·25   3·00
1713   **588**   1f. multicoloured .... 4·00   3·75

(Des Marco Nescher. Litho Cartor)

2015 (1 June). Nature Reserves in Liechtenstein. T **594** and similar horiz designs. Multicoloured. P 13½.
1722   1f. Type **594** .... 4·00   3·75
        a. Pair. Nos. 1722/1723 .... 9·00

	b. Block of 4. Nos. 1722/1725	17·00	
1723	1f. Pond (right)	4·00	3·75
1724	1f. Meadow (left)	4·00	3·75
	a. Pair. Nos. 1724/1725	9·00	
1725	1f. Meadow (right)	4·00	3·75
1722/1725	Set of 4	14·50	13·50

Nos. 1722/1723 and 1724/1725 were printed, *se-tenant*, in horizontal pairs, within blocks of four (No. 1722b), within the sheet, each pair forming a composite design

595 Pelican

596 Sand Lizard

(Des Armin Hoop. Litho Cartor)

2015 (1 June). Cathedral of St Florin Vaduz. T **595** and similar vert designs showing keystone images. Multicoloured. P 13.

1726	1f. Type **595**	4·00	3·75
1727	1f.40 Lamb of God	5·50	5·00
1728	1f.90 Eagle	7·25	6·75
1729	2f. Lion	7·50	7·00
1726/1729	Set of 4	22·00	20·00

(Des Silvia Ruppen. Litho Gutenberg AG)

2015 (1 June). Reptiles. T **596** and similar square designs. Multicoloured. Self-adhesive. Die-cut perf 12½.

1730	1f.80 Type **596**	7·25	6·75
1731	2f. Smooth Snake	7·50	7·00
1732	5f. Common Lizard	20·00	18·00
1730/1732	Set of 3	31·00	29·00

597 Kaiser Auto Tractor

598 Malbuntal, Liechtenstein

(Des Mark Heine. Litho and gold foil die-stamped Cartor)

2015 (7 Sept). Collections in Liechtenstein. Commercial Vehicles. T **597** and similar horiz designs. Multicoloured. P 13½×13.

1733	85c. Type **597**	3·25	3·00
1734	1f. Raimündle Tractor	4·00	3·75
1735	1f.40 Unimog	5·50	5·00
1736	1f.90 Fordson Tractor	7·25	6·75
1733/1736	Set of 4	18·00	17·00

(Des Tomo Jesenični̇k, Slovenia or Marco Nescher, Liechtenstein. Litho Enschedé)

2015 (7 Sept). The Alps. T **598** and similar horiz design. Multicoloured. P 14×13½.

1737	1f.40 Type **598**	5·50	5·00
	a. Pair. Nos. 1737/1738	11·50	10·50
1738	1f.40 Velika Planina, Slovenia	5·50	5·00

Nos. 1737/1738 were printed, *se-tenant*, in horizontal pairs within the sheet.
Stamps of a similar design were issued by Slovenia.

599 Triesenberger Weinapfel

(Des Angelo Boog. Litho Gutenberg AG)

2015 (7 Sept). Old Fruit Varieties. Apples. Sheet 146×208 mm containing T **599** and similar hexagonal designs. Multicoloured. Self-adhesive. Die-cut perf 12½.

MS1739	1f.40×8, Type **599**; Damason Reinette; Leuser, Bohnapfel; Berlepsch; Rollapfel; Goldparmäne; Rösli Marie	44·00	41·00

600 Red Jasper Cameo

(Des Sven Beham. Litho, embossed and silver foil die-stamped Cartor)

2015 (16 Nov). Archaeological Finds in Liechtenstein. Jewellery. T **600** and similar horiz designs. Multicoloured. P 13½.

1740	85c. Type **600**	3·25	3·00
1741	1f. Gold ring with white chalcedony cameo	4·00	3·75
1742	1f.30 Green glass cameo	5·25	5·00
1740/1742	Set of 3	11·50	10·50

No. 1742 is inscribed 'SEPAC' and was issued for the Small European Postal Administrations.

601 Lo, How a Rose E'er Blooming

602 Adoration of the Shepherds

(Des Oskar Weiss. Litho)

2015 (16 Nov). Christmas. Christmas Carols. T **601** and similar horiz designs. Self-adhesive. Die-cut perf 12×12½.

1743	85c. Type **601**	3·25	3·00
1744	1f. Silent Night	4·00	3·75
1745	1f.40 Oh, How Joyfully	5·50	5·00
1746	1f.90 Come, All Ye Shepherds	7·25	6·75
1743/1746	Set of 4	18·00	17·00

(Des Hans Peter Gassner. Litho and embossed Cartor)

2015 (16 Nov). Princely Treasures. Paintings by Jacques Jordaens. T **602** and similar horiz designs. Multicoloured. P 13×13½.

1747	1f. Type **602**	4·00	3·75
1748	1f.40 As the Old Ones Sing, So The Young Ones Pipe	5·50	5·00
1749	1f.90 Meleager and Atalante	7·25	6·75
1747/1749	Set of 3	15·00	14·00

The face values of Nos. 1747/1749 are embossed.

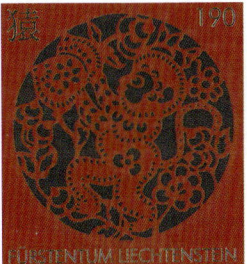
603 Monkey

(Des Stefan Erne. Litho and gold foil die-stamped Gutenberg AG)

2015 (16 Nov). Chinese New Year. Year of the Monkey. Sheet 146×205 mm. Scarlet and gold. Self-adhesive. Die-cut perf 12½.

MS1750	1f.90×4, Type **603**×4	33·00	31·00

The design of T **603** is laser cut through the backing paper.
No. **MS**1750 is cut around in the shape of a Monkey.

LIECHTENSTEIN 2016

604 Oak Tree

(Des Stefan Erne. Litho Gutenberg AG, Schaan)

2016 (7 Mar). Trees. T **604** and similar square designs. Multicoloured. P 13½×14.

1751	85c. Type **604**	3·25	3·00
1752	1f. Weeping Willow	4·00	3·75
1753	1f.50 Walnut	6·00	5·50
1754	1f.70 Aspen	6·50	6·25
1755	2f. Birch	7·50	7·00
1751/1755	Set of 5	25·00	23·00

605 Knife

(Des Sven Beham. Litho, embossed and silver foil die-stamped Cartor)

2016 (7 Mar). Archaeological Finds in Liechtenstein. Utensils. T **605** and similar horiz designs. Multicoloured. P 13½.

1756	1f. Type **605**	4·00	3·75
1757	1f.50 Razor	6·00	5·50
1758	2f. Axe head	7·50	7·00
1756/1758	Set of 3	16·00	14·50

606 Ruggeller Riet

(Des Stefan Erne. Litho Enschedé)

2016 (7 Mar). Painters from Liechtenstein. Alois Ritter Commemoration. T **606** and similar horiz design. Multicoloured. P 13½×14.

1759	1f. Type **606**	4·00	3·75
1760	2f. Im Bofel	7·50	7·00

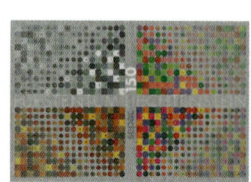 

607 The Four Seasons **608** Green and Polluted Earth

(Des Hans Peter Gassner. Litho Enschedé)

2016 (7 Mar). SEPAC (small European mail services). P 13½×14.

1761	**607** 1f.50 multicoloured	6·00	5·50

(Des Aurora Corrado (No. 1762) or Doxia Sergidou (No. 1763))

2016 (7 Mar). Europa. Think Green. Multicoloured. T **608** and similar multicoloured design.

(a) Ordinary gum. Litho. Gutenberg AG, Schaan. P 14×13½.

1762	1f.50 Type **608**	6·00	5·50

(b) Self-adhesive. Litho. Cartor. Die-cut perf 12×12½

1763	1f.50 Roller painting contaminated landscape green (*horiz*)	6·00	5·50

609 Herbstlängler

(Des Angelo Boog. Litho Gutenberg AG)

2016 (6 June). Old Fruit Varieties. Pears. Sheet 146×208 mm containing T **609** and similar hexagonal designs. Multicoloured. Self-adhesive. Die-cut perf 12½.

MS1764	1f.×8, Type **609**; Kugeläugstler; Hermannsbirne, Rote Holzbirne; Sulser Längler; Sülibirne; Wolfsbirne; Tollbirne	32·00	29·00

610 Pond

(Des Dietmar Walser. Litho Cartor)

2016 (6 June). Nature Reserves in Liechtenstein. Ruggeller Riet. T **610** and similar horiz designs. Multicoloured. P 13½.

1765	1f. Type **610**	4·00	3·75
	a. Pair. Nos. 1765/1766	9·00	
	b. Block of 4. Nos. 1765/1768	17·00	
1766	1f. Pond (right)	4·00	3·75
1767	1f. Meadow (left)	4·00	3·75
	a. Pair. Nos. 1767/1768	9·00	
1768	1f. Meadow (right)	4·00	3·75
1765/1768	Set of 4	14·50	13·50

Nos. 1765/1766 and 1767/1768 were printed, *se-tenant*, in horizontal pairs, within blocks of four (No. 1765b), within the sheet, each pair forming a composite design

611 Ship on Wheels Drinking Vessel   **612** Archery

(Des Silvia Ruppen. Litho and silver foil Enschedé)

2016 (6 June). Princely Treasures. Silversmithing. T **611** and similar vert designs. Multicoloured. P 14×13½.

1769	1f. Type **611**	4·00	3·75
1770	1f.50 Diana riding Stag	6·00	5·50
1771	2f. Nautilus cup	7·50	7·00
1769/1771	Set of 3	16·00	14·50

(Des Romero Britto. Litho and silver foil die-stamped Gutenberg AG)

2016 (6 June). Olympic Games. Rio 2016. T **612** and similar vert designs. Multicoloured. Self-adhesive. Die-cut perf 12½×12.

1772	1f. Type **612**	4·00	3·75
1773	2f. Judo	7·50	7·00

613 M. Thun 490 cc. Motorcycle, 1928

(Des Mark Heine. Litho and gold foil die-stamped Cartor)

2016 (5 Sept). Collections in Liechtenstein. Motorcycles. T **613** and similar horiz designs. Multicoloured. P 13.

1774	85c. Type **613**	3·25	3·00
1775	1f. Harley-Davidson 1000 cc., 1920	4·00	3·75
1776	1f.50 Norton Königswellen single-cylinder 30 HP motorcycle and Type Stolz sidecar, 1948	6·00	5·50
1777	2f. Rudge, 1933	7·50	7·00
1774/1777	Set of 4	19·00	17·00

614 Maria Hilf Fraternity, Balzers

(Des Stéphanie Keiser. Litho Cartor)

2016 (5 Sept). Fraternities in Liechtenstein. T **614** and similar horiz designs. Multicoloured. P 14½.

1778	1f. Type **614**	4·00	3·75
1779	1f.50 St Anna Fraternity, Vaduz	6·00	5·50
1780	2f. St Sebastian Fraternity, Nendeln	7·50	7·00
1778/1780	Set of 3	16·00	14·50

615 Woman **616** *Young Woman on a Balcony (Gerrit Dou)*

(Des Erich Allgäuer. Litho Gutenberg AG)

2016 (5 Sept). Artistic Photography. Erich Allgäuer. T **615** and similar vert designs showing images photographed in Plane tree bark. Multicoloured. P 13½.

1781	1f. Type **615**	4·00	3·75
1782	1f.50 Man	6·00	5·50
1783	2f. Woman wearing hat	7·50	7·00
1781/1783	Set of 3	16·00	14·50

(Des Václav Fajt. Eng Václav Fajt. Recess Gutenberg AG)

2016 (5 Sept). Art. P 12.

1784	**616**	1f.50 multicoloured	6·00	5·50

A stamp of a similar design was issued by Czech Republic.

617 Lamplight **618** Badger and Mile Stone

(Des Stefan Erne. Litho Gutenberg AG, Schaan)

2016 (14 Nov). Christmas. Nostalgic Christmas Cards. T **617** and similar multicoloured designs. Self-adhesive. Die-cut perf 12×12½ (horiz) or 12½×12 (vert).

1785	85c. Type **617**	3·25	3·00
1786	1f. Exchanging Christmas presents (*vert*)	4·00	3·75
1787	1f.50 City scene (*vert*)	6·00	5·50
1788	2f. Winter walk	7·50	7·00
1785/1788	Set of 4	19·00	17·00

(Des Angelo Boog. Litho Enschedé)

2016 (14 Nov). Liechtenstein without Us. Sheet 180×381 mm containing T **618** and similar square designs. Multicoloured. P 14½×13½.

MS1789 2f.×3, Type **618**; Eagle; Parrots in flight .... 24·00 22·00

No. **MS**1789 is folded into three panes, each 180×127 mm, showing the area after 20 years, 100 years and 500 years, respectively, without the presence of man.

619 Rooster **620** Oats

(Des Stefan Erne. Litho and gold foil die-stamped Gutenberg AG)

2016 (14 Nov). Chinese New Year. Year of the Rooster. Scarlet and gold. Self-adhesive. Die-cut perf 12½.

MS1790 2f.×4, Type **619**×4 .... 33·00 31·00

The design of T **619** is laser cut through the backing paper.

(Des Armin Hoop. Litho Gutenberg AG, Schaan)

2017 (6 Mar). Crop Plants. Grains. T **620** and similar square designs. Multicoloured. Self-adhesive. Die-cut perf 12½.

1791	85c. Type **620**	3·25	3·00
1792	1f. Barley	4·00	3·75
1793	1f.50 Maize	5·75	5·25
1794	2f. Millet	7·50	7·00
1791/1794	Set of 4	18·00	17·00

 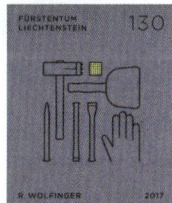

621 Snowboarding **622** Stonemason

(Des Julius Tiefenthaler and Yannick Oberhofer. Litho Cartor)

2017 (6 Mar). Outdoor Sports. T **621** and similar horiz designs. Multicoloured. P 13½.

1795	85c. Type **621**	3·25	3·00
1796	1f. Windsurfing	4·00	3·75
1797	2f. Ski-jump	7·50	7·00
1795/1797	Set of 3	13·50	12·50

(Des René Wolfinge. Litho Gutenberg AG, Schaan)

2017 (6 Mar). Trades and Crafts. P 12½×12.

1798	1f.30 lilac, black and chrome	5·00	4·75
1799	1f.80 azure, black and cerise	7·00	6·50
1800	2f. orange-yellow and emerald	7·50	7·00
1798/1800	Set of 3	18·00	16·00

Designs: 1f.30 T **622**; 1f.80 Tailor; 2f. Goldsmith.
No. 1800 is inscribed 'sepac'.

623 Vaduz Castle

(Des Angelo Boog. Litho Cartor)

2017 (6 Mar). Europa. Castles. T **623** and similar horiz designs. Multicoloured. P 14½.

1801	1f.50 Type **623**	5·75	5·25
1802	1f.50 Gutenberg Castle	5·75	5·25

LIECHTENSTEIN 2017

624 *Request for Admission*

625 *Multicoloured Handprints*

(Des Silvia Ruppen. Litho and gold foil die-stamped Enschedé)

2017 (5 June). Princely Treasures. Paintings by Peter Fendi. T **624** and similar vert designs. Multicoloured. P 14×13½.

1803	85c. Type **624**	3·25	3·00
1804	1f. *Sneaking a Peek*	4·00	3·75
1805	1f.50 *A Child's Prayer*	5·75	5·25
1803/1805	Set of 3	11·50	11·00

(Des Karin Beck. Litho Gutenberg AG, Schaan)

2017 (5 June). Diversity. 50th Anniversary of HPZ Remedial Education Centre. Self-adhesive. Die-cut perf 12×12½.

1806	**625**	1f. multicoloured	4·00	3·75

626 *Summer*

(Des Xaver Roser and Sepp Köppel. Litho Cartor)

2017 (5 June). Nature Reserves in Liechtenstein. Gampriner Seelein. T **626** and similar horiz designs. Multicoloured. P 13½.

1807	1f. Type **626**	4·00	3·75
	a. Pair. Nos. 1807/1808	9·00	
	b. Block of 4. Nos. 1807/1810	17·00	
1808	1f. Summer (right)	4·00	3·75
1809	1f. Winter (left)	4·00	3·75
	a. Pair. Nos. 1809/1810	9·00	
1810	1f. Winter (right)	4·00	3·75
1807/1810	Set of 4	14·50	13·50

Nos. 1807/1808 and 1809/1810 were printed, *se-tenant*, in horizontal pairs, within blocks of four (No. 1807b), within the sheet, each pair forming a composite design.

627 *Vaduz Castle*

628 *Apricot Mombacher Früprikose*

(Des Stéphanie Keiser and Angelo Boog)

2017 (5 June). Golden Wedding of Prince Hans-Adam II and Princess Marie of Liechtenstein. Sheet 116×80 mm containing T **627** and similar vert designs. Multicoloured. P 14½.

MS1811 1f.30 Type **627**; 2f.20 Royal couple (45×62 *mm*); 2f.80 Twin wedding rings (45×62 *mm*) .... 26·00 24·00

(Des Angelo Boog. Litho Gutenberg AG)

2017 (4 Sept). Old Fruit Varieties. Stone Fruit. Sheet 146×208 mm containing T **628** and similar hexagonal designs. Multicoloured. Self-adhesive. Die-cut perf 12½.

MS1812 1f.×8, Type **628**; Greengage Reine Claude Verte; Plum Kirkespflaume; Plum Hauszwetschge; Cherry Schauenburger Kirsche; Apricot Ungarische Beste; Plum Mirabelle von Nancy; Cherry Gelbe Denise .... 32·00 29·00

629 *Postman and Child*

630 *Settlement Area*

(Des Christine Böhmwalder. Litho and gold foil die-stamped Enschedé)

2017 (4 Sept). Bicentenary of Post ('K K Briefsammelstelle Balzers'). Sheet 111×55 mm containing T **629** and similar vert designs. Multicoloured. P 14×14½.

MS1813 1f.30 Type **629**; 2f.20 Posthorn; 2f.80 Early Horse-drawn mail coach .... 26·00 24·00

(Des Hans Peter Gassner. Litho Enschedé)

2017 (4 Sept). Settlement Area of Liechtenstein. P 14×13½.
1814	**630**	1f.50 multicoloured	5·75	5·25

631 *Rappastein*

(Des Hans Peter Gassner (after Helmut Ditsch). Litho Enschedé)

2017 (4 Sept). Mountain Painting. Helmut Ditsch. P 14×13½.
1815	**631**	3f.80 multicoloured	14·50	13·50

632 *Castor fiber* (Beaver)

633 *Star of Bethlehem*

(Des Angelo Boog. Litho Gutenberg AG, Schaan)

2017 (13 Nov). Fauna. Returnees. Animals believed to have been Extinct. T **632** and similar horiz designs. Multicoloured. P 12×12½.

1816	85c. Type **632**	3·25	3·00
1817	1f. *Lynx lynx*	4·00	3·75
1818	1f.30 *Canis lupus* (Wolf)	5·75	5·25
1819	1f.50 *Ciconia ciconia* (Stork)	7·50	7·00
1816/1819	Set of 4	18·00	17·00

(Des Eliane Schädler. Litho Gutenberg AG, Schaan)

2017 (13 Nov). Christmas. T **633** and similar vert designs. Multicoloured. P 12½×12.

1820	85c. Type **633**	3·25	3·00
1821	1f. Winter Forest	3·75	3·50
1822	1f.50 Moonshine on house	5·75	5·25
1823	2f. Church and full moon	7·50	7·00
1820/1823	Set of 4	18·00	17·00

634 Nordic Skiing

(Des Sojung Kim-McCarthy. Litho Gutenberg AG, Schaan)
2017 (13 Nov). Winter Olympic Games, Pyeongchang. T **634** and similar horiz design. P 12×12½.
1824	1f.70 Type **634**	6·50	6·00
1825	2f. Alpine Skiing	7·50	7·00

635 Dog

(Des Stefan Erne. Litho and gold foil die-stamped Gutenberg AG)
2017 (13 Nov). Chinese New Year. Year of the Dog. Sheet 146×208 mm. Scarlet and gold. Self-adhesive. Die-cut perf 12½.
MS1826 2f.×4, Type **635**×4 .... 33·00 31·00
The design of T **635** is laser cut through the backing paper. No. **MS**1826 is cut around in the shape of a Dog.

 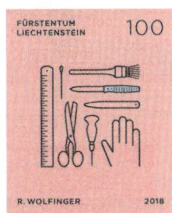

636 Aubergine   **637** Bookbinder

(Des Armin Hoop. Litho Gutenberg AG, Schaan)
2018 (5 Mar). Crop Plants. Vegetables. T **636** and similar square designs. Multicoloured. Self-adhesive. Die-cut perf 12½.
1827	85c. Type **636**	3·25	3·00
1828	1f. Radish	4·00	3·75
1829	1f.50 Courgette	5·75	5·25
1830	2f. Sweet Pepper	7·50	7·00
1827/1830 Set of 4		18·00	17·00

(Des René Wolfinger. Litho Gutenberg AG, Schaan)
2018 (5 Mar). Trades and Crafts. T **637** and similar vert designs. P 12½×12.
1831	1f. flesh, black and azure	3·75	3·50
1832	1f.30 chrome-yellow, black and violet	5·00	4·50
1833	1f.80 pale dull green, black and orange	6·75	6·25
1831/1833 Set of 3		14·00	13·00
Designs: 1f. T **637**; 1f.30 Instrument maker; 1f.80 Shoemaker.

638 Old Rhine Bridge, Vaduz

(Des Roland Rick. Litho Enschedé)
2018 (5 Mar). Europa. Bridges. T **638** and similar horiz design. Multicoloured. P 14×13½.
1834	1f.50 Type **638**	5·75	5·25
1835	1f.50 Balzers Footbridge	5·75	5·25

639 The Kiss   **640** '100', Pen and Cross

(Des Silvia Ruppen. Litho and gold foil Cartor)
2018 (5 Mar). Death Centenary of Gustav Klimt. T **639** and similar vert design. Multicoloured. P 15×14½.
1836	2f.60 Type **639**	9·75	9·00
1837	3f.70 Death and Life	14·50	13·50

(Des Hans Peter Gassner. Litho Enschedé)
2018 (4 June). Centenary of Direct Electoral System. P 14×13½.
1838 **640** 1f. multicoloured .... 3·75 3·50

641 Spring (left)

(Des Dietmar Walser and Johannes Frigg. Litho Cartor)
2018 (4 June). Nature Reserves in Liechtenstein. Hälos. T **641** and similar horiz designs. Multicoloured. P 13½.
1839	1f. Type **641**	3·75	3·50
	a. Pair. Nos. 1839/1940	7·75	7·25
	b. Block of 4. Nos. 1839/1842	16·00	
1840	1f. Spring (right)	3·75	3·50
1841	1f. Summer (left)	3·75	3·50
	a. Pair. Nos. 1841/1842	7·75	7·25
1842	1f. Summer (right)	3·75	3·50
1839/1842 Set of 4		13·50	12·50
Nos. 1839/1840 and Nos. 1841/1842 were printed, *se-tenant*, in horizontal pairs, within blocks of four (No. 1839b), within the sheet, each pair forming a composite design.

642 Kelchle   **643** Green Crown and '1968–2018'

(Des Marco Nescher. Litho Cartor)
2018 (4 June). Summit Crosses. T **642** and similar horiz designs. Multicoloured. P 13½.
1843	1f. Type **642**	3·75	3·50
1844	1f.50 Kläusli	5·75	5·25
1845	2f. Mittlerspitz	7·50	7·00
1846	2f.60 Hubel	9·00	8·50
1843/1846 Set of 4		23·00	22·00
No. 1844 is inscribed 'sepac'.

(Des Hans Peter Gassner. Recess and litho Enschedé)
2018 (11 June). 50th Birth Anniversary of Hereditary Prince Alois von und zu Liechtenstein. Sheet 111×55 mm containing T **643** and similar multicoloured designs. P 14½×14.
MS1847 1f.30 Type **643**; 2f.20 Prince Alois (30×36 mm); 2f.80 Red crown .... 26·00 24·00

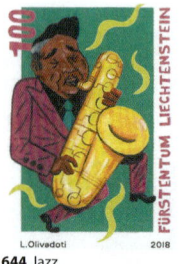 

644 Jazz **645** Grey Heron

(Des Luigi Olivadoti. Litho Cartor)

2018 (3 Sept). Music for Dancing. Sheet 210×146 mm containing T **644** and similar vert designs. Multicoloured. P 14.
MS1848 1f.×8, Type **644**; Flamenco; Hip Hop; Electro; Folk Music; Country; Samba; Classical .... 32·00 29·00

(Des Sven Beham and Hans Peter Gassner. Litho, embossed and varnish Cartor)

2018 (3 Sept). Artistic Photography. Bird's Eyes. T **645** and similar horiz designs. Multicoloured. P 14.
1849	1f. Type **645**	3·75	3·50
1850	1f.30 Great Crested Grebe	5·25	5·00
1851	1f.50 Cormorant	6·00	5·50
1849/1851	Set of 3	13·50	12·50

646 The Tea Ceremony

(Des Hans Peter Gassner. Litho Cartor)

2018 (3 Sept). Princely Treasures. Tapestries (manufactured by Jean Barraband II) *The Chinese Series*. T **646** and similar multicoloured designs. P 13½.
1852	1f. Type **646**	3·75	3·50
1853	1f.50 Audience with the Emperor of China (60×42 mm)	6·00	5·50
1854	1f.80 The Scholar before the Great Mogul (41×36 mm)	6·75	6·25
1852/1854	Set of 3	15·00	13·50

647 Biedermann House

(Des Karin Beck. Litho and embossing Enschedé)

2018 (3 Sept). 500th Anniversary of Biedermann House (two-storey wooden building, insulated with lichens and mosses, with each beam numbered to allow the house to be moved). P 13½×14.
| 1855 | **647** | 2f. multicoloured | 7·50 | 7·00 |

648 The Wise Men from the East

(Des Manfred Näscher. Litho Gutenberg AG, Schaan)

2018 (12 Nov). Christmas. T **648** and similar horiz designs. Multicoloured. Self-adhesive. Die-cut perf 12×12½.
1856	85c. Type **648**	3·25	3·00
1857	1f. The Star shows the Way	3·75	3·50
1858	1f.50 Peace on Earth	5·75	5·25
1859	2f. Birth of Jesus	7·50	7·00
1856/1859	Set of 4	18·00	17·00

 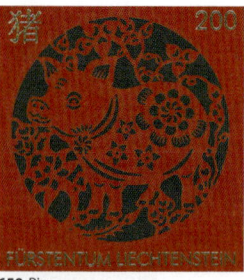

649 Hope **650** Pig

(Des Peter Vetsch. Litho Enschedé)

2018 (12 Nov). Migration. T **649** and similar vert designs. P 14½×14.
1860	85c. Type **649**	3·25	3·00
1861	1f. Departure	3·75	3·50
1862	1f.30 New Beginning	5·00	4·50
1860/1862	Set of 3	11·00	10·00

(Des Stefan Erne. Litho and gold foil die-stamped Gutenberg AG)

2018 (12 Nov). Chinese New Year. Year of the Pig. Sheet 208×146 mm. Scarlet and gold. Self-adhesive. Die-cut perf 12½.
MS1863 2f.×4, Type **650**×4 .... 32·00 29·00
The design of T **650** is laser cut through the backing paper. No. MS1863 is cut around in the shape of a Pig.

MACHINE LABELS

A Vaduz **B** Vaduz

1995 (4 Dec). Commune Arms. Horiz designs as T **A** showing Commune Arms. Multicoloured. Face values 10r. to 99f.90 in 10r. steps.
Fixed values:
4.12.95 60r., 80r., 1f., 1f.80 (Type **A**, Balzars, Eschen, Gamprin, Mauren, Planken, Rugell, Schaan, Sehellenberg, Triesen, Triesenberg)
1.1.96 70r., 90r., 1f.10, 1f.80 (Type **A**, Balzars, Eschen, Gamprin, Mauren, Planken, Rugell, Schaan, Sehellenberg, Triesen, Triesenberg)
1.7.00 70r., 90r., 1f.20, 1f.30 (Type **A**, Balzars, Eschen, Gamprin, Mauren, Planken, Rugell, Schaan, Sehellenberg, Triesen, Triesenberg)

2003 (2 June). Towns. Horiz designs as T **B** showing streets and buildings from the named town. Multicoloured. Face values 10r. to 99f.90 in 5r. steps.
Fixed values:
2.6.03 70r., 90r., 1f.20, 1f.30 (Type **B**, Balzars, Eschen, Gamprin-Bendern, Mauren, Nerdeln, Ruggell, Schaan, Schaanwald, Schellenburg, Triesen, Triesenburg)
1.1.04 85r., 1f., 1f.20, 1f.30 (Type **B**, Balzars, Eschen, Gamprin-Bendern, Mauren, Nerdeln, Ruggell, Schaan, Schaanwald, Schellenburg, Triesen, Triesenburg)

DESIGN INDEX

This index provides in a condensed form a key to the designs and subjects of portrait and pictorial stamps of Liechtenstein. In order to save space, portrait stamps are listed under surname only, views under the name of the town or area and works of art under the name of the artist. In cases of difficulty part of the inscription has been used to identify the stamp. Where the same name or subject appears on more than one stamp in a set, only the first appearance is indexed.

AIR 150, 176, 259, 395
Official Stamps O118A, O126, O150, O174, O255, O287, O495, O652
Overprinted stamps 14, 17, 46, 63A, 150, 308, 324, 1624
Postage Due D43, D84, D189

1848 Revolutions in Europe 1181
1921 Constitution 537

A
Abstract (painting) 726
Actors 1660
Advent Windows 1530
Aeroplanes 110
Agricultural Propaganda 195
Agriculture 933, 1541
Airmail stamps 395
Alois II 217
Alpha and Omega 472
Alpine Animals 1646
Alpine Association 1512
Alpine Flowers 1652
Alpine Marmot 256
Alpine pastures 1382, 1410, 1448, 1470
Alpine Rhine 1590
Alpine Skier 1537
Alpine Skiing 1825
Ammonite 1299, 1363
Amphibians 1683
Andean Condor 1072
Angel 685, 808, 1111
Animals 252, 255, 283, 1061, 1816
Anniversaries 816, 1008, 1070, 1192, 1550
Annunciation 1530, 1564
Ants 1508
Archaeological finds 1756
Archangel Gabriel 1315
Archangel Michael 906
Architectural Heritage 617
Arctic Hare 253
Arms 7, 14, 17, 20, 42, 47*a*A, 77, 118, 127, 246, 344, 433, 443, 498, 506, 581, 922, **MS**1036
Arms of Bailiffs 740, 763, 788
Arms of Triesen Families 458
Art 503, 557, 1588, 1650, 1663, 1759, 1784, 1803, 1836
Art Museum 1231
Aspen 1754
Aston Martin 1655
Astronomy 502
Athletics 340
Athletics, volleyball and cycling 1573
Aubergine 1827
Autumn customs 962
Avalanche rescue dogs 1637
Axe head 1758
Aztecs 1030

B
Badger 1061
Badminton cabinet 1523
Ballet 1659
Balzers Footbridge 1835
Bargalla 1382
Barley 1792
Barn Swallows 892
Base Clef and woman 1405
Basket of Roses 1160
Bats 1388
Beaver 1816
Bee 1445
Bendern **MS**553, 1329
Bendern-Haag Bridge 1675
Bicentenary of Sovereignty 1401
Biedermann House 1855
Biology 500
Bird **MS**1589
Birds 176, 892
Bird's Eyes 1849
Bishop Marxer 600
Bishop Ortlieb von Brandis 651
Black Grouse 284
Black-headed Gulls 176
Bog Flowers 1686
Bookbinder 1831
Boy cutting loaf 287
Boy Scouts 358
Bridges .... 836, 1298, 1398 , 1834
Bridges between Switzerland and Liechtenstein 1642, 1671
Bronze Age 1130
Bronze Boar 529
Brussels International Exhibition 367
Büchel 475
Buchs-Schaan Bridge 1673
Buildings 691, 1570
Busch 1483
Butterflies 1518, 1553, 1586
Butterfly and flower 1518

C
Cabbage 903
Cameos 1740
Campaign emblem 489
Candle wreath 1492
Capercaillie 254
Car 1619, 1655, 1689, 1698
Cardinal Virtues 869
Carols 1743
Castle of Vaduz 27, 72
Castles 677, 1596, 1801
Cathedrals 1726
Chamois 255, 1647
Champion 505
Championship 1479
Chapel of St Mamerta 1526
Chapel of St Mamertus 1042
Charter 1606
Child drinking 722
Children's Books 1561
Children's Drawings **MS**1618
Children's games 952
Chinese New Year **MS**1600, **MS**1633, **MS**1670, **MS**1706, **MS**1750, **MS**1790, **MS**1826, **MS**1863
Christian symbols 472
Christianity **MS**1216
Christmas 360, 372, 392, 419, 438, 528, 543, 560, 586, 602, 625, 647, 685, 717, 735, 758, 783, 808, 829, 858, 880, 906, 924, 946, 981, 999, 1021, 1042, 1064, 1087, 1111, 1145, 1160, 1182, 1209, 1235, 1260, 1286, 1315, 1360, 1390, 1422, 1455, 1492, 1530, 1564, 1593, 1629, 1665, 1699, 1743, 1785, 1820, 1856
Christmas cards 1785
Church Patrons 506
City Palace 919
City scene 1787
Clasped hands 413
Classic cars 1619
Clown 1032, 1174
Cogwheels 467
Coins 674, 707, 1680
Colonnade 499
Coloured ribbons 1106
Commercial Vehicles 1733
Composers 1413
Constitution Charter 923
Contemporary Art 1049
Co-operation in Europe 1234
Cormorant 1851
Costumes 751
Council of Europe 726, 1192
County of Vaduz 922, 1041
Courgette 1829
Courtyard 886
Cow 1318
Crayfish 630
Crested Newt 1684
Cribs 1235, 1593
Crops 1791, 1827
Cross-country skiing 539, 1024, 1163
Crossbow 748
Crown **MS**1847
Crown Prince Alois 1045
Crown Prince Alois and Princess Sophie 1284
Crown Prince Johann Adam Pius (Prince Hans Adam) 243, 336, 405, **MS**471, 795, **MS**938
Crucible 1130
Crystallography 1695
Cup 1771
Curta Calculator 1425
Cycling 942

D
Dahlia 1609
Dancers 1661
de Loyola 1008
Decorated Easter Eggs 1581
Denar 1680
Development Aid 727
Dish aerial 931
Diversity 1806
Dog **MS**1825
Domain of Schellenberg 280
Door 1212
Dove 1010, 1094, 1234
Dragon **MS**1600
Drinking vessel 1769
Drum 1678
Duchess Sophie of Bavaria **MS**1056

E
Eagle 1728
Earth 1090
Easter 581
Easter eggs 1243
Electoral System 1838
Elephant with letter 1075
Emblem 414, 476, 1217, 1247, 1273, 1522, 1713, 1717
Endangered animals 955
Endangered Bird species **MS**1589
Ender 820
Envelopes 1018
Eschen 1115, **MS**1189
Eulogy of Madness (painting) 1079
Eurasian Badger 285
EURO 2008 Football 1479
Europa 404, 412, 413, 427, 437, 462, 467, 490, 499, 523, 536, 552, 576, 587, 609, 628, 664, 689, 720, 738, 761, 786, 811, 836, 861, 892, 912, 931, 952, 987, 1006, 1030, 1049, 1094, 1131, 1150, 1170, 1190, 1223, 1246, 1271, 1294, 1371, 1398, 1434, 1469, 1506, 1561, 1585, 1608, 1639, 1678, 1715, 1762, 1801, 1834
European Campaign for Rural Areas 933
European Free Trade Association 476
European Small States Games 1195/1203
Exchanging gifts 1786
EXPO 2000 1220
Expo 2010, Shanghai **MS**1547

F
Falknis 965
False Ringlet (Butterfly) 582
Famous Visitors to Liechtenstein 779, 804, 832
Famous Women 1131
Farming implements 745
Fauna 582, 596
Faust (play) 1207
Fendi 1803
Ferns 1037
Ferrari 1656
Fibonacci sequence 1634
Field crops 903
Figure supporting roof 1550
Finger print 1552
Fire fighters 1467
First Aid 248, 1502
Fish 915, 959
Flags 1551
Flood relief 80
Flowers 532, 548, 1057, 1609, 1686, 1719
Foot and Cycle Bridge 1672
Football 320, 593, 990, 1074, 1276, 1409
Forest 1508, 1585
Fossils 1363
Francis Joseph II 183, 186, 899
Frankincense 880
Fraternities 1778
Freedom from Hunger 423
Frommelt 1099
Fruit **MS**1739, **MS**1764, **MS**1812
Fungi 1153, 1238

G
Game Birds 996
Gamprin Primary School building 912
Gantner 1046
Gehr 1136
Geometric shape 1707
Girl vintager 96A
Glass painting 602
Glass tree decorations 1160
Goalkeeper 1173
Goat 1716
Goethe 1207
Golden Eagle 145, 257
Golden Wedding **MS**1811
Goldsmith 1800
Government building 73
Graf Zeppelin 116
Grebe 1850
Green and Polluted Earth 1762
Greeting Cards 1436

LIECHTENSTEIN / Design Index

Greeting Stamps........ 1032, 1075, 1102, 1174, 1241
Gulden........ 1681
Gutenberg........ 1215
Gutenberg Castle........ 226, 775, 1596, 1802
Gymnastics........ 351, 544, 1133

H

Hands........ 1321
Hare........ 1649
Harley-Davidson........ 1775
Harvester........ 386
Hat........ 1712
Headphones........ 936
Heart........ 1102
Helicopter........ 395
Heraldic windows........ 728
Heron........ 1849
Hill........ 495
Hillside farming........ 1541
Hindenburg (airship)........ 151
Historical Association........ 1248
Historical Environment........ 1250, 1274, 1292, 1358, 1386, 1428, 1462, 1498
Holy Year........ 825
Homage to Liechtenstein........ 1114, 1159, 1166
Honeggar........ 1263
Honeycomb........ 404
Horse........ **MS**1670
Hot air balloon........ 1322
Houses........ 1274
Hubel........ 1846
Hunting........ 900
Hunting weapons........ 748
Hydropower........ 1558

I

Ibex........ 1646
Imperial Insignia........ 611, 670
Inn Signs........ 1289, 1376
Insects........ 1445, 1474
Instrument maker........ 1832
International Radio Consultative Committee........ 725
International Scout Conference........ 313
International Telecommunications Union........ 452
International Year of Disabled Persons........ 769
International Year of Light........ 1718
International Year of Mountains........ 1265
International Year of the Child........ 722
Irrigation canal........ 221

J

Jaguar (car)........ 1657, 1692
Jazz........ **MS**1848
Joseph and Mary........ 946
Judo........ 636, 1195
Justice........ 869

K

Kaiser........ 441
Kaufmann........ 1267
Kelchle........ 1843
Key........ 490
Klausli........ 1844
Kliemand........ 1650
Klimt........ 1839
Knife........ 1756
Koalas........ 1227

L

Lamb........ 1727
Land Register........ 1507
Landscapes........ 561
Lawena Springs........ 561
Legends........ 838
Lent customs........ 813
Lenten Fast........ 894
LIBA 02........ 1273, 1282, 1318
LIBA 2012........ **MS**1618
LIBA 72........ **MS**553
LIBA 82........ 795
LIBA 92........ 1018, **MS**1036
Liechtenstein........ 1641, **MS**1789
Liechtenstein Land Bank........ 898
Liechtenstein Museum........ 1372, 1400, 1523, 1548, 1567
Liechtenstein Philatelic Exhibition........ **MS**153, **MS**251*a*, **MS**279*a*
Liechtenstein Philatelic Society........ 1522
Liechtenstein Sagas........ 468, 492, 516
Liechtenstein stamps........ 1601
Liechtenstein–Singapore........ 1707
Liechtenstein Traditional Costume Association........ 1712
Lifestyle Museum........ 1527
Lindenberg........ 504
Linocuts........ 1503
Lion........ 1729
Literary characters........ **MS**1623
Lizard........ 1732
Lord Baden-Powell........ 313, 358
Lynx........ 1817

M

Mace quartz........ 984
Madonna........ 43A
Madonna (wood sculpture)........ 442
Madonna and Child........ 200, 327, 1152
Magician........ 1662
Maize........ 1793
Malaria eradication........ 414
Man........ 1782
Map of Europe........ 1366
Map of Liechtenstein........ 367
Marathon........ 1477
Marian Year........ 327
Marmot........ 1648
Marsh land........ 221
Martial arts........ 1472
Mary and Joseph........ 1286
Mathematical symbols........ 1354
Mathematics and Nature........ 1634
Meadow........ 1724, 1725, 1767, 1768
Meadow Flowers........ 1719
Medicinal plants........ 1107
Menzinger........ 801
Mercedes........ 1658
Migration........ 1860
Milk and Bread........ 423
Milking pail........ 745
Millenary of Austria........ 1141
Millet........ 1794
Minerals........ 984, 1084
Minnesingers........ 407, 415, 428
Missionary Work........ 1054
Mittlerspritz........ 1845
Modern Olympic Games........ 1133
Monasteries........ 863
Monkey........ **MS**1750
Monoplane........ 110
Mosses and lichens........ 771
Motorcycle........ 1774
Mount Naafkopf........ 121
Mountain Chapels........ 1699
Mountain hut and inn........ 1616
Mountain sports........ 332
Mountains........ 965/979, 1671, 1815
Mounted courier........ 1005
Mozart........ 1421
Multicoloured handprints........ 1806
Museum of Art........ 1567
Music........ 861, 1430, **MS**1848
Musical Instruments........ 1678
Music score........ 954

N

NASA Space Technology and Research Students Project........ 1270
National Costumes........ 681
National Day Procession........ 761
National Flags........ 1172
National Historical Society........ 634
National Identity........ 1464, 1527
National Museum........ 317, 529, 1299
Natural Gas Filling Station........ 1545
Nature Conservation Year........ 519
Nature Protection........ 453
Nature Reserves........ 1722, 1765, 1807, 1839
Nendeln........ 1442
New Parliament Building........ 1461
Nigg........ 448
Nordic Skiing........ 1824
Norway Spruce (tree)........ 355

O

Oak Tree........ 1751
Oats........ 1791
Oberdendern........ 1386
Occupations........ 844/855
Old Rhine Bridge........ 1642, 1643, 1834
Old Toys........ 1715
Olympic Games, Athens........ 1350
Olympic Games, Barcelona........ 1027
Olympic Games, Beijing........ 1472
Olympic Games, Los Angeles........ 841
Olympic Games, Montreal........ 636
Olympic Games, Munich........ 544
Olympic Games, Seoul........ 942
Olympic Games, Sydney........ 1227
Olympic Games, Tokyo........ 432
Olympic torch........ 1350
Orange Lily........ 519
Orchids........ 1279, 1351
Organisation for Security and Ornamental disc........ 317
Outdoor sports........ 1795

P

Paintings........ 269, 299, 305, 609, 714, 801, 820, 874, 981, 991, 999, 1014, 1021, 1046, 1051, 1099, 1115, 1136, 1142, 1166, 1204, 1218, 1224, 1253, 1267, 1374, 1468, 1548, 1650, 1663, 1747, 1759, 1836
Paintings from Prince's Collection........ 309
Palm Sunday........ 895
Papal Arms........ **MS**873
Papal Visit........ **MS**873
Paralympics, Beijing........ 1477
Parliament and Constitution........ 1606
Patron Saints........ 731
Patrons of the Church........ 477
Peace 2000........ 1224
Pelican........ 1726
Pen and Cross........ 1838
Penny Black........ 989, 1714
Pepper........ 1830
Performing Arts........ 1659
Pfennig........ 1682
Pheasant........ 996
Photography........ 1781
Photovoltaic cells........ 1578
Physics........ 501
Pierce Arrow........ 1690
Pig........ **MS**1863
Pioneers of Flight........ 259
Pioneers of Philately........ 495, 504, 554
Planken........ 227, 278
Planken and Schaan........ **MS**1617
Polar Bear........ 1715
Pole vaulting........ 841
Pond........ 1722, 1723, 1765, 1766
Pope John Paul II........ 825, **MS**1679
Pope Pius XII........ 378
Porcelain........ 1702
Portrait........ 305
Portrait of a Young Lady (painting, da Cottignola)........ 1435
Portrait of a Young Man........ 309
Postal Museum........ 744, 1379
Postal service........ 1217, 1499
Postal vehicles........ 1639
Posthorn........ 279, 576, 594
Postman........ 1241, 1499
Postman and child........ **MS**1813
Preservation of Historical Environment........ 1185
Presidency of Council of Europe........ 1247
Prince Alois........ 918
Prince Constantin........ 606
Prince Francis I........ 92, 109B, 124, 174,
Prince Francis Joseph II........ 241, 302A, 346, 406, 422, 526, 601, **MS**635, 703, **MS**767, 824
Prince Franz Joseph........ 457
Prince Hans Adam........ 201, 1278, 1709, **MS**1710
Prince John Charles........ 210
Prince John II........ 1, 9, 15, 18, 28, 43A, 74, 84, 88, 189, **MS**412*a*
Prince Karl I........ **MS**1491
Prince Nikolaus........ 1583*a*
Prince Wenzel........ 524
Princes and Princesses........ 1583*a*
Princess Elsa........ 119, 258
Princess Georgina........ 214, 330
Princess Gina........ 404*a*, 601, 823, 994
Princess Gina and Prince Franz........ 451
Princess Marie........ 856, 1019, 1277
Princess Tatjana........ 684
Printer's Art........ 1503, 1627, 1693
Puppets........ 883

Q

Quick Response Code........ 1576

R

Radish........ 1828
Railway Bridge........ 1644, 1645
Railways........ 1156
Rainbow........ 1458
Razor........ 1757
Red Cross........ 248, 336, 424, 524, 616, 866
Red Deer........ 252
Relay race........ 1027
Relief........ 1625
Religious Festivals........ 895, 1558, 1578
Reptiles........ 1730
Rheinberger........ 175, 954, 1256, 1677
Rhine Bridge........ 1674
Ritter........ 1759
River bank........ 816
Road makers........ 168
Roadway........ 1556
Roebuck........ 283, 900
Rolls Royce........ 1689

LIECHTENSTEIN / Design Index

Roman Castle 437
Rooster **MS**1790
Rossauer Castle 280
Royal Wedding **MS**471, **MS**1056
Rubens 640
Rural industries 797

S

Saints 1307, 1323, 1367
Salamander 1685
Samaritan Volunteers 1502
Sand Lizard 1730
Satellite 1006
Scenes 1115/1128
Schaan-Vaduz Rail Station 1570
Schadler Ceramics Building 1498
Schellenberg 1267
Schellenberg Castle 160
Schellenberg Convent 1482
Schubert 1149
Schuepp 1396
Science 1354
Scouts 768, 1434
SEPAC (small European mail services) 1454,
  1526, 1592, 1761
Settlement Area 1814
Sheep **MS**1706
Ship 462
Shoemaker 1833
Silver Fir 909
Silver Wedding Anniversary 491
Silversmithing 1769
Ski Jump 1797
Ski slope 732, 1067
Skier 1393
Small European State's Games 1573
Snake 1190, **MS**1633, 1731
Snow flake 826
Snowboarding 1795
Soldiers 1011
Space shuttle 1270
Speed skating 621
Sports 363
Spring 1080, 1839, 1840
St Barbara's Shrine 939
St Elisabeth Convent 863
St Fridolin Parish Church 1292
St Lucius 205, 251
St Mamertus Chapel 55, 360
St Matthew 924, 1145
St Nicholas 1002
St Theodul 770
St Theresa's Chapel 1250
Staircase 919
Stamp 744
Star 829
State Arms 1140
Steam train 1156
Steck 991
Stonemason 1798
Stork 1819
Studebaker 1691
Summer 1807, 1808, 1841, 1842
Summit Crosses 1843
Super Nova 1506
Swimming 1614
Swiss Confederation 1014
Swiss Currency 47aA
Switzerland 1640

T

T 515
Tailor 1799
Tapestries 1852
Technical Innovations 1425, 1451, 1495
Telecommunications symbols 452
Telegraph System 515
Telephone 1188
Text 537
The Alps 1737
The Annunciation (painting) 735, 999, 1209,
  1260, 1360, 1422
The Black Hatter (painting) 1055
The Four Elements 1090
The Letter (painting) 949
The Magic Flute (Mozart) 1413
The Rhine 1439
The Wild Gnomes 1150
Theatre 883
Think Green 1762
Tightrope walker 1271
Title page 1070
Toad 1683
Tourism 1329, 1373, 1405, 1439, 1442
Tractor 797, 1733
Trades and Crafts 1798, 1831
Traditional crafts 1178, 1257

Treasures from Prince's Collection ... 578, 589, 1625,
  MS1669, 1702, 1747, 1769, 1803, 1852
Tree 453, 1585
Tree bark 909
Tree of Life 1054
Trees 754, 1751
Trees and bushes 355, 369, 375, 401
Triesenberg 1373

U

United Nations emblem 1010
United Nations flag 1096
United Nations Membership 1010, 1717
Universal Postal Union 279, 594
University of Applied Science 1534
Unterland **MS**1189

V

Vaduz 62, 1439, **MS**1547
Vaduz Castle 225, 304, 379, 886, 1516,
  1562, 1801, **MS**1811
Vaduz Parish Church 463
Veldkirch 1141
Verling 1204
Vine-dresser 67
Vines 1080, 1295
Violinist 1430
Virgin Mary 1182
Visit Liechtenstein 1608
Viticulture 1295, 1301, 1304, 1312
Volunteer Civil Protection 1539, 1637
Volunteer Fire Service 1467
von Eschenbach **MS**525
von Flüe 914
von Humboldt 1072

W

Waiter and chef 1371
Wall Covering **MS**1669
Walled settlement 318
Walnut 1753
Walser Identification Marks 1212
Wave field 725
Wayside shrines 939
Weapons and Armour 877
Weeping Willow 1752
Wheel, boat and Donkey 1697
White Storks 1311
Windsurfing 1796
Wine press 195
Winged Altar **MS**1676
Winter 1809, 1810
Winter customs 1002
Winter Olympic Games, Albertville 1024
Winter Olympic Games, Calgary 928
Winter Olympic Games, Innsbruck 621
Winter Olympic Games, Lake Placid 732
Winter Olympic Games, Lillehammer 1067
Winter Olympic Games, Nagano 1163
Winter Olympic Games, Pyeongchang 1824
Winter Olympic Games, Sapporo 539
Winter Olympic Games, Sarajevo 826
Winter Olympic Games, Sochi 1671
Winter Olympic Games, Turin 1393
Winter Olympic Games, Vancouver 1537
Winter Walk 1788
Wolf 1818
Woman 1781
Wood carvings 1390
Wooden milk vat 1178
Workers' Issue 168
World Cup Football Championship 593, 792,
  990, 1074, 1173, 1276, 1409
World Map 279
World Refugee Year 399
World Wildlife Fund 630
Wright 259

Y

Year of the Dog **MS**1826
Year of the Dragon **MS**1600
Year of the Horse **MS**1717
Year of the Monkey **MS**1750
Year of the Pig **MS**1863
Year of the Rooster **MS**1790
Year of the Sheep **MS**1706
Year of the Snake **MS**1633
Youth Charities 118

Z

Zodiac 643, 666, 710
Zotow 1142

United Nations Office at Geneva

The following issues, many in the designs of the stamps for the New York Headquarters but with values in Swiss currency, can only be used on mail from the Palais des Nations, Geneva.
They differ from those listed after Switzerland by being issues of the United Nations Postal Administration, and not the Swiss PTT.

G **1** UN Headquarters, New York, and World Map

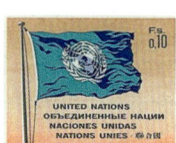

G **2** UN Flag

G **3** Three Figures on Globe (Races United)

G **4** Palms des Nations, Geneva

G **5** Palais des Nations, Geneva

G **6** Opening Words of UN Charter

G **7** UN Emblem across Globe

G **8** UN and Emblem

G **9** Birds in Flight

G **10** Emblem and New York Headquarters

G **12** UN Emblem

G **11** Flags

G **13** Globe and Weather Vane

G **14** Starcke's Statue

G **15** UN Emblem

(Des J. Vertel (5c.), G. Hannon (20c.), O. Mathesen (50c., 60c.), L. Holdandwicz and M. Freudenreich (70c.), V. Pierre-Noel (80c.), H. Sanborn (90c.), Rashid-ud-Din (1f.), M. El Mekki (2f.), Adapted from statue (3f.), J. Doeve (10f.), O. Hamann (others) Litho and embossed West German State Pig Wks, Berlin (1f.), Recess State Bank Note Ptg Wks, Helsinki (10f.), Photo State Bank Note Ptg Wks, Helsinki (5c., 70c., 80c., 90c., 2f.), Austrian State Ptg Wks, Vienna (75c.) or Courvoisier (others))

1969 (4 Oct)–**72**. P 13 (5c., 70c., 90c.), 12½ (10c.), 11½×12 (75c., 10f.), 14 (80c., 1f.), 12×11½ (2f.), 11½ (others).

G1	G **1**	5c. multicoloured	20	20
		a. Yellow-green omitted	£800	
G2	G **2**	10c. multicoloured	25	25
G3	G **3**	20c. multicoloured	30	30
G4	G **4**	30c. multicoloured	35	35
G5	G **5**	40c. multicoloured (5.1.72)	70	70
G6	G **6**	50c. multicoloured	70	70
G7	G **7**	60c. gold, orange-red and deep red brown (17.4.70)	70	70
G8	G **8**	70c. red, gold and black (22.9.70)	70	70
G9	G **9**	75c. multicoloured	70	70
G10	G **10**	80c. multicoloured (22.9.70)	75	75
G11	G **11**	90c. multicoloured (22.9.70)	95	95
G12	G **12**	1f. deep blue-green and light blue-green	1·10	1·10
G13	G **13**	2f. multicoloured (22.9.70)	2·20	2·20
G14	G **14**	3f. multicoloured	3·25	3·25
G15	G **15**	10f. deep ultramarine (17.4.70)	9·00	9·00
G1/G15 *Set of 15*			20·00	20·00

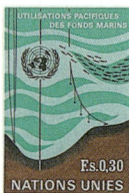

G **16** UN Emblem on Seabed

G **17** Refugees

(Des P. Rahikainen. Recess and photo State Bank Note Ptg Wks, Helsinki)

1971 (25 Jan). Peaceful Uses of the Seabed. P 13.
G16   G **16**   30c. multicoloured 70   70

(Des K. Nygaard and M. Weber. Litho Enschedé)

1971 (12 Mar). United Nations Work with Refugees. P 13×12½.
G17   G **17**   50c. black, orange and carmine-red.... 1·10   1·10

G **18** Wheatsheaf on Globe

G **19** New UPU Headquarters Building

164

1971 UNITED NATIONS OFFICE AT GENEVA

(Des O. Mathiesen. Photo Heraclio Fournier, Spain)
1971 (13 Apr). World Food Programme. P 14.
G18 G 18   50c. multicoloured .... 1·10   1·10

(Des O. Mathiesen. Photo Courvoisier)
1971 (28 May). Opening of New Universal Postal Union Headquarters Building, Berne. P 11½.
G19 G 19   75c. multicoloured .... 1·40   1·40

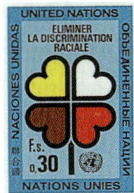

G **20** Four-leafed Clover   G **21** Linked Globes

(Des D. Gonzague (30c.), O. Hamann (50c.). Photo Japanese Govt Ptg Wks, Tokyo)
1971 (21 Sept). Racial Equality Year. P 13½.
G20 G 20   30c. multicoloured 55   55
G21 G 21   50c. multicoloured 80   80

G **22** *Maia* (Picasso)   G **23** X over Atomic Explosion

(Des O. Hamann. Photo Courvoisier)
1971 (19 Nov). United Nations International Schools. P 11½.
G22 G 22   1f.10 multicoloured .... 1·60   1·60

(Des A. Johnson. Photo Heraclio Fournier, Spain)
1972 (14 Feb). Non-Proliferation of Nuclear Weapons. P 13½.
G23 G 23   40c. multicoloured .... 1·10   1·10

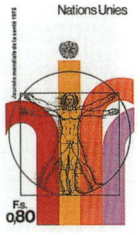 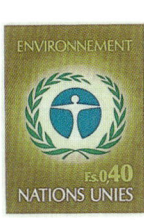

G **24** *Proportions of Man* (Leonardo da Vinci)   G **25** Environmental Emblem

(Des G. Hamori. Recess and litho State Bank Note Ptg Wks, Helsinki)
1972 (7 Apr). World Health Day. P 13.
G24 G 24   80c. multicoloured .... 1·40   1·40

(Des R. Perrot. Litho and embossed Enschedé)
1972 (5 June). UN Environmental Conservation Conference, Stockholm. P 12½×14.
G25 G 25   40c. multicoloured 70   70
G26 G 26   80c. multicoloured .... 1·30   1·30

G **26** Europe Flower   G **27** World United (part of Sert mural, Geneva)

(Des A. Medina. Litho Japanese Govt Ptg Wks, Tokyo)
1972 (11 Sept). Economic Commission for Europe (ECE). P 13×13½.
G27 G 26   1f.10 multicoloured .... 2·20   2·20

(Des O. Hamann. Photo Courvoisier)
1972 (17 Nov). United Nations Art. P 12½.
G28 G 27   40c. multicoloured 70   70
G29   80c. multicoloured .... 1·40   1·40

G **28** Laurel and Broken Sword   G **29** Skull on Poppy

(Des K. Plowitz. Litho Ajans-Türk Matbaasi, Ankara)
1973 (9 Mar). Disarmament Decade. P 13.
G30 G 28   60c. multicoloured 80   80
G31   1f.10 multicoloured .... 1·50   1·50

(Des G. Hamori. Photo Heraclio Fournier, Spain)
1973 (13 Apr). No Drugs Campaign. P 14×13½.
G32 G 29   60c. multicoloured .... 1·10   1·10

G **30** Emblems in Honeycomb   G **31** Namibia

(Des Courvoisier staff artists. Photo Heraclio Fournier, Spain)
1973 (25 May). UN Volunteers Programme. P 14.
G33 G 30   80c. multicoloured .... 1·40   1·40

(Des G. Hamori. Photo Heraclio Fournier, Spain)
1973 (1 Oct). Namibia (South West Africa). P 14.
G34 G 31   60c. multicoloured .... 1·10   1·10

G **32** Emblem and Flame   G **33** Headquarters Building

(Des A. Guerra. Photo Japanese Govt Ptg Wks, Tokyo)
1973 (16 Nov). 25th Anniversary of Declaration of Human Rights. P 13×13½.
G35 G 32   40c. multicoloured 55   55
G36   80c. multicoloured .... 1·10   1·10

(Des H. Bencsath. Photo Heraclio Fournier, Spain)
1974 (11 Jan). Inauguration of New International Labour Organisation Headquarters, Geneva. P 14.
G37 G 33   60c. multicoloured 90   90
G38   80c. multicoloured .... 1·10   1·10

G **34** Globe within Posthorn   G **35** Children's Choir (Candido Portinari)

UNITED NATIONS OFFICE AT GENEVA 1974

(Des A. Johnson. Photo Ashton-Potter, Canada)
1974 (22 Mar). Centenary of Universal Postal Union. P 12½.
G39 G 34 30c. multicoloured 55 55
G40   60c. multicoloured .... 1·10 1·10

(Des adapted by O. Hamann. Photo Heraclio Fournier, Spain)
1974 (6 May). Brazilian Peace Mural. P 14.
G41 G 35 60c. multicoloured 80 80
G42   1f. multicoloured .... 1·40 1·40

G **36** Young Children with Globe

G **37** Ship and Fish

(Des H. Bencsath. Photo Heraclio Fournier, Spain)
1974 (18 Oct). World Population Year. P 14.
G43 G 36 60c. multicoloured 80 80
G44   80c. multicoloured .... 1·10 1·10

(Des A. Kalderon. Photo Heraclio Fournier, Spain)
1974 (22 Nov). UN Conferences on Law of the Sea. P 14.
G45 G 37 1f.30 multicoloured .... 1·70 1·70

G **38** Satellite, Globe and Symbols

G **39** Sex Equality

(Des H. Bencsath. Litho State Bank Note Ptg Wks, Helsinki)
1975 (14 Mar). Peaceful Uses of Outer Space. P 13.
G46 G 38 60c. multicoloured 80 80
G47   90c. multicoloured .... 1·20 1·20

(Des E. Kurti and A. Kalderon. Litho Questa)
1975 (9 May). International Women's Year. P 14.
G48 G 39 60c. multicoloured 80 80
G49   90c. multicoloured .... 1·20 1·20

G **40** The Hope of Mankind

G **41** Cupped Hand

(Des A. Kalderon. Litho Ashton-Potter, Toronto)
1975 (26 June). 30th Anniversary of United Nations Organisation. P 13×13½.
G50 G 40 60c. multicoloured 75 75
G51   90c. multicoloured .... 1·10 1·10
MSG52 92×70 mm. Nos. G50/G51, Imperf .... 2·30 2·30

(Des H. Bencsath. Photo Heraclio Fournier)
1975 (22 Sept). Namibia. UN Direct Responsibility. P 13½.
G53 G 41 50c. multicoloured 60 60
G54   1f.30 multicoloured .... 1·50 1·50

G **42** Wild Rose and Barbed Wire

G **43** Linked Ribbands

(Des E. Olvio. Recess State Bank Note Ptg Wks, Helsinki)
1975 (21 Nov). UN Peacekeeping Operations. P 12½.
G55 G 42 60c. turquoise-blue 75 75
G56   70c. reddish violet .... 1·00 1·00

(Des G. Hannon. Photo Heraclio Fournier)
1976 (12 Mar). World Federation of UN Associations. P 14.
G57 G 43 90c. multicoloured .... 1·20 1·20

G **44** Globe and Crate

G **45** Houses bordering Globe

(Des H. Bencsath. Photo Courvoisier)
1976 (23 Apr). UN Trade and Development Conference. P 11½.
G58 G 44 1f.10 multicoloured .... 1·40 1·40

(Des E. Weisshoff. Photo Heraclio Fournier)
1976 (28 May). UN Human Settlements Conference. P 14.
G59 G 45 40c. multicoloured 50 50
G60   1f.50 multicoloured .... 1·80 1·80

G **46** UN Emblem within Posthorn

G **47** Stylised Ear of Wheat

(Des H. Viola. Photo Courvoisier)
1976 (8 Oct). 25th Anniversary of UN Postal Administration. P 11½.
G61 G 46 80c. multicoloured .... 2·40 2·40
G62   1f.10 multicoloured .... 3·00 3·00

(Des E. Weisshoff. Litho Questa)
1976 (19 Nov). World Food Council Publicity. P 14½.
G63 G 47 70c. multicoloured .... 1·10 1·10

G **48** WIPO Headquarters

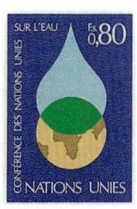
G **49** Rain Drop and Globe

1977 UNITED NATIONS OFFICE AT GENEVA

(Des E. Weishoff. Photo Heraclio Fournier)
1977 (11 Mar). World Intellectual Property Organisation Publicity. P 13½×14.
G64   G **48**   80c. multicoloured .... 1·20   1·20

(Des E. Tomei. Photo Japanese Govt Ptg Wks, Tokyo)
1977 (22 Apr). UN Water Conference. P 13.
G65   G **49**   80c. multicoloured .... 1·10   1·10
G66   1f.10 multicoloured .... 1·50   1·50

G **50** Protective Hands

(Des G. Hamori. Photo Heraclio Fournier)
1977 (27 May). Security Council Commemoration. P 14.
G67   G **50**   80c. multicoloured .... 1·10   1·10
G68   1f.10 multicoloured .... 1·50   1·50

G **51** Intertwining of Races

(Des M. A. Munnawar. Litho State Bank Note Ptg Wks, Helsinki)
1977 (19 Sept). Combat Racism. P 13½×13.
G69   G **51**   40c. multicoloured 55   55
G70   1f.10 multicoloured .... 1·50   1·50

G **52** Atoms and Laurel Leaf   G **53** Tree and Birds

(Des W. Janowski and M. Freudenreich. Photo Heraclio Fournier)
1977 (18 Nov). Peaceful Uses for Atomic Energy. P 14.
G71   G **52**   80c. multicoloured 95   95
G72   1f.10 multicoloured .... 1·50   1·50

(Des M. Hioki. Litho Questa)
1978 (27 Jan). P 14½.
G73   G **53**   35c. multicoloured 70   70
   A stamp of a similar design was also issued by United Nations (Vienna).

 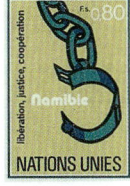

G **54** Smallpox Bacilli and Globe   G **55** Broken Manacle

(Des E. Weishoff. Photo Courvoisier)
1978 (31 Mar). Global Eradication of Smallpox. P 11½.
G74   G **54**   80c. multicoloured .... 1·10   1·10
G75   1f.10 multicoloured .... 1·50   1·50

(Des C. Tomei. Photo State Ptg Wks. Vienna)
1978 (5 May). Namibia. Liberation, Justice, Co-operation. P 12.
G76   G **55**   80c. multicoloured .... 1·10   1·10

G **56** Aircraft Flight Paths   G **57** Globe, Flags and General Assembly Interior

(Des T. R. Savrda. Photo Heraclio Fournier)
1978 (12 June). International Civil Aviation Organisation. Safety in the Air. P 14.
G77   G **56**   70c. multicoloured .... 1·00   1·00
G78   80c. multicoloured .... 1·20   1·20

(Des H. Bencsath. Photo Mitsubishi Corporation, Japan)
1978 (15 Sept). General Assembly. P 13.
G79   G **57**   70c. multicoloured .... 1·00   1·00
G80   1f.10 multicoloured .... 1·60   1·60

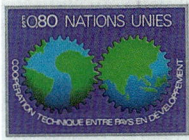 

G **58** Hemispheres within Cogwheels   G **59** Disaster

(Des S. Keter and D. Pesach. Photo Heraclio Fournier)
1978 (17 Nov). Technical Co-operation among Developing Countries. P 14.
G81   G **58**   80c. multicoloured .... 1·30   1·30

(Des M. Klutmann. Photo Heraclio Fournier)
1979 (9 Mar). UN Disaster Relief Co-ordinator. P 14.
G82   G **59**   80c. multicoloured .... 1·20   1·20
G83   1f.50 multicoloured .... 2·20   2·20

G **60** Children and Rainbow   G **61** Olive Branch and Map of Namibia

(Des A. Glaser. Photo Heraclio Fournier)
1979 (4 May). International Year of the Child. P 14.
G84   G **60**   80c. multicoloured .... 1·10   1·10
G85   1f.10 multicoloured .... 1·50   1·50

(Des E. Weishoff. Litho Ashton-Potter)
1979 (5 Oct). For a Free and Independent Namibia. P 13.
G86   G **61**   1f.10 multicoloured .... 1·40   1·40

G **62** International Court of Justice and Scales   G **63** Key symbolising Unity of Action

(Des K. Maeno. Litho State Bank Note Ptg Wks, Helsinki)
1979 (9 Nov). International Court of Justice. P 13.
G87   G **62**   80c. multicoloured .... 1·10   1·10
G88   1f.10 multicoloured .... 1·50   1·50

UNITED NATIONS OFFICE AT GENEVA 1980

(Des J.-P. Meuer. Litho Questa)
1980 (11 Jan). New International Economic Order. P 14½.
G89   G **63**   80c. multicoloured .... 1·10   1·10

G **64** Emblem

G **65** Helmet

(Des M. A. Munnawar. Litho Questa)
1980 (7 Mar). UN Decade for Women. P 14½.
G90   G **64**   40c. multicoloured 55   55
G91   70c. multicoloured 95   95

(Des B. Wiese. Litho Enschedé)
1980 (16 May). Peacekeeping Operations. P 14×12½.
G92   G **65**   1f.10 new blue and blue-green .... 1·50   1·50

G **66** Dove and 35

G **67** 35 composed of Flags

(Des G. Sagi (40c.), C. Mutver (70c.), O. Hamann (No. **MS**G95). Litho Ashton-Potter, Toronto)
1980 (26 June). 35th Anniversary of United Nations. P 13.
G93   G **66**   40c. grey-black and turquoise-blue 55   55
G94   G **67**   70c. multicoloured 95   95
MSG95 92×73 mm. Nos. G93/G94 Imperf .... 1·60   1·60

G **68** Various Emblems forming Bunch of Flowers   G **69** Figures ascending Graph

(Des D. Kowall (40c.), A. Medina (70c.). Litho Ashton-Potter, Toronto)
1980 (21 Nov). Economic and Social Council. P 13.
G96   G **68**   40c. multicoloured 55   55
G97   G **69**   70c. blue, dull vermilion and black 95   95

G **70** Text and UN Emblem

(Des D. Dewhurst. Photo Courvoisier)
1981 (30 Jan). Inalienable Rights of the Palestinian People. P 11½.
G98   G **70**   80c. multicoloured .... 1·10   1·10

G **71** Disabled Person

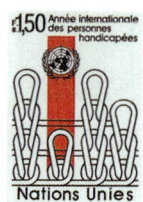
G **72** Knot Pattern

(Des G. P. van der Hyde (40c.), S. van Heeswyck (1f.50). Photo Heraclio Fournier)
1981 (6 Mar). International Year of Disabled Persons. P 14.
G99   G **71**   40c. black and greenish blue 55   55
G100   G **72**   1f.50 black and bright scarlet .... 2·00   2·00

G **73** Sebastocrator Kaloyan and his wife Desislava (13th-century Bulgarian fresco)

G **74** Sun and Sea

(Des O. Hamann. Photo Courvoisier)
1981 (15 Apr). Art. P 11½.
G101   G **73**   80c. multicoloured .... 1·10   1·10

(Des U. Dreyer. Litho State Bank Note Ptg Wks, Helsinki)
1981 (29 May). New and Renewable Sources of Energy. P 13.
G102   G **74**   1f.10 multicoloured .... 1·50   1·50

G **75** Grafted Plant

G **76** Emblems of Science, Agriculture and Industry

(Des G. Nussgen (40c.), B. Mirbach (70c.). Litho Walsall Security Printers)
1981 (13 Nov). Tenth Anniversary of UN Volunteers Programme. P 13½×13.
G103   G **75**   40c. multicoloured 55   55
G104   G **76**   70c. multicoloured 95   95

G **77** Anti-apartheid

G **78** Flags

(Des T. Savrda (30c.), D. Kowall (1f.). Photo Courvoisier)
1982 (22 Jan). P 11½.
G105   G **77**   30c. multicoloured 40   40
G106   G **78**   1f. multicoloured .... 1·40   1·40

G **79** Leaves

G **80** Hand holding Seedling

(Des S. Brunner (40c.), P. Hartert (1f.20). Litho Enschedé)
1982 (19 Mar). Human Environment. P 13½×13.
G107   G **79**   40c. multicoloured 55   55
G108   G **80**   1f.20 multicoloured .... 1·60   1·60

1982 UNITED NATIONS OFFICE AT GENEVA

 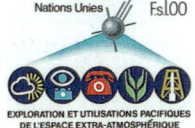

G **81** Olive Branch and UN Emblem

G **82** Satellite and Emblems

(Des W. C. Nerwinski (80c.), G. Hamori (1f.). Litho Enschedé)

1982 (11 June). Second United Nations Conference on Exploration and Peaceful Uses of Outer Space. P 13½.
G109	G **81**	80c. bright violet, rose-pink and light green	1·10	1·10
G110	G **82**	1f. multicoloured	1·40	1·40

G **83** Bird

G **84** Snake (reptiles)

(Des G. Hamori. Photo Heraclio Fournier)

1982 (19 Nov). Conservation and Protection of Nature. P 14.
G111	G **83**	40c. multicoloured	55	55
G112	G **84**	1f.50 multicoloured	2·00	2·00

G **85** Cable Network

(Des L. Berengo. Litho Walsall Security Printers Ltd)

1983 (28 Jan). World Communications Year. P 13½×13.
G113	G **85**	1f.20 multicoloured	1·60	1·60

G **86** Ship and Buoy

G **87** Radar Screen within Lifebelt

(Des J. M. Lenfant (40c.), V. Wurnitsch (80c.). Litho Questa)

1983 (18 Mar). Safety at Sea. International Maritime Organisation. P 14½.
G114	G **86**	40c. multicoloured	55	55
G115	G **87**	80c. multicoloured	1·10	1·10

G **88** Giving Food

(Des M. Kwiatkowski. Recess Govt Ptg Wks, Tokyo)

1983 (22 Apr). World Food Programme. P 13½.
G116	G **88**	1f.50 blue	2·00	2·00

G **89** Coins and Cogwheels

G **90** Exports

(Des D. Braklow (80c.), W. Brykczynski (1f.10). Litho Carl Ueberreuter, Vienna)

1983 (6 June). Trade and Development. P 14.
G117	G **89**	80c. multicoloured	1·10	1·10
G118	G **90**	1f.10 multicoloured	1·50	1·50

G **91** Homo Humus Humanitas

G **92** Droit de Creer

(Des F. Hundertwasser. Recess and photo State Ptg Wks, Vienna)

1983 (9 Dec). 35th Anniversary of Universal Declaration of Human Rights. P 14.
G119	G **91**	40c. multicoloured	55	55
G120	G **92**	1f.20 multicoloured	1·60	1·60

G **93** World Housing

(Des Marina Langer-Rosa and H. Langer. Litho State Ptg Wks, Berlin)

1984 (3 Feb). International Conference on Population, Mexico City. P 14.
G121	G **93**	1f.20 multicoloured	1·60	1·60

G **94** Fish in net

G **95** Planting Saplings

(Des A. Vanooijen. Litho Walsall Security Printers Ltd)

1984 (15 Mar). World Food Day. P 14½.
G122	G **94**	50c. multicoloured	70	70
G123	G **95**	80c. multicoloured	1·10	1·10

G **96** Fort St Angelo, Malta

G **97** Los Glaciares, Argentina

(Des R. J. Callan and T. Lee. Litho Harrison)

1984 (18 Apr). World Heritage. UN Educational, Scientific and Cultural Organisation. P 14½.
G124	G **96**	50c. multicoloured	80	80
G125	G **97**	70c. multicoloured	1·10	1·10

No. G124 is wrongly described as Valetta.

UNITED NATIONS OFFICE AT GENEVA 1984

G **98** Man and Woman   G **99** Head of Woman

(Des H. Erni. Photo Courvoisier)
1984 (29 May). Future for Refugees. P 11½.
G126 G **98**   35c. black and yellow-olive................. 55   55
G127 G **99**   1f.50 black and reddish brown............. 2·00 2·00

G **100** Heads

(Des E. Weishoff. Litho J.W.)
1984 (15 Nov). International Youth Year. P 13½.
G128 G **100** 1f.20 multicoloured.............................. 1·80 1·80

G **101** Turin Centre Emblem   G **102** U Thant Pavilion

(Des R. J. Callari and T. Lee. Eng M. Iwakuni and H. Ozaki (80c.), H. Sasaki and K. Uematsu (1f.20). Recess Govt Ptg Wks, Tokyo)
1985 (1 Feb). 20th Anniversary of Turin Centre of International Labour Organisation. P 13½.
G129 G **101** 80c. brown-red.................................... 1·10 1·10
G130 G **102** 1f.20 deep blue-green........................... 1·60 1·60

G **103** Ploughing and Group of People

(Des H. Geluda and M. Pereg. Photo Courvoisier)
1985 (15 Mar). Tenth Anniversary of United Nations University, Tokyo. Granite paper. P 11½.
G131 G **103** 50c. multicoloured............................... 70   70
G132   80c. multicoloured............................... 1·10 1·10

G **104** Postman   G **105** Doves

(Des A. Glaser (20c.), K. Sliwka (1f.20). Litho Carl Ueberreuter, Vienna)
1985 (10 May). P 14.
G133 G **104** 20c. multicoloured............................... 25   25
G134 G **105** 1f.20 new blue and black....................... 1·60 1·60

G **106** Snow Scene (Andrew Wyeth)   G **107** Harvest Scene (Andrew Wyeth)

(Photo Courvoisier)
1985 (26 June). 40th Anniversary of United Nations Organisation. Granite paper. P 11½.
G135 G **106** 50c. multicoloured............................... 70   70
G136 G **107** 70c. multicoloured............................... 95   95
MSG137 76×81 mm. Nos. G135/G136 Imperf............... 2·75 2·75

G **108** Children   G **109** Child Drinking

(Des M. Harris (50c.). A. Vanooijen (1f.20). Recess and photo Govt Ptg Wks, Tokyo)
1985 (22 Nov). UNICEF Child Survival Campaign. P 13½.
G138 G **108** 50c. multicoloured............................... 70   70
G139 G **109** 1f.20 multicoloured.............................. 1·60 1·60

G **110** Children raising Empty Bowls to Weeping Mother   G **111** Herring Gulls

(Des Alemayehou Gabremedhiu. Photo Courvoisier)
1986 (31 Jan). Africa in Crisis. Granite paper. P 11½.
G140 G **110** 1f.40 multicoloured.............................. 1·90 1·90

(Des R. Alcantara Rodriguez. Litho Questa)
1986 (14 Mar). P 15×14½.
G141 G **111** 5c. multicoloured................................. 40   40

G **112**/G **115** Timber Production

(Des T. Lee. Photo Govt Ptg Wks, Tokyo)
1986 (14 Mar). Development Programme. P 13½.
G142 G **112** 35c. multicoloured............................... 2·75 2·75
              a. Block of 4 Nos. G142/G145........ 11·50
G143 G **113** 35c. multicoloured............................... 2·75 2·75
G144 G **114** 35c. multicoloured............................... 2·75 2·75
G145 G **115** 35c. multicoloured............................... 2·75 2·75
G142/G145 *Set of 4*.. 10·00 10·00
    Nos. G142/G145 were issued together in *se-tenant* blocks of four within the sheet, each block forming the composite design illustrated.

1986 UNITED NATIONS OFFICE AT GENEVA

G **116** Magnifying Glass and Stamp

(Des G. Mathieu: photo Courvoisier (90c.). Recess and photo Govt Ptg Wks, Tokyo (1f.40))
1987 (30 Jan). P 11½×12 (90c.) or 13½ (1f.40).
G152 G **122** 90c. multicoloured.................... 1·20 1·20
G153 G **123** 1f.40 multicoloured.................. 1·90 1·90

G **117** United Nations Stamps

(Des I. Axelsson. Eng C. Slania. Recess Swedish Stamp Ptg Office)
1986 (22 May). Philately. P 12½.
G146 G **116** 50c. slate-green and scarlet-vermilion............................... 80 80
G147 G **117** 80c. black and orange............... 1·50 1·50

G **124** Mixing Cement and Carrying Bricks

G **125** Fitting Windows and Painting

(Des W. Brykczynski. Litho Enschedé)
1987 (13 Mar). International Year of Shelter for the Homeless. P 13½×12.
G154 G **124** 50c. deep olive and black............ 1·10 1·10
G155 G **125** 90c. blue, greenish blue and black... 1·60 1·60

G **118** Ribbon forming Dove

G **119** Peace and Olive Branch

(Des R. Ferrini (45c.), S. Kanidinc (1f.40). Photo and embossed Govt Ptg Wks, Tokyo)
1986 (20 June). International Peace Year. P 13½.
G148 G **118** 45c. multicoloured....................... 70 70
G149 G **119** 1f.40 multicoloured.................... 2·00 2·00

G **126** Mother and Baby   G **127** Workers in Paddy field

(Des Susan Borgen, N. Werret and C. M. Dudash. Litho Questa)
1987 (12 June). Anti-drugs Campaign. P 14½×15.
G156 G **126** 80c. multicoloured....................... 1·40 1·40
G157 G **127** 1f.20 multicoloured.................... 1·90 1·90

G **120** *(Illustration reduced, actual size 120×65 mm)*

(Litho Enschedé)
1986 (14 Nov). 40th Anniversary of World Federation of United Nations Associations. Sheet 120×65 mm. Multicoloured. P 13×13½.
MS G150 G **120** 35c. Birds (Benigno Gomez); 45c. Circle and prisms (Alexander Calder); 50c. Eye (Joan Miró); 70c. Dove and musical instruments (Ole Hamann)............................... 10·00 10·00

G **128** People in Boat and Palms des Nations, Geneva

G **129** Dancers

(Des Elisabeth von Janota-Bzowski (35c.), F. H. Oerter (50c.). Litho Questa)
1987 (23 Oct). United Nations Day. P 14½×15.
G158 G **128** 35c. multicoloured....................... 80 80
G159 G **129** 50c. multicoloured....................... 1·40 1·40

G **121** Trygve Lie (after Harald Dal)

(Eng W. Seidel. Recess and photo State Ptg Wks, Vienna)
1987 (30 Jan). Ninth Death Anniversary of Trygve Lie (first UN Secretary-General). P 13½×14.
G151 G **121** 1f.40 multicoloured.................... 1·90 1·90

G **130** Whooping Cough

G **131** Tuberculosis

(Des S. Chwast. Litho Questa)
1987 (20 Nov). Immunise Every Child. P 15×14½.
G160 G **130** 90c. multicoloured....................... 1·40 1·40
G161 G **131** 1f.70 multicoloured.................... 2·75 2·75

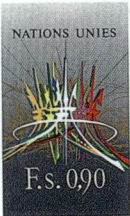

G **122** Abstract

G **123** Armillary Sphere, Geneva Centre

G **132** Goatherd

G **133** Women and Baskets of Fruit

171

UNITED NATIONS OFFICE AT GENEVA 1988

(Des S. Arolas. Litho CPE Australia Ltd, Melbourne)
1988 (29 Jan). International Fund for Agricultural Development For a World Without Hunger Campaign. P 13½.
G162	G **132**	35c. multicoloured	70	70
G163	G **133**	1f.40 multicoloured	2·30	2·30

G **141** Flame

(Des R. Callari. Photo Courvoisier)
1988 (9 Dec). 40th Anniversary of Declaration of Human Rights. Granite paper. P 11½.
G171	G **141**	90c. multicoloured	1·40	1·40
MSG172	120×79 mm. Type G **141** 2f. multicoloured		3·75	3·75

G **142** Communications	G **143** Industry	G **144** Blue Helmet Soldier

G **134** People G **135**/G **136** Pine Forest

(Des B. Wiinblad. Photo Heraclio Fournier)
1988 (29 Jan). P 14.
G164	G **134**	50c. multicoloured	80	80

(Des B. Bralds. Litho Questa)
1988 (18 Mar). Survival of the Forests. P 14×15.
G165	G **135**	50c. multicoloured	6·00	6·00
		a. Vert pair Nos. G165/G166	12·50	12·50
G166	G **136**	1f.10 multicoloured	6·00	6·00

Nos. G165/G166 were issued together in sheetlets of 12 stamps comprising six vertical *se-tenant* pairs, each pair forming the composite design illustrated.

(Des S. Lumboy. Litho Enschedé)
1989 (27 Jan). World Bank. P 13×14.
G173	G **142**	80c. multicoloured	1·40	1·40
G174	G **143**	1f.40 multicoloured	2·00	2·00

(Des T. Bland. Litho CPE Australia Ltd. Melbourne)
1989 (17 Mar). Award of Nobel Peace Prize to United Nations Peacekeeping Forces. P 14×13½.
G175	G **144**	90c. multicoloured	1·50	1·50

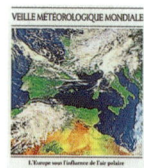 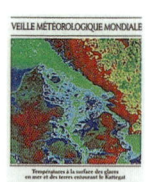

G **145** Cold Arctic Air over Europe G **146** Surface Temperatures of Kattegat

G **137** Instruction in Fruit Growing	G **138** Teaching Animal Husbandry

(Des C. Magadini. Litho Enschedé)
1988 (6 May). International Volunteer Day. P 13×14 (80c.) or 14×13 (90c.).
G167	G **137**	80c. multicoloured	1·20	1·20
G168	G **138**	90c. multicoloured	1·50	1·50

(Des R. Callari and R. Stein. Litho Enschedé)
1989 (21 Apr). 25th Anniversary of World Weather Watch. P 13×14.
G176	G **145**	90c. multicoloured	1·60	1·60
G177	G **146**	1f.10 multicoloured	2·20	2·20

G **147** Tree and Birds G **148** Woman and Flower

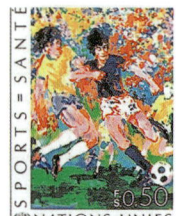

G **139** Football G **140** Swimming

(Des L. Neiman. Litho Govt Ptg Wks, Tokyo)
1988 (17 June). Health in Sports. P 13½×13 (50c.) or 13×13½ (1f.40).
G169	50c. multicoloured	80	80
G170	1f.40 multicoloured	2·20	2·20

(Des A. Lehmden (50c.) Des A. Brauer, eng W. Seidel (2f.) Photo (50c.) or recess and photo (2f.) State Ptg Wks, Vienna)
1989 (23 Aug). Tenth Anniversary of United Nations Vienna International Centre. P 14.
G178	G **147**	50c. multicoloured	95	95
G179	G **148**	2f. multicoloured	3·75	3·75

1989 UNITED NATIONS OFFICE AT GENEVA

G **149** *Young Mother sewing* (Mary Cassatt) (Article 3)

G **150** *Runaway Slave* (Albert Mangones) (Article 4)

(Des R. Callari, R. Stein and A. Gaines. Litho Enschedé)

1989 (17 Nov). Universal Declaration of Human Rights (1st series). P 13½.
G180	G **149**	35f. multicoloured	70	70
G181	G **150**	80f. multicoloured	1·20	1·20

Nos. G180/G181 were each issued with *se-tenant* label giving the text of the Article in English, French or German, in sheets of 12 stamps and 12 labels.
See also Nos. G193/G194, G209/G210, G224/G225 and G234/G235.

G **151** *Port Activities*

G **152** *Palais des Nations*

(Des R. Bernstein. Litho Questa)

1990 (2 Feb). International Trade Centre. P 14½×15.
G182	G **151**	1f.50 multicoloured	2·50	2·50

(Des G. Breniaux and Elizabeth White. Photo Heraclio Fournier)

1990 (2 Feb). P 14.
G183	G **182**	5f. multicoloured	6·50	6·50

G **153** *AIDS*

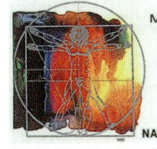
G **154** *Vitruvian Man* (Leonardo da Vinci)

(Des J. Tofil (50c.), Lee Keun Moon (80c.). Litho Enschedé)

1990 (16 Mar). Anti-AIDS Campaign. P 13½×12½.
G184	G **153**	50c. multicoloured	1·10	1·10
G185	G **154**	80c. multicoloured	1·60	1·60

G **155** *Frangipani* (*Plumena rubra*)

G **156** *Cinchona officinalis*

(Photo Courvoisier)

1990 (4 May). Medicinal Plants. Granite paper. P 11½.
G186	G **155**	90c. multicoloured	1·40	1·40
G187	G **156**	1f.40 multicoloured	2·00	2·00

G **157** *Projects forming 45*

G **158** *Dove and 45*

(Des Ruth Schmidthammer (90c.), M. Mertens (1f.10), R. Stein (No. **MS**G190) Litho Enschedé)

1990 (26 June). 45th Anniversary of United Nations Organisation. P 14½×13.
G188	G **157**	90c. multicoloured	1·60	1·60
G189	G **158**	1f.10 multicoloured	1·90	1·90
MSG190	100×73 mm. Nos. G188/G189		5·75	5·75

G **159** *Men making Deal over Painting*

G **160** *Man spilling Waste from Cart*

(Des J. Ryzec. Litho Heraclio Fournier)

1990 (13 Sept). Crime Prevention. P 14.
G191	G **159**	50c. multicoloured	80	80
G192	G **160**	2f. multicoloured	3·25	3·25

G **161** *Prison Courtyard* (Vincent van Gogh) (Article 9)

G **162** *Katho's Son Redeems the Evil Doer from Execution* (Albrecht Dürer) (Article 10)

(Des R. Callari, R. Stein and A. Gaines. Litho Enschedé)

1990 (16 Nov). Universal Declaration of Human Rights (2nd series). P 13½.
G193	G **161**	35c. multicoloured	55	55
G194	G **162**	90c. black and pale flesh	1·50	1·50

Nos. G193 and G194 were each issued with *se-tenant* label giving the text of the Article in English, French or German, in sheets of 12 stamps and 12 labels.

G **163**/G **166** *Lake*

(Des C. Ochagavia. Litho Heraclio Fournier)

1991 (15 Mar). Economic Commission for Europe. For a Better Environment. P 14.
G195	G **163**	90c. multicoloured	2·40	2·40
		a. Block of 4 Nos. G195/G198	9·75	
G196	G **164**	90c. multicoloured	2·40	2·40
G197	G **165**	90c. multicoloured	2·40	2·40
G198	G **166**	90c. multicoloured	2·40	2·40
G195/G198 Set of 4			8·75	8·75

Nos. G195/G198 were issued together in *se-tenant* blocks of four within the sheet, each block forming the composite design illustrated.

G **167** *Mountains*

G **168** *Baobab*

173

UNITED NATIONS OFFICE AT GENEVA 1991

(Des R. Callari and R. Stein. Litho Heraclio Fournier)
1991 (10 May). First Anniversary of Namibian independence. P 14.
G199 G **167** 70c. multicoloured .... 1·40 1·40
G200 G **168** 90c. multicoloured .... 1·90 1·90

G **169** Papers and Ballot Box

G **170** UN Emblem

(Des R. Mawilmada (80c.). M. Goujou (1f.50). Litho Questa)
1991 (10 May). P 15×14½.
G201 G **169** 80c. multicoloured .... 1·20 1·20
G202 G **170** 1f.50 multicoloured .... 2·20 2·20

G **171** Baby in Open Hands (Ryuta Nakalima)

G **172** Children playing amongst Flowers (David Popper)

(Litho Questa)
1991 (14 June). 30th Anniversary (1989) of UN Declaration on the Rights of the Child and 1990 World Summit on Children. New York Children's Drawings. P 14½.
G203 G **171** 80c. multicoloured .... 1·50 1·50
G204 G **172** 1f.10 multicoloured .... 1·90 1·90

G **173** Bubble of Toxin, City and Drums

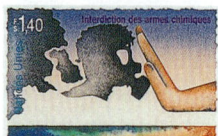
G **174** Hand pushing back Gas Mask

(Des O. Asboth (80c.), M. Granger (1f.40). Litho Heraclio Fournier)
1991 (11 Sept). Banning of Chemical Weapons. P 13½×14.
G205 G **173** 80c. multicoloured .... 1·50 1·50
G206 G **174** 1f.40 multicoloured .... 2·50 2·50

G **175** UN (New York) 1951 15c. Stamp

G **176** UN (New York) 1951 50c. Stamp

(Des R. Callari. Litho Questa)
1991 (24 Oct). 40th Anniversary of United Nations Postal Administration. P 14½×15.
G207 G **175** 50c. blue and deep lilac/*cream* 80 80
G208 G **176** 1f.60 indigo/*cream* .... 2·50 2·50

G **177** Early Morning in Ro, 1925 (Paul Klee) (Article 15)

G **178** The Marriage of Arnolfini (Jan van Eyck) (Article 16)

(Des R. Callari, R. Stein and A. Gaines. Litho Enschedé)
1991 (20 Nov). Universal Declaration of Human Rights (3rd series). P 13½.
G209 G **177** 50c. multicoloured 80 80
G210 G **178** 90c. multicoloured .... 1·60 1·60
Nos. G209/G210 were each issued with *se-tenant* label giving the text of the Article in English, French or German, in sheets of 12 stamps and 12 labels.

G **179** Sagarmatha National Park, Nepal

G **180** Stonehenge, United Kingdom

(Des R. Stein. Litho Cartor)
1992 (24 Jan). 20th Anniversary of UNESCO World Heritage Convention. P 13.
G211 G **179** 50c. multicoloured .... 1·20 1·20
G212 G **180** 1f.10 multicoloured .... 2·50 2·50

G **181** UN Headquarters, New York

G **182**/G **183** Sea Life

(Des N. Martin. Litho Questa)
1992 (24 Jan). P 15×14½.
G213 G **181** 3f. multicoloured .... 4·50 4·50

(Des B. Bralds. Litho Questa)
1992 (13 Mar). Clean Oceans. P 14×15.
G214 G **182** 80c. multicoloured .... 1·80 1·80
　　　　　　　　a. Vert pair. Nos. G214/G215........... 3·75 3·75
G215 G **183** 80c. multicoloured .... 1·80 1·80
Nos. G214/G215 were issued together in sheetlets of 12 stamps comprising six vertical *se-tenant* pairs, each pair forming the composite design illustrated.

1992 UNITED NATIONS OFFICE AT GENEVA

G **184**/G **187** Planet Earth

(Des P. Max. Photo Courvoisier)

1992 (22 May). Second United Nations Conference on Environment and Development, Rio de Janeiro. Granite paper. P 11½.

G216	G **184**	75c. multicoloured	1·60	1·60
		a. Block of 4 Nos. G216/G219	6·75	
G217	G **185**	75c. multicoloured	1·60	1·60
G218	G **186**	75c. multicoloured	1·60	1·60
G219	G **187**	75c. multicoloured	1·60	1·60
G216/G219	Set of 4		5·75	5·75

Nos. G216/G219 were issued together in *se-tenant* blocks of four within the sheet, each block forming the composite design illustrated.

G **188**/G **189** Mission Planet Earth

(Des A. Hejja. Photo Courvoisier)

1992 (4 Sept). International Space Year. Granite paper. Rouletted.

G220	G **188**	1f.10 multicoloured	2·00	2·00
		a. Horiz pair Nos. G220/G221	4·25	4·25
G221	G **189**	1f.10 multicoloured	2·00	2·00

Nos. G220/G221 were issued together in horizontal *se-tenant* pairs within the sheet, each pair forming the composite design illustrated.

G **190** Women in Science and Technology
G **191** Graduate using VDU

(Des S. Mandel. Litho Unicover Corp, Cheyenne, USA)

1992 (2 Oct). Commission on Science and Technology for Development. P 13½×14.

G222	G **190**	90c. multicoloured	1·60	1·60
G223	G **191**	1f.60 multicoloured	2·75	2·75

G **192** The Oath of the Tennis Court (Jacques-Louis David) (Article 21)
G **193** Rocking Chair I (Henry Moore) (Article 22)

(Des R. Stein and A. Gaines. Litho Enschedé)

1992 (20 Nov). Universal Declaration of Human Rights (4th series). P 13½.

G224	G **192**	50c. multicoloured	70	70
G225	G **193**	90c. multicoloured	1·40	1·40

Nos. G224/G225 were each issued with *se-tenant* label giving the text of the Article in English, French or German, in sheets of 12 stamps and 12 labels.

G **194** Voluntary Work
G **195** Security of Employment

(Des C. Dudash. Litho Cartor)

1993 (5 Feb). Ageing. Dignity and Participation. Tenth Anniversary (1992) of International Plan of Action on Ageing. P. 13.

G226	G **194**	50c. multicoloured	95	95
G227	G **195**	1f.60 multicoloured	2·75	2·75

G **196** Gorilla
G **197** Peregrine Falcon (*Falco peregrinus*)

G **198** Amazon Manatee (*Trichechus inunguts*)
G **199** Snow Leopard (*Panthers, uncia*)

(Des Betina Ogden. Litho Enschedé)

1993 (3 Mar). Endangered Species (1st series). P 12½.

G228	G **196**	80c. multicoloured	1·40	1·40
		a. Block of 4. Nos. G228/G231	5·75	
G229	G **197**	80c. multicoloured	1·40	1·40
G230	G **198**	80c. multicoloured	1·40	1·40
G231	G **199**	80c. multicoloured	1·40	1·40
G228/G231	Set of 4		5·00	5·00

Nos. G228/G231 were issued together in *se-tenant* blocks of four within the sheet.

See also Nos. G246/G249, G264/G267, G290/G293, G308/G311, G333/G336, G372/G375, G389/G392, G409/G412, G433/G436, G460/G463, G476/G479, G498/G501, G520/G523, G544/G547, G571/G574, G617/G620a, G653/G656, G716/G719, G732/G735, G766/G769, G795/G798 and G809/G812.

G **200** Neighbourhood and Community Environment
G **201** Urban Environment

(Des M. Glaser. Litho Leigh-Mardon Pty Ltd, Melbourne)

1993 (7 May). 45th Anniversary of World Health Organisation. P 15×14½.

G232	G **200**	60c. multicoloured	1·40	1·40
G233	G **201**	1f. multicoloured	2·00	2·00

G **202** Three Musicians (Pablo Picasso) (Article 27)
G **203** Voice of Space (Rene Magritte) (Article 28)

UNITED NATIONS OFFICE AT GENEVA 1993

(Des A. Gaines and R. Stein. Litho Enschedé)
1993 (11 June). Declaration of Human Rights (5th series). P 13½.
G234	G **202**	50c. multicoloured	70	70
G235	G **203**	90c. multicoloured	1·40	1·40

Nos. G234/G235 were each issued with *se-tenant* label giving the text of the Article in English, French or German, in sheets of 12 stamps and 12 labels.

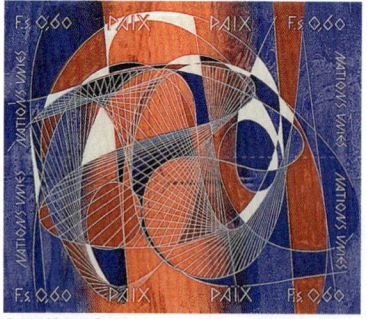

G **204**/G **207** Peace

(Des H. Erni. Recess and litho PTT, Bern)
1993 (21 Sept). International Peace Day. Rouletted.
G236	G **204**	60c. multicoloured	1·40	1·40
		a. Block of 4 Nos. G236/G239.	5·75	
G237	G **205**	60c. multicoloured	1·40	1·40
G238	G **206**	60c. multicoloured	1·40	1·40
G239	G **207**	60c. multicoloured	1·40	1·40
G236/G239 Set of 4			5·00	5·00

Nos. G236/G239 were issued together in *se-tenant* blocks of four within the sheet, each block forming the composite design illustrated.

G **208** Polar Bears   G **209** Whale in Melting Ice

G **210** Elephant Seal   G **211** Adélie Penguins

(Des B. Bralds. Litho Questa)
1993 (29 Oct). The Environment. Climate. P 14½.
G240	G **207**	1f.10 multicoloured	1·90	1·90
		a. Horiz strip of 4. Nos. G240/G243	7·75	
G241	G **209**	1f.10 multicoloured	1·90	1·90
G242	G **210**	1f.10 multicoloured	1·90	1·90
G243	G **211**	1f.10 multicoloured	1·90	1·90
G240/G243 Set of 4			6·75	6·75

Nos. G240/G243 were issued together in horizontal *se-tenant* strips of four within the sheet, each strip forming a composite design.

 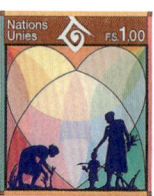

G **212** Father calling Child   G **213** Three Generations

(Des R. Callari. Litho Cartor)
1994 (4 Feb). International Year of the Family. P 13.
G244	G **212**	80c. multicoloured	1·60	1·60
G245	G **213**	1f. multicoloured	2·40	2·40

G **214** Mexican Prairie Dogs (*Cynomys mexicanus*)   G **215** Jabiru (*Jabiru mycteria*)

G **216** Blue Whale (*Balaenoptera musculus*)   G **217** Golden Lion Tamarin (*Leontopithecus rosalia*)

(Des L. Parson. Litho Enschedé)
1994 (18 Mar). Endangered Species (2nd series). P 12½.
G246	G **214**	80c. multicoloured	1·40	1·40
		a. Block of 4 Nos. G246/G249.	5·75	
G247	G **215**	80c. multicoloured	1·40	1·40
G248	G **216**	80c. multicoloured	1·40	1·40
G249	G **217**	80c. multicoloured	1·40	1·40
G246/G249 Set of 4			5·00	5·00

Nos. G246/G249 were issued together in *se-tenant* blocks of four within the sheet.

G **218** Hand delivering Refugee to New Country

(Des Francoise Peyroux. Litho Leigh-Mardon Pty Ltd, Melbourne)
1994 (29 Apr). United Nations High Commissioner for Refugees. P 14½×15.
G250	G **218**	1f.20 multicoloured	2·75	2·75

G **219**/G **222** Shattered Globe and Evaluation

(Des K. Koga. Litho Questa)
1994 (24 May). International Decade for Natural Disaster Reduction. P 14×14½.
G251	G **219**	60c. multicoloured	1·80	1·80
		a. Block of 4. Nos. G251/G254	7·50	
G252	G **220**	60c. multicoloured	1·80	1·80
G253	G **221**	60c. multicoloured	1·80	1·80
G254	G **222**	60c. multicoloured	1·80	1·80
G251/G254 Set of 4			6·50	6·50

Nos. G251/G254 were issued together in *se-tenant* blocks of four stamps within the sheet, each block forming the composite design illustrated.

G **223** Mobilisation of Resources in Developing Countries

G **224** Internal Migration of Population

(Des J. Smath. Litho Enschedé)

1994 (1 Sept). International Population and Development Conference, Cairo. P 13½×14.
G255	G **223**	60c. multicoloured	1·10	1·10
G256	G **224**	80c. multicoloured	1·60	1·60

G **225** Palais des Nations, Geneva

G **226** Creation of the World (detail of tapestry, Oili Mäki)

G **227** Palais des Nations

(Des R. Callari. Litho Questa)

1994 (1 Sept). P 14½×15.
G257	G **225**	60c. multicoloured	80	80
G258	G **226**	80c. multicoloured	1·20	1·20
G259	G **227**	1f.80 multicoloured	2·75	2·75
G257/G259		Set of 3	4·25	4·25

G **228** Map and Linked Ribbons

G **229** Map and Ribbons

(Des L. Sardá. Litho Enschedé)

1994 (28 Oct). 30th Anniversary of United Nations Conference or Trade and Development. P 13½×14.
G260	G **228**	80c. multicoloured	1·60	1·60
G261	G **229**	1f. multicoloured	1·90	1·90

G **230** Anniversary Emblem

G **231** Social Summit 1995

(Des R. Callari. Recess and litho PTT, Bern)

1995 (1 Jan). 50th Anniversary of United Nations Organisation (1st issue). P 13½.
G262	G **230**	80c. multicoloured	1·60	1·60

See also Nos. G270/**MS**G272 and G275/G286.

(Des F. Hundertwasser. Eng W. Seidel. Recess and photo State Ptg Wks, Vienna)

1995 (3 Feb). World Summit for Social Development, Copenhagen. P 13½×14.
G263	G **231**	1f. multicoloured	2·75	2·75

1994 UNITED NATIONS OFFICE AT GENEVA

G **232** Crowned Lemur (*Lemur coronatus*)

G **233** Giant Scops Owl (*Otus gurneyi*)

G **234** Painted Frog (*Atelopus varius zeteki*)

G **235** American Wood Bison (*Bison bison athabascae*)

(Des Sibylle Erni. Litho Enschedé)

1995 (24 Mar). Endangered Species (3rd series). P 13×12½.
G264	G **232**	80c. multicoloured	1·40	1·40
		a. Block of 4. Nos. G264/G267	5·75	
G265	G **233**	80c. multicoloured	1·40	1·40
G266	G **234**	80c. multicoloured	1·40	1·40
G267	G **235**	80c. multicoloured	1·40	1·40
G264/G267		Set of 4	5·00	5·00

Nos. G264/G267 were issued together in *se-tenant* blocks of four stamps within the sheet.

G **236** Field in Summer

G **237** Field in Winter

(Des G. Kumpf. Litho Questa)

1995 (26 May). Youth Our Future. Tenth Anniversary of International Youth Year. P 14½×15.
G268	G **236**	80c. multicoloured	1·60	1·60
G269	G **237**	1f. multicoloured	2·20	2·20

G **238** Signing UN Charter

G **239** Veteran's Memorial Hall and Opera House, San Francisco (venue for signing of Charter)

(Des P. and C. Calle. Eng Inge Madlé Recess (Nos. G270/G271) or recess and litho (No. **MS**G272) Enschedé)

1995 (26 June). 50th Anniversary of United Nations Organisation (2nd issue). P 13½×14.
G270	G **238**	60c. maroon	1·10	1·10
G271	G **239**	1f.80 blackish green	3·25	3·25
MSG272		92×70 mm. Nos. G270/G271. Imperf	4·75	4·75

G **240** Woman and Cranes

G **241** Women Worshipping

UNITED NATIONS OFFICE AT GENEVA 1995

(Des Ting Shao Kuang. Photo Postage Stamp Ptg Wks, Peking)
1995 (5 Sept). Fourth World Conference on Women, Peking. P 12½.
G273	G **240**	60c. multicoloured	1·20	1·20
G274	G **241**	1f. multicoloured	2·20	2·20

G **242**/G **244**

G **245**/G **247**

G **248**/G **250**

G **251**/G **253**

(Des B. Verkaaik. Litho Questa)
1995 (24 Oct). 50th Anniversary of United Nations Organisation (3rd issue). P 14.
G275	G **242**	30c. multicoloured	70	70
		a. Sheetlet of 12. Nos. G275/G286	8·75	
		b. Block of 6. Nos. G275/G280	4·50	
		c. Booklet pane. Nos. G275/G277.	2·20	
G276	G **243**	30c. multicoloured	70	70
G277	G **244**	30c. multicoloured	70	70
G278	G **245**	30c. multicoloured	70	70
		c. Booklet pane. Nos. G278/G280.	2·20	
G279	G **246**	30c. multicoloured	70	70
G280	G **247**	30c. multicoloured	70	70
G281	G **248**	30c. multicoloured	70	70
		b. Block of 6. Nos. G281/G286	4·50	
		c. Booklet pane. Nos. G281/G283.	2·20	
G282	G **249**	30c. multicoloured	70	70
G283	G **250**	30c. multicoloured	70	70
G284	G **251**	30c. multicoloured	70	70
		c. Booklet pane Nos. G284/G286..	2·20	
G285	G **252**	30c. multicoloured	70	70
G286	G **253**	30c. multicoloured	70	70
G275/G286 Set of 12			7·50	7·50

Nos. G275/G277 and G278/G280 form the left and right halves respectively of a composite design, and Nos. G281/G283 and G284/G286 another composite design, the two composites being issued together (separated by a gutter) in a *se-tenant* sheetlet of 12 stamps.

The booklet panes have a perforated white margin on three sides of the block.

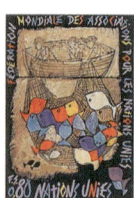

G **254** Catching Fish

(Des R. Mirer. Litho Enschedé)
1996 (2 Feb). 50th Anniversary of World Federation of United Nations Associations. P 13×13½.
G287	G **254**	80c. multicoloured	1·80	1·80

G **255** *Galloping Horse treading on a Flying Swallow* (Chinese bronze sculpture, Han Dynasty)

G **256** Palais des Nations, Geneva

(Des L. Bianco (40c.). Catherine Charbonnier Casile (70c.). Litho Questa)
1996 (2 Feb). P 14½×15.
G288	G **255**	40c. multicoloured	70	70
G289	G **256**	70c. multicoloured	1·40	1·40

1996 UNITED NATIONS OFFICE AT GENEVA

G **257** *Paphropedilum delenatii*   G **258** *Pachypodium baronii*

G **259** Yellow Amaryllis   G **260** Cobra Plant
(*Sternbergia lutea*)   (*Darlingtonia californica*)

(Des Diane Bruyninckx. Litho Enschedé)

1996 (14 Mar). Endangered Species (4th series). P 13×12½.
G290	G **257**	80c. multicoloured	1·40	1·40
		a. Block of 4 Nos. G290/G293	5·75	
G291	G **258**	80c. multicoloured	1·40	1·40
G292	G **259**	80c. multicoloured	1·40	1·40
G293	G **260**	80c. multicoloured	1·40	1·40
G290/G293 *Set of 4*			5·00	5·00

Nos. G290/G293 were issued together in *se-tenant* blocks of four stamps within the sheet.

G **261** Family on   G **262** Women in
Verandah of House   Traditional Dress in
    Gardens

G **263** Produce Seller   G **264** Boys playing on
and City   Riverside

G **265** Elderly Couple
reading Newspaper

(Des Teresa Fasolino. Litho Enschedé)

1996 (3 June). Habitat II. Second United Nations Conference on Human Settlements, Istanbul, Turkey. P 14×13½.
G294	G **261**	70c. multicoloured	1·60	1·60
		a. Horiz strip of 5. Nos. G294/G298	8·25	
G295	G **262**	70c. multicoloured	1·60	1·60
G296	G **263**	70c. multicoloured	1·60	1·60
G297	G **264**	70c. multicoloured	1·60	1·60
G298	G **265**	70c. multicoloured	1·60	1·60
G294/G298 *Set of 5*			7·25	7·25

Nos. G294/G298 were issued together in *se-tenant* strips of five stamps within the sheet, each strip forming a composite design.

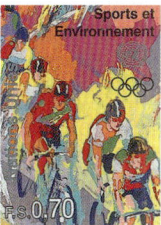

G **266** Cycling   G **267** Running

(Des L. Neiman. Litho Questa)

1996 (19 July). Sport and the Environment. Centenary of Modern Olympic Games. P 14×14½ (70c.) or 14½×14 (1f.10).
G299	G **266**	70c. multicoloured	1·40	1·40
G300	G **267**	1f.10 multicoloured	2·40	2·40
MSG301	88×78 mm. Nos. G299/G300		4·00	4·00

G **268** Birds in   G **269** Flowers
Treetop   growing from Bomb

(Des Chen Yu (90c.). Zhou Jing (1f.10). Litho Questa)

1996 (17 Sept). A Plea for Peace. Winning Entries in China Youth Design Competition. P 15×14½.
G302	G **268**	90c. multicoloured	1·90	1·90
G303	G **269**	1f.10 multicoloured	2·40	2·40

G **270** The Sun and the   G **271** Ananse (African
Moon (South American   spider tale)
legend)

(Des Walt Disney Co. Litho Questa)

1996 (20 Nov). 50th Anniversary of United Nations Children's Fund Children's Stories. P 14½×15.
G304	G **270**	70c. multicoloured	1·40	1·40
G305	G **271**	1f.80 multicoloured	3·50	3·50

Each issued in sheets of eight stamps and one label bearing the anniversary emblem.

G **272** UN Flag   G **273** Building Palais des
    Nations (detail of fresco,
    Massimo Campigli)

(Litho Questa)

1997 (12 Feb). P 14½×15.
G306	10c. multicoloured	25	25
G307	1f.10 multicoloured	1·90	1·90

UNITED NATIONS OFFICE AT GENEVA 1997

G **274** Polar Bear (*Ursus maritimus*)   G **275** Blue Crowned Pigeon (*Goura cristata*)

G **276** Marine Iguana (*Amblyrhynchus cristatus*)   G **277** Guanaco (*Lama guanicoe*)

(Des Daniela Costa. Litho Enschedé)

1997 (13 Mar). Endangered Species (5th series). P 13×12½.

G308	G **274**	80c. multicoloured	1·40	1·40
		a. Block of 4. Nos. G308/G311	5·75	
G309	G **275**	80c. multicoloured	1·40	1·40
G310	G **276**	80c. multicoloured	1·40	1·40
G311	G **277**	80c. multicoloured	1·40	1·40
G308/G311		Set of 4	5·00	5·00

Nos. G308/G311 were issued together in *se-tenant* blocks of four within the sheet.

G **278**/G **281** Sunrise over Mountains

(Des P. Max. Photo Courvoisier)

1997 (30 May). Earth Summit +5. Fifth Anniversary of United Nations Conference on Environment and Development. Granite paper. P 11½.

G312	G **278**	45c. multicoloured	1·10	1·10
		a. Block of four. Nos. G312/G315	4·50	
G313	G **279**	45c. multicoloured	1·10	1·10
G314	G **280**	45c. multicoloured	1·10	1·10
G315	G **281**	45c. multicoloured	1·10	1·10
G312/G315		Set of 4	4·00	4·00

MSG316 90×75 mm. 1f.10, Motifs as Nos. G312/G315. Imperf .... 2·75 2·75

Nos. G312/G315 were issued together in *se-tenant* blocks of four stamps within the sheet, each block forming the composite design illustrated.

G **282** Fokker F.IX and Zeppelin   G **283** Lockheed Constellation and Boeing 314 Clipper

G **284** de Havilland DH.106 Comet and Boeing 747   G **285** Ilyushin Il-62 and Boeing 747

G **286** Concorde

(Des M. Cockcroft. Litho Questa)

1997 (29 Aug). 50th Anniversaries of Economic Commission for Europe and Economic and Social Commission for Asia and the Pacific. P 14×14½.

G317	G **282**	70c. multicoloured	1·60	1·60
		a. Horiz strip of 5. Nos. G317/G321	8·25	
G318	G **283**	70c. multicoloured	1·60	1·60
G319	G **284**	70c. multicoloured	1·60	1·60
G320	G **285**	70c. multicoloured	1·60	1·60
G321	G **286**	70c. multicoloured	1·60	1·60
G317/G321		Set of 5	7·25	7·25

Nos. G317/G321 were issued together in horizontal *se-tenant* strips of five stamps within the sheet, each strip forming a composite design.

G **287** 1986 50c. Philately Stamp   G **288** 1986 80c. Philately Stamp

(Des R. Stein. Litho Enschedé)

1997 (14 Oct). Tribute to Philately. P 13½×14.

G322	G **287**	70c. multicoloured	1·40	1·40
G323	G **288**	1f.10 multicoloured	1·80	1·80

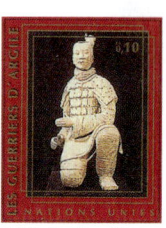 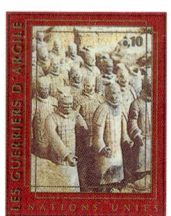

G **289** Kneeling Warrior   G **290** Ranks of Armoured Warriors

1997 UNITED NATIONS OFFICE AT GENEVA

G **291** Head

G **292** Group in Wrap-over Tunics

G **293** Head and Shoulders

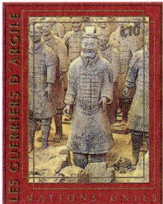
G **294** Group in Armour

(Des R. Stein. Litho Austrian State Ptg Wks, Vienna)

1997 (19 Nov). 25th Anniversary of World Heritage Convention. Terracotta Warriors from Emperor Qin Shi Huang's Tomb, Xian, China. P 13½.

(a) Booklet stamps

G324	G **289**	10c. multicoloured	55	55
		a. Booklet pane. No. G324×4	2·30	
G325	G **290**	10c. multicoloured	55	55
		a. Booklet pane. No. G325×4	2·30	
G326	G **291**	10c. multicoloured	55	55
		a. Booklet pane. No. G326×4	2·30	
G327	G **292**	10c. multicoloured	55	55
		a. Booklet pane. No. G327×4	2·30	
G328	G **293**	10c. multicoloured	55	55
		a. Booklet pane. No. G328×4	2·30	
G329	G **294**	10c. multicoloured	55	55
		a. Booklet pane. No. G329×4	2·30	

(b) Sheet stamps

G330	G **291**	45c. multicoloured	80	80
G331	G **292**	70c. multicoloured	1·60	1·60
G324/G331 Set of 8			5·25	5·25

G **295** Palais des Nations, Geneva

(Litho Questa)

1998 (13 Feb). P 14½×15.
G332   G **295**   2f. multicoloured.................. 3·50   3·50

G **296** Tibetan Stump-tailed Macaques (*Macaca thibetana*)

G **297** Greater Flamingoes (*Phoenicopterus ruber*)

G **298** Queen Alexandra's Birdwings (*Ornithoptera alexandrae*)

G **299** Fallow Deer (*Cervus dama*) *mesopotamica*

(Des Suzanne Duranceau. Litho Enschedé)

1998 (13 Mar). Endangered Species (6th series). P 13×12½.

G333	G **296**	80c. multicoloured	1·40	1·40
		a. Block of 4. Nos. G333/G336	5·75	
G334	G **297**	80c. multicoloured	1·40	1·40
G335	G **298**	80c. multicoloured	1·40	1·40
G336	G **299**	80c. multicoloured	1·40	1·40
G333/G336 Set of 4			5·00	5·00

Nos. G333/G336 were issued together in *se-tenant* blocks of four stamps within the sheet.

G **300** Walrus   G **301** Orangutan with Young

(Des J. Ellis. Litho Enschedé)

1998 (20 May). International Year of the Ocean. T G **300** and similar horiz designs. Multicoloured. P 14×13½.

G337		45c. Type G **300**	80	80
		a. Sheetlet of 12. Nos G337/G348	9·75	
G338		45c. Polar Bears	80	80
G339		45c. Polar Bear, Musk Oxen, Penguins and Seal on ice	80	80
G340		45c. Diver	80	80
G341		45c. Seals	80	80
G342		45c. Narwhal	80	80
G343		45c. Fish and Shark	80	80
G344		45c. Shark's tail, Seal and Puffin	80	80
G345		45c. Fish and Penguin's back	80	80
G346		45c. Fish and Jellyfish	80	80
G347		45c. Seal, Penguin and Squid	80	80
G348		45c. Penguin hunting fish	80	80
G337/G348 Set of 12			8·75	8·75

Nos. G337/G348 were issued together in *se-tenant* sheetlets of 12 stamps.

(Des R. Garcia. Litho Govt Ptg Wks, Tokyo, Japan)

1998 (19 June). Rainforest Preservation. P 13×13½.

G349	G **301**	70c. multicoloured	1·40	1·40
MSG350 82×70 mm. Type G **301** 3f. multicoloured			5·25	5·25

G **302** Soldier with Children   G **303** Soldier holding Baby

(Des A. Davidson. Photo Courvoisier)

1998 (15 Sept). 50 Years of United Nations Peacekeeping. Granite paper. P 12.

G351	G **302**	70c. multicoloured	1·40	1·40
G352	G **303**	90c. multicoloured	1·60	1·60

G **304** Birds   G **305** Hand releasing Birds

(Des J.-M. Folon. Litho Cartor)

1998 (27 Oct). 50th Anniversary of Universal Declaration of Human Rights. P 13½×13.

G353	G **304**	90c. multicoloured	1·60	1·60
G354	G **305**	1f.80 multicoloured	3·00	3·00

Stamps of a similar design were issued by Italy.

UNITED NATIONS OFFICE AT GENEVA 1998

G **306** Palace Façade

G **307** Great Palm House

G **308** Gloriette

G **309** Blue and White Vase (Mirror Room) G **310** Detail of Wall Hanging (Johann Wenzl Bergl)

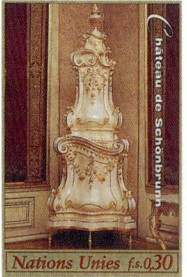
G **311** Porcelain Stove

(Des R. Stein. Litho Questa)

1998 (4 Dec). World Heritage Site. Schönbrunn Palace, Vienna. P 14×13½ (horiz) or 13½×14 (vert).

(a) Booklet stamps

G355	G **306**	10c. multicoloured	40	40
		a. Booklet pane. No. G355×4	1·70	
G356	G **307**	10c. multicoloured	40	40
		a. Booklet pane. No. G356×4	1·70	
G357	G **308**	10c. multicoloured	40	40
		a. Booklet pane. No. G357×4	1·70	
G358	G **309**	30c. multicoloured	1·00	1·00
		a. Booklet pane. No. G358×3	3·25	
G359	G **310**	30c. multicoloured	1·00	1·00
		a. Booklet pane. No. G359×3	3·25	
G360	G **311**	30c. multicoloured	1·00	1·00
		a. Booklet pane. No. 360×3	3·25	

(b) Sheet stamps

G361	G **307**	70c. multicoloured	1·40	1·40
G362	G **309**	1f.10 multicoloured	2·00	2·00
G355/G362	*Set of 8*		6·75	6·75

G **312** Palais Wilson, Geneva

(Photo Courvoisier)

1999 (5 Feb). Headquarters of United Nations High Commissioner for Human Rights. Granite paper. P 11½.

G363	G **312**	1f.70 brown-red	3·00	3·00

G **313** Tasmanian Wilderness G **314** Wet Tropics, Queensland

G **315** Great Barrier Reef G **316** Uluru-Kata Tjuta National Park

 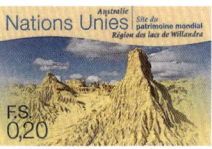
G **317** Kakadu National Park G **318** Willandra Lakes Region

(Des Passmore Design. Litho Questa)

1999 (19 Mar). World Heritage Sites in Australia. P 13.

(a) Booklet stamps

G364	G **313**	10c. multicoloured	40	40
		a. Booklet pane. No. G364×4	1·70	
G365	G **314**	10c. multicoloured	40	40
		a. Booklet pane. No. G365×4	1·70	
G366	G **315**	10c. multicoloured	40	40
		a. Booklet pane. No. G366×4	1·70	
G367	G **316**	20c. multicoloured	80	80
		a. Booklet pane. No. G367×4	3·50	
G368	G **317**	20c. multicoloured	80	80
		a. Booklet pane. No. G368×4	3·50	
G369	G **318**	20c. multicoloured	80	80
		a. Booklet pane. No. G369×4	3·50	

(b) Sheet stamps

G370	G **317**	90c. multicoloured	1·60	1·60
G371	G **315**	1f.10 multicoloured	2·20	2·20
G364/G371	*Set of 8*		6·75	6·75

G **319** Asiatic Wild Ass (*Equus hemionus*) G **320** Hyacinth Macaw (*Anodorhynchus hyacinthinus*)

1999 UNITED NATIONS OFFICE AT GENEVA

G **321** Jamaican Boa (*Epicrates subflavus*)
G **322** Bennett's Tree Kangaroo (*Dendrolagus bennettianus*)

(Des T. Barrall. Litho Enschedé)

1999 (22 Apr). Endangered Species (7th series). P 13×12½.

G372	G **319**	90c. multicoloured	1·40	1·40
		a. Block of 4. Nos. G372/G375	5·75	
G373	G **320**	90c. multicoloured	1·40	1·40
G374	G **321**	90c. multicoloured	1·40	1·40
G375	G **322**	90c. multicoloured	1·40	1·40
G372/G375 Set of 4			5·00	5·00

Nos. G372/G375 were issued together in *se-tenant* blocks of four stamps within the sheet.

G **323**/G **324** Satellite-aided Agriculture

(Des A. Hejja. Litho Courvoisier)

1999 (7 July). Third Conference on Exploration and Peaceful Uses of Outer Space, Vienna. Granite paper. Rouletted.

G376	G **323**	45c. multicoloured	70	70
		a. Horiz pair. Nos. G376/G377	1·50	1·50
G377	G **324**	45c. multicoloured	70	70
MSG378 90×75 mm. 2f. Combined design as Nos. G376/G377 (71×29 *mm*). P 14½			4·00	4·00
MSG379 90×75 mm. 2f. As No. **MS**G378 but additionally inscr 'PHILEXFRANCE 99 LE MONDIAL DU TIMBRE PARIS 2 AU 11 JUILLET 1999' in bottom margin			5·50	5·50

Nos. G376/G377 were issued together in horizontal *se-tenant* pairs within the sheet, each pair forming the composite design illustrated.

G **325**/G **328** Early 20th-century Mail Transport

(Des M. Hess. Litho Courvoisier)

1999 (23 Aug). 125th Anniversary of Universal Postal Union. Granite paper. P 11½.

G380	G **325**	70c. multicoloured	1·40	1·40
		a. Block of 4. Nos. G380/G383	5·75	
G381	G **326**	70c. multicoloured	1·40	1·40
G382	G **327**	70c. multicoloured	1·40	1·40
G383	G **328**	70c. multicoloured	1·40	1·40
G380/G383 Set of 4			5·00	5·00

Nos. G380/G383 were issued together in *se-tenant* blocks of four stamps within the sheet, each block forming the composite design illustrated.

G **329** Palais des Nations, Geneva

G **330** (*Illustration reduced, actual size 90×75 mm*)

(Des R. Stein. Litho Walsall Security Printers Ltd)

1999 (21 Sept). In Memoriam. Fallen in the Cause of Peace. P 14½×14.

G384	G **329**	1f.10 multicoloured	1·90	1·90
MSG385 90×75 mm. Type G **330** 2f. multicoloured			4·00	4·00

G **331** Couple on Globe

G **332** Environment

(Des R. Britto. Litho Austrian State Ptg Wks, Vienna)

1999 (18 Nov). Education. Keystone to the 21st-century. P 13½×14.

G386	G **331**	90c. multicoloured	1·60	1·60
G387	G **332**	1f.80 multicoloured	3·25	3·25

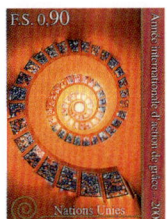

G **333** Glory Window (Gabrielle Loire), Chapel of Thanksgiving, Dallas

UNITED NATIONS OFFICE AT GENEVA 2000

(Des R. Katz. Litho and thermography Cartor)
2000 (1 Jan). International Year of Thanksgiving. P 13½.
G388　G **333**　90c. multicoloured .... 1·60　1·60

G **334** Hippopotamus
(*Hippopotamus amphibius*)

G **335** Coscoroba Swan
(*Coscoroba coscoroba*)

G **336** Emerald Monitor
(*Varanus prasinus*)

G **337** Sea Otter (*Enhydra lutris*)

(Des R. Hynes. Litho Enschedé)
2000 (6 Apr). Endangered Species (8th series). P 13×12½.
G389　G **334**　90c. multicoloured .... 1·60　1·60
　　　　　a. Block of 4. Nos. G389/G392 .... 6·75
G390　G **335**　90c. multicoloured .... 1·60　1·60
G391　G **336**　90c. multicoloured .... 1·60　1·60
G392　G **337**　90c. multicoloured .... 1·60　1·60
G389/G392 *Set of* 4 .... 5·75　5·75
　Nos. G389/G392 were issued together in *se-tenant* blocks of four stamps within the sheet.

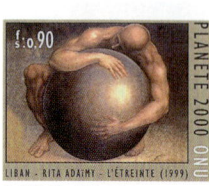
G **338** The Embrace
(Rita Adaïmy)

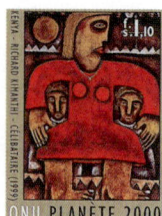
G **339** Living Single
(Richard Kimanthi)

(Des R. Stein. Litho Cartor)
2000 (30 May). Our World 2000 International Art Exhibition, New York. Entries in Millennium Painting Competition. P 13×13½ (90c.) or 13½×13 (1f.10).
G393　G **338**　90c. multicoloured .... 1·60　1·60
G394　G **339**　1f.10 multicoloured .... 2·00　2·00

G **340** Corner Stone Dedication, 1949

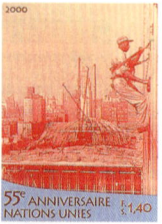
G **341** Window Cleaner, Secretariat Building, 1951

(Des R. Katz. Litho Cartor)
2000 (7 July). 55th Anniversary of the United Nations and 50th Anniversary of Opening of UN Headquarters, New York. P 13½×13.
G395　G **340**　90c. scarlet-vermilion, cobalt and
　　　　　　　yellow-ochre .... 1·60　1·60
G396　G **341**　1f.40 scarlet-vermilion, cobalt and
　　　　　　　yellow-ochre .... 2·75　2·75
MSG397 67×86 mm. Nos. G395/G396 .... 4·25　4·25

G **342** Two Women

G **343** (*Illustration reduced, actual size* 141×165 *mm*)

(Des W. McLean. Litho Austrian State Ptg Wks, Vienna)
2000 (15 Sept). The United Nations in the 21st-century. Sheet 141×165 mm containing T G **342** and similar horiz designs, forming an overall design T G **343**. Multicoloured. P 14.
MSG398 50c. Type G **342**; 50c. Man carrying bricks on head; 50c. Soldier and villagers; 50c. Dam and Doves; 50c. Men digging; 50c. Men damming irrigation channel.. 6·75　6·75

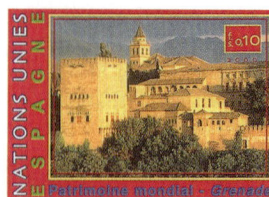
G **344** Granada

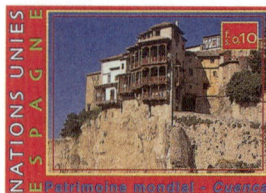
G **345** Cliff-top Houses, Cuenca

G **346** Roman Aqueduct, Segovia

2000 UNITED NATIONS OFFICE AT GENEVA

G **347** Archaeological Site, Mérida

G **348** Toledo

G **349** Güell Park, Barcelona

(Des R. Stein. Litho Questa)
2000 (6 Oct). World Heritage Sites in Spain. P 15×14½.

		(a) Booklet stamps		
G399	G **344**	10c. multicoloured	30	30
		a. Booklet pane. No. G399×4............	1·30	
G400	G **345**	10c. multicoloured	30	30
		a. Booklet pane. No. G400×4............	1·30	
G401	G **346**	10c. multicoloured	30	30
		a. Booklet pane. No. G401×4............	1·30	
G402	G **347**	20c. multicoloured	70	70
		a. Booklet pane. No. G402×4............	3·00	
G403	G **348**	20c. multicoloured	70	70
		a. Booklet pane. No. G403×4............	3·00	
G404	G **349**	20c. multicoloured	70	70
		a. Booklet pane. No. G404×4............	3·00	
		(b) Sheet stamps		
G405	G **345**	1f. multicoloured	1·90	1·90
G406	G **348**	1f.20 multicoloured	2·40	2·40
G399/G406 *Set of 8*			6·50	6·50

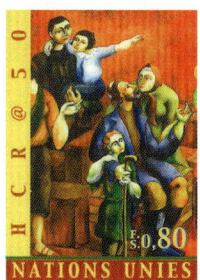
G **350** Family of Refugees

G **351** (*Illustration reduced, actual size* 121×82 *mm*)

(Des Yu. Gevorgian. Litho Enschedé)
2000 (9 Nov). 50th Anniversary of United Nations High Commissioner for Refugees. P 13½×13.

G407	G **350**	80c. multicoloured	1·60	1·60
MSG408 121×82 mm. Type G **351** 1f.80, multicoloured			3·75	3·75

G **352** Lynx (*Felis lynx canadensis*)

G **353** Green Peafowl (*Pavo muticus*)

G **354** Galapagos Tortoise (*Geochelone elephantopus*)

G **355** Lemur (*Lepilemur* sp.)

(Des Higgins Bond. Litho Enschedé)
2001 (1 Feb). Endangered Species (9th series). P 13×12½.

G409	G **352**	90c. multicoloured	1·60	1·60
		a. Block of 4. Nos. G409/G412........	6·75	
G410	G **353**	90c. multicoloured	1·60	1·60
G411	G **354**	90c. multicoloured	1·60	1·60
G412	G **355**	90c. multicoloured	1·60	1·60
G409/G412 *Set of 4*			5·75	5·75

Nos. G409/G412 were issued together in *se-tenant* blocks of four stamps within the sheet.

G **356** Hands forming Heart (Ernest Pignon-Ernest)

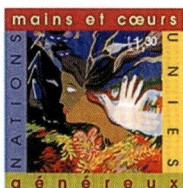
G **357** Women's Head and White Dove (Paul Siché)

(Des R. Stein and Rorie Katz. Litho Enschedé)
2001 (29 Mar). United Nations International Year of Volunteers. P 13½.

G413	G **356**	90c. multicoloured	1·60	1·60
G414	G **357**	1f.30 multicoloured	2·75	2·75

G **358** Pagoda, Kyoto

UNITED NATIONS OFFICE AT GENEVA 2001

G 359 Imperial Palace, Nara

G 360 Himeji Castle

G 361 Shirakawa-go and Gokayama Villages

G 362 Itsukushima Shinto Shrine

G 363 Temple, Nikko

(Des R. Katz. Litho Enschedé)

2001 (1 Aug). World Heritage Sites in Japan. P 13×13½.

(a) Booklet stamps

G415	G **358**	10c. multicoloured	25	25
		a. Booklet pane. No. G415×4	1·10	
G416	G **359**	10c. multicoloured	25	25
		a. Booklet pane. No. G416×4	1·10	
G417	G **360**	10c. multicoloured	25	25
		a. Booklet pane. No. G417×4	1·10	
G418	G **361**	30c. multicoloured	70	70
		a. Booklet pane. No. G418×4	3·00	
G419	G **362**	30c. multicoloured	70	70
		a. Booklet pane. No. G419×4	3·00	
G420	G **363**	30c. multicoloured	70	70
		a. Booklet pane. No. G420×4	3·00	

(b) Sheet stamps

G421	G **359**	1f.10 multicoloured	2·00	2·00
G422	G **362**	1f.30 multicoloured	2·30	2·30
G415/G422	*Set of 8*		6·50	6·50

G 364 Hammarskjöld

(Des O. Mathiesen. Recess Banknote Corporation of America Inc)

2001 (18 Sept). 40th Death Anniversary of Dag Hammarskjöld (United Nations Secretary General, 1953–1961). P 11×11½.

G423	G **364**	2f. deep carmine	3·75	3·75

G 365 Postman and Stamps   G 366 Trumpets and Stamps

G 367 Emblem

(Des R. Katz. Litho Enschedé)

2001 (18 Oct). 50th Anniversary of United Nations Postal Administration. P 13½.

G424	G **365**	90c. multicoloured	1·60	1·60
G425	G **366**	1f.30 multicoloured	2·40	2·40
MSG426	102×102 mm. Type G **367** 1f.30, 1f.80, cobalt and bright carmine. P 13		5·75	5·75

G 368 Flowers and Coastline   G 369 Wind-powered Generators and Brick Making

G 370 Power Station inside Glass Dome   G 371 Couple sitting beside Lake

(Des R. Giusti. Litho Walsall Security Printers Ltd)

2001 (16 Nov). Climate Change. P 13½.

G427	G **368**	90c. multicoloured	1·80	1·80
		a. Horiz strip of 4. Nos. G427/G430	7·50	
G428	G **369**	90c. multicoloured	1·80	1·80
G429	G **370**	90c. multicoloured	1·80	1·80
G430	G **371**	90c. multicoloured	1·80	1·80
G427/G430	*Set of 4*		6·50	6·50

Nos. G427/G430 were issued together in horizontal *se-tenant* strips of four stamps, each strip forming a composite design.

2001 UNITED NATIONS OFFICE AT GENEVA

G **372** United Nations Flag

(Des R. Stein. Litho Cartor)

2001 (10 Dec). Kofi Annan, Winner of Nobel Peace Prize, 2001. P 13½.
G431   G **372**   90c. multicoloured .... 1·80   1·80

G **373** Armillary Sphere,
Ariana Park

(Des R. Stein. Litho Austrian State Ptg Wks, Vienna)

2002 (1 Mar). P 14.
G432   G **373**   1f.30 multicoloured .... 2·40   2·40

G **374** Bald Uakari (*Cacajao calvus*)   G **375** Ratel (*Mellivora capensis*)

G **376** Pallas's Cat (*Otocolobus manul*)   G **377** Savannah Monitor (*Varanus exanthematicus*)

(Des Lori Anzalone. Litho Enschedé)

2002 (4 Apr). Endangered Species (10th series). P 13×12½.
G433   G **374**   90c. multicoloured .... 1·80   1·80
       a. Block of 4. Nos. G433/G436 .... 7·50
G434   G **375**   90c. multicoloured .... 1·80   1·80
G435   G **376**   90c. multicoloured .... 1·80   1·80
G436   G **377**   90c. multicoloured .... 1·80   1·80
G433/G436 Set of 4 .... 6·50   6·50

Nos. G433/G436 were issued together in *se-tenant* blocks of four stamps within the sheet.

G **378** Wooden Statue   G **379** Carved Wooden Container

(Des Karen Kelleher. Litho Questa)

2002 (20 May). East Timor Independence. P 14×14½.
G437   G **378**   90c. multicoloured .... 1·80   1·80
G438   G **379**   1f.30 multicoloured .... 2·75   2·75

G **380** Weisshorn, Switzerland   G **381** Mount Fuji, Japan

G **382** Vinson Massif, Antarctica   G **383** Kamet, India

(Des R. Stein and R. Katz. Litho Cartor)

2002 (24 May). International Year of Mountains. P 13×13½.
G439   G **380**   70c. multicoloured .... 1·20   1·20
       a. Block or vert strip of 4. Nos. G439/G442 .... 7·00
G440   G **381**   70c. multicoloured .... 1·20   1·20
G441   G **382**   1f.20 multicoloured .... 2·20   2·20
G442   G **383**   1f.20 multicoloured .... 2·20   2·20
G439/G442 Set of 4 .... 6·00   6·00

Nos. G439/G442 were issued together either in *se-tenant* blocks or vertical strips of four stamps within sheetlets of 12.

G **384** Sun, Water, Birds and Flowers   G **385** Figure's wearing Fashionable Dress

G **386** Women's Profile   G **387** Yacht

(Des P. Max. Litho Questa)

2002 (27 June). World Summit on Sustainable Development, Johannesburg. P 14½×14.
G443   G **384**   90c. multicoloured .... 1·60   1·60
       a. Block or vert strip of 4. Nos. G443/G446 .... 9·50
G444   G **385**   90c. multicoloured .... 1·60   1·60
G445   G **386**   1f.80 multicoloured .... 3·00   3·00
G446   G **387**   1f.80 multicoloured .... 3·00   3·00
G443/G446 Set of 4 .... 8·25   8·25

Nos. G443/G446 were issued together either in *se-tenant* blocks or vertical strips of four stamps in sheetlets of 12.

G **388** Duomo di Sant'Andrea, Amalfi Coast

UNITED NATIONS OFFICE AT GENEVA 2002

G **389** View across Islands, Aeolian Islands

G **390** Del Moro Fountain, Rome

G **391** Santa Maria del Fiore, Florence

G **392** Leaning Tower, Pisa

G **393** The Forum, Pompeii

(Des R. Katz. Litho Cartor)

2002 (30 Aug). World Heritage Sites in Italy. P 13½×13.

(a) Booklet stamps

G447	G 388	10c. multicoloured	40	40
		a. Booklet pane. No. G447×4	1·70	
G448	G 389	10c. multicoloured	40	40
		a. Booklet pane. No. G448×4	1·70	
G449	G 390	10c. multicoloured	40	40
		a. Booklet pane. No. G449×4	1·70	
G450	G 391	20c. multicoloured	80	80
		a. Booklet pane. No. G450×4	3·50	
G451	G 392	20c. multicoloured	80	80
		a. Booklet pane. No. G451×4	3·50	
G452	G 393	20c. multicoloured	80	80
		a. Booklet pane. No. G452×4	3·50	

(b) Sheet stamps

G453	G 392	90c. multicoloured	1·80	1·80
G454	G 389	1f.30 multicoloured	3·00	3·00
G447/G454	*Set of 8*		7·50	7·50

Stamps of a similar design were issued by Italy.

G **394** AIDS Symbol on UN Secretariat Building, New York

G **395** AIDS Symbol on UN Secretariat Building, New York at Night (*Illustration reduced, actual size 80×80 mm*)

(Des R. Katz. Litho Walsall Security Printers Ltd)

2002 (24 Oct). AIDS Awareness Campaign. P 13½.

G455	G **394**	1f.30 multicoloured	2·75	2·75
MSG456	80×80 mm. Type G **395** 90c.+30c. P 14½		2·75	2·75

The premium was for AIDS charities.

G **396** Doves

(Des T. Clauson. Litho Questa)

2002 (24 Oct). P 14½×15.

G457	G **396**	3f. multicoloured	5·75	5·75

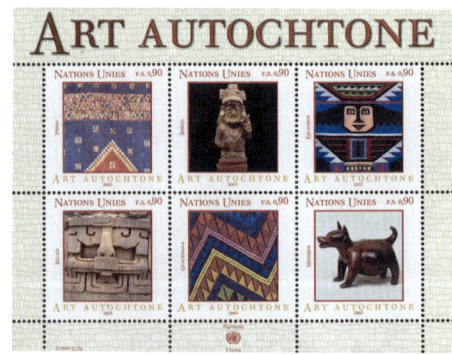
G **397** Artefacts (*Illustration reduced, actual size 125×97 mm*)

(Des R. Katz and R. Stein. Litho Questa)

2003 (31 Jan). Indigenous Art (1st series). Sheet 125×97 mm. Multicoloured. P 14½.

MSG458 90c. Inca poncho, Peru; 90c. Bahia statue, Brazil; 90c. Blanket, Ecuador; 90c. Mayan stone sculpture, Xunantunich, Belize; 90c. Embroidered fabric, Guatemala; 90c. Colima terracotta sculpture, Mexico .... 11·50 11·50

See also Nos. **MS**G480 and **MS**G518.

2003 UNITED NATIONS OFFICE AT GENEVA

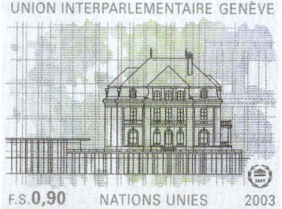

G **398** Headquarters Building

(Des C. Wursten. Litho Questa)

2003 (20 Feb). Inauguration of New Inter-Parliamentary Union Headquarters, Geneva. P 14½×14.
G459 G **398** 90c. multicoloured .... 1·90 1·90

G **399** Red-breasted Goose (*Branta ruficollis*)   G **400** Bald Ibis (*Geronticus calvus*)

G **401** Fulvous Whistling Duck (*Dendrocygna bicolor*)   G **402** Channel-billed Toucan (*Ramphastos vitellinus*)

(Des J. Hautman. Litho Enschedé)

2003 (3 Apr). Endangered Species (11th series). 30th Anniversary of Convention on International Trade in Endangered Species (CITES). P 13×12½.
G460 G **399** 90c. multicoloured .... 1·80 1·80
           a. Block of 4. Nos. G460/G463 .... 7·50
G461 G **400** 90c. multicoloured .... 1·80 1·80
G462 G **401** 90c. multicoloured .... 1·80 1·80
G463 G **402** 90c. multicoloured .... 1·80 1·80
G460/G463 Set of 4 .... 6·50 6·50
  Nos. G460/G463 were issued in *se-tenant* block of four stamps within the sheet.

G **403** Autumnal Trees and Stream   G **404** Depleted Lake

(Des R. Garcia. Litho De La Rue)

2003 (20 June). International Year of Freshwater. P 14×14½.
G464 G **403** 70c. multicoloured .... 1·40 1·40
           a. Horiz pair. Nos. G464/G465 .... 4·00 4·00
G465 G **404** 1f.30 multicoloured .... 2·40 2·40
  Nos. G464/G465 were issued in horizontal *se-tenant* pairs within the sheet, each pair forming a composite design.

G **405** Ralph Bunche

(Des L. Cherne and R. Katz. Litho and die-stamped Enschedé)

2003 (7 Aug). Ralph Bunche (politician) Commemoration. P 13½×14.
G466 G **405** 1f.80 multicoloured .... 3·50 3·50

G **406** Yosemite National Park

G **407** Smoky Mountains

G **408** Olympic National Park

G **409** Hawaii Volcanoes

G **410** Everglades

G **411** Yellowstone National Park

(Litho De La Rue)

2003 (24 Oct). World Heritage Sites in USA. P 14½.

(a) Booklet stamps
G467 G **406** 10c. multicoloured 25 25
           a. Booklet pane. No. G467×4 .... 1·10
G468 G **407** 10c. multicoloured 25 25
           a. Booklet pane. No. G468×4 .... 1·10
G469 G **408** 10c. multicoloured 25 25
           a. Booklet pane. No. G469×4 .... 1·10
G470 G **409** 30c. multicoloured 80 80
           a. Booklet pane. No. G470×4 .... 3·50
G471 G **410** 30c. multicoloured 80 80
           a. Booklet pane. No. G471×4 .... 3·50
G472 G **411** 30c. multicoloured 80 80
           a. Booklet pane. No. G472×4 .... 3·50

(b) Sheet stamps
G473 G **410** 90c. multicoloured .... 1·80 1·80
G474 G **411** 1f.30 multicoloured .... 2·50 2·50
G467/G474 Set of 8 .... 6·75 6·75
  Nos. G467/G474 have chestnut bands at top and bottom edges.

UNITED NATIONS OFFICE AT GENEVA 2003

G **412** Flag at Half-mast

(Des R. Stein. Litho Cartor)

2003 (24 Oct). In Memoriam. Support for United Nations Staff Killed or Injured in Terrorist Attacks. P 13½×13.
G475 G 412 85c. multicoloured .... 1·80 1·80

G **413** Asiatic Black Bear (*Ursus thibetanus*)   G **414** Northern Andean Deer (*Hippocamelus antisensis*)

G **415** Lion-tailed Macaque (*Macaca silenus*)   G **416** Guar (*Bos Gaurus*)

(Des Yuan Lee. Litho Enschedé)

2004 (29 Jan). Endangered Species (12th series). P 13.
G476 G 413 1f. multicoloured .... 1·80 1·80
            a. Block of 4. Nos. G476/G479 .... 7·50
G477 G 414 1f. multicoloured .... 1·80 1·80
G478 G 415 1f. multicoloured .... 1·80 1·80
G479 G 416 1f. multicoloured .... 1·80 1·80
G476/G479 *Set of 4* .... 6·50 6·50

Nos. G476/G479 were issued in *se-tenant* block of four stamps within the sheet.

G **417** Artefacts (*Illustration reduced, actual size 125×96 mm*)

(Des R. Katz and R. Stein. Litho Enschedé)

2004 (4 Mar). Indigenous Art (2nd series). Sheet 125×96 mm. Multicoloured. P 13½.
MSG480 1f.×6, Cow's decorative headgear, Switzerland; Seated woman (sculpture). Cirna Woda, Romania; Butter pats, France; Herald's embroidered tabard, United Kingdom; Medieval woodcut, Cologne; Mother and child (sculpture), Drenovac, Serbia and Montenegro .... 11·50 11·50

G **418** Hand enclosing Pedestrian (pedestrians awareness campaign)   G **419** Seatbelt enclosing Body as Map (seatbelt campaign)

(Des M. Granger. Litho Cartor)

2004 (7 Apr). Road Safety Campaign. P 13×13½ (horiz) or 13½×13 (vert).
G481 G 418 85c. multicoloured .... 1·50 1·50
G482 G 419 1f. multicoloured .... 1·90 1·90

G **420** Peace Bell, United Nations Headquarters, New York

(Des and eng M. Mörck. Recess and litho)

2004 (7 Apr). 50th Anniversary of Japanese Peace Bell. P 13½.
G483 G 420 1f.30 multicoloured .... 2·40 2·40

G **421** Acropolis, Athens

G **422** Ruins, Delphi

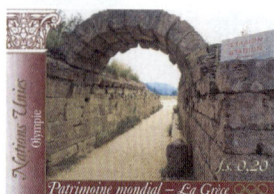

G **423** Tunnel, Olympia

G **424** Lions, Delos

G **425** Pythagoreion and Heraion, Samos

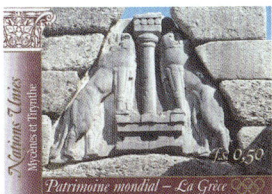

G **426** Relief, Mycenae and Tiryns

(Litho Enschedé)

2004 (12 Aug). World Heritage Sites in Greece. P 14½.

(a) Booklet stamps

G484	G **421**	20c. multicoloured	55	55
		a. Booklet pane. No. G484×4	2·30	
G485	G **422**	20c. multicoloured	55	55
		a. Booklet pane. No. G485×4	2·30	
G486	G **423**	20c. multicoloured	55	55
		a. Booklet pane. No. G486×4	2·30	
G487	G **424**	50c. multicoloured	1·20	1·20
		a. Booklet pane. No. G487×4	5·00	
G488	G **425**	50c. multicoloured	1·20	1·20
		a. Booklet pane. No. G488×4	5·00	
G489	G **426**	50c. multicoloured	1·20	1·20
		a. Booklet pane. No. G489×4	5·00	

(b) Sheet stamps

G490	G **422**	1f. multicoloured	1·90	1·90
G491	G **425**	1f.30 multicoloured	2·40	2·40
G484/G491 *Set of 8*			8·50	8·50

Nos. G484/G491 have brown-lake bands at left and bottom edges.

G **427** Globe as Face enclosed in Dove and Hands (Anggun Sita Rustinya)

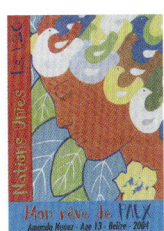

G **428** Woman with Hair of Doves (Amanda Nunez)

(Litho Austrian State Printing Wks, Vienna)

2004 (21 Sept). My Dream of Peace. Winning Designs in Children's Painting Competition. P 14.

G492	G **427**	85c. multicoloured	1·60	1·60
G493	G **428**	1f.20 multicoloured	2·20	2·20

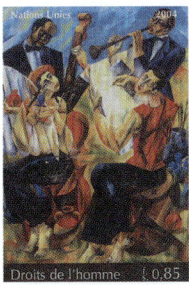

G **429** Woman holding Blue Rose and Musicians

G **430** Family and Large Blue Rose

(Des Yuri Gevorgian (Yuroz). Litho Austrian State Printing Wks, Vienna)

2004 (14 Oct). International Decade of Human Rights' Education. P 11½.

G494	G **429**	85c. multicoloured	1·60	1·60
G495	G **430**	1f.30 multicoloured	2·40	2·40

The stamps of United Nations Headquarters in New York, Geneva and Vienna form a composite design.

G **431** General Assembly

(Des and eng C. Slania, Recess and litho (1f.30) or litho (3f.) Banknote Corporation of America Inc, Browns Summit, North Carolina)

2005 (4 Feb). 60th Anniversary of United Nations. P 11½.

G496	G **431**	1f.30 multicoloured	2·40	2·40
MSG497	100×80 mm. Type G **431** 3f. multicoloured. Imperf		6·50	6·50

Nos. G496/**MS**G497 have deep rose-lilac borders.

G **432** *Laelia milleri* G **433** *Psygmorchis pusilla*

G **434** *Dendrobium cruentum* G **435** *Orchis purpurea*

(Des B. Zlotsky. Litho Enschedé)

2005 (13 Mar). Endangered Species (13th series). P 13.

G498	G **432**	1f. multicoloured	1·80	1·80
		a. Block of 4. Nos. G498/G501	7·50	
G499	G **433**	1f. multicoloured	1·80	1·80
G500	G **434**	1f. multicoloured	1·80	1·80
G501	G **435**	1f. multicoloured	1·80	1·80
G498/G501 *Set of 4*			6·50	6·50

Nos. G498/G501 were issued together in *se-tenant* blocks of four stamps within the sheet.

G **436** Children collecting Water, India

G **437** *Ophioderma rubicundum*, Bahamas

UNITED NATIONS OFFICE AT GENEVA 2005

(Des R. Stein. Litho Cartor)
2005 (21 Apr). EXPO 2005 World Exhibition, Aichi, Japan. P 14×13½.
G502	G **436**	1f. multicoloured	2·20	2·20
G503	G **437**	1f.30 multicoloured	2·75	2·75

G **438** Wheelchair Racer   G **439** Cyclists

(Des R. Hirter. Litho Cartor)
2005 (3 June). International Year of Sport. P 13×13½.
G504	G **438**	1f. multicoloured	2·20	2·20
G505	G **439**	1f.30 multicoloured	2·75	2·75

G **440** Sphinx, Necropolis, Memphis

G **441** Castle, Philae

G **442** Abu Mena

G **443** Head, Necropolis, Thebes

G **444** Mosque, Cairo

G **445** Saint Catherine Monastery

(Des R. Katz. Litho Enschedé)
2005 (4 Aug). World Heritage Sites in Egypt. P 14×13½ (Nos. G506/G511) or 13×13½ (Nos. G512/G513).

(a) Booklet stamps
G506	G **440**	20c. multicoloured	45	45
		a. Booklet pane. No. G506×4	1·90	
G507	G **441**	20c. multicoloured	45	45
		a. Booklet pane. No. G507×4	1·90	
G508	G **442**	20c. multicoloured	45	45
		a. Booklet pane. No. G508×4	1·90	
G509	G **443**	50c. multicoloured	1·20	1·20
		a. Booklet pane. No. G509×4	5·00	
G510	G **444**	50c. multicoloured	1·20	1·20
		a. Booklet pane. No. G510×4	5·00	
G511	G **445**	50c. multicoloured	1·20	1·20
		a. Booklet pane. No. G511×4	5·00	

(b) Sheet stamps
G512	G **441**	1f. multicoloured	2·20	2·20
G513	G **444**	1f.30 multicoloured	2·75	2·75
G506/G513		Set of 8	9·00	9·00

G **446** Hands enclosing Globe and Dove (Marisa Harun)   G **447** Globe and Flags as Dream-catcher (Carlos Teixido)

(Litho Austrian State Ptg Wks, Vienna)
2005 (21 Sept). My Dream of Peace One Day. Winning Designs in Children's Painting Competition. P 14.
G514	G **446**	1f. multicoloured	2·20	2·20
G515	G **447**	1f.30 multicoloured	2·75	2·75

G **448** Food Aid Delivery by Aircraft and Camels

G **449** Women and Lorries carrying Food

(Des A. Davidson. Litho Austrian State Ptg Wks, Vienna)
2005 (20 Oct). Food for Life. P 13½×14.
G516	G **448**	1f. black, deep carmine-red and dull violet-blue	2·20	2·20
G517	G **449**	1f.30 black, deep carmine-red and dull violet-blue	2·75	2·75

2006 UNITED NATIONS OFFICE AT GENEVA

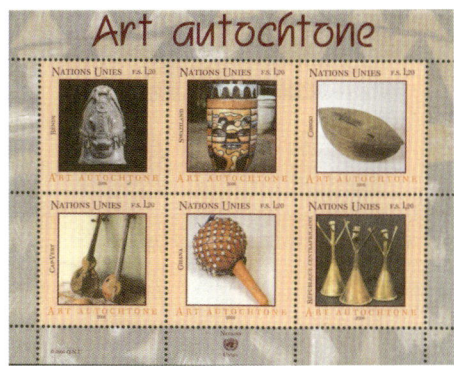

G **450** Musical Instruments (*Illustration reduced, actual size 125×96 mm*)

(Des R. Katz and R. Stein. Litho Enschedé)

2006 (3 Feb). Indigenous Art (3rd series). Sheet 125×96 mm. Multicoloured. P 13½.
MSG518 1f.20×6, Horse head bell, Benin; Drum, Swaziland; Stringed instrument (Sanza), Congo; Stringed instruments (Cavaquinho and Cimbo), Cape Verde; Gourd Caixixi, Ghana; General de Gaulle shaped bells, Central African Republic............ 13·00 13·00

G **451** Armillary Sphere, Geneva Headquarters

(Des R. Katz. Litho and holography Cartor)

2006 (3 Feb). P 13.
G519 G **451** 1f.30 multicoloured........................ 2·40 2·40

G **452** Tomato Frog (*Dyscophus antonglii*) G **453** Flap-necked Chameleon (*Chamaeleo dilepis*)

G **454** Emerald Tree Boa (*Corallus caninus*) G **455** Golfodulcean Poison Frog (*Phyllobates vittatus*)

(Des J. Dawson. Litho Enschedé)

2006 (16 Mar). Endangered Species (14th series). P 13.
G520 G **452** 1f. multicoloured........................ 1·80 1·80
    a. Block of 4. Nos. G520/G523............ 7·50
G521 G **453** 1f. multicoloured........................ 1·80 1·80
G522 G **454** 1f. multicoloured........................ 1·80 1·80
G523 G **455** 1f. multicoloured........................ 1·80 1·80
G520/G523 Set of 4 .... 6·50 6·50
Nos. G520/G523 were issued together in *se-tenant* blocks of four stamps within the sheet.

G **456** Family reading G **457** Family riding Motor Scooter

(Des Shelly Bartek. Litho Enschedé)

2006 (27 May). International Day of Families. P 13×13½.
G524 G **456** 1f. multicoloured........................ 2·20 2·20
G525 G **457** 1f.30 multicoloured........................ 2·75 2·75

G **458** Banks of the Seine

G **459** Provins

G **460** Carcassonne

G **461** Pont du Gard

G **462** Mont Saint Michel

UNITED NATIONS OFFICE AT GENEVA 2006

G **463** Château de Chambord

(Des R. Stein. Litho and foil embossed Cartor)

2006 (17 June). World Heritage Sites in France. P 14×13½ (Nos. G526/G531) or 13×13½ (Nos. G523/G523).

(a) Booklet stamps
G526	G 458	20c. multicoloured	45	45
		a. Booklet pane. No. G526×4	1·90	
G527	G 459	20c. multicoloured	45	45
		a. Booklet pane. No. G527×4	1·90	
G528	G 460	20c. multicoloured	45	45
		a. Booklet pane. No. G528×4	1·90	
G529	G 461	50c. multicoloured	1·20	1·20
		a. Booklet pane. No. G529×4	5·00	
G530	G 462	50c. multicoloured	1·20	1·20
		a. Booklet pane. No. G530×4	5·00	
G531	G 463	50c. multicoloured	1·20	1·20
		a. Booklet pane. No. G531×4	5·00	

(b) Sheet stamps
G532	G 459	1f. multicoloured	2·20	2·20
G533	G 462	1f.30 multicoloured	2·75	2·75
G526/G533		Set of 8	9·00	9·00

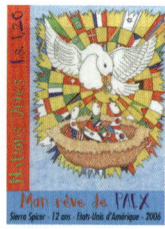

G **464** Globe and Dove (Ariam Boaglio)

G **465** Dove with Flag covered Chicks (Sierra Spicer)

(Litho Cartor)

2006 (21 Sept). My Dream of Peace One Day. Winning Designs in Children's Painting Competition. P 14.
G534	G 464	85c. multicoloured	1·60	1·60
G535	G 465	1f.20 multicoloured	2·40	2·40

G **466** Uganda
G **467** Luxembourg

G **468** Italy
G **469** New Zealand

G **470** Cape Verde
G **471** Belgium

G **472** Switzerland
G **473** Lebanon

(Des Rorie Katz. Litho Cartor)

2006 (5 Oct). Coins and Flags of Member Countries (1st series). P 13.
G536	G 466	85c. multicoloured	1·60	1·60
		a. Sheetlet of 8. Nos. G536/G543	13·50	
		b. Block of 4. Nos. G536/G539	6·75	
G537	G 467	85c. multicoloured	1·60	1·60
G538	G 468	85c. multicoloured	1·60	1·60
G539	G 469	85c. multicoloured	1·60	1·60
G540	G 470	85c. multicoloured	1·60	1·60
		b. Block of 4. Nos. G540/G543	6·75	
G541	G 471	85c. multicoloured	1·60	1·60
G542	G 472	85c. multicoloured	1·60	1·60
G543	G 473	85c. multicoloured	1·60	1·60
G536/G543		Set of 8	11·50	11·50

Nos. G536/G539 and G540/G543, respectively were issued in se-tenant blocks of four stamps within sheets of eight, the blocks separated by a central gutter divided by a line of rouletting.

See also G548/G555, G575/G582, G645/G652, G700/G707, G722/G729, G771/G777 and G799/G806.

G **474** Gelada Baboon (*Theropithecus gelada*)

G **475** De Brazza's Monkey (*Cercopithecus neglectus*)

G **476** Ruffed Lemur (*Varecia varigata*)

G **477** Javan Gibbon (*Hylobates moloch*)

(Des J. Dawson. Litho Enschedé)

2007 (16 Mar). Endangered Species (15th series). P 13.
G544	G 474	1f. multicoloured	1·80	1·80
		a. Block of 4. Nos. G544/G547	7·50	
G545	G 475	1f. multicoloured	1·80	1·80
G546	G 476	1f. multicoloured	1·80	1·80
G547	G 477	1f. multicoloured	1·80	1·80
G544/G547		Set of 4	6·50	6·50

Nos. G544/G547 were issued together in se-tenant blocks of four stamps within the sheet.

G **478** Burkina Faso

G **479** France

G **480** Bolivia

G **481** Myanmar

G **482** Moldova

G **483** Papua New Guinea

G **484** Mali

G **485** Tunisia

(Des Rorie Katz. Litho Cartor)

2007 (3 May). Coins and Flags of Member Countries (2nd series). P 13.

G548	G **478**	85c. multicoloured	1·60	1·60
		a. Sheetlet of 8. Nos. G548/G555	13·50	
		b. Block of 4. Nos. G548/G551	6·75	
G549	G **479**	85c. multicoloured	1·60	1·60
G550	G **480**	85c. multicoloured	1·60	1·60
G551	G **481**	85c. multicoloured	1·60	1·60
G552	G **482**	85c. multicoloured	1·60	1·60
		b. Block of 4. Nos. G552/G555	6·75	
G553	G **483**	85c. multicoloured	1·60	1·60
G554	G **484**	85c. multicoloured	1·60	1·60
G555	G **485**	85c. multicoloured	1·60	1·60
G548/G555 *Set of 8*			11·50	11·50

Nos. G548/G551 and G552/G555, respectively were issued in *se-tenant* blocks of four stamps within sheets of eight, the blocks separated by a central gutter divided by a line of rouletting.

G **486** Women with Apples

G **487** Women with Doves

(Des Slavka Kolestar. Litho Lowe-Martin Group)

2007 (1 June). Peaceful Visions. P 14.

G556	G **486**	1f.20 multicoloured	2·20	2·20
G557	G **487**	1f.80 multicoloured	3·25	3·25

G **488** Tiwanaku, Bolivia

G **489** Iguacu, Brazil

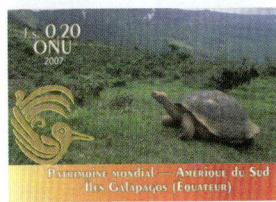
G **490** Galapagos Islands

G **491** Rapa Nui, Chile

G **492** Cueva de las Manos, Argentina

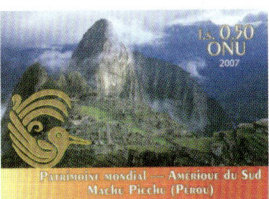
G **493** Machu Pichu, Peru

(Des Rorie Katz. Litho Lowe-Martin Group)

2007 (9 Aug). World Heritage Sites in South America. P 13.

(a) Booklet stamps

G558	G **488**	20c. multicoloured	35	35
		a. Booklet pane. No. G558×4	1·50	
G559	G **489**	20c. multicoloured	35	35
		a. Booklet pane. No. G559×4	1·50	

G560	G 490	20c. multicoloured	35	35
		a. Booklet pane. No. G560×4	1·50	
G561	G 491	50c. multicoloured	95	95
		a. Booklet pane. No. G561×4	4·00	
G562	G 492	50c. multicoloured	95	95
		a. Booklet pane. No. G562×4	4·00	
G563	G 493	50c. multicoloured	95	95
		a. Booklet pane. No. G563×4	4·00	

(b) Sheet stamps

G564	G 488	1f. multicoloured	1·80	1·80
G565	G 493	1f.80 multicoloured	3·25	3·25
G558/G565		Set of 8	8·00	8·00

G **494** Flying Postman and Hands

(Des Rorie Katz. Litho Lowe-Martin Group)

2007 (6 Sept). Humanitarian Mail. P 13.
G566	G 494	1f.80 multicoloured	3·00	3·00

G **495** Astronaut   G **496** Jupiter and Spacecraft

G **497** Space Walk

(Des Donato Giancola. Litho Enschedé)

2007 (25 Oct). 50th Anniversary of Space Exploration. P 13.
G567	G 495	1f. multicoloured	1·80	1·80
G568	G 496	1f.80 multicoloured	3·25	3·25
MSG569		100×80 mm. Type G **497** 3f. multicoloured	5·50	5·50

G **498** Barbed Wire becoming Flowers

(Des Matias Delfino. Litho Lowe-Martin)

2008 (27 Jan). International Holocaust Remembrance Day. P 14.
G570	G 498	85c. multicoloured	1·60	1·60

No. G570 was issued in sheetlets of nine stamps with enlarged inscribed top margin.

A stamp of a similar design was issued by Israel, United Nations (New York and Vienna).

G **499** Pacific Walrus   G **500** Brain Coral (*Platygyra daedalea*)
(*Odobenus rosmarus*)

G **501** Pygmy Seahorse   G **502** Beluga Whale
(*Hippocampus bargibanti*)   (*Delphinapterus leucas*)

(Des Suzanne Duranceau. Litho Enschedé)

2008 (6 Mar). Endangered Species (16th series). P 13.
G571	G 499	1f. multicoloured	1·80	1·80
		a. Block of 4. Nos. G571/G574	7·50	
G572	G 500	1f. multicoloured	1·80	1·80
G573	G 501	1f. multicoloured	1·80	1·80
G574	G 502	1f. multicoloured	1·80	1·80
G571/G574		Set of 4	6·50	6·50

Nos. G571/G574 were issued in *se-tenant* blocks of four stamps within the sheet.

G **503** Madagascar   G **504** Rwanda

G **505** Namibia   G **506** Maldives

G **507** Benin   G **508** Iran

G **509** Albania   G **510** Turkey

(Des Rorie Katz. Litho Cartor)

2008 (8 May). Coins and Flags of Member Countries (3rd series).
G575	G 503	85c. multicoloured	1·60	1·60
		a. Sheetlet of 8. Nos. G575/G582	13·50	
		b. Block of 4. Nos. G575/G578	6·75	
G576	G 504	85c. multicoloured	1·60	1·60
G577	G 505	85c. multicoloured	1·60	1·60
G578	G 506	85c. multicoloured	1·60	1·60
G579	G 507	85c. multicoloured	1·60	1·60
		b. Block of 4. Nos. G579/G582	6·75	

G580	G **508**	85c. multicoloured	1·60	1·60
G581	G **509**	85c. multicoloured	1·60	1·60
G582	G **510**	85c. multicoloured	1·60	1·60
G575/G582	Set of 8		11·50	11·50

Nos. G575/G578 and G579/G582, respectively were issued in *se-tenant* blocks of four stamps within sheets of eight, the blocks separated by a central gutter divided from the stamps by a line of rouletting.

G **511** 'Rein á Notre Sujet Sans Nous' (nothing about us without us)

G **512** 'Langue des Signes' (sign language)

(Des Rorie Katz. Litho Enschedé)

2008 (8 Aug). Convention on the Rights of People with Disabilities. P 13.

G583	G **511**	1f. multicoloured	2·00	2·00
G584	G **512**	1f.80 multicoloured	3·75	3·75

G **513** Gymnastics

G **514** Tennis

(Des Romero Britto. Litho and gold foil)

2008 (8 Aug). Olympic Games, Beijing. P 13.

G585	G **513**	1f. multicoloured	2·00	2·00
G586	G **514**	1f.80 multicoloured	3·75	3·75
MSG587	92×83 mm. 3f. As Type G **513**		6·50	6·50

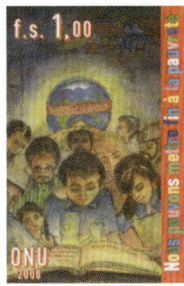 

G **515** Reading and Education (Ranajoy Banerjee)

G **516** Children sharing (Elizabeth Elaine Chun Ning Au)

(Litho Sweden Post Stamps)

2008 (18 Sept). We Can End Poverty. Winning Designs in Children's Painting Competition. P 13.

G588	G **515**	1f. multicoloured	2·00	2·00
G589	G **516**	1f.80 multicoloured	3·75	3·75

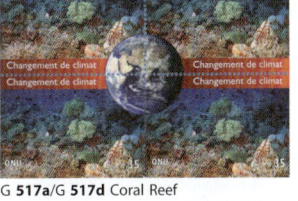

G **517a**/G **517d** Coral Reef

G **518a**/G **518d** Ice Floes

G **519a**/G **519d** Pollution

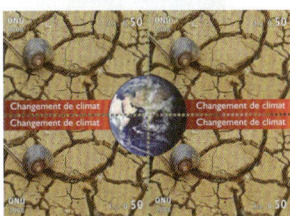

G **520a**/G **520d** Desert

G **521a**/G **521d** Polar Bear

G **522a**/G **522d** Deforestation

(Des Rorie Katz. Litho Lowe-Martin Group)

2008 (23 Oct). Action on Climate Change. Phosphor markings. P 13.

G590	G **517a**	35c. multicoloured	70	70
		a. Booklet pane. Nos. G590/G593.	3·00	
G591	G **517b**	35c. multicoloured	70	70
G592	G **517c**	35c. multicoloured	70	70
G593	G **517d**	35c. multicoloured	70	70

UNITED NATIONS OFFICE AT GENEVA 2009

G594	G **518a**	35c. multicoloured	70	70
		a. Booklet pane. Nos. G594/G597.	3·00	
G595	G **518b**	35c. multicoloured	70	70
G596	G **518c**	35c. multicoloured	70	70
G597	G **518d**	35c. multicoloured	70	70
G598	G **519a**	35c. multicoloured	70	70
		a. Booklet pane. Nos. G598/G601.	3·00	
G599	G **519b**	35c. multicoloured	70	70
G600	G **519c**	35c. multicoloured	70	70
G601	G **519d**	35c. multicoloured	70	70
G602	G **520a**	50c. multicoloured	1·10	1·10
		a. Booklet pane. Nos. G602/G605.	4·75	
G603	G **520b**	50c. multicoloured	1·10	1·10
G604	G **520c**	50c. multicoloured	1·10	1·10
G605	G **520d**	50c. multicoloured	1·10	1·10
G606	G **521a**	50c. multicoloured	1·10	1·10
		a. Booklet pane. Nos. G606/G609.	4·75	
G607	G **521b**	50c. multicoloured	1·10	1·10
G608	G **521c**	50c. multicoloured	1·10	1·10
G609	G **521d**	50c. multicoloured	1·10	1·10
G610	G **522a**	50c. multicoloured	1·10	1·10
		a. Booklet pane. Nos. G610/G613.	4·75	
G611	G **522b**	50c. multicoloured	1·10	1·10
G612	G **522c**	50c. multicoloured	1·10	1·10
G613	G **522d**	50c. multicoloured	1·10	1·10
G590/G613 *Set of 24*			19·00	19·00
MSG614 120×90 mm. 1f.20×4, As Type G **521a**/G **521d** (Polar Bear)			9·50	9·50
MSG615 120×90 mm. 1f.80×4, As Type G **518a**/G **521d** (Ice floes)			15·00	15·00

G **523** U Thant

(Litho Enschedé)

2009 (6 Feb). Birth Centenary of U Thant (United Nations Secretary General 1961–1971). P 14×13½.

G616	G **523**	1f.30 multicoloured	2·75	2·75

G **524** *Maculinea arion* (Large Blue Butterfly) G **525** *Dolomedes plantarius* (Fen Raft Spider)

G **526** *Cerambyx cerdo* (Great Capricorn Beetle) G **527** *Coenagrion mercuriale* (Southern Damselfly)

(Des Roger Kent. Litho Enschedé)

2009 (16 Apr). Endangered Species (17th series). Phosphor markings. P 14½.

G617	G **524**	1f. multicoloured	1·90	1·90
		a. Block of 4. Nos. Nos. G617/G620	7·75	
G618	G **525**	1f. multicoloured	1·90	1·90
G619	G **526**	1f. multicoloured	1·90	1·90
G620	G **527**	1f. multicoloured	1·90	1·90
G617/G620 *Set of 4*			6·75	6·75

Nos. G617/G620 were printed, *se-tenant*, in blocks of four stamps within the sheet.

G **528** Town Hall and Roland on the Marketplace of Bremen

G **529** Wartburg Castle

G **530** Palaces and Parks of Potsdam and Berlin

G **531** Aachen Cathedral (Cathedrale d'Aix-la-Chapelle)

G **532** Monastic Island of Reichenau

G **533** Luther Memorials in Eisleben and Wittenberg

(Des Grit Fielder. Litho Enschedé)

2009 (7 May). World Heritage Sites in Germany. P 13.

(a) Booklet stamps

G621	G **528**	30c. multicoloured	80	80
		a. Booklet pane. No. G621×4	3·50	
G622	G **529**	30c. multicoloured	80	80
		a. Booklet pane. No. G622×4	3·50	

2009 UNITED NATIONS OFFICE AT GENEVA

G623	G **530**	30c. multicoloured	80	80
		a. Booklet pane. No. G623×4	3·50	
G624	G **531**	50c. multicoloured	1·20	1·20
		a. Booklet pane. No. G624×4	5·00	
G625	G **532**	50c. multicoloured	1·20	1·20
		a. Booklet pane. No. G625×4	5·00	
G626	G **533**	50c. multicoloured	1·20	1·20
		a. Booklet pane. No. G626×4	5·00	
		(b) Sheet stamps		
G627	G **529**	1f. multicoloured	2·20	2·20
G628	G **532**	1f.30 multicoloured	3·00	3·00
G621/G628	*Set of 8*		10·00	10·00

G **534** Mother and Child (Maternal health)

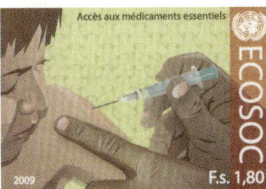

G **535** Vaccination (Access to essential medicines)

2009 (6 Aug). United Nations Economic and Social Council (ECOSOC). P 13.

G629	G **534**	85c. multicoloured	1·90	1·90
G630	G **535**	1f.80 multicoloured	3·75	3·75

G **536** Bowl of Food (Eradicate extreme poverty and hunger)

G **537** Pencil (Achieve universal primary education)

G **538** Female Symbol (Promote gender equality and empower women)

G **539** Teddy Bear (Reduce child mortality)

G **540** Female Figure enclosing Heart (Improve maternal health)

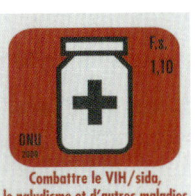

G **541** Medicine Jar (Combat HIV/AIDS, malaria and other disases)

G **542** Stylised Tree (Ensure environmental sustainability)

G **543** Stylised Figures (Develop a global partnership for development)

2009 (25 Sept). Millennium Development Goals. P 13.

G631	G **536**	1f.10 chrome-yellow, black and new blue	2·30	2·30
		a. Sheetlet of 8. Nos. G631/G638	19·00	
G632	G **537**	1f.10 bright yellow-green, black and red	2·30	2·30
G633	G **538**	1f.10 orange-red, black and red	2·30	2·30
G634	G **539**	1f.10 pale turquoise-blue, black and red	2·30	2·30
G635	G **540**	1f.10 pale bright rose, black and red	2·30	2·30
G636	G **541**	1f.10 scarlet-vermilion, black and red	2·30	2·30
G637	G **542**	1f.10 apple-green, black and red	2·30	2·30
G638	G **543**	1f.10 blue, black and red	2·30	2·30
G631/G638	*Set of 8*		17·00	17·00

Nos. G631/G638 were printed, *se-tenant*, in sheetlets of eight stamps.

G **544** New Caledonia

G **545** Namibia

G **546** Namibia

G **547** United Republic of Tanzania

G **548** Thailand

G **549** French Polynesia

(Des Stephen Bennett)

2009 (8 Oct). Indigenous Peoples. P 13.

G639	G **544**	1f.30 multicoloured	2·75	2·75
		a. Sheetlet of 6. Nos. G639/G644	18·00	
G640	G **545**	1f.30 multicoloured	2·75	2·75
G641	G **546**	1f.30 multicoloured	2·75	2·75
G642	G **547**	1f.30 multicoloured	2·75	2·75
G643	G **548**	1f.30 multicoloured	2·75	2·75
G644	G **549**	1f.30 multicoloured	2·75	2·75
G639/G644	*Set of 6*		15·00	15·00

Nos. G639/G644 were printed, *se-tenant*, in sheetlets of six stamps.

UNITED NATIONS OFFICE AT GENEVA 2010

G **550** Equitorial Guinea

G **551** Laos

G **552** Argentine

G **553** Morocco

G **554** Seychelles

G **555** Mauritania

G **556** Sudan

G **556a** Brunei Darussalam

(Des Rorie Katz. Litho Cartor)

2010 (5 Feb). Coins and Flags of Member Countries (4th series).

G645	G **550**	85c. multicoloured	1·60	1·60
		a. Sheetlet of 8. Nos. G645/G652	13·50	
		b. Block of 4. Nos. G645/G648	6·75	
G646	G **551**	85c. multicoloured	1·60	1·60
G647	G **552**	85c. multicoloured	1·60	1·60
G648	G **553**	85c. multicoloured	1·60	1·60
G649	G **554**	85c. multicoloured	1·60	1·60
		b. Block of 4. Nos. G549/G652	6·75	
G650	G **555**	85c. multicoloured	1·60	1·60
G651	G **556**	85c. multicoloured	1·60	1·60
G652	G **556a**	85c. multicoloured	1·60	1·60
G645/G652 Set of 8			11·50	11·50

Nos. G645/G648 and G549/G652, respectively were printed *se-tenant* in blocks of four stamps within sheets of eight, the blocks separated by a central gutter divided from the stamps by a line of rouletting.

G **557** *Fouquieria columnaris* (Boojum Tree)

G **558** *Aloe arborescens* (Krantz Aloe)

G **559** *Galanthus krasnovii* (Snowdrop)

G **560** *Dracaena draco* (Dragon Tree)

(Des Rosie Saunders. Litho Enschedé)

2010 (15 Apr). Endangered Species (18th series). P 13×12½.

G653	G **557**	1f. multicoloured	1·90	1·90
		a. Block of 4. Nos. G653/G656	7·75	
G654	G **558**	1f. multicoloured	1·90	1·90
G655	G **559**	1f. multicoloured	1·90	1·90
G656	G **560**	1f. multicoloured	1·90	1·90
G653/G656 Set of 4			6·75	6·75

Nos. G653/G656 were printed, *se-tenant*, in blocks of four stamps within the sheet.

G **561** Arachnid

G **562** Starfish

(Des Deborah Halperin. Litho L.M.G.)

2010 (15 Apr). International Year of Biodiversity. Art from Nature by Ernst Heinrich. Multicoloured. P 13.

G657	G **561**	1f.60 multicoloured	3·50	3·50
G658	G **562**	1f.90 multicoloured	4·00	4·00

G **563** Turtle, Eel, Fish and Coral

G **564** Turtle, Eel, Fish and Coral

G **565** Turtle, Eel, Fish and Coral

G **566** Turtle, Eel, Fish and Coral

G 567 Dolphins, Shark and Fish

G 568 Dolphins, Shark and Fish

G 569 Dolphins, Shark and Fish

G 570 Dolphins, Shark and Fish

G 571 Turtle, Hammerhead Shark and Coral

G 572 Turtle, Hammerhead Shark and Coral

G 573 Turtle, Hammerhead Shark and Coral

G 574 Turtle, Hammerhead Shark and Coral

G 575 Dolphin, Fish and Turtle

G 576 Dolphin, Fish and Turtle

G 577 Dolphin, Fish and Turtle

G 578 Dolphin, Fish and Turtle

G 579 Two Dolphins, Shark, Ray and Turtle

G 580 Two Dolphins, Shark, Ray and Turtle

UNITED NATIONS OFFICE AT GENEVA 2010

G **581** Two Dolphins, Shark, Ray and Turtle

G **582** Two Dolphins, Shark, Ray and Turtle

G **583** Dolphin Pod, Shark, Ray and Coral

G **584** Dolphin Pod, Shark, Ray and Coral

G **585** Dolphin Pod, Shark, Ray and Coral

G **586** Dolphin Pod, Shark, Ray and Coral

(Des Robert Wyland. Litho Enschede)

2010 (6 May). One Planet, One Ocean. 50th Anniversary of Intergovernmental Oceanographic Commission. Multicoloured. P 13½×13 (booklet stamps) or 14×13½ (Nos. **MS**G683/**MS**G684).

G659	G **563**	30c. multicoloured	40	40
		a. Block of 4. Nos. G659/G662	1·70	
G660	G **564**	30c. multicoloured	40	40
G661	G **565**	30c. multicoloured	40	40
G662	G **566**	30c. multicoloured	40	40
G663	G **567**	30c. multicoloured	40	40
		a. Block of 4. Nos. G663/G666	1·70	
G664	G **568**	30c. multicoloured	40	40
G665	G **569**	30c. multicoloured	40	40
G666	G **570**	30c. multicoloured	40	40
G667	G **571**	30c. multicoloured	40	40
		a. Block of 4. Nos. G667/G670	1·70	
G668	G **572**	30c. multicoloured	40	40
G669	G **573**	30c. multicoloured	40	40
G670	G **574**	30c. multicoloured	40	40
G671	G **575**	50c. multicoloured	1·10	1·10
		a. Block of 4. Nos. G671/G674	4·75	
G672	G **576**	50c. multicoloured	1·10	1·10
G673	G **577**	50c. multicoloured	1·10	1·10
G674	G **578**	50c. multicoloured	1·10	1·10
G675	G **579**	50c. multicoloured	1·10	1·10
		a. Block of 4. Nos. G675/G678	4·75	
G676	G **580**	50c. multicoloured	1·10	1·10
G677	G **581**	50c. multicoloured	1·10	1·10
G678	G **582**	50c. multicoloured	1·10	1·10
G679	G **583**	50c. multicoloured	1·10	1·10
		a. Block of 4. Nos. G679/G682	4·75	
G680	G **584**	50c. multicoloured	1·10	1·10
G681	G **585**	50c. multicoloured	1·10	1·10
G682	G **586**	50c. multicoloured	1·10	1·10
G659/G682 *Set of 24*			16·00	16·00
MSG683 180×110 mm. 85c.×4, As Types G **579**/G **582**			7·50	7·50
MSG684 180×110 mm. 1f.×4, As Type G **583**/G **586**			8·75	8·75

Nos. G659/G662, G663/G666, G667/G670, G671/G674, G675/G678 and G679/G682, respectively were printed, *se-tenant*, in blocks of four, one block per booklet page, each block forming a composite design.

G **587** '65'

(Des Rorie Katz. Litho and die-stamped gold foil L.M.G.)

2010 (28 June). 65th Anniversary of United Nations. P 13½.
G685	G **587**	1f.90 bright scarlet and gold	4·00	4·00
MSG686 80×80 mm. 1f.90×2, Type G **587**×2			8·25	8·25

G **588** Large Forklift Truck

G **589** Small Forklift Truck

G **590** Land Rover with truck back

G **591** Flatbed truck carrying Crane

G **592** Armed Personnel Carrier

2010 UNITED NATIONS OFFICE AT GENEVA

(Des Simon Williams. Litho UAB Garsu Pasaulis, Lithuania)
2010 (2 Sept). United Nations Transport. Land. Multicoloured. P 13½×13.

G687	G **588**	1f. multicoloured	2·20	2·20
		a. Horiz strip of 5. Nos. G687/G691	11·50	
G688	G **589**	1f. multicoloured	2·20	2·20
G689	G **590**	1f. multicoloured	2·20	2·20
G690	G **591**	1f. multicoloured	2·20	2·20
G691	G **592**	1f. multicoloured	2·20	2·20
G687/G691 Set of 5			10·00	10·00

Nos. G687/G691 were printed, *se-tenant*, in horizontal strips of five stamps, each strip forming a composite design.

G **593** Australia

G **594** Brunei

G **595** United Republic of Tanzania

G **596** French Polynesia

G **597** United Republic of Tanzania

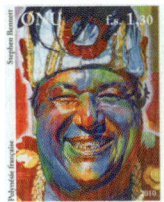
G **598** French Polynesia

(Des Stephen Bennett. Litho L.M.G.)
2010 (21 Oct). Indigenous Peoples. P 13.

G692	G **593**	1f.30 multicoloured	2·75	2·75
		a. Sheetlet of 6. Nos. G692/G697..	18·00	
G693	G **594**	1f.30 multicoloured	2·75	2·75
G694	G **595**	1f.30 multicoloured	2·75	2·75
G695	G **596**	1f.30 multicoloured	2·75	2·75
G696	G **597**	1f.30 multicoloured	2·75	2·75
G697	G **598**	1f.30 multicoloured	2·75	2·75
G692/G697 Set of 6			15·00	15·00

Nos. G692/G697 were printed, *se-tenant*, in sheets of six stamps with enlarged upper margin.

G **599** Aerial View of UN Headquarters Geneva

G **600** UN Headquarters Geneva Building Façade

(Des Scott Solberg. Litho Cartor)
2011 (4 Feb). UN Building. P 13.

G698	G **599**	10c. multicoloured	25	25
G699	G **600**	50c. multicoloured	1·10	1·10

G **601** Mongolia

G **602** Senegal

G **603** Egypt

G **604** Republic of the Congo

G **605** Nicaragua

G **606** Central African Republic

G **607** Algeria

G **608** Ukraine

(Des Rorie Katz. Litho Cartor)
2011 (3 Mar). Coins and Flags of Member Countries (5th series). Multicoloured. P 13½×13.

G700	G **601**	85c. multicoloured	1·80	1·80
		a. Sheet of 8. Nos. G700/G707	15·00	
		b. Block of 4. Nos. G700/G703	7·50	
G701	G **602**	85c. multicoloured	1·80	1·80
G702	G **603**	85c. multicoloured	1·80	1·80
G703	G **604**	85c. multicoloured	1·80	1·80
G704	G **605**	85c. multicoloured	1·80	1·80
		b. Block of 4. Nos. G704/G707	7·50	
G705	G **606**	85c. multicoloured	1·80	1·80
G706	G **607**	85c. multicoloured	1·80	1·80
G707	G **608**	85c. multicoloured	1·80	1·80
G700/G707 Set of 8			13·00	13·00

Nos. G700/G707 were printed, *se-tenant*, in two blocks of four stamps within sheet of eight, the blocks separated by a central gutter.

UNITED NATIONS OFFICE AT GENEVA 2011

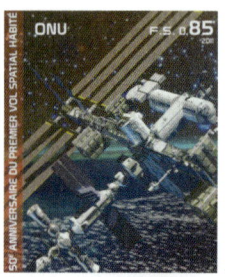

G **609** Space Station (left)   G **610** Space Station (right)

G **611** Saturn

G **612** Shuttle, Space Station, Satellites and Astronauts (*Illustration reduced, actual size 40×30 mm*)

(Des Peter Bollinger. Litho L.M.G.)

2011 (12 Apr). 50th Anniversary of Space Flight. P 13×13½.
G708	G **609**	85c. multicoloured	2·00	2·00
		a. Pair. Nos. G708/G709	4·50	4·50
G709	G **610**	1f. multicoloured	2·30	2·30
MSG710		180×155 mm. Size 40×30 mm. 50c.×16, Type G **611** and 15 other horiz designs forming the overall design Type G **612**	19·00	19·00

Nos. G708/G709 were printed, *se-tenant*, in horizontal pairs within the sheet each pair forming a composite design.

G **613** Kronborg Castle, Denmark

G **614** Suomenlinna Fortress, Finland

(Des Rorie Katz. Litho Enschedé)

2011 (5 May). World Heritage Sites. Nordic Countries. P 14×13½.
G711	G **613**	85c. multicoloured	2·00	2·00
G712	G **614**	1f. multicoloured	2·30	2·30

G **615** AIDS Ribbon

(Des Rorie Katz. Litho L.M.G.)

2011 (3 June). 30 Years of a World living with AIDS. Self-adhesive. Die-cut.
G713	G **615**	1f.30 scarlet and orange	3·00	3·00

No. G713 was die-cut around the design and printed in sheets of four stamps.

G **616** Girls writing (Achieve equality by 2015)

G **617** Women using PCs (Developing earning and knowledge among young people and adults)

(Des Rorie Katz. Litho Cartor)

2011 (1 July). ECOSOC (Economic and Social Council). Education. P 14½.
G714	G **616**	1f. multicoloured	2·30	2·30
G715	G **617**	1f.30 multicoloured	3·00	3·00

G **618** *Strigops habroptilus* (Kakapo)

G **619** *Lophophorus impejanus* (Himalayan Monal)

G **620** *Ciconia nigra* (Black Stork)

G **621** *Pithecophaga jefferyi* (Philippine Eagle)

(Des Wendy Wray. Litho Enschedé)

2011 (7 Sept). Endangered Species (19th series). P 13×12½.
G716	G **618**	1f. multicoloured	2·30	2·30
		a. Block of 4. Nos. G716/G719	9·50	
G717	G **619**	1f. multicoloured	2·30	2·30

2011 UNITED NATIONS OFFICE AT GENEVA

G718	G **620**	1f. multicoloured	2·30	2·30
G719	G **621**	1f. multicoloured	2·30	2·30
G716/G719 *Set of 4*			8·25	8·25

Nos. G716/G719 were printed, *se-tenant*, in blocks of four stamps within the sheet.

G **622** Birds and Butterflies in Flight and Tree Canopy

G **623** Undersea 'forest'

(Des Sergio Baradat. Litho and foil L.M.G.)

2011 (13 Oct). International Year of Forests. Multicoloured. P 12½.

G720	G **622**	85c. multicoloured	1·90	1·90
		a. Pair. Nos. G720/G721	5·50	5·50
G721	G **623**	1f.40 multicoloured	3·25	3·25

Nos. G720/G721 were printed, *se-tenant*, in vertical pairs within the sheet, each pair forming a composite design.

G **624** Saudi Arabia

G **625** Georgia

G **626** Democratic People's Republic of Korea

G **627** Lesotho

G **628** Serbia

G **629** Djibouti

G **630** Belize

G **631** Liechtenstein

(Des Rorie Katz. Litho Cartor)

2012 (5 Feb). Coins and Flags of Member Countries (6th series). Multicoloured. P 13½×13.

G722	G **624**	85c. multicoloured	1·90	1·90
		a. Sheetlet of 8. Nos. G722/G729	16·00	
		b. Block of 4. Nos. G722/G725	7·75	
G723	G **625**	85c. multicoloured	1·90	1·90
G724	G **626**	85c. multicoloured	1·90	1·90
G725	G **627**	85c. multicoloured	1·90	1·90
G726	G **628**	85c. multicoloured	1·90	1·90
		b. Block of 4. Nos. G726/G729	7·75	
G727	G **629**	85c. multicoloured	1·90	1·90
G728	G **630**	85c. multicoloured	1·90	1·90
G729	G **631**	85c. multicoloured	1·90	1·90
G722/G729 *Set of 8*			13·50	13·50

Nos. G722/G729 were printed, *se-tenant*, in two blocks of four stamps within sheets of eight, the blocks separated by a central gutter.

G **632** Circles

G **633** Symbols

(Litho Enschedé)

2012 (2 Apr). World Autism Awareness Day. P 14×13½.

G730	G **632**	1f.40 multicoloured	3·25	3·25
		a. Pair. Nos. G730/G731	6·75	6·75
G731	G **633**	1f.40 multicoloured	3·25	3·25

G **634** Tiger (*Panthera tigris*)

G **635** Painted Tiger-parrot (*Psittacella picta*)

G **636** Green Iguana (*Iguana iguana*)

G **637** Golden-crowned Sifaka (*Propithecus tattersalli*)

(Des Diana Marques. Litho Enschedé)

2012 (19 Apr). Endangered Species (20th series). P 13×12½.

G732	G **634**	1f. multicoloured	2·30	2·30
		a. Block of 4. Nos. G732/G735	9·50	
G733	G **635**	1f. multicoloured	2·30	2·30
G734	G **636**	1f. multicoloured	2·30	2·30
G735	G **637**	1f. multicoloured	2·30	2·30
G732/G735 *Set of 4*			8·25	8·25

Nos. G732/G735 were printed, *se-tenant*, in blocks of four stamps within the sheet.

G **638** Symbols of Healthy Environment

UNITED NATIONS OFFICE AT GENEVA 2012

(Des Shailesh Khandeparkar. Litho Lowe-Martin Group, Canada)

2012 (1 June). Rio+20 United Nations Conference on Sustainable Development. P 13.
G736 G **638** 1f.40 multicoloured .... 3·50 3·50

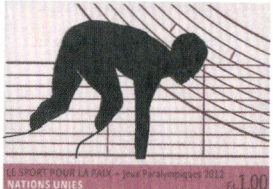
G **639** Runner

G **640** Archer

(Des Daniel Stolle. Litho and foil die-stamped Cartor)

2012 (17 Aug). Sport for Peace. Paralympic Games, London 2012. P 14½.
G737 G **639** 1f. silver, carmine and pale magenta .... 2·40 2·40
G738 G **640** 1f.40 silver, carmine and pale magenta .... 3·25 3·25
MSG739 92×83 mm. 1f.40 As Type G **640** .... 3·50 3·50

G **641** Gorilla, Virunga National Park

G **642** El Jem Amphitheatre, Tunisia

(Litho Lowe-Martin Group Canada)

2012 (5 Sept). World Heritage Africa. Virunga National Park. P 13.
G740 G **641** 85c. multicoloured .... 2·20 2·20
G741 G **642** 1f. multicoloured .... 2·40 2·40

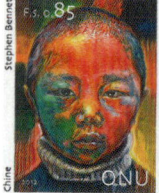
G **643** Boy, China

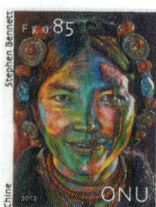
G **644** Woman, China

G **645** Man, Mongolia

G **646** Woman, Mexico

G **647** Man, Papua New Guinea

G **648** Girl, Haiti

(Des Stephen Bennett. Litho Lowe-Martin Group Canada)

2012 (11 Oct). Indigenous Peoples. P 13½.
G742 G **643** 85c. multicoloured .... 2·00 2·00
             a. Sheetlet of 6. Nos. G742/G747.. 12·50
G743 G **644** 85c. multicoloured .... 2·00 2·00
G744 G **645** 85c. multicoloured .... 2·00 2·00
G745 G **646** 85c. multicoloured .... 2·00 2·00
G746 G **647** 85c. multicoloured .... 2·00 2·00
G747 G **648** 85c. multicoloured .... 2·00 2·00
G742/G747 Set of 6 .... 11·00 11·00

Nos. G742/G747 were printed, *se-tenant*, in sheets of six stamps with enlarged upper margin.

G **649** Radio Operator in the Field

G **650** Transmission Desk

(Des Rorie Katz. Litho Lowe-Martin Group, Canada)

2013 (13 Feb). UN Radio. World Radio Day 2013. P 13×13½.
G748 G **649** 1f.40 multicoloured .... 3·50 3·50
G749 G **650** 1f.90 multicoloured .... 4·75 4·75

G **651** Leaf containing Figure

G **652** Dove and Figures

(Des Sergio Baradat. Litho Enschedé)

2013 (5 Mar). Humanity. P 14×13.
G750 G **651** 1f. multicoloured .... 2·30 2·30
G751 G **652** 1f.40 multicoloured .... 3·50 3·50

2013 UNITED NATIONS OFFICE AT GENEVA

G **653** Mogao Caves

G **654** Potala Palace, Lhasa

G **655** Great Wall

G **656** Imperial Palace, Beijing

G **657** Mount Huangshan

G **658** Qin Dynasty Terracotta Warriors

G756	G **657**	50c. multicoloured	1·40	1·40
		a. Booklet pane. Nos. G756×4	5·75	
G757	G **658**	50c. multicoloured	1·40	1·40
		a. Booklet pane. Nos. 757×4	5·75	
		(b) Sheet stamps		
G758		1f.40 As Type G **654**	3·50	3·50
G759		1f.90 As Type G **657**	4·50	4·50
G752/G759 Set of 8			12·50	12·50

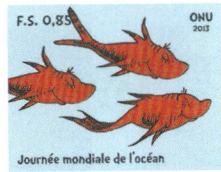
G **659** Three Fish

G **660** Fish (*Illustration reduced, actual size 140×170 mm*)

(Des Dr Seuss. Litho Lowe-Martin Group, Canada)

2013 (31 May). World Oceans' Day. Sheet 140×170 mm containing T G **659** and forming the overall design T G **660**. P 13½.
MSG760 85c.×12 Type G **659**; Green Fish; Three red Fish; Two green Fish; Large red Fish; Yellow Fish; Red Fish; Yellow Fish; Two green Fish; Small red Fish; Two green and one red Fish; Yellow Fish in car. 26·00 26·00

G **661** Helix Nebula   G **662** NGC 1850 Nebula

G **663** Eagle Nebula

UNITED NATIONS OFFICE AT GENEVA 2013

(Des Sergio Baradat. Litho UAB Garsu Pasaulis, Lithuania)
2013 (9 Aug). World Space Week. Nebulae. P 14.

G761	G 661	1f.40 multicoloured	3·25	3·25
		a. Pair. Nos. G761/G762	6·75	6·75
G762	G 662	1f.40 multicoloured	3·25	3·25
MSG763	81×81 mm. Type G 663 1f. multicoloured		2·40	2·40

 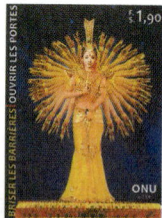

G **664** See the Girl with Red Dress On (Sargy Mann) G **665** China Disabled Peoples Performing Arts Troupe

(Des Rorie Katz. Litho UAB Garsu Pasaulis, Lithuania)
2013 (20 Sept). Break Barriers. Open Doors. P 14.

G764	G 664	1f.40 multicoloured	3·50	3·50
G765	G 665	1f.90 multicoloured	4·50	4·50

G **666** Pangolin (*Smutsia temminckii*)   G **667** Potto (*Perodicticus potto*)

G **668** Philippine Tarsier (*Tarsius (Carlito) syrichta*)   G **669** Livingstone's Fruit Bat (*Pteropus livingstonii*)

(Des Sara Menon. Litho Enschedé)
2013 (10 Oct). Endangered Species (21st series). P 12½×13.

G766	G 666	1f.40 multicoloured	3·00	3·00
		a. Block of 4. Nos. G766/G769	12·50	
G767	G 667	1f.40 multicoloured	3·00	3·00
G768	G 668	1f.40 multicoloured	3·00	3·00
G769	G 669	1f.40 multicoloured	3·00	3·00
G766/G769	Set of 4		11·00	11·00

Nos. G766/G769 were printed, *se-tenant*, in blocks of four stamps within the sheet.

G **670** Ivory Coast   G **671** Marshall Islands

G **672** Andorra   G **673** Guinea Bissau

G **674** Kenya   G **675** Antigua and Barbuda

G **676** Tajikistan   G **677** Micronesia

(Des Rorie Katz. Litho Cartor)
2013 (6 Nov). Coins and Flags of Member Countries (7th series). Multicoloured. P 13.

G770	G 670	1f.40 multicoloured	3·25	3·25
		a. Sheet of 8. Nos. G770/G777	27·00	
		b. Block of 4. Nos. G770/G737	13·50	
G771	G 671	1f.40 multicoloured	3·25	3·25
G772	G 672	1f.40 multicoloured	3·25	3·25
G773	G 673	1f.40 multicoloured	3·25	3·25
G774	G 674	1f.40 multicoloured	3·25	3·25
		b. Block of 4. Nos. G774/G777	13·50	
G775	G 675	1f.40 multicoloured	3·25	3·25
G776	G 676	1f.40 multicoloured	3·25	3·25
G777	G 677	1f.40 multicoloured	3·25	3·25
G770/G777	Set of 8		23·00	23·00

Nos. G770/G777 were printed, *se-tenant*, in two blocks of four stamps within sheets of eight, the blocks separated by a central gutter.

G **678** 'Smiling' Dog   G **679** Two Girls forming Heart

(Des Rorie Katz. Litho Lowe-Martin Group, Canada)
2014 (17 Mar). International Day of Happiness. P 13½.

G778	G 678	1f. multicoloured	2·50	2·50
G779	G 679	1f.40 multicoloured	3·25	3·25

2014 UNITED NATIONS OFFICE AT GENEVA

G **680** Singer

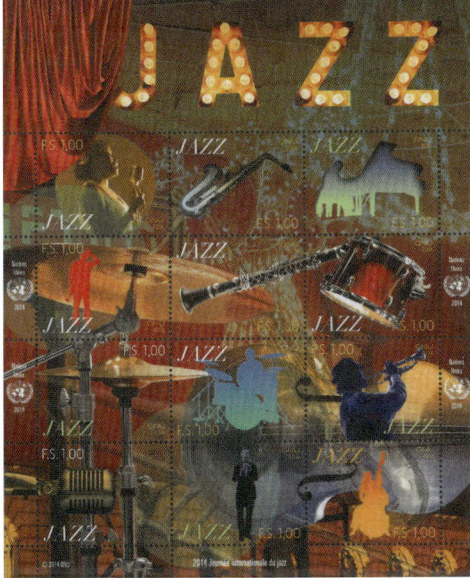

G **681** Jazz (*Illustration reduced, actual size* 140×170 mm)

(Des Sergio Baradat. Litho Cartor)

2014 (30 Apr). International Jazz Day. Sheet 140×170 mm containing T G **680** and forming the overall design T G **681**. P 13×13½.
MSG780 1f.×12, Type G **680**; Saxophone; Pianist; Cymbal and stand, partial; Cymbal and Clarinet; Clarinet and Drum; Stand and Cymbals; Drummer; Trumpeter; Microphone and stands; Clarinetist; Double base .... 31·00   31·00

The stamps and margins of No. **MS**G780 form a composite design of instruments and musicians.

G **682** Building and Spirals

G **683** Peacock and Spirals

(Des Sergio Baradat. Litho Lowe-Martin Group, Canada)

2014 (6 June). Spirals. P 13.
G781   G **682**   2f.20 multicoloured .... 5·25   5·25
G782   G **683**   2f.60 multicoloured .... 6·25   6·25

G **684** Taj Mahal

G **685** Taj Mahal in the Evening

G **686** Taj Mahal and Camel

G **687** Taj Mahal and Water

G **688** Taj Mahal from End of Canal

G **689** Taj Mahal and Elephant

(Des Rorie Katz. Litho Enschedé)

2014 (11 July). World Heritage Sites. Taj Mahal. P 14.

(a) Booklet stamps
G783   G **684**   30c. multicoloured 55   55
                   a. Booklet pane. Nos. G783×4 .... 2·30
G784   G **685**   30c. multicoloured 55   55
                   a. Booklet pane. Nos. G784×4 .... 2·30
G785   G **686**   30c. multicoloured 55   55
                   a. Booklet pane. Nos. G785×4 .... 2·30
G786   G **687**   50c. multicoloured .... 1·40   1·40
                   a. Booklet pane. Nos. G786×4 .... 5·75
G787   G **688**   50c. multicoloured .... 1·40   1·40
                   a. Booklet pane. Nos. G787×4 .... 5·75
G788   G **689**   50c. multicoloured .... 1·40   1·40
                   a. Booklet pane. Nos. G788×4 .... 5·75

(b) Sheet stamps
G789   1f.40 As Type G **685** .... 3·50   3·50
G790   1f.90 As Type G **688** .... 4·75   4·75
G783/G790 *Set of 8* .... 12·50   12·50

UNITED NATIONS OFFICE AT GENEVA 2014

G **690** Women and Artichoke   G **691** Farm and Family

(Des Sergio Baradat. Litho Lowe-Martin Group, Canada)
2014 (21 Aug). International Year of Family Farming. Cultivating Hope. P 13.
G791 G **690** 1f.30 multicoloured .... 3·00 3·00
G792 G **691** 1f.60 multicoloured .... 4·00 4·00

(Des Oamul Lu. Litho Lowe-Martin Group, Canada)
2014 (18 Sept). Education First. Multicoloured. P 13.
G793 1f.90 Children seated in museum .... 4·75 4·75
MSG794 40×140 mm. 1f.90 Child reading in library (32×32 mm) .... 5·00 5·00
Types G **692**/G **693** are unavailable.

G **694** *Arapaima gias*   G **695** *Cetorhinus maximus* (Basking Shark)

G **696** *Pristis pristis* (Large-tooth Sawfish)   G **697** *Acipenser baerii* (Siberian Sturgeon)

(Des Rocco J Callari. Litho Enschedé)
2014 (23 Oct). Endangered Species (22nd series). P 12½×13.
G795 G **694** 1f.40 multicoloured .... 3·25 3·25
              a. Block of 4. Nos. G795/G798 .... 13·50
G796 G **695** 1f.40 multicoloured .... 3·25 3·25
G797 G **696** 1f.40 multicoloured .... 3·25 3·25
G798 G **697** 1f.40 multicoloured .... 3·25 3·25
G795/G798 Set of 4 .... 11·50 11·50
Nos. G795/G798 were printed, *se-tenant*, in blocks of four stamps within the sheet.

G **698** Vanuatu   G **699** Nauru

G **700** Eritrea   G **701** El Salvador

G **702** Mozambique   G **703** Burundi

G **704** Turkmenistan   G **705** Guinea

(Des Rorie Katz. Litho Cartor)
2015 (6 Feb). Coins and Flags of Member Countries (8th series). Multicoloured. P 13.
G799 G **698** 90c. multicoloured .... 2·75 2·75
              a. Sheetlet of 8. Nos. G799/G806.. 23·00
              b. Block of 4. Nos. G799/G802....... 11·50
G800 G **699** 90c. multicoloured .... 2·75 2·75
G801 G **700** 90c. multicoloured .... 2·75 2·75
G802 G **701** 90c. multicoloured .... 2·75 2·75
G803 G **702** 90c. multicoloured .... 2·75 2·75
              b. Block of 4. Nos. G803/G806....... 11·50
G804 G **703** 90c. multicoloured .... 2·75 2·75
G805 G **704** 90c. multicoloured .... 2·75 2·75
G806 G **705** 90c. multicoloured .... 2·75 2·75
G799/G806 Set of 8 .... 20·00 20·00
Nos. G799/G806 were printed, *se-tenant*, in two blocks of four stamps within sheets of eight, the blocks separated by a central gutter.

G **706** Pen Nib

G **707** Li Bai (*Illustration reduced, actual size* 177×127 *mm*)

2015 UNITED NATIONS OFFICE AT GENEVA

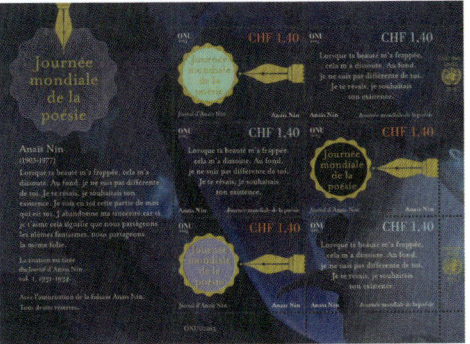

G **708** Anais Nin (*Illustration reduced, actual size 177×127 mm*)

(Des Sergio Baradat. Litho Cartor)

2015 (20 Mar). World Poetry Day. Li Bai and Anais Nin. Two sheets each 177×127 mm containing T G **706** and forming the overall designs Types G **707** and G **708**. P 14½.

MSG807 1f.×6 Li Bai. Type G **706**; Chinese characters; Chinese characters; As Type G **706**; As Type G **706**; Chinese characters .... 17·00 17·00

MSG808 1f.40×6, Anais Nin. As Type G **706**; 'Lorsque to beauté m'a frappée...'; 'Lorsque to beauté m'a frappée...'; As Type G **706**; 'Lorsque to beauté m'a frappée...';" .... 26·00 26·00

The stamps and margins of **MS**G807 and **MS**G808 form composite designs.

G **709** Wilson's Bird-of-Paradise (*Diphyllodes respublica*) G **710** Paradise Riflebird (*Ptiloris paradiseus*)

G **711** Wallace's Standardwing (*Semioptera wallacii*) G **712** Goldie's Bird-of-Paradise (*Paradisaea decora*)

(Des Rorie Katz and Sergio Baradat. Litho Enschedé)

2015 (16 Apr). Endangered Species (23rd series). P 12½×13.
G809	G **709**	1f.40 multicoloured	4·00	4·00
		a. Block of 4. Nos. G809/G812	17·00	
G810	G **710**	1f.40 multicoloured	4·00	4·00
G811	G **711**	1f.40 multicoloured	4·00	4·00
G812	G **712**	1f.40 multicoloured	4·00	4·00
G809/G812		Set of 4	14·50	14·50

Nos. G809/G812 were printed, *se-tenant*, in blocks of four stamps within the sheet.

Types G **713**/G **714** and Nos. G813/G814 are vacant.

G **715** Luang Prabang, Laos

G **716** Ankor Wat, Cambodia

G **717** Ayttaya, Thailand

G **718** Borobudur Temple, Indonesia

G **719** Banaue Rice Terraces, Philippines

G **720** Huê Monument, Vietnam

(Des Sergio Baradat. Litho Enschedé)

2015 (5 June). World Heritage Sites. South East Asia. P 14.

(a) Booklet stamps
G815	G **715**	30c. multicoloured	80	80
		a. Booklet pane. Nos. G815×4	3·50	
G816	G **716**	30c. multicoloured	80	80
		a. Booklet pane. Nos. G816×4	3·50	
G817	G **717**	30c. multicoloured	80	80
		a. Booklet pane. Nos. G817×4	3·50	
G818	G **718**	50c. multicoloured	1·50	1·50
		a. Booklet pane. Nos. G818×4	6·25	
G819	G **719**	50c. multicoloured	1·50	1·50
		a. Booklet pane. Nos. G819×4	6·25	
G820	G **720**	50c. multicoloured	1·50	1·50
		a. Booklet pane. Nos. G820×4	6·25	

(b) Sheet stamps
G821		1f.40 As Type G **716**	4·00	4·00
G822		1f.90 As Type G **719**	5·50	5·50
G815/G822		Set of 8	15·00	15·00

UNITED NATIONS OFFICE AT GENEVA 2015

G **721** Wolf wooing Child ('Child Marriage')

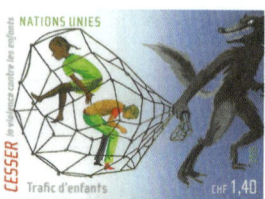

G **722** Wolf dragging Children Away ('Child Trafficking')

(Des Chris Sharp. Litho Cartor)

2015 (20 Aug). End Violence against Children. P 13.
G823	G **721**	1f. multicoloured	2·75	2·75
G824	G **722**	1f.40 multicoloured	4·00	4·00

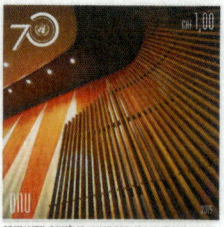

G **723** ECOSOC Chamber

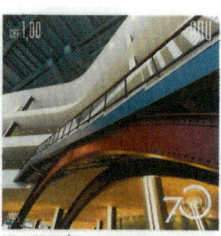

G **724** Visitors Lobby

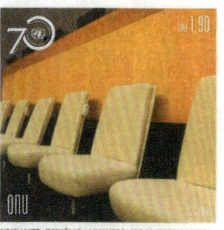

G **725** Chairs ECOSOC Chamber

G **726** Secretariat Façade

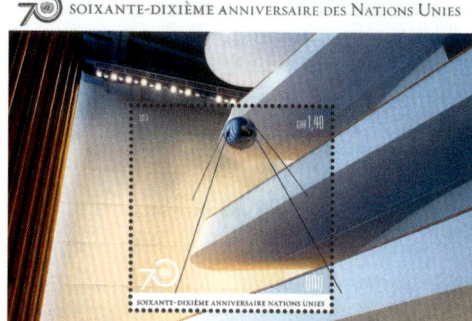

G **727** Visitors Lobby (*Illustration reduced, actual size* 105×81 mm)

(Des Rorie Katz. Litho Cartor)

2015 (23 Oct). 70th Anniversary of the United Nations. P 13.
G825	G **723**	1f. multicoloured	2·75	2·75
		a. Pair. Nos. G825/G826	5·75	5·75
G826	G **724**	1f. multicoloured	2·75	2·75
G827	G **725**	1f.90 multicoloured	5·50	5·50
		a. Nos. G827/G828	11·50	11·50
G828	G **726**	1f.90 multicoloured	5·50	5·50
G825/G828 *Set of 4*			15·00	15·00
MSG829 105×81 mm. Type G **727** 1f.40 multicoloured			4·50	4·50

Nos. G825/G826 and G827/G828, respectively were printed, *se-tenant*, in horizontal pairs within sheets of eight stamps with enlarged illustrated margins.

G **728** Emblem

(Des Charles Haumont. Litho I.T.V.F.)

2015 (24 Nov). COP21 Climate Change Conference, Paris.
G830	G **728**	1f.40 multicoloured	4·00	4·00

G **729** Two Women

G **730** Family

2016 UNITED NATIONS OFFICE AT GENEVA

(Des Sergio Baradat. Litho Cartor)

2016 (5 Feb). Free and Equal. United Nations Campaign for Sexual Minorities. P 13.
G831	G 729	1f. multicoloured	2·75	2·75
G832	G 730	1f.50 multicoloured	4·00	4·00

G **731** Boy

G **732** Girl

(Des Sergio Baradat and Mirko Ilić. Litho Lowe-Martin Group, Canada)

2016 (8 Mar). HeforShe. Gender Equality. P 12½×13.
G833	G 731	1f. multicoloured	2·75	2·75
G834	G 732	2f. multicoloured	5·50	5·50

Stamps of a similar design were issued by India.

G **733** Two Male Dancers

G **734** Swedish Dance (*Illustration reduced, actual size* 140×170 mm)

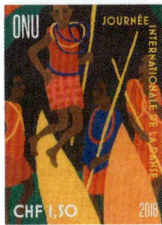
G **735** Leaping Dancer

G **736** African Dance (*Illustration reduced, actual size* 140×170 mm)

(Des Karin Rönmark. Litho Cartor)

2016 (29 Apr). International Dance Day. Two sheets, each 140×170 mm, one containing T G **733** and forming the overall design T G **734**; and the other containing T G **735** and forming the overall design T G **736**. P 13×13½.

MSG835 1f.×6 Sweden. Type G **733**; Couple, man kneeling; Couple, woman on left; Couple, woman on right; Circle dance, left; Circle dance, right............ 17·00 17·00
MSG836 1.50×6, Africa. Type G **735**; Three dancers, yellow leaf; Three dancers, pink leaf; Totem; Two dancers wearing headdresses; Dancer wearing horned headdress.. 26·00 26·00

G **737** Peacekeepers

G **738** Speaking to Women

(Des Sergio Baradat. Litho and gold foil die-stamped Lowe-Martin Group, Canada)

2016 (29 May). International Day of United Nations Peacekeepers. P 13½.
G837	G 737	1f. multicoloured	2·75	2·75
G838	G 738	1f.50 multicoloured	4·00	4·00

Stamps of a similar design were issued by Austria.

G **739**/G **740** Rowers (*Illustration reduced, actual size* 100×35 mm)

UNITED NATIONS OFFICE AT GENEVA 2016

G **741**-G **742** Gymnastic Dance (*Illustration reduced, actual size 100×35 mm*)

(Des Nick Iluzada. Litho and varnish Cartor).
2016 (22 July). Sport for Peace. Olympic Games 2016. P 14½.

G839	G **739**	1f. multicoloured	2·75	2·75
		a. Pair. Nos. G839/G840	5·75	5·75
G840	G **740**	1f. multicoloured	2·75	2·75
G841	G **741**	2f. multicoloured	5·50	5·50
		a. Pair. Nos. G841/G842	11·50	11·50
G842	G **742**	2f. multicoloured	5·50	5·50
G839/G842 *Set of 4*			15·00	15·00

Nos. G839/G840 and G841/G842, respectively, were printed, se-tenant, in horizontal pairs within the sheet, each pair forming a composite design.

G **743** UN Building, left

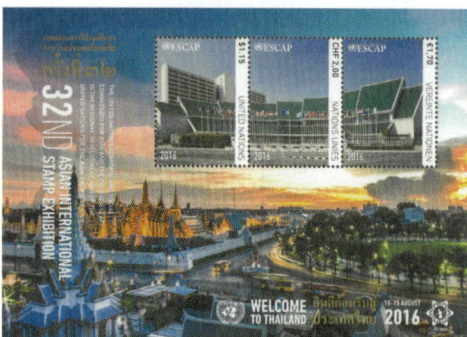

G **744** UN Building and Bangkok (*Illustration reduced, actual size 150×105 mm*)

2016 (10 Aug). Asian International Stamp Exhibition, Bangkok. Sheet 150×105 mm containing T G **743** and forming the overall design T G **744**. P 13½.
MSG843 1f.15 Type G **743**; 1f.70 UN Building, right;
2f. UN Building, centre .... 27·00 27·00

No. **MS**G843 contains three stamps, one valid for each of the United Nations Headquarters (Geneva, New York and Vienna).

G **745** Bridges of Prague

G **746** Gardens and Castle at Kroměříž

G **747** Historic Centre, Kutna Hora

G **748** City Centre, Olomouc

G **749** Lednice-Valtice Cultural Landscape

G **750** Historic Centre, Český Krumlov

(Des Sergio Baradat. Litho Cartor)
2016 (8 Sept). World Heritage Sites. Czech Republic. P 13½.

(a) Booklet stamps

G844	G **745**	30c. multicoloured	80	80
		a. Booklet pane. Nos. G844×4	3·50	
G845	G **746**	30c. multicoloured	80	80
		a. Booklet pane. Nos. G845×4	3·50	
G846	G **747**	30c. multicoloured	80	80
		a. Booklet pane. Nos. G846×4	3·50	
G847	G **748**	50c. multicoloured	1·50	1·50
		a. Booklet pane. Nos. G847×4	6·25	
G848	G **749**	50c. multicoloured	1·50	1·50
		a. Booklet pane. Nos. G848×4	6·25	
G849	G **750**	50c. multicoloured	1·50	15·00
		a. Booklet pane. Nos. G849×4	6·25	

(b) Sheet stamps

G850	1f. As Type G **746**	2·75	2·75
G851	1f.50 As Type G **749**	4·00	4·00
G844/G851 *Set of 8*		12·50	12·50

Stamps of a similar design were issued by Czech Republic.

2016 UNITED NATIONS OFFICE AT GENEVA

G **751** Grey Crowned Crane

G **752** African Fauna and Flora (*Illustration reduced, actual size 100×80 mm*)

(Des Sergio Baradat. Litho Cartor)

2016 (24 Sept). Eyes on Africa. CITES COP17. Sheet 100×80 mm Containing T G **751** and forming the overall design T G **752**. P 13½.

MSG852 2f.×4, Type G **751**; *Mantella madagascariensis* (Madagascar Golden Frog); Mountain Gorilla; *Avonia quinaria*..................... 23·00   23·00

G **753** No Poverty

G **754** Zero Hunger

G **755** Good Health and Well Being

G **756** Quality Education

G **757** Gender Equality

G **758** Clean Water and Sanitation

G **759** Clean and Affordable Energy

G **760** Decent Work and Economic Growth

G **761** Industry Innovation and Infrastructure

G **762** Reduced Inequalities

G **763** Sustainable Cities and Communities

G **764** Responsible Consumption and Production

G **765** Action of Climate Change

G **766** Life below Water

G **767** Life on Land

G **768** Peace Justice and Strong Institutions

G **769** Partnerships for the Realisation of the Goals

UNITED NATIONS OFFICE AT GENEVA 2016

(Des Lindsey Thoeng. Litho Lowe-Martin Group, Canada)

2016 (24 Oct). Sustainable Development Goals. P 13½.

G853	G 753	1f. multicoloured	2·75	2·75
		a. Sheet of 17. Nos. G853/G869, plus label	48·00	
G854	G 754	1f. multicoloured	2·75	2·75
G855	G 755	1f. multicoloured	2·75	2·75
G856	G 756	1f. multicoloured	2·75	2·75
G857	G 757	1f. multicoloured	2·75	2·75
G858	G 758	1f. multicoloured	2·75	2·75
G859	G 759	1f. multicoloured	2·75	2·75
G860	G 760	1f. multicoloured	2·75	2·75
G861	G 761	1f. multicoloured	2·75	2·75
G862	G 762	1f. multicoloured	2·75	2·75
G863	G 763	1f. multicoloured	2·75	2·75
G864	G 764	1f. multicoloured	2·75	2·75
G865	G 765	1f. multicoloured	2·75	2·75
G866	G 766	1f. multicoloured	2·75	2·75
G867	G 767	1f. multicoloured	2·75	2·75
G868	G 768	1f. multicoloured	2·75	2·75
G869	G 769	1f. multicoloured	2·75	2·75
G853/G869 Set of 17			42·00	42·00

Nos. G853/G869 were printed, *se-tenant*, in sheets of 17 stamps and one stamp-size label.

G **770** Monkey King and Tiger

G **773** The Quadrille (*Illustration reduced, actual size 140×170 mm*)

G **771** Monkey King (*Illustration reduced, actual size 150×105 mm*)

2016 (24 Oct). Asian International Stamp Exhibition, Nanning, China. Sheet 150×105 mm containing T G **770** and forming the overall design T G **771**. P 13½.

MSG870 1f.15 Type G **770**; 1f.70 Monkey King; 2f. Monkey King (*different*) .... 24·00 24·00

No. **MS**G870 contains three stamps, one valid for each of the United Nations Headquarters (Geneva, New York and Vienna).

G **774** Woman

G **772** Woman

G **775** The Japanese Fan Dance (*Illustration reduced, actual size 140×170 mm*)

(Des Sergio Baradat and Jean François Martin. Litho Cartor)

2017 (23 Mar). International Dance Day. Two sheets, each 140×170 mm, one containing T G **772** and forming the overall design T G **773**; and the other containing G **774** and forming the overall design T G **775**. P 13×13½.

MSG871 1f.×6 Carnival of Venice. The Quadrille.
Type G **772**; Harlequin; Man, facing right; Woman, facing left; Woman, head and shoulders; Man, head and shoulders .... 17·00 17·00
MSG872 1.50×6, Japan. Japanese Fan Dance. Type G **774**; Dancer with left hand raised; Head of dancer; Dancer, head and shoulders; Hand holding fan; Head of dancer (*different*).. 26·00 26·00

STAMP BOOKLETS

The following checklist covers, in simplified form, booklets issued by the United Nations Geneva Headquarters. It is intended that it should be used in conjunction with the main listings and details of stamps and panes listed there are not repeated.

Prices are for complete booklets

Booklet No.	Date	Contents and Cover Price	Price
SBG1	24.10.95	50th Anniversary of UNO 4 panes, Nos. G275c, G278c, G281c and G284c (3f.60)...	9·00
SBG2	19.11.97	Terracotta Warriors 6 panes, Nos. G324a, G325a, G326a, G327a, G328a and 329a (2f.40)................	14·50
SBG3	04.12.98	Schönbrunn Palace 6 panes, Nos. G355a, G356a, G357a, G358a, G359a and G360a (3f.90)............	16·00
SBG4	19.3.99	Australia 6 panes, Nos. G364a, G365a, G366a, G367a, G368a and G369a, (3f.60)...........	17·00
SBG5	06.10.00	Spain 6 panes, Nos. G399a, G400a, G401a, G402a, G403a and G404a (3f.60)............	13·50
SBG6	01.8.01	Japan 6 panes, Nos. G415a, G416a, G417a, G418a, G419a and G420a (4f.80)............	13·00
SBG7	30.8.02	Italy 6 panes, Nos. G447a, G448a, G449a, G450a, G451a and G452a (3f.60)............	17·00
SBG8	24.10.03	USA 6 panes, Nos. G467a, G468a, G469a, G470a, G471a and G472a (4f.80)............	14·50
SBG9	12.8.04	Greece 6 panes, Nos. G 484a, G485a, G486a, G487a, G488a and G489a (4f.80)............	23·00
SBG10	04.8.05	Egypt 6 panes, Nos. G506a, G507a, G508a, G509a, G510a and G511a (8f.40)............	22·00
SBG11	17.6.06	France 6 panes, Nos. G526a, G527a, G528a, G529a, G530a and G531a (8f.40)............	22·00
SBG12	09.8.07	South America 6 panes, Nos. G558a, G559a, G560a, G561a, G562a and G563a (8f.40)............	18·00
SBG13	23.10.08	Climate Change 6 panes. Nos. G590a, G594a, G598a, G602a, G606a and G610a (4f.80)............	24·00
SBG14	07.7.09	Germany 6 panes. Nos. G621a, G622a, G623a, G624a, G625a and G626a (9f.60)............	27·00
SBG15	6.5.10.	One Planet, One Ocean. 50th Anniversary of Intergovernmental Oceanographic Commission 6 panes, Nos. G659/G662; G663/G666; G667/G670; G671/G674; G675/G678; G679/G682 (8f.60).....................	20·00
SBG16	11.4.13	World Heritage. China 6 panes, Nos. G752a; G753a; G754a; G755a; G756a; G757a (4f.80)..............	25·00
SBG17	11.7.14	World Heritage. Taj Mahal 6 panes, Nos. G783a; G784a; G785a; G786a; G787a; G788a (4f.80)................	25·00
SBG18	5.6.15	World Heritage. South East Asia 6 panes, Nos. G815a; G816a; G817a; G818a; G819a; G820a (4f.80)................	30·00
SBG19	8.9.16	World Heritage. Czech Republic 6 panes, Nos. G844a; G845a; G846a; G847a; G848a; G849a (4f.80)................	30·00

Switzerland Order Form

YOUR ORDER

Stanley Gibbons account number

Condition (mint/UM/ used)	Country	SG No.	Description	Price	Office use only
			POSTAGE & PACKING	£3.60	
			TOTAL		

The lowest price charged for individual stamps or sets purchased from Stanley Gibbons Ltd, is £1.

Payment & address details

Name
Address (We cannot deliver to PO Boxes)

Postcode
Tel No.
Email

PLEASE NOTE Overseas customers MUST quote a telephone number or the order cannot be dispatched. Please complete ALL sections of this form to allow us to process the order.

☐ Cheque (made payable to Stanley Gibbons Ltd)
☐ I authorise you to charge my
☐ Mastercard ☐ Visa ☐ Diners ☐ Amex ☐ Maestro

Card No. (Maestro only)
Valid from   Expiry date   Issue No. (Maestro only)   CVC No. (4 if Amex)
CVC No. is the last three digits on the back of your card (4 if Amex)

Signature   Date

4 EASY WAYS TO ORDER

Post to
Mark Pegg,
Stamp Mail Order Department,
Stanley Gibbons Ltd,
399 Strand, London,
WC2R 0LX, England

Call
020 7836 8444
+44 (0)20 7836 8444

Fax
020 7557 4499
+44 (0)20 7557 4499

Click
mpegg@stanleygibbons.com

Put Simply...

UPA is a 'trade disruptor' and has been successfully so for the past twenty years

If you wish to discover an altogether different selling experience, whether you sell to my company – or if valuable enough we sell for you upon a commission basis – you will benefit from the fact that my philatelic auctions company sells to more collectors (in 49 different countries) than any other stamp auction in the UK, and for that matter, most of the rest of the world.

In the following double page spread advertisement you will discover the reasons why …

If you like what you see, please contact Universal using the contact details upon the following right-hand page. Thank you,

Andrew McGavin,
Managing Director UPA
Philatelic Author & Expert

Experience **Philatelic Passion**, *Contact* **UPA NOW**

Creating a (Successful) *Stamp*

Hi,
That's me Promoting Philately with Alan Titchmarsh on UK National TV

'We canvassed trade opinion – Dealers told us it wouldn't work!'

It was 1999. We had a good stamp business. I'd started by supplying stamps on approval. In fact, just like Victor Kiam of Remington Razors fame, I bought the stamp 'Approvals' Company called Omniphil that sent me stamps on approval when I was in my teens, but that's another story...

After a few years I decided that a 'one-legged' stamp approvals business, should stand on two feet(!), so I added a 'Buy One, Take One Free' off-paper world mixtures department which soon became a big success thanks to a loyal following of collectors who loved sorting through unsorted mixtures, and still do.

Meanwhile buying stamp collections at auction had created a pleasant problem. We had accumulated better stamps which we felt were too valuable to be sent to clients on approval through the mail. Determining how best to handle these my wife and I came to the conclusion that just like a stool, a good stamp business should not stand on two feet alone... so we decided to add a third leg to our stamp business ...

...Yes, a stamp auction, which (you may have already guessed) had to be unlike any other by including the best features of other auctions, whilst eliminating the worst features such as 'caveat emptor' (buyer beware) and buyer's premiums which instinctively, we reasoned not to be in the best interests of collectors. We wrote to existing stamp auctions for their latest catalogues which we thoroughly analysed. And soon, we named our new stamp auction - Universal Philatelic Auctions and christened it UPA.

But Could We Solve the Stamp Trade's BIGGEST Problem...?

It was common knowledge in the trade that the trade's biggest problem was not what sold – but what didn't sell. That's the reason why you see the same overpriced stamps year in, year out with some dealers and auctions. Nowadays dealers and auctions are more sophisticated – for example they may sell on eBay as well as conventionally – but twenty years ago auctions would parcel up their unsold auction lots and sell them/swop them with other auctions, in order to 're-fresh' each other's stock, thereby offering 'NEW' stock to (hopefully) new collector clients. Other auctions would go to the lengths of re-describing their old unsold auction lots in order to disguise them. Just imagine, for a moment ... the Importance of Selling Your Unsold Lots – unless you are unscrupulous, your unsold lots represent your profit tied up in stale stock, not cash!

The 'break-through' took a fair bit of 'head-scratching' – but would it *work*...?

Twenty years later the answer seems simple, but it didn't feel simple then. The future health of our new UPA 'baby' depended upon getting it right. We had to break through moribund stamp industry practices which were obviously sticking a plaster on the 'unsolds' wound, whilst not facing up to the fact that if it wasn't selling it simply wasn't worth the price being asked...

ACCEPT YOUR 1st £55 GBP FREE TRIAL OFFER

...and therein lies the 'clue'. As soon as we thought of the solution, it seemed so simple that we questioned would it work? Why had no other auction – even to this very day not thought of, or deployed a structured Reducing Estimate (and Reserve) Price System each time an unsold lot was re-offered, and instead of trying to hide what wouldn't sell – we'd make a virtue out of a reduced price lot and tell collectors that (sin